The Official LSAT
SuperPrep™

A Publication of the Law School Admission Council
Newtown, PA

Introduction to the LSAT

The LSAT is a half-day standardized test required for admission to all 202 LSAC-member schools. It provides a standard measure of acquired reading and verbal reasoning skills that law schools can use as one of several factors in assessing applicants.

The test consists of five 35-minute sections of multiple-choice questions. Four of the five sections contribute to the test taker's score. These sections include one reading comprehension section, one analytical reasoning section, and two logical reasoning sections. The unscored section typically is used to pretest new test questions and to preequate new test forms. The placement of this section, which is commonly referred to as the variable section, varies for different administrations of the test. A 30-minute writing sample is administered at the end of the test. The writing sample is not scored by LSAC, but copies are sent to all law schools to which you apply. The score scale for the LSAT is 120 to 180.

The LSAT is designed to measure skills that are considered essential for success in law school: the reading and comprehension of complex texts with accuracy and insight; the organization and management of information and the ability to draw reasonable inferences from it; the ability to think critically; and the analysis and evaluation of the reasoning and arguments of others.

Scoring

Your LSAT score is based on the number of questions answered correctly (the raw score). There is no deduction for incorrect answers, and all questions count equally. In other words, there is no penalty for guessing.

■ Test Score Accuracy—Reliability and Standard Error of Measurement

Candidates perform at different levels on different occasions for reasons quite unrelated to the characteristics of a test itself. The accuracy of test scores is best described by the use of two related statistical terms, reliability and standard error of measurement.

Reliability is a measure of how consistently a test measures the skills being assessed. The higher the reliability coefficient for a test, the more certain we can be that test takers would get very similar scores if they took the test again. LSAC reports an internal consistency measure of reliability for every test form. Reliability can vary from 0.00 to 1.00, and a test with no measurement error would have a reliability coefficient of 1.00 (never attained in practice). Reliability coefficients for past LSAT forms have ranged from .90 to .95, indicating a high degree of consistency for these tests. LSAC expects the reliability of the LSAT to continue to fall within the same range.

LSAC also reports the amount of measurement error associated with each test form, a concept known as the standard error of measurement (SEM). The SEM, which is usually about 2.6 points, indicates how close a test taker's observed score is likely to be to his or her true score. True scores are theoretical scores that would be obtained from perfectly reliable tests with no measurement error—scores never known in practice. Score bands, or ranges of scores that contain a test taker's true score a certain percentage of the time, can be derived using the SEM. LSAT score bands are constructed by adding and subtracting the (rounded) SEM to and from an actual LSAT score (e.g., the LSAT score, plus or minus 3 points). Scores near 120 or 180 have asymmetrical bands. Score bands constructed in this manner will contain an individual's true score approximately 68 percent of the time.

Measurement error also must be taken into account when comparing LSAT scores of two test takers. It is likely that small differences in scores are due to measurement error rather than to meaningful differences in ability. The standard error of score differences provides some guidance as to the importance of differences between two scores. The standard error of score differences is approximately 1.4 times larger than the standard error of measurement for the individual scores.

Thus, a test score should be regarded as a useful but approximate measure of a test taker's abilities as measured by the test, not as an exact determination of his or her abilities. LSAC encourages law schools to examine the range of scores within the interval that probably contains the test taker's true score (e.g., the test taker's score band) rather than solely interpret the reported score alone.

■ Adjustments for Variation in Test Difficulty

All test forms of the LSAT reported on the same score scale are designed to measure the same abilities, but one test form may be slightly easier or more difficult than another. The scores from different test forms are made comparable through a statistical procedure known as equating. As a result of equating, a given scaled score earned on different test forms reflects the same level of ability.

■ Research on the LSAT

Summaries of LSAT validity studies and other LSAT research can be found in member law school libraries.

How These PrepTests Differ from an Actual LSAT

These sample tests are made up of the scored sections and writing sample from actual LSATs administered in February 1996, February 1999, and February 2000. However, none of these sample tests contain the extra, variable section that is used to pretest new test questions of one of the three question types. Also, you are likely to encounter the three LSAT question types in a different order when you take an actual LSAT than they are in these PrepTests. This is because the order of the question types is intentionally varied for each administration of the test.

The Question Types

The multiple-choice questions that make up most of the LSAT reflect a broad range of academic disciplines and are intended to give no advantage to candidates from a particular academic background.

The five sections of the test contain three different question types. The following material presents a general discussion of the nature of each question type and some strategies that can be used in answering them.

■ Logical Reasoning Questions

Logical reasoning questions evaluate a test taker's ability to understand, analyze, criticize, and complete arguments. The arguments are contained in short passages taken from a variety of sources, including letters to the editor, speeches, advertisements, newspaper articles and editorials, informal discussions and conversations, as well as articles in the humanities, the social sciences, and the natural sciences.

Each logical reasoning question requires the examinee to read and comprehend the argument or the reasoning contained in the passage, and answer one or two questions about it. Further discussion of logical reasoning questions, including a discussion of different varieties of these questions and strategies for answering them, can be found on pages 15–39.

■ Reading Comprehension Questions

The purpose of reading comprehension questions is to measure your ability to read, with understanding and insight, examples of lengthy and complex materials similar to those commonly encountered in law school work. The reading comprehension section of the test consists of four passages, each approximately 450 words long, followed by five to eight questions that test your reading and reasoning abilities. Passages for reading comprehension questions draw from subjects such as the humanities, the social sciences, biological and physical sciences, and issues related to the law.

Reading comprehension questions require test takers to read carefully and accurately, to determine the relationships among the various parts of the passage, and to draw reasonable inferences from the material in the passage. Further discussion of reading comprehension questions, including a discussion of different varieties of these questions and strategies for answering them, can be found on pages 40–54.

■ Analytical Reasoning Questions

Analytical reasoning questions are designed to measure the ability to understand a structure of relationships and to draw conclusions about the structure. The examinee is asked to make deductions from a set of statements, rules, or conditions that describe relationships among entities such as persons, places, things, or events. They simulate the kinds of detailed analyses of relationships that a law student must perform in solving legal problems. For example, a passage might describe four diplomats sitting around a table, following certain rules of protocol as to who can sit where. The test taker must answer questions about the implications of the given information, for example, who is sitting between diplomats X and Y.

The passage used for each group of questions describes a common relationship such as the following:

■ Assignment: Two parents, P and 0, and their children, R and S, must go to the dentist on four consecutive days, designated 1,2, 3, and 4;

■ Ordering: X arrived before Y but after Z;

■ Grouping: A manager is trying to form a project team from seven staff members—R, S, T, U, V, W, and X. Each staff member has a particular strength—writing, planning, or facilitating;

■ Spatial: A certain country contains six cities and each city is connected to at least one other city by a system of roads, some of which are one-way.

Further discussion of analytical reasoning questions, including a discussion of different varieties of these questions and strategies for answering them, can be found on pages 4–14.

The Writing Exercise

Test takers are given 30 minutes to complete the brief writing exercise, which is not scored but is used by law school admission personnel to assess writing skill. Read the topic carefully. You will probably find it best to spend a few minutes considering the topic and organizing your thoughts before you begin writing. Do not write on a topic other than the one specified. Writing on a topic of your own choice is not acceptable.

There is no "right" or "wrong" position on the writing sample topic. Law schools are interested in how skillfully you support the position you take and how clearly you express that position. How well you write is much more important than how much you write. No special knowledge is required or expected. Law schools are interested in organization, vocabulary, and writing mechanics. They understand the short time available to you and the pressure under which you are writing.

Confine your writing to the lined area following the writing sample topic. You will find that you have enough space if you plan your writing carefully, write on every line, avoid wide margins, and keep your handwriting a reasonable size. Be sure that your handwriting is legible.

Scratch paper is provided for use during the writing sample portion of the test only. Scratch paper cannot be used in other sections of the LSAT.

The writing sample is photocopied and sent to law schools to which you direct your LSAT score. A pen will be provided at the test center, which must be used (for the writing sample only) to ensure a photocopy of high quality.

Some writing sample prompts, or variations of them, may be given at more than one LSAT administration. A collection of 50 representative writing prompts is included in *LSAT: The Official TriplePrep Plus*, published by LSAC.

Taking the PrepTests Under Simulated LSAT Conditions

One important way to prepare for the LSAT is to take a sample test under the same requirements and time limits you will encounter in taking an actual LSAT. This helps you to estimate the amount of time you can afford to spend on each question in a section and to determine the question types on which you may need additional practice.

Since the LSAT is a timed test, it is important to use your allotted time wisely. During the test, you may work only on the section designated by the test supervisor. You cannot devote extra time to a difficult section and make up that time on a section you find easier. In pacing yourself, and checking your answers, you should think of each section of the test as a separate minitest.

Be sure that you answer every question on the test. When you do not know the correct answer to a question, first eliminate the responses that you know are incorrect, then make your best guess among the remaining choices. Do not be afraid to guess, as there is no penalty for incorrect answers.

When you take a sample test, abide by all the requirements specified in the directions and keep strictly within the specified time limits. Work without a rest period. When you take an actual test you will have only a short break—usually 10–15 minutes—after SECTION III. When taken under conditions as much like actual testing

conditions as possible, a sample test provides very useful preparation for taking the LSAT.

Official directions for the four multiple-choice sections and the writing sample are included in these PrepTests so that you can approximate actual testing conditions as you practice.

To take a test:

- Set a timer for 35 minutes. Answer all the questions in SECTION I of a PrepTest. Stop working on that section when the 35 minutes have elapsed.

- Repeat, allowing yourself 35 minutes for each of the other three sections.

- Set the timer for 30 minutes, then prepare your response to the writing sample for the PrepTest.

- Refer to "Computing Your Score" for the PrepTest for instruction on evaluating your performance. An answer key is provided for that purpose.

How to Approach Analytical Reasoning Questions

In working through an Analytical Reasoning section of the LSAT, you'll want to do two things: get the answer to the questions right and use your time efficiently. In this section, you'll get advice on how to do both.

Analytical Reasoning questions test your ability to reason within a given set of circumstances. These circumstances are described in the "setup." A setup consists of sets of elements (people, places, objects, tasks, colors, days of the week, and so on) along with a list of conditions designed to impose some sort of structure, or organization, on these elements (for example, putting them into an ordered sequence from first to last, or selecting subgroups from a larger group, or pairing elements from one set with elements from another set). The different structures allowed by the setup are the "outcomes."

Consider the following setup:

Each of five students—Hubert, Lori, Paul, Regina, and Sharon—will visit exactly one of three cities—Montreal, Toronto, or Vancouver—for the month of March, according to the following conditions:
    Sharon visits a different city than Paul.
    Hubert visits the same city as Regina.
    Lori visits Montreal or else Toronto.
    If Paul visits Vancouver, Hubert visits Vancouver with him.
    Each student visits one of the cities with at least one of the other four students.[1]

This setup features two sets of elements: a set of students and a set of cities. There are five conditions that constrain how the members of these two sets are associated with each other. The kind of structure that is to be imposed on the elements is this: each student must be paired with exactly one of the cities in strict accordance with the conditions.

> **Note.** Analytical Reasoning setups all have one crucial property in common: there is always more than one acceptable outcome. For example, in the example involving students and the cities they visit, the conditions do not work together to restrict each of the students to visiting a particular city and no other. Instead, there is more than one structure that satisfies all of the requirements of the setup.

Analytical Reasoning questions test your ability to determine what is necessary, what is possible, and what is impossible within the circumstances of the setup.

Questions that you are likely to be asked, based on setups such as the one above, are questions like these:

Which one of the following must be true for March?
Which one of the following could be false in March?
If Sharon visits Vancouver, which one of the following must be true for March?
If Hubert and Sharon visit a city together, which one of the following could be true in March?

In other words, you'll need to determine what can or must happen, either in general or else in specified circumstances (such as Sharon visiting Vancouver or Hubert and Sharon visiting a city together). And now we'll look at how you go about doing this:

■ Figuring Out the Setup

The first thing you need to get very clear about is what exactly is supposed to happen to the elements in the setup. So first you need to recognize which parts of the setup serve only as background information.

In the example above, the five students and the three cities are the things you have to associate with one another. What happens to them makes the difference between one outcome and another. But the month of March, which is mentioned both in the original setup and in each of the questions cited, is merely background information, as is the fact that the visitors are all students. The overall setup allows for a number of different arrangements for the visits. But none of the differences is in any way related to the fact that the visits happen in March, just as none of the differences is in any way related to the fact that the visitors are students. The month could just as well have been April, and the visitors could just as well have been professors or tourists. Changing these things would not change the way the setup and the questions function.

Now, what happens to the elements in the setup? Looking at the students first, we find that each of them is to visit just one of the cities. Looking at the cities, you might at first assume that each city will be visited by at least one of the students. However, notice that there is actually nothing that says that each of the cities has to be visited. Consider the implications of the last condition. This condition essentially says that no student can visit a city alone. This means that, for all three cities to be visited by at least two students, there would have to be at least six students. In actual fact, there are only five. So we know that there cannot be student visitors in all three cities. And the first of the conditions tells us that the students cannot all visit the same city, since Sharon and Paul cannot visit the same city as each other.

So we now know, in general outline, what an acceptable outcome will look like: one of the three cities will be visited by three of the students, one of them by two, and one of them by none. This is the type of implication that can be very useful to work out as you read the conditions, even before you start to answer the questions. It underscores the importance of reading through the setup carefully in order to work through its implications and understand how it works.

How to Represent What Happens (Some Time-saving Tips)

Because we have worked out some of the implications of the setup, we now have an idea of the basic shape of the acceptable outcomes. At this point, it might be possible for some people to figure out the answers to individual questions in their heads. Generally, however, this requires enormous powers of concentration and creates opportunities for error. For most people, trying to work these problems in their heads would be an extremely bad idea. Virtually everyone is well advised to use pencil and paper in solving Analytical Reasoning questions.

The time allotted for Analytical Reasoning questions gives you an average of less than 1½ minutes per question. Time management, therefore, is important. Since it does take time to sketch out solutions on paper, you should do whatever you can to use your time economically. Here are some time-saving tips that many people find useful:

- Abbreviate the elements by using just their initials. The elements in lists of names or places or objects will usually have different initials. When elements such as days of the week don't have different initials, be ready to devise abbreviations that will allow you to distinguish them. (For example, in a set of questions involving days of the week, you might use "T" for "Tuesday" and "Th" for "Thursday.")

- Just as you would use initials to represent the elements, you should work with shorthand versions of the conditions. Familiarize yourself with the most common types of conditions and devise your own shorthand way of representing them. For example, one frequent kind of condition stipulates that something that happens to one member of a pair of elements also happens to the other member. In the example above, the condition saying that "Hubert visits the same city as Regina" is of this type. You might decide that your shorthand for this condition will be "H = R." And for the condition that reads, "If Paul visits Vancouver, Hubert visits Vancouver with him," you might use "if Pv then Hv" or "P(V) → H(V)."

  Your shorthand versions of the conditions are the versions that you will be working with, so make sure that they correctly represent what the original conditions actually mean. The time spent in setting the conditions down in this way is more than offset by the time you'll save through the economy of working with the conditions in a form in which they can be quickly and easily taken in at a glance.

 Note. It doesn't matter whether anyone else would be able to look at your abbreviations and make sense of them. All that matters is that you yourself become fully fluent in using your abbreviations, so that you can save time when you put things down on paper. Practice doing Analytical Reasoning questions using your own abbreviations. Pick abbreviations that make sense to you. Pick abbreviations that are distinct enough that you won't mistake one for another, especially under the time pressure of taking the test.

- A quick check of the abbreviated setup conditions will sometimes show that one or more of the elements in the setup isn't mentioned in any of the conditions. Don't take this as an indication that there must be a mistake somewhere. Rather, take it at face value: those elements are not specifically constrained. You might devise a special notation for this situation. For example, you could circle those initials and include them at the bottom of your list of setup conditions. Or you might just make a shorthand list of all the elements, whether they are mentioned in the conditions or not.

- In your shorthand system, find a striking way to represent what **cannot** happen. For example, if you encounter a condition of the form "Greg cannot give the first presentation," this might be simply abbreviated as "G not 1" or even "*G(1)," where the asterisk is the symbol you use to represent "not."

- You might find it useful to represent certain conditions in more than one form. For example, you may decide that whenever you find a condition like "If Paul is selected, Raoul is also selected," you will automatically put down, as your shorthand version, both "P → R" and "not R → not P," since (as we'll see later) the two are logically equivalent and you might find it helpful to be reminded of this fact when you're answering the questions.

- You will very likely use certain elementary diagramming techniques, for example, using the elements in one set as headers and the elements in the other as entries under those headers. Try to think a bit about which diagramming techniques are effective for you. For example, in the case of the setup involving students and cities, you might diagram an outcome as follows:

<u>M</u>   <u>T</u>   <u>V</u>
H, R, S   L, P

Or you might diagram it like this:

M: H, R, S
T: L, P
V:

But you might not want to end up with this diagram:

<u>H</u> <u>L</u> <u>P</u> <u>R</u> <u>S</u>
M T T M M

Although this last diagram presents the same information as the other two, you might well feel that it does so less usefully. For example, the last diagram does not capture the fact that one of the cities will not be visited by any of the students as graphically as the other two diagrams do. Develop strategies ahead of time that will lead you to create diagrams that you work with easily and well. There is no one way to do this, just as there is no one right way to abbreviate conditions. The only way to find out what works for you is to practice diagramming a number of setups before taking the test.

- For some questions, you might find that it is helpful to quickly write out your abbreviations for the active elements in the set—H R P L S, for example—before you begin to work out the solution. Then you can cross out each element as you satisfy yourself that you have accounted for it in the current solution. This method is especially helpful if the list of elements is too long for you to keep track of in your head or if you have already marked up your original list of elements.

Orientation Questions

Most Analytical Reasoning sets begin with a question in which each answer choice represents a complete possible outcome, or sometimes just part of an outcome. The question asks you to select the answer choice that is an acceptable outcome (one that doesn't violate any part of the setup). You can think of questions of this kind as "orientation questions" since they do a good job of orienting you to the setup conditions.

For such questions, probably the most efficient approach is to take each condition in turn and check to see whether any of the answer choices violates it. As soon as you find an answer choice that violates a condition, you should eliminate that answer choice from further consideration—perhaps by crossing it out in your test booklet. When you have run through all of the setup conditions in this fashion, one answer choice will be left that you haven't crossed out: that is the correct answer.

Here's an orientation question relating to the setup in our example:

Which one of the following could be true for March?

(A) *Hubert, Lori, and Paul visit Toronto, and Regina and Sharon visit Vancouver.*
(B) *Hubert, Lori, Paul, and Regina visit Montreal, and Sharon visits Vancouver.*
(C) *Hubert, Paul, and Regina visit Toronto, and Lori and Sharon visit Montreal.*
(D) *Hubert, Regina, and Sharon visit Montreal, and Lori and Paul visit Vancouver.*
(E) *Lori, Paul, and Sharon visit Montreal, and Hubert and Regina visit Toronto.*

Let's take the setup conditions in order from first to last. First, check the first condition against each option:

Condition 1: *Sharon visits a different city than Paul.*

Condition 1 is met in (A) through (D) but violated in (E), since in (E) Sharon is scheduled to visit the same city as Paul. So you cross out (E) and do not check it any further. Now take the second condition:

Condition 2: *Hubert visits the same city as Regina.*

Condition 2 is violated in (A), since in (A) Hubert is scheduled to visit a different city than Regina. Cross out (A) and don't consider it any further. Condition 2 is not violated in (B), (C), or (D). (Remember, you don't need to check (E) since you've already ruled it out.) Proceed in the same way with the rest of the conditions:

Condition 3: *Lori visits Montreal or else Toronto.*

Condition 4: *If Paul visits Vancouver, Hubert visits Vancouver with him.*

Condition 5: *Each student visits one of the cities with at least one of the other four students.*

Condition 3 is violated in (D), since in (D) Lori is scheduled to visit Vancouver. Cross out (D). Condition 4 is violated in neither (B) nor (C), the only answer choices you are still checking. (The fact that condition 4 is violated in (D) is irrelevant at this point: you've already crossed out (D)). This leaves condition 5 to decide between (B) and (C). Condition 5 is violated in (B), since in (B) Sharon is scheduled to be the lone student visitor to Vancouver. Thus (B) gets crossed out. The only answer choice not crossed out is (C), which is consequently the correct answer. No further checking of (C) is needed. You've already checked (C) against each of the setup conditions. You are done. With this sort of question, there is no need for diagramming; all you needed to refer to was your abbreviated list of the conditions.

Another way of approaching an orientation question is to consider each answer choice in turn to see whether it violates any of the conditions. This will lead you to the correct answer relatively quickly if the correct answer is (A), and less quickly the further down the correct answer is. On balance, this is probably a less efficient way of finding the answer to orientation questions. Efficiency matters, because the more time you can save doing relatively straightforward questions such as these, the more time you have available to solve more challenging questions.

> **Caution.** The method of checking each condition against the answer choices is what you want to use with orientation questions. However, as we'll see below, this is generally **not** the approach you'll want to take with other types of questions. Keep in mind that your objective in answering the questions is to select the correct answer and move on to the next question, not to prove that the incorrect answer choices are wrong. (Also remember that not every set of questions includes an orientation question. When there is an orientation question, it will always be the question right after the setup.)

Questions That Include the Phrase "Any One of Which"

Another kind of question is concerned with complete and accurate lists of elements "any one of which" has some specific characteristic. A question of this kind might ask:

Which one of the following is a complete and accurate list of students any one of which could visit Vancouver in March?

The answer choices might be:

(A) Hubert, Lori, Regina
(B) Hubert, Regina, Sharon
(C) Paul, Regina, Sharon
(D) Hubert, Paul, Regina, Sharon
(E) Hubert, Lori, Paul, Regina, Sharon

What this question asks you to do is take each of the students in the setup and ask, "Could he/she visit Vancouver in March?" It doesn't matter whether any of the other students on the list could also visit Vancouver at the same time. You just need to ask whether there is an acceptable outcome in which the student you're considering visits Vancouver. If the answer is yes, that student needs to be included on the list, and if the answer is no, that student needs to stay off the list. If you do this systematically and correctly, the list you eventually end up with will be complete: no student who belongs on that list will have been left out. And it will be accurate: the list will not include any student who does not belong there. The correct answer is the list of all the students for whom the answer is "yes."

Sometimes the task of checking individually whether each element in the setup belongs on this list may seem daunting, but the task can often be simplified. For example, looking at the setup conditions, you notice that the third condition bars Lori from visiting Vancouver. So the two answer choices that include Lori—(A) and (E)—can immediately be crossed out.

Similarly, the second condition directly rules out (C). Condition 2 requires that Hubert visit the same city as Regina, so if we know that it is possible for one of them to visit Vancouver, it must be possible for the other to visit Vancouver too. This is what the condition requires. So (C), which includes Regina but not Hubert, is either incomplete or inaccurate.

This leaves us with (B) and (D). They both include Hubert, Regina, and Sharon. **Don't waste time checking these elements**. Since you have already determined that they are bound to be part of the correct answer, none of them will help you determine which of the remaining two answer choices is the correct one.

> **Note.** In general, when dealing with questions that include the phrase "any one of which" there is no point in checking an element that appears in all of the answer choices that you are still considering. It can't help you tell the correct answer from the incorrect ones.

Since the only thing that distinguishes (B) from (D) is that (D) includes Paul, the only point you need to check is whether Paul can visit Vancouver. Since he can, (B) is incomplete and thus incorrect. The correct answer is (D). In this case, when it came down to just (B) and (D), it turned out that checking one element was enough to allow you to identify the correct answer. If it had turned out that Paul could not visit Vancouver, then the correct answer would have been (B). As this case illustrates, it is generally worth your while to use time-saving strategies.

> **Note.** In questions that include the phrase "any one of which," if some element appears in only one of the answer choices still under consideration, check that element first. That way, if this element does belong on the list, you are done. Since any list, in order to be complete, would have to include this element, the answer choice that contains this element is the correct answer. On the other hand, if it turns out that the element doesn't belong on the list, then any remaining answer choices that include it should be crossed off.

Questions That Ask About What Must Be True

Many Analytical Reasoning questions ask about what must be true. Something that must be true is something that is true of every single acceptable outcome. In other words, there **cannot** be an acceptable outcome in which this thing is false. But this does not mean—and this is an important point—that to find the correct answer you should somehow mechanically draw up all of the acceptable outcomes and then look through them to identify the one answer choice that these outcomes all have in common. Don't try to do this.

The reason you should avoid determining all of the acceptable outcomes is not that it will give incorrect results. If used with care and without error, it will lead you to the correct answer. The problem is that it is usually far too time-consuming.

So what should you do instead? This depends on the form of the question. Does the question ask what must be true under certain specified circumstances, or does it ask what must be true on the basis of the setup alone, no matter what the circumstances are? Let's take a look at each of these two possibilities separately.

■ What Must Be True Under Certain Specified Circumstances

Consider the following example:

If Sharon visits Vancouver, which one of the following must be true for March?

The answer choices are:

(A) Hubert visits Montreal.
(B) Lori visits Montreal.
(C) Paul visits Montreal.
(D) Lori visits the same city as Paul.
(E) Lori visits the same city as Regina.

In this question, we start with the supposition that Sharon visits Vancouver and then we ask if anything follows from that. In fact, something does follow. Consider the first condition, which tells us that Sharon visits a different city than Paul. From these two pieces of information, we can conclude that Paul visits either Montreal or Toronto, but not Vancouver (because Sharon visits Vancouver and Paul cannot visit the same city that she does). This is our first result, and checking this result against the answer choices, we find that we can't answer the question yet. In particular, we don't know whether (C) has to be true. We have only determined that it **can** be true.

Next, note that Paul is not the only one who visits Montreal or Toronto, but not Vancouver. The third condition tells us that this is true of Lori as well. And from the discussion in *Figuring Out the Setup* we know that only two cities will be visited by any of the students. Vancouver is one of those cities, since we are supposing that Sharon visits Vancouver. We don't know whether the other city is Montreal or Toronto. But we do know that whichever it is, it has to be the city that both Paul and Lori visit, since neither of them visits Vancouver.

Checking this second result against the answer choices, we find that we are done. Our second result guarantees the truth of answer choice (D) ("Lori visits the same city as Paul"). There is an unbroken chain of inference that takes us from the specific supposition of the question to (D). There was no need to check the other answer choices. Nor was there any need to work out even a single complete acceptable outcome. The moral of the story is: use your time wisely.

> **Note.** A check of the incorrect answer choices, if one had been done, would have revealed a situation that is fairly typical in the case of questions about what must be true. Some of the answer choices—(B) and (C)—are things that can be true but don't have to be true, and some of them—(A) and (E)—are things that can't be true. Among the incorrect answer choices, you might encounter any combination of things that can't be true and things that can be true but don't have to be.

So what generally applicable strategies can be extracted from the way the question above was answered?

When approaching a question about what must be true under certain specified circumstances, the first thing to do is to see what inferences, if any, you can draw on the basis of the setup conditions and how they interact with the specified circumstances. Having drawn any immediately available inferences, check them against the answer choices. If, on the basis of those inferences, one of the answer choices has to be true, you're done. Remember that your objective is to select the correct answer and move on to the next question, not to prove that the incorrect answer choices are wrong.

If none of the immediately available inferences matches any of the answer choices, try to see what can be inferred from the inferences you've already made (in conjunction with the setup conditions). Check this second round of inferences against the answer choices. If any of these inferences match one of the answer choices, you're done. This is what happened in the example above. Keep doing this until you're done.

As you work through the rest of the questions, keep trying to draw further inferences. There is a complementary strategy to pursue as you go along: Look for any answer choices that you can eliminate on the basis of inferences you have already established by working on previous questions. Cross out any incorrect answer choices that you come across in this way.

When considering "what must be true," sometimes it is possible to rule out an incorrect answer choice by constructing an acceptable outcome in which that answer choice is not true. To see how this would work, consider the example above, which asks what must be true if Sharon visits Vancouver. Suppose you were trying to rule out (B) ("Lori visits Montreal") by constructing an acceptable outcome in which (B) is false. You'd start with the following partial diagram:

$$\underline{M} \qquad \underline{T} \qquad \underline{V}$$
$$\qquad \quad L \qquad \quad S$$

The starting point for the question is that Sharon visits Vancouver, so we represent this in the diagram. Now, to

have an outcome in which (B) is false, Lori has to visit either Toronto or Vancouver. But Lori visiting Vancouver is ruled out by the third condition, so if Lori doesn't visit Montreal, she must visit Toronto. Since we then have Lori visiting Toronto and Sharon visiting Vancouver, the city visited by none of the students must be Montreal. This is how we established the partial diagram above.

Continue by drawing further inferences from the conditions. From the first condition we can infer that Paul has to visit Toronto. We add Paul to the diagram as follows:

$$\underline{M} \qquad \underline{T} \qquad \underline{V}$$
$$\qquad \quad L, P \qquad S$$

From the second condition we know that Hubert and Regina have to visit the same city. But that city can't be Toronto, because that would mean that only one person would visit Vancouver, contrary to the fifth condition. So Hubert and Regina must visit Vancouver, along with Sharon. This gives us the following outcome:

$$\underline{M} \qquad \underline{T} \qquad \underline{V}$$
$$\qquad \quad L, P \qquad H, R, S$$

This is an outcome in which (B) is false but that satisfies all the setup conditions plus the specific circumstance introduced in the question. So (B) does not have to be true and can thus be eliminated.

■ What Must Be True on the Basis of the Setup Conditions Alone

Not all of the questions that ask about what must be true ask what must be true under particular circumstances specified in the question. Some questions ask about what must be true merely on the basis of the setup.

An example of a question that asks about what must be true on the basis of the setup alone is the following:

Which one of the following must be true for March?

A correct answer would be:

Hubert visits a different city than Lori.

This follows directly from the setup conditions. Hubert cannot visit the same city as Lori, because if he did, that city would receive visits from four of the students: Hubert, Regina (who, by the second condition, visits the same city as Hubert), Lori, and either Paul or Sharon (since only two cities get visited, and Paul and Sharon cannot visit the same city, on account of the first condition). But that would mean that only one student—either Paul or Sharon—would visit one of the cities, and the fifth condition would then be violated. So we know that Hubert must visit a different city than Lori.

Questions that ask about what must be true on the basis of the setup alone have an interesting property:

you can add the correct answer to what you have already inferred from the setup. Something that must be true on the basis of the setup alone is nothing but a logical consequence of how the setup conditions interact. Of course, before you use this result to help you answer other questions, you want to be very sure that the answer you selected is indeed the correct one.

Note that by contrast—and this is very important—suppositions that are introduced into individual questions, such as the supposition "if Sharon visits Vancouver" in the question discussed above, **never** carry over to any other questions. The correct answer to that question depended on the supposition, but in moving from one question to another, suppositions are not brought along. This is why it is possible for the suppositions in different questions to be inconsistent with each other.

> **Note.** In addition to questions about what must be true, you may encounter questions such as the following:
>
> *Which one of the following must be false?*
> *Which one of the following CANNOT be true?*
> *Each of the following could be true EXCEPT:*
>
> In all of these cases, the correct answer is something that is not true in even a single acceptable outcome. So among the incorrect answer choices you will find things that must be true as well as things that could be true.

■ Questions That Ask About What Could Be True

Many Analytical Reasoning questions ask about what could be true rather than about what must be true. Something that could be true is something that is true in at least one acceptable outcome, even if there are many acceptable outcomes in which it is false. This means that the incorrect answer choices are all things that **cannot** be true in any acceptable outcome.

As with questions about what must be true, some questions ask what could be true under certain specified circumstances and others ask what could be true on the basis of the setup alone.

■ What Could Be True Under Certain Specified Circumstances

Consider the following question:

If Regina visits Toronto, which one of the following could be true in March?

The five answer choices are:

(A) *Lori visits Toronto.*
(B) *Lori visits Vancouver.*
(C) *Paul visits Toronto.*
(D) *Paul visits Vancouver.*
(E) *Sharon visits Vancouver.*

How do you approach a question like this? A first step is to quickly check to see if any of the answer choices can be immediately ruled out as being in direct violation of one of the setup conditions. In this case, you would rule out (B) as directly violating the third condition, which requires that Lori visit either Montreal or Toronto. (There's no need to methodically go through each condition to see if any of the answer choices violate one of the conditions. That's a good strategy for orientation questions, but not usually for other questions. For non-orientation questions that ask for what can be true, just give the answer choices a quick look to see if any of them obviously violate something in the setup.)

Next, turn to the circumstance specified in the question—in this case, that Regina visits Toronto—and work from that. If Regina visits Toronto, Hubert also visits Toronto, as required by the second condition. Since by the first condition Sharon visits a different city than Paul, either Sharon or Paul will also visit Toronto, because only two cities are visited by any of the students. Toronto will thus be visited by three of the students.

So which city will be visited by just two students, Montreal or Vancouver? Since one of those two students must be Lori, it has to be Montreal; it cannot be Vancouver, because of the third condition. This means that none of the students visits Vancouver. So the answer choices specifying a visit to Vancouver (that is, (B), (D), and (E)) cannot be true. That leaves us with (A) and (C). But since we also know that Lori visits Montreal, we know that (A) cannot be true. So we know that (C) has to be the correct answer.

The approach above is to start with the setup conditions and then turn to the specific circumstance specified in the question and see what can be inferred from it in conjunction with the setup conditions. The emphasis here is not on what can be inferred to be the case, but on what **cannot** be the case, because the goal is to eliminate the incorrect answer choices and find the one that can be true. All of the incorrect answer choices must be false.

It is also possible to arrive at the correct answer by a different method. Assume that the answer choices, each in turn, are true. In four of the five cases, this assumption will lead you into a contradiction, thereby showing that the answer choice cannot be true.

Using this method to answer the question above, you would start by assuming that (A) is true. That is, you would assume that Lori visits Toronto. So Toronto would be visited by both Lori and Regina. By the second condition, if Regina visits Toronto, so does Hubert. That means that the other city visited would be visited by Paul and Sharon. But the first condition rules this out.

So under the circumstance specified by the question—that Regina visits Toronto—Lori cannot visit Toronto.

Next you assume that (B) is true—namely, that Lori visits Vancouver. But this is immediately ruled out by the third condition.

You then assume that (C) is true—that Paul visits Toronto. So Toronto would be visited by Paul, Regina (as specified in the question), and Hubert (as specified by the second condition). That leaves Sharon and Lori to visit Montreal. This outcome satisfies all of the setup conditions, and is thus acceptable. Thus you know that (C) could be true, and you're done.

■ What Could Be True on the Basis of the Setup Conditions Alone

An example of a question that asks about what could be true on the basis of the setup alone is the following:

Which one of the following could be true for March?

The answer choices are:

(A) *Hubert and Lori both visit Toronto.*
(B) *Paul and Sharon both visit Vancouver.*
(C) *Regina and Sharon both visit Montreal.*
(D) *Hubert visits Toronto and Paul visits Vancouver.*
(E) *Regina visits Montreal and Sharon visits Vancouver.*

The first step, as usual, is to check if any of the answer choices can be immediately ruled out as being in direct violation of one of the setup conditions. In this case, (B) can be eliminated on those grounds, because it is in direct violation of the first condition. In addition, (D) can be eliminated as being in violation of the fourth condition.

That leaves us with (A), (C), and (E). You will have to evaluate these three answer choices one by one to see which one cannot be eliminated.

So assume that (A) is true. If Hubert and Lori both visit Toronto, then by the second condition Regina must visit Toronto as well. That leaves Paul and Sharon to visit a city together, which is ruled out by the first condition. So (A) cannot be true.

Assume, then, that (C) is true. If Regina and Sharon both visit Montreal, then by the second condition Hubert must visit Montreal as well. That leaves Paul and Lori to visit a city together, and nothing prevents them from visiting Toronto. This outcome satisfies all of the setup conditions, and is thus acceptable. Thus you know that (C) could be true, and you're done. There is no need to evaluate (E).

> **Note.** In addition to questions about what could be true, you may encounter questions such as the following:
>
> *Which one of the following could be false?*
> *Each of the following must be true EXCEPT:*
>
> In both of these cases, the correct answer is something that is not true in at least one acceptable outcome. Thus, all of the incorrect answer choices will be things that must be true.
>
> You might also encounter a question that asks:
>
> *Which one of the following could be, but need not be, true?*
>
> In these cases, the correct answer is something that is true in at least one acceptable outcome but which is also false in at least one acceptable outcome. Both things that must be true and things that **cannot** be true are incorrect answer choices for this sort of question.

Conditional Statements

Often one or more of the setup conditions is in the form of a conditional statement. Conditional statements say that if something is the case, then something else is the case. For example, "If Theo is on the committee, then Vera is also on the committee." To work efficiently and effectively with Analytical Reasoning questions it is important to have a clear understanding of how to reason correctly with conditional statements and to know what errors to avoid.

> **Cross-reference:** The topic of conditional statements is discussed from a slightly different perspective in the section on "Necessary Conditions and Sufficient Conditions" in the Guide to Logical Reasoning Questions, pages 24–25.

Conditional relationships ("conditionals") can be expressed in a variety of ways. The following are all equivalent ways of stating the same conditional:

(1) *If Theo is on the committee, then Vera is also on the committee.*
(2) *If Vera is not on the committee, then Theo is not on the committee.*
(3) *Theo is not on the committee if Vera is not on the committee.*
(4) *Theo is not on the committee unless Vera is on the committee.*
(5) *Theo is on the committee only if Vera is on the committee.*

All of these, despite the differences in their formulation, express exactly the same conditional relationship between Theo's being on the committee and Vera's being on the committee. What they all tell you is that Theo's being on the committee guarantees that Vera is on the committee. But none of them tells you that Vera's being on the committee guarantees that Theo is on the committee.

> **Note.** The fact that all of the formulations displayed above are logically equivalent is not intuitively obvious. For most people, there is a marked difference in focus between some of these. For example, (1) seems to invite getting the facts about Theo straight first and if it turns out that Theo is on the committee, this tells you something about Vera. By contrast, (4) seems to invite finding out whether Vera is on the committee and if it turns out that she is not, this tells you that Theo is not on the committee either. Looking at things this way, it is easy to miss the underlying equivalence. But familiarity with, and automatic reliance on, this equivalence is crucial for dealing effectively with many Analytical Reasoning questions. So time that you spend now becoming thoroughly familiar with these equivalences is time well spent. Come test day, you'll be able to handle conditionals no matter how they're worded.

How does a conditional—regardless of how it happens to be formulated—work in drawing inferences? What are the kinds of additional information that, taken in conjunction with a conditional, yield proper inferences? Let's look at an example. Take the conditional "If Theo is on the committee, then Vera is on the committee." There are basically four cases to consider: 1. Theo is on the committee; 2. Theo is not on the committee; 3. Vera is on the committee; and 4. Vera is not on the committee. Each of these cases is discussed in turn below:

1. **Theo is on the committee**. If this is true, then given the conditional (in any of its formulations), it's guaranteed that Vera is also on the committee. The conditional says as much. This case is straightforward.

2. **Theo is not on the committee**. If this is true, you cannot use the conditional (regardless of how it is formulated) to derive any legitimate inferences about Vera. In particular, you **cannot** conclude that Vera is not on the committee. As far as the conditional goes, Theo's not being on the committee is consistent both with Vera's being on the committee and with her not being there. The conditional is simply silent about whether or not Vera is on the committee.

3. **Vera is on the committee**. If this is true, you cannot use the conditional (regardless of how it is formulated) to derive any legitimate inferences about Theo. In particular, you **cannot** conclude that Theo is also on the committee.

In fact, we have just made this point in the discussion of point 2 above. As we said there, Theo's not being on the committee is consistent with Vera's being on the committee. In the same way, Vera's being on the committee is consistent with Theo's not being on the committee.

4. **Vera is not on the committee**. If this is true, you can use the conditional (in any of its formulations) to derive a legitimate inference about Theo. You can infer that Theo is not on the committee either. This is because if Theo were on the committee without Vera also being on the committee, then the conditional, "If Theo is on the committee, Vera must also be on the committee," would be violated. So, to sum this up, if Vera is not on the committee, the only way not to violate the conditional is for Theo not to be on the committee either.

> **Note.** Sometimes Analytical Reasoning questions call for inferences involving more than one conditional. Suppose you're given two conditionals like the following:
>
> *If Theo in on the committee, Vera is on the committee.*
>
> *If Vera is on the committee, Ralph is on the committee.*
>
> From these you can legitimately infer
>
> *If Theo is on the committee, Ralph is on the committee.*
>
> and
>
> *If Ralph is not on the committee, Theo is not on the committee.*
>
> Note that these inferences can be derived no matter how the conditionals on which they are based are formulated. So for example, from these versions:
>
> *If Vera is not on the committee, then Theo is not on the committee.*
>
> *Unless Ralph is on the committee, Vera is not on the committee.*
>
> you can make the same two inferences as above:
>
> *If Theo is on the committee, Ralph is on the committee.*
>
> and
>
> *If Ralph is not on the committee, Theo is not on the committee.*

Wordings Used in Analytical Reasoning Questions

In Analytical Reasoning questions, the language used in presenting the setup and asking the questions must be precise and unambiguous. As a result, many things are spelled out at greater length and in more detail than they would be in most other kinds of writing. For example, in a setup that talks about a group of people who will give presentations at a meeting, it will probably be stated explicitly that each person makes only one presentation and that the people give their presentations one after another. Here are some other examples:

- **at some time before/immediately before**

These expressions typically occur in place of "before" alone. This is because if you were simply told that "Smith's presentation comes before Jeng's presentation," it might be unclear whether someone else's presentation could occur between them. And so it might not be clear whether some outcome is acceptable or not. The use of phrases like "immediately before" is intended to avoid such ambiguity.

If you're told, "Smith's presentation comes **immediately before** Jeng's presentation," you know that no other presentation can occur between those two. On the other hand, if you're told, "Smith's presentation comes **at some time before** Jeng's presentation," you know that another presentation can, but doesn't have to, occur between those two. If another presentation had to occur between Smith's and Jeng's presentations, this would have to be said explicitly.

Similarly, you may be told that Smith's office is on "a higher floor" than Jeng's office (which allows for the possibility that the two offices are on adjacent floors and for the possibility that they are on nonadjacent floors), or you may be told that Smith's office is on the floor "immediately above" Jeng's office (which ensures that there are no other floors between the ones on which Smith's office and Jeng's office are located).

Or you might be told that within a row of offices, Smith's office is "the office" between Jeng's office and Robertson's office. This would tell you something different than if you were told that Smith's office is "an office" between Jeng's office and Robertson's office. In the first case, the use of the definite article "the" indicates that there is only one office between Jeng's and Robertson's offices, namely, Smith's office. In the second case, however, it is left open whether there are any offices in addition to Smith's office between those of Jeng and Robertson.

- **at least/at most/exactly**

There are times when simply being told that there must be three people on a certain committee would leave you uncertain whether this means that there can be more than three people on the committee or that there must be exactly three people on the committee. This kind of uncertainty is avoided by using precise language to talk about numbers. If the point is that three is the minimum number of committee members, you would typically be told that there must be **at least** three people on the committee. If three is the maximum number of committee members, then typically you would be told that there are **at most** three people on the committee. Otherwise, you would typically be told that there are **exactly** three people on the committee.

- **respectively/not necessarily in that order**

If you were asked to evaluate whether the statement "If Y is performed first, the songs performed second, third, and fourth could be T, X, and O," you might wonder what is meant. Does this mean (1) T, X, and O in some order or other, or does it mean (2) T second, X third, and O fourth? In Analytical Reasoning questions this potential uncertainty is avoided by saying, "If Y is performed first, the songs performed second, third, and fourth could be T, X, and O, **not necessarily in that order**," if (1) is what is meant. And by saying, "If Y is performed first, the songs performed second, third, and fourth, **respectively**, could be T, X, and O," if (2) is what is meant.

More Points to Consider

Here are several points to keep in mind. Some have been mentioned earlier and some are additional notes and tips.

- Always keep in mind that your objective is to select the correct answer, not to produce a comprehensive account of all of the logical possibilities available under the circumstances specified in the question. Arriving at the correct answer almost never requires working out all of the possible outcomes.

- As you draw inferences on the basis of how the question-specific circumstances interact with the setup conditions, keep checking the answer choices. At any

point, you might be able to identify the correct answer. Or you might be able to eliminate some answer choices as incorrect. If you have succeeded in identifying the correct answer, you are done even if there are still further inferences you could draw or if there are some answer choices that you have not yet been able to eliminate. There is no need for you to prove that those answer choices are incorrect. By the same token, if you have succeeded in eliminating all but one answer choice, you are done even if you have not independently shown that the remaining answer choice is correct.

- Remember that when dealing with Analytical Reasoning questions, anything is acceptable that is not prohibited by the setup conditions or by what is implied by the setup conditions along with any circumstances specified in the question. Do not make any unwarranted assumptions, however natural they might seem. For example, if you are told that a committee must include an expert on finance and an expert on marketing, do not take it for granted that the committee's expert on finance must be a different person from the committee's expert on marketing.

- In Analytical Reasoning questions, careful and literal reading is of critical importance. Even though time management is important, it is even more important not to read too quickly. To give a specific example of the kind of problem that can arise, consider the following two statements: "F and G cannot both go on vacation during July" and "Neither F nor G can go on vacation during July." There are a number of superficial resemblances between them. However, the two are not equivalent, and mistaking one for the other would almost certainly lead to errors. If F goes on vacation in July and G does not, the first condition is not violated, but the second one is.

- Recall the earlier discussion of active elements in the setup that aren't mentioned in any of the conditions. It isn't necessary for *all* of the individual elements to be explicitly constrained by the setup conditions. If a particular element is not explicitly mentioned in the conditions, this means that the element is constrained only by what happens with the other elements. It does not mean that the set of setup conditions is incomplete or otherwise defective.

- Suppose you are asked a question like, "Which one of the following must be advertised during week 2," based on a setup involving seven products to be advertised during a four-week period. Suppose fur-

ther that you determine that product H must be advertised during week 2, but that H does not appear among the answer choices. Does this mean that the question is defective? No. In this case it could be that G is also a product that must be advertised during week 2, and G is one of the answer choices. Keep in mind that there can only be one correct answer among the answer choices, but there can be more than one correct answer to the question.

- There are occasionally questions that ask about acceptable outcomes but only present partial outcomes in the answer choices. For example, the setup might be concerned with dividing a group of people into subgroups 1 and 2. The question might ask which one of the answer choices is an acceptable subgroup 1. In a case like this, if you look for violations of setup conditions only within the group that actually appears in the answer choices, you might find more than one that seems acceptable. But remember that what has to be acceptable is an outcome as a whole—the composition of **both** subgroup 1 and subgroup 2. So, even though subgroup 2 is not displayed in any of the answer choices, you still need to check it for violations of the setup conditions. That is, you would need to work out the outcome for subgroup 2 for those answer choices that you cannot otherwise eliminate as incorrect.

Recall the earlier discussion of what must be true on the basis of the setup conditions alone. It is extremely important that you keep in mind the point made there—that circumstances specified in an individual question hold for that question only. Very occasionally, a question will direct you to suppose that one of the original setup conditions were replaced with a different one. Such changes to the setup conditions also apply **only** to the question in which they are described, and never carry over to any other questions.

What Is an Argument?

Most Logical Reasoning questions focus on arguments, which are sets of statements that present evidence and draw a conclusion on the basis of that evidence. These arguments are generally short and self-contained.

Consider this basic example:

Sarah is well-qualified, and the hiring committee is very familiar with her work. Therefore, she will probably receive a job offer.

This is a simple argument. Two pieces of evidence are presented. These are the **premises** of the argument. These premises are offered in support of the view that Sarah will probably receive a job offer. This is the **conclusion** of the argument.

Let's look at a second case:

Computer Whiz *is a well-respected magazine with a large readership, so its product endorsements carry a lot of weight in the computer electronics marketplace. The X2000 display monitor was recently endorsed by* Computer Whiz. *It is therefore likely that sales of the X2000 monitor will increase dramatically.*

In this argument, information about the magazine's reputation and large readership serves as a basis for reaching an **intermediate, or subsidiary, conclusion**: that its endorsements are very influential in the marketplace. This intermediate conclusion in conjunction with a premise that reports that the X2000 was recently endorsed by the magazine provides the grounds for the prediction of an increase in sales. This prediction is the **main, or overall, conclusion** of the argument.

■ Identifying the Parts of an Argument

An argument can be analyzed by identifying its various parts and the roles that those parts play. The most basic parts of an argument are premises and conclusions. As we have already seen, an argument may have one or more intermediate conclusions in addition to its overall conclusion.

Premises come in a variety of forms. Some premises are specific matters of fact, some are definitions, and others are broad principles or generalizations. What all premises have in common is that they are put forward as true without support. That is, there is no attempt within the argument to prove or justify them. In contrast, a conclusion is **not** simply asserted. A conclusion is presented as being justified by certain premises. Thus, the conclusion of an argument is open to the challenge that it is not adequately supported by the premises. (Premises, of course, can also be challenged, on grounds such as factual accuracy, but such challenges are not matters of logic.)

One thing to remember about premises and conclusions is that they can come in any order. Premises are presented in support of a conclusion, but this does not mean that premises always precede the conclusion. A conclusion may be at the beginning, middle, or end of an argument. Consider the following examples:

Dolores is far more skillful than Victor is at securing the kind of financial support the Volunteers for Literacy Program needs, and Dolores does not have Victor's propensity for alienating the program's most dedicated volunteers. Therefore, the Volunteers for Literacy Program would benefit if Dolores took Victor's place as director.

Dolores is far more skillful than Victor is at securing the kind of financial support the Volunteers for Literacy Program needs. Therefore, the program would benefit if Dolores took Victor's place as director, especially since Dolores does not have Victor's propensity for alienating the program's most dedicated volunteers.

The Volunteers for Literacy Program would benefit if Dolores takes Victor's place as director, since Dolores is far more skillful than Victor is at securing the kind of financial support the program needs and Dolores does not have Victor's propensity for alienating the program's most dedicated volunteers. [September 1995 LSAT, section 2, question 19]

These three examples all present the same argument. In each example, the conclusion is that the Volunteers for Literacy Program would benefit if Dolores took Victor's place as director, and this conclusion is supported by the same two premises. But each example expresses the argument in a different way, with the conclusion appearing in the final, middle, and initial position, respectively. It is important, then, to focus on the role each statement plays in the argument as a whole. Position within the argument simply doesn't matter.

Another thing to keep in mind is the presence of indicator words that mark the roles that statements play in arguments. For example, "therefore" often precedes a conclusion; it is a common conclusion indicator. So are "thus," "hence," "consequently," "it follows that," "it can be concluded that," and various others. Similarly, premises are often preceded by indicator words, the most typical being "since" and "because." However, do not rely uncritically on these indicator words. They can be misleading, especially in the case of complex arguments, which might contain one or more subarguments. There is no completely mechanical way of identifying the roles that various statements play within an argument.

It is worth noting that people, in making arguments, often do not confine themselves to presenting just the conclusion and the statements that support it. Likewise, the short arguments in Logical Reasoning questions often include statements that are neither premises nor conclusions. This includes statements that indicate the motivation for making the argument, statements that convey background information, and statements that identify the position the argument comes out against. So don't assume that everything that is not part of the argument's conclusion must be functioning as support for that conclusion.

■ How the Argument Goes

Once you have identified the premises and the conclusion, the next step is to get clear about exactly how the argument is meant to go; that is, how the grounds offered for the conclusion are actually supposed to bear on the conclusion. Understanding how an argument goes is a crucial step in answering many questions that appear on the LSAT. This includes questions that ask you to identify a reasoning technique used within an argument, questions that require you to match the pattern of reasoning used in two separate arguments, and of a variety of other question types.

Determining how an argument goes involves discerning how the premises are supposed to support the overall conclusion. Consider, for example, the argument presented earlier about the Volunteers for Literacy Program, which concludes that the program would benefit if Dolores took Victor's place as director. Two considerations in support of this conclusion are offered: one asserting Dolores's superiority in securing financial support and the other charging that Victor is more prone to alienating dedicated volunteers. These two considerations are both relevant to the conclusion since, all other things being equal, a program benefits from having a director who is both better at fund-raising and less likely to alienate volunteers. Each of these considerations provides some support for the conclusion, and the support provided by one is completely independent of the support provided by the other.

In other arguments, the way in which premises support a conclusion can be much more complex. Consider this example:

The years 1917, 1937, 1956, 1968, 1979, and 1990 are all notable for the occurrence of both popular uprisings and near-maximum sunspot activity. During heavy sunspot activity, there is a sharp rise in positively charged ions in the air people breathe, and positively charged ions are known to make people anxious and irritable. Therefore, it is likely that sunspot activity has actually been a factor in triggering popular uprisings.[2]

The conclusion of this argument, signaled by "Therefore," is that it is likely that sunspot activity has been a factor in triggering popular uprisings. There are three premises. The first tells us about specific years in which both heavy sunspot activity and popular uprisings occurred. The other two are generalizations: that there is a sharp rise

in positively charged ions in the air during heavy sunspot activity, and that positively charged ions make people anxious and irritable.

So how does this argument go? The first premise provides some direct support for the conclusion, but this support is very weak, circumstantial evidence. The second and third premises do not support the conclusion directly, but only in conjunction with each other. If these two premises are true, they work together to establish that sunspots are a causal factor in increased irritability. Notice that there is still no link between sunspots and popular uprisings. There is some plausibility, however, to the idea that increased irritability makes popular uprisings more likely, and the argument tacitly assumes that this is in fact so.

If we make this assumption then, we can see the connection between sunspot activity and popular uprisings. This greatly enhances the evidence that the first premise provides.

> **Cross-reference:** You can learn more about the role of assumptions in arguments in the discussion starting on pages 28–31.

■ Questions About How the Argument Goes

Your test may include questions that ask you about how an argument proceeds overall, or about the logical role played by a particular part of an argument, or about the logical move one participant in a dialogue makes in responding to the other. Understanding how the relevant argument goes puts you in a position to answer these questions. Three examples are briefly discussed below.

Example 1

Red squirrels are known to make holes in the bark of sugar maple trees and to consume the trees' sap. Since sugar maple sap is essentially water with a small concentration of sugar, the squirrels almost certainly are after either water or sugar. Water is easily available from other sources in places where maple trees grow, so the squirrels would not go to the trouble of chewing holes in trees just to get water. Therefore, they are probably after the sugar.[3]

The question based on this argument is simply:

The argument proceeds by

---

[2]   February 1995 LSAT, section 4, question 8.

[3]   June 2002 LSAT, section 4, question 10.

The conclusion of this argument is quite easy to identify: red squirrels, in making holes in the bark of sugar maple trees, are probably after the sugar contained in the trees' sap. The argument arrives at this conclusion by first noting that since maple tree sap is essentially just water and sugar, the squirrels must be after either the one or the other. The argument goes on to reject the idea that it is the water that the squirrels are after, on the grounds that water is readily available for less effort where maple trees grow.

Once you have figured out how the argument goes, you're ready to check the answer choices to find the best characterization of the argument's reasoning. In this particular case, the best characterization is:

> *rejecting a possible alternative explanation for an observed phenomenon*

This is not the only way to describe how the argument proceeds, and it may not be the description you would have given. But it is an accurate characterization and is thus the correct answer. So keep in mind when checking the answer choices that the correct answer may be just one of several acceptable ways of putting things.

Example 2

> *In order to determine automobile insurance premiums for a driver, insurance companies calculate various risk factors; as the risk factors increase, so does the premium. Certain factors, such as the driver's age and past accident history, play an important role in these calculations. Yet these premiums should also increase with the frequency with which a person drives. After all, a person's chance of being involved in a mishap increases in proportion to the number of times that person drives.*[4]

The question based on this argument is:

> *The claim that insurance premiums should increase as the frequency with which a driver drives increases plays which one of the following roles in the argument?*

The first step in determining how this argument goes is identifying the conclusion. To do this, find the position for which the argument offers support.

The short phrase "after all" at the beginning of the fourth sentence indicates that the statement that follows functions as a premise. This premise essentially says that the frequency with which a person drives is a factor in their risk of being involved in a traffic accident. We know from the first sentence that risk factors matter in

determining a driver's automobile insurance premiums: as certain risk factors increase, the premium increases. Putting all of this together, we see that the argument is constructed to support the position stated in the third sentence: "…these premiums should also increase with the frequency with which the person drives."

So the claim that insurance premiums should increase as the frequency with which a driver drives increases is the conclusion of the argument. That is its role in the argument. The answer choice that expresses this, in some way or other, is the correct one.

Example 3

> *Zachary: The term "fresco" refers to paint that has been applied to wet plaster. Once dried, a fresco indelibly preserves the paint that a painter has applied in this way. Unfortunately, additions known to have been made by later painters have obscured the original fresco work done by Michelangelo in the Sistine Chapel. Therefore, in order to restore Michelangelo's Sistine Chapel paintings to the appearance that Michelangelo intended them to have, everything except the original fresco work must be stripped away.*

> *Stephen: But it was extremely common for painters of Michelangelo's era to add painted details to their own fresco work after the frescos has dried.*[5]

The corresponding question is:

Stephen's response to Zachary proceeds by

Zachary tells us that Michelangelo's frescoes in the Sistine Chapel had additions made to them by later painters. On the basis of this he argues that everything except Michelangelo's original fresco work has to be stripped away if the paintings are to have the appearance Michelangelo intended them to have.

Stephen's response makes clear that for painters of Michelangelo's era, the frescoes as originally executed did not necessarily have the appearance that those painters intended them to have. So Stephen's response points to and casts doubt on an assumption of Zachary's argument. This assumption is that Michelangelo did not make additions to his own fresco work in order to give the paintings the appearance that he wanted them to have.

Turning to the answer choices, you find this statement among them:

> *calling into question an assumption on which Zachary's conclusion depends*

---

[4] October 2002 LSAT, section 1, question 18.
[5] October 2001 LSAT, section 4, question 25.

This statement correctly characterizes how Stephen's response to Zachary proceeds.

A Point to Consider

■ Arguments vary widely in their strength, that is, in the extent to which their conclusions are justified by their premises. In the extreme case—the case of a "deductively valid" (i.e., conclusive) argument—the truth of the conclusion is completely guaranteed by the truth of the premises. In other words, anyone who accepts those premises is thereby committed to accepting the conclusion. In most cases, however, the relationship of the premises to the conclusion is less strict: the premises provide some grounds for accepting the conclusion, but these grounds are not airtight. In other words, someone might accept all of the premises of such an argument yet still be logically justified in not accepting its conclusion.

■ Identifying the Main Conclusion of an Argument

Some questions present you with an argument and ask you to identify its main conclusion. In questions of this kind, the conclusion is actually drawn in the argument, but it is often stated somewhat indirectly and it is sometimes not signaled by any of the standard conclusion—indicator words such as "therefore" or "thus." To identify the conclusion, therefore, you also need to look at what the statements in the argument mean, and how they are related to each other. Look for a position that the argument as a whole is trying to establish, and rule out any statements that, either directly or indirectly, give reasons for that position. You should also eliminate statements that merely establish a context or supply background information.

An Example

Journalist: Obviously, though some animals are purely carnivorous, none would survive without plants. But the dependence is mutual. Many plant species would never have come to be had there been no animals to pollinate, fertilize, and broadcast their seeds. Also, plants' photosynthetic activity would deplete the carbon dioxide in Earth's atmosphere were it not constantly being replenished by the exhalation of animals, engine fumes, and smoke from fires, many set by human beings.[6]

The question asks:

Which one of the following most accurately expresses the main conclusion of the journalist's argument?

So, how do you tackle this question? First, read the argument through. You might immediately recognize that the argument is of a familiar sort. The argument is directed toward a position that has two sides to it: a very straightforward one that is simply asserted and a less obvious one that the argument goes to some trouble to establish. The first sentence presents the straightforward side of the position being argued for. The second sentence states the entire position. The third and fourth sentences make the case for the less obvious side of the position.

Suppose that after reading the argument you are not sure exactly how it goes. What do you do then? It might be helpful to go through the argument statement by statement and ask about each statement in turn, "Does this statement receive support from some other statement?" If so, the statement is either a subsidiary conclusion drawn to support the main conclusion or it is itself the main conclusion. If the statement does not receive support from anything else in the argument, ask whether it provides support for some other statement. If it does, it's a premise of the argument, and whatever statement it provides support for is either the main conclusion or a subsidiary conclusion.

In the journalist's argument, the first statement does not receive support from anything else that is said in the argument. It does, however, provide support for the second statement by establishing one side of the dependence that the second statement refers to. So the second statement is a candidate for being the main conclusion of the argument. If you go on to analyze the third and fourth statements, you'll find that neither receives any support from anything else in the argument and that each independently supports the second statement by establishing the other side of the mutual dependence. Since everything else in the argument goes toward supporting the second statement, it is clear that the second statement expresses the main conclusion of the argument.

The second statement states the main conclusion in a somewhat abbreviated way in that it doesn't spell out what is meant by "dependence." But having worked through the argument, we can recognize that the following is an accurate statement of the conclusion:

Just as animals are dependent on plants for their survival, plants are dependent on animals for theirs.

The incorrect answer choices often restate a premise or part of a premise. For example, the following incorrect answer is a partial restatement of the fourth sentence of the journalist's argument:

---

[6] October 2002 LSAT, section 4, question 3.

Human activity is part of what prevents plants from depleting the oxygen in Earth's atmosphere on which plants and animals alike depend.

Other incorrect answer choices may state something that can be inferred from statements in the argument but that is not the argument's main conclusion. Here is an example of this, based on the journalist's argument:

The chemical composition of Earth and its atmosphere depends, at least to some extent, on the existence and activities of the animals that populate Earth.

Some Points to Consider

- If there is a "thus" or "therefore" in the argument, do not assume that these words introduce the main conclusion of the argument. They often indicate a subsidiary conclusion rather than the main conclusion.

- With questions that ask you to identify the main conclusion, it is generally possible to form a fairly precise idea of what the correct answer will be like before considering the answer choices. Doing so makes it possible to select the correct answer very efficiently. You should also try to get a precise idea of the main conclusion, because some of the incorrect answer choices may be only slightly inaccurate. For example, if the actual conclusion is that something is likely to be true, an incorrect answer choice may say that it is definitely true. This choice is incorrect because it goes beyond the actual conclusion.

■ Matching Patterns of Reasoning in Arguments

There is another kind of question that tests your ability to determine how an argument goes. It begins with an argument and then asks you to choose one argument from among the answer choices that is most similar in its reasoning to the initial (or reference) argument. The questions themselves are worded in a variety of ways, including:

The pattern of reasoning in which of the following arguments is most similar to that in the argument above?

Which one of the following arguments is most similar in its reasoning to the argument above?

You don't need to come up with a verbal description of the pattern of reasoning in order to answer these questions. All you need is a solid intuitive grasp of the logical

structure of the reference argument: what its conclusion is, and how the premises fit together to support the conclusion.

These questions are asking for a match in logical structure, that is, the way the premises fit together to support the conclusion. So do not pay any attention to similarity or dissimilarity in subject matter, or to background material that is not part of the premises or the conclusion. Nor should you concern yourself with anything about the particular way the argument is laid out, such as the order in which the premises and the conclusion are presented.

An Example

All known deposits of the mineral tanzanite are in Tanzania. Therefore, because Ashley collects only tanzanite stones, she is unlikely ever to collect a stone not originally from Tanzania.[7]

The question asks:

Which one of the following is most similar in its reasoning to the argument above?

So what is the structure of the reasoning in the reference argument? There are two premises, the one about tanzanite deposits and the one about Ashley's collecting habits. And there is a conclusion: Ashley is unlikely ever to collect a stone not originally from Tanzania. Note that the conclusion merely says that something is unlikely, not that it will definitely not happen. The conclusion is probably qualified in this way because the premise about tanzanite deposits speaks only about the known deposits of that mineral, thereby leaving open the possibility that there are undiscovered tanzanite deposits outside of Tanzania.

But also note that the argument is a fairly strong one. The premises give a reasonable basis for accepting the conclusion: if the premises are true, the only way in which Ashley would ever collect a stone that is not originally from Tanzania is if tanzanite is someday discovered outside of Tanzania or if she begins to collect some different type of stone in the future.

The next step is to check the answer choices and to find the one with the same pattern of reasoning.

So let's try this answer choice:

Frogs are the only animals known to live in the lagoon on Scrag Island. The diet of the owls on Scrag Island consists of nothing but frogs from the island. Therefore, the owls are unlikely ever to eat an animal that lives outside the lagoon.

---

[7] June 2002 LSAT, section 2, question 26.

Does this follow the same pattern of reasoning as the argument about tanzanite? The conclusion has the right shape: it says that something is unlikely ever to happen, just as the conclusion of the reference argument does. In addition, this argument, like the reference argument, has a premise that limits itself to speaking about what is known to be true, thereby leaving open the possibility of cases unlike those now known. Plus, the second premise is exclusionary in nature: where the reference argument uses "only," this argument says "nothing but." So there are a number of resemblances between important parts of the two arguments.

However, whereas the reference argument is fairly strong, this argument is seriously flawed. Notice that the two premises do not rule out the possibility there are frogs on Scrag Island that do not live in the lagoon. So there seems to be a strong possibility that the owls on Scrag Island eat frogs that aren't from the lagoon. The conclusion of this argument thus receives little or no support from the premises. If the reasoning in this argument were closely parallel to that in the reference argument, its premises would provide similarly strong support for its conclusion. So this answer choice cannot be correct.

Let's try another one of the answer choices:

The only frogs yet discovered on Scrag Island live in the lagoon. The diet of all the owls on Scrag Island consists entirely of frogs on the island, so the owls will probably never eat an animal that lives outside the lagoon.

Here, too, the conclusion has the right shape: it says that something is unlikely ever to happen. In addition, this argument has a premise that limits itself to speaking about what is known to be the case. Plus, the second premise is exclusionary in nature.

In this case, the premises provide support for the conclusion in just the same way that the premises in the reference argument do for the conclusion of that argument. This argument can be paraphrased in a way that is parallel to the reference argument: All known frogs on Scrag Island live in the lagoon. Scrag Island owls eat only frogs. It is therefore unlikely that an owl on Scrag Island will ever eat an animal that does not live in the lagoon. Thus, the pattern of reasoning in the two arguments is essentially the same.

What Can Be Concluded From the Information Provided

Many Logical Reasoning questions test your ability to determine what is supported by a body of available evidence. These questions ask you to pick one statement that can in some way or another be inferred from the available evidence. So, in effect, you are asked to distinguish between positions that are supported by the information that you have been given and positions that are not supported by that information. These questions come in a variety of forms.

■ Identifying a Position That Is Conclusively Established by Information Provided

Some questions test your ability to identify what follows logically from certain evidence or information. For these questions, you will be presented with information that provides **conclusive** support for one of the answer choices. Typical wordings for these questions include:

If the statements above are true, which one of the following must also be true?

Which one of the following logically follows from the statements above?

With these questions, you are looking for something that is **guaranteed** to be true by the information you have been given. That is, the correct answer will be a statement that **must** be true if the given information is true. Incorrect answer choices may receive some support from the information but that support will be inconclusive. In other words, an incorrect answer choice could be false even if the information provided is true.

An Example

Any sale item that is purchased can be returned for store credit but not for a refund of the purchase price. Every home appliance and every piece of gardening equipment is on sale along with selected construction tools.[8]

The question asks:

If the statements above are true, which one of the following must also be true?

Notice that the statements have a common element: they talk about sale items. This common element allows you to combine bits of information to draw conclusions. For example, since all home appliances are sale items, you could conclude that any home appliance that is purchased can be returned for store credit. Because several conclusions like this can be drawn from these statements, you cannot determine the correct answer without reading the answer choices. So you need to go through the answer choices to find one that must be true if the statements are true.

One choice reads:

No piece of gardening equipment is returnable for a refund.

We are told that every piece of gardening equipment is a sale item and sale items are **not** returnable for a refund. So it must be true that gardening equipment is not returnable for a refund. This is the correct answer choice.

For the sake of comparison, consider another answer choice:

Some construction tools are not returnable for store credit.

To rule out this answer choice, you need to see that it does not have to be true if the statements in the passage are true. It obviously doesn't have to be true for construction tools that are on sale—the statements guarantee that those construction tools are returnable for store credit. As for the rest of the construction tools, those that aren't on sale, nothing indicates that they are not returnable for store credit. Based on what the statements say, it is possible, and even likely, that these tools are returnable for store credit. The answer choice is therefore incorrect.

In this example, you were given a set of statements that do not seem to be designed to lead to any particular conclusion. It was up to you to determine the implications of those statements. In other cases, however, the information may appear to be designed to lead the reader to a specific unstated conclusion. In such cases, the correct answer could be the unstated conclusion, if it logically follows from the information provided, or it could be some other statement that logically follows from that information.

Some Points to Consider

- For some claim to logically follow from certain information, that information has to guarantee that the claim is true. It isn't enough for the information to strongly support the claim; it has to conclusively establish the claim.

- Incorrect answers to questions about what logically follows can be claims that receive some support from the information but that nevertheless **could** be false even though all of the information is correct.

- Answer choices are often incorrect because they take things one step beyond what the evidence supports. They might make claims that are too sweeping; for example, they might say "all" when the evidence supports only a "most" statement. Or where a statement about what "is likely to be" is warranted, an incorrect answer choice might say "is." Or where a statement about "all known cases" is warranted, an incorrect answer choice might say "all cases."

- Remember that a modest or limited claim can be a correct answer even if the information also supports a stronger claim. If the information supports drawing the conclusion that there will be a festival in every month, then it also supports the conclusion that there will be a festival in June.

■ Identifying a Position Supported by Information Provided

Some questions ask you to identify a position that is supported by a body of evidence, but not supported conclusively. These questions might be worded as follows:

Which one of the following is most strongly supported by the information above?

Which one of the following can most reasonably be concluded on the basis of the information above?

The statements above, if true, most strongly support which one of the following?

For these questions, you will generally not be presented with an argument, but merely with some pieces of information. Your task is to evaluate that information and distinguish between the answer choice that receives strong support from that information (the correct answer) and answer choices that receive no significant support (the incorrect answer choices).

An Example

Consider the following pieces of information:

People should avoid taking the antacid calcium carbonate in doses larger than half a gram, for despite its capacity to neutralize stomach acids, calcium carbonate can increase the calcium level in the blood and thus impair kidney function. Moreover, just half a gram of it can stimulate the production of gastrin, a stomach hormone that triggers acid secretion.[9]

You are asked,

Which one of the following is most strongly supported by the information above?

With questions of this kind you shouldn't expect the correct answer to follow in a strict logical sense from the information, but you should expect the information to provide a strong justification for the correct answer. When you begin work on a question of this sort, you should note any obvious interconnections among the facts given, but there is no point in formulating a precise prediction of what the correct answer will look like. A sensible approach is to read the passage carefully, and make a mental note of any implications that you spot. Then go on to consider each answer choice in turn and determine whether that answer choice gets any support from the information you have been given.

Let's follow this approach with the question above. Reading the passage, you find that a certain antacid is described as having the obvious intended effect of neutralizing stomach acid but as also having adverse side effects if the dosage is too high. One of these adverse effects results in impaired kidney function and other results in acid secretion in the stomach.

There is a suggestion in the passage that doses exceeding half a gram are necessary for the first effect to be triggered to any serious extent. The passage also suggests that doses of half a gram or more will trigger the second effect. No other implications of this passage stand out. At this point, it is probably a good idea to consider each answer choice in turn.

One answer choice is:

Doses of calcium carbonate smaller than half a gram can reduce stomach acid more effectively than much larger doses do.

Is this choice supported by the information? The passage does give reasons as to why this might be true. It tells us that doses of half a gram or more can stimulate the production of a stomach hormone that triggers acid secretion. This hormone might counteract any extra acid-neutralization that comes from additional calcium carbonate over and above a half-gram dose; but then again it might not. Perhaps the extra calcium carbonate neutralizes more stomach acid than it triggers. For this reason, this answer choice is not strongly supported by the information.

Another answer choice is:

Half a gram of calcium carbonate can causally contribute to both the secretion and the neutralization of stomach acids.

Is there support for this choice in the information provided? We have noted that at half a gram the secretion of acid in the stomach is triggered. The passage mentions the drug's "capacity to neutralize stomach acids," strongly suggesting that some acid-neutralizing effect occurs at any dosage level. So there is strong support in the passage for both parts of this answer choice.

Some Points to Consider

- In answering questions dealing with support for conclusions, base your judgment about whether or not a particular answer choice is supported strictly on the information that is explicitly provided in the passage. If the passage concerns a subject matter with which you are familiar, ignore any information you might have about the subject that goes beyond what you have been told.

- Keep in mind that the support for the correct answer does not have to involve all of the information provided. For instance, in the example about calcium carbonate, an adverse effect on the kidneys is mentioned, but this information plays no role in the support for the correct answer.

■ Identifying Points on Which Disputants Hold Conflicting Views

You may also encounter questions involving two speakers where the first speaker puts forward a position and the second responds to that position. You will then be asked something like:

The main point at issue between Sarah and Paul is whether

Which one of the following most accurately expresses the point at issue between Juan and Michiko?

On the basis of their statements, Winchell and Trent are committed to disagreeing over whether

An Example

Mary: Computers will make more information available to ordinary people than was ever available before, thus making it easier for them to acquire knowledge without consulting experts.

Joyce: As more knowledge became available in previous centuries, the need for specialists to synthesize and explain it to nonspecialists increased. So computers will probably create a greater dependency on experts.[10]

The question asks,

The dialogue most strongly supports the claim that Mary and Joyce disagree with each other about whether

In answering questions of this kind, you may find it useful to read the dialogue closely enough to form a clear mental picture of each person's stance and then go on to the answer choices.

Now consider this answer choice:

computers will make more information available to ordinary people

Does what Joyce and Mary say show that they disagree about this? Mary straightforwardly says that computers will make more information available to ordinary people. But what about Joyce? She predicts that computers will create a greater dependency on experts because of a historical trend of an increasing dependency on experts whenever more knowledge becomes available to ordinary people. So she seems to assume that computers will make more information become available to ordinary people. So she probably agrees with Mary on this point.

Now consider a second answer choice:

dependency on computers will increase with the increase of knowledge

Nothing either Mary or Joyce says commits either of them to a particular view on this position. This is because neither of them explicitly discusses the issue of people's dependency on computers. But there is certainly no indication at all that they hold opposing views on whether dependency on computers will increase with the increase of knowledge.

Finally, consider a third answer choice:

computers will increase the need for ordinary people seeking knowledge to turn to experts

Based on what she says, Mary straightforwardly disagrees with this claim. Computers, she says, will make it easier for ordinary people to acquire knowledge without consulting experts. Joyce, on the other hand, concludes that computers will create a greater dependency on experts. The precedent from past centuries that she cites in support of this conclusion makes it clear that nonspecialists—that is, ordinary people—will depend more on experts when knowledge increases. So Mary and Joyce disagree on whether the need for ordinary people to turn to experts will be increased by computers.

Some Points to Consider

- The evidence that two speakers disagree about a particular point always comes from what they explicitly say. Sometimes there is a direct conflict between something that one of the speakers says and something that the other speaker says. The phrasing of the question indicates that you should be looking for a direct conflict when it says something straightforward like "Max and Nina disagree over whether." At other times the point of disagreement must be inferred from the explicit positions that the speakers take. The phrasing of the question will indicate that this inference needs to be made. For example, a question like "The dialogue provides the most support for the claim that Nikisha and Helen disagree over whether" does not suggest that they disagree explicitly, only that there is some evidence that they disagree.

- Do not try to derive a speaker's likely position on a topic from a psychological stereotype. It may be true that a speaker who takes a certain position would be the kind of person who would likely hold certain other positions as well, but you should not rely on this sort of association. Rely only on what a speaker explicitly says and on what can be properly inferred from that.

- The incorrect answer choices are not necessarily positions that the two speakers can be shown to agree on. In many cases, the views of at least one of the speakers on a given position cannot be determined from what has been said.

---

[10] December 2001 LSAT, section 3, question 4.

Necessary Conditions and Sufficient Conditions

Suppose you read the following statements:

You don't deserve praise for something unless you did it deliberately.

Tom deliberately left the door unlocked.

Does it follow from these statements that Tom deserves praise for leaving the door unlocked? You can probably see that this doesn't follow. The first statement says that you have to do something deliberately in order to deserve praise for doing it. It doesn't say that any time you do something deliberately you thereby deserve praise for doing it. So the mere fact that Tom did something deliberately is not enough to bring us to the conclusion that Tom deserves praise for doing it.

To put it in a slightly more technical way, the first statement expresses a **necessary condition**. Doing something deliberately is a necessary condition for deserving praise for doing it. In Logical Reasoning questions, it can be very important to recognize whether something expresses a necessary condition or whether it expresses what is called a **sufficient condition**. If the first statement had said "If you do something deliberately then you deserve praise for doing it," it would be saying that doing something deliberately is a sufficient condition for deserving praise for doing it.

> **Cross-reference:** Reasoning involving necessary and sufficient conditions is also covered, from a slightly different perspective, in the discussion of "Conditional Statements" in the Analytical Reasoning section, pages 11–12.

In the example above, it is fairly easy to see that the first statement expresses a necessary condition and not a sufficient condition. This may be because it would be quite strange to say that doing something deliberately is a sufficient condition for deserving praise. That would imply that you deserve praise for anything you do deliberately, even if it is an immoral or criminal act. But the content of a statement doesn't always help you determine whether it expresses a necessary condition or a sufficient condition. For this reason, it pays to devote very close attention to the precise wording of any statements that express conditions. And it pays to have a clear idea in your mind about how statements that express necessary conditions function in arguments and about how statements that express sufficient conditions function in arguments.

There are many ways to express a necessary condition. The necessary condition above could have been stated just as accurately in several different ways, including:

You deserve praise for something only if you did it deliberately.

You don't deserve praise for something if you didn't do it deliberately.

To deserve praise for something, you must have done it deliberately.

If you think carefully about these statements, you should see that they all mean the same thing. And you can see that none of them says that doing something deliberately is a sufficient condition for deserving praise. Sufficient conditions can also be expressed in several different ways:

If it rains, the sidewalks get wet.

Rain is all it takes to get the sidewalks wet.

The sidewalks get wet whenever it rains.

These statements each tell us that rain is a sufficient condition for the sidewalks getting wet. It is sufficient, because rain is all that it takes to make the sidewalks wet. But notice that these statements do not say that rain is the only thing that makes the sidewalks wet. They do not rule out the possibility that the sidewalks can get wet from melting snow or from being sprayed with a garden hose. So these statements do not express necessary conditions for wet sidewalks, only sufficient conditions.

■ How Necessary Conditions Work in Inferences

We've already noted one thing about basing inferences on statements that express necessary conditions, such as

N: You deserve praise for something only if you did it deliberately.

If we are also given a case that satisfies the necessary condition, such as

Tom deliberately left the door unlocked

we cannot legitimately draw an inference. Specifically, the conclusion that Tom deserves praise for leaving the door unlocked does not follow.

Statements that express necessary conditions can play a part in legitimate inferences, of course, but only in combination with the right sort of information. Suppose that in addition to statement N we are told

Tom deserves praise for leaving the door unlocked.

This allows us to conclude that Tom deliberately left the door unlocked. Since statement N says that you have to do something deliberately in order to deserve praise for doing it, Tom must have deliberately left the door unlocked if he deserves praise for what he did.

Or, suppose that in addition to statement N we are told

Tom did not leave the door unlocked deliberately.

This allows us to conclude that Tom does not deserve praise for leaving the door unlocked. This follows because statement N insists that only deliberate actions deserve praise, and because we are told clearly that Tom's action is not deliberate.

So in general, when you have a statement that expresses a necessary condition, it allows you to infer something in just two cases: (1) you can infer from knowing that the necessary condition is **not** met that the thing it is the necessary condition for does **not** occur; (2) you can infer that the necessary condition is met from knowing that the thing it is the necessary condition for occurs.

■ How Sufficient Conditions Work in Inferences

Statements that express sufficient conditions can also serve as a basis for inferences. Let's revisit one of the earlier statements of a sufficient condition:

S: If it rains, the sidewalks get wet.

If we are told that the sufficient condition is satisfied (i.e., told that it is raining), then we can legitimately draw the inference that the sidewalks are getting wet. This should be quite obvious.

We can also draw another conclusion from a statement of a sufficient condition, provided that we have the right sort of additional information. Suppose that in addition to statement S we are told that the sidewalks did not get wet. Since the sidewalks get wet whenever it rains, we can conclude with complete confidence that it didn't rain.

So in general, when you have a statement that expresses a sufficient condition, it allows you to infer something in just two cases: (1) if you know that the sufficient condition is met, then you can infer that the thing it is the sufficient condition for occurs; (2) you can infer that the sufficient condition is **not** met from knowing that the thing it is the sufficient condition for does **not** occur.

Though it may sometimes seem that there are other ways to draw an inference from a statement of a sufficient condition, there are none. Suppose that in addition to statement S, we are told that the sidewalks are wet. Can we legitimately conclude that it rained? No, because statement S does not rule out the possibility that something other than rain, such as melting snow, can make the sidewalks wet. Or suppose that in addition to statement S, we are told that it didn't rain. Can we legitimately conclude that the sidewalks did not get wet? Again no, and for the same reason: statement S does not rule out the possibility that something other than rain can make the sidewalks wet.

Understanding the Impact of Additional Information

The LSAT typically includes several questions that test your ability to see how additional facts bear on an argument. These questions may focus on facts that strengthen an argument, they may focus on facts that weaken the argument, or they may merely ask what additional information, if it were available, would be useful in evaluating the strength of the argument. Typical wordings of such questions are:

Which one of the following, if true, most strengthens the argument?

Which one of the following, if true, most weakens the argument?

In order to evaluate the argument, which one of the following would it be most useful to determine?

Tip: When the qualifier "if true" appears in this kind of question, it tells you not to be concerned about the actual truth of the answer choices. Instead, you should consider each answer choice as though it were true. Also, consider each answer choice independently of the others, since it is not necessarily the case that the answer choices can all be true together.

Questions of this kind are based on arguments that—like most real-life arguments—have premises that provide some grounds for accepting the conclusion, but that fall short of being decisive arguments in favor of the conclusion. For an argument like this, it is possible for additional evidence to make the argument stronger or weaker. For example, consider the following argument:

A survey of oil-refinery workers who work with MBTE, an ingredient currently used in some smog-reducing gasolines, found an alarming incidence of complaints about headaches, fatigue, and shortness of breath. Since gasoline containing MBTE will soon be widely used, we can expect an increased incidence of headaches, fatigue, and shortness of breath.[11]

The incidence of complaints about headaches, fatigue, and shortness of breath among oil-refinery employees who work with MBTE is, on the face of it, evidence for the conclusion that widespread use of gasoline containing MBTE will make headaches, fatigue, and shortness of breath more common. However, additional information could, depending on what this information is, make the argument stronger or weaker.

For example, suppose it is true that most oil-refinery workers who do not work with MBTE also have a very high incidence of headaches, fatigue, and shortness of breath. This would provide evidence that it is not MBTE but some other factor that is primarily responsible for these symptoms. But if we have evidence that something other than MBTE is causing these symptoms, then the argument provides only very weak support, if any, for its conclusion. That is, the argument's original premises, when combined with the additional information, make a much weaker case for the argument's conclusion than those premises did alone. In other words, the new information has made the argument weaker.

Of course, different additional evidence would make the argument stronger. For example, suppose that gasoline containing MBTE has already been introduced in a few metropolitan areas, and since it was first introduced, those areas have reported increased complaints about headaches, fatigue, and shortness of breath. This would provide evidence that when MBTE is used as a gasoline additive, it increases the incidence of these symptoms not just among refinery workers who work closely with it but also among the general public. So we now have evidence that is more directly relevant to the argument's conclusion. Thus, we now have a stronger case for the argument's conclusion; in other words, the new evidence has made the argument stronger.

We have seen that when new information makes an argument stronger, that information, together with the argument's original premises, makes a stronger case for the argument's conclusion than do the original premises alone. There are several ways in which this could work. The additional information could eliminate an obvious weak spot in the original argument. Alternatively, there may be no obvious weak spot in the original argument; the case for the argument may simply become even stronger with the addition of the new evidence. In some cases, the additional information will be something that helps establish the argument's conclusion but only when combined with the argument's existing premises. In other cases, the new information will provide a different line of reasoning in addition to that provided by the original premises. The information that strengthens the argument about MBTE is an example of something that provides a different line of reasoning for the conclusion. In still other cases, the additional information will strengthen the argument by ruling out something that would have weakened the argument. And of course, additional information may weaken an argument in corresponding ways.

An Example

Consider this argument:

A recent study reveals that television advertising does not significantly affect children's preferences for breakfast cereals. The study compared two groups of children. One group had watched no television, and the other group had watched average amounts of television and its advertising. Both groups strongly preferred the sugary cereals heavily advertised on television.[12]

The conclusion of the argument is that television advertising does not significantly affect children's preferences for breakfast cereals. As evidence for this conclusion, the argument presents the results of a study comparing two groups of children: the study found that children in both groups—those who watched no television and those who watched average amounts of television and its advertising—strongly preferred the sugary cereals heavily advertised on television. On the face of it, the study results do seem to provide some support, although not conclusive support, for the argument's conclusion; if television advertising did significantly affect children's preferences, then we'd expect the children who watched television to have different preferences than the children who didn't watch television.

Here is the question:

Which one of the following statements, if true, most weakens the argument?

Let's consider an answer choice:

Most of the children in the group that had watched television were already familiar with the advertisements for these cereals.

Does this information weaken the argument? It suggests that even if the television advertising influenced the preferences of the children who watched television, this influence occurred some time ago. But this does not really imply anything about whether the advertising did influence the children's preferences. So the information provided by this answer choice neither strengthens nor weakens the argument.

Let's consider another answer choice:

> *Both groups rejected cereals low in sugar even when these cereals were heavily advertised on television.*

This information may well be relevant to the argument's conclusion since it suggests that if a cereal is unappealing to children, then even a great deal of television advertising will not change the children's preferences. But this would provide additional evidence **in favor of** the argument's conclusion that television advertising does not significantly affect children's cereal preferences. So this answer choice strengthens the argument rather than weakens it.

> **Tip:** In questions that ask what weakens an argument, often one or more incorrect answer choices will provide evidence that strengthens the argument (or vice versa in the case of questions that ask for a strengthener). By the time you've read several answer choices, it is easy to forget what the question is asking for and pick an answer choice because it is clearly relevant—even though it's the opposite of what the question is asking for. It is important to keep the question clearly in mind in order to guard against making this kind of mistake.

Consider a third answer choice, then:

> *The preferences of children who do not watch television advertising are influenced by the preferences of children who watch the advertising.*

How does this information affect the argument? Well, the reason originally offered for the conclusion is that the two groups of children do not differ in their preferences. But if the preferences of the children who do not watch television advertising are influenced by the preferences of those who do watch it, then the fact that the two groups do not differ in their preferences provides little, if any, reason to think that none of the children's preferences were affected by television advertising. After all, it could well be that the preferences of the children who watched television were strongly influenced by the advertising, and these children's preferences in turn

strongly influenced the preferences of those who did not watch television, with the result that the two groups had the same preferences. So when combined with the additional information, the argument's original premises make a much weaker case for the argument's conclusion than they did alone. Thus, this is the correct answer.

More Points to Consider

- The additional pieces of information that weaken an argument generally do not challenge the truth of the argument's explicit premises. They are pieces of information that call into question whether the conclusion is strongly supported by those premises.

- Keep in mind that additional information may strengthen (or weaken) an argument only to a small extent or it may do so to a large extent. When the question asks for a strengthener, an answer choice will be correct even if it strengthens the argument only slightly, provided that none of the other answer choices strengthen the argument significantly. On the other hand, if one answer choice strengthens the argument a great deal, then answer choices that strengthen only slightly are incorrect. For most questions that ask for weakeners, the correct answer will weaken the argument to some extent, but the premises will still provide some support for the conclusion. However, for some of these questions, the correct answer will eliminate all or almost all of the argument's original strength.

- Beware of answer choices that are relevant to the general subject matter, but not relevant to the way the argument supports its conclusion. A weakener or strengthener must affect the support for the conclusion. For example, consider the argument about gasoline containing MBTE. Suppose that adding MBTE to gasoline dramatically increased the price of gasoline. This information would be relevant if the argument's conclusion were broader, for example, if it concluded that gasoline containing MBTE should be widely used. Since the argument, however, is narrowly focused on whether widespread use of gasoline containing MBTE will increase the incidence of headaches, fatigue, and shortness of breath, the increased cost resulting from adding MBTE to gasoline is irrelevant and thus would neither strengthen nor weaken the argument.

- Similarly, for new information to weaken an argument, it must reduce the support that the premises provide for the conclusion. A fact may have negative connotations in the context of an argument but do nothing to weaken that argument. For example, consider the argument about television advertising and cereal preferences. Suppose that children who watch average amounts of television, unlike children who watch no television, do not get enough exercise. This would clearly be a negative aspect of watching television. But it doesn't weaken the support that the argument provides for the conclusion that television

advertising does not significantly affect children's preferences for breakfast cereal.

Assumptions

The Logical Reasoning section typically includes several questions that test your ability to identify assumptions of arguments. An assumption of an argument plays a role in establishing the conclusion. However, unlike a premise, an assumption is not something that the arguer explicitly asserts to be true; an assumption is instead just treated as true for the purposes of the argument.

Although assumptions can be stated explicitly in an argument, Logical Reasoning questions that ask about assumptions ask only about unstated assumptions. Unstated (or tacit) assumptions can figure only in arguments that are not entirely complete, that is, in arguments in which some of the things required to establish the conclusion are left unstated. There is thus at least one significant gap in such an argument.

Assumptions relate to the gaps in an argument in two different ways. An assumption is a **sufficient** one if adding it to the argument's premises would produce a conclusive argument, that is, an argument with no gaps in its support for the conclusion. An assumption is a **necessary** one if it is something that must be true in order for the argument to succeed. It is possible for an assumption to be both necessary and sufficient.

■ Sufficient Assumptions

Typical wordings of questions that ask you to identify sufficient assumptions are:

Which one of the following, if assumed, enables the conclusion of the argument to be properly drawn?

The conclusion follows logically from the premises if which one of the following is assumed?

An Example

Vague laws set vague limits on people's freedom, which makes it impossible for them to know for certain whether their actions are legal. Thus, under vague laws people cannot feel secure.[13]

The question you're asked about this argument is:

The conclusion follows logically if which one of the following is assumed?

In order to approach this question, you first have to identify the conclusion of the argument and the premises offered in its support. In this case, the conclusion is signaled by the conclusion indicator "thus" and reads "…under vague laws people cannot feel secure." Two considerations are explicitly presented in support of this conclusion. First, that vague laws set vague limits on people's freedom, and second, that having vague limits set on their freedom makes it impossible for people to know for certain whether their actions are legal. Note that the premises, though they tell us certain things about vague laws, make no explicit reference to whether people feel secure, and not feeling secure is what the conclusion is about. For the conclusion to follow logically, this gap has to be bridged.

At this point, you are ready to look at the answer choices. Here are two of them:

(A) *People can feel secure only if they know for certain whether their actions are legal.*

(B) *If people know for certain whether their actions are legal, they can feel secure.*

Your task is to identify the answer choice that, together with the premises you've been given, will provide conclusive support for the conclusion.

So is (A) that answer choice? The explicit premises of the argument tell you that under vague laws people cannot know for certain whether their actions are legal. (A) tells you that if people do not know for certain whether their actions are legal, they cannot feel secure. So putting the explicit premises and (A) together, you can infer that under vague laws people cannot feel secure. And this is, in fact, the conclusion of the argument. So the conclusion follows logically if (A) is assumed.

Now, let's consider why assuming (B) is not sufficient to ensure that the argument's conclusion follows logically. (B) tells us about one circumstance in which people **can** feel secure. However, the argument's conclusion will not follow logically without the right kind of information about the circumstances in which people

---

[13] December 2001 LSAT, section 3, question 12.

cannot feel secure. (B) does not give us any such information directly. Moreover, we cannot infer such information from what (B) does tell us. After all, it's perfectly compatible with (B) that people can feel secure in some circumstances in addition to the one (B) describes. For example, perhaps people can feel secure if they know for certain that they will not be prosecuted for their actions. Thus, since (B) tells us nothing about circumstances in which people cannot feel secure, it has nothing to contribute to reaching the argument's conclusion that people cannot feel secure under vague laws.

Some Points to Consider

- In answering sufficient assumption questions, you need to find a link between the stated premises and the conclusion. Try to determine from the explicit parts of the argument what logical work that link needs to do. Finally, look among the answer choices for one that can do that logical work and that, taken along with the explicit premises, allows the conclusion to be properly inferred.

- In trying to figure out what logical work the link needs to do, don't get too specific. For example, what can be said about the logical work required of the link in the argument about vague laws analyzed above? It has to link something that has been explicitly connected with vague laws to an inability to feel secure. But there are two things like that: vague limits on people's freedom, and the impossibility of knowing for certain whether one's actions are legal. What this means is that answer choice (A) was not the only possible sufficient assumption here. An equally acceptable sufficient assumption would have been, "People cannot feel secure if they have vague limits on their freedom." So don't approach the answer choices with too specific a view of what you're looking for.

- When trying to identify a sufficient assumption, keep in mind that the correct answer must, when added to the argument's explicit premises, result in a conclusive argument; that is, in an argument that fully establishes its conclusion (provided that the explicit premises and the added assumption are all true).

■ Necessary Assumptions

Typical wordings of questions that ask you to identify necessary assumptions include the following:

The argument relies on assuming which one of the following?

The argument depends on the assumption that

Which one of the following is an assumption required by the argument?

Questions about necessary assumptions refer to arguments that, while not completely spelled out, do present a comprehensible case for accepting their conclusion on the strength of evidence explicitly presented. But if you look closely at the grounds offered for the conclusion and at the conclusion itself, you find that the evidence explicitly presented falls short of establishing the conclusion. That is, there is at least one significant gap in the argument.

Example 1

Since Mayor Drabble always repays her political debts as soon as possible, she will almost certainly appoint Lee to be the new head of the arts commission. Lee has wanted that job for a long time, and Drabble owes Lee a lot for his support in the last election.[14]

As far as its explicit premises go, this argument leaves important matters unresolved. In order for the argument to show that Lee is the likely appointee, there can't be anyone else to whom Drabble has owed a such a large and long-standing political debt and for whom this appointment would be adequate repayment. This idea of there being no one ahead of Lee in line is the sort of unstated but indispensable link in the support for the conclusion that we mean when we speak of a necessary assumption of an argument.

It can readily be shown that the assumption sketched above is in fact indispensable to the argument. Suppose the situation were otherwise and there were a person to whom Mayor Drabble owed a political debt that is of longer standing than her debt to Lee, and suppose further that the appointment could reasonably be viewed as paying off that debt. In this hypothetical circumstance, the fact that Mayor Drabble always repays her political debts as soon as possible would no longer point to Lee as the likely choice for the appointment. In fact, the argument above would fail. If the argument is to succeed, there cannot be another, better-positioned candidate for the appointment. And the argument depends on the assumption that there isn't any better-positioned candidate.

---

[14] June 2004 LSAT, section 2, question 24.

A Test for Necessary Assumptions

Necessary assumption questions, then, require you to identify tacit assumptions. The method for testing necessary assumptions that was introduced above in analyzing Mayor Drabble's situation is quite generally applicable, and for good reason. A necessary assumption is an indispensable link in the support for the conclusion of an argument. Therefore, an argument will be ineffective if a necessary assumption is deemed to be false. This points to a useful test: to see whether an answer choice is a necessary assumption, suppose that what is stated in that answer choice is **false**. If under those circumstances the premises of the argument fail to support the conclusion, the answer choice being evaluated is a necessary assumption.

Example 2

The test for necessary assumptions can be used with the following argument:

Advertisement: Attention pond owners! Ninety-eight percent of mosquito larvae in a pond die within minutes after the pond has been treated with BTI. Yet BTI is not toxic to fish, birds, animals, plants, or beneficial insects. So by using BTI regularly to destroy their larvae, you can greatly reduce populations of pesky mosquitoes that hatch in your pond, and can do so without diminishing the populations of fish, frogs, or beneficial insects in and around the pond.[15]

The question asks:

Which one of the following is an assumption on which the argument depends?

Before you look for a necessary assumption, you need to get clear about the structure of the argument. The conclusion is that regular applications of BTI in a pond can, without reducing populations of assorted pond life, greatly reduce the numbers of mosquitoes that emerge from the pond. The evidence is that BTI kills almost all of the mosquito larvae in the pond, but does not kill (or even harm) other pond life.

The case that the argument makes for its conclusion is straightforward. Applications of BTI, by killing mosquito larvae, prevent the adult mosquito population from being replenished, but they have no direct effect on the other populations. So the argument concludes that, of the populations under consideration, only the mosquito populations will decline.

The first answer choice reads:

The most effective way to control the numbers of mosquitoes in a given area is to destroy the mosquito larvae in that area.

Now we apply the test for necessary assumptions by asking whether the argument would fail if this answer choice were false. That is, would it fail if the destruction of mosquito larvae were not the most effective way to control the numbers of mosquitoes? Definitely not. For one thing, the argument is not concerned with mosquito control alone, but speaks to a dual purpose, that of controlling mosquitoes while leaving other creatures unaffected. So the potential existence of any mosquito-control regimen, however effective, that did not spare other pond creatures would be beside the point. For another thing, the argument merely concludes that the use of BTI works, not that it works better than all other methods. So the denial of this answer choice does not interfere with the support that the conclusion receives from the evidence presented. But if this answer choice were a necessary assumption, denying it would interfere with that support.

Now consider a second answer choice:

The fish, frogs, and beneficial insects in and around a pond-owner's pond do not depend on mosquito larvae as an important source of food.

Applying the test, we ask whether the argument would fail if this answer choice were false (that is, if these creatures did depend on mosquito larvae for food). Yes it would; after all, if the use of BTI means that fish, frogs, and so forth will be deprived of a food that is important for them (mosquito larvae), then there is no reason to conclude that these creatures will survive in undiminished numbers. So denying the answer choice under consideration would cause the argument to fail; we have found a necessary assumption.

Some Points to Consider

▪ As you can see from the characterization of necessary assumptions given above, they are (unstated) constituents of arguments. Whether or not the author of the argument had a particular assumption in mind is not relevant to the issue. It is important to remember that identifying necessary assumptions is a matter of logically analyzing the structure of an argument, not a matter of guessing the beliefs of the arguer.

---

[15] February 1994 LSAT, section 4, question 18.

- For the purpose of *identifying* a necessary assumption, it is not necessary or even useful to evaluate whether that assumption is actually true, or how likely it is to be true. Identifying an assumption is a matter of probing the structure of an argument and recognizing hidden parts of that structure.

- An argument may have more than one necessary assumption. For example, the argument in Example 2 ignores the fact that a small proportion of mosquito larvae in a pond are not killed by BTI. But if there is a genetic basis for their not being killed, one might imagine that regular applications of BTI in a given pond will make it more and more likely that the mosquitoes left to breed with one another will be BTI-resistant ones that will likely produce BTI-resistant offspring. This population of BTI-resistant mosquitoes might then grow, without being kept in check by further applications of BTI, contrary to the drift of the argument. So the argument also depends on assuming that the two percent of mosquito larvae not killed by an initial application of BTI do not constitute an initial breeding pool for a BTI-resistant population of mosquitoes.

  An argument can thus have more than one necessary assumption. Of course, only one of them will appear among the answer choices. But the one that does appear may not be one that occurred to you when you analyzed the argument. So it is a good idea not to prejudge what the correct answer will be. Instead, keep an open mind and examine each of the answer choices in turn.

- As indicated above, an argument may have more than one gap. Any one necessary assumption will address only one such gap. Moreover, a necessary assumption will often address only some aspects of a gap. In Example 2, the gap addressed by the necessary assumption—*The fish, frogs, and beneficial insects in and around a pond-owner's pond do not depend on mosquito larvae as an important source of food*—is, broadly speaking, that BTI does not kill the fish, frogs, and beneficial insects indirectly. But food deprivation is not the only way that BTI might kill those creatures indirectly. For example, as the mosquito larvae killed by applications of BTI decay, they might harm fish, frogs, and beneficial insects.

  So do not reject an answer choice as a necessary assumption merely on the grounds that the argument, even if you make that necessary assumption, is still not a strong argument.

Principles

Some Logical Reasoning questions test your ability to apply general rules and principles and to understand their use. These questions can involve the use of principles in arguments, or they can involve applying principles to actions or states of affairs.

Principles are broad guidelines concerning what kinds of actions, judgments, policies, and so on are appropriate. Most principles spell out the range of situations to which they apply. Within that range of situations, principles often serve to justify the transition from claims about what is the case to conclusions regarding what should be done.

There are several kinds of questions involving principles. You may be given a principle and be asked which action conforms to it, or which judgment it justifies, or which argument relies on it. Alternatively, the question may present a judgment, decision, or argument and ask which principle is appealed to in making that judgment, decision, or argument. Logical Reasoning questions may also involve principles in various other ways. For example, a question could ask which action violates a principle. You may also see Logical Reasoning items that ask you to recognize two situations as involving the same underlying principle, where that principle is not stated.

■ Applying a Principle That Is Given

An Example

People who receive unsolicited advice from someone whose advantage would be served if that advice is taken should regard the proffered advice with skepticism unless there is good reason to think that their interests substantially coincide with those of the advice giver in the circumstance in question.[16]

The following question refers to this principle:

This principle, if accepted, would justify which one of the following judgments?

The correct answer is provided by the judgment that is presented below.

While shopping for a refrigerator, Ramón is approached by a salesperson who, on the basis of her personal experience, warns him against the least expensive model. However, the salesperson's commission increases with the price of

---

the refrigerator sold, so Ramón should not reject the least expensive model on the salesperson's advice alone.

The task here is to check how well the particulars of the situation fit with the principle. Do the general terms in which the principle is expressed cover the specific circumstances of the situation?

So first you should ask, "Does someone in this situation receive unsolicited advice from someone whose advantage would be served if that advice is taken?" If the answer is "yes," then the case under consideration falls within the range of situations to which the principle applies. If the answer is "no," then the principle offers no guidance. In this situation, someone—Ramón—does receive advice. If Ramón took the advice, this would be to the advantage of the advice giver (the salesperson), because the salesperson would receive a higher commission than she would otherwise. Is the advice unsolicited? Yes, because the salesperson approached Ramón without his asking for help.

The next question you should ask is, "Does the situation culminate in a judgment that the advice should be regarded with skepticism?" The answer is again "yes." The judgment that Ramón should not reject the least expensive model solely on the salesperson's advice is a judgment that treats the advice given—to avoid buying the least expensive model—skeptically.

You are not quite done at this point. The principle restricts itself to situations in which the person giving the advice and the person receiving the advice do not have interests that coincide. So you need to ask one more question: "Is there reason to think that the interests of Ramón and those of the salesperson substantially coincide in this matter?" Since Ramón probably wants to spend no more than he has to and since the salesperson probably wants Ramón to spend freely, there is reason to think that in this matter their interests do **not** coincide. So the principle applies to the situation and justifies the judgment.

■ Identifying a Guiding Principle

In the example above, the passage contained a principle and you were asked which judgment it justified. There are also questions that present a judgment or argument in the passage and ask which principle justifies it.

An Example

Marianne is a professional chess player who hums audibly while playing her matches, thereby distracting her opponents. When ordered by chess officials to cease humming
or else be disqualified from professional chess, Marianne protested the order. She argued that since she was unaware of her humming, her humming was involuntary and that therefore she should not be held responsible for it.[17]

The question that is based on this passage is:

Which one of the following principles, if valid, most helps to support Marianne's argument against the order?

To answer this question, you need to compare the specific circumstances presented in the passage with the principle presented in each answer choice. First, consider the following answer choice:

Of a player's actions, only those that are voluntary should be used as justification for disqualifying that player from professional chess.

Does this principle apply to Marianne's situation? Well, it is clear that the principle concerns which of a chess player's actions can appropriately be used as justification for disqualifying that player from professional chess. Since the argument in the passage is concerned with whether one of Marianne's actions—humming while playing—should disqualify her from professional chess, it definitely falls under the range of situations to which the principle applies.

The principle will help support Marianne's argument if it leads to a judgment that Marianne's humming while playing should not be used as justification for disqualifying her from playing. According to a subsidiary conclusion of Marianne's argument, her humming is involuntary (this is supported by the claim that she was unaware of it). The principle asserts that only voluntary actions should be used as justification for disqualifying a player from professional chess, so this principle, together with the subsidiary conclusion of Marianne's argument, leads to the judgment that Marianne's humming should not be used as justification for disqualifying her. Thus the principle does help support Marianne's argument.

For the sake of comparison, consider one of the other answer choices:

Chess players should be disqualified from professional chess matches if they regularly attempt to distract their opponents.

Does this principle apply to Marianne's situation? Yes, it apparently does since it is also about the conditions under which chess players should be disqualified from professional chess matches. So now you need to ask, does the principle establish, or help establish the conclusion that

---

Marianne should not be disqualified for humming during matches? The answer is no. This principle just gives one condition under which a chess player should be disqualified—when that player regularly attempts to distract opponents. Since Marianne's humming is, she argues, involuntary, we can conclude that she is not trying to distract her opponents. Thus the principle does not lead to the judgment that Marianne should be disqualified for humming. But this does not mean that the principle leads to the judgment that Marianne should not be disqualified. After all, it is compatible with the principle that there are other conditions under which a player should be disqualified, and such conditions could include humming while playing. So the principle does not lead to the conclusion that Marianne should not be disqualified from professional matches and thus does not provide any support for Marianne's argument.

> **Cross-reference:** Making a common reasoning error known as confusion between "sufficient conditions" and "necessary conditions" could lead one to pick this answer choice. There are many opportunities for this confusion to arise in principles questions. Further discussion of sufficient and necessary conditions, and of correct and incorrect ways of reasoning with conditions, can be found on pages 24–25.

Note that the process of finding the correct answer to a question that asks you to identify a guiding principle is basically the same as it is for a question that asks you to apply a given principle. The task is to make sure that a principle, which will be couched in general terms, fits the particulars of the situation. The only difference is that in the one case you need to check five different situations against one principle, and in the other case you need to check a single situation against five different principles. But the way you determine the best fit is the same. You check the principle for applicability, and you check to see whether the judgment, decision, recommendation, or action is in line with what the principle says.

Some Points to Consider

- Although principles always go beyond the particular case, they can vary enormously in degree of generality and abstractness. For example, the principle in the question about Ramón's refrigerator shopping is very general, applying to anyone who receives unsolicited advice. In contrast, the principle in the question about Marianne the chess player is more specific, applying only to professional chess players. And some questions have principles that can be even more specific than this. So be sure not to reject a principle as a correct answer solely because it seems to be too specific.

- When answering questions involving principles, it is always a good idea to check all of the answer choices. There is no sure way to determine whether a given answer choice provides the best fit except by considering and comparing all of the answer choices.

- Don't reject a principle as providing justification for an argument merely because it seems to do no more than spell out what the argument takes for granted. For example, someone might say, "Gerry sees very poorly without glasses. Therefore, Gerry should always wear glasses when driving." A principle justifying this judgment might be "Anyone who needs glasses to see well should always wear glasses when driving."

- Don't worry about the legitimacy of any of the principles you are presented with. Do not reject an answer because the principle involved is one that you personally would not accept.

Flaws in Arguments

▪ Identifying Argument Flaws

The Logical Reasoning section includes a number of questions that ask you to identify a flaw of reasoning that has been committed in an argument. Questions of this kind are worded in a variety of ways. Here are some examples:

The reasoning in the argument is flawed because the argument

The argument commits which one of the following errors of reasoning?

The argument's reasoning is questionable because the argument fails to rule out the possibility that

The reasoning above is most vulnerable to criticism on the grounds that it

Test questions about flawed reasoning require you to recognize in what way an argument is defective in its reasoning. They will not require you to decide whether or not the argument is flawed. That judgment is already made and is expressed in the wording of the question. Your task is to recognize which one of the answer choices describes an error of reasoning that the argument makes.

When an argument is flawed, the argument exemplifies poor reasoning. This is reasoning in which the premises may appear to provide support for the conclusion but actually provide little or no real support. Poor reasoning of this sort can be detected by examining the argument itself, without considering any factual issues that aren't mentioned in the argument.

Tip: Logical Reasoning questions in the LSAT test your skills in reasoning and analysis, not what you know about any particular subject matter. Whether a premise is factually accurate is not relevant. So don't pay attention to the factual accuracy of an argument's premises. Focus instead on logical connections between the premises that the argument sets out and the conclusion that it draws.

Since the flaws that you'll be looking for are not specific to the subject matter but relate to the argument's logical structure, the characterization of those flaws can be quite general. That is to say, the flawed reasoning in an argument might be described in terms that also apply to other arguments that commit the same error of reasoning. So once you detect where a particular argument has gone wrong, you may then have to figure out which of several quite general descriptions covers the case.

Example 1

Consider the following brief exchange:

Physicist: The claim that low-temperature nuclear fusion can be achieved entirely by chemical means is based on chemical experiments in which the measurements and calculations are inaccurate.

Chemist: But your challenge is ineffectual, since you are simply jealous at the thought that chemists might have solved a problem that physicists have been unable to solve.[18]

Here is the question that is based on this exchange:

Which one of the following is the strongest criticism of the chemist's response to the physicist's challenge?

Before looking at the answer choices, briefly consider what appears to be wrong with the chemist's response. Notice that the chemist claims that the physicist's challenge

is ineffectual but doesn't actually engage the substance of the physicist's challenge. Instead, the chemist accuses the physicist of professional jealousy and dismisses the physicist's challenge purely on that basis. But there is no reason to think that a challenge, even if it is fueled by jealousy, cannot be on target. So the chemist's response can rightly be criticized for "getting personal."

Now consider two of the answer choices. One of them reads,

It fails to establish that perfect accuracy of measurements and calculations is possible.

This statement is certainly true about the chemist's response. The chemist does not establish that perfect accuracy is possible. But this is not a good criticism of the chemist's response because it is entirely beside the point. Establishing that perfect accuracy is possible would have, if anything, damaged the chemist's position. So the chemist's response cannot be legitimately criticized for failing to establish this.

Another answer choice reads,

It is directed against the proponent of a claim rather than against the claim itself.

This criticism goes to the heart of what is wrong with the chemist's response. The chemist dismisses the physicist's challenge because of the physicist's alleged motives for making it and never actually discusses the merits of the challenge itself. It is directed against the person rather than against the position.

In this example, the chemist's response is clearly irrelevant to the substance of the physicist's claim. The argument that the chemist presents seems more like a rhetorical ploy than a serious argument. Many arguments are flawed in much less dramatic ways, however. They may contain only a small logical lapse that undermines the integrity of the argument, like the following two examples.

Example 2

Morris High School has introduced a policy designed to improve the working conditions of its new teachers. As a result of this policy, only one-quarter of all part-time teachers now quit during their first year. However, a third of all full-time teachers now quit during their first year. Thus, more full-time than part-time teachers at Morris now quit during their first year.[19]

[18] June 1995 LSAT, section 2, question 2.
[19] October 1994 LSAT, section 2, question 14.

Notice that the argument uses proportions to indicate the degree to which first-year teachers are quitting. It says that **one-quarter** of part-time first-year teachers quit and that **one-third** of full-time first-year teachers quit. The conclusion of the argument is not expressed in terms of proportions, however, but in terms of a comparison between quantities: **more** full-timers than part-timers quit during their first year.

Your task is to accurately complete the following statement:

The argument's reasoning is questionable because the argument fails to rule out the possibility that

Note that we are looking for a possibility that needs to be ruled out in order for the conclusion to be well supported. So let's consider one of the answer choices:

before the new policy was instituted, more part-time than full-time teachers at Morris High School used to quit during their first year

How would the argument be affected by this information? It tells us something about the way things were before the new policy went into effect, but it doesn't shed much light on the effects of the new policy. And there is no way to infer anything about how many part-time and full-time teachers are quitting now, after the policy was instituted. So this information has no effect on the support for the conclusion, and there would be no reason for the argument to rule it out. Failing to rule it out, then, would not make the reasoning questionable.

Let's go on to consider another answer choice:

Morris High School employs more new part-time teachers than new full-time teachers

So how would the argument be affected if there were more new part-time teachers than new full time teachers? If there were more new part-timers than full-timers, then one-quarter of the new part-timers could outnumber one-third of the new full-timers. So it could be true that more part-timers than full-timers quit during their first year. Since the argument concludes that more full-timers than part-timers quit in their first year, this possibility needs to be ruled out in order for the conclusion to be well supported. Thus, this choice is the correct answer.

Example 3

If Blankenship Enterprises has to switch suppliers in the middle of a large production run, the company will not

show a profit for the year. Therefore, if Blankenship Enterprises in fact turns out to show no profit for the year, it will also turn out to be true that the company had to switch suppliers during a large production run.[20]

The question asks:

The reasoning in the argument is most vulnerable to criticism on which one of the following grounds?

This question tells you that you should be looking for a problem with the argument. When you analyze the argument, you can identify the problem if you recognize that there may well be other reasons for not showing a profit besides having to switch suppliers in the middle of a large production run. This points to a major oversight in the argument. At this point, you are ready to review the answer choices.

One answer choice says:

The argument is a circular argument made up of an opening claim followed by a conclusion that merely paraphrases that claim.

This gives a general account of an argument flaw, but close inspection shows that the Blankenship argument does not have this flaw. That argument's conclusion says something quite different from what was said in the argument's premise. The conclusion says "If there is no profit, then there was a switch in suppliers." The premise is superficially similar, but it says "If there is a switch in suppliers, then there will be no profit." So this answer choice is not a legitimate criticism.

Another answer choices reads:

The argument fails to establish that a condition under which a phenomenon is said to occur is the only condition under which that phenomenon occurs.

This is the correct answer. The argument could only succeed if it showed that switching suppliers in the middle of a large production run is the only condition under which the company will show no profit for the year. But the argument fails to establish this point. Note that this answer choice points out what is wrong with this particular argument using general terms that could cover many different arguments.

---

[20] December 1994 LSAT, section 2, question 26.

> **Cross-reference:** This is an example of a common reasoning error: confusion between "sufficient conditions" and "necessary conditions." A more detailed discussion of sufficient and necessary conditions, and of correct and incorrect ways of reasoning with conditions, can be found on pages 24–25.

Some Points to Consider

- When you begin a flawed reasoning question, you should first try to get fairly clear about just where the argument goes wrong. If you have a reasonably clear sense of what is wrong with the reasoning, you can then look for the answer choice that describes the kind of error you have identified. Keep in mind that the descriptions offered may be very general—ones that could also apply to arguments very different in subject matter from the one you're considering.

- Keep in mind that for an answer to be the correct answer, it is not enough that it describe some aspect of the argument correctly. The correct answer must describe a flaw in the reasoning of the particular argument under consideration.

- When dealing with a flawed argument that contains quantitative or statistical information, always check to see that the reference groups mentioned in the argument are appropriate and consistent. An argument may, for example, present information about the percentage of primary school teachers who have degrees in education and go on to draw a conclusion about the percentage of people who receive degrees in education and go on to teach primary school. Detecting this shift in reference groups is the key to identifying the flaw in this argument. It is not unusual for argument flaws to involve subtle shifts such as this.

- Some flawed arguments involve errors in reasoning about the relationship between proportions and quantities. Example 2 is a case in point. That argument involves a shift from talk about proportions in the premises to a statement about relative quantities in the conclusion. In some other argument, there might be an illicit shift from quantities in the premises to proportions in the conclusion. So pay close attention to any shifts like these.

■ Matching Argument Flaws

In your test you will sometimes encounter logical reasoning questions like the following:

Which one of the following arguments is most similar in its flawed reasoning to the argument above?

It is best to approach these questions in a straightforward way. First, try to determine in what way the reasoning in the reference argument is flawed. Then go over the arguments in the answer choices until you find the one whose reasoning is flawed in just the same way.

The wording of the question tells you that the reference argument is in fact flawed in its reasoning and that at least one other argument is, too. There is no need to worry about the precise wording of that flaw: the question does not hinge on it. But you do need to get a reasonably clear idea of the kind of reasoning error committed, because you will be making a judgment about whether one of the answer choices matches that error.

For this type of question, incorrect answer choices can be of two kinds. Some present arguments that are perfectly good, so they don't contain any flaw at all, let alone one that matches the one in the reference argument. Others do present flawed arguments, but the reasoning errors in those arguments are clearly different from the one in the reference argument.

An Example

Consider the following argument:

If the majority of the residents of the apartment complex complain that their apartments are infested with ants, then the management of the complex will have to engage the services of an exterminator. But the majority of the residents of the complex indicate that their apartments are virtually free of ants. Therefore, the management of the complex will not have to engage the services of an exterminator.[21]

The question you are asked about this argument is

Which one of the following arguments contains a flawed pattern of reasoning parallel to that contained in the argument above?

This question directs us to look for a flawed **pattern** of reasoning in the reference argument and to look for an answer choice that contains a similarly flawed pattern. This means that we should look for an argument that takes the same flawed approach to establishing its conclusion as the

---

[21] June 1994 LSAT, section 4, question 20.

reference argument does, even though the two arguments might not share other characteristics, such as subject matter.

So what exactly is the flaw in the reference argument? One of the argument's premises says that under a certain condition the exterminator will have to come, and the second premise says that this condition is not met. The argument concludes that the exterminator will not have to be hired. But it is not difficult to see that something is wrong with this way of arguing: the problem is that there may be other conditions under which the exterminator has to be hired. To use a concrete example, it may also be true that if there is a rodent infestation in the apartment complex, the management has to call in an exterminator. So the fact that the condition about ants is not met is not a good enough reason for concluding that the exterminator will not have to be hired. Without offering any reasons for doing so, the argument treats one circumstance that would produce a certain result as though it were the only circumstance under which this result comes about.

The next step is to check the answer choices and to find the one that exhibits the same flawed pattern of reasoning. So let's consider the following choice:

The number of flights operated by the airlines cannot be reduced unless the airlines can collect higher airfares. But people will not pay higher airfares, so it is not the case that the number of flights will be reduced.

Is this an instance of the same flawed pattern? This argument is like the reference argument in that one of its premises asserts that under a certain condition (airlines cannot collect higher airfares) something will happen (schedules will not be cut). But this argument is unlike the reference argument in that its second premise actually meets the condition set out in the first premise. We are told that "people will not pay higher airfares," so it stands to reason that airlines cannot collect higher airfares. And thus the conclusion—that the number of flights will not be reduced—follows from these premises. So this argument does not exhibit the same pattern of flawed reasoning as the reference argument. In fact, it does not exhibit flawed reasoning at all.

Let's try another one of the answer choices:

Most employees will attend the company picnic if the entertainment committee is successful in getting a certain band to play at the picnic. But that band will be out of the country on the day of the picnic, so it is not true that most employees will attend.

Is this an instance of the pattern you are trying to match? Again, there is a conditional statement: if a certain band plays at the picnic, most employees will attend. So again, under a certain condition, something will happen. In this argument, the second premise indicates that the condition will not be met. The band, being out of the country, will certainly not play at the picnic. The argument goes on to conclude that most employees won't attend the picnic. So, as in the reference argument, this conclusion says that the thing that would happen under the original condition will not happen.

This is an exact match of the pattern of reasoning in the reference argument, hence it is an exact match of the flaw. As with the reference argument, the flaw can be illustrated concretely. Suppose, for example, that if the entertainment committee hires a certain well-known comedian to perform at the picnic, most employees will attend. This shows that the conclusion could be true even if what the argument tells us about the band is true.

Some Points to Consider

- For this type of question, there is no need to decide whether the reference argument is flawed. You are told that there is a flawed pattern of reasoning underlying the argument. It is sometimes useful, however, to determine whether or not an argument in an answer choice is flawed. If such an argument is **not** flawed, it cannot be the correct answer, because it will not be a relevant match for the reference argument.

- Remember that, although you need to get a reasonably clear fix on the kind of reasoning error committed in the reference argument, you do not need to come up with a precise formulation of that error. Since you are not asked to put your understanding of the reasoning error into words, all you need is a solid intuitive grasp of where the reasoning goes wrong.

- With this type of question, you look for the argument that most closely matches the reference argument in terms of its flawed reasoning. So other similarities with the reference argument, such as in the way the argument is expressed or in its subject matter, are irrelevant. Two arguments can be expressed in very different ways, or be about very different things, even though they exhibit the same pattern of reasoning.

Cross-reference: For a more extensive discussion of this point, see "Identifying the Parts of an Argument" on pages 15–16.

Explanations

Some of the questions in the Logical Reasoning section require you to identify a potential explanation for some state of affairs that is described to you. Broadly speaking, these questions come in two types: one in which you need to find an explanation for one particular situation, and another in which you need to explain how two seemingly conflicting elements of a given situation can both be true.

In the first sort of case, the phenomenon to be explained will merely be something that one would not ordinarily expect, the kind of thing that makes people say, "There must be an explanation for this." Imagine, for example, that it is discovered that domestic cats with purely gray coats are, on average, significantly heavier than those with multicolored coats. A fact like this calls for an explanation. The wording of a corresponding question would be along the lines of:

Which one of the following, if true, most helps to explain the difference in average weights?

In the second sort of case, the phenomenon to be explained is more complex. You are not simply presented with one fact that seems to require an explanation. Rather, you are presented with statements that appear to conflict with one another, and your task is to identify the answer choice that most helps to resolve this apparent discrepancy. That is, you are to select an answer choice that explains not just one or the other of the apparently conflicting elements but explains how they can both be true. With this sort of question, the passage might say, for example, that people spend much less time reading today than they did 50 years ago, and yet many more books are sold per year now than were sold 50 years ago. A typical wording for this sort of question is:

Which one of the following, if true, most helps to resolve the apparent discrepancy in the information given above?

Example 1

The situation that follows seems to call for an explanation. In this case, a software production company's decision to refrain from prosecuting people who illegally copy its program raises questions regarding the company's reasons.

The company that produces XYZ, a computer spreadsheet program, estimates that millions of illegally reproduced copies of XYZ are being used. If legally purchased, this number of copies would have generated millions of dollars

in sales for the company, yet despite a company-wide effort to boost sales, the company has not taken available legal measures to prosecute those who have copied the program illegally.[22]

The question that is based on this situation reads as follows:

Which one of the following, if true, most helps to explain why the company has not taken available legal measures?

Incorrect answer choices such as

XYZ is very difficult to copy illegally, because a sophisticated anticopying mechanism in the program must first be disabled.

do nothing to help us understand the company's decision. They may, however, be relevant to some aspect of the situation. The answer choice above, for example, does suggest that those who do the illegal copying are knowledgeable about computers and computer software, but it doesn't throw any light on the company's decision not to prosecute.

The correct answer,

Many people who purchase a software program like XYZ are willing to purchase that program only after they have already used it.

on the other hand, does suggest a reason for the company to tolerate the use of illegal copies of its program: those copies happen to serve as effective marketing aids in many cases and lead to legal sales of the program. The company may think that it has more to lose than to gain from going to court in order to stop the illegal copying. At the very least, the correct answer tells us that there is a disadvantage for the company in stopping the illegal copying, and this helps to explain why no legal measures are taken.

Example 2

Of the five bill collectors at Apex Collection Agency, Mr. Young has the highest rate of unsuccessful collections. Yet Mr. Young is the best bill collector on the agency's staff.[23]

This situation has an air of paradox. It seems clear that a superior ability to bring a collection effort to a success-

[22] December 1994 LSAT, section 4, question 2.
[23] June 1995 LSAT, section 2, question 5.

ful conclusion is what makes one bill collector better than another. So how can Mr. Young, who has the lowest rate of successful collections, be the best bill collector? This is the focus of the question that goes along with this situation:

Which one of the following, if true, most helps to resolve the apparent discrepancy?

Consider the following answer choice:

Mr. Young's rate of collections per year has remained fairly steady in the last few years.

This gives us information that is pertinent to Mr. Young's performance as a bill collector. But it gives us no reason to think that Mr. Young could be the best bill collector at the agency despite having the lowest collection rate. It only gives us more reason to think Mr. Young is a poor bill collector, because it allows us to infer that his collection rate has been low for years.

Now consider another choice:

Mr. Young is assigned the majority of the most difficult cases at the agency.

This gives us reason to think more highly of Mr. Young's ability as a bill collector, because it makes sense to assign the most difficult cases to Mr. Young if he is very good at collecting bills. And if his rate of success is relatively low, this is not really a surprise, because his cases tend to be more difficult. So this answer makes it clear how two facts that seemed to be difficult to recon-cile with one another can in fact both be true. This resolves the apparent discrepancy in a satisfying way.

Some Points to Consider

- The correct answers to these questions do not generally offer complete and detailed explanations. Rather, they present crucial information that plays an important part within an adequate explanation.

- Pay close attention to what you are asked to explain. In the case of simple explanations of a particular factual matter, the wording of the question will direct you specifically to the fact to be explained. In the case of explanations that resolve an apparent conflict, however, it is generally up to you to develop a clear picture of that conflict.

- In most cases, there is more than one way to explain a set of facts or resolve an apparent conflict. So it is generally not a good idea to work out several explanatory stories in your head before examining the answer choices. Go to the answer choices instead and, for each choice, determine whether it helps to explain or resolve the situation.

- Note that these questions are qualified by the expression "if true." This indicates that you do not have to be concerned about the actual truth of the answer choices. Simply consider each answer choice as though it were true.

How to Approach Reading Comprehension Passages

The Reading Comprehension section is intended to assess your ability to read, with understanding and insight, passages comparable in terms of level of language and complexity to materials you are likely to have to deal with in the study of law. The passages are selected so that they can be adequately understood simply on the basis of what they say; you won't need any specialized prior knowledge to understand Reading Comprehension passages. Any technical terms that you need to understand to answer the questions are explained in the passages and all of the questions can be answered on the basis of information given in the passages.

Typically, a passage has a single main point. Sometimes the main point of a passage is to present a controversial position and either attack or defend it. Sometimes it is to examine and critique someone else's view. Sometimes it is to explain a puzzling phenomenon. Sometimes it is to give an accurate historical account of some important development. All passages will present a number of considerations that are relevant to the main point of the passage; the roles these considerations play are largely determined by the nature of that main point.

So how should you approach a Reading Comprehension passage? The single most important thing is to get clear about the main thrust of the passage: what is the passage mainly trying to get across to the reader? Occasionally, a passage will contain a particular sentence that explicitly states the main point. Even when there is such a statement, however, it does not necessarily come at the beginning of the passage; it could occur anywhere in the passage. More often, a passage will just present its position, critique, account, or explanation and rely on the reader to see where the passage is going. So what you should do as you work through a passage is read attentively, but at the same time you should be aware that it is not necessary to absorb and retain all of the descriptive detail that the author presents along the way. Try to remain focused on the main business of the passage, because the entire passage is organized around that. Without a clear sense of what the passage is about, you are likely to make mistakes about the relative significance of the various subsidiary points that the passage raises in support of its central point.

■ Be Aware of Paragraphs and Transition Words

Shifts in focus and perspective occur frequently in Reading Comprehension passages. A passage might shift from one concern to another, from the particular to the general, from a positive view of a topic to a negative one, or from one person to another. To get a solid grasp of how a given passage works, you must be aware of what the different ideas presented in the passage are and, more importantly, how the ideas relate to one another.

A reader therefore needs to track the ideas presented by the author and the nature of the transition from one to another in order to grasp the significance, within the passage as a whole, of what is being said at any given point in the passage.

One feature of passages that can be extremely helpful in determining exactly how they work is their division into paragraphs. Paragraphs tend to have a relatively narrow focus and often play well-defined roles within the passage as a whole. So, for example, when an author switches from citing support for a position to defending the position against a challenge, the switch is typically marked by starting a new paragraph. Consequently, by asking yourself what each paragraph does you can put together a fairly accurate picture of the structure of the passage as a whole.

Still, not all shifts in focus or perspective coincide with the transition from one paragraph to the next; one or more shifts might occur within a given paragraph, or conversely, two or more paragraphs might share the same basic focus. Another useful indicator of significant shifts in Reading Comprehension passages is the use of words or phrases such as "however," "nevertheless," "on the other hand," "by contrast," "and yet," and others. If you pay close attention to these sorts of signals, they will help orient you to what the significant parts of the passage are, and they will alert you to when a significant shift in focus or perspective is taking place. Incidentally, authors often provide helpful signals of continuity as well as shifts; continuity is frequently signaled by means of words or phrases like "for example," "by the same token," "furthermore," "in the same vein," "moreover," "similarly," and others.

One final caution about understanding the author's point of view: many times authors compare competing positions or theories and ultimately endorse one position or theory over its competitors. A common technique used by authors in this type of passage is to present the ideas they ultimately intend to reject in the best light possible, at least initially. One advantage of this approach is that criticisms are much more damaging if they work against an idea that has been presented in its strongest form; another advantage is that an author who takes pains to be as fair and evenhanded as possible to his or her opponents gains greatly in credibility. But what this means for you is that it can be quite difficult to follow such passages if you do not monitor the author's stance very carefully. When the author of a passage presents an opponent's point of view in the best light possible, it can appear to the unwary reader that the author endorses a position that he or she actually rejects. All of the techniques discussed above so far in this section can help you keep oriented to where the author actually stands in passages like these.

■ Should You Read the Questions First?

Some of you may be wondering at this point about a commonly heard piece of advice—that you should read the questions first, and only then turn to the passage. You should, of course, feel free to try this strategy and use it if you find it helpful. It is our opinion, however, that most people will find this strategy to be unhelpful. There are several reasons for this.

First, all of the questions associated with LSAT passages fit into standard question types—questions that ask for the main point or main purpose of the passage, questions that ask what the author would agree or disagree with, questions that ask what can be inferred from the information in the passage, and so on. We will say more about these and other question types in the sections that follow; what matters here is that many of these questions, though based on very different passages, look similar from one Reading Comprehension set to the next. Through study and practice, you can familiarize yourself with the types of questions that are typically written for an LSAT passage. You will then be able to anticipate what many of the questions will look like without having to spend your valuable time reading them before you read the passage.

Of course, some of the questions that follow a given passage might not look exactly like others of the same type; some even appear to be quite unique. But even in these cases, you will probably still gain very little from reading the questions first: it takes work to remember

questions as you read the passage, and your mental energy is probably better spent on simply trying to comprehend the passage. As we have discussed already, LSAT reading passages can be quite difficult, involving sophisticated ideas and complex relationships. Answering the questions correctly requires you to get a firm grasp of the big picture in the passage. If you read everything in the passage with an eye to answering questions about particular details rather than with full attention to the thrust of the passage as a whole, you can easily miss the main point of the passage, and you run the risk of failing to grasp what the author agrees and disagrees with as well. So though you might do well on the questions that ask about those details, you might very well increase your chances of getting other questions in the set wrong.

Finally, it is important to remember that in the actual testing situation you have to read four passages and answer some 27 questions in 35 minutes. Time is of the essence. You can read the questions before you read the passages, but you still have to read the questions again when you are ready to answer them (you won't remember precisely what every question asks). Assume for the sake of argument that it takes roughly five seconds to read each question without reading the responses. That adds up to more than two minutes just to read the questions in a single Reading Comprehension section. If you read them twice, you double that to more than four minutes.

How to Approach Reading Comprehension Questions

After reading through the passage once, you should turn to the questions. At this point you will probably have a fairly good sense of what the passage as a whole is trying to say, how the passage is organized, and roughly where in the passage specific points are made or particular facts are mentioned. But even if you do not feel all that confident of your understanding of the passage, you should proceed to the questions anyway rather than rereading the whole passage. In most cases, the first question in a set will ask you about the main point or the main purpose of a passage. If you don't think you have a handle on the passage, you might be able to recognize the main point or purpose of the passage when you see it, and answering this first question will in turn help orient you to the passage as a whole and to the questions that follow.

Either way, you should not feel that you need to remember the passage in great detail in order to begin working on the questions. For example, a passage might talk about two theoretical accounts of the rationale for incarceration, rehabilitative and punitive, and provide detail, even important detail, about both. In reading this passage, you should try to develop a clear sense of the difference between the two accounts and a

general sense of where each is discussed. But there would be no point in trying to commit all of the detail in the passage to memory. First, not everything—not even every important thing—in the passage is going to be asked about. Second, if you have a general idea of the structure of the passage and of where its key elements are located, it is easy to check on the relevant details by rereading just portions of the passage. In fact, even if you are fairly confident that you remember everything you need to answer a particular question, it usually is a good idea to confirm your answer by checking the relevant portions of the passage anyway. Only if you have absolutely no doubt about the answer to a question is it advisable to respond without consulting the passage at least briefly.

When you read the questions, you should carefully attend to how each question is worded. Many questions contain detail that is intended to direct you to the relevant information in the passage. For example, one passage in the June 2000 LSAT discussed the conflict between philosophers who subscribe to a traditional, subjective approach to studying the mind and philosophers who support a new "objectivist" approach. According to the passage, the "subjectivists" believe that the mind should be explored by means of investigating individual subjective experiences such as consciousness, pain, emotions, and the like; "objectivists" find this approach outdated, however, and they believe the study of the mind should be limited to "hard" data such as the transmission of nerve impulses in the brain. One question in this set asks,

According to the passage, subjectivists advance which one of the following claims to support their claim that objectivism is faulty?[24]

The first thing this question tells you is that the correct response will be a claim attributed in the passage to the subjectivists. Other claims in the passage are attributed to the objectivists, and the author also makes a few claims of his or her own; obviously, none of these can be the correct answer. Moreover, the question tells you that the correct answer must be the claim made by the subjectivists as part of their argument that objectivism is faulty. At this point most test takers will recall that the views of subjectivists regarding the problems with objectivism are described in the first half of the passage, and more specifically, in the second paragraph. A quick glance at that portion of the passage will enable you to identify the correct response.

In this case, the views being asked about are not the author's view, but many questions do in fact focus on what the author says, believes, or might agree with. At the same time, as we noted above, authors of passages used in the LSAT often mention other people as making claims, presenting evidence, holding beliefs, or taking positions about whatever it is that the question is asking about. Again, it is important to pay very close attention to whether a question focuses on the views or claims of the author, or those of another person or group discussed by the author.

There is one additional piece of advice that applies to all Reading Comprehension questions: in general, even if you are fairly sure you have found the correct answer, you should probably take at least a quick look at any answer choices that you have not already eliminated. Incorrect answer choices are often partially correct, and as a result incorrect choices can sometimes appear to be correct when you first read them. Sometimes, a consideration of the full set of answer choices will lead you to reject a wrong answer that you initially thought to be correct.

Questions About the Passage as a Whole (Main Idea, Primary Purpose, Overall Organization)

As we said earlier, the first question in most Reading Comprehension sets will ask you to identify the statement that best expresses the central idea, main idea, or the main point that the passage as a whole is designed to convey. These question come in three main varieties. A few will take the following form: "Which one of the following most accurately **summarizes** the contents of the passage?" As the question implies, you should try to identify the response that summarizes the passage most accurately.

The thing to remember about questions like this is that the correct response will be the one that covers the important material in the passage most completely. That is not to say that the correct answer is necessarily the longest one, but it does mean that the correct answer will be most inclusive of the major steps in the discussion in the passage. The thing to keep in mind is that for questions that ask for the best **summary** of the passage, the correct answer will be the most comprehensive and inclusive of the steps taken in the passage. This variant of main idea questions is fairly rare, however. We use them infrequently, and you may not encounter any when you take the test.

The second, and by far most common, variant asks you to identify the **main point**, **main idea**, **or central idea** of the passage. Rather than asking you to identify the answer that summarizes the passage the best, these questions ask you to identify the idea or point that is at the heart of the passage. The important thing to know about these questions is that they have a much narrower focus than summary questions do. To answer them correctly, you have to be able to recognize what is the most important idea that the passage is trying to establish, the idea to which all other ideas in the passage are subordinated.

The third variant offers five potential titles for the passage and asks you to identify the answer that would be the **best title**. This variant is related to the main point/main idea question inasmuch as the best title will be the one that touches most directly on the central idea or point of the passage. These questions are also relatively rare. If you come across one, focus on finding the title that contains the content you would expect to see in a standard statement of the main idea of the passage.

One important thing to know about main idea or main point questions is that an answer choice that captures something that is true about the passage is still not necessarily the correct answer. For one thing, that answer choice may also say something that is not true about the passage, in which case it cannot be, on the whole, taken as correctly expressing the main idea of the passage. On the other hand, an answer choice may even be accurate in its entirety in stating something said in the passage, but be

---

[24] June 2000 LSAT, Section 4, Question 24.

about something that is only a side issue in the passage rather than the main idea of the passage.

It is also worth noting that that there is more than one way of saying what the main idea of a passage is; as a result, you may not find an answer choice that expresses the main point the way you would have put it. But if you have a good grasp of the passage, the correct answer should come closer to the way you would put it than the other responses do. What this means, however, is that the advice we mentioned earlier—namely, that you should check all the answer choices before moving on to the next question—is especially important for main point questions. As you review all the answer choices, keep in mind that each of the incorrect answer choices will either say something about the passage that is simply false or will describe something that is in the passage and might even contribute to establishing the main point but is not itself that main point. And again, the correct answer will be the only answer choice that is both entirely accurate in its statement of what is in the passage **and** on target in terms of hitting on the most important idea in the passage.

In addition to questions about the main point, which deal with the content that the passage is intended to convey, there is another kind of question that deals with the function of the passage as a whole. This kind of question asks about the way the author proceeds in developing the main idea; that is, they are questions about how the passage is structured. Such questions ask how the passage proceeds, or how the passage is organized, or what the passage is primarily meant to convey, or what the primary purpose of the passage is. For example, a passage might present a puzzling phenomenon and offer an explanation for it. Or it might contrast two opposing views and develop a case for preferring one to the other. Or it might summarize the history of a scientific dispute. The answer choices for questions of this sort won't track every twist and turn of the author's development of the main point but will instead be very broad characterizations of the way the main point is developed. So don't be concerned if the correct answer seems to contain very little detail. The incorrect answer choices will be at a similar level of generality but will clearly fail to capture how the passage as a whole is organized. An incorrect answer choice might describe something that goes on in a portion of the passage or it might not fit anything about the passage at all. In any event, though, it will not get at the main structural blueprint of the passage as a whole.

Note that questions about the structure or organization of the author's text are not all concerned with the passage as a whole. Occasionally there are questions that ask you about the organization of a single paragraph. To answer these, it is a good idea to reread the specific paragraph that the question asks about.

Questions About What the Passage Says or Implies

For each Reading Comprehension passage, you will be asked questions about the various ideas conveyed by the passage. These questions can range from very basic and straightforward questions (what does the passage say, literally?) to more sophisticated questions (what does the author imply without saying it explicitly?) to quite complex and advanced questions (what can be inferred from evidence presented in the passage, independently of whether or not the author intended the implication?). We will discuss all of these types of questions, starting with those at the basic end of the spectrum.

Perhaps the most basic component of Reading Comprehension is simply that of grasping what the text says on a literal level, and some Reading Comprehension questions are designed to make sure that you have processed the passage accurately at this fundamental level. Questions that assess this skill might ask, "Which one of the following is stated in the passage?", "The author says which one of the following about X?", "The passage asserts which one of the following regarding X?", "According to the passage, what is true about X?", or something similar. Even though these questions are fairly straightforward, the correct answer will not be an exact word-for-word repetition of something stated in the passage; it will, however, typically consist of a very close paraphrase of some part of the passage. The idea is that you should be able to identify not the exact wording of something said in the passage, but rather the gist of it.

For example, one of the questions following a passage about muralism, a Mexican artistic movement, reads

Which one of the following does the author explicitly identify as a characteristic of Mexican mural art?

(A) Its subject matter consisted primarily of current events.
(B) It could be viewed outdoors only.
(C) It used the same techniques as are used in easel painting.
(D) It exhibited remarkable stylistic uniformity.
(E) It was intended to be viewed from more than one angle.[25]

In the passage the author asserts that the muralists' works "were designed to be viewable from many different vantage points." The correct answer is therefore (E), "It was intended to be viewed from more than one angle." Notice that the correct answer is a fairly close paraphrase of what the author had stated in the passage.

A similar example occurs after a passage that says at one point, "the lower regions of the Earth's mantle have roughly the same composition as meteorites." The question reads,

According to the passage, the lower regions of the Earth's mantle are characterized by.

(A) *a composition similar to that of meteorites*
(B) *the absence of elements found in rocks on the Earth's crust*
(C) *a greater stability than that of the upper regions*
(D) *the presence of large amounts of carbon dioxide*
(E) *a uniformly lower density than that of the upper regions*[26]

The correct answer is (A), "a composition similar to that of meteorites." Again, the phrase "similar to" is a straightforward equivalent of "roughly the same as." Recognition of what the author says is all that is required in this question; there is no need for any significant interpretation. Questions like this one might seem unexpectedly easy, especially to test takers for whom Reading Comprehension is a relative strength. Don't be put off by how easy such questions might seem, however, and in particular, don't assume that some sort of trick must be lurking in such easy-seeming questions. Just remember that some LSAT questions are designed to test fairly basic skills, and are therefore necessarily easy.

Of course, the process of reading also typically depends on skills that are considerably more advanced than this basic skill of comprehension of the literal content of a text, and other Reading Comprehension questions are designed to test these skills. Any complex piece of writing conveys much more to the attentive reader than what it explicitly states. Authors rely on this, and without having to think about it, readers typically process texts at the level of what they convey implicitly as well as at the level of what they say explicitly. In some cases, much of what a writer leaves out and relies on the reader to supply is subject matter knowledge that the writer assumes the reader to possess. This is especially true when the writer and the intended readers are all thoroughly familiar with the same specialized subject matter: articles in professional journals are good examples of texts that rely on this sort of shared knowledge. It is important to note, however, that **the LSAT does not presuppose any specialized subject matter knowledge**, so none of the questions in it test this kind of specialized reading.

There are, however, many other types of information that a writer leaves out and relies on the reader to supply: things whose inclusion in the reader's comprehension of a text is supported by what the text does explicitly state. Suppose, for example, that a writer states, "The closing of the factory caused additional damage to a regional economy already experiencing high unemployment." In saying this, the writer has not explicitly said that the closing of the factory occurred before the additional damage to the regional economy, but a reader who fails to understand that the closing preceded the damage has probably failed to understand the sentence as a whole. In fact, it is probably safe to say that a reader who lacks the ability to supply such inferences cannot be said to understand what he or she reads in general.

There are a variety of Reading Comprehension questions that assess this ability. For example, you might be asked what can be inferred from a passage or from some specific portion of the passage, what the passage suggests or indicates about some particular matter addressed explicitly in the passage, or what, according to the passage, is true of some particular matter.

Other questions might ask about what a passage conveys or implies about people's beliefs—for example, "It can most reasonably be inferred that the author would agree with which one of the following statements?" or "It can be inferred from the passage that the author most clearly holds which one of the following views?" or "It can be inferred from the passage that Ellison most clearly holds which one of the following views regarding an audience's relationship to works of art?" or "Given the information in the passage, the author is LEAST likely to believe which one of the following?" In approaching such questions, you need to pay close attention to specifically whose beliefs the question asks about. The incorrect answer choices will often be beliefs held by people other than those that the question is about.

What the correct answers to all such questions have in common—whether the questions ask about beliefs or about information—is that they are justified by something that is explicitly stated in the passage. Sometimes this may be no more than a single sentence; on the other hand, sometimes you may have to pull together information from various parts of the passage to identify the correct answer. In some cases, locating the part of the passage that justifies an inference is straightforward. In other cases, the relevant justifying information might not be where one would most naturally expect to find it. In still other cases, there is no single part of the passage that contains all the relevant justifying information.

Questions also vary widely in how closely the correct answers match the part of the passage that justifies them.

Sometimes, the correct answer does not go much beyond a slight rephrasing of the explicit content of the passage. For example, one passage discusses Richard A. Posner's critique of the law-and-literature movement, a movement that advocates the use of "techniques of literary analysis for the purpose of interpreting laws and in the reciprocal use of legal analysis for interpreting literary texts." One question for this passage asks:

The passage suggests that Posner regards legal practitioners as using an approach to interpreting law that

(A) *eschews discovery of multiple meanings*
(B) *employs techniques like deconstruction*
(C) *interprets laws in light of varying community standards*
(D) *is informed by the positions of literary critics*
(E) *de-emphasizes the social relevance of the legal tradition*[27]

The correct answer is (A), "eschews discovery of multiple meanings." What the passage explicitly says is that Posner asserts that "legal interpretation is aimed at discovering a single meaning." The reasoning involved in answering this question is quite straightforward: the passage does not come right out and say that Posner believes that legal practitioners eschew discovery of multiple meanings, but on the other hand it does not take much work to see that "eschew[ing] the discovery of multiple meanings" is the flip side of "to aim at discovering a single meaning." If you can remember the relevant part of the passage or find it quickly, you will find this question and others like it to be quite easy.

Other questions involve identifying the implicit ideas underlying a particular assertion made in a passage. In such cases, the connection between what the passage says and what the correct answer says is often less direct than in the last example, though the connection may still be somewhat easy to see. For example, after a passage concerning harmful bacteria that attack crops, one question reads:

It can be inferred from the passage that crop rotation can increase yields in part because

(A) *moving crop plants around makes them hardier and more resistant to disease*
(B) *the number of Pseudomonas fluorescens bacteria in the soil usually increases when crops are rotated*
(C) *the roots of many crop plants produce compounds that are antagonistic to phytopathogens harmful to other crop plants*

(D) *the presence of phytopathogenic bacteria is responsible for the majority of plant diseases*
(E) *phytopathogens typically attack some plant species but find other species to be unsuitable hosts*[28]

The correct answer is (E), "phytopathogens typically attack some plant species but find other species to be unsuitable hosts." The support for this answer is found in the first paragraph, where the author states:

Cultivation of a single crop on a given tract of land leads eventually to decreased yields. One reason for this is that harmful bacterial phytopathogens, organisms parasitic on plant hosts, increase in the soil surrounding plant roots. The problem can be cured by crop rotation, denying the pathogens a suitable host for a period of time.

Note that the passage says that crop rotation denies pathogens a suitable host for a period of time, but it does not provide an explanation as to why that strategy would work. It is left to the reader to fill in the gap by inferring what the relevant explanation is—namely, because crop rotation involves planting different crops in succession, and because pathogens that attack particular plants typically find other plants to be unsuitable hosts. This idea is not actually stated in the passage; it is instead an implicit assumption. In other words, this is a case in which the reader has to supply missing information in order to fully understand what the author says.

Some of you may have found that you supplied the missing information so quickly and so automatically that it hardly seemed like you drew an inference at all; as a result, you might think it odd that the question asks what can be inferred from the passage. But do not be thrown off if filling the relevant gap required little conscious effort for you. First, what was automatic and effortless for you may in fact require conscious effort on the part of other test takers. Second, questions like this one are designed to test your skill at high-level reading, and part of what defines that skill is the ability to supply relevant presuppositions when the author relies on you to do so. In short, even if, in your subjective experience of this question, the inference was so automatic that it seemed that little or no actual reasoning was required, logically speaking, you still had to draw an inference. This is a genuine skill that this type of Reading Comprehension question is designed to test.

Of course, there are questions in which the connection between the correct answer and the part of the passage that supports it is not so close. The following question involves a relatively large inference to get from the

[27] December 1992 LSAT, Section 3, Question 3.
[28] February 1993 LSAT, Section 3, Question 18.

passage to the correct answer. A second question associated with the passage on Posner and the law-and-literature movement reads:

According to the passage, Posner argues that legal analysis is not generally useful in interpreting literature because

(A) use of the law in literature is generally of a quite different nature than use of the law in legal practice
(B) law is rarely used to convey important ideas in literature
(C) lawyers do not have enough literary training to analyze literature competently
(D) legal interpretations of literature tend to focus on legal issues to the exclusion of other important elements
(E) legal interpretations are only relevant to contemporary literature[29]

The correct answer is (A), "use of the law in literature is generally of a quite different nature than use of the law in legal practice."

Here is the part of the passage that supports this answer:

Critiquing the movement's assumption that lawyers can offer special insights into literature that deals with legal matters, Posner points out that writers of literature use the law loosely to convey a particular idea, or as a metaphor for the workings of the society envisioned in their fiction. Legal questions per se, about which a lawyer might instruct readers, are seldom at issue in literature.

According to Posner, therefore, lawyers can be expected to be helpful about specific technical legal questions, but detailed analysis of technical legal questions is rarely at issue when the law is invoked, as it typically is in literature, to convey an idea or serve as a metaphor. So for Posner the law as it figures in legal practice is very different from the law as it figures in literature. The correct answer, then, is justified by the text of the passage but is by no means a simple restatement of anything that is actually said there. A certain amount of interpretation is required to arrive at this answer.

Similarly, the following is an example of the more typical case of questions that ask what can be inferred from, or what is suggested by, the passage. The question asks:

It can be inferred from the passage that the author's view of Watteau's works differs most significantly from that of most late-nineteenth-century Watteau admirers in which one of the following ways?

The correct answer is:

In contrast to most late-nineteenth-century Watteau admirers, the author finds it misleading to see Watteau's work as accurately reflecting social reality.[30]

There is no statement of precisely this point anywhere in the passage. There are two points in this answer, and they have to be established separately. The first of these points is that most late-nineteenth-century Watteau admirers saw Watteau's work as accurately reflecting social reality. The clearest statement of this position comes in the first paragraph, in which we are told that nineteenth-century writers accepted as genuine the image Watteau had presented of his age (the early eighteenth century). Underscoring this point, the first paragraph ends with the statement that by 1884, the bicentenary of Watteau's birth, it was standard practice for biographers to refer to him as "the personification of the witty and amiable eighteenth century."

The second point contained in the correct answer is that the author does not see Watteau's work as accurately reflecting social reality. Watteau's work is characterized as lyrical and charming, and the century that it portrays as witty and amiable. But the author tells us in the second paragraph that the eighteenth century's first decades, the period of Watteau's artistic activity, were "fairly calamitous ones." The author goes on to say that the year of Watteau's first Paris successes was marked by military defeat and a disastrous famine. For this question, then, justifying the correct answer requires you to identify as relevant, and then put together, various pieces of information that in the passage are interspersed among other pieces of information that have no bearing on the specific question asked.

One final comment on the general category of question we have been discussing in this section. We have been making a distinction between recognizing a paraphrase of something said in the passage and answering questions that require some interpretation or inference. But it may have occurred to some of you that this line can get quite blurry, especially if the paraphrase looks quite different from the original, or the inference seems fairly obvious. For example, think back to the question about crop rotation we discussed earlier (page 45). This question asks what can be inferred from the passage, and the correct answer is indeed an inference inasmuch as it is not stated explicitly, but is rather left implicit in the relevant part of the passage. But on the other hand, the implication is not really very far from the surface of the passage; as a result, identifying it may seem unexpectedly easy to some people.

---

[29] December 1992 LSAT, Section 3, Question 6.
[30] December 1994 LSAT, Section 3, Question 18.

As this example shows, it can be risky to judge answer choices by whether they are easier (or harder) than you expect the correct answer to be. The important thing to remember is that, whatever form the relationship between the passage and the correct answer takes, the correct answer is always the only answer choice that is truly supported by the passage. The incorrect answer choices might appear to be right at first glance, but they will always be found on closer inspection to have something about them that is wrong. Perhaps they are not really supported by the passage, or perhaps they even contradict the passage. As with all Reading Comprehension questions, you should judge the answer choices in questions about what the passage says or implies only by whether or not they are supported by the passage.

Questions That Require Using Context to Refine Meaning (Meaning in Context)

Another skill a good reader brings to a text is the ability to interpret words and phrases not just as a dictionary would define them, but in a more specific sense identifiable from the way in which the author is using them in the particular text. In a given text, words and phrases do not appear in isolation but are embedded in the context of a narrative, an argument, an explanation, and so on. What this wider context does, among other things, is clarify ambiguous expressions, narrow the meaning of vague expressions, or supply a definition for idiosyncratic uses of an expression.

Accordingly, the Reading Comprehension section typically contains questions that test the reading skill of ascertaining the contextually appropriate meanings of words and phrases. In some cases, this task is not very involved. For example, in a passage concerned with offshore oil production, the second paragraph ends by saying:

researchers have discovered that because the swirl of its impeller separates gas out from the oil that normally accompanies it, significant reductions in head can occur as it [a centrifugal pump] operates.

One of the questions following this passage reads:

Which one of the following phrases, if substituted for the word "head" in line 47, would LEAST change the meaning of the sentence?

(A) the flow of the crude inside the pump
(B) the volume of oil inside the pump
(C) the volume of gas inside the pump
(D) the speed of the impeller moving the crude
(E) the pressure inside of the pump[31]

The word "head" is used here in a specialized sense not accessible to the ordinary reader. But the attentive reader of the passage at issue would have noticed that the previous paragraph ended with this sentence:

This surge in gas content causes loss of "head," or pressure inside a pump, with the result that a pump can no longer impart enough energy to transport the crude mixture through the pipeline and to the shore.

In other words, the precise sense in which the word "head" is used in this passage in connection with the operation of pumps has been explicitly clarified. Accordingly, the answer to the question that deals with the meaning of the word "head" here is "the pressure inside of the pump," or (E).

There are cases where contextual clarification is not as clear cut. Take as an example the opening sentence of the passage about the French painter Watteau:

Late-nineteenth-century books about the French artist Watteau (1684 1721) betray a curious blind spot: more than any single artist before or since, Watteau provided his age with an influential image of itself, and nineteenth-century writers accepted this image as genuine.

One of the questions about this passage reads as follows:

The phrase "curious blind spot" (lines 2–3) can best be interpreted as referring to which one of the following?

(A) some biographers' persistent inability to appreciate what the author considers a particularly admirable quality
(B) certain writers' surprising lack of awareness of what the author considers an obvious discrepancy
(C) some writers' willful refusal to evaluate properly what the author considers a valuable source of information about the past
(D) an inexplicable tendency on the part of some writers to undervalue an artist whom the author considers extremely influential
(E) a marked bias in favor of a certain painter and a concomitant prejudice against contemporaries the author considers equally talented[32]

---

[31] February 1994 LSAT, Section 3, Question 4.
[32] December 1994 LSAT, section 3, question 17.

The correct answer turns out to be (B), "certain writers' surprising lack of awareness of what the author considers an obvious discrepancy." You can see that the sentence in which the phrase "curious blind spot" actually appears does not provide nearly enough information to establish the correctness of this answer. No obvious discrepancy is revealed in that sentence, and also no indication that anyone was unaware of this discrepancy. All that can be inferred from the opening sentence of the passage is that the blind spot has to do with nineteenth-century writers accepting as genuine the image Watteau had provided of his age. It is not until we find, at the end of the first paragraph, a nineteenth-century description of Watteau as "the personification of the witty and amiable eighteenth century" that we can tell that the image that Watteau has provided was overwhelmingly positive. In the second paragraph we are told that "The eighteenth century's first decades, the period of [Watteau's] artistic creativity, were fairly calamitous ones." So here the "obvious discrepancy" is finally revealed. Given its obviousness, the fact that late-nineteenth-century writers were evidently not aware of it can reasonably be seen as surprising, or "curious." Notice, however, that a phrase that is introduced in the first sentence of the passage cannot be given the fully specific sense intended for it by the author until the end of the second paragraph has been reached.

Questions About How Things the Author Says Function in Context

A skilled reader has to be able to cope with the fact that writers, even good writers, do not make explicit why they say certain things in certain places. The reader has to be able to extract the function that certain expressions, phrases, sentences, or even paragraphs, have in the context of a larger piece of writing. Sometimes the writer does use conventional cues to guide the reader in how to take what is being said. Such cues, though conventional, can be quite subtle. A good reader picks up on those cues and uses them in interpreting the piece of text to which they are relevant.

An example of a textual connection not made explicit at all occurs in the following lengthy excerpt from a passage about women medical practitioners in the Middle Ages. First, a little background to place the excerpt in context: it begins with the phrase, "This common practice," which refers back to a practice discussed earlier in the same paragraph. According to the author, the typical practice among historians studying the Middle Ages is to take the term "woman medical practitioner," whenever it appears in medieval records, to mean "midwife." The relevant excerpt, then, reads:

> This common practice obscures the fact that, although women were not represented on all levels of medicine equally, they were represented in a variety of specialties throughout the broad medical community. A reliable study by Wickersheimer and Jacquart documents that, of 7,647 medical practitioners in France during the twelfth through fifteenth centuries, 121 were women; of these, only 44 were identified as midwives, while the rest practiced as physicians, surgeons, apothecaries, barbers, and other healers.

There is no explicit statement in this passage of why the author chooses to cite the study by Wickersheimer and Jacquart. The sentence about that study simply follows the one preceding it. The reader is not specifically told how to connect the information in that sentence with information presented either earlier or later. For a skilled reader, though, the connection is obvious: the study presents scholarly, documented support for a claim that is made in the preceding sentence, namely that women were represented in a variety of specialties throughout the broad medical community.

So for a question that asks:

> The author refers to the study by Wickersheimer and Jacquart in order to
>
> (A) demonstrate that numerous medical specialties were recognized in Western Europe during the Middle Ages
> (B) demonstrate that women are often underrepresented in studies of medieval medical practitioners
> (C) prove that midwives were officially recognized as members of the medical community during the Middle Ages
> (D) prove that midwives were only a part of a larger community of women medical practitioners during the Middle Ages
> (E) prove that the existence of the midwives can be documented in Western Europe as early as the twelfth century[33]

the correct answer is (D),

> prove that midwives were only a part of a larger community of women medical practitioners during the Middle Ages

This is so even though the author has not said anything like "As proof of this, the study by Wickersheimer and

---

[33] June 1994 LSAT, Section 3, Question 26.

Jacquart may be cited." It is probably safe to say that a reader who does not make this connection on his or her own did not comprehend this part of the passage. For such a reader, the author's reference to the study by Wickersheimer and Jacquart will probably appear to come of out nowhere.

Now consider an example of a question that requires you to understand the way an author uses subtle cues to indicate the function of a piece of text. The passage on which the question is based reads, in part:

Critics have long been puzzled by the inner contradictions of major characters in John Webster's tragedies . . . The ancient Greek philosopher Aristotle implied that such contradictions are virtually essential to the tragic personality, and yet critics keep coming back to this element of inconsistency as though it were an eccentric feature of Webster's own tragic vision.

This question asks:

The author's allusion to Aristotle's view of tragedy in lines 11–13 serves which one of the following functions in the passage?

(A) It introduces a commonly held view of Webster's tragedies that the author plans to defend.
(B) It supports the author's suggestion that Webster's conception of tragedy is not idiosyncratic.
(C) It provides an example of an approach to Webster's tragedies that the author criticizes.
(D) It establishes the similarity between classical and modern approaches to tragedy.
(E) It supports the author's assertion that Elizabethan tragedy cannot be fully understood without the help of recent scholarship.[34]

The correct answer is (B), "It supports the author's suggestion that Webster's conception of tragedy is not idiosyncratic." The author's allusion to Aristotle's view of tragedy introduces the idea that a vision of tragedy similar to Webster's can be traced back to the ancient Greeks. So Webster's view cannot be regarded as idiosyncratic unless the critics are essentially prepared to

dismiss Aristotle's view as unimportant. But what the author does is let Aristotle's view stand as authoritative by using it to portray the critics as wrongheaded. What the author says is that the critics view the element of inconsistency in Webster's characters "as though it were" eccentric. By using the phrase "as though it were" the author suggests that the critics are wrong. The author further says that the critics "keep coming back" to this element, thereby signaling a certain impatience with the stubbornness with which the critics hold on to their mistaken view. And the author says "and yet," thereby signaling that the critics hold on to their mistaken view in the face of clear evidence to the contrary, provided by Aristotle.

To understand how this type of question works, note that the author provides a variety of cues to indicate to the reader that the allusion to Aristotle is introduced to support the position, endorsed by the author, that Webster's conception of tragedy is not idiosyncratic. The cues are recognizable, but they are relatively subtle. There is no explicit statement of the author's position or of how the allusion to Aristotle bears on it.

In approaching questions about what the author's purpose is in using a certain word, phrase, or sentence, remember that, unless that word, phrase, or sentence left you puzzled, you probably already understood the author's purpose as you made your way through the passage. The process involved here is essential and often subtle, but good readers typically exercise this skill automatically and unconsciously. One conclusion to be drawn from this fact is that you should not look for far-fetched interpretations of what the author's purpose was. Most probably the purpose that you automatically supplied in the process of reading is the correct one. If you were not able to appreciate immediately what the purpose of using a particular word, phrase, or sentence was, reread the immediate context. In a well-written text, the author generally supplies all the cues you need to understand the purpose of any part of the text right around that text. An author is not likely to hide hints as to the purpose of a particular choice of word two or three paragraphs away. A close reading of the immediate context will usually reveal what the author's purpose was.

Questions That Require the Recognition of Analogous Patterns or Features in Different Factual Settings

One way for a reader to demonstrate an understanding of a fact pattern that is presented in a text (or of the way someone has made a case for a position) is by recognizing another fact pattern (or argument) as structurally similar. Questions that test this ability are typically included in the Reading Comprehension section.

Questions of this kind will direct you to something specific in the text and ask you to find something similar to it among the answer choices. The relevant part of the passage can be characterized insightfully in general terms, and this characterization has to fit the correct

---

[34] February 1993 LSAT, Section 3, Question 10.

answer as well. What sorts of general terms? Typically, things of the following sort:

- One thing is a cause of another.

- One thing is a subset of another.

- One thing is mistaken for another.

- Some type of behavior is irresponsible.

- Something falls short of a particular standard.

- An action has consequences that are the opposite of those intended.

These examples are given only to illustrate roughly the kind of similarity that you will typically be looking for. They are not meant to suggest that you should first try to restate what is going on in the passage in such terms. What is crucial is a clear understanding of the relevant part of the passage. You don't need an explicit formulation; in fact, attempting to come up with such an explicit formulation may be a waste of your time.

To see what is involved here, let us consider a very simple case first. The question asks,

Which one of the following is most closely analogous to the error the author believes historians make when they equate the term "woman medical practitioner" with "midwife"?

(A) equating pear with apple
(B) equating science with biology
(C) equating supervisor with subordinate
(D) equating member with nonmember
(E) equating instructor with trainee[35]

As we saw earlier when we considered another question from this set (page 48), the author asserts that historians do in fact equate the term "woman medical practitioner," whenever they encounter it in medieval records, with "midwife." But the wording of the question further alerts us to the fact that historians who equate the two terms are committing a particular kind of error. The author's account of this error is presented in the following words: "This common practice obscures the fact that, although women were not represented on all levels of medicine equally, they were represented in a variety of specialties throughout the broad medical community." The author elaborates on

this by saying that in a study of medical practitioners that included 121 women, only 44 of those women were midwives, whereas the rest practiced as physicians, surgeons, apothecaries, barbers, and other healers. So the error, stated in general terms, lies in equating a category with one of its subcategories. What you are asked to do is select the answer choice that presents the same error.

The correct answer is (B), "equating science with biology." Someone who equates science with biology would be ignoring the fact that the category of science includes many subcategories in addition to biology. Such a person would commit an error analogous to the one that the author believes historians make.

Notice that not everything about (B) is closely analogous to the historians' equating of woman medical practitioners with midwives. For example, the terms equated in (B) refer to academic subjects and not to people. On the other hand, the terms equated in (C) and (E) do refer to people, just as do those equated by the historians. So why does the similarity in terms of people being referred to not matter? Because it is no part of what makes the historians' practice an error that they happen to be talking about people.

When you focus on finding errors analogous to the historians' error, you find that none of answer choices (A), (C), (D), and (E) make such an error. They all do make an error, and it happens to be the same kind of error in each case. They all equate terms, neither of which includes the other, whereas the historians equate terms, one of which—but only one of which—includes the other. What the historians get wrong is that they fail to see that not all woman medical practitioners were midwives, even though all midwives were medical practitioners. By contrast, what (A), for example, gets wrong in equating pears with apples is that it lumps together two categories, neither of which includes the other even partially.

Now let's look at a more complex example. In a passage concerned with certain interactions between the United States Bureau of Indian Affairs and the Oneida tribe of Wisconsin, we are told that the Oneida were offered a one-time lump-sum payment of $60,000 in lieu of the $0.52 annuity guaranteed in perpetuity to each member of the tribe under the Canandaigua Treaty. We are then further informed that

The offer of a lump-sum payment was unanimously opposed by the Oneida delegates, who saw that changing the terms of a treaty might jeopardize the many pending land claims based upon the treaty.

---

[35] June 1994 LSAT, Section 3, Question 23.

There is a question that is based on this rejection of the lump-sum offer and which reads as follows:

Which one of the following situations most closely parallels that of the Oneida delegates in refusing to accept a lump-sum payment of $60,000?

(A) A university offers a student a four-year scholarship with the stipulation that the student not accept any outside employment; the student refuses the offer and attends a different school because the amount of the scholarship would not have covered living expenses.

(B) A company seeking to reduce its payroll obligations offers an employee a large bonus if he will accept early retirement; the employee refuses because he does not want to compromise an outstanding worker's compensation suit.

(C) Parents of a teenager offer to pay her at the end of the month for performing weekly chores rather than paying her on a weekly basis; the teenager refuses because she has a number of financial obligations that she must meet early in the month.

(D) A car dealer offers a customer a $500 cash payment for buying a new car: the customer refuses because she does not want to pay taxes on the amount, and requests instead that her monthly payments be reduced by a proportionate amount.

(E) A landlord offers a tenant several months rent-free in exchange for the tenant's agreeing not to demand that her apartment be painted every two years, as is required by the lease; the tenant refuses because she would have spend her own time painting the apartment.[36]

What precisely is the situation of the Oneida delegates in refusing the lump-sum payment? It is an action (refusing the offer) that is motivated by a specific reason, namely concern that not taking that action might have undesirable legal ramifications. This is a rather broad characterization of the situation in which the Oneida delegates find themselves, but it turns out to be a description that applies equally well to the correct answer, and **only** to the correct answer. The correct answer is (B), "A company seeking to reduce its payroll obligations offers an employee a large bonus if he will accept early retirement; the employee refuses because he does not want to compromise an outstanding worker's compensation suit." What is parallel is the reason why an otherwise generous-seeming offer is refused.

Notice that there are some clear differences between the situation of the Oneida delegates and that of the employee. For example, in one case it is delegates refusing on behalf of a large group that would be affected by that decision, and in the other case a single individual refuses on his own behalf alone. But this difference plays no role in selecting the correct answer, even though it might be seen as a significant difference between the two situations. First, the fact that this important decision affecting the Oneida people as a whole was made by Oneida delegates, although mentioned in the passage, is not given any prominence anywhere in the passage. What the passage does focus on, in discussing the refusal of the lump-sum offer, is the reasons the delegates had for their refusal. So as the passage presents the situation, the reasons for the refusal are the central feature of the situation, and for another situation to be parallel, it would have to be parallel in this respect. Only the correct answer meets this requirement. Moreover, notice that all of the answer choices are like the correct answer in focusing on an individual, which means that it is not the case that any of the incorrect answers are more parallel to the passage even in this regard.

In fact, any scenario that is analogous or parallel to another one **has to be different** in some ways. Otherwise it would be identical to the first scenario, and not just analogous to it. So it is important to keep in mind that the correct answer to this type of question will be the one that is **most closely parallel** or **most analogous** or **most similar** to something discussed in the passage, even though it will necessarily be dissimilar in many respects.

Questions About the Author's Attitude

Authors write things for a variety of reasons. They may just write to report, simply putting down what they take to be the facts, giving no indication of their own feelings, either positive or negative, about those facts. Or they may set down what someone else has reported as fact, without giving any indication of how that person feels about them or how they themselves feel about them. But often authors write with other purposes in mind. For example, they may write to persuade the reader of the merits of some position, in which case they typically write in such a way that the reader can tell that they have positive feelings with respect to that position. By contrast, they may write to warn the reader that a view has no merit, in which case they often make evaluative comments that allow the reader to infer what their attitude toward the matter is. Thus, one feature of a text that

---

[36] October 1993 LSAT, Section 1, Question 13.

careful readers pay attention to is whether the author, by taking a certain tone, or by certain word choices, betrays any attitude other than bland neutrality toward the material he or she is presenting. Also of interest is whether any of the people mentioned by the author in the passage are presented as having any particular attitude toward anything that figures in the passage. These things are potentially important in evaluating what has been read. For example, if an author's attitude is one of boundless enthusiasm, a careful reader might take what that author says with a grain of salt.

In the Reading Comprehension section, you will encounter questions that ask directly about what the author's attitude is, or the attitude of people that the author discusses. Another kind of question may ask you to consider words or phrases that appear in the passage and to identify those that indicate the attitude of the author, or of people mentioned in the passage, toward some specific thing that is discussed in the passage.

When you are dealing with a question that asks directly about attitude, you should assess the passage with an eye to whether it contains indicators of tone or evaluative terms. For example, sometimes an initially positive tone is tempered later by an expression of reservations; or an initially rather dismissive tone might be moderated later by a grudging admission of something worthwhile. The description of the author's attitude overall will reflect this and you should choose among the answer choices accordingly. An example will illustrate this point. The question reads:

The attitude of the author of the passage toward Breen and Innes's study can best be described as one of

(A) *condescending dismissal*
(B) *wholehearted acceptance*
(C) *contentious challenge*
(D) *qualified approval*
(E) *sincere puzzlement*[37]

The correct answer is (D), "qualified approval." The first reference to Breen and Innes occurs early in the passage, in the sentence

In Myne Owne Ground, *T. H. Breen and Stephen Innes contribute significantly to a recent, welcome shift from a white-centered to a black-centered inquiry into the role of African Americans in the American colonial period.*

The word "welcome" indicates approval, and since Breen and Innes are said to have significantly contributed to something that is welcome, the approval extends to them and their study. But this is not the only sign of the author's attitude. Much later in the passage, the author says that Breen and Innes "underemphasize much evidence that customary law, only gradually embodied in statutory law, was closing in on free African Americans well before the 1670's . . ." The verb "underemphasize" expresses a criticism of Breen and Innes' work, and so the approval indicated by "welcome" can no longer be regarded as unqualified. The correct answer, "qualified approval," does justice to both expressions of the author's attitude.

Sometimes you may be asked to identify the words or phrases in a passage that are indicative of the author's attitude toward something. A question of this sort might ask,

The author's attitude toward the "thesis" mentioned in line 56 is revealed in which one of the following pairs of words?

(A) *"biases" (line 5) and "rhetorical" (line 6)*
(B) *"wield" (line 7) and "falsification" (line 17)*
(C) *"conjectures" (line 16) and "truck with" (line 19)*
(D) *"extremism" (line 20) and "implausible" (line 24)*
(E) *"naïve" (line 35) and "errors" (line 42)*[38]

The correct answer is (D), "extremism" (line 20) and "implausible" (line 24). As the term "extremism" is used in line 20, it applies to the authors of the thesis mentioned in line 56, and thus indirectly to the thesis itself. In line 24 the author uses the term "implausible" to characterize one aspect of the thesis, its rejection of a traditional belief. Taken together, these two words reveal a strongly negative attitude on the part of the author toward the thesis at issue. By contrast, in the incorrect answer choices, at least one of the terms presented, though it may reveal an attitude of the author's, does not apply to the thesis in line 56. For example, one of the incorrect answer choices is "naïve" (line 35) and "errors" (line 42).

Both words are good candidates for indicating attitude, and both are used by the author to express an attitude. However, when you look at line 35, you discover that the author uses "naïve" to characterize a view that is an extreme opposite of the thesis at issue, and so does not express the author's attitude toward the thesis itself. Having discovered this much, you know that you can rule out this answer choice, whatever it is that "errors" applies to.

---

[37] December 1994 LSAT, Section 3, Question 12.
[38] December 1992 LSAT, Section 3, Question 15.

Questions About the Significance of Additional Information

Good readers read critically. That is to say, as they read the particular case an author makes for taking a certain position, they do not just passively take in what is on the page. Rather, they evaluate the plausibility, coherence, and strength of the claims and arguments advanced by the author. As they go along, they evaluate the strength of the author's case. They may think of objections to the way an author supports a position. Alternatively, they may think of things that the author hasn't mentioned that would have strengthened the author's case. Or they may think of questions to which they don't know the answer but that would be relevant questions to raise.

The test does not require you to think up considerations that would either strengthen or undercut the case an author has made for a position, but it includes questions that require you to recognize such considerations. You will be asked to determine whether new information strengthens or weakens a particular argument made in the passage. Often, the question will use the words **strengthen** or **weaken** themselves. But questions might also use analogous expressions such as to **support**, **bolster**, or **reinforce** a given claim or position; or to **undermine**, **challenge**, or **call into question** a given claim or position.

The following is an example of how a question might be phrased that requires you to recognize a difficulty with an explanation that has been proposed:

Which one of the following, if true, would most seriously undermine the explanation proposed by the author in the third paragraph?

(A) A number of songbird species related to the canary have a shorter life span than the canary and do not experience neurogenesis.

(B) The brain size of several types of airborne birds with life spans similar to those of canaries has been shown to vary according to a two-year cycle of neurogenesis.

(C) Several species of airborne birds similar to canaries in size are known to have brains that are substantially heavier than the canary's brain.

(D) Individual canaries that have larger-than-average repertoires of songs tend to have better developed muscles for flying.

(E) Individual canaries with smaller and lighter brains than the average tend to retain a smaller-than-average repertoire of songs.[39]

Notice that the proviso "if true" means that you are told to treat each answer choice as if it is true, at least for the purposes of this question. You do not have to concern yourself with whether it is actually true. The explanation in the

third paragraph to which the question refers is an explanation of a phenomenon called neurogenesis (the growth of new neurons) that has been observed in canaries:

A possible explanation for this continual replacement of nerve cells may have to do with the canary's relatively long life span and the requirements of flight. Its brain would have to be substantially larger and heavier than might be feasible for flying if it had to carry all the brain cells needed to process and retain all the information gathered over a lifetime.

In other words, neurogenesis is held to be explained by the hypothesized need to keep the canaries' brains small and light so that the birds can fly. This explanation would have to be abandoned, or at least greatly modified, if the correct answer, (C), were true: "Several species of airborne birds similar to canaries in size are known to have brains that are substantially heavier than the canary's brain." In other words, assuming that this answer choice is true, it seems unlikely that canaries would have any difficulty flying even if their brains were a good bit heavier than they are. In that case, the requirements of flight would not appear to be what dictates the small brain size in canaries and thus could not be invoked to explain neurogenesis, the mechanism by which canary brains are kept small.

In this example, the explanation depended on a certain supposition's being true. The additional information suggests that this supposition might well not be true. In other questions that ask about what would weaken or strengthen something in the passage, the additional information given in the correct answer might be related to the passage in other ways. For example, the additional information might suggest that something is true that would have been predicted given what the passage says, thereby strengthening the case made in the passage. Or it might tell you that something that would have been predicted given what the passage says doesn't, or isn't likely to, happen, in which case the argument advanced in the passage would be weakened. Or it might suggest that a generalization that the passage relied on does not hold up in the particular case under consideration. Or it might suggest that a claim made in the passage is unlikely to be true.

What you have to keep in mind is that what you're looking for is information that has an impact on the plausibility of the position, explanation, claim, evidence, and so on that the question specifically asks you about. It is not enough that a piece of information is about something that the passage is concerned with or even about the particular thing that the question is about. The correct answer has to have a real effect on the strength of the position being asked about.

On the other hand, the correct answer does not have to conclusively establish or definitively refute the position being asked about. Given that these questions ask about what would **strengthen** or **weaken** something said in the passage, it is enough for the correct answer to increase (for **strengthen** questions) or decrease (for **weaken** questions) the likelihood that the argument or position in question is right.

On the following pages, you will find answers and explanations for all the questions that appear in the PrepTests A, B, and C in this book. Each question has been assigned a level of difficulty. We recommend that you read the guides on pages 4–54 before reading the explanations since some of the explanations presuppose that you have read the guides.

■ Level of Difficulty

The difficulty categories are based on a measure designed to represent how hard it is to solve the questions without guessing. For each question type (Analytical Reasoning, Logical Reasoning, and Reading Comprehension), the questions for the three tests in this book are divided into five groups according to their difficulty, from 1 (easiest) to 5 (hardest). So, for example, an Analytical Reasoning question with a difficulty level of 1

is among the easiest fifth of the Analytical Reasoning questions, a Logical Reasoning question with a difficulty level of 1 is among the easiest fifth of the Logical Reasoning questions, and so on.

■ Organization

The explanations are divided into sets of questions corresponding to the sections of each test—first PrepTest A (February 1996), then PrepTest B (February 2000), and finally PrepTest C (February 2000). The explanations appear here in the same order as they appear on the test. Page numbers corresponding to the passage or question under discussion appear in italics.

General Directions for the LSAT Answer Sheet

The actual testing time for this portion of the test will be 2 hours 55 minutes. There are five sections, each with a time limit of 35 minutes. The supervisor will tell you when to begin and end each section. If you finish a section before time is called, you may check your work on that section only; do not turn to any other section of the test book and do not work on any other section either in the test book or on the answer sheet.

There are several different types of questions on the test, and each question type has its own directions. Be sure you understand the directions for each question type before attempting to answer any questions in that section.

Not everyone will finish all the questions in the time allowed. Do not hurry, but work steadily and as quickly as you can without sacrificing accuracy. You are advised to use your time effectively. If a question seems too difficult, go on to the next one and return to the difficult question after completing the section. MARK THE BEST ANSWER YOU CAN FOR EVERY QUESTION. NO DEDUCTIONS WILL BE MADE FOR WRONG ANSWERS. YOUR SCORE WILL BE BASED ONLY ON THE NUMBER OF QUESTIONS YOU ANSWER CORRECTLY.

ALL YOUR ANSWERS MUST BE MARKED ON THE ANSWER SHEET. Answer spaces for each question are lettered to correspond with the letters of the potential answers to each question in the test book. After you have decided which of the answers is correct, blacken the corresponding space on the answer sheet. BE SURE THAT EACH MARK IS BLACK AND COMPLETELY FILLS THE ANSWER SPACE. Give only one answer to each question. If you change an answer, be sure that all previous marks are erased completely. Since the answer sheet is machine scored, incomplete erasures may be interpreted as intended answers. ANSWERS RECORDED IN THE TEST BOOK WILL NOT BE SCORED.

There may be more questions noted on this answer sheet than there are questions in a section. Do not be concerned but be certain that the section and number of the question you are answering matches the answer sheet section and question number. Additional answer spaces in any answer sheet section should be left blank. Begin your next section in the number one answer space for that section.

LSAC takes various steps to ensure that answer sheets are returned from test centers in a timely manner for processing. In the unlikely event that an answer sheet(s) is not received, LSAC will permit the examinee to either retest at no additional fee or to receive a refund of his or her LSAT fee. THESE REMEDIES ARE THE EXCLUSIVE REMEDIES AVAILABLE IN THE UNLIKELY EVENT THAT AN ANSWER SHEET IS NOT RECEIVED BY LSAC.

Score Cancellation

Complete this section only if you are absolutely certain you want to cancel your score. A CANCELLATION REQUEST CANNOT BE RESCINDED. IF YOU ARE AT ALL UNCERTAIN, YOU SHOULD NOT COMPLETE THIS SECTION; INSTEAD, YOU SHOULD CONSIDER SUBMITTING A SIGNED SCORE CANCELLATION FORM, WHICH MUST BE RECEIVED AT LSAC WITHIN 9 CALENDAR DAYS OF THE TEST.

To cancel your score from this administration, you **must**:

A. fill in both ovals here ..... ◯◯
   AND

B. read the following statement. Then sign your name and enter the date.
   YOUR SIGNATURE ALONE IS NOT SUFFICIENT FOR SCORE CANCELLATION. BOTH OVALS ABOVE MUST BE FILLED IN FOR SCANNING EQUIPMENT TO RECOGNIZE YOUR REQUEST FOR SCORE CANCELLATION.

I certify that I wish to cancel my test score from this administration. I understand that my request is irreversible and that my score will not be sent to me or to the law schools to which I apply.

_____
Sign your name in full

_____
Date

HOW DID YOU PREPARE FOR THE LSAT?
(Select all that apply.)

Responses to this item are voluntary and will be used for statistical research purposes only.

◯ By studying the sample questions in the *LSAT Registration and Information Book.*
◯ By taking the free sample LSAT in the *LSAT Registration and Information Book.*
◯ By working through *The Official LSAT Prep Test(s) and/or TriplePrep.*
◯ By using a book on how to prepare for the LSAT **not** published by LSAC.
◯ By attending a commercial test preparation or coaching course.
◯ By attending a test preparation or coaching course offered through an undergraduate institution.
◯ Self study.
◯ Other preparation.
◯ No preparation.

CERTIFYING STATEMENT

Please write (DO NOT PRINT) the following statement. Sign and date.

I certify that I am the examinee whose name appears on this answer sheet and that I am here to take the LSAT for the sole purpose of being considered for admission to law school. I further certify that I will neither assist nor receive assistance from any other candidate, and I agree not to copy or retain examination questions or to transmit them in any form to any other person.

_____
_____
_____
_____
_____
_____
_____
_____
_____
_____

SIGNATURE: _____   TODAY'S DATE: ____/____/____
                                                                      MONTH DAY YEAR

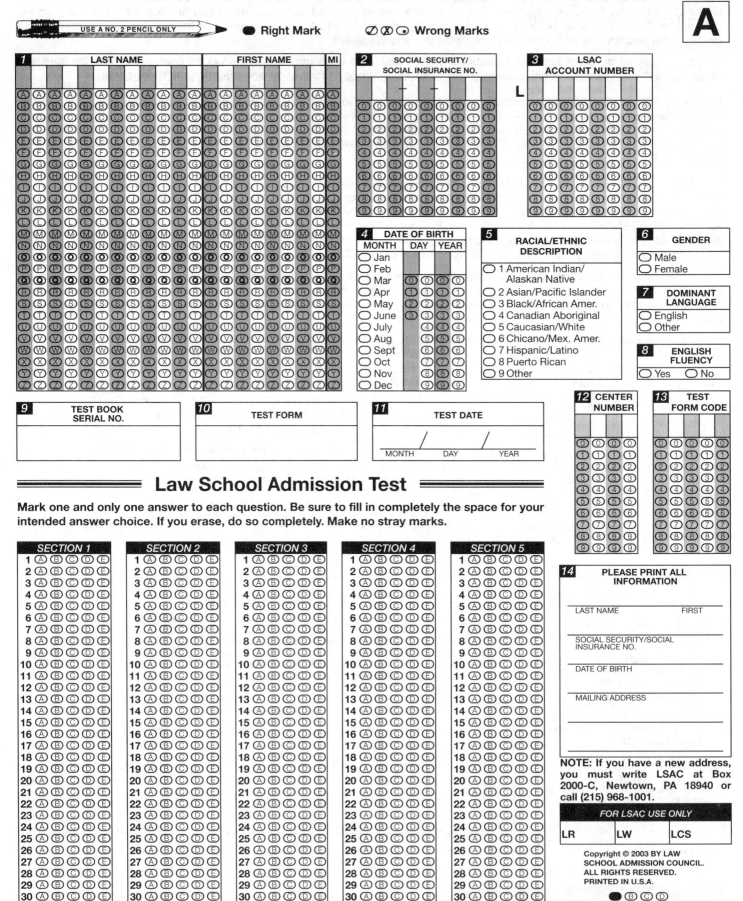

PrepTest A Table of Contents

SECTION I

Time—35 minutes

25 Questions

<u>Directions:</u> The questions in this section are based on the reasoning contained in brief statements or passages. For some questions, more than one of the choices could conceivably answer the question. However, you are to choose the <u>best</u> answer; that is, the response that most accurately and completely answers the question. You should not make assumptions that are by commonsense standards implausible, superfluous, or incompatible with the passage. After you have chosen the best answer, blacken the corresponding space on your answer sheet.

1. Frequently, people who diet to lose weight become trapped in a vicious cycle. When those people diet, they not only lose weight, but their bodies become used to fewer calories and become accustomed to functioning at that lower rate of caloric intake. As a result, when they stop dieting and go back to eating amounts of food that would have just maintained their weight in the days before the diet, they take in far more calories than they need. Those excess calories produce excess weight.

   The passage above best supports which one of the following conclusions about people who diet to lose weight?

   (A) They are bound to end up weighing more than when they started dieting.
   (B) They should not diet if they desire to maintain their reduced weight.
   (C) They must not go back to eating pre-diet amounts of food if they are to maintain their weight at the reduced level resulting from dieting.
   (D) They will have to eat even less than the amount of food allowed by their diets if they are to avoid gaining weight after they stop dieting.
   (E) They never can go back to their pre-diet caloric intake without regaining all of the weight lost by dieting.

2. The *gu*, the *hu*, and the *jue* are types of bronze libation vessels that were produced in China during the Shang dynasty, almost 4,000 years ago. Close examination of authentic *gu*, *hu*, and *jue* vessels reveals that they all bear incised patterns symbolizing the *taotie*, a mythological beast of greed. It must be true then that any bronze libation vessel that does not bear incised patterns symbolizing the *taotie* is not an authentic vessel produced in China during the Shang dynasty.

   The argument makes which one of the following errors of reasoning?

   (A) basing a generalization on claims that contradict each other
   (B) basing a generalization on examples that the argument itself admits are atypical
   (C) treating the fact that some members of a given category possess a certain characteristic as sufficient evidence that other objects that possess the characteristic are also members of that category
   (D) treating the fact that some members of a category possess a certain characteristic as sufficient evidence that possession of the characteristic is necessary for membership in that category
   (E) treating the facts that certain specific objects belong to a given category and that some other objects belonging to that category possess a certain characteristic as sufficient evidence that the former objects also possess that characteristic

GO ON TO THE NEXT PAGE.

3. In a democratic society, when a political interest group exceeds a certain size, the diverse and sometimes conflicting economic interests that can be found in almost any large group of people tend to surface. Once these conflicting interests have surfaced, they can make it impossible for the political interest group to unite behind a common program. Yet to have the political impact necessary to influence legislation, a group must be united.

The statements above, if true, most strongly support which one of the following views?

(A) Political interest groups are generally less influential when their membership is expanding than when it is numerically stable.

(B) For a democratic society to function effectively, it is necessary for political groups within that society to make compromises with each other.

(C) Politicians can ignore with impunity the economic interests of very large groups of people.

(D) A political interest group can become ineffective by expanding to include as wide a membership as possible.

(E) Political interest groups generally start out effectively but lose their effectiveness over time.

4. Safety inspector: The number of laboratory samples of rabies virus sent through the university delivery service has recently grown dangerously high. We need to limit this use of the service.

Biologist: There is no need for a limit. The university delivery service has been handling rabies virus samples for 20 years with no accidents.

As a rebuttal of the safety inspector's claim, the biologist's reasoning is flawed in that it

(A) fails to explain why the number of samples sent through the service has increased

(B) fails to focus specifically on the issue of rabies virus samples

(C) overlooks the possibility that there has been a change in the hazardousness of the rabies virus samples themselves

(D) offers no defense of the university's need for continued delivery of rabies virus samples

(E) does not address the potential for harm that is posed by the recent increase in the number of samples sent through the service

5. Manager: One reason productivity in our office is not as high as it could be is that office workers spend too much time taking unauthorized breaks. Since the number of office workers assigned to each manager will soon be reduced, managers will be able to supervise workers more closely in the future to make sure that they are not taking unauthorized breaks. Therefore, productivity in our office will soon increase.

Which one of the following is an assumption on which the manager's argument depends?

(A) The best way to improve productivity is to reduce the number of employees and give more work to employees who remain on the job.

(B) Office workers are spending more time now taking unauthorized breaks than they used to.

(C) Giving financial incentives to workers whose divisions increase their productivity would not have any significant effect on overall office productivity.

(D) Supervising employees more closely to reduce unauthorized breaks is the most efficient way of increasing overall office productivity.

(E) The gain in productivity that will result from reducing unauthorized breaks will exceed any loss in productivity caused by closer supervision.

GO ON TO THE NEXT PAGE.

Questions 6–7

Tom: Executives in this country make around 85 times what the average worker earns. This is an extraordinarily large disparity, and therefore public resentment over the size of executives' salaries is justified.

Martha: Such resentment is not justified, since wealth is created by taking risks and making decisions, actions most people prefer to avoid. Generous rewards for those who choose not to avoid these actions are both fair and necessary.

Tom: I think you misunderstood me. I'm not saying that people resent that there is a large disparity here between executives' salaries and workers' salaries, but rather they resent that it is atypically large: in other countries executives earn only 20 or 30 times what the average worker earns.

6. Which one of the following most accurately expresses the main point at issue between Tom and Martha?

(A)   whether executives in this country make 85 times the average worker's salary

(B)   whether public resentment of the size of executive salaries is justified

(C)   whether a wage gap between executives and workers is necessary to promote the creation of wealth

(D)   whether executives deserve higher salaries than workers deserve

(E)   whether executives in this country create as much wealth as do those in other countries

7. Tom responds to Martha's critique in which one of the following ways?

(A)   He strengthens his own position by tacitly agreeing to drop one of his original premises and introduces a new line of argument defending his original conclusion.

(B)   He introduces evidence showing that a generalization Martha has made regarding the creation of wealth is unwarranted because it is not based on any evidence.

(C)   He undermines Martha's position by pointing out that Martha has made two contradictory assertions in support of the same claim.

(D)   He undermines the relevance of Martha's objection by making explicit his grounds for judging that the disparity at issue is unjustifiably large.

(E)   He raises considerations that call into question the grounds on which Martha bases her conclusion.

8. Fossilized bones from the hominids *Australopithecus robustus* and *Homo erectus* were chemically analyzed. The *robustus* bones contained a lower ratio of strontium to calcium than did the *erectus* bones. The lower the ratio of strontium to calcium in fossilized hominid bones, the more meat the hominid had in its diet. *H. erectus* is known to have eaten meat.

The statements above, if true, most strongly support which one of the following?

(A)   The diet of *A. robustus* included at least some meat.

(B)   The meat in the diet of *H. erectus* was higher in strontium than was the meat in the diets of other hominids.

(C)   The diet of *H. erectus* was richer in calcium than was the diet of *A. robustus*.

(D)   The diets of *A. robustus* and *H. erectus* both contained less strontium than calcium.

(E)   The process of fossilization altered the ratio of strontium to calcium in the bones of both *A. robustus* and *H. erectus*.

GO ON TO THE NEXT PAGE.

Questions 9–10

Letter to the editor: I was shocked to learn that Judge
    Mosston was convicted of criminal assault, but I
    disagree with my fellow citizens who believe that he
    should be forced to resign. I have played cards with
    Judge Mosston for many years, and he has always shown
    himself to be fair toward me and our fellow cardplayers.
    Our judicial system simply cannot afford to lose any just
    and fair judges.

9. Which one of the following most accurately expresses
    the main conclusion of the letter writer's argument?

    (A)   Judge Mosston is a fair judge.
    (B)   Judge Mosston should not be forced to resign.
    (C)   Fairness is the most important quality in a judge.
    (D)   A conviction for criminal assault is never
          sufficient grounds for damaging anyone's
          professional career.
    (E)   Individuals who have interacted with a judge
          outside that judge's courtroom are the most
          objective assessors of that judge's fairness.

10. The reasoning in the letter is most vulnerable to the
    criticism that it

    (A)   confuses duties specific to legal professionals
          with the responsibilities of private citizens
    (B)   insists upon a distinction between "fair" and
          "just" which cannot plausibly be maintained
    (C)   makes a general claim about an individual's
          professional competence based on an
          unrepresentative sampling of the individual's
          behavior
    (D)   treats the violent crime of criminal assault as if its
          consequences were no more serious than
          winning or losing at cards
    (E)   asserts a conclusion based on popular opinion
          rather than on argumentation

11. Building a space station, in which astronauts would live
    for a considerable time, is essential even if the space
    station project were to contribute no new knowledge
    about space or Earth that could not otherwise be
    obtained. For future missions to explore Mars, we will
    need the medical knowledge that the space station
    project will give us about the limits of human capacities
    to live in spacecraft for an extended time.

    The argument makes the assumption that

    (A)   the exploration of Mars will be carried out by
          people traveling in spacecraft and not by robots
          alone
    (B)   the capacities of astronauts are typical of those of
          ordinary human beings
    (C)   no unforeseen medical problems will arise on the
          first mission to explore Mars
    (D)   a mission to Mars will be the first of many
          missions that will explore the solar system
    (E)   living in a spaceship for an extended time
          presents insurmountable medical problems

12. The hearts of patients who are given vitamin E before
    undergoing heart surgery are less susceptible to certain
    postoperative complications than are the hearts of
    patients who are not given vitamin E before heart
    surgery. From six hours after surgery onward, however,
    the survivors from both groups show the same level of
    heart function, on average, and also recover equally well.
    Despite this lack of long-term effect, doctors often
    recommend vitamin E for patients about to undergo heart
    surgery.

    Which one of the following, if true, most helps to
    explain the doctors' recommendation?

    (A)   Postoperative complications pose the greatest
          threat to patients during the first six hours after
          heart surgery.
    (B)   Postoperative complications occur six or more
          hours after surgery for some patients who have
          not been given vitamin E.
    (C)   It sometimes takes less than six hours for a
          patient's heart function to return to normal after
          heart surgery.
    (D)   Certain categories of patients are inherently less
          likely to develop postoperative complications
          than other patients are.
    (E)   Many patients who are told that they are being
          given vitamin E actually receive a medically
          inert substance.

13. Architect: Obviously, a dirty stone building is less
          attractive than a clean one. But the process of
          cleaning stone buildings with water drives the
          water deep into the stone, eventually causing
          irreparable damage. Dirt also damages stone
          buildings, but less than water does. So I am afraid
          stone buildings must remain dirty if they are to last
          as long as possible.

    Engineer: Not so fast. Advances in technology make it
          possible to clean stone buildings without water,
          using mild chemicals that do not penetrate the
          stone.

    The engineer responds to the architect by doing which
    one of the following?

    (A)   disputing the accuracy of the evidence that the
          architect cites in support of the conclusion
    (B)   showing that the architect's argument is internally
          inconsistent
    (C)   describing undesirable consequences that follow
          from accepting the architect's conclusion
    (D)   adducing facts selected to show that the
          architect's conclusion is false
    (E)   using the evidence cited by the architect to draw
          an alternative conclusion

GO ON TO THE NEXT PAGE.

14. Anthropologist: The culture responsible for the inscriptions at the site must have used fire to fashion iron implements. Of the Xa, Ye, and Zi, the three cultures known to have inhabited the area surrounding this site, the Xa could obtain iron but could not use fire to fashion implements and the Ye had no access to iron. Therefore the Zi is the only culture known to be from the surrounding area that could have made these inscriptions.

The reasoning in which one of the following arguments most closely parallels the reasoning used in the argument above?

(A)   Whoever committed the burglary wore size nine shoes. Of the three suspects in custody, Jensen, Kapp, and Lomax, neither Jensen nor Lomax could have worn size nine shoes. Of the three suspects in custody, therefore, nobody but Kapp could be the burglar.

(B)   Anyone wishing to file a claim must first send a check and then visit the bureau. Of Quinn, Robins, and Su, Robins and Su each sent a check and visited the bureau, so Robins and Su can each file a claim.

(C)   The person who designed the Ultra 180 must have been a very patient person. Of three well-known designers, Morris, Nieves, and Ott, who worked for Ultra's manufacturer when the Ultra 180 was designed, Morris and Ott were both impatient people. Therefore, Nieves is the only person who could have designed the Ultra 180.

(D)   Anyone aspiring to public office must have a quick wit and a ready smile. Of my friends Gail, Harry, and Ida, only Harry and Ida are aspiring to public office, so only Harry and Ida could have both a quick wit and a ready smile.

(E)   Whoever wrote this letter to me signed it "Tony." Since I do not know anyone who signs letters with that name, the writer of this letter could only have been someone whom I do not know.

15. Antiwhaling activist: Not all species of whales are threatened with extinction. Nevertheless, given the highly mechanized technology used in whaling, a ban on the whaling of endangered species cannot be enforced without banning the whaling of all other species. Hence, since hunting endangered whale species should be banned, all whale-hunting should be banned.

Which one of the following principles, if established, would do the most to justify the conclusion drawn by the antiwhaling activist?

(A)   The fishing industry has a right to hunt members of species that are not endangered.

(B)   If a certain activity ought to be prohibited, so should any other activity that interferes with the enforcement of that prohibition.

(C)   No industry should adopt new technologies if the adoption of those technologies would create new ethical problems.

(D)   All actions that are instrumental in achieving ends that are permissible are themselves permissible.

(E)   If a commercial form of a certain activity ought to be prohibited, then so should all noncommercial forms of that activity.

GO ON TO THE NEXT PAGE.

Questions 16–17

Giordano Bruno, the Renaissance philosopher, must have been a spy for England during the time he served in the French embassy there. English state records show that a spy who foiled at least two assassination plots against Queen Elizabeth of England was in place in the French embassy in London at that time. Since the spy is identified in confidential English state documents only as "the only clergyman working at the French embassy" at that time, Bruno must have been the spy: Bruno had been ordained a member of the clergy long before he started work at the French embassy.

16. Which one of the following, if true, most weakens the force of the evidence advanced in the argument?

   (A)   Long before his employment at the embassy, Bruno had been excommunicated from his church and thereafter neither dressed nor functioned as a member of the clergy.

   (B)   During Bruno's tenure in the French embassy, a high degree of tension and an atmosphere of mutual suspicion prevailed between France and England.

   (C)   English records show that the spy sometimes transmitted information to the English government in French, which was not the language Bruno knew best.

   (D)   The French ambassador at the time was a man who trusted Bruno implicitly, often defending him from the criticisms of others on the embassy staff.

   (E)   During the Renaissance, well-educated members of the clergy often served in nonclerical roles as tutors, secretaries, and personal assistants to wealthy aristocrats.

17. Which one of the following, if true, provides the most support for the argument?

   (A)   During the Renaissance the staff of each French embassy always included at least one member of the clergy to officiate as chaplain for the ambassador and his staff.

   (B)   Several years after his embassy service ended, Bruno was condemned for his philosophical ideas by the pope, who was at that time generally hostile to England and sympathetic to France.

   (C)   Like the rest of the diplomatic staff at the French embassy, Bruno was introduced to many English aristocrats by the French ambassador.

   (D)   Bruno was known to his contemporaries as a teacher, and that is how he first gained employment with the king of France, who later recommended him to the French ambassador in England.

   (E)   The period of Bruno's tenure at the French embassy corresponds exactly to the period during which, according to English records, the spy was transmitting information.

18. Theories in certain scientific fields may be in flux today, but this unsettled state must be attributed to scientific progress, not to a lack of theoretical rigor. Several decades of scientific research have recently culminated in a wealth of new discoveries in these fields, and whenever many new facts come to light in a field, the ways in which that field organizes its knowledge inevitably need adjustment.

The argument proceeds by

   (A)   presenting the situation to be explained as part of a general pattern

   (B)   referring to the unacceptable consequences of adopting a particular explanation

   (C)   showing that two alternate explanations for a situation are equally probable

   (D)   citing a law of nature to explain a particular kind of change

   (E)   explaining why a situation came about by referring to the intended outcome of a course of action

19. All art criticism is political because all art has political implications. Clearly, the critic who chooses to address overtly an artwork's political implications is engaged in political discourse. But those critics who attempt a purely aesthetic evaluation of a work, and therefore ignore the work's political implications, necessarily, though perhaps inadvertently, end up endorsing the politics of the artist.

If the statements above are all true, which one of the following must also be true?

   (A)   Critics who overtly address an artwork's political implications rarely endorse art for art's own sake.

   (B)   Critics who are politically naïve always attempt purely apolitical critiques of art.

   (C)   Art that makes an overt social or political statement is the sort of art with which critics are typically concerned.

   (D)   A political critique of a work of art has more value than any other sort of critique of that work.

   (E)   Art criticism that is intended to evaluate a work on purely aesthetic grounds never ends up rejecting the politics of the artist whose work is under review.

GO ON TO THE NEXT PAGE.

20. In the country of Boldavia at present, only 1 percent of 80-year-olds are left-handed, whereas 10 percent of 50-year-olds and 15 percent of 20-year-olds are left-handed. Yet over the past 80 years, the proportion of Boldavians who are born left-handed has not increased, nor have Boldavian attitudes toward left-handedness undergone any important changes.

Which one of the following, if true, most helps to explain the variation in incidence of left-handedness among Boldavians?

(A) In Boldavia, where men have a shorter average life expectancy than do women, left-handedness is less common among women than among men.

(B) In Boldavia, left-handed people are no more likely than right-handed people to be involved in accidents.

(C) Ambidexterity is highly valued in Boldavia.

(D) The birthrate in Boldavia has decreased slowly but steadily over the course of the past 80 years.

(E) Left-handed people have never accounted for more than 18 percent of the population of Boldavia.

21. Eugenia: Reliable tests have shown that Koolair brand refrigerators are the best-made of any of the major brands because they last longer and, on the whole, require fewer repairs than do refrigerators of any other major brand.

Neil: That is impossible. I have owned refrigerators of several different major brands, including Koolair, and the Koolair needed more repairs than did any of the others.

The reasoning in Neil's response is flawed because he

(A) uses a different notion of a product's quality from that used by Eugenia

(B) contradicts Eugenia's claim on the basis of a snap judgment and without making any attempt to offer supporting argumentation

(C) rejects a generalization on the basis of a single negative instance when that generalization has reasonable support and is not universal

(D) uses a pretense of authority in a technical field as the only support for his claim

(E) concludes that what holds true of each member of a group taken individually must also hold true of that group taken collectively

22. Advertisement: RediMed is the cold treatment to choose. People who treat their colds with RediMed have symptoms half as severe as those suffered by people who leave their colds untreated.

The flawed pattern of reasoning in which one of the following is most similar to that in the advertisement above?

(A) When cooking spaghetti, you should add the salt to the water when the water is already boiling, since the spaghetti takes on a bitter flavor otherwise.

(B) National Financial is the place for your everyday banking, since it has more checking account customers than any other bank.

(C) Tuff-Grip tires are the ones to choose, since in trials by a consumer magazine they were found to be the most durable and the safest.

(D) The lubricant to select for locks is graphite, since unlubricated locks are stiffer than locks lubricated with graphite and sometimes freeze completely.

(E) If you are not going to use butter for frying, you should use olive oil, since European chefs use olive oil.

GO ON TO THE NEXT PAGE.

23. Health association: In certain studies, most volunteers who used to eat meat have permanently excluded meat from their diets and now eat only vegetables and fruits. These volunteers suffered no ill effects and many even prefer the new regimen. So people who eat meat can change their diets to meatless ones and not suffer as a result.

   Critic: Participants in these studies were all favorably disposed to the substitution before they started, and even so, many of them failed to make a complete transition to a vegetarian diet.

   The critic's response would most seriously call into question which one of the following conclusions, if that conclusion were drawn on the basis of the evidence given by the health association?

   (A)   The diets of most people who eat meat would be improved if those people ate only vegetables and fruits instead.
   (B)   Among those who make the attempt to exclude meat from their diets, the more favorably disposed to the meatless regimen a person is the more likely that person is to succeed in the attempt.
   (C)   The number of people who have adopted a strictly vegetarian diet has increased in the last few years.
   (D)   Participants in the study who failed to make the transition to a vegetarian diet do not regret the attempt.
   (E)   Most people, if told by their physicians to exclude meat from their diets and eat only vegetables and fruits, would succeed in doing so.

24. The shoe factory in Centerville is the town's largest firm, and it employs more unskilled workers on a full-time basis than all of the other businesses in town combined. Therefore, if the shoe factory closes down and ceases all operations, more than half of Centerville's residents who are unskilled workers with full-time jobs in Centerville will lose their jobs.

   The conclusion above logically follows from the premises if which one of the following is assumed?

   (A)   More people who now are residents of Centerville are employed than are unemployed.
   (B)   Centerville has more unskilled workers among its population than it has skilled workers.
   (C)   The shoe factory in Centerville employs more unskilled workers than skilled workers.
   (D)   The shoe factory in Centerville employs no one who is not a resident of Centerville.
   (E)   There are no factories in Centerville other than the shoe factory.

25. In one-round sealed-bid auctions, each prospective buyer submits in strict confidence a single bid, and the sale goes to the highest bidder. A reserve price—a minimum price below which there will be no sale—can be set by the seller as protection against a token bid, which is an unreasonably low bid sometimes made by a bidder who gambles that there will be no other bid. Paradoxically, such protection is most needed when extremely desirable items are auctioned off this way.

   Which one of the following, if true about one-round sealed-bid auctions, most helps to explain why the generalization characterized above as paradoxical holds?

   (A)   The bidder who submitted the winning bid on an item cannot, on being informed of this fact, decline acceptance of the item in favor of the next-highest bidder.
   (B)   The identity of unsuccessful bidders is not disclosed unless those bidders themselves choose to disclose it.
   (C)   The reserve price on an extremely desirable item is generally set high enough to yield a profit for the seller even if the winning bid just matches it.
   (D)   Prospective buyers of an extremely desirable item can often guess quite accurately who at least some of the other prospective buyers are.
   (E)   Prospective buyers tend to believe that, in order to be successful, a bid on an extremely desirable item would have to be so high as not to make economic sense.

S T O P

IF YOU FINISH BEFORE TIME IS CALLED, YOU MAY CHECK YOUR WORK ON THIS SECTION ONLY.
DO NOT WORK ON ANY OTHER SECTION IN THE TEST.

SECTION II

Time—35 minutes

27 Questions

Directions: Each passage in this section is followed by a group of questions to be answered on the basis of what is stated or implied in the passage. For some of the questions, more than one of the choices could conceivably answer the question. However, you are to choose the best answer; that is, the response that most accurately and completely answers the question, and blacken the corresponding space on your answer sheet.

Historians of medieval marriage practices ascribe particular significance to Pope Alexander III's twelfth-century synthesis of existing ecclesiastical and legal opinion concerning marriage. Alexander produced a
(5) doctrine that treated marriage as a consensual union rather than as an arrangement made by parents for reasons of economic expediency: under Alexandrine doctrine, a couple could establish marriage by words of mutual consent and without the consent of parents.
(10) These contracts were of two kinds. On the one hand, a binding and immediately effective union was created through the exchange of words of present consent (*per verba de praesenti*). Neither the prior announcement of the intention to wed nor the solemnization conferred by
(15) Church ritual added anything to the validity and permanence of such a contract. On the other hand, a promise to marry was expressed by words of future consent (*per verba de futuro*); such a contract might be terminated by the agreement of the parties or by a
(20) subsequent *de praesenti* contract.

Although Alexandrine doctrine accepted the secular legal validity of those contracts that lacked public announcement and ritual solemnization, it nonetheless attempted to discourage such clandestine
(25) unions and to regulate marriage procedures. According to the doctrine, a marriage was to be preceded by the publication of the marriage announcements, or banns, on three successive Sundays to allow community members to raise any legal objections to the intended
(30) union. Those couples ignoring this requirement were to be excommunicated, and any priest solemnizing an unpublicized union could be suspended for up to three years. However, the essential secular legal validity of the marriage was in no way impaired.
(35) The presence or absence of the banns became the acid test to determine whether a contract was considered clandestine. Consequently, the very term "clandestine" came to cover a multitude of sins. It could apply just as much to the publicly solemnized
(40) marriage that violated Church law with regard to the time and place of the banns as it could to the informal *de praesenti* contract.

Historian Charles Donahue has stressed the controversial nature of Alexander's view that the
(45) consent of the individuals concerned was sufficient to produce a legally binding marriage; so long as they acted in accordance with established bann procedures, a couple could marry without parental consent and still enjoy the blessing of the Church. Furthermore,
(50) Donahue suggests that Alexandrine doctrine can be

seen as encouraging marriage as a spiritual union rather than as a merely pragmatic arrangement: marriages of love were to be promoted at the expense of those of economic convenience, and the Church was made the
(55) guardian of individual freedom in this area. This interpretation is indeed a radical one, given traditional perceptions of the medieval Church as the most potent authoritarian force in a rigidly hierarchical society.

1. Which one of the following best states the main idea of the passage?

(A) The doctrine of marriage by Pope Alexander III represented a synthesis of traditional ecclesiastical and legal opinion and, according to at least one commentator, encouraged clandestine marriages.

(B) The doctrine of marriage promulgated by Pope Alexander III was based on the mutual consent of the persons involved and, according to at least one commentator, encouraged marriages based on love.

(C) Though ostensibly intended to promote marriages based on love rather than on expediency, the doctrine of marriage promulgated by Pope Alexander III in fact represented a tightening of Church authority.

(D) The spoken marriage contracts legitimized by Pope Alexander III were of two kinds: words of present consent and words of future consent.

(E) According to at least one interpretation, the doctrine of marriage promulgated by Pope Alexander III stated that couples who married without ritual solemnization were to be excommunicated from the Church.

GO ON TO THE NEXT PAGE.

2. Which one of the following can be inferred about the role of parents in medieval marriage practices?

    (A) Parents were more likely to bow to the dictates of the Church than were their children.

    (B) Parents were likely to favor the *de praesenti* rather than the *de futuro* contract.

    (C) Parents were more concerned with the ecclesiastical sanction of a marriage than with its legal validity.

    (D) Parents did not have the power, under Alexandrine doctrine, to prohibit a marriage based on the mutual consent of the couple rather than an economic expediency.

    (E) Parents' concern over the prevalence of clandestine marriages helped bring about the Alexandrine synthesis.

3. According to the passage, which one of the following placed couples at risk of being excommunicated under Alexandrine doctrine?

    (A) violation of laws requiring ritual solemnization of vows

    (B) violation of established banns procedures

    (C) marrying without parental consent

    (D) marrying without the blessing of a priest

    (E) replacing a *de futuro* contract with a *de praesenti* contract

4. Which one of the following best defines "clandestine" as that word is used in the second paragraph of the passage?

    (A) legal, but unrecognized by the Church

    (B) legal, but unrecognized by a couple's parents

    (C) recognized by the Church, but legally invalid

    (D) recognized by the Church, but arranged for reasons of economic expediency

    (E) arranged by *de futuro* contract, but subsequently terminated

5. The primary purpose of the passage is to

    (A) question the legitimacy of a scholarly work by examining the facts on which it is based

    (B) trace the influence of an important legal doctrine through several historical periods

    (C) call for a renewed commitment to research into a neglected field

    (D) summarize the history of an era and endorse a new scholarly approach to that era

    (E) explain a historically important doctrine and describe a controversial interpretation of that doctrine

6. Which one of the following can be inferred from the passage concerning the differences between Charles Donahue's interpretation of medieval marriage practices and other interpretations?

    (A) Most other studies have deemphasized the importance of Pope Alexander III.

    (B) Most other studies have seen in Alexandrine doctrine the beginning of modern secular marriage laws.

    (C) Most other studies have not emphasized the medieval Church's promotion of individual choice in marriage.

    (D) Most other studies have misread the complicated legal and ecclesiastical rituals involved in the public announcement and ritual solemnization of marriage.

    (E) Most other studies have concentrated on the ecclesiastical rather than the secular aspects of Alexandrine doctrine.

7. According to the passage, which one of the following distinguished the *de futuro* contract from the *de praesenti* contract?

    (A) One was recognized by Alexandrine doctrine, while the other was considered a secular contract.

    (B) One required the permission of parents, while the other concerned only the couple involved.

    (C) One required the announcement of marriage banns, while the other could be entered into solely through a verbal contract.

    (D) One expressed future intent, while the other established an immediate, binding union.

    (E) One allowed the solemnization of Church ritual, while the other resulted in excommunication.

8. Which one of the following best describes the function of the second paragraph of the passage?

    (A) It presents an interpretation of facts that diverges from the interpretation given in the first paragraph.

    (B) It identifies an exception to a rule explained in the first paragraph.

    (C) It elaborates upon information presented in the first paragraph by presenting additional information.

    (D) It summarizes traditional interpretations of a topic, then introduces a new interpretation.

    (E) It states the objections of the author of the passage to the argument presented in the first paragraph.

GO ON TO THE NEXT PAGE.

Nontraditional black women filmmakers share with the broader community of radical filmmakers a problematic relation to mainstream, realist cinematic practice. Realist filmmakers manipulate the use of the
(5) camera and techniques of editing and lighting in ways that create the illusion that cinema is like life, that it may indeed be the same as life. In contrast, avant-garde and many minority and feminist filmmakers who seek to tell new stories resist the conventions of cinematic
(10) realism precisely because these practices conceal the artificiality of the filmmaking process, thereby implying that narrative structures, and thus social relations, are inevitable, and that circumstances are as they should be. For example, precisely because one
(15) might expect that a scene depicting a family dinner would entail a continuous view of several people seated together eating and conversing, an avant-garde filmmaker might intersperse images of the dining family with a seemingly arbitrary image—people
(20) standing in a breadline during the Depression of the 1930s, for example. The outcome, according to many film theorists, is that our notion of reality is violated: the images do not make immediate sense, and we are therefore forced to question our convictions about the
(25) "reality" to which we are committed. The very techniques that create the illusion of visual continuity, some theorists say, smooth over contradictions and incoherences that might reflect a reality that Hollywood—and the majority culture that is its
(30) audience—does not want to admit or know.

The ideological content of these conservative cinematic techniques notwithstanding, some nontraditional black women filmmakers do tend to explore the formal possibilities of realism in
(35) documentaries instead of experimenting with more daring modes. They may choose to work within the realist form because it is more accessible to a broad audience, or because of the financial constraints under which they labor. It is important to emphasize,
(40) however, that the prevailing notion that such filmmakers cannot be called experimental, because only technical experimentation counts as "experimental," places an undue emphasis on form at the expense of content. A realist work that centers on a
(45) nontraditional subject might rightfully be called experimental in its own way.

For example, *Fannie's Film* (1981) by Fronza Woods provides the opportunity for a working woman to tell her own story. This film belongs to a group of
(50) films that, by presenting the stories of "ordinary" women whose experiences have usually been trivialized or ignored by mainstream media, expose the thematic assumptions and stylistic conventions of realistic filmmaking. Documentaries have also
(55) attracted these directors because documentaries provide opportunities for revising the list of traditionally acknowledged prominent figures by creating more accounts of black public figures. Films like Michelle Parkerson's . . . *But Then, She's Betty Carter* (1980),
(60) by examining and preserving the lives and works of the visual and performing artists who are their subjects, urge their audiences to question their own expectations about who gains public recognition and why.

9. Which one of the following best states the main idea of the passage?

(A) Nontraditional black women filmmakers share with the broader community of radical filmmakers a problematic relation to conservative techniques of editing and lighting.

(B) Some nontraditional black women filmmakers successfully use what are commonly regarded as mainstream cinematic techniques to make experimental films.

(C) Experimental filmmakers manipulate techniques of editing and lighting in order to dispel the illusion that cinema is like life.

(D) Mainstream and experimental filmmakers have not acknowledged the impact of black women filmmakers on cinematic practice.

(E) Mainstream filmmakers prefer to avoid dealing with controversial topics in their films.

10. It can be inferred that the author of the passage believes which one of the following about the "prevailing notion" (line 40) of what constitutes an experimental film?

(A) The notion mistakenly relies upon a narrow definition of technical experimentation espoused by mainstream filmmakers.

(B) The notion fails to acknowledge the unique potential of conservative cinematic techniques for expressing radical ideas.

(C) The notion pays insufficient attention to the way nontraditional black women filmmakers exploit experimental cinematic techniques in their films.

(D) The notion ignores the fact that the content of a cinematic work may be as crucial to the work's experimental character as is the work's form.

(E) The notion ignores the fact that the form of a cinematic work may not be as important to the work's mainstream character as is the work's content.

GO ON TO THE NEXT PAGE.

11. Each of the following is accomplished by one of the documentary films described by the author of the passage EXCEPT:

   (A) calling the thematic assumptions of realistic filmmaking into question

   (B) examining the lives of black public figures who have not received substantial public recognition

   (C) examining the lives of women neglected by mainstream media

   (D) influencing how women are portrayed in mainstream media

   (E) moving audiences to question their assumptions about why certain people are denied public recognition

12. It can be inferred from the passage that the theorists referred to in line 27 would most probably agree with which one of the following statements about mainstream filmmakers?

   (A) Most of them cater to audiences who are not sufficiently knowledgeable to be able to appreciate films that employ experimental techniques.

   (B) Some of them seek to combat majority culture ignorance about minority cultures.

   (C) Many of them make films whose techniques conceal from audiences what those audiences would prefer not to know.

   (D) They usually do not exploit the documentary form because this form relies less on techniques that create illusions of visual continuity.

   (E) They do not make many experimental films because they are not knowledgeable about the techniques of experimental filmmaking.

13. The primary purpose of the passage is to

   (A) contrast and assess some of the works of nontraditional black women filmmakers

   (B) critique the subjects and techniques of realist filmmaking

   (C) define which black women filmmakers can be considered experimental

   (D) examine the relationship of nontraditional black women filmmakers to realist cinematic practice

   (E) contextualize and categorize the works of avant-garde and feminist filmmakers

GO ON TO THE NEXT PAGE.

Like Charles Darwin, Alfred Wegener revolutionized an entire science. Unlike Darwin's ideas, which still stir up much controversy, Wegener's theory of drifting continents is accepted almost without
(5) question, but it did not succeed without a struggle.

In 1912 Wegener suggested that Africa and South America are estranged pieces of a single, ancient supercontinent, Pangaea, that had drifted apart, leaving the Atlantic Ocean between them. However, even
(10) Wegener believed that geological wear and tear over the ages would have damaged the fine detail of ancient coastlines, destroying the best evidence for drift. He never tested the fit between the African and South American coastlines with any exactitude, and for a time
(15) his ideas were virtually ignored. In 1924 Harold Jeffreys, who would become one of the strongest critics of the theory, dismissed it in his landmark book *The Earth*. Apparently after casually observing the shorelines on a globe, Jeffreys concluded that the fit
(20) between Africa and South America was very poor.

Disturbed by Jeffreys' obviously perfunctory observation, S. W. Carey used careful techniques of geometric projection to correct, better than most maps do, for the fact that the continents' margins lie on a
(25) sphere rather than on a flat surface. He found a remarkably close fit. At about the same time, Keith Runcorn found other evidence for drift. When volcanic lava cools and hardens into basalt, it is magnetized by the earth's own magnetic field. The rock's poles
(30) become aligned with the earth's magnetic poles. Though the planet's poles have wandered over the past few hundred million years, the magnetic field of each basalt fragment is still aligned the way the earth's poles were at the time the rock was formed. Although one
(35) would expect that the magnetic fields of rocks of the same age from any continent would all be aligned the way the earth's magnetic field was aligned at that time, the magnetic fields of basalts in North America are now aligned quite differently from rocks formed in the
(40) same epoch in Europe. Thus, the rocks provided clear evidence that the continents had drifted with respect to each other. True to form, Jeffreys brusquely rejected Runcorn's studies. His casual disdain for such observational data led some field geologists to suggest
(45) that his classic should be retitled *An Earth*.

In 1966 compelling proof that the seafloor spreads from the midocean ridges confirmed the hypothesis that molten rock wells up at these ridges from deep within the earth and repaves the seafloor as giant
(50) crustal plates move apart. Thus, seafloor spreading not only explained the long-standing puzzle of why the ocean basins are so much younger than the continents, but also provided evidence that the plates, and so the continents on them, move. Overnight, plate
(55) tectonic theory, with continental drift, became the consensus view.

14. Which one of the following best expresses the main idea of the passage?

(A) Confirmation of Wegener's theory of continental drift came from unexpected sources.

(B) Critics of Wegener's theory of continental drift provided information that contributed to its final acceptance.

(C) The history of the theory of continental drift is similar in a number of ways to the history of Darwin's most important theory.

(D) Though Wegener's theory of continental drift is now generally accepted, Wegener himself was unable to provide any evidence of its accuracy.

(E) Though Wegener's theory of continental drift had significant implications, many years and much effort were required to win its acceptance.

15. Jeffreys' approach to Wegener's theory is most like the approach of which one of the following?

(A) a botanist who concludes that two species are unrelated based on superficial examination of their appearance

(B) a driver who attempts to find a street in an unfamiliar city without a map

(C) a zoologist who studies animal behavior rather than anatomy

(D) a politician who bases the decision to run for office on the findings of a public opinion poll

(E) a psychiatrist who bases treatment decisions on patients' past histories

GO ON TO THE NEXT PAGE.

16. According to the passage, evidence of seafloor spreading helped to explain which one of the following?

    (A) the reason for the existence of the giant crustal plates on which the continents are found

    (B) the reason basalts retain their magnetic field alignment

    (C) the reason the earth's poles have wandered

    (D) the composition of the giant crustal plates on which the continents are found

    (E) the disparity between the age of the continents and that of the ocean basins

17. Which one of the following phrases, as used in context, most clearly reveals the author's opinion about Jeffreys?

    (A) "virtually ignored" (line 15)

    (B) "very poor" (line 20)

    (C) "obviously perfunctory" (line 21)

    (D) "careful techniques" (line 22)

    (E) "consensus view" (line 56)

18. The author's mention of the fact that some field geologists suggested calling Jeffreys' work *An Earth* (line 45) serves to

    (A) contrast two of Jeffreys' ideas

    (B) justify criticisms of Jeffreys' work

    (C) emphasize an opinion of Jeffreys' work

    (D) explain the reasons for Jeffreys' conflict with Wegener

    (E) support an assertion about Jeffreys' critics

19. It can be inferred that Carey believed Jeffreys' 1924 appraisal to be

    (A) authoritative and supported by indirect evidence

    (B) obvious but in need of interpretation

    (C) accurate but in need of validation

    (D) unquestionably based on insufficient research

    (E) so deficient as to be unworthy of investigation

20. The information in the passage suggests that which one of the following findings would most clearly undermine evidence for the theory of continental drift?

    (A) It is discovered that the ocean basins are actually older than the continents.

    (B) New techniques of geometric projection are discovered that make much more accurate mapping possible.

    (C) It is determined that the magnetic fields of some basalts magnetized in Europe and North America during the twentieth century have the same magnetic field alignment.

    (D) It is found that the magnetic fields of some contemporaneous basalts in Africa and South America have different magnetic field alignments.

    (E) It is determined that Jeffreys had performed careful observational studies of geological phenomena.

GO ON TO THE NEXT PAGE.

To some scholars, the European baroque is not merely an aesthetic style characterized by extravagant forms and elaborate ornamentation, but also a political, social, and cultural mentality prevalent in Europe from
(5) approximately 1600 to 1680. This larger view was held by the late Spanish historian José Antonio Maravall, whose writings trace aspects of the modern world—especially the principle of individual liberty in opposition to the state's power—back to the baroque
(10) era as it unfolded in Spain.

Maravall argues that the baroque period was characterized by "monarchical absolutism": monarchs, having suppressed the worst excesses of aristocratic disorder, could now ally themselves with their
(15) nobilities to defend traditional order and values in societies unsettled by the Renaissance's liberating forces of criticism and opposition. These forces appeared especially threatening because deteriorating economic conditions heightened conflict among
(20) different elements of society. For Maravall, baroque culture was the response of the ruling class (including crown, Church, and nobility) to the European social and economic crisis, although that crisis was more acute, and the social structure more frozen, in imperial
(25) Spain than elsewhere. Maravall regards the baroque as a culture of control and containment, or, more dynamically, as a directive culture, designed to reintegrate and unite a society living under the shadow of social and intellectual disruption.
(30) Maravall suggests that even though all the political controls were centralized in the monarchical system, this system of authority was not simply repressive. It was also enticing, promoting a public delight in grandiose artifice by means of devices that ranged from
(35) fireworks displays to theater to religious festivals. Operating upon an urban culture that already possessed characteristics of modern mass culture, these enticements deflected the desire for novelty into areas of life where it represented no challenge to the political
(40) order. Maravall concludes that every aspect of the baroque emerged from the necessity, as public opinion grew increasingly important, of manipulating opinions and feelings on a broad public scale.

Perhaps, however, Maravall's interpretation is
(45) overly influenced by his quest for baroque foreshadowings of "modernity" and by his experience of living under the Spanish dictator Franco. He tends to exaggerate the capacity of those in authority to manipulate a society for their own ideological ends. A
(50) look at the seventeenth-century courts of Charles I in England or Philip IV in Spain suggests that efforts at manipulation were at times wholly counterproductive. In England and Spain during the 1630s, the rulers themselves, not the subjects, succumbed to the illusions
(55) carefully sustained by ceremony, theater, and symbol. The result was that members of the ruling class became dangerously isolated from the outside world, and as the gulf between illusion and reality widened, the monarchy and aristocracy fell headlong into a
(60) credibility gap of their own creation.

21. Which one of the following best expresses the main idea of the passage?

(A) Until recently, the baroque has been regarded simply as an aesthetic style; however, Maravall has shown that it was a cultural mentality serving to reinforce monarchical absolutism.

(B) Maravall views baroque culture as a strategy for dissipating opposition and managing public opinion; however, he overestimates the strategy's success.

(C) Maravall interprets European baroque culture as an expansion of the social and intellectual developments of the Renaissance; however, his view of the seventeenth century is colored by his focus on Spain.

(D) Maravall's theory about the intent of the ruling class to control society via baroque culture is refuted by the examples of specific baroque-era monarchies.

(E) According to the historian Maravall, baroque culture was a political construct designed essentially to control society and repress dissent.

22. Which one of the following phrases, in the context in which it occurs, most accurately indicates the author's attitude toward Maravall's concept of baroque culture?

(A) "This larger view" (line 5)
(B) "grandiose artifice" (line 34)
(C) "tends to exaggerate" (lines 47–48)
(D) "own ideological ends" (line 49)
(E) "wholly counterproductive" (line 52)

23. Which one of the following words best expresses the meaning of "directive" as that word is used in line 27 of the passage?

(A) straightforward
(B) evolving
(C) codified
(D) guiding
(E) compelling

GO ON TO THE NEXT PAGE.

24. It can be inferred from the passage that Maravall regarded monarchs of the baroque era as

   (A) increasingly indifferent to unfavorable public opinion
   (B) concerned with the political threat posed by the aristocracy
   (C) captivated by the cultural devices designed to control their subjects
   (D) somewhat successful in countering the disruptive legacy of the Renaissance
   (E) preoccupied with the goal of attaining cultural preeminence for their respective countries

25. In Maravall's view, baroque theater was intended to

   (A) spur economic growth
   (B) echo the consensus of public opinion
   (C) entertain and divert the urban population
   (D) express the emerging principle of individual liberty
   (E) terrify the citizenry with the threat of monarchical repression

26. The main purpose of the passage is to

   (A) contrast two competing theories and offer an evaluation
   (B) challenge a widely accepted viewpoint by means of a counterexample
   (C) explicate an interpretation and introduce a qualification
   (D) articulate opposing arguments and propose a reconciliation
   (E) explain the unprecedented consequences of a political construct

27. Which one of the following pieces of evidence, if it existed, would most weaken Maravall's interpretation of baroque culture?

   (A) confirmation that Maravall himself participated in opposing Franco's authoritarian regime
   (B) the discovery that baroque-era nobility commissioned far more works of art than did the monarchs
   (C) an analysis of baroque art that emphasizes its idealized depiction of the monarchy and aristocracy
   (D) documents indicating that many baroque-era works of art expressed opposition to the monarchy
   (E) documents indicating a conscious attempt on the part of Franco to control Spanish society by cultural means

S T O P

IF YOU FINISH BEFORE TIME IS CALLED, YOU MAY CHECK YOUR WORK ON THIS SECTION ONLY.
DO NOT WORK ON ANY OTHER SECTION IN THE TEST.

SECTION III

Time—35 minutes

24 Questions

Directions: Each group of questions in this section is based on a set of conditions. In answering some of the questions, it may be useful to draw a rough diagram. Choose the response that most accurately and completely answers each question and blacken the corresponding space on your answer sheet.

Questions 1–5

A contractor is scheduling construction of seven decks—F, G, H, J, K, L, and M—during a seven-week period: week 1 through week 7. Because of customers' requirements, exactly one deck must be built each week according to the following conditions:

G must be built at some time before K is built.

L must be built either immediately before or immediately after M is built.

F must be built during week 5.

J must be built during week 2 or week 6.

1. Which one of the following is an acceptable construction schedule for the decks, in order from the deck built in week 1 to that built in week 7 ?

(A) G, K, H, M, F, J, L
(B) H, G, L, M, F, K, J
(C) H, J, G, F, M, L, K
(D) H, M, L, G, F, J, K
(E) K, J, H, G, F, M, L

2. If G is built at some time after F is built, which one of the following must be true?

(A) G is built during week 7.
(B) H is built during week 1.
(C) J is built during week 6.
(D) L is built during week 3.
(E) M is built during week 1.

3. Which one of the following is a complete and accurate list of the weeks any one of which could be the week in which K is built?

(A) 2, 3, 6
(B) 2, 3, 7
(C) 2, 5, 6, 7
(D) 1, 2, 3, 6, 7
(E) 2, 3, 4, 6, 7

4. Which one of the following is a complete and accurate list of decks any one of which could be the deck built in week 3 ?

(A) K, L, M
(B) F, G, H, K
(C) F, H, K, M
(D) G, H, K, L, M
(E) H, J, K, L, M

5. If G is built during week 4, then there are exactly how many acceptable orders any one of which could be the order in which the seven decks are built?

(A) one
(B) two
(C) three
(D) four
(E) five

GO ON TO THE NEXT PAGE.

Questions 6–10

Each of five salespeople—F, G, H, I, and J—will present a different one of a company's products—L, M, N, O, and P—at a convention running from Monday through Wednesday. Exactly two products will be presented on Monday, exactly one on Tuesday, and exactly two on Wednesday. The scheduling of presentations is governed by the following conditions:

F cannot present a product on the same day as H.
Either I or else J must present product N on Tuesday.
G must present a product on the day that product O is presented, whether or not G is the salesperson who presents product O.

6. Which one of the following must be true?

(A) If F presents a product on Monday, then G presents product O.
(B) If I presents a product on Tuesday, then J presents a product on Monday.
(C) If J presents a product on Tuesday, then G presents a product on Monday.
(D) If both F and J present products on Monday, then H presents product O.
(E) If both H and I present products on Wednesday, then product O is presented on Monday.

7. If salespeople H and I present products on Monday, which one of the following must be true?

(A) F presents product M.
(B) G presents product L.
(C) I presents product N.
(D) Product O is presented on Wednesday.
(E) Product P is presented on Wednesday.

8. If G presents product P on Wednesday, then any of the following could be true EXCEPT:

(A) H presents product O.
(B) I presents product N.
(C) I presents product O.
(D) F makes a presentation on Monday.
(E) F makes a presentation on Wednesday.

9. If products M and P are presented on Monday, which one of the following could be true?

(A) G presents product P.
(B) I presents product O.
(C) J presents product L.
(D) F presents a product on Monday.
(E) G presents a product on Monday.

10. If product O is presented on the same day as product P, which one of the following must be true?

(A) F presents product O or else product P.
(B) F presents neither product O nor product P.
(C) H presents product O or else product P.
(D) I presents product O or else product P.
(E) J presents neither product O nor product P.

GO ON TO THE NEXT PAGE.

Questions 11–17

The seven members of an academic department are each to be assigned a different room as an office. The department members are professors F and G, lecturers Q, R, and S, and instructors V and W. The available rooms are seven consecutive rooms along one side of a straight hallway numbered sequentially 101 through 107. The assignment must conform to the following conditions:

Neither instructor is assigned a room next to a professor's room.

Neither professor is assigned room 101 and neither professor is assigned room 107.

G is not assigned a room next to R's room.

W is not assigned a room next to V's room unless R is also assigned a room next to V's room.

11. If F and G are assigned rooms that have exactly one room between them, which one of the following is the list of department members each of whom could be assigned to the intervening room?

(A) Q, R
(B) Q, S
(C) Q, V
(D) R, W
(E) S, V

12. Which one of the following is a possible assignment of rooms for members R, V, and W ?

(A) 101: V; 102: W; 103: R
(B) 101: V; 102: W; 104: R
(C) 101: V; 103: W; 104: R
(D) 103: W; 104: V; 106: R
(E) 105: R; 106: W; 107: V

13. If R is assigned room 104, which one of the following must be assigned either room 103 or else room 105 ?

(A) F
(B) G
(C) Q
(D) V
(E) W

14. What is the greatest number of rooms that could be between the rooms to which F and G are assigned?

(A) one
(B) two
(C) three
(D) four
(E) five

15. Which one of the following CANNOT be assigned room 104 ?

(A) F
(B) G
(C) Q
(D) S
(E) V

16. If no two faculty members of the same rank are assigned adjacent rooms, which one of the following must be true?

(A) F is assigned either room 103 or else room 104.
(B) Q is assigned either room 102 or else room 106.
(C) R is assigned either room 102 or else room 105.
(D) S is assigned either room 104 or else room 105.
(E) V is assigned either room 101 or else room 107.

17. If F and G are not assigned rooms that are next to each other, which one of the following CANNOT be assigned room 107 ?

(A) W
(B) V
(C) S
(D) R
(E) Q

GO ON TO THE NEXT PAGE.

Questions 18–24

The coordinator of an exhibition will select at least four and at most six rugs from a group of eight rugs made up of two oval wool rugs, three rectangular wool rugs, one oval silk rug, and two rectangular silk rugs according to the following conditions:

At least two oval rugs must be selected.

The number of wool rugs selected can be neither less than two nor more than three.

If the oval silk rug is selected, at least one rectangular silk rug must be selected.

18. Which one of the following is an acceptable selection of rugs for the exhibition?

(A) one oval silk rug, one oval wool rug, and two rectangular wool rugs

(B) one oval silk rug, one rectangular wool rug, and two rectangular silk rugs

(C) two oval wool rugs, one rectangular silk rug, and two rectangular wool rugs

(D) two oval wool rugs, one rectangular silk rug, and one rectangular wool rug

(E) two rectangular silk rugs and three rectangular wool rugs

19. If three wool rugs are selected, then any of the following could be a complete and accurate list of the other rugs selected EXCEPT:

(A) one oval silk rug

(B) one rectangular silk rug

(C) two rectangular silk rugs

(D) one oval silk rug and one rectangular silk rug

(E) one oval silk rug and two rectangular silk rugs

20. The rugs selected for the exhibition can include any of the following EXCEPT:

(A) one oval silk rug

(B) two oval wool rugs

(C) three oval rugs

(D) two rectangular wool rugs

(E) three rectangular wool rugs

21. If only one silk rug is selected for the exhibition, then the other rugs selected must be a group made up of

(A) one oval rug and two rectangular rugs

(B) two oval rugs and one rectangular rug

(C) two oval rugs and two rectangular rugs

(D) two oval rugs and three rectangular rugs

(E) three rectangular rugs

22. If exactly four rugs are selected, then the rugs selected could be

(A) one oval rug and three rectangular wool rugs

(B) two oval rugs and two rectangular wool rugs

(C) three oval rugs and one rectangular silk rug

(D) three oval rugs and one rectangular wool rug

(E) two rectangular silk rugs and two rectangular wool rugs

23. If all three silk rugs are selected, then each of the following could be a complete and accurate list of the other rugs selected EXCEPT:

(A) one oval wool rug

(B) two oval wool rugs

(C) one oval wool rug and one rectangular wool rug

(D) one oval wool rug and two rectangular wool rugs

(E) two oval wool rugs and one rectangular wool rug

24. If exactly six rugs are selected, they must include

(A) exactly one of the oval rugs

(B) the two oval wool rugs

(C) the two rectangular silk rugs

(D) exactly three of the rectangular rugs

(E) all three rectangular wool rugs

S T O P

IF YOU FINISH BEFORE TIME IS CALLED, YOU MAY CHECK YOUR WORK ON THIS SECTION ONLY.
DO NOT WORK ON ANY OTHER SECTION IN THE TEST.

SECTION IV

Time—35 minutes

25 Questions

<u>Directions:</u> The questions in this section are based on the reasoning contained in brief statements or passages. For some questions, more than one of the choices could conceivably answer the question. However, you are to choose the <u>best</u> answer; that is, the response that most accurately and completely answers the question. You should not make assumptions that are by commonsense standards implausible, superfluous, or incompatible with the passage. After you have chosen the best answer, blacken the corresponding space on your answer sheet.

1. Preschool children who spend the day in day-care nurseries are ill more often than those who do not. They catch many common illnesses, to which they are exposed by other children in the nurseries. However, when these children reach school age they tend to be ill less often than their classmates who did not spend the day in day-care nurseries during their preschool years.

    Which one of the following, if true, best explains the discrepancy in the information above?

    (A) There are many common infectious illnesses that circulate quickly through a population of school-age children, once one child is infected.

    (B) Those children who have older siblings are likely to catch any common infectious illnesses that their older siblings have.

    (C) By school age, children who have been in day-care nurseries have developed the immunities to common childhood illnesses that children who have not been in such nurseries have yet to develop.

    (D) The number of infectious illnesses that children in a day-care nursery or school develop is roughly proportional to the number of children in the facility, and day-care nurseries are smaller than most schools.

    (E) Although in general the illnesses that children contract through contact with other children at day-care nurseries are not serious, some of those illnesses if untreated have serious complications.

2. The vision test for obtaining a driver's license should not be limited to measuring the adequacy of vision in daylight conditions, as is the current practice. Many people whose daylight vision is adequate have night vision that is inadequate for safe night driving. Most car accidents occur at night, and inadequate vision plays a role in 80 percent of these accidents.

    The main point of the argument is that

    (A) the vision test for obtaining a driver's license should measure the adequacy of vision in night conditions

    (B) inadequate vision does not play a role in most of the accidents that occur in daylight

    (C) most drivers who have adequate vision in daylight conditions also have adequate vision in night conditions

    (D) inadequate vision is the primary factor in the majority of car accidents that occur at night

    (E) the current vision test for obtaining a driver's license ensures that most licensed drivers have adequate vision for night driving

GO ON TO THE NEXT PAGE.

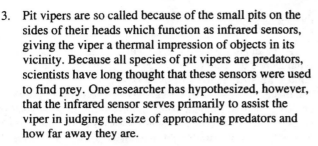

3. Pit vipers are so called because of the small pits on the sides of their heads which function as infrared sensors, giving the viper a thermal impression of objects in its vicinity. Because all species of pit vipers are predators, scientists have long thought that these sensors were used to find prey. One researcher has hypothesized, however, that the infrared sensor serves primarily to assist the viper in judging the size of approaching predators and how far away they are.

Which one of the following, if true, would most support the researcher's hypothesis?

(A) Pit vipers of both sexes have infrared sensors, and both sexes exhibit aggressive and defensive behaviors.

(B) Pit vipers do not differ in their predatory behavior from closely related vipers without pits, but they do differ markedly from these other species in their strategies of defense against predators.

(C) Pit vipers are distinguishable from other viper species not only by their pits but also by the chemical composition of their venom.

(D) Pit vipers have a well-developed sense of smell that they use to supplement the thermal impressions they receive from their infrared sensors.

(E) The rattle of the diamondback rattlesnake, one of the most common kinds of pit viper, functions as a defense mechanism to intimidate predators.

Questions 4–5

Many scholars believe that official medieval persecutions of various minority groups were undertaken very reluctantly by medieval authorities and only in order to soothe popular unrest caused by underlying popular hostility to the groups in question. This belief is highly questionable. For one thing, there are few indications of any profound underlying popular hostility toward persecuted groups in cases where persecutions were particularly violent and sustained. For another, the most serious and widespread persecutions carried out by medieval authorities seem to have had as targets exactly those groups that most effectively disputed these authorities' right to govern.

4. The argument proceeds by

(A) referring to the large numbers of scholarly adherents of a certain view to support the claim that the view is correct

(B) providing reasons to suspect the reliability of any conclusions based on evidence concerning the distant past

(C) attempting to make a particular comparison seem absurd by adducing evidence that suggests that the events compared share only traits that are irrelevant to the claim the comparison is intended to support

(D) citing both a lack of evidence supporting a particular explanation and further evidence that suggests an alternative explanation

(E) establishing a general principle and using the principle to justify a conclusion about a particular category of cases

5. Which one of the following, if true, most strengthens the argument that the scholars' belief is questionable?

(A) Official persecutions in medieval times were usually preceded by officially sanctioned propaganda campaigns vilifying the groups to be persecuted.

(B) Medieval minority communities often existed under the direct protection of official institutions.

(C) Some groups, such as those accused of witchcraft, were the victims of spontaneous mob violence as well as of occasional official persecution.

(D) Many medieval leaders refused to authorize the dissemination of information misrepresenting the religious practices of officially protected minorities.

(E) Convicted felons were often legally excluded from participation in medieval society, but this practice was seen as a form of punishment and not of persecution.

GO ON TO THE NEXT PAGE.

6. The frozen, well-preserved body of a man was recently discovered in a glacier as the glacier melted. Artifacts found on the body reveal that the man lived at least 4,000 years ago. The nature of the glacier indicates that the man died on virtually the same spot where his body was discovered. If the body had not been sealed in the glacier shortly after the man died, or if the body had thawed in the intervening millennia, it would not still be preserved.

Which one of the following is most strongly supported if all of the statements above are true?

(A) None of the artifacts found on the body were more than 4,000 years old.
(B) The man whose body was discovered in the glacier did not freeze to death.
(C) The glacier that melted to reveal the ancient body is at least 4,000 years old.
(D) The artifacts found on the frozen body would not have been preserved if they had not also been frozen.
(E) The global climate is, on average, warmer now than it was 4,000 years ago.

7. One hundred people listened to a single musical composition, "Study I," on a certain morning. Later that day, they listened to "Study I" again and to another musical composition, "Study II," and were asked which they preferred. A substantial majority preferred "Study I." These results support the hypothesis that people prefer music they have heard on an earlier occasion to music they are hearing for the first time.

Which one of the following, if true, most strengthens the argument?

(A) Half of the members of a large group of people who heard only "Study II" in the morning and heard both "Study I" and "Study II" later the same day preferred "Study I."
(B) Ninety percent of the members of a large group of people who listened to "Study I" and "Study II" without having heard either of the compositions on any earlier occasion preferred "Study I."
(C) The group of 100 people who listened to "Study I" in the morning and to both "Study I" and "Study II" later the same day included some professional music critics.
(D) Of 80 people who heard only "Study II" in the morning and heard both "Study I" and "Study II" later the same day, 70 preferred "Study II."
(E) Many of the 100 people who in the morning listened only to "Study I" complained afterward that they had not been able to hear well from where they had been seated.

Questions 8–9

After an area has been hit by a natural disaster, there is often a great demand for plywood for repairing damaged homes. Retailers in the area often raise prices on new shipments of plywood to well above their predisaster prices, and some people denounce these retailers for taking advantage of a disaster to make more money on each sheet of plywood they sell. In fact, however, these retailers do not make more money on each sheet of plywood than before the disaster, because transporting the plywood into devastated areas is difficult and expensive, and therefore the plywood's cost to retailers is higher than it was before the disaster.

8. Which one of the following is an assumption on which the argument depends?

(A) Residents of areas affected by natural disasters are often unable to pay the prices the retailers in those areas set for scarce necessities.
(B) Retailers must pay the full amount of any increase in shipping costs.
(C) No retailer makes enough money on each sheet of plywood sold to absorb for long an increase in shipping costs without raising prices.
(D) Suppliers of plywood do not transport as much plywood to an area after it has been affected by a natural disaster as they did before it was so affected.
(E) The increase in the prices charged by retailers for plywood following a natural disaster does not exceed the increase in cost to those retailers.

9. The clause "the plywood's cost to retailers is higher than it was before the disaster" serves in the argument as which one of the following?

(A) a counterexample to a claim
(B) the main conclusion toward which the argument as a whole is directed
(C) a subsidiary conclusion used to support the main conclusion of the argument
(D) an example used to illustrate the implausibility of the position argued against
(E) background information used to provide a context for the argument

GO ON TO THE NEXT PAGE.

10. Industrial scientists have hypothesized that much of the nitrous oxide that contributes to air pollution originates from the burning of organic matter in forest fires. The results of one extensive study in which smoke samples taken from forest fires were bottled and then analyzed in a research laboratory support this hypothesis, since the analysis showed that all of the samples contained high concentrations of nitrous oxide.

Which one of the following, if true, most undermines the argument?

(A) The production of synthetic products such as nylon is responsible for up to 10 percent of the nitrous oxide present in the atmosphere.

(B) Many of the pollutants that are present in the atmosphere are produced by the combustion of fossil fuels, such as petroleum, which are derived from organic matter.

(C) Soil bacteria that feed on ammonium compounds present in organic ash are thought by some scientists to excrete small amounts of nitrous oxide that then enter the atmosphere.

(D) When in a closed container, the gases in smoke produced by forest fires quickly react with each other thereby producing high concentrations of nitrous oxide.

(E) By using gas-analyzing devices mounted on helicopters, researchers can perform on-site analyses of smoke instead of sending smoke samples to laboratories for analysis.

11. By examining the fossilized leaves of any prehistoric plant it is possible to determine the climate in which that specimen grew because the size and shape of a leaf are unique to a given climate. Since the climate at a given location depends on the altitude at that location, it follows that the size and shape of a fossilized leaf also indicates the altitude at which the plant grew.

The reasoning in the argument is vulnerable to criticism on the grounds that it

(A) fails to demonstrate that no species of plant can long survive a violent change in its environment

(B) overlooks the possibility that locations at different altitudes can have the same climate

(C) treats the size and shape of a leaf as if they were the only physical characteristics of a leaf that depend on climate

(D) relies on a weak analogy between a leaf and the fossil of a leaf as evidence for the claims advanced

(E) ignores the possibility that the location at which a fossilized leaf was found is not the location at which the original plant grew

12. Box office receipts at movie theaters increased 40 percent last year over the previous year. Thus, the film industry overall evidently is prospering. Yet twice as many movie theaters went bankrupt last year as in the preceding two years combined.

Which one of the following, if true, most helps to resolve the apparent discrepancy in the information above?

(A) Films cost, on average, twice as much to produce today as they did ten years ago.

(B) Ticket prices at some theaters fell last year.

(C) Those of last year's films that were successful were very profitable films that were shown by exclusive engagement at only a selection of the largest theaters.

(D) The amount of money spent on film advertising increased greatly last year over the year before, and the majority of this expense was absorbed by the producers and the distributors of films, not by the theater owners.

(E) In general, an increase in a theater's box office receipts for any year is accompanied by an increase in that theater's profits from snack-food and soft-drink sales for that year.

GO ON TO THE NEXT PAGE.

13. Suffering from kidney failure and having fallen into a coma, Mr. Smith urgently required a kidney transplant. When Mr. Smith's cousin volunteered to donate a kidney, Mr. Smith's daughter had to decide whether to sign the consent form permitting the transplant. She knew that her father strongly objected to transplantation of organs from live donors on the grounds that these operations caused serious disability to the organ donor. Although she knew her father's objection was based on a mistaken belief about the danger to kidney donors, she decided not to consent to the surgery.

Mr. Smith's daughter's decision conforms to which one of the following principles?

(A) A son or a daughter must do everything possible to protect the life and health of a parent unless the parent has prohibited the son or daughter from doing so.

(B) Anyone called on to make a medical decision concerning another person should always treat the interests of that person as paramount and decide according to what would most help promote that person's health, regardless of that person's age, mental condition, or physical disabilities.

(C) A person has no obligation to permit medically advisable surgery for an unconscious relative if that surgery is not likely to prolong the life of the patient.

(D) Withholding a medically advisable treatment from an unconscious patient is justified if securing that treatment would result in another person's becoming seriously disabled.

(E) A patient's rights to self-determination impose an obligation on others to accede to the patient's preferences concerning treatment, even when those preferences can only be inferred from a general knowledge of the patient's commitments, beliefs, and desires.

Questions 14–15

Letter to the editor: According to last Thursday's editorial, someone who commits a burglary runs almost no risk of being caught. This is clearly false. Police reports show that at least 70 percent of people who commit crimes are caught. All burglars are criminals, so although some burglars will undoubtedly escape, a large percentage of them will eventually be caught.

14. Which one of the following arguments exhibits a flawed pattern of reasoning parallel to that exhibited in the argument that a large percentage of burglars will be caught?

(A) A large percentage of professional persons are self-employed. Thus, since nurses are professional persons, a large percentage of nurses are self-employed.

(B) Psychiatrists have medical training, and a large percentage of them also have social-work training. Therefore, some people who have social-work training also have medical training.

(C) Since a large percentage of professional persons have changed their careers, and since career changes require new training, all professional persons who have changed their careers required new training.

(D) A large percentage of doctors are specialists. Since anyone who is a specialist must have training beyond the usual medical curriculum, it follows that many doctors have training beyond the usual medical curriculum.

(E) Many engineers are employed in management positions, and since anyone in a management position needs training in management, many engineers need training in management.

15. The claim that some burglars will undoubtedly escape plays which one of the following roles in the letter writer's argument?

(A) It is evidence presented in support of the letter writer's conclusion.

(B) It is the conclusion of a subsidiary argument.

(C) It provides an example of the kind of case under discussion.

(D) It restates the position against which the letter writer's argument as a whole is directed.

(E) It concedes a point that does not undermine the letter writer's conclusion.

GO ON TO THE NEXT PAGE.

16. Scientists have recently discovered that, in doses massive enough to kill cells, almost any chemical is carcinogenic because cell death causes rapid division among surviving cells, promoting cancer-causing mutations. A few chemicals are also carcinogenic without causing cell death. Until now studies of the carcinogenicity of food additives have always involved administering to test animals doses of additives larger than the largest possible human exposure levels and massive enough to kill large numbers of cells in the animals, and then observing the animals' cancer rates.

If the statements above are true, which one of the following conclusions is most strongly supported by them?

(A) In the doses heretofore used in carcinogenicity studies of food additives, cell death often does not occur in test animals.

(B) Until now results of carcinogenicity studies encouraged overestimation of the degree to which some food additives are carcinogenic.

(C) Truly carcinogenic chemicals usually cause some immediate cell death, even in small doses.

(D) Carcinogenic chemicals are usually absorbed in small doses in the natural environment.

(E) Most of the food additives that are now banned because of carcinogenicity could safely be used in human foods.

17. Drivers in the country of Holston want highway tolls eliminated. The cost of maintaining the highways is paid entirely out of revenue from the highway tolls. Holston must maintain its highways. Thus, it follows that if the tolls are eliminated, then the entire cost of maintaining the highways will have to be paid for by an increase in general taxes.

Which one of the following is an assumption made by the argument?

(A) Work on highway maintenance can be authorized only if the money needed to pay for it has already been collected.

(B) The amount of money saved by eliminating the costs associated with toll collection would not be available to pay part of the total cost of maintaining the highways.

(C) If the highway tolls are eliminated and the general taxes are increased to pay for maintaining the highways, there will be less emphasis on preventive maintenance.

(D) The total cost of maintaining the highways will be less if the highway tolls rather than the general taxes pay for the maintenance.

(E) If the highway tolls are not eliminated, there will be no need to increase the general taxes.

Questions 18–19

Efraim: The popular press continually advises people to avoid various health risks. Yet by seeking to avoid health risks, people inevitably become anxious, and anxiety, in turn, poses a major health risk. Thus, paradoxical as it seems, simply disregarding journalists' advice about reducing health risks is bound to pose less of a health risk than does trying to follow any such advice.

Felicity: But history shows that you are wrong. It was articles in the popular press that made people aware of the health risks posed by smoking cigarettes. Many people stopped smoking in response, and they led longer and healthier lives than they would have otherwise.

18. Which one of the following most accurately expresses the point at issue between Efraim and Felicity?

(A) whether products and practices described by journalists as posing health risks do in fact pose health risks

(B) whether the people most likely to suffer anxiety in stressful situations are also the ones most likely to try to avoid health risks

(C) whether there are any people who ignore journalists' advice about avoiding health risks

(D) whether people can reduce risks to their health by heeding the advice of articles in the popular press

(E) whether the sort of anxiety that results from efforts to avoid health risks can be overcome

19. Which one of the following is an assumption on which Efraim's argument depends?

(A) A significant proportion of the people who, following journalists' advice, seek to avoid specific health risks cannot avoid those risks completely.

(B) Journalists who advise people to avoid various health risks render their advice in needlessly alarming language.

(C) The popular press is not unanimous in its recommendations to people wishing to avoid various health risks.

(D) The anxiety, if any, produced by disregarding journalists' advice to avoid health risks is less than that produced by attempting to heed this advice.

(E) Most strategies for dealing with sources of personal anxiety are themselves anxiety inducing.

GO ON TO THE NEXT PAGE.

20. All orchid species that are pollinated solely by insects have features that attract insects. The flower of a recently discovered orchid species contains edible tendrils that invariably attract insects to the inside of the flower. Hence, it follows that this orchid species is one that is pollinated solely by insects.

The argument is flawed because it

(A) makes an unwarranted assumption that a characteristic that is shared by two classes of things is their only common feature

(B) assumes without warrant that a characteristic that distinguishes one class of things from another is the only characteristic that distinguishes that class from the other

(C) mistakes a characteristic that is unique to one particular class of things for a characteristic that is unique to an unrelated class of things

(D) treats a characteristic known to be true of one class of things as if that characteristic were unique to that class

(E) makes broad generalizations about all members of a particular class of things on the basis of what is known about a member of an unrelated class of things

21. In 1578 Moroccan troops defeated a Portuguese army on Moroccan soil. Accounts written by Portuguese contemporaries report the defeat but omit mention of the fact that King Sebastian of Portugal was killed in the battle. Such omissions cannot simply be the result of ignorance of Sebastian's death. Sebastian's death is not even mentioned in the battle accounts written by two captured Portuguese officers while waiting to be ransomed from a Moroccan prison. These two officers actually shared their cells with the Portuguese soldiers who identified the king's body to Moroccan officials. The omissions therefore had to have had a psychological cause: the Portuguese evidently found Sebastian's death so humiliating that they could not bring themselves to write about it.

The discussion about the two Portuguese officers advances the argument by

(A) providing grounds for eliminating an alternative explanation

(B) supplying indirect evidence that a disputed death actually occurred

(C) resolving an apparent contradiction between two of the argument's main premises

(D) giving evidence supporting a general psychological principle on which the main conclusion is explicitly based

(E) offering grounds for doubting the reliability of historical reports that conflict with the argument's main conclusion

22. A tiny, tree-living thrips is the first species identified that can reproduce both by laying eggs and by bearing live young, although for any one instance of reproduction, a given female will use only one of the two methods. Interestingly, biologists have observed that all of the offspring of this insect that are hatched from eggs are females, and all of the offspring that are live-born are males. It has also been noted that any particular live-born brood will comprise fewer individuals than any particular brood hatched from eggs. However, a much larger proportion of male offspring than of female offspring survives to adulthood, and among thrips reaching adulthood the ratio of males to females is about even.

Which one of the following can be properly inferred about the species of thrips described in the passage?

(A) It is the only species capable of using two different methods of reproduction.

(B) Any female of the species that can reproduce by laying eggs can also reproduce by bearing live young but not necessarily vice versa.

(C) On average, across the species, more of the offspring are born by hatching from eggs than are born live.

(D) For the species as a whole, there are, over time, about as many instances of live-born broods as there are broods hatched from eggs.

(E) There are females that use only one of the two methods of reproduction over the course of their lives.

GO ON TO THE NEXT PAGE.

23. Since the zoo has more animals than enclosures, and every animal lives in an enclosure, it must be true that at least one of the enclosures contains more than one animal.

   The argument above exhibits a pattern of reasoning that is most closely paralleled by which one of the following?

   (A) Every person has two biological parents, so some people who have no brothers or sisters have more parents than their parents have children.

   (B) Since every year there are more marriages than divorces, there must be some marriages that will not end in divorce.

   (C) Since boys under ten slightly outnumber girls under ten and since some families have more than one child under ten, it follows that at least one girl under ten has more than one brother under ten.

   (D) At least one of the families in Herndon has more than one child, since in Herndon, there are fewer families than children and every child is a member of a family.

   (E) There must be fewer families that include teenagers than there are teenagers belonging to such families, since there is at least one family that includes more than one teenager.

24. In the Hartshorn Building, most but not all of the third-floor offices are larger than any office on the second floor. The fourth-floor offices are all larger than any office on the second floor. However, all the second-floor offices are larger than any office on the first floor.

   If the statements above are true, which one of the following must also be true?

   (A) Some first-floor offices are as large as the smallest fourth-floor offices.

   (B) Some first-floor offices are as large as the smallest third-floor offices.

   (C) Some third-floor offices are not as large as the largest first-floor offices.

   (D) Some third-floor offices are not as large as the smallest fourth-floor offices.

   (E) Some fourth-floor offices are not as large as the largest third-floor offices.

25. Louis: People's intentions cannot be, on the whole, more bad than good. Were we to believe otherwise, we would inevitably cease to trust each other, and no society can survive without mutual trust among its members.

   The argument is most vulnerable to which one of the following criticisms?

   (A) It fails to rule out the possibility that a true belief can have deleterious consequences.

   (B) It mistakenly assumes that if two claims cannot at the same time both be true, then they cannot at the same time both be false.

   (C) It challenges the truth of a claim merely by calling into question the motives of those who profess that they believe it to be true.

   (D) It assumes without warrant that in any situation with two possible outcomes, the most negative one will inevitably occur.

   (E) It provides no reason to believe that a statement that is true of a given group of individuals is also true of any other group of individuals.

S T O P

IF YOU FINISH BEFORE TIME IS CALLED, YOU MAY CHECK YOUR WORK ON THIS SECTION ONLY.
DO NOT WORK ON ANY OTHER SECTION IN THE TEST.

SIGNATURE _____ __/__/__
DATE

LSAT WRITING SAMPLE TOPIC

An oil tanker has spilled its cargo near the economically depressed town of Gull Point, which is situated near a pristine wetlands area. The town is selecting an environmental contractor to clean up the spill; the oil company will underwrite the cost. Write an argument supporting one contractor over the other based on the following criteria:

- Gull Point wants to provide income to local residents whose livelihoods were affected by the spill.
- Gull Point needs a fast and effective cleanup of the oil spill to protect the wetlands and its wildlife.

BayTech, a local biotechnology company with 50 full-time employees, has developed a chemical product that in laboratory tests rapidly consumes crude oil. These tests predict that this product would be 90% effective in eliminating oil from salt water and would minimize oil reaching the shore, but the product is too new to have been tested on an actual oil spill in the open ocean. BayTech promises to use as many town residents as possible to assist in the cleanup, which it estimates will take four to six months. If BayTech's chemical product proves effective in the ocean, the scientific community believes it will be a significant advance in environmental technology.

Clear Waters is a national environmental consulting firm with a solid reputation for environmental cleanup work. Clear Waters proposes to contain and absorb the offshore spill using technology of booms and suction that it developed 20 years ago. The Clear Waters technology is 70% effective in eliminating oil from the open ocean. This contractor claims that the cleanup can be accomplished in four months and would employ 100 town residents full time to mop up oil from the shore and clean oil from affected wildlife.

Directions:

1. Use the Answer Key on the next page to check your answers.

2. Use the Scoring Worksheet below to compute your raw score.

3. Use the Score Conversion Chart to convert your raw score into the 120-180 scale.

Scoring Worksheet

1. Enter the number of questions you answered correctly in each section.

Number Correct

Section I . . . . _____

Section II . . . . _____

Section III . . . . _____

Section IV . . . . _____

2. Enter the sum here: _____
   This is your Raw Score.

Conversion Chart

For Converting Raw Score to the 120-180 LSAT Scaled Score

LSAT Form 6LSS31

Reported Score	Raw Score Lowest	Raw Score Highest
180	100	101
179	99	99
178	98	98
177	97	97
176	--*	--*
175	96	96
174	95	95
173	94	94
172	--*	--*
171	93	93
170	92	92
169	90	91
168	89	89
167	88	88
166	87	87
165	85	86
164	84	84
163	82	83
162	80	81
161	79	79
160	77	78
159	75	76
158	73	74
157	71	72
156	69	70
155	67	68
154	66	66
153	64	65
152	62	63
151	60	61
150	58	59
149	56	57
148	55	55
147	53	54
146	51	52
145	50	50
144	48	49
143	46	47
142	45	45
141	43	44
140	41	42
139	40	40
138	38	39
137	37	37
136	35	36
135	34	34
134	32	33
133	31	31
132	30	30
131	28	29
130	27	27
129	26	26
128	25	25
127	24	24
126	23	23
125	22	22
124	21	21
123	20	20
122	19	19
121	18	18
120	0	17

* There is no raw score that will produce this scaled score for this form

SECTION I

1. C	8. A	15. B	22. D
2. D	9. B	16. A	23. E
3. D	10. C	17. E	24. D
4. E	11. A	18. A	25. E
5. E	12. A	19. E	
6. B	13. D	20. A	
7. D	14. A	21. C	

SECTION II

1. B	8. C	15. A	22. C
2. D	9. B	16. E	23. D
3. B	10. D	17. C	24. D
4. A	11. D	18. C	25. C
5. E	12. C	19. D	26. C
6. C	13. D	20. A	27. D
7. D	14. E	21. B	

SECTION III

1. D	8. C	15. E	22. C
2. B	9. D	16. E	23. A
3. E	10. E	17. D	24. C
4. D	11. B	18. D	
5. D	12. C	19. A	
6. E	13. A	20. E	
7. D	14. A	21. B	

SECTION IV

1. C	8. E	15. E	22. C
2. A	9. C	16. B	23. D
3. B	10. D	17. B	24. D
4. D	11. B	18. D	25. A
5. A	12. C	19. D	
6. C	13. E	20. D	
7. D	14. A	21. A	

Logical Reasoning: Questions 1–25

Question 1

Overview: The passage gives an account of a vicious cycle that confronts dieters. Notice that this vicious cycle only occurs when people come to the end of their weight-loss diet and then go back to "eating amounts of food that would have just maintained their weight in the days before the diet." It is that practice of going back to eating as much as before that sets the vicious cycle in motion and then perpetuates it.

The Correct Answer:

C People who have lost weight through dieting do not need as many calories to maintain their new weight as they needed to maintain their pre-diet weight. So as the passage explains, if they return to their pre-diet caloric intake, they will be consuming excess calories, which will cause them to gain weight. Thus, if such people are to maintain the reduced weight they have achieved through dieting, they must not go back to eating as much as they did before the diet.

The Incorrect Answer Choices:

A The passage does not support (A) even for people who, having dieted, go back to eating as much as before. Clearly, those people will regain weight. But the passage does not go into enough detail to let us calculate how much they will gain, so we cannot conclude that they will end up weighing more than they did when they started dieting. Also, the term "Frequently" in the first sentence suggests that not everyone who diets to lose weight gets trapped in the vicious cycle.

B The passage says that after successfully dieting, people use up fewer calories. So if people wish to maintain their reduced weight, they need to maintain a reduced caloric intake. That is, once people have achieved the desired weight loss, they need to settle on a maintenance diet to keep their weight at the new level. So, contrary to (B), the passage does not support the conclusion that people should not diet if they want to maintain their reduced weight.

D As the discussion of the correct answer shows, we can conclude from the passage that people who lost weight by dieting will have to eat less than pre-diet amounts of food if they are to avoid gaining weight after they stop dieting. How much they can eat without gaining weight is not examined in any detail. It is consistent with what the passage says that a weight-maintenance diet following weight loss might allow larger amounts of food than the weight-loss diet itself. Thus the passage provides no support for (D).

E The passage supports the view that people who lose weight by dieting and who then go back to their pre-diet caloric intake will gain some weight. However, the passage does not provide any information about how much weight they will gain back. It is perfectly consistent with the passage that they will gain back some but not all of the weight they lost. So (E) is not strongly supported by the passage.

- *Difficulty Level: 2*

Question 2

Overview: The argument's conclusion is given in the last sentence: bronze libation vessels lacking the *taotie* pattern are not authentic vessels produced during China's Shang dynasty. This conclusion is inferred from the claim that all *gu, hu,* and *jue* vessels are from the Shang era together with the claim that all *gu, hu,* and *jue* vessels bear the taotie pattern.

But note that although the passage states that the *gu,* the *hu,* and the *jue* are types of authentic Shang-era bronze libation vessels, it does not say that these are the **only** types of authentic Shang-era vessels. For all we have been told, there might be dozens of other types of authentic Shang-era vessels. And it could well be that some, or even all, of these other types of Shang-era vessels do not have the *taotie* pattern. So we cannot reasonably conclude, just from the fact that all *gu, hu,* and *jue* vessels have the taotie pattern, that all vessels without that pattern are not authentic Shang-era bronze libation vessels.

The Correct Answer:

D   The argument deals with a category—authentic Shang-era bronze vessels—and claims that some members of that category—the *gu, hu,* and *jue* vessels—possess a certain characteristic: they bear the *taotie* pattern. The argument concludes from this that, for a bronze libation vessel to be an authentic Shang-era vessel, it must bear that pattern. But it is an error to draw that conclusion. It is an error because it is possible, judging only from the information given, for there to be authentic Shang-era bronze libation vessels—those that are neither *gu, hu,* nor *jue*—that do not bear the *taotie* pattern. Answer choice (D) is a description, in general terms, of the error of reasoning the argument makes.

The Incorrect Answer Choices:

A   The argument does not present any claims that contradict each other, so it cannot base any generalization on such mutually contradictory claims. Thus, (A) cannot be a correct description of an error of reasoning that the argument makes.

B   The argument's conclusion is a generalization to the effect that all authentic Shang-era bronze libation vessels bear the *taotie* pattern. And this generalization is based on examples—the *gu, hu,* and *jue* vessels—which may, for all we know, be atypical. But the argument itself says nothing about these vessels being atypical. Thus, there is no indication that the argument is basing a generalization on examples that are admitted to be atypical.

C   If the argument had proceeded along the lines of (C), it would have gone as follows: the fact that some authentic Shang-era vessels—the *gu, hu,* and *jue* ones—possess the characteristic of bearing the *taotie* pattern is sufficient evidence that other Shang-era vessels bearing that pattern are also authentic. So if the argument had gone like this, its conclusion would have been that other Shang-era vessels bearing the *taotie* pattern are authentic. But this is not what the argument concludes. So (C) cannot be a correct description of an error of reasoning that the argument makes.

E   (E) says that the argument concludes that certain specific objects belonging to a given category have a certain characteristic on the grounds that some other objects belonging to that category have the characteristic in question. But the argument does not draw a conclusion about specific objects; it draws a conclusion about **any** bronze libation vessel that lacks the *taotie* pattern, even one that has not yet been discovered. So (E) cannot be a correct description of an error of reasoning that the argument makes.

■ *Difficulty Level: 1*

Question 3

Overview: The passage tells us that political interest groups will not be able to influence legislation if they are not united behind a common program. It also tells us that achieving such unity can be impossible when conflicting interests surface in a political interest group. It further tells us that when groups get too large, conflicting interests tend to surface.

The Correct Answer:

D The passage indicates that conflicting interests tend to surface in a political interest group when the group becomes too large. So if a political interest group expands to include as wide a membership as possible, the group could become so large that conflicting interests arise. These conflicting interests, according to the passage, can render the political interest group ineffective. Therefore, the expansion of a political interest group to include as wide a membership as possible can render the group ineffective. (D) is thus supported by the passage.

The Incorrect Answer Choices:

A The passage tells us that large size can make a political interest group unable to influence legislation. It is only the size of the group, however, rather than how the size is changing, that is mentioned in the passage. So the passage indicates that a large political interest group can, as a result of the group's size, lack influence. But the passage gives no indication that a group with a small but expanding membership would, as a result of the group's expanding membership, lack influence. (A) is thus not supported by the passage.

B The passage does not consider what it takes for a democratic society to function effectively, nor does it consider how political interest groups need to interact with one another to that end. What the passage says about loss of effectiveness applies to political interest groups, not to society as a whole. So the passage does not support the view expressed in (B).

C The passage deals solely with people who have organized themselves into political interest groups, and it does not say whether a political interest group that is too large to be influential is necessarily a very large group of people. Moreover, even though the passage talks about cases in which some large political interest groups fail to influence politicians, it does not say that the politicians can ignore the interests of people in those groups with impunity.

E The passage discusses one way in which political interest groups can lose their effectiveness. But it does not connect this loss of effectiveness to the passage of time, so (E) is not supported.

■ *Difficulty Level: 2*

Question 4

Overview: The safety inspector makes an argument whose conclusion is that use of the university delivery service for sending samples of rabies virus needs to be limited. The grounds given for this conclusion are that the number of such deliveries has risen recently to dangerously high levels. The biologist argues against the safety inspector's conclusion, on the grounds that for 20 years the university delivery system has been accident-free in delivering such virus samples.

The Correct Answer:

E   The safety inspector does not say that it is generally too dangerous to send virus samples through the university delivery service. Instead, the safety inspector says that this practice has become too dangerous because of a significant change, namely that the number of samples has reached a dangerously high level. The biologist's response—that there have been 20 years of accident-free deliveries of such samples—fails to address this change. So the biologist's evidence is not good evidence that at the recent unprecedented level of use the delivery service is still safe. (E) points out this shortcoming in the biologist's response.

The Incorrect Answer Choices:

A   If the safety inspector is correct in judging the number of samples currently being sent through the service to be unacceptably high, that number would be too high no matter why it got to be so high. So if the biologist had explained why so many more samples are being sent through the service, this would not have touched on the issue of whether the numbers now sent are unacceptably high. So (A) does not describe a flaw in the biologist's reasoning.

B   The biologist, in responding to the safety inspector, does talk specifically about the safety of sending rabies virus samples through the university delivery service. Thus (B), as a description of the biologist's response, is false. So it cannot be a description of what the biologist does wrong.

C   The safety inspector is concerned that the number of rabies virus samples being sent is now dangerously high. But the safety inspector never asserts that the hazardousness of the samples has increased. Indeed, nothing the safety inspector says even suggests that the hazardousness of the samples might have changed. Thus, in rebutting the safety inspector's claims, there is no need for the biologist to address the possibility that the hazardousness of the samples has changed. Therefore, (C) does not describe a flaw in the biologist's reasoning.

D   In arguing for limits on, rather than the elimination of, the use of the university delivery service, the safety inspector acknowledges a legitimate need for continued delivery of rabies virus samples. Since the safety inspector does not contest the university's continuing need in this area, it would have been pointless for the biologist to offer a defense of that need. And not doing what it would have been pointless to do is not a sign of flawed reasoning.

■ *Difficulty Level: 1*

Question 5

Overview: The argument bases its conclusion on two considerations. First, productivity in the office is lower than it could be, because of a specific cause. And second, changes are about to be made that will eliminate that cause. The argument concludes that, once those changes are made, productivity will soon increase.

The question asks you to identify an assumption on which the argument for the predicted increase in office productivity depends.

The Correct Answer:

E   It is possible that supervising workers more closely will have some unintended consequence that tends to reduce productivity. For example, workers who are supervised too closely might become resentful and find ways of resisting supervisory control, perhaps by working more slowly. Such a slowdown would reduce productivity. For the plan to succeed, any loss in productivity resulting from closer supervision must be less than the gain in productivity resulting from the elimination of unauthorized breaks. And this is equivalent to what (E) says.

The Incorrect Answer Choices:

A, C, D   The argument lays out a plan for increasing productivity and concludes that it will work. Success of the plan in increasing productivity does not depend on whether or not the manager has hit on the best possible way of achieving an increase. Nor does it depend on some other way of trying to increase productivity not working very well. Nor does it depend on whether or not the manager has hit on the most efficient way possible of achieving an increase. So neither (A) nor (C) nor (D) is assumed.

B   The manager's plan obviously cannot succeed if workers are not spending any time taking unauthorized breaks. But for the plan to succeed it does not have to be true that workers now spend more time taking unauthorized breaks than they used to. So (B) is not assumed.

- *Difficulty Level: 4*

Questions 6–7

Overview: Tom gives an argument concluding that public resentment over the size of executives' salaries is justified, and Martha counters by arguing that it is not. Tom then defends his conclusion by claiming that, and showing how, Martha has misconstrued his argument.

Tom bases his argument on the observation that the disparity between the salaries earned by executives and those earned by average workers is extraordinarily large. Martha explains why she thinks that it is acceptable for this disparity to be large. But this does not fully engage Tom's point. Tom counters Martha's response by pointing out that the key fact for him is that the disparity is atypically large in their country.

Question 6

The Correct Answer:

B   Tom's conclusion is directly contradicted by Martha's conclusion, so clearly the main point at issue between the two lies here. Tom concludes that public resentment over the size of executives' salaries is justified, and Martha concludes that it is not. So the main point at issue between them is stated in (B).

The Incorrect Answer Choices:

A   Tom claims that executives in their country make 85 times the average worker's salary. But since Martha does not dispute this claim, the main point at issue between them cannot lie here.

C, D   Martha says, in essence, that it is necessary and fair to reward generously those who take the kinds of action that create wealth. Tom appears to grant Martha's point. Tom's complaint is that in their country those rewards are overly generous. So neither (C) nor (D) expresses the main point at issue between Tom and Martha.

E   Neither Tom nor Martha compares the wealth created by executives in their country with the wealth created by executives in other countries. Since neither of them even raises this issue, (E) does not express the main point at issue between them.

- *Difficulty Level: 1*

Question 7

The Correct Answer:

D Martha's objection is essentially an argument in favor of there being a salary gap. For Tom, however, the issue is not the existence of a salary gap but what he sees as its excessive size in their country. In his response to Martha, Tom compares the salary gap in their country to that in other countries, thereby making explicit his reason for thinking the gap is excessively large. Since Martha has argued only that some gap is justified, Tom's response undermines the relevance of her objection. Thus (D) is a good description of how Tom responds to Martha's critique.

The Incorrect Answer Choices:

A Tom initially argues on the basis of two premises: the fact that executives in their country make 85 times what the average worker earns, and the judgment that this salary gap is extraordinarily large. In responding to Martha, he drops neither premise. Rather, he cites further facts in support of the judgment that the size of the salary gap in their country is uncommonly large. (A) does not, therefore, describe how Tom responds to Martha's critique.

B Tom questions the relevance of Martha's generalizations to his main point, but he does not question whether those generalizations are warranted. (B), therefore, misdescribes Tom's response to Martha's critique.

C Although Martha's conclusion contradicts Tom's, her conclusion is not itself based on contradictory assertions, nor does Tom claim that she has made any such contradictory assertions. So (C) does not describe how Tom responds to Martha's critique.

E Although Tom raises considerations that call into question Martha's conclusion, he says nothing to challenge any of the grounds she offers in support of that conclusion. What Tom does is give a fuller account of the grounds on which he bases his own conclusion. So (E) misdescribes Tom's response to Martha's critique.

- *Difficulty Level: 3*

Question 8

Overview: The passage provides information relevant to a comparison between two kinds of hominids: *Australopithecus robustus* and *Homo erectus*. The question asks you to determine what conclusion is most strongly supported by the information provided in the passage.

The Correct Answer:

A The passage tells us that *H. erectus* ate meat. Since the fossilized bones of *A. robustus* had a lower ratio of strontium to calcium than those of *H. erectus* and since a lower strontium-to-calcium ratio indicates greater meat consumption, *A. robustus* can be inferred to have had more meat in its diet than *H. erectus* did. So the passage strongly supports the conclusion that the diet of *A. robustus* included meat.

The Incorrect Answer Choices:

B, C, D Each of these responses presents a conclusion that concerns the amount of strontium or calcium in the **diets** of *H. erectus* or *A. robustus*. But the passage only presents information about the ratio of strontium to calcium in **fossilized bones** and doesn't say anything to connect the amounts of strontium or calcium in fossilized bones to strontium or calcium in the diet. Therefore, (B), (C), and (D) are not supported by the passage.

E The passage gives information about what the ratio of strontium to calcium was at the time the bones were analyzed. Nothing is said or even suggested about how the process of fossilization might have affected that ratio. So (E) is not supported by the passage.

- *Difficulty Level: 3*

Questions 9–10

Overview: The letter writer concludes that Judge Mosston should not be forced to resign and offers two considerations that, taken together, are supposed to support that conclusion. First, within the circle of people he plays cards with, Judge Mosston has always shown himself to be fair. Second, the judicial system cannot afford to spare any just and fair judges.

Question 9

The Correct Answer:

B The letter writer expresses disagreement with the belief that Judge Mosston should be forced to resign. The other statements in the letter are offered in support of this position. Thus the letter as a whole is directed to establishing the conclusion that Judge Mosston should not be forced to resign.

The Incorrect Answer Choices:

A The letter writer apparently does implicitly conclude that Judge Mosston is a fair judge. But this conclusion is not the main conclusion of the argument. Rather, it is part of the letter writer's support for the main conclusion—that Judge Mosston should not be forced to resign.

C The letter writer clearly takes fairness to be an important quality in a judge but gives no indication of taking it to be the single most important quality. In any event, the letter writer's argument is not directed toward the issue of how important fairness is in a judge. It is directed toward whether Judge Mosston should be forced to resign.

D The letter writer's argument is concerned with the impact of a conviction for criminal assault on a specific career, not with the broader question of what impact on professional careers such a conviction should have, in general.

E The letter writer does refer to interactions with Judge Mosston outside the courtroom and does assess the judge's fairness on the basis of those interactions. However, the argument is not directed to whether the letter writer's assessment is objective, and even less to the issue of what kinds of individuals, in general, can most objectively assess a judge's fairness.

■ *Difficulty Level: 3*

Question 10

The Correct Answer:

C The letter writer's main conclusion is based in part on the premise that the judicial system cannot afford to lose any just and fair judges. As mentioned in the "Overview," in order for this premise to support the main conclusion, the letter writer must infer from the other premise—that within the circle of people he plays cards with, Judge Mosston has shown himself to be fair—that Mosston is a just and fair judge. So the letter writer has inferred a conclusion about Judge Mosston's professional competence based on his behavior within a circle of people who play cards together. But a person's behavior in a circle of cardplayers is an extremely narrow, and thus unrepresentative, sample of that person's behavior. In particular, it is not a reliable indicator of how that person discharges his or her professional duties. (C) describes this weakness.

The Incorrect Answer Choices:

A The reasoning in the letter relates what might be called a responsibility of private citizens—to be fair when playing cards—to a duty specific to a certain legal professional—for a judge to be just and fair in judging a case. But even though the reasoning relies on a questionable inference from the first of these to the second, there is no indication that it confuses the two.

B The reasoning in the letter treats "fair" and "just" as distinguishable attributes of judges, but it does not insist on drawing a specific distinction between them. Therefore, with respect to the letter writer's reasoning, the question of whether a particular distinction between "fair" and "just" can be plausibly maintained does not arise.

D The letter writer's conclusion is not based on an attempt to minimize the crime of assault by comparing it to winning or losing at cards. Instead, the conclusion is based on a claim that Judge Mosston is a just and fair judge, as revealed by his behavior as a cardplayer. That is, the issue of card playing is introduced to argue that Judge Mosston is just and fair, not to minimize the seriousness of Judge Mosston's crime. Since the reasoning does not make the comparison that (D) describes, it is not vulnerable to criticism on that point.

E To the extent that there is something like "popular opinion" involved here, it is the opinion of the letter writer's fellow citizens, and their opinion is that Judge Mosston should be forced to resign. The argument, far from basing its conclusion on that opinion, draws a conclusion that is directly opposed to that opinion. So the reasoning in the letter is not vulnerable to the criticism in (E).

- *Difficulty Level: 1*

Question 11

Overview: The argument concludes that it is necessary to develop a space station with astronauts aboard. This is necessary, according to the argument, because medical knowledge about the ability of human beings to tolerate an extended stay in a spacecraft is needed for future missions to Mars, and a space station can provide this medical knowledge.

The Correct Answer:

A The argument would not succeed if future missions to Mars were carried out exclusively by robots and did not involve people traveling in spacecraft. Medical knowledge concerning the limits of human capacities to live in a spacecraft would not be needed if the spacecraft transported only robots. But the argument, by saying that such knowledge needs to be gained, assumes that future explorations of Mars will involve people traveling in spacecraft.

The Incorrect Answer Choices:

B The people who would be sent on missions to explore Mars would undoubtedly be astronauts. It is thus appropriate for the medical knowledge to be acquired through the space station project to be knowledge about the capacities of astronauts, not ordinary human beings. So the argument would be unaffected if, contrary to (B), astronauts' capacities greatly exceeded the capacities of ordinary people in many respects.

C The argument makes a case for undertaking a project that is precautionary in nature. In an area as complex as medicine, it is not generally expected that precautionary measures will be so successful that all medical problems they are intended to guard against will have been anticipated. Nothing in this argument indicates that there is any expectation that they would reach such a level of success in this case. So there is no reason to suppose that the argument assumes (C).

D What is important to the argument is the idea that there will be future space missions involving human astronauts spending extended periods of time traveling by spacecraft. But the argument does not depend on the idea that there will be many missions that will explore the solar system. If only one such mission were contemplated, the space station project would be no less essential.

E The argument needs to assume that there is something about living in spacecraft that needs to be learned. But it need not assume that what will be learned is that living in spacecraft for an extended time presents insurmountable problems. The argument can still succeed if living in spacecraft for an extended time presents problems that can be overcome by taking appropriate measures. So the argument does not assume (E).

- *Difficulty Level: 4*

Question 12

Overview: Two groups of heart patients are compared: those who are given vitamin E before undergoing heart surgery and those who are not given vitamin E before undergoing heart surgery. The incidence of certain postoperative complications is lower among those who are given vitamin E. However, the comparison seems to show that in the long term, survivors from both groups fare equally well. The passage then raises the question of why doctors bother to recommend vitamin E for patients about to undergo heart surgery.

The Correct Answer:

A If (A) is true, then the risk that a patient will die is likely to be greatest during the first six hours after heart surgery. So (A) suggests that vitamin E might make the difference between a patient surviving or not surviving the first six hours after surgery. Thus (A) explains how, in spite of the statistic according to which survivors from both groups do equally well in the long run, vitamin E can improve long-term outcomes. This is because the statistic holds true only for patients who have survived the first six hours after surgery. So (A) helps to explain why doctors recommend vitamin E.

The Incorrect Answer Choices:

B Postoperative complications that occur six or more hours after surgery are among the kinds of things that would have been considered when arriving at the judgment that from six hours after surgery onward people in both groups do equally well. That judgment gives doctors no reason to recommend taking vitamin E.

C, D Neither (C) nor (D) tell us anything about differences between patients who take vitamin E and those who do not, so they cannot help explain why doctors recommend vitamin E.

E If (E) is true, then the group of patients who were not given vitamin E includes many patients who believed falsely that they did receive vitamin E. If this belief, though false, had an effect on a patients' recovery, then (E) makes the statistics cited in the passage more difficult to evaluate but does not help explain why doctors recommend vitamin E. If this belief has no such effect, then (E) adds nothing of relevance to the information given in the passage and thus does not help explain why doctors recommend vitamin E.

- *Difficulty Level: 2*

Question 13

Overview: The architect produces an argument that concludes that stone buildings must remain dirty if they are to last as long as possible. This conclusion is based on the fact that, although dirt damages stone, cleaning stone buildings with water is more damaging to those buildings than leaving them dirty is. The engineer objects to the architect's argument by pointing out that stone buildings can be cleaned without water.

The Correct Answer:

D   The engineer responds to the architect's argument by bringing in an additional fact, namely, that it is possible to clean stone buildings without water and without damaging penetration of the stone, by using mild chemicals. The description of the chemicals as mild strongly suggests that these chemicals do not damage the stone chemically. And since those chemicals would remove dirt, there would be no continuing damage from dirt. Taken together, these facts strongly suggest that cleaning with mild chemicals is the best way to ensure that stone buildings last as long as possible and that, therefore, the architect's conclusion is false.

The Incorrect Answer Choices:

A   The engineer does not take issue with any of the evidence that the architect has cited but, rather, introduces significant new evidence that the architect had not mentioned. In so doing, the engineer does not dispute the accuracy of the architect's evidence but rather its completeness.

B   The engineer does not show, or even attempt to show, that some of the evidence used by the architect is contradicted by other evidence that the architect uses. Rather, what the engineer points out is that there is highly relevant evidence that the architect does not use at all.

C   The engineer does not describe any of the consequences, desirable or undesirable, that would follow from accepting the architect's conclusion.

E   The engineer does imply an alternative conclusion: stone buildings do not have to remain dirty for them to last as long as possible. But this alternative conclusion is not based on the evidence cited by the architect. Rather, the support for this conclusion comes from evidence that is introduced by the engineer.

- *Difficulty Level: 5*

Question 14

Overview: There is evidence that some culture in a certain area used fire to fashion iron implements. There are exactly three cultures that are known to have inhabited that area. One of them did not know enough about fire to use it to fashion implements, and another one had no iron. So neither of these two can have been the culture that used fire to fashion iron implements. Therefore, if one of the three cultures known to have inhabited the area was the culture that used fire to fashion iron implements, it had to be the third.

You should bear in mind here that you need to focus squarely on how the argument goes, and not on how good an argument it is. You are only being asked to find another argument with reasoning that is parallel.

Stated in more general terms, the pattern of reasoning in this argument runs as follows: We want to know who was responsible for a given action. Exactly three candidates are being considered. Two can be eliminated from consideration. Therefore, of the three, the only one who could have done it is the third.

The Correct Answer:

A   This argument goes: There are exactly three people in custody who are suspected of having committed a certain burglary. Two of them could not have worn shoes the size the burglar was wearing. Therefore, out of the three suspects now in custody, the only one who could have committed the burglary is the third.

You can see that the anthropologist's reasoning and the reasoning in (A) are both instances of the same general pattern of reasoning outlined above.

The Incorrect Answer Choices:

B   This argument goes: Anyone who wishes to take a certain action must first do both of two things. Out of one group of three people, two have done both of those things. Therefore, they are free to take the action at issue.

The reasoning in (B) is not parallel to the anthropologist's reasoning: (B) does not set up a group of three as candidates for something, eliminate two from consideration, and conclude that the only candidate remaining from that group is the third.

C   This argument goes: Three particular designers worked for a certain manufacturer when a certain product was designed. Two of them were not patient enough to have designed the product. Therefore, the only person who could have designed that product is the third.

The reasoning in (C) is superficially very close to the reasoning in the anthropologist's argument, but one giveaway is in the conclusion. The conclusion is not qualified the way it would have to be in order to be parallel to the conclusion in the anthropologist's argument. The conclusion of (C) does not say, as it would have to, that **out of the three designers being considered**, the only one who could have designed that product is the third. Also note that (C) differs from the anthropologist's argument in that it doesn't rule out the possibility that the manufacturer may have employed other designers besides the three.

D   This argument goes: Anyone who wishes to reach a certain goal must satisfy two criteria. Of a certain group of three people, only two wish to reach the goal. Therefore, those two are the only ones who could satisfy both criteria.

The reasoning in (D) is not parallel to the anthropologist's reasoning: (D) does not set up a group of three as candidates for something, eliminate two from consideration, and conclude that the only candidate remaining from that group is the third.

E   This argument goes: A letter signed "Tony" was written. All people in a certain category—those known to the recipient of the letter—are immediately eliminated from consideration. Therefore, someone not belonging to that category has to have signed that letter.

The argument in (E) does not arrive at its conclusion in the same way that the anthropologist's argument arrives at its conclusion. (E) does not eliminate from consideration all but one from a list of candidates and then conclude that the one not eliminated is the only remaining candidate.

▪ *Difficulty Level: 5*

Question 15

Overview: The argument's conclusion is that all whale hunting should be banned. Two claims are offered in support of this conclusion: (1) the hunting of endangered whale species should be banned; (2) a ban on the whaling of endangered species cannot be enforced without banning the whaling of all other species.

You can analyze the conclusion as consisting of two parts: the hunting of endangered whale species should be banned and the hunting of nonendangered whale species should be banned. The part of this conclusion that needs further justification is the second part. Claim (2) above tells you only that a choice has to be made: either we do without an effective ban on the hunting of endangered species or else we ban the hunting of nonendangered species. The argument comes down in favor of banning the hunting of nonendangered species. But, strictly speaking, it provides no justification for preferring this choice over the alternative. So what you are looking for is a principle that would supply that justification.

The Correct Answer:

B   The principle in (B) supplies a justification for banning the whaling of nonendangered species. As you can see from the "Overview," claim (1) tells you that the hunting of endangered whales is an activity that ought to be prohibited. Claim (2) tells you that the whaling of nonendangered species is an activity that interferes with the enforcement of that prohibition. So, according to the principle in (B), that interfering activity should be prohibited.

The Incorrect Answer Choices:

A   The principle in (A) would run directly counter to the conclusion of the argument. It would justify the choice of doing without an effective ban on the hunting of endangered whale species because it would rule out a ban on the whaling of nonendangered species. So the conclusion that all whale hunting should be banned could not be drawn.

C   According to the passage, highly mechanized technology has already been adopted by the whaling industry. The argument does not mention any new technologies that might be adopted and that might create new ethical problems. So there is nothing in this argument for the principle in (C) to be applied to. In any event, the principle in (C) could, at most, tell us whether new technologies should be adopted and not how to solve problems created by their adoption. In particular, it would not tell us how to choose between the two alternatives that the argument presents us with.

D The argument turns on the choice between doing without an effective ban on the hunting of endangered whale species and banning the hunting of nonendangered whale species. Unless one of these alternatives is not permissible, the mere permissibility of the other one does not justify choosing one over the other. The principle in (D) would at most show that banning the hunting of nonendangered species is permissible. But it does nothing to show that doing without an effective ban on the hunting of endangered species is not permissible. So (D) does not justify the argument's conclusion.

E The principle in (E) would justify moving from a ban on commercial whaling to a completely general ban. But what needs to be justified is moving from a ban on the whaling of endangered species to a ban on whaling in general. Since the argument does not even distinguish between commercial and noncommercial whaling, (E) does nothing to justify its conclusion.

- *Difficulty Level: 1*

Questions 16–17

Overview: The argument concludes that Giordano Bruno was a spy for England while serving in the French embassy in London. The evidence is twofold. First, there is documentary evidence that a spy who foiled at least two assassination attempts against Queen Elizabeth was the only clergyman working at the French embassy at the time. Second, there is evidence that Bruno had become a member of the clergy well before joining the French embassy.

Question 16

The Correct Answer:

A This answer choice tells us that at the relevant time Bruno was not in fact a member of the clergy. It tells us, in addition, that Bruno did not do the kinds of things that could have given the impression that he was a member of the clergy. So (A) makes it likely that whoever described the spy as "the only clergyman working at the French embassy" was referring to someone other than Bruno. Thus the case for concluding that Bruno was a spy essentially collapses if (A) is true.

The Incorrect Answer Choices:

B This answer choice suggests that during Bruno's tenure in the French embassy, the two countries were probably spying heavily on the other. This sort of observation about the general state of affairs, however, neither strengthens nor weakens the specific case made for Bruno being a spy for England in the French embassy.

C There could be many reasons why Bruno would sometimes transmit information to the English in French even if it wasn't his best language. For example, it may have been the only language he had in common with the English. So the claim that the spy sometimes communicated in French provides no reason to think that Bruno was not the spy.

D This answer choice tells us that Bruno, if he was a spy while serving in the French embassy, managed not to arouse suspicion in the French ambassador. The argument suggests that the spy, whoever he or she might have been, was very successful, and it is likely that such success would not have been possible if that person had aroused suspicion in the French ambassador. So (D) does not cast any doubt on the argument that Bruno was a spy.

E   We do not know whether Bruno was one of the "well-educated members of the clergy." In addition, even if he was, it is not clear that Bruno served in a nonclerical role while serving in the French embassy. In short, (E) does not weaken the case for considering Bruno a spy because it is not even clear that (E) has anything to do with the relevant phase of Bruno's life and career.

- *Difficulty Level: 2*

Question 17

The Correct Answer:

E   For the evidence cited in the argument to support the conclusion drawn, it is important that none of the spy's known activity should have occurred either before or after Bruno's tenure at the French embassy. (E) tells us that this is so. Thus, (E) provides support for the argument.

The Incorrect Answer Choices:

A   The argument depends on there being only one clergyman working at the French embassy at the time. For (A) to support the argument, it would have to provide evidence that there was indeed only one clergyman working there at the time. But (A) tells that there was at least one, and possibly more. So (A) provides no support for the argument.

B   This answer choice suggests that the pope's political sympathies might well have been the opposite of Bruno's—if Bruno was indeed the spy. However, (B) says nothing to suggest that the pope's condemnation of Bruno was motivated by political rather than philosophical differences of opinion. So (B) does nothing to support the argument.

C   For Bruno to have been a spy for England, he would have needed to have contact with the English, and (C) could explain how he made such contact. But since (C) would also explain how everyone else on the diplomatic staff at the French embassy could have made contact with the English, (C) provides no support for the conclusion that it was Bruno in particular who spied for the English.

D   (D) partly explains how Bruno came to serve in the embassy, but it does not provide any reason to think that Bruno was a spy. Thus, (D) does not support the argument.

- *Difficulty Level: 1*

Question 18

Overview: The argument claims that a certain general pattern holds: "whenever many new facts come to light in a field, the ways in which that field organizes its knowledge inevitably need adjustment." It further claims that in certain scientific fields, there has recently been "a wealth of new discoveries"; in other words, many new facts have come to light in those fields. These two claims are used to argue for a particular explanation of why theories in these scientific fields are in flux today. This explanation is used as a basis for accepting one account of the current unsettled state and for rejecting another.

The Correct Answer:

A   The argument shows that the situation to be explained—the present state of flux of theories in certain scientific fields—is just what always happens when many new facts come to light in a field. So the argument presents the current situation as part of a general pattern.

The Incorrect Answer Choices:

B   The argument does not consider the consequences of the explanation that it favors ("scientific progress"), nor does it consider the consequences of the explanation that it rejects ("lack of theoretical rigor"). So it does not do what (B) says it does.

C   The argument does consider two alternate explanations for a situation, but far from showing that the two are equally probable, it argues that one of them ("scientific progress") is correct, and the other ("lack of theoretical rigor") is not.

D   The argument does rely on one general observation: that the discovery of many new scientific facts in a field makes a reorganization of knowledge in that field necessary. But this is not a law of nature. Rather, it is an observation said to hold true in a field of human endeavor, namely the pursuit of scientific knowledge.

E   The scientific research mentioned in the argument was very likely carried out with the intention of producing new discoveries. But the argument, in presenting its explanation, does not refer to the intended outcome of the research. The explanation would work just the same if the particular new discoveries had all come about as the result of lucky accidents.

■ *Difficulty Level: 3*

Question 19

Overview: For questions like this that ask you to figure out what has to be true if all the statements in the passage are true, efforts to analyze the structure of the passage are often not the best use of your time. Simply read the passage carefully and then turn to the answer choices to see which of them is fully supported by information in the passage. Typically, you will find that you can eliminate some answer choices very quickly, leaving you with just two or three to consider in detail.

The Correct Answer:

E   If a purely aesthetic evaluation of a work of art necessarily ends up endorsing the politics of the artist, then it never ends up rejecting the politics of the artist. Thus Choice (E) must be true if the third sentence of the passage is true.

The Incorrect Answer Choices:

A   The only claim made in the passage about critics who overtly address an artwork's political implications is that they are engaged in political discourse. Nothing is stated or implied about whether such critics might also endorse art for art's own sake, or about how common such endorsement might be.

B   The passage makes no explicit mention of critics who are politically naïve. There is some suggestion that critics who attempt purely aesthetic evaluations of a work might be politically naïve since they are said to end up endorsing the politics of the artist, though perhaps inadvertently. But there is no indication that politically naïve critics do not sometimes attempt political critiques of art.

C   The passage does say that all art has political implications. If this statement is true, then it must also be true that the artworks with which art critics are concerned are works with political implications. But from this it does not follow that they are works that make an **overt** social or political statement.

D   The passage does not compare the value of a political critique of a work of art with that of any other kind of critique. So (D) has no support from the statements in the passage.

■ *Difficulty Level: 3*

Question 20

Overview: The passage first presents a somewhat puzzling fact: there are surprisingly large differences among Boldavians in the incidence of left-handedness by age group. The explanation of this fact is what is at issue in the question. The passage itself rules out two possible lines of explanation.

The Correct Answer:

A If Boldavian men have a shorter average life expectancy than Boldavian women do, it is plausible, as one goes from one age group to the next, in ascending order of age, that a smaller proportion of people in each successive age group are men. This would mean that any quality—such as left-handedness, or being more than 6 feet tall—that is more common among men than it is among women would be less prevalent in successively older age groups. (A) says that Boldavian men live less long, on average, than Boldavian women and also says that left-handedness is more common among men. (A) therefore helps to explain the observed variation, by age, of left-handedness among Boldavians.

The Incorrect Answer Choices:

B If it were true that left-handed Boldavians were more likely than right-handed ones to be the victims of fatal accidents, then accidents could very well have the effect, over time, of increasing the proportion of right-handers in the population. But (B) says that there is no difference between left-handed and right-handed people in terms of how likely they are to be involved in accidents. So (B) does nothing to help explain the age-related variation in left-handedness among Boldavians.

C (C) might give rise to a tendency for Boldavians who are not strongly right-handed or left-handed to declare themselves ambidextrous. But even if there were such a tendency, it would not explain the variation in incidence of left-handedness by age group.

D A decreasing birthrate affects population size and relative numerical strength of age groups. But with nothing further having been said, a decrease in the birthrate has no implications for the distribution of specific characteristics, such as left-handedness, within an age group. Therefore, (D) by itself does not help explain the variation in incidence of left-handedness by age group.

E This statement suggests that the proportion of left-handed people in the overall population of Boldavia may fluctuate somewhat. This may indicate that the disparities in left-handedness across age groups are not necessarily constant. But this does not help explain why those sorts of disparities exist in the first place.

- *Difficulty Level: 4*

Question 21

Overview: Eugenia reports on a comparative study of refrigerators, according to which the Koolair brand is the best-made of all major brands. This result is based on two findings. First, Koolair refrigerators last longer and, second, they require fewer repairs, on the whole, than any other major brand. Neil denies that this could be so. He justifies his denial by citing his own experience with refrigerators of several different brands. He found that, of all of his refrigerators, the Koolair was the one needing the most repairs.

The Correct Answer:

C Eugenia claims that reliable tests have shown that, on the whole, Koolair refrigerators require the fewest repairs of any major brand. That is, Eugenia has stated a generalization and has offered reasonable support for it (the reliable tests). Moreover, the generalization is not universal; Eugenia claims only that, **on the whole**, Koolair refrigerators require fewer repairs. Neil counters by saying that, of the several major brand refrigerators he has owned, the Koolair needed the most repairs. That is, Neil has cited a single incidence of unreliability as grounds for rejecting the generalization made by Eugenia. So (C) correctly describes a flaw in Neil's reasoning.

The Incorrect Answer Choices:

A Neil does not use a different notion of a product's quality than Eugenia. She uses low frequency of repair as an indicator of good quality, and he uses high frequency of repair as an indicator of poor quality. In other words, they both rely on a notion like *a good refrigerator rarely needs repair*. Since (A) does not accurately describe what Neil does, it cannot be a description of how his reasoning goes wrong.

B Neil does contradict Eugenia's claim, but not on the basis of a snap judgment. Rather, he makes an effort to offer supporting evidence for his position, by citing his own experiences with various brands of refrigerators. Thus (B) misdescribes a central aspect of Neil's disagreement with Eugenia. So (B) cannot correctly describe how Neil's reasoning goes wrong.

D Neil does not claim any special expertise in a technical field. He supports his position using everyday experiences. So (D) does not describe a flaw in Neil's reasoning.

E What (E) describes is not necessarily a flaw: if each Koolair refrigerator were poorly made, then it would be proper to conclude that Koolair refrigerators are poorly made. Moreover, (E) is not even a good description of what Neil does. Neil draws his conclusion on the basis of what holds true for just one member of a group, not what holds true for each member of that group.

- *Difficulty Level: 4*

Question 22

Overview: The advertisement says that RediMed is "the cold treatment to choose"; in other words, that RediMed is preferable to all other cold treatments. The basis for this claim is that cold sufferers who use RediMed suffer symptoms half as severe as people who do not treat their colds at all.

The evidence that the argument in the advertisement offers would justify the conclusion that cold sufferers are better off treating their cold with RediMed than not treating their cold at all. The evidence does nothing to show that RediMed is more effective than other cold treatments. So the conclusion of the advertisement—that RediMed is preferable to all other cold treatments—is entirely unsupported.

Stated in more general terms, the flawed pattern of reasoning in this argument runs as follows: evidence shows that in a particular kind of situation, doing a certain thing is better than not doing anything at all. The argument concludes from this that in such situations, doing that thing is better than doing anything else.

The Correct Answer:

D Evidence shows that lubricating locks with graphite is better than leaving them unlubricated. From this the argument concludes that graphite is a better lubricant for locks than any other lubricant.

You can see that the reasoning in the advertisement and the reasoning in (D) are both instances of the same flawed pattern of reasoning outlined in the "Overview."

The Incorrect Answer Choices:

A The argument claims that spaghetti tastes bitter when cooked in water that has had salt added before it came to a boil. From this it concludes that when cooking spaghetti, you should add salt when the water is already boiling.

If the claim the argument makes is true, it provides very strong support for the conclusion. Thus the reasoning in this argument is not flawed, and it cannot be an instance of the same flawed pattern of reasoning as that in the advertisement.

B Evidence is offered that might provide some support for the conclusion that National Financial is the bank with the best checking accounts. The argument concludes from this that National Financial is the best bank for everyday banking of all kinds.

The reasoning flaw in (B) is that of concluding that something is best in all respects because it is best in one respect. So the reasoning in (B) is not an instance of the same flawed pattern as the reasoning in the advertisement.

C The argument in (C) bases a conclusion that one tire brand is superior to all others on a comparison among tire brands in terms of two clearly relevant criteria. The evidence offered is thus good evidence, though it may not be complete. So while (C) is not a conclusive argument, it involves no flawed pattern of reasoning.

E Evidence is offered that might provide some support for concluding that olive oil is a good oil to use for frying. What the argument actually concludes, though, is that if you are not going to use butter for frying, you should use olive oil.

Stated in more general terms, this argument goes: evidence is given that something is good, and the conclusion is drawn that it is, therefore, a good alternative to something else. Therefore, although flawed, this argument is flawed in a very different way from the argument in the advertisement.

- *Difficulty Level: 3*

Question 23

Overview: There is tension between what the health association says and what the critic says. The health association cites studies that suggest that people have no difficulty switching from a diet that includes meat to a vegetarian diet. Of the people in those studies, most were successful in making the change, none suffered ill effects as a result, and many prefer the new regimen to the old. The critic points out that the people in the studies were all favorably disposed towards making the change, and the critic further observes that despite this favorable predisposition, many did not in fact make a complete transition.

The Correct Answer:

E If the health association concluded (E) on the basis of the evidence it presents, it would be taking the fact that most of a group of volunteers were able to exclude meat from their diets as adequate evidence that most people in general would be able to exclude meat from their diets if told by their doctors to do so. However, according to the critic, all of the study volunteers were favorably disposed to the dietary change before the study began. It seems likely that people who are favorably disposed to eliminating meat from their diet would find it easier to make that change than the average person would. So the critic's response provides evidence that people in general would be less likely than the study volunteers to succeed in eliminating meat from their diet. That is, the critic's response casts doubt on the adequacy of the health association's evidence as a basis for inferring (E).

The Incorrect Answer Choices:

A If the health association concluded (A) from the evidence it gives, it would be equating the absence of ill effects with improvement. So anything that would challenge this equation would call the conclusion into question. But the critic's response does not address this matter. Neither does the critic directly challenge the truth of (A). Thus, the critic says nothing to call (A) into question.

B The health association, in presenting its evidence, does not even consider the issue of attitudes toward a meatless regimen among the study volunteers. So the health association's evidence provides no basis for concluding (B). But suppose the health association did conclude (B). The specific point of (B)—that having a favorable disposition toward eliminating meat from one's diet is closely connected to succeeding at eliminating meat—is not addressed, and thus not challenged, by the critic.

C If the health association concluded that the number of strict vegetarians has increased in recent years, the critic's response would not call that conclusion into question. The critic tacitly grants that people are able to switch to a meatless diet, so the critic's response is consistent with there having been an increase in the number of strict vegetarians.

D (D) is not supported by the evidence given by the association. But neither is it challenged by anything that the critic says. The critic provides information about the participants' attitude prior to the study but no information about how any of them felt at the end of the study.

■ *Difficulty Level: 5*

Question 24

Overview: The entire second sentence, beginning with the word "Therefore," is the conclusion of the argument. This conclusion is based on information about the proportion of full-time unskilled workers employed in Centerville who are employed in the shoe factory. The point about the shoe factory being the town's largest firm is merely background information and does not provide any additional support for the conclusion.

As it stands, the argument is far from conclusive. The information intended to support the conclusion is about full-time unskilled workers employed by businesses in Centerville. As far as this information goes, it is possible that none of the full-time unskilled workers employed in Centerville actually live in Centerville. The conclusion, however, is about **residents** of Centerville who are unskilled workers and who have full-time jobs in Centerville.

The question asks you to identify information that, if added to the argument, would make the argument conclusive.

The Correct Answer:

D The first sentence of the passage tells us that the shoe factory employs more than half of all full-time unskilled workers employed in Centerville. (D) says that everyone employed by the shoe factory is also a resident of Centreville. This means that the shoe factory employs more than half of all Centerville residents who are full-time unskilled workers employed in Centerville. From this, it follows that most of the Centerville residents who are full-time unskilled workers employed in Centerville would lose their jobs if the factory closed. That is, the conclusion of the passage follows logically if (D) is assumed.

The Incorrect Answer Choices:

A Suppose that more Centerville residents are employed than are unemployed, as (A) says. It could still be true that a high proportion of full-time, unskilled workers employed at the Centerville shoe factory are not residents of Centerville. Thus, (A) leaves the argument as inconclusive as before.

B This statement does not tell us anything about where Centerville residents who are unskilled workers are employed. So even if Centerville has more unskilled workers among its population than it has skilled workers, it could still be true that a high proportion of full-time, unskilled workers employed at the Centerville shoe factory are not residents of Centerville. Thus, (B) leaves the argument as inconclusive as before.

C Even if the shoe factory in Centerville employs more unskilled workers than skilled workers, as (C) says, most of those unskilled workers might not be Centerville residents. Thus, (C) leaves the argument as inconclusive as before.

E This statement tells us that any full-time unskilled worker who works in a factory in Centerville works in the shoe factory. But it does not tell us anything about where these workers live. So (E) leaves the argument as inconclusive as before.

- *Difficulty Level: 4*

Question 25

Overview: The passage describes a certain type of auction that does not allow bidders to raise their bid if they are outbid. If the item up for auction is extremely desirable, you might reasonably expect there to be a number of bidders who genuinely wish to acquire the item and who, in order to increase their chances of winning, would submit a bid for the maximum amount that they are prepared to pay for the item. In such a case, therefore, you would expect there to be many reasonably high bids, and so there would seem to be no need to set a reserve price. A reserve price, after all, would merely prevent the item from being sold at an unreasonably low price. The passage, however, states that it is especially in such cases that the protection of a reserve price is most needed.

You are asked to select a statement that helps to explain why this seemingly paradoxical generalization holds. Thus, the statement to be selected would have to make the generalization appear distinctly less paradoxical.

The Correct Answer:

E If (E) is true, it suggests that, with extremely desirable items, many people might refrain from bidding because they believe that the highest bid they are willing to make would stand no chance of being high enough to win. This would increase the probability that the only bids received would be from bidders who gamble on there being no serious bids. So (E) would help explain why, in one-round sealed-bid auctions, sellers have the greatest need to protect themselves by setting a reserve price when the items being auctioned off are extremely desirable.

The Incorrect Answer Choices:

A The fact about one-round sealed-bid auctions noted in (A) would explain why prospective buyers would need to consider the bid they submit very carefully. It does not, however, explain why any item should attract only unreasonably low bids, let alone why extremely desirable items should be especially likely to attract only unreasonably low bids.

B It is possible that some people would refrain from bidding on certain items if they knew that the identity of unsuccessful bidders would be disclosed. (B) tells us, however, that unsuccessful bidders can decide whether their identity is disclosed or not. So (B) does not explain why people would refrain from bidding on items that they consider exceptionally worth having.

C The fact mentioned in (C) establishes that sellers who opt for the protection of a reserve price do so in order to make sure of at least some profit in the event of a sale, even if the highest bid turns out to be disappointingly low and to just match the reserve price. Sellers could reasonably be expected to want this level of protection regardless of the desirability of the item they put up for auction. But (C) does not explain why a seller would most need such protection when offering an extremely desirable item for auction.

D Having a fairly accurate idea of who some of the other bidders might be could enter into a prospective buyer's calculations of how high to bid or even whether to bid. But it does not explain why, particularly with extremely desirable items, there would be no serious bids from any of the potential bidders.

- *Difficulty Level: 5*

Questions 1–8

Synopsis: This passage discusses Pope Alexander III's twelfth-century doctrine regarding marriage. The author begins by describing the doctrine as a synthesis of existing ecclesiastical and secular legal opinion. The first paragraph addresses the legal side of this synthesis. It explains that under Alexandrine doctrine, a legally valid marriage is established by words of mutual consent on the part of the couple and requires neither the consent of the parents nor the approval of the Church.

The second paragraph addresses the ecclesiastical side of the synthesis. It makes clear that, although under Alexandrine doctrine the Church has no authority over the secular legal validity of a marriage, couples who ignore Church requirements still face severe consequences. The third paragraph elaborates on one issue raised in the second paragraph—namely, the church's standards regarding what defines a marriage as "clandestine."

Up to this point the author has simply presented the content of Alexandrine doctrine. In the final paragraph, however, the author introduces an interpretation of the Alexandrine doctrine advanced by historian Charles Donahue. This interpretation, which the author describes as radical, focuses on one aspect of Alexandrine doctrine, namely that a marriage entered into without parental consent could be fully solemnized by the Church. Donahue concludes that because of Alexandrine doctrine, the church became a guarantor of individual freedoms in the area of marriage.

Question 1

Overview: This question asks you to identify the statement that best expresses the idea that the passage as a whole is designed to convey. You should keep in mind that an answer choice that says something that is true of the passage is not necessarily the correct answer. For one thing, the answer choice may also say something that is not true of the passage, in which case it cannot, taken as a whole, correctly express the main idea of the passage. Likewise, an answer choice that is completely accurate in its description of some of the content of the passage may nonetheless be wrong because what it describes is not the main focus of the passage.

The Correct Answer:

B The first paragraph establishes that Alexander's doctrine treated marriage as a consensual union of the individuals involved, and in the second paragraph we are told that the mutual consent of the couple was all that was required for the secular legal validity of a marriage. The final paragraph states that, according to historian Charles Donahue, Alexandrine doctrine promoted marriages based on love rather than those based on economic convenience. So, of the five answer choices, (B) best expresses the main focus of the passage.

The Incorrect Answer Choices:

A The first sentence of the passage introduces the Alexandrine doctrine of marriage as a "synthesis of existing ecclesiastical and legal opinion." So the first part of (A) correctly reflects an important idea that is in the passage. But the second part of (A) is inaccurate since the only commentator cited by the author, Charles Donahue, does not, according to the passage, claim that Alexandrine doctrine encouraged clandestine marriages. Moreover, the author explicitly says that the Alexandrine doctrine was intended to discourage clandestine marriages (lines 23–25).

C Contrary to what (C) says, the passage does not claim that Alexander's doctrine represented a tightening of Church authority. According to the doctrine, the Church had no authority whatsoever with respect to the "essential secular legal validity" (line 33) of a marriage. With respect to Church law, of course, the Church had considerable authority; it could, for example, excommunicate couples and suspend priests who failed to abide by its marriage regulations (lines 30–33). Still, nothing in the passage suggests that the Church's authority was tightened even in this respect as a result of the doctrine. Indeed, the passage might be taken as suggesting that the church relinquished some of its former authority in deciding to recognize the legal validity of marriages it did not solemnize.

D The passage does discuss these two types of verbal marriage contracts in the first paragraph, so the statement in (D) correctly captures a detail from the passage. But this detail is not one that the passage develops to any extent. Thus (D) misrepresents the focus of the passage.

E The passage does state that couples who married without observing the church's bann requirement were, under Alexandrine doctrine, subject to excommunication (lines 30–33). But the passage represents the issue of excommunication as a matter of straightforward historical fact, and not, as (E) has it, as a matter subject to differing interpretations. More importantly, the central focus of the passage has to do with Alexandrine doctrine in general, and not with specific regulations concerning what kinds of marriage could result in excommunication.

■ *Difficulty Level: 3*

Question 2

The Correct Answer:

D According to the passage (line 7), "under Alexandrine doctrine, a couple could establish marriage by words of mutual consent and without the consent of parents." This statement clearly supports the inference that Alexandrine doctrine denies parents the power to prohibit a marriage that was based on the mutual consent of the couple.

The Incorrect Answer Choices:

A, B Parents are mentioned in the passage only in connection with the limits placed by Alexander's doctrine on their power to control who their children would marry. The passage does not provide any information relating to how the attitudes of parents and their children toward Church dictates might compare, so there is nothing in the passage to suggest that (A) might be true. Neither is there anything to suggest that parents were likely to favor one type of verbal marriage contract over the other, and thus (B) cannot be inferred from the passage.

C The passage provides no information on parents' views about the importance of the ecclesiastical sanction of a marriage. However, the passage strongly suggests that parents were concerned about the economic implications of a marriage, and thus it seems likely that the legal validity of a marriage would be a major concern of parents. On these grounds one might think that the **reverse** of (C) is possibly true. In any case, it is not possible to infer (C) from the passage.

E The passage provides no grounds for believing that clandestine marriages were prevalent prior to the Alexandrine synthesis. On the other hand, the passage makes it clear that clandestine marriages could easily occur given the Alexandrine doctrine. There is, therefore, no basis to infer that there was any parental concern about clandestine marriages prior to the Alexandrine synthesis, much less that such concern helped to bring about that synthesis.

■ *Difficulty Level: 1*

Question 3

Overview: To answer this question, you need first to look for any information provided by the passage regarding the excommunication of couples. The passage contains exactly one reference to this topic: lines 30–31 say, "Those couples ignoring this requirement were to be excommunicated." To understand what is being said, however, you need to know what requirement is being referred to; thus, to answer this question you need to take the preceding sentence into account as well. In that sentence (lines 25–30), we read, "a marriage was to be preceded by the publication of the marriage announcements, or banns, on three successive Sundays to allow community members to raise any legal objections to the intended union."

The Correct Answer:

B   As the excerpts from the passage quoted above make clear, under Alexandrine doctrine it is violating established banns procedures that places couples at risk of being excommunicated.

The Incorrect Answer Choices:

A, D   It is important to note that the passage distinguishes between the prior announcement of an intended marriage on the one hand, and the solemnization conferred on the marriage by Church ritual (lines13–16), which is performed by a priest (line 31), on the other hand. A violation of the solemnization requirement (A)—which is essentially marrying without the ritually conferred blessing of a priest (D)—is not something the passage says would have resulted in the excommunication of the couple. The only thing that the passage presents as exposing a couple to the risk of being excommunicated is failure to comply with the requirement of prior announcement of the intention to wed.

C   Lines 46–49 of the passage say that "so long as they acted in accordance with established bann procedures, a couple could marry without parental consent and still enjoy the blessing of the Church." So according to the passage, marrying without parental consent would not expose couples to the risk of being excommunicated.

E   Both *de futuro* contracts and *de praesenti* contracts have to do with the secular validity of a marriage and not with Church ritual or Church law. And excommunication has nothing to do with the secular side of a marriage; it is presented as a punishment meted out by the Church for failure to comply with its bann procedures. So according to what the passage says, the action described in (E) would not have exposed couples to the risk of excommunication.

■ *Difficulty Level: 1*

Question 4

Overview: The word "clandestine" appears in the sentence beginning on line 21: "Although Alexandrine doctrine accepted the secular legal validity of those contracts that lacked public announcement and ritual solemnization, it nonetheless attempted to discourage such clandestine unions and to regulate marriage procedures." In this context, the word "unions" refers to the marriages created by the "contracts" referred to in line 22. The question essentially asks you to pick out which answer choice best describes the kind of marriage that the phrase "clandestine unions" refers to.

The Correct Answer:

A　We know that the marriages in question are legal because they are described as being formed by contracts that have "secular legal validity" (line 22). The passage also states that "clandestine unions" are not recognized by the church because they lack public announcement and ritual solemnization. So the "clandestine unions" referred to in the second paragraph are the type of marriage described in (A).

The Incorrect Answer Choices:

B　Lines 21–23 characterize the clandestine unions at issue in two respects: their legal status and their standing in the eyes of the Church. No reference is made in this context to parental attitudes or reactions, which would in any event, according to Alexandrine doctrine, have no effect on either the legal status of these marriages or their recognition by the Church. So being unrecognized by the couple's parents is not what makes a marriage a clandestine union.

C, D　As we noted in the discussion of the correct answer, clandestine unions are marriages that are not recognized by the Church. Both (C) and (D) are therefore incorrect because they describe clandestine unions as recognized by the church.

E　As clandestine unions are characterized in the second paragraph of the passage, they are real marriages; in fact, they have secular legal validity. What (E) describes, however, is not actually a marriage. Rather, (E) describes a promise to marry that is not kept.

- *Difficulty Level: 2*

Question 5

The Correct Answer:

E　The first three paragraphs of the passage provide fairly detailed accounts of Pope Alexander III's twelfth-century doctrine of marriage. According to the author, this is a doctrine that historians regard as significant (lines 1–4). The final paragraph describes an interpretation of that doctrine that the author characterizes as a radical interpretation. Therefore, (E) correctly describes the purpose of the passage.

The Incorrect Answer Choices:

A　The only particular scholarly work mentioned in the passage is that of historian Charles Donahue. The author states that Donahue's interpretation is a "radical one" (line 56) but does not question its legitimacy. Moreover, the author does not identify, much less examine, the facts on which Donahue's interpretation is based.

B　The author outlines what could properly be described as an important legal doctrine. But while the author states that historians ascribe particular significance to this doctrine (lines 1–4), the passage says nothing about any influence the doctrine might have had in subsequent historical periods. So (B) misrepresents what the passage actually does.

C　The passage gives us no reason to believe that the field of medieval marriage practices is a neglected field of research. In fact, the first sentence, which refers to "[h]istorians of medieval marriage practices," suggests that the field is receiving scholarly attention. In any case, the author gives no indication of being concerned about any possible neglect, nor does the passage call for any such situation to be remedied.

D　The passage focuses on a single legal and ecclesiastical doctrine and makes no attempt to summarize the entire history of the era in question. So while the author's description of Charles Donahue's work might possibly be construed as an endorsement of a new scholarly approach, (D) cannot be the correct answer because the first part of it is very far off the mark.

- *Difficulty Level: 1*

Question 6

The Correct Answer:

C According to the final paragraph, Donahue presented the medieval Church as the guardian of individual freedom in the area of marriage. The author contrasts Donahue's "radical" view with "traditional perceptions of the medieval Church as the most potent authoritarian force in a rigidly hierarchical society" (lines 55–58). Thus the passage suggests that far from emphasizing the Church's promotion of individual choice, as Donahue does, traditional interpretations portray the church as restricting individual freedoms.

The Incorrect Answer Choices:

A According to the first sentence of the passage, historians of medieval marriage practices ascribe particular significance to Pope Alexander III's doctrine concerning marriage. Thus the passage does not suggest that those other historians consider Pope Alexander III to be any less historically important than Donahue does.

B The passage does not mention modern secular marriage laws, or their connection to Alexandrine doctrine, at all. In any case, since both Alexandrine doctrine and modern secular marriage laws treat marriage as a consensual union, both Donahue and traditional historians of medieval marriage practices would probably grant that Alexandrine doctrine could be considered a forerunner of modern marriage laws.

D The passage does not indicate what particular views Donahue or any other historians might have regarding how to read the "complicated legal and ecclesiastical rituals involved in the public announcement and ritual solemnization of marriage." So the passage gives us no reason to think that a difference between Donahue and other historians is that he reads those rituals correctly and they do not.

E The passage does not tell us enough about Donahue's views or those of any other historians to indicate whether any of them concentrated more on one aspect of Alexandrine doctrine than on another. So there is no reason to think that (E) gets at a difference between Donahue's interpretation and other historians' interpretations.

■ *Difficulty Level: 3*

Question 7

Overview: The passage gives an account of two kinds of verbal contract recognized by Alexandrine doctrine. One kind, the *de futuro* contract, was a promise to marry in the future (lines 17–18); the other kind, the *de praesenti* contract, created a binding and immediately effective marriage contract through the exchange of words of consent (lines 11–12).

The Correct Answer:

D As noted above, what distinguished the *de futuro* contract from the *de praesenti* contract is that the de futuro contract expresses an intent to marry in the future, while the *de praesenti* contract established an immediate, binding union.

The Incorrect Answer Choices:

A According to the passage, Alexandrine doctrine recognized both types of contract (lines 4–10). Furthermore, both types of contract were secular. Thus (A) does not describe a distinction between the two kinds of contract.

B The passage states that couples could enter into marriage contracts "by words of mutual consent and without the consent of parents" (lines 8–9). The passage adds, "These contracts were of two kinds," and it goes on to describe *de praesenti* and *de futuro* contracts (lines 10–20). So (B) does not correctly describe a difference between the two kinds of contract.

C In lines 13–16, the passage says that the prior announcement of the intention to wed added nothing to the validity and permanence of marriages established by *de praesenti* contracts. The passage does not explicitly discuss the public announcement of the intention to wed in connection with *de futuro* contracts. But inasmuch as both types of contracts are secular contracts, and inasmuch as the marriage banns pertain to Church solemnization of marriages rather than to their secular legal validity, the same can be inferred regarding *de futuro* contracts. So (C) does not correctly describe a difference between the two kinds of contract as they are presented in the passage.

E The only discussion of excommunication to be found in the passage says that couples who married without prior public announcement "were to be excommunicated" (lines 30–31). Since the *de futuro* contract formalized the intent to marry without establishing an actual marriage, the passage tells us in effect that only the establishment of a *de praesenti* contract could result in excommunication. With regard to solemnization by Church ritual, the situation is the same: the passage only talks about the solemnization of actual marriages. Since both parts of (E) apply to *de praesenti* contracts only, (E) does not describe a difference between the two types of contract.

- *Difficulty Level: 1*

Question 8

Overview: The first paragraph begins by characterizing Alexandrine doctrine as a "synthesis of existing ecclesiastical and legal opinion concerning marriage" (lines 3–4). The rest of the paragraph goes on to present in some detail the purely secular, legal side of that synthesis. The second paragraph gives an account of how ecclesiastical concerns figured in Alexandrine doctrine.

The Correct Answer:

C As we just noted, Alexandrine doctrine is described as a synthesis. But most of the first paragraph is concerned only with the legal, secular side, and insists that the Church had no authority over the secular legal validity of marriages created through the exchange of words of present consent (lines 13–16). The second paragraph addresses the other side of the synthesis. It shows that under Alexandrine doctrine the Church nevertheless had considerable authority with respect to marriage. Thus the second paragraph presents additional information that elaborates on information presented in the first paragraph.

The Incorrect Answer Choices:

A To the extent that the second paragraph deals with the same facts as the first paragraph—the secular legal validity of certain verbal marriage contracts without the blessing of the Church—it essentially restates those facts. The other information presented in the second paragraph is new information that the passage presents as supplementing, rather than as diverging from, the information given in the first paragraph.

B The first paragraph explains that under Alexandrine doctrine a couple could establish a legally binding marriage without parental consent and without any regard to Church requirements. It also describes the actions through which couples could establish *de praesenti* and *de futuro* contracts. Any of these might conceivably be construed as rules, but to the extent that they are, the second paragraph confirms the validity of those rules. The second paragraph does not identify any exceptions to any rule identified in the passage.

D The matters discussed in the second paragraph are presented as straightforward matters of historical fact. The second paragraph does not attempt to present any particular interpretations, traditional or new, of its topic.

E The first paragraph is primarily concerned with giving an account of one side of the doctrine that the author has introduced as a synthesis. The second paragraph is primarily concerned with giving an account of the other side of that synthesis. So the second paragraph is a supplement rather than an objection to the first paragraph.

- *Difficulty Level: 5*

Questions 9–13

Synopsis: This passage discusses the work of certain nontraditional black women filmmakers who challenge the assumptions of mainstream cinema while using the realist cinematic techniques of mainstream filmmakers. The central claim made by the author is that their work is experimental even though it uses mainstream techniques.

The first paragraph describes the relation of experimental films to mainstream cinema. According to the author, the stories told by mainstream filmmakers present a world that contains nothing that the majority culture finds unacceptable. Mainstream films create the illusion that what you are seeing in the cinema is actually what real life is like. Radical filmmakers who want to expose this illusion try to force people to see that the way things appear in the cinema has very little to do with the way things are in real life. And filmmakers can achieve this effect—according to film theorists cited by the author—by rejecting realist techniques that "create the illusion of visual continuity" in favor of experimental techniques that produce images that "do not make immediate sense."

At this point, the passage might be taken to suggest that nontraditional black women filmmakers who want to expose the misrepresentations of mainstream cinema would have to reject realist cinematic techniques. But in the second paragraph the author tells us that in fact some of these filmmakers choose to work within the realist form and do not use experimental cinematic techniques. So what, one might ask, makes these filmmakers nontraditional? The author answers this challenge by questioning the prevailing notion that a filmmaker cannot be both realist and experimental. The author argues that films can also legitimately be called experimental if they focus on subjects that have been ignored or trivialized by mainstream realist cinema.

The final paragraph offers support for this position by discussing two films by nontraditional black women filmmakers as examples of "experimental" films in which nontraditional subjects are treated realistically. The point being made is that these films also expose mainstream cinema's misrepresentation of the way things are in real life, but the films do so by their choice of content rather than by using antirealist techniques.

Question 9

The Correct Answer:

B   The second paragraph tells you that some nontraditional black women filmmakers use mainstream cinematic techniques. As discussed above, the author's thesis is that the films made by these women filmmakers are legitimately described as experimental even though they use mainstream techniques because their subject matter is nontraditional. Thus (B) is the best answer.

The Incorrect Answer Choices:

A   According to the first paragraph, many radical filmmakers refuse to use conservative (i.e., mainstream) cinematic techniques. However, the central focus of the passage is the work of nontraditional black women filmmakers who make experimental films using these very techniques. So (A) fails to capture the main idea of the passage.

C   According to the first paragraph of the passage, (C) is true for many experimental filmmakers. But the author focuses on experimental filmmakers who achieve their goals by making films about nontraditional subjects, not by means of technical experimentation.

D   The passage doesn't comment on the impact that black women filmmakers have had on cinematic practice. Nor does it say anything about whether mainstream and experimental filmmakers have acknowledged or ignored any impact black women filmmakers might have had. Thus, (D) cannot be the correct answer.

E   The passage suggests that (E) is likely to be true, especially if "controversial topics" means those that are likely to upset mainstream audiences. But the main focus of the passage is nontraditional black women filmmakers, not the preferences of mainstream filmmakers.

- *Difficulty Level: 5*

Question 10

Overview: In line 40 the author refers to a "prevailing notion" that filmmakers who use mainstream cinematic techniques cannot be called experimental. The question asks you what the author most likely believes about this notion.

The Correct Answer:

D   The author says that prevailing notion "places an undue emphasis on form at the expense of content" (lines 43–44). The author also claims that a film can be considered experimental because of its content, even if it uses mainstream techniques. These two claims together allow us to infer that the author holds that the content of a cinematic work may be as crucial to the work's experimental character as its form is.

The Incorrect Answer Choices:

A   The author thinks that the prevailing notion of what makes a film experimental is too narrow in that it focuses exclusively on technical experimentation. The author does not suggest that the prevailing definition of technical experimentation is itself too narrow.

B   The tension in the passage arises from the fact that filmmakers who wish to express radical ideas typically do so by means of radical cinematic techniques. So while the author believes that conservative filmmaking techniques do have some potential for expressing radical ideas (for example, in the works of the black women filmmakers discussed in the last paragraph), we cannot infer that the author believes that these techniques have a **unique** potential for expressing radical ideas. The work of most radical filmmakers shows that radical techniques have that potential as well.

C   The author's criticism of the prevailing notion is not that it pays insufficient attention to the cinematic techniques used by nontraditional black women filmmakers, but rather that it pays insufficient attention to the experimental nature of the **content** of their films. Thus (C) cannot be inferred from the passage.

E   According to the prevailing notion, films made using mainstream cinematic techniques cannot be considered **experimental**. The author argues that they can, depending on their content. But neither the prevailing notion nor the author's argument discusses in any way whether form or content is more important to a film's **mainstream** character.

- *Difficulty Level: 5*

Question 11

Overview: What you are looking for in this question is the answer choice that describes something **not** accomplished by any of the documentary films described by the author. The only place where the author describes specific documentary films is in the third paragraph, so you should concentrate on that paragraph in answering this question. Since it might be easier to identify what the passage **does** say (in other words, the wrong answers) than it is to identify what the passage doesn't say, a good approach to questions like this one might be to eliminate the wrong answers first.

The Correct Answer:

D In discussing documentary films, the author, does not say, or even suggest, that they have any effect on mainstream media.

The Incorrect Answer Choices:

A Lines 52–54 say of *Fannie's Film* that it belongs to a group of films that "expose the thematic assumptions ... of realistic filmmaking." So according to the author, at least one of the documentary films discussed could be said to call these assumptions into question.

B Lines 55–58 say that "documentaries provide opportunities for revising the list of traditionally acknowledged prominent figures by creating more accounts of black public figures." So according to the author, some of the documentaries can be said to examine the lives of black public figures who have not received substantial recognition.

C Lines 50–52 refer to a group of films that present the stories of women "whose experiences have usually been trivialized or ignored by mainstream media." So according to the author, some of the documentaries examine the lives of such women.

E The author describes Michelle Parkerson's film *... But Then, She's Betty Carter* (lines 59–63) as being one of those films that "urge their audiences to question their own expectations about who gains public recognition and why." So according to the author, one of the documentaries does this.

■ *Difficulty Level: 5*

Question 12

The Correct Answer:

C The author describes the features of "mainstream, realist cinematic practice" at the beginning of the first paragraph, stating that realist filmmakers "manipulate the use of the camera and techniques of editing and lighting in ways that create the illusion that cinema is like life ..." (lines 4–6). Meanwhile, lines 25–30 state, "The very techniques that create the illusion of visual continuity, **some theorists say**, smooth over contradictions and incoherences that might reflect a reality that Hollywood—and the majority culture that is its audience—does not want to admit or know" [emphasis added]. The phrase "the very techniques that create the illusion of visual continuity" refers back to the description of mainstream cinematic practice at the beginning of the paragraph. So if we put these two statements together, we can infer that the theorists would indeed be likely to agree that mainstream filmmakers use techniques that conceal what audiences would prefer not to know.

The Incorrect Answer Choices:

A The passage suggests that, at least in the eyes of the theorists, mainstream audiences might not be open-minded enough to appreciate experimental films. But the theorists do not, according to anything said in the passage, attribute this possible dislike for experimental films to a lack of knowledge on the part of mainstream audiences. So nothing that the author says about the theorists would support the inference that the theorists would agree with (A).

B There is no indication that the theorists believe that mainstream filmmakers aim to educate their audience about minority cultures. In fact, there is perhaps a slight suggestion that the theorists might believe the opposite.

D The passage does not say or suggest anything regarding how the theorists might view the use of the documentary form by mainstream filmmakers. So the passage provides no justification for inferring that the theorists would agree with (D).

E Mainstream filmmakers' use of conventional realist techniques is presented in the passage as the result of calculated strategy, not as the result of ignorance of more experimental alternatives. And the passage gives us no reason to think that the theorists would believe any differently. So the passage provides no justification for inferring that the theorists would agree with (E).

■ *Difficulty Level: 3*

Question 13

The Correct Answer:

D As indicated in the "Synopsis," the primary aim of the passage is to examine how certain nontraditional black women filmmakers can use realist cinematic techniques and still produce experimental films. Thus (D) most accurately describes the purpose of the passage.

The Incorrect Answer Choices:

A The final paragraph describes two films by nontraditional black women filmmakers in which nontraditional subjects are treated realistically. But the author does not contrast these films. Instead, the author examines what they have in common—namely, a conventional, realist approach to nontraditional subjects—in order to argue that this is what ultimately makes them experimental films. So (A) does not describe the primary purpose of the passage.

B The first paragraph does, to some extent, provide a critique of the subjects and techniques of realist filmmaking. However, this critique is not the main focus of the passage, but is instead part of the background for the primary focus of the passage: the experimental character of films made by certain nontraditional black women filmmakers. So (B) does not describe the primary purpose of the passage.

C The author is not concerned with black women filmmakers in general and how to tell which of them are experimental and which are not. Consequently, (C) does not capture the primary purpose of the passage.

E The author mentions avant-garde and feminist filmmakers in the first paragraph of the passage, but only in passing, as filmmakers who resist the conventions of cinematic realism. The primary focus of the passage, however, is the work of certain black women filmmakers who use those conventions. So (E) is inaccurate.

- *Difficulty Level: 2*

Questions 14–20

Synopsis: This passage summarizes the history of Alfred Wegener's theory of continental drift, from its initial formulation in 1912 to its virtually unanimous acceptance some 50 years later. The passage opens with a very short introductory paragraph comparing Wegener to Darwin (note, however, that this comparison plays no further role in the passage). The second paragraph briefly sets out Alfred Wegener's 1912 theory of continental drift, according to which Africa and South America were once pieces of a single supercontinent that gradually drifted apart. The author notes that Wegener never carefully tested the fit between the African and South American coastlines because he assumed that geological wear and tear would have destroyed the evidence for his theory. The author also observes that Wegener's theory was largely ignored until 1924, when Harold Jeffreys dismissed it in a landmark book called *The Earth*.

Up to this point (line 18), the author has simply been setting out the facts, and the passage has remained essentially neutral in its tone. But the final sentence of the second paragraph and the first sentence of the third paragraph mark a shift in the passage. Here, the author's choice of words in describing Jeffreys's book is far from neutral. Telling turns of phrase such as "Apparently after casually observing ..." reveal that the author actually has little patience for Jeffreys.

The third paragraph reports subsequent findings that supported Wegener's theory. First there is a brief account of the work of S. W. Carey, whose use of "careful techniques of geometric projection" (note the pointed contrast with Jeffreys's "obviously perfunctory observation") showed "a remarkably close fit" between the coastlines of Africa and South America. The rest of the paragraph is taken up by the author's discussion of the findings of Keith Runcorn. Runcorn examined the orientation of the magnetic poles in a type of magnetic rock called basalt. Comparing the orientation of these poles in basalt of roughly the same age in what are now North America and Europe, he found clear evidence that the continents had drifted with respect to each other. The last two sentences of the paragraph comment critically on Jeffreys's careless rejection of this new evidence.

The final paragraph of the passage talks about a 1966 finding that revealed the mechanism underlying continental drift—namely that continents rest on massive plates that move over time. This finding immediately led to widespread acceptance of Wegener's theory.

Question 14

The Correct Answer:

E The author begins the passage by saying that Wegener's theory is comparable to Darwin's theory of evolution inasmuch as it revolutionized an entire science. Thus the theory clearly had significant implications. The rest of the passage recounts objections to the theory, together with a series of discoveries that provided mounting evidence in favor of the theory, culminating in its acceptance more than 50 years after it was first proposed. Thus (E) expresses the main idea of the passage.

The Incorrect Answer Choices:

A The author describes evidence that supported Wegener's theory, but there is no indication that the author is interested in assessing whether there was anything unexpected about where the evidence was found or about who provided it. So (A) is not supported by the passage.

B The passage mentions only one critic of Wegener's theory, Harold Jeffreys, who is presented as persistently hostile to the theory and remarkably careless in his approach to scientific evidence. In other words, the passage portrays Jeffreys as consistently ignoring relevant evidence, rather than providing evidence in favor of the theory.

C Darwin's theory is mentioned only in the brief introductory paragraph, where it serves as a point of comparison indicating how scientifically significant Wegener's theory is. Beyond that, the histories of the two theories appear to be quite different, since Darwin's is described as still controversial, whereas Wegener's is said to be accepted almost without question. In any case, the author is clearly not interested in exploring whatever similarities there might be since Darwin's theory is not mentioned again after the second sentence of the passage.

D Although the author suggests (lines 12–14) that Wegener himself did not test the fit between the African and South American coastlines, this is a fairly minor point in the overall scheme of the passage. The author is far more concerned with subsequent developments relating to reactions to Wegener's theory on the part of his scientific peers. So although what (D) says is suggested by the passage, it does not express the main idea of the passage.

■ *Difficulty Level: 2*

Question 15

Overview: Each of the answer choices in this question describes a person who acts in a certain way in a specific context. You are asked to select the one who acts in a way that is most similar to the way Jeffreys is described as acting in his response to Wegener's theory. According to lines 17–20, Jeffreys dismissed the theory after "casually observing the shorelines on a globe," an approach that is further characterized as "obviously perfunctory" in line 21.

The Correct Answer:

A The botanist in (A) reaches a scientific judgment based on an examination that is described as superficial. In dismissing Wegener's theory, Jeffreys is presented as relying on observations that are characterized as casual. Thus both Jeffreys and the botanist base a substantive judgment on superficial appearances.

The Incorrect Answer Choices:

B The driver in (B) is presented as completely lacking a potentially useful source of information—a suitable map. Jeffreys, on the other hand, evidently had a source of information—a globe. Thus, unlike the driver, Jeffreys did not lack relevant information; he simply declined to make more than perfunctory use of it.

C For the zoologist in (C), choosing to study animal behavior rather than anatomy is a choice of professional specialization. There is no indication that this decision is made casually. Thus it does not correspond to anything in the passage's negative characterization of Jeffreys' response to Wegener's theory.

D The politician in (D) who decides to run for office on the basis of the findings of a public opinion poll is not presented as ignoring relevant information, or as being careless or cavalier in assessing the information.

E The psychiatrist in (E) who bases treatment decisions on a patient's past history can be presumed to be using appropriate information, and there is no indication that this information is being treated casually. The psychiatrist is therefore unlike Jeffreys in both respects.

■ *Difficulty Level: 1*

Question 16

Overview: This question asks you to identify what the evidence of seafloor spreading helped to explain, according to the passage. Since the passage discusses seafloor spreading only in the last paragraph, you should focus on that paragraph in answering this question.

The Correct Answer:

E In lines 51–53, the passage says that seafloor spreading explained "why the ocean basins are so much younger than the continents." (E) paraphrases this portion of the passage.

The Incorrect Answer Choices:

A, D In lines 47–50 the author says that proof that the seafloor spreads from the midocean ridges confirms the hypothesis that molten rock repaves the seafloor as giant crustal plates move apart. There is no other mention of giant crustal plates. So there is nothing in the passage to suggest that seafloor spreading explains either the reason for the existence of these plates or their composition.

B According to the passage (lines 32–34), the magnetic poles of a given fragment of basalt are fixed from the time that fragment of basalt was formed. The evidence regarding seafloor spreading described in the last paragraph does nothing to explain why that orientation is retained.

C Although the passage mentions (lines 31–32) that the earth's poles have wandered, no explanation for this phenomenon is presented or discussed anywhere in the passage.

■ *Difficulty Level: 3*

Question 17

The Correct Answer:

C The author uses the phrase "obviously perfunctory" in line 21 to suggest that Jeffreys was hasty and lax in his evaluation of Wegener's theory. The author emphasizes this point by contrasting Jeffreys's "obviously perfunctory observation" with the "careful techniques" that S. W. Carey used to in obtain his evidence. As it is used in context, therefore, the phrase "obviously perfunctory" reveals a great deal about the author's opinion about Jeffreys.

The Incorrect Answer Choices:

A The phrase "virtually ignored" in line 15 is used to characterize the **general** reaction to Wegener's ideas around the time he proposed them in 1912. Furthermore, the first mention of Jeffreys occurs in connection with the discussion of his book of 1924 in which he explicitly rejected, rather than ignoring, Wegener's theory. Thus, "virtually ignored," as it is used in context, does not apply to Jeffreys, hence it does not reveal the author's opinion of Jeffreys.

B The phrase "very poor" conveys a judgment attributed **to** Jeffreys, rather than the author's judgment **about** Jeffreys. It expresses how Jeffreys viewed the fit between the shorelines of Africa and South America. As the author's description of S. W. Carey's "careful techniques" suggests (line 22), the fit of the shorelines, as they appeared on an ordinary globe, would probably have seemed poor to any observer. Thus, while the phrase "very poor" is a paraphrase of Jeffreys's mistaken judgment, it does not actually reveal the author's opinion of Jeffreys.

D In line 22, the phrase "careful techniques" characterizes how S. W. Carey, a critic of Jeffreys, approached the problem of determining the fit between the shorelines of Africa and South America. In this description there is an implicit comparison with Jeffreys's approach, but the phrase does not apply to Jeffreys directly. To the extent that it suggests anything about the author's view of Jeffreys, it does so only by means of contrast with phrases (such as "obviously perfunctory") that do directly reveal the author's opinion of Jeffreys. Thus, (D) can't be the answer choice that most clearly reveals the author's opinion of Jeffreys.

E The author uses the phrase "consensus view" in line 56 to describe the eventual acceptance of Wegener's theory. The passage does not mention Jeffreys at all in connection with the emergence of the consensus view.

- *Difficulty Level: 2*

Question 18

Overview: This question asks you to identify the rhetorical purpose served by the author's allusion to a comment made by certain field geologists. According to the author, Jeffreys's "casual disdain for such observational data led some field geologists to suggest that his classic should be retitled *An Earth*" (lines 43–45). This suggestion is mentioned in the last sentence of a paragraph describing strong empirical evidence for continental drift, which the author describes Jeffreys as, characteristically, having "brusquely rejected."

The Correct Answer:

C The definite article in Jeffrey's title *The Earth* implies that the book is about the concrete, objectively known earth studied by field geologists. But Jeffreys is presented as having little interest in the kind of empirical evidence valued by scientists. Accordingly, the indefinite article in the title *An Earth* suggests that the work is not about **the** earth, but rather about some other, quasi-imaginary earth. In other words, by mentioning the field geologists' satiric suggestion, the author expresses disapproval of Jeffreys's cavalier disregard for empirical evidence.

The Incorrect Answer Choices:

A Jeffreys is discussed in the passage only because of his opposition to Wegener's theory; he is not represented as having any other views. Thus, while the geologists' suggestion does implicitly contrast Jeffreys's approach with a more scientific approach, it can't be said to contrast two of Jeffreys's ideas.

B A humorous comment like that of the field geologists cannot really be said to justify anyone's position. Jokes can belittle or ridicule, but they cannot be taken as evidence or arguments. Thus the author refers to the geologists' suggestion in order to make his or her own criticism of Jeffreys's approach to empirical evidence more vivid, not as an additional justification for the author's, or for anyone else's, criticisms.

D The reference to the geologists' suggestion emphasizes Jeffreys's casual approach to empirical evidence. This tendency on Jeffreys's part is certainly a major factor contributing to his conflict with Wegener, but the geologists' suggestion can hardly be said to **explain** the reasons for that conflict. The suggestion is a satiric characterization of Jeffreys's approach, not an explanation of anything.

E   Carey and the field geologists who made the suggestion in question are all critics of Jeffreys. The author makes no assertions about the field geologists, other than to say that they made their satirical suggestion. And while the author makes several assertions about Carey in lines 21–26, none of them are in any way supported by the mention of the geologists' suggestion.

- *Difficulty Level: 3*

Question 19

The Correct Answer:

D   At the beginning of the third paragraph, the author asserts that Carey was disturbed by the "obviously perfunctory observation" on which Jeffreys apparently based his dismissal of Wegener's theory. In response, Carey did careful research of his own that resulted in evidence that contradicted Jeffreys's conclusion and strongly supported Wegener's theory. Thus, it can be inferred that Carey believed that Jeffreys' 1924 appraisal was unquestionably based on insufficient research.

The Incorrect Answer Choices:

A, C   For the reasons discussed in the explanation of the correct answer, Carey clearly did not believe that Jeffreys's appraisal was either authoritative or accurate. Thus it can be inferred that Carey did not believe either (A) or (C).

B   The passage clearly indicates that Carey regarded Jeffreys's appraisal as wrong, but not as requiring any interpretation.

E   The passage indicates that Carey did indeed believe Jeffreys's appraisal to be deficient. However, since he went on to conduct research aimed at undermining Jeffreys's position, we must infer that Carey did not view Jeffreys's appraisal as unworthy of further investigation.

- *Difficulty Level: 1*

INSTRUCTIONS FOR COMPLETING THE BIOGRAPHICAL AREA ARE ON THE BACK COVER OF YOUR TEST BOOKLET.
USE ONLY A NO. 2 OR HB PENCIL TO COMPLETE THIS ANSWER SHEET. DO NOT USE INK.

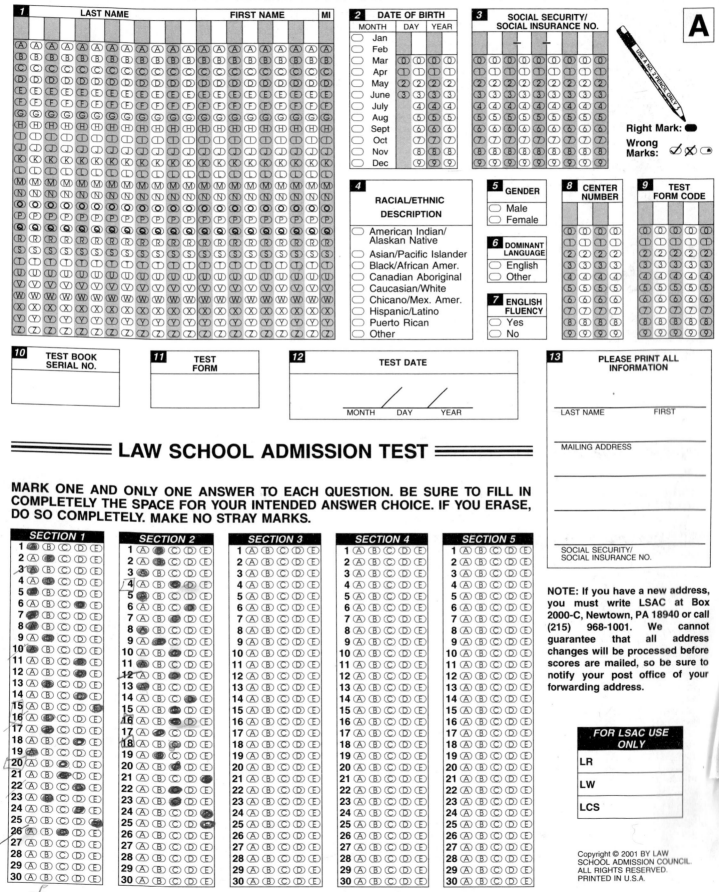

LAW SCHOOL ADMISSION TEST

MARK ONE AND ONLY ONE ANSWER TO EACH QUESTION. BE SURE TO FILL IN COMPLETELY THE SPACE FOR YOUR INTENDED ANSWER CHOICE. IF YOU ERASE, DO SO COMPLETELY. MAKE NO STRAY MARKS.

NOTE: If you have a new address, you must write LSAC at Box 2000-C, Newtown, PA 18940 or call (215) 968-1001. We cannot guarantee that all address changes will be processed before scores are mailed, so be sure to notify your post office of your forwarding address.

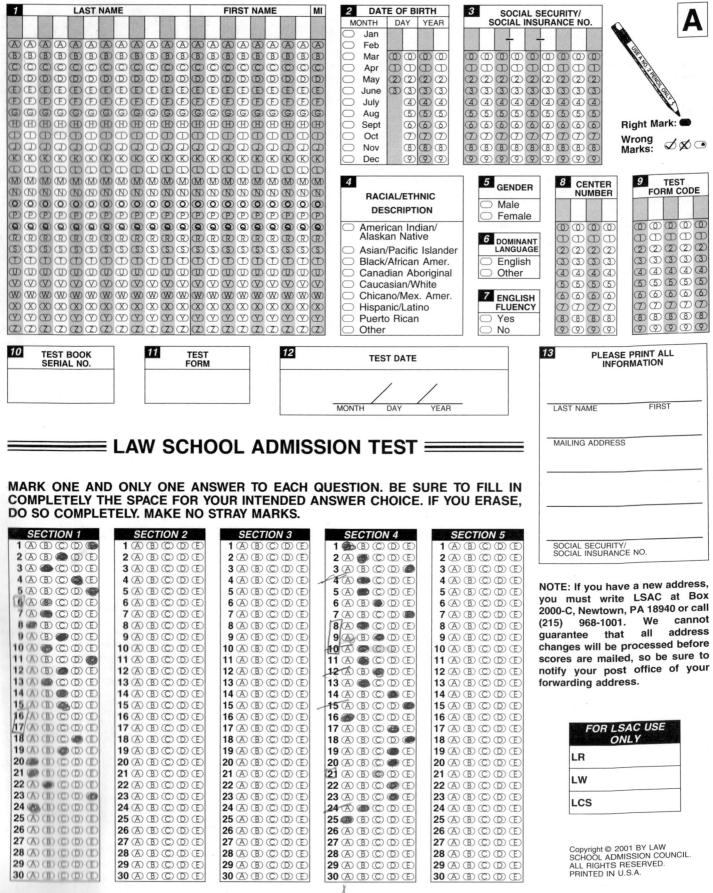

Question 20

Overview: According to the passage, the theory of continental drift claims that what are now the two continents of Africa and South America had originally been parts of a single, ancient supercontinent that drifted apart, leaving the Atlantic Ocean between them. One of the key pieces of evidence for this theory is described in the last paragraph: "In 1966 compelling proof that the seafloor spreads from the midocean ridges confirmed the hypothesis that molten rock wells up at these ridges from deep within the earth and repaves the seafloor as giant crustal plates move apart" (lines 46–50). The author adds that this evidence solved the long-standing puzzle of why ocean basins are so much younger than the continents. This question asks you to pick out the answer choice that is most clearly inconsistent with the evidence for continental drift, and the correct answer focuses on this piece of evidence.

The Correct Answer:

A   According to the theory, the Atlantic Ocean came into existence as what had originally been a single land mass drifted apart into separate continents. Consequently, one would expect the basin of the Atlantic Ocean to be younger than the continents surrounding it, and this is what the evidence described in the last paragraph confirms. If (A) were true, however, the ocean basin would be older than the continents, and thus the truth of (A) would undermine evidence for the theory of continental drift.

The Incorrect Answer Choices:

B   As (B) is stated, we cannot tell whether more accurate mapping would yield a closer fit between Africa and South America or a fit that is not as close as earlier mappings found. So (B) can be ruled out on the grounds that we cannot determine whether it would strengthen or weaken evidence for the theory.

C   According to the passage, an important source of evidence for continental drift comes from the way magnetic fields of basalt in different continents are aligned. That evidence depends on the expectation that "the magnetic fields of rocks of the same age from any continent would all be aligned the way the earth's magnetic field was aligned at that time" (lines 35–37). (C) would show this expectation to be true with respect to some basalts magnetized during the twentieth century. Therefore, (C) is consistent with key evidence for the theory of continental drift.

D   Lines 27–42 describe the significance, for the theory of continental drift, of evidence derived from the magnetic field alignment of basalts. The significant evidence comes from basalts formed before the continents drifted apart. (D) refers to basalts found in Africa and South America that were formed at about the same time, but it does not tell whether that was before or after the continents began to drift apart. So the impact of (D) on evidence for the theory of continental drift cannot be determined.

E   The observational studies referred to in (E) might well have concerned geological evidence that is irrelevant to the theory of continental drift. Since (E) doesn't tell us what phenomena Jeffreys observed carefully, we cannot conclude that (E) undermines evidence for the theory of continental drift.

■ *Difficulty Level: 4*

Questions 21–27

Synopsis: The passage describes and criticizes Spanish historian José Antonio Maravall's interpretation of baroque culture. The first paragraph includes Maravall among those scholars who regard the European baroque (1600–1680) as a political, social, and cultural mentality and not just an aesthetic style. The second paragraph introduces Maravall's view that baroque culture was created by the European ruling classes as a strategy for containing the liberating and destabilizing forces unleashed by the Renaissance. The third paragraph describes this strategy more specifically as one that relied on enticement, with rulers attempting to redirect the public's desire for novelty into politically harmless channels by means of grand spectacles, an attempt that Maravall clearly regards as having largely succeeded. In the fourth paragraph the author, who has up to now merely described Maravall's views, becomes more critical, arguing that Maravall exaggerated the ability of rulers to manipulate society for their own ends and using the examples of England and Spain in the 1630s to show that these rulers in fact sometimes fell victim to the illusions they created.

Question 21

The Correct Answer:

B   The passage focuses on Maravall's view that baroque culture was an attempt to distract people from challenging the political order (lines 39–40) by manipulating opinions and feelings on a broad public scale (lines 42–43) and argues (last paragraph) that Maravall overestimated the success of this strategy. Thus (B) expresses the main idea of the passage.

The Incorrect Answer Choices:

A   In the first, introductory paragraph, the author positions Maravall among scholars of the European baroque, using language similar to that used in (A), but these introductory remarks do not express the main idea of the passage. Moreover, (A) goes beyond the passage in ascribing both novelty ("Until recently ... however, Maravall") and success ("has shown") to Maravall.

C   Maravall presents European baroque culture as a reaction to the "Renaissance's liberating forces of criticism and opposition" (lines 16–17), not as an expansion of the social and intellectual developments of the Renaissance. So (C) misrepresents what the passage says about the relationship between baroque culture and the Renaissance. And, in any case, this is not the chief concern of the passage. Nor is the passage particularly concerned with the fact that Maravall focused on Spain, though it does mention that fact.

D   The author's examples of specific baroque-era monarchies—England and Spain—are used to argue against Maravall's belief that the ruling class was **successful** in controlling society by means of baroque culture. But these examples do not call into question the **intention** of the ruling class to achieve such control. Indeed, in presenting these examples, the author presupposes that there was such an intent. Thus (D) is factually wrong about the passage and so cannot express its main idea.

E   Part of the main concern of the passage is to present Maravall's view that baroque culture was not simply repressive but was also enticing (lines 32–33), relying on people's going voluntarily where they were being led. Thus (E) gives an unbalanced picture of what the passage says about Maravall's view and so cannot express the main idea of the passage. And, unlike the correct answer (B), it ignores the critical stance taken by the passage.

■ *Difficulty Level: 5*

Question 22

The Correct Answer:

C The phrase "tends to exaggerate" occurs in lines 47–48 as part of the sentence "He [Maravall] tends to exaggerate the capacity of those in authority to manipulate a society for their own ideological ends." This is clearly a criticism of Maravall's view of baroque culture, which the author backs up with examples. Thus this phrase indicates an attitude of the author toward Maravall's view, namely, disagreement.

The Incorrect Answer Choices:

A In the first sentence of the passage, the author contrasts the view of the European baroque as merely an aesthetic style with the view of it as both an aesthetic style and "a political, social, and cultural mentality." It is the latter to which the author applies the phrase "this larger view" in line 5. In calling it larger, the author is making the factual claim that it encompasses a wider range of phenomena, not a value judgment. So, although this phrase does apply to Maravall's view, it does not indicate an attitude of the author toward it.

B The phrase "grandiose artifice" in line 34 refers to such things as fireworks, theater, and religious festivals that could be staged as big spectacles to delight the public. Thus it refers to things Maravall discusses, not to his views. And in any case, the phrase as it is used in line 34 does not express an attitude, only a factual judgment about the size of the spectacles.

D The phrase "own ideological ends" occurs within the larger phrase "the capacity of those in authority to manipulate a society for their own ideological ends" (lines 48–49). The phrase is in a paragraph in which the author's own opinions are presented, but the phrase is used in a descriptive way to refer to a phenomenon that both the author and Maravall are interested in. To the extent that it conveys an attitude, it is an attitude toward "those in authority," and not toward Maravall.

E The phrase "wholly counterproductive" in line 52 is used to express the author's opinion of the effectiveness of the efforts of Charles I and Philip IV to manipulate their respective societies. Thus, while it does express an attitude, it is an attitude toward these efforts and not toward Maravall's concept of baroque culture.

■ *Difficulty Level: 3*

Question 23

Overview: This question asks you to pick the word that could best be used to replace "directive" in line 27 while retaining the overall meaning of the sentence in which it occurs. To do this, you need to interpret the sentence within the larger context of the author's account of Maravall's position. The term "directive culture" is neither self-explanatory nor explained in the sentence that introduces it.

The Correct Answer:

D The word "directive" occurs in line 27 as part of the sentence "Maravall regards the baroque as a culture of control and containment, or, more dynamically, as a directive culture, designed to reintegrate and unite a society living under the shadow of social and intellectual disruption." The larger context of the passage tells us that, according to Maravall, this culture worked through enticement and manipulation of opinions and feelings. In other words, the sort of control that is being exercised is not simply repressive or coercive but relies on people voluntarily going where they are being led. Of the answer choices available, the one that comes closest to capturing this idea is "guiding."

The Incorrect Answer Choices:

A "Straightforward" is not a possible meaning of "directive" (though it is a possible meaning of "direct"). Moreover, we would not normally describe a culture, let alone one that relies on enticement and manipulation, as "straightforward."

B The point of calling a culture "directive" is to indicate how those in authority attempt to exercise control, whether or not the culture in fact is changing, or evolving. So "evolving" does not express the meaning of "directive" in this context.

C "Directive" and "codify" are far apart in meaning. To codify something is to reduce it to a set of rules. It is not clear that a culture is the sort of thing that can be codified, but even if it is, this is clearly not what the author means in calling baroque culture "directive."

E The word "compelling" may be taken in two senses. One of them, that of compulsion or coercion, is the opposite of "directive" in the sense at issue here, that of enticing people so that they voluntarily go where you want them to go. The other sense of "compelling"—as in "compelling performance" or "compelling proof"—refers to an effect that has been achieved. Since "directive" in the sense at issue here is used to refer to the way in which the culture exercises control, "compelling" in this second sense does not express the meaning of "directive" either.

- *Difficulty Level: 3*

Question 24

Overview: This question is about an inference concerning Maravall's views. The passage both reports Maravall's views and gives the author's opinion of them. So it is important to know whose point of view any particular piece of the passage expresses.

The Correct Answer:

D Maravall argues that monarchs in the baroque period attempted to "defend traditional order and values in societies unsettled by the Renaissance's liberating forces of criticism and opposition" (lines 11–17). In lines 37–40, where the author is still presenting Maravall's views, we are told that the enticements used by monarchs "deflected the desire for novelty into areas where it represented no challenge to the political order." So we can infer that Maravall believed that the monarchs of the baroque era achieved a certain measure of success in countering the disruptive legacy of the Renaissance.

The Incorrect Answer Choices:

A According to lines 40–43, Maravall concludes that "every aspect of the baroque emerged from the necessity, as public opinion grew increasingly important, of manipulating opinions and feelings on a broad public scale." From this we can infer that Maravall regarded monarchs of the baroque era as increasingly sensitive to unfavorable public opinion, not increasingly indifferent to it.

B According to lines 11–15, Maravall argues that the baroque period was characterized by monarchs who, "having suppressed the worst excesses of aristocratic order, could now ally themselves with their nobilities to defend traditional order." From this we can infer that Maravall regarded monarchs of the baroque era as facing no significant threat from the aristocracy.

C In the last paragraph of the passage, monarchs of the baroque era are indeed characterized as being captivated by the cultural devices designed to control their subjects (see especially lines 53–55). However, this characterization is a point made by the author of the passage in criticism of Maravall's view, as something that Maravall failed to recognize.

E   As presented in the passage, Maravall was concerned solely with the relationship between the ruling class in a country and the people of that country. So nothing can be inferred from the passage about Maravall's view on whether or not monarchs of the baroque era were preoccupied with the goal of attaining cultural preeminence for their respective countries.

- *Difficulty Level: 5*

Question 25

The Correct Answer:

C   The only place in which the passage mentions theater is in line 35, where it figures in a list along with fireworks displays and religious festivals. All of these are said by Maravall to be devices used by the system of authority for "promoting a public delight in grandiose artifice." Also according to Maravall, the system's goal in employing these devices was to deflect "the desire for novelty into areas of life where it represented no challenge to the political order" (lines 38–40). Thus Maravall believed that baroque theater was intended to entertain and divert the urban population.

The Incorrect Answer Choices:

A   The passage suggests that Maravall viewed baroque culture as a response to deteriorating economic conditions that heightened conflict among different elements of society (lines 17–23). But as Maravall seems to see it, the response of baroque culture was not to tackle the underlying causes of the economic crisis, but to distract the public's attention from that crisis. Baroque theater, according to Maravall, was one of the means used to deflect the public's attention, not an economic stimulus.

B   Maravall believed that baroque theater was intended, along with other devices, to manipulate public opinion, not to reflect it. It was one of the tools baroque monarchs relied on in "manipulating opinions and feelings on a broad public scale" (lines 42–43).

D   According to Maravall, the baroque period was characterized by monarchs who were intent on defending traditional order and values against the Renaissance's liberating forces. Baroque theater was one of the tools used in mounting this defense. Thus it is not the case that, in Maravall's view, the baroque theater was intended to express the emerging principle of individual liberty.

E   As noted in the discussion of (C), Maravall believed that the theater's purpose was to entice and delight, not to terrify.

- *Difficulty Level: 4*

Question 26

The Correct Answer:

C   As the synopsis of the passage shows, the main purpose of the passage is to set out Maravall's interpretation of baroque culture and, without challenging it wholesale, to argue that it needs to be modified in at least one important respect.

The Incorrect Answer Choices:

A, D   The passage discusses only one position, namely Maravall's, and raises one specific objection. No position competing with Maravall's is presented. So neither (A) nor (D) correctly describes the main purpose of the passage.

B   (B) is not a correct description of the passage for two reasons: first, the author says nothing to suggest that Maravall's interpretation is a widely accepted one; and secondly, the author does not challenge the main features of Maravall's interpretation but only a specific aspect of it.

E   While baroque culture can perhaps be called a political construct, (E) misses the fact that the passage concerns not just baroque culture itself but Maravall's interpretation of it, an aspect of which the author also criticizes. Moreover, the passage doesn't characterize any consequences of baroque culture as "unprecedented."

■ *Difficulty Level: 5*

Question 27

The Correct Answer:

D   According to the passage, Maravall believed that during the baroque period art was one of the means by which the ruling class "deflected the desire for novelty into areas of life where it represented no challenge to the political order" (lines 38–40). If it turned out that many baroque-era works of art expressed opposition to the monarchy, art would have been an area of life that presented a challenge to the political order. Evidence of the kind described in (D), therefore, would seriously weaken Maravall's interpretation of baroque culture.

The Incorrect Answer Choices:

A, E   The author somewhat tentatively suggests (lines 46–47) that Maravall's experience of living under the Spanish dictator Franco influenced his interpretation of baroque culture. This question, however, is about the validity of this interpretation, not what caused Maravall to hold it. Answering it thus requires evidence about the baroque period itself, not evidence about Franco. (This is true even if the experience of living under Franco biased Maravall's judgment, since a biased judgment can still be correct.)

B   As Maravall saw it, the ruling class in the baroque period included the nobility as well as the monarch. Maravall's analysis is concerned with how the ruling class as a whole used art in responding to the existing social and economic crisis. Hence, whether the nobility commissioned more works of art than the monarchy is irrelevant, since they were both on the same side.

C   The passage gives an account of Maravall's interpretation of the use to which art was put by the ruling class in defending traditional order and values. Nothing in this account suggests that art that presented an idealized picture of the monarchy and aristocracy would have been unsuited to this purpose. So an analysis of baroque art such as that described in (C) would not raise any problems for Maravall's interpretation.

■ *Difficulty Level: 4*

Questions 1–5

What the setup tells you: This group of questions is about the sequencing of seven elements. The elements are deck-construction jobs: in each of seven consecutive weeks, one (and only one) deck is to be built. For the different jobs, there are different degrees of flexibility in scheduling. For deck F, there is no flexibility at all; according to the third condition, it must be built during week 5. There is slightly more flexibility with respect to deck J. According to the fourth condition, there are two scheduling alternatives for deck J: week 2 or week 6.
None of the other decks' construction is directly tied to any particular week or weeks. The first two conditions, however, do put constraints on the construction of pairs of decks relative to each other. The first condition says that K cannot be built until after G has been built. (So the first condition tells you that K can't be scheduled to be built during week 1 and that G can't be scheduled to be built during week 7.) And the second condition requires some block of two consecutive weeks to be set aside for the construction of decks L and M, although it doesn't matter which of the two is built first. None of the conditions explicitly mentions deck H, so H can be constructed during any week not required for the construction of one of the other decks.

Question 1

Overview: This question asks you to select a schedule that satisfies all of the setup conditions. Note that the question itself doesn't add any further constraints to the basic setup conditions. As mentioned in "A Guide to Analytical Reasoning Questions," for orientation questions like this, probably the most efficient approach is to take each condition in turn and check to see whether any of the answer choices violates it. It is also possible, though perhaps less efficient, to consider each answer choice in turn and check to see whether it violates any of the conditions. In either case, as soon as you find that an answer choice violates a condition, you should eliminate that answer choice from further consideration—perhaps by crossing it out in your test booklet. You can identify the correct answer simply by finding the one construction schedule that doesn't violate any of the conditions.

The Incorrect Answer Choices:

A   The second condition requires decks L and M to be constructed during two consecutive weeks. But if, as in (A), L is scheduled to be constructed during week 7 and M during week 4, then this condition is violated.

B   Here you have deck J scheduled for construction during week 7. But the fourth condition requires J to be scheduled either for week 2 or for week 6. So (B) is not an acceptable construction schedule.

C   The third condition requires deck F to be built during week 5. Since (C) has F scheduled for week 4, it violates this condition.

E   In (E), deck K is scheduled for construction during week 1 and deck G is scheduled for week 4. Since the first condition requires G to be built before K is built, (E) violates the first condition.

The Correct Answer:

D   The schedule in (D) is the only one that violates none of the conditions. It has deck K scheduled for construction during week 7, safely after G is constructed in week 4, thus satisfying the first condition. Decks M and L are scheduled for construction during weeks 2 and 3, thus satisfying the second condition. Deck F is scheduled for construction during week 5, as required by the third condition. And deck J is scheduled for week 6, thus satisfying the fourth condition. (D) is therefore an acceptable construction schedule.

■ *Difficulty Level: 1*

Question 2

Overview: Deck F must be built during week 5. So for deck G to be built after F is built, G would have to be scheduled either for week 6 or for week 7. But since, to satisfy the first condition, deck K cannot be built until after G has been built, G must be scheduled for week 6 and K for week 7. That means that to satisfy the fourth condition, deck J has to be scheduled for week 2. That leaves weeks 1, 3, and 4. Since (by the second condition) two consecutive weeks are required for the construction of decks L and M, decks L and M have to be scheduled for weeks 3 and 4. That leaves week 1 for the construction of deck H. So for deck G to be built at some time after deck F, the construction schedule must be as follows:

Week 1	Week 2	Week 3	Week 4	Week 5	Week 6	Week 7
H	J	L or M	M or L	F	G	K

The Correct Answer:

B As you can see from the construction schedule worked out in the "Overview" above, deck H must be scheduled for week 1. So (B) must be true.

The Incorrect Answer Choices:

A, C, E From the construction schedule worked out in the "Overview," you can see that answer choices (A), (C), and (E) are false.

D As the construction schedule worked out in the "Overview" shows, deck L could be built during either week 3 or week 4. So, although (D) can be true, (D) does not **have** to be true.

- *Difficulty Level: 1*

Question 3

What you should keep in mind for this question: Think of a "complete and accurate list of the weeks any one of which could be the week in which K is built" as a list that has been constructed in the following way: First, ask: Is there an acceptable construction schedule that has K scheduled to be built during week 1? If there is, then week 1 has to be put on the list; if there isn't, then week 1 cannot be on the list. Next ask: Is there an acceptable construction schedule for the seven decks that has K scheduled to be built during week 2? If there is, then week 2 has to be put on the list; if there isn't, then week 2 cannot be on the list. And so on for each of the seven weeks. What this means is that a list can **fail** to be complete and accurate (and thus can be eliminated from consideration) in either of two ways: if it **includes** a week during which K **cannot** be scheduled, or if it **leaves out** a week in which K **can** be scheduled.

(For a more general discussion of questions such as this one, see the section titled "Questions that Include the Phrase 'any one of which'" in "A Guide to Analytical Reasoning Questions.")

Overview: Often, there are time-saving ways of tackling this sort of question.

First, try to eliminate all of the answer choices that directly violate one of the conditions. For example, it follows from the first condition that K cannot be built during week 1. Consequently, answer choice (D) can be ruled out. Similarly, it follows from the third condition that K cannot be built during week 5, so answer choice (C) can be ruled out.

Second, don't bother to check any week that all of the remaining answer choices have in common, because these weeks won't distinguish the remaining choices. In this question, the remaining answer choices—(A), (B), and (E)—all include weeks 2 and 3. Don't waste time checking these possibilities: since they are bound to be part of the correct answer, all you will find out by checking is that they are indeed acceptable possibilities.

Third, see if one of the elements that hasn't yet been checked appears in only one of the remaining answer choices. If there is such an element, check that element first. That way, if this element is an acceptable possibility, you are done, since any list, to be complete, would have to include this element, and only one of the lists still under consideration does.

With this in mind, try scheduling the construction of K for week 4, since only the list in answer choice (E) includes week 4:

Week 1	Week 2	Week 3	Week 4	Week 5	Week 6	Week 7
H	J	G	K	F	L	M

The above is an acceptable schedule with K scheduled for week 4. There are various other schedules with K scheduled for week 4, but you do not need to check those. You have already established that scheduling K for week 4 is an acceptable possibility.

You have now finished. Since any complete list would have to include week 4 as one of the acceptable possibilities, and since only the list in (E) includes week 4, answer choice (E) is the correct answer. To prove **exhaustively** that (E) is the correct answer, you would also have to show that weeks 2, 3, 6, and 7 are acceptable possibilities. But to do so would be to waste time and energy, because your task is only to **select** the correct answer, and you have been able to do that without checking any of weeks 2, 3, 6, or 7.

The Correct Answer:

E   Answer choice (E) lists all of the weeks in which it would be permissible to build K, and only those weeks.

The Incorrect Answer Choices:

A, B   Answer choices (A) and (B) each include weeks in which K could be built, but they fail to be correct because each is incomplete (that is, not all of the weeks in which K could be built are listed).

C   Answer choice (C) is incorrect, since the third condition requires that F be built during week 5. So K cannot be built in week 5.

D   Answer choice (D) is incorrect for two reasons. First, the first condition requires that K not be built in week 1, since G must be built in an earlier week than K. Second, the list of weeks does not include week 4, but K could be built in week 4.

- *Difficulty Level: 1*

Question 4

Overview: As explained in connection with the previous question, there are frequently timesaving ways of tackling this sort of question.

Again, first try to eliminate all of the answer choices that include an element whose inclusion is in direct violation of a condition. For example, it follows from the third condition that F cannot be built during week 3. Consequently, answer choices (B) and (C) can be eliminated. Furthermore, it follows from the fourth condition that J cannot be built during week 3, so answer choice (E) can be eliminated.

Second, since the remaining answer choices—(A) and (D)—have the elements K, L, and M in common, do not bother to check these elements. None of them can give you information useful in determining which of the remaining two answer choices is the correct one.

Third, since neither of the elements remaining to be checked—decks G and H—are included in the list in answer choice (A), all you have left to do is to check one of them. If either deck G or deck H can be built in week 3, then you know that (A) can be eliminated because it leaves out an acceptable possibility. On the other hand, if either G or H fails to be an acceptable possibility, you are also done, because (D) would include an element that is not an acceptable possibility.

So (since deck G is more constrained than deck H) check to see whether deck G can be built in week 3:

Week 1	Week 2	Week 3	Week 4	Week 5	Week 6	Week 7
		G		F		

It turns out that you know the answer to this question. You have already developed a suitable schedule with G in week 3 in responding to question 3. (Note, however, that the fact that you already had this schedule worked out is a lucky break. You should not count on such lucky breaks, but you should certainly take advantage of any that come your way. Without this break, you would have had to fall back on the setup conditions in trying to complete the partial schedule above.)

You have now finished question 4. The correct answer is (D), not because (A) includes any elements that are in error but because (A) fails to include elements that are part of the complete list of acceptable possibilities. As far as (D) is concerned, remember that you save time and energy by confining yourself to selecting the correct answer. You don't have to demonstrate exhaustively the correctness of that answer.

The Correct Answer:

D   Answer choice (D) is the correct answer. Any of the decks listed could be the one built in week 3, and no deck that could be built in week 3 is missing from this list.

The Incorrect Answer Choices:

A Answer choice (A) does not include G or H, but each of these decks could be the one built in week 3, as the following schedules show:

Week 1	Week 2	Week 3	Week 4	Week 5	Week 6	Week 7
H	J	G	K	F	L	M
G	J	H	K	F	L	M

B, C Each of these answer choices is incorrect because it includes F, which must be built in week 5. (Each of these answer choices also fails to include some of the decks that could be built in week 3.)

E This answer choice includes J, which can only be built in week 2 or week 6. It also fails to include G, which could be built in week 3.

▪ *Difficulty Level: 1*

Question 5

Overview: You need to determine how many acceptable construction schedules there are that have deck G built during week 4. The third condition requires that deck F be built during week 5. So in order to satisfy the first condition, any schedule that has G built during week 4 must have K built during either week 6 or week 7. However, if K is built during week 6, J would have to be built during week 2 (to satisfy the fourth condition). The resulting schedule would look like this:

Week 1	Week 2	Week 3	Week 4	Week 5	Week 6	Week 7
—	J	—	G	F	K	—

But in that case, L and M could not be built during two consecutive weeks, as the second condition requires. So if G is to be built during week 4, then K must be built during week 7 and J during week 6. This leaves weeks 1, 2, and 3 for decks H, L, and M. Since two consecutive weeks have to be reserved for L and M, H would have to be built either during week 1 or during week 3. Each of these possibilities (H in week 1 and H in week 3) permits two different complete schedules, since L and M can be constructed in either order. Thus, the acceptable schedules for G being built during week 4 are as follows:

Week 1	Week 2	Week 3	Week 4	Week 5	Week 6	Week 7
H	L	M	G	F	J	K
H	M	L	G	F	J	K
L	M	H	G	F	J	K
M	L	H	G	F	J	K

The correct answer is therefore (D).

The Correct Answer:

D As shown in the "Overview," if G is built in week 4, then J has to be built in week 6 (so that L and M can be built in consecutive weeks), and that means that K must be built in week 7. There are then four possible schedules: two in which H is built in the first week, and two in which H is built in the third week.

The Incorrect Answer Choices:

A, B, C These answer choices are all incorrect because they indicate fewer schedules than what is in fact possible.

E Answer choice (E) is incorrect because it indicates a greater number of schedules than what is actually possible.

▪ *Difficulty Level: 2*

Questions 6–10

What the setup tells you: This group of questions is about arranging for five products to be presented over a three-day period. Each of the five products is to be presented by a different one of five salespeople, with two of these five presentations to take place on Monday, one on Tuesday, and the remaining two on Wednesday. Thus you might diagram this setup in the following way:

Mon	Tues	Wed
S1 : P1	S3 : P3	S4 : P4
S2 : P2		S5 : P5

The individual questions are going to be about which of the salespeople will be salesperson S1 and which of the products will be product P1, and so forth.

The way you fill in the diagram is constrained by three conditions. The first condition tells you that salespeople F and H can't both do their presenting on Monday and they can't both do their presenting on Wednesday. And since the second condition says that the only salespeople who can present on Tuesday are I and J, you know that one of F and H will present on Monday and the other will present on Wednesday. The second condition also tells you that N has to be the product presented on Tuesday (so you know that the third presentation (P3) is always going to be of product N). The third condition ties the day G presents a product to the day product O is presented (and because of the second condition, we know that this day will be either Monday or Wednesday).

It is worth noticing that only two of the products (N and O) are constrained in any way by the setup conditions. This means that, as far as the setup itself is concerned, products L, M, and P are indistinguishable from one another. It is also worth noticing that, as far as the setup itself is concerned, salespeople F and H are indistinguishable from each other, and salespeople I and J are indistinguishable from each other. So you know that, as far as the setup is concerned, anything salesperson F can do, salesperson H could do instead (and vice versa), anything salesperson I can do, salesperson J could do instead (and vice versa), and anything that's true of any of products L, M, or P could equally well be true of either of the other two. Also, as far as the setup is concerned, whatever is true of Monday could equally well be true of Wednesday instead (and vice versa).

Question 6

Overview: This question asks you to figure out what **must** be true on the basis of the setup alone.

However, all of the answer choices are conditional. That means that each answer choice, in effect, asks a different question, and each will have to be considered independently. (A) asks: Does F's presenting a product on Monday make it necessary for G to present product O? (B) asks: Does I's presenting a product on Tuesday make it necessary for J to present a product on Monday? And so on. If the answer is "yes," then you have found the correct answer. If the answer is "no," then that answer choice is incorrect.

The Incorrect Answer Choices:

A F's presenting on Monday forces H to present on Wednesday, but leaves it open on which of these two days G presents. So G could present on Monday, in which case product O has to be presented on Monday. But O could then be presented by F while G presents any one of products L, M, or P. So having F present a product on Monday **does not make it necessary** for G to present product O, as the following diagram of one acceptable schedule shows.

Mon	Tues	Wed
F : O	I : N	H : M
G : L		J : P

B I's presenting a product on Tuesday forces J to present either on Monday or on Wednesday, but leaves it open on which of these two days J presents. So I's presenting a product on Tuesday **does not make it necessary** for J to present a product on Monday as can be seen from the same diagram given above for (A).

C J's presenting a product on Tuesday forces I to present on either Monday or Wednesday, but leaves it open on which of those days I presents. So I's presentation could be on Monday. From the setup you know that either F or H must also present on Monday. So I's presenting on Monday means that G presents on Wednesday. Therefore, J's presenting on Tuesday **does not make it necessary** for G to present a product on Monday, as can be seen from the following diagram:

Mon	Tues	Wed
F : L	J : N	H : P
I : M		G : O

D   If both F and J present products on Monday, then H and G must present products on Wednesday. And one of the products presented on Wednesday must be product O. But G could present O, and H could present any one of products L, M, or P. So having F and J both present products on Monday **does not make it necessary** for H to present product O, as can be seen from the following diagram:

Mon	Tues	Wed
F : L	I : N	H : P
J : M		G : O

The Correct Answer:

E   If both H and I present products on Wednesday, then it has to be J who presents product N on Tuesday. That leaves F and G, and both of them will have to present products on Monday. So, since product O **must** be presented on the day G gives a presentation, O has to be presented (either by F or by G) on Monday. Thus, having H and I both present products on Wednesday **does make it necessary** for product O to be presented on Monday.

■ *Difficulty Level: 2*

Question 7

Overview: There are a couple of shortcuts you could take to get the correct answer for this question. The first shortcut takes advantage of a lucky break of a kind that very rarely occurs:

Getting the correct answer to the preceding question (question 6) also, in effect, gives you the correct answer to question 7. All you have to do is to notice that, as far as the setup conditions are concerned, anything that happens on Wednesday could just as well have happened on Monday. A quick glance at the answer choices will then let you pick out (D) as the correct answer without having to do any further work.

The second shortcut involves a strategy that can often be useful. Question 7 puts additional restrictions on salespeople but not on products, and it asks what **must** be true, given those restrictions. So, if you have noticed that, as far as the setup is concerned, anything true of one of products L, M, and P could equally well be true of either of the others, you can immediately eliminate answer choices (A), (B), and (E) from consideration.

Of course, you can also consider each answer choice and see whether assigning H and I to give their presentations on Monday forces that answer choice to be true.

The Incorrect Answer Choices:

A, B, E   If H and I give their presentations on Monday, then the second condition forces J to present product N on Tuesday, leaving F and G to present products on Wednesday. The third condition then forces product O to be presented on Wednesday, but leaves it open which of F or G does the presenting. And whichever one does not present O can present any of products L, M, or P. So, although F **could** present M (as long as G presents O), F **doesn't have to** present M. And although G **could** present L (as long as F presents O), G **doesn't have to** present L. So neither (A) nor (B) have to be true. And since M and O (or L and O) could be the products presented by F and G on Wednesday, (E) doesn't have to be true, either.

C   The second condition requires product N to be presented on Tuesday. So if I's presentation is on Monday, I cannot present N. Therefore, (C) cannot be true.

The Correct Answer:

D   If H and I present products on Monday, then J has to present product N on Tuesday. That forces F and G to give their presentations on Wednesday. So, by the third condition, O has to be one of the products presented on Wednesday. Thus, (D) has to be true.

■ *Difficulty Level: 1*

Question 8

What you need to keep in mind for this question: Be careful to note that this question requires you to find something that can be **ruled out** by the setup conditions whenever G presents product P on Wednesday.

Overview: Product O must be presented on the same day that G gives a presentation. So you know that if G presents product P on Wednesday, then the other salesperson who gives a presentation on Wednesday will have to present product O. And that salesperson must be either F or H, for reasons explained above in "What the setup tells you."

The Correct Answer:

C   From the "Overview" above, it follows that salesperson I cannot present product O, no matter when G gives a presentation or what product G presents. So (C) cannot be true.

The Incorrect Answer Choices:

A   A look at the "Overview" for this question shows that H **can** be the salesperson presenting product O. So (A) can't be ruled out.

B   G's presenting product P on Wednesday puts no special restriction on who can present product N. Since that person can be either I or J, (B) can't be ruled out.

D, E   As explained in the "Overview" for this question, either F or H could be the salesperson presenting product O on Wednesday. Whichever of the two does not present product O on Wednesday has to present a product—either L or M—on Monday. Therefore F, in particular, could present a product either on Monday or on Wednesday. So neither (D) nor (E) can be ruled out.

- *Difficulty Level: 2*

Question 9

Overview: If products M and P are presented on Monday, the products presented on Wednesday must be L and O. Since O is presented on Wednesday, G's presentation must also be on Wednesday. The other presentation on Wednesday must be given either by F or by H.

The Correct Answer:

D   If products M and P are presented on Monday, O must be presented on Wednesday. So G has to give one of the presentations on Wednesday and the other has to be given either by F or by H. So G and H could be the salespeople giving presentations on Wednesday. And, in that case, F would have to give one of the presentations on Monday since whichever one of F or H does not present a product on Wednesday must present a product on Monday. Thus, (D) could be true, as the following diagram shows.

Mon	Tues	Wed
F : M	I : N	G : L
J : P		H : O

The Incorrect Answer Choices:

A, E   You know from the "Overview" for this question that G must present a product on Wednesday, and that the products presented on Wednesday are L and O. So G cannot present product P, and G cannot present a product on Monday. Thus both (A) and (E) can be eliminated.

B, C   Again, from the "Overview," you can see that the products presented on Wednesday must be L and O, that G must present one of these products and that the other must be presented either by F or by H. So I cannot present product O, and J cannot present product L.

- *Difficulty Level: 2*

Question 10

Overview: If product O is presented on the same day as product P, then one of those two products (though not necessarily product O) must be presented by G, and the other product presented on that day must be presented by either F or H.

The Correct Answer:

E From the "Overview" above, you can see immediately that J **cannot** give either of the presentations on a day on which O and P are both presented. Thus (E) **must** be true.

The Incorrect Answer Choices:

A, B, C If product O is presented on the same day as product P, then the presentations that day will be given either by F and G or by H and G. If F and G are the ones giving the presentations, then (A) will be true, and both (B) and (C) will be false. But the presentations could equally well be given by H and G. And in that case, (A) will be false and both (B) and (C) will be true. So although (A) **could** be true, or (B) and (C) **could** be true, none of the three answer choices **must** be true.

D If product O is presented on the same day as product P, then one of those two must be presented by G and the other by either F or H. That means that I cannot present either O or P. So (D) has to be false.

■ *Difficulty Level: 3*

Questions 11–17

What the setup tells you: This set of questions is about assigning seven people to seven rooms, one person per room. The rooms are next to each other in a row:

Room 101	Room 102	Room 103	Room 104	Room 105	Room 106	Room 107

The people—all members of an academic department—are divided into three groups: professors, lecturers, and instructors. (These academic titles might suggest that these groups are in some sort of rank order, with professors at the highest rank and instructors at the lowest, but as far as the setup is concerned, all that matters is that the seven people are divided into three groups.)

The four setup conditions by themselves don't fix the assignment of any particular person to any particular room. And they don't reserve any particular room to people of just one academic rank. When combined, however, the first and second conditions quite strongly constrain the assignment of professors and instructors to rooms.

The first three conditions are relatively straightforward. The fourth condition is a little more complicated. What it tells you is this: It doesn't matter (as far as the fourth condition is concerned) where R's room is as long as W's room is **not** next to V's room. However, if W **does** have a room next to V's room, then there has to be a string of three rooms that are assigned in one of the following ways:

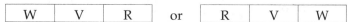

Question 11

Overview: The "Overview" for Questions 3 and 4 provide some strategies for questions of this general kind. Here are some things to keep in mind for this question in particular.

This question can be represented by the following diagram:

What the question asks for is a list of all of the people who could be assigned to the room between F and G.

F and G are both professors, and V and W are both instructors. So the first condition tells you that neither V nor W can be assigned to the room between F and G. Thus, since neither V nor W can be on the list, you can immediately rule out answer choices (C), (D), and (E).

That leaves Q, R, and S to check. All three are lecturers, so each satisfies the first condition. Since the remaining two answer choices both include Q, you can take it for granted that Q is on the list.

That leaves R and S to check. None of the conditions have anything to say about S (or about Q) in particular, but the third condition says that R's room can't be next to G's room. So you know that R can't be on the list. Thus, you can rule out (A) as well.

Therefore, since (B) is the only answer choice left, you know that (B) must be the correct answer.

You could also tackle this question from the opposite direction. Reflecting on the setup conditions shows you that Q and S are the two department members who are the least constrained (especially with respect to F and G). Indeed, as far as the setup conditions are concerned, Q and S are indistinguishable. So if only two people can be assigned to the room between F and G, it is very likely that those two people are going to be Q and S—and thus very likely that the correct answer is (B). Thus, your first move might be to test (B) by trying to produce a complete diagram like one of those above.

The Correct Answer:

B   If there is exactly one room between F and G, that room could be assigned to either Q or S. The following two diagrams show that such an overall assignment is possible and thus that (B) is the correct answer.

101	102	103	104	105	106	107
V/W	R	F	Q/S	G	S/Q	W/V

101	102	103	104	105	106	107
V/W	S/Q	G	Q/S	F	R	W/V

The Incorrect Answer Choices:

A   R cannot be assigned to a room next to G's room, so (A) is incorrect.

C, D, E   F and G are both professors, and no instructor can be assigned to a room next to a professor's room. V and W are instructors, so any answer choice that includes either V or W is incorrect.

■ *Difficulty Level: 1*

Question 12

What you need to keep in mind for this question: If V's room is **not** next to W's, then (as far as the fourth condition is concerned) it doesn't matter where R's room is. It's only when V and W are next to each other that you need to worry about where R's room is.

Overview: This question doesn't add any additional constraints to the basic setup conditions. Since both the question and the answer choices mention only R, V, and W, your first move should be to use the fourth condition to try to eliminate the incorrect answer choices.

The Incorrect Answer Choices:

A, B, E   The fourth condition tells you that V and W cannot be assigned to rooms next to each other unless there is a string of three rooms that are assigned in one of the following ways:

W	V	R	or	R	V	W

One point, then, is immediately obvious: W and V can't have rooms next to each other if V is in a room at either end of the row. That is, if V and W are next to each other, V **cannot** be assigned either to room 101 or to room 107, because in that case R could not be assigned to a room next to V's. Three of the answer choices—(A), (B), and (E)—have V assigned to an end room and W assigned to the room next to V's. So all three can be eliminated.

D   In (D), W is in room 103, next to V in room 104. So to satisfy the fourth condition, R would have to be in room 105, the room next to V on the other side. But R is in room 106, not room 105. So (D) can be eliminated.

The Correct Answer:

C In (C), R and W are assigned to adjacent rooms but the room to which V is assigned is **not** next to W's room. Thus, the assignment in (C) does not violate the fourth condition. Having eliminated all the other answer choices, you can stop here. You have done enough to show that (C) is the correct answer. However, let's take a further look here just to make the point clear that (C)'s assignment for R, V, and W meets all the setup conditions, and is thus a possible assignment. The following complete assignment of department members to rooms, which has R and W assigned to adjacent rooms but V not next to W's room, is possible:

101	102	103	104	105	106	107
V	Q	W	R	F	G	S

- *Difficulty Level: 3*

Question 13

Overview: You could approach this question in two ways. You could try to eliminate each listed department member in turn by trying to produce a complete assignment with R in room 104 and that department member in some room other than 103 or 105. Or you could work out the implications of assigning R to room 104 before turning to the answer choices.

Since this question asks who **must** be assigned either to room 103 or to room 105 if R is assigned to room 104, you can be sure that assigning R to room 104 puts serious constraints on other room assignments. And since room 104 is the middle room in the row, you know that rooms 103 and 105 are mirror images of each other, as are rooms 101 and 107, and rooms 102 and 106. So this is a case where working out at least some of the implications first is likely to pay off.

If R is assigned to room 104, the third condition prevents G from being assigned either to room 103 or to room 105. Note that this immediately rules out answer choice (B). Since G is a professor, the second condition prevents G from being assigned to either of the end rooms. So if R is assigned to room 104, G has to be assigned either to room 102 or to room 106.

Consider the first case, with G assigned to room 102. Then (by the first condition) neither V nor W can be assigned either to room 101 or to room 103. But (by the second condition) F can't be assigned to room 101 either. That means that either Q or S must be assigned to room 101.

101	102	103	104	105	106	107
Q/S	G	not V not W	R			

So that leaves either F or whichever of S or Q is not assigned to room 101 to be assigned to room 103. But if F is **not** assigned to room 103, F would have to be assigned either to room 105 or room 106 and thus end up next to either V or W (or both), thereby violating the first condition. So F must be assigned to room 103.

101	102	103	104	105	106	107
Q/S	G	F	R			

That leaves V, W, and either S or Q for rooms 105, 106, and 107. So in the case where G is assigned to room 102, F must be assigned to room 103.

The second case, with G assigned to room 106, is the mirror image of the first case, and by an analogous line of reasoning, if G is assigned to room 106, then F must be assigned to room 105.

101	102	103	104	105	106	107
			R	F	G	Q/S

The Correct Answer:

A   There are only two cases. In one, F must be assigned to room 103, and in the other F must be assigned to room 105.

The Incorrect Answer Choices:

B, C   As the diagrams above show, if R is assigned to room 104, G must be assigned either to room 102 or to room 106 and Q can be assigned either to room 101 or to room 107. So neither G nor Q **has** to be assigned to room 103 or room 105.

D, E   To see that neither V nor W **has to be** assigned either to room 103 or to room 105, consider the following completed assignments for the case where G is assigned to room 102:

101	102	103	104	105	106	107
Q/S	G	F	R	W	S/Q	V

101	102	103	104	105	106	107
Q/S	G	F	R	V	W	S/Q

Taken together, these two diagrams show that, with G in room 102, **either V or W** has to be in room 105. However, the first of these assignments shows that **V can** be assigned to room 107 (and so does **not** have be assigned either to room 103 or to room 105). And the second diagram shows that **W can** be assigned to room 106 (and so does **not** have be assigned either to room 103 or to room 105).

- *Difficulty Level: 3*

Question 14

Overview: For this question, F and G have to be assigned to rooms that are as far apart as possible. Then you have to count the number of rooms (rooms assigned to other people) there are between F's room and G's room.

The Incorrect Answer Choices:

D, E   Between the two end rooms, 101 and 107, there are five rooms. However, the second condition tells you that neither F nor G can be assigned to either of rooms 101 or 107. So (considering only the second condition) the farthest apart F and G can be is for one to be in room 102 and the other to be in room 106. And between rooms 102 and 106 there are only three rooms.

C   But could professors F and G be assigned to rooms 102 and 106 and so have three rooms between them?

101	102	103	104	105	106	107
	F				G	

If they were, none of rooms 101, 103, 105, and 107 can be assigned to instructors. So all four of these rooms would have to be assigned to lecturers. But there are only three lecturers. So there can't be three rooms between F's room and G's room.

B   Could there be two rooms?

101	102	103	104	105	106	107
		F			G	

Well, one consequence of excluding F and G from the end rooms is that any room to which either F or G is assigned will be next to two other rooms. That means that even if F and G are separated by only two rooms, four lecturers would still be required for the first condition to be satisfied. But there are only three lecturers.

The Correct Answer:

A   So no more than one room can separate the rooms to which F and G are assigned. Therefore, you know that (A) must be the correct answer.

And indeed it is. To see that there can, in fact, be one room between F's room and G's room, consider the following possible assignment:

101	102	103	104	105	106	107
W	R	F	S	G	Q	V

- *Difficulty Level: 3*

Question 15

What you need to keep in mind for this question: Be careful to note that this question asks you to find someone who **cannot** be assigned to room 104.

Overview: This question asks you to figure out who is prevented from being assigned to room 104 by the setup conditions alone. So anyone who can be assigned to room 104 as part of a complete assignment of department members to rooms can be eliminated from consideration. That means that before considering the answer choices in turn, you might find it worthwhile to glance very briefly over any complete assignments you filled out in the course of answering previous questions to see whether they will allow you to eliminate any of the answer choices. (For this reason, it might be a good idea, as part of your general strategy in working these questions, to put a check mark beside any complete assignment you have determined to be consistent with the setup conditions, and to cross out assignments that violate the conditions. This will allow you to refer back to your earlier work efficiently to find just the information you need.)

The Incorrect Answer Choices:

A, B   The following assignment shows that either F or G can be assigned to room 104:

101	102	103	104	105	106	107
V	R	Q	F/G	G/F	S	W

C, D   The following assignment shows that either Q or S can be assigned to room 104:

101	102	103	104	105	106	107
W	S/Q	G	Q/S	F	R	V

The Correct Answer:

E   Since (A), (B), (C), and (D) have been eliminated, the correct answer must be (E).

To show that V, in fact, cannot be assigned to room 104, consider the following: Neither F nor G can be in one of the end rooms (by the second condition). So if V, an instructor, is assigned to room 104, F and G have to be in rooms 102 and 106 to avoid violating the first condition.

101	102	103	104	105	106	107
	F/G		V		G/F	

All the unassigned rooms are either next to F's room or next to G's room, and one of those rooms must be assigned to W. But if W is assigned to a room that is next to F's room or to G's room, the first condition will be violated. Thus V cannot be assigned to room 104, and (E) is confirmed as the correct answer.

Answering this question by considering each answer choice in turn, though effective, is time-consuming. Time spent answering a question can sometimes be considerably reduced by reflecting briefly about which answer is most likely to be correct.

Note that as far as the setup conditions are concerned, Q and S are interchangeable. That makes it unlikely that one of them can be assigned to room 104 while the other cannot. Since both are among the answer choices, neither is a good bet to check first. F and G are also both among the answer choices. And although F is not quite interchangeable with G, they are similar enough to suggest that V is probably the one who cannot be assigned to room 104. This line of reasoning would lead you to check out answer choice (E) first.

■ *Difficulty Level: 3*

Question 16

Overview: Suppose that no two faculty members of the same academic rank are assigned to adjacent rooms. Consider the professors first. By the first condition neither F nor G can have rooms adjacent to rooms that are assigned to instructors. And by the second condition, F and G cannot be in either of the end rooms. So if F and G are not in adjacent rooms, they must each be assigned to rooms flanked on both sides by lecturers. But there are only three lecturers. (And as you already know from the discussion of Question 14, F and G can be separated by at most one room.) Therefore, some section of the row of rooms must be assigned according to the following pattern:

Lecturer	Professor (F/G)	Lecturer	Professor (G/F)	Lecturer

By the third condition, G can't be next to R, so R can't be the lecturer assigned to the middle room. And to avoid having the two instructors assigned to adjacent rooms, they will have to be assigned to rooms 101 and 107. Thus, the only possible assignments are given in the following diagrams:

101	102	103	104	105	106	107
V/W	R	F	Q/S	G	S/Q	W/V

and

101	102	103	104	105	106	107
V/W	Q/S	G	S/Q	F	R	W/V

All that is left to do is to check each of the answer choices against the two assignment diagrams.

The Incorrect Answer Choices:

A The second diagram shows that F can be assigned to room 105. So F does **not** have to be assigned to either room 103 or room 104.

B Both diagrams show that Q can be assigned to room 104. So Q does **not** have to be assigned to either room 102 or room 106.

C The second diagram shows that R can be assigned to room 106. So R does **not** have to be assigned to either room 102 or room 105.

D The first diagram shows that S can be assigned to room 106, and the second diagram shows that S can be assigned to room 102. So S does **not** have to be assigned to either room 104 or room 105.

The Correct Answer:

E   V (like W) can be assigned either to room 101 or to room 107 and to no other room. So V **must** be assigned either to room 101 or to room 107.

- *Difficulty Level: 4*

Question 17

What you need to keep in mind for this question: Be careful to note that this question is about assignments in which F and G are **not** assigned to adjacent rooms. And it asks you to find someone who **cannot** be assigned to room 107 in such an assignment.

Overview: By the second condition, neither F nor G can be assigned to an end room. Thus, by the first condition, if they are not assigned to rooms that are next to each other, their rooms must each be flanked on both sides by rooms assigned to lecturers. Since there are only three lecturers, this means that one of the lecturers must be assigned to a room that is next to F's room on one side and next to G's room on the other side.

Lecturer	(F/G)	Lecturer	(G/F)	Lecturer

By the third condition, this lecturer can't be R. Thus, five adjacent rooms must be assigned in one of the following ways:

R	F	Q/S	G	S/Q

or

Q/S	G	S/Q	F	R

By the fourth condition, if V and W are assigned to adjacent rooms, V's room must be between R's room and W's room. So the assignments have to be completed in one of the following ways:

101	102	103	104	105	106	107
V/W	R	F	Q/S	G	S/Q	W/V

101	102	103	104	105	106	107
W	V	R	F	Q/S	G	S/Q

101	102	103	104	105	106	107
W/V	Q/S	G	S/Q	F	R	W/V

101	102	103	104	105	106	107
Q/S	G	S/Q	F	R	V	W

The Incorrect Answer Choices:

A, B, C, E   By looking at the four possible diagrams for assignments where F and G are **not** assigned to adjacent rooms, you can see that V, W, S, and Q are the only department members who **can** be assigned to room 107.

The Correct Answer:

D   None of the four diagrams has R assigned to room 107. And since no other assignments in which F's room is not next to G's room are possible, you know that R **cannot** be assigned to room 107.

You could also approach this question by first considering which answer choice is most likely to be the correct answer and trying that first. Here, as in question 15, you are looking for the one department member who cannot be assigned to a particular room. Q and S are both listed, and you know that Q and S are interchangeable. So neither is a likely choice. V and W are both listed. And although V and W are not quite interchangeable, you know by this time that in most cases they are. So neither V nor W is a likely choice. (Besides, you may remember from working out the diagrams for question 16 that both V and W **can**, in fact, be assigned to room 107 when F and G are not in adjacent rooms.) So that leaves R as the best bet and (D) as the answer choice to consider first.

■ *Difficulty Level: 5*

Questions 18–24

What the setup tells you: This set of questions is about the selection of a group of rugs for an exhibition. There are eight rugs from which to make the selection. And of those eight, four rugs or five rugs or six rugs can be selected, but no other number of rugs can be selected. All we know about the rugs is their shape—either oval or rectangular—and the material of which they are made—either silk or wool.

Besides the basic restriction on the total number of rugs selected (four to six), there are just three conditions that have to be met for a selection to be acceptable.

The first condition is straightforward: at least two oval rugs (regardless of their material) must be selected. Since there is only one oval silk rug available, any acceptable selection will have to include at least one of the oval wool rugs.

The second condition tells you that in an acceptable selection the total number of wool rugs (no matter what their shape) can be equal to two, or can be equal to three, but no other number of wool rugs is acceptable. So you know that to get enough rugs, an acceptable selection has to include both silk and wool rugs.

The third condition tells you that the oval silk rug cannot be the only silk rug selected. So you know that if only one silk rug is selected, it has to be a rectangular one.

Question 18

Overview: Each of the selections includes a total of either four or five rugs, so they are all of an acceptable size. That means that each of the incorrect answer choices will violate at least one of the three setup conditions. So by checking each answer choice in turn against the conditions, you can eliminate incorrect answers. When you find an answer choice that can't be eliminated, that answer choice will satisfy all three conditions and is the correct answer.

The Incorrect Answer Choices:

A   This selection includes the oval silk rug but doesn't include either of the rectangular silk rugs. It thus violates the third condition.

B   This selection includes only one oval rug and only one wool rug. It thus violates the first condition, which rules out any selection with fewer than two oval rugs. And it also violates the second condition, which rules out any selection in which there are fewer than two wool rugs.

C   This selection includes a total of four wool rugs. So it violates the second condition, in this case by including more than the permitted maximum of three wool rugs.

E   In this selection all of the rugs are rectangular rugs. The selection therefore violates the first condition.

The Correct Answer:

D   Having eliminated all of the other answer choices, you know that (D) is the correct answer. And here's a demonstration that (D) is in fact correct: The selection in (D) includes two oval rugs and thus satisfies the first condition. It includes a total of three rectangular wool rugs, and therefore satisfies the second condition. And although it includes only one silk rug, that silk rug is rectangular, not oval, so the third condition is also satisfied.

- *Difficulty Level: 1*

Question 19

What you need to keep in mind for this question: Be careful to note that this question requires you to find the rug, or group of rugs, that **cannot** be added to three wool rugs to make up an acceptable selection **no matter which three of the five available wool rugs are selected**. So if the rug, or group of rugs, listed in an answer choice plus some combination of three wool rugs would make up a selection that satisfies all of the setup conditions, that answer choice is **incorrect**.

Remember also that for each answer choice, what you are considering is the possible acceptability of a selection consisting of some group of three wool rugs plus **all** of the rugs on that list **and no other rugs**.

Overview: Here three wool rugs (whose shape is unspecified) have been selected. That means that a group of between one and three additional rugs must be added to those rugs to make up a selection of the right size. It also means that none of the additional rugs can be wool rugs (to avoid violating the second condition). However, a quick glance at the answer choices will show you that none of the answer choices either lists more than three rugs or includes a wool rug. So they are all the right size, and all satisfy the second condition. Since the three already selected wool rugs could include the two oval wool rugs, no further rugs have to be added for the first condition to be satisfied. So none of the answer choices will violate the first condition either. Thus all you have left to work with is the third condition, which is only about silk rugs. Finding the correct answer, then, means finding the list of silk rugs that violates the third condition. And what the third condition says, in effect, is that the oval silk rug cannot be the only rug in the list.

The Correct Answer:

A   The list in (A) would produce a selection consisting of three wool rugs plus an oval silk rug. That oval silk rug would be the only silk rug in the selection, so the selection violates the third condition. Therefore, an acceptable overall selection of rugs **cannot** be produced by adding the rug listed in (A) to three wool rugs.

The Incorrect Answer Choices:

B, C   The third condition is satisfied as long as the oval silk rug is not the only silk rug selected. Therefore, since the oval silk rug is not included at all in either (B) or (C), both satisfy the third condition. Thus both would be acceptable completions of the selection, provided that the three wool rugs already selected include the two oval wool rugs.

D, E   Any selection that includes both an oval silk rug and at least one rectangular silk rug satisfies the third condition. Thus both (D) and (E) would be acceptable completions of the selection, provided that the three wool rugs already selected include at least one of the two oval wool rugs.

- *Difficulty Level: 2*

Question 20

What you need to keep in mind for this question: What you are looking for is a rug, or group of rugs that **cannot** be part of any acceptable selection. That is, you are looking for a rug, or group of rugs, that, once selected, makes it **impossible** to complete the selection without violating one or more of the conditions, **no matter which other rugs are also included**.

Overview: Since the question itself doesn't add any further constraints to the basic setup conditions, probably the most efficient strategy is simply to consider each answer choice in turn and try to add to that list of rugs to produce an acceptable selection. Any answer choice that you **can** complete in this way should be rejected as an **incorrect** answer.

The Incorrect Answer Choices:

A   To the oval silk rug, add one rectangular silk rug to satisfy the third condition. To this add the two oval wool rugs, satisfying simultaneously the first and the second condition while bringing the total number of rugs selected up to four. The result is an acceptable selection, so (A) can be rejected.

B   The acceptable selection arrived at for (A) above included two oval wool rugs, so (B) is shown to be an incorrect answer choice by the same overall selection that allowed (A) to be rejected.

C   The acceptable selection arrived at for (A) above included all three oval rugs, so (C) is shown to be an incorrect answer choice by the same overall selection that allowed both (A) and (B) to be rejected.

D   To two rectangular wool rugs, add one oval wool rug (thereby reaching the maximum number of wool rugs, namely three) and one oval silk rug (in order to satisfy the first condition). Since the oval silk rug cannot be the only silk rug selected, add a rectangular silk rug (thereby satisfying the third condition). This brings the total number of rugs selected to five. The result is an acceptable overall selection, so (D) can be rejected.

The Correct Answer:

E   Since here you are starting with three rectangular **wool** rugs, the second condition rules out adding any more wool rugs. Only silk rugs can be added. But the first condition requires that at least two oval rugs be included in the selection, and there is only one oval silk rug available. So it is impossible to arrive at an acceptable overall selection that includes three rectangular wool rugs.

- *Difficulty Level: 2*

Question 21

Overview: In effect, this question asks which wool rugs must be included in any acceptable selection that includes only one silk rug. As you will probably see right away, limiting a selection to one silk rug puts a lot of constraints on the selection as a whole. Therefore, this question is one where doing some preliminary thinking before examining the answer choices is likely to pay off handsomely.

You know immediately that if only one silk rug is selected, it has to be a rectangular silk rug to avoid violating the third condition. That means that the selection has to include both of the oval wool rugs, in order to satisfy the first condition. The selection also has to include at least one rectangular wool rug, to bring the total up to the minimum of four rugs, but it can't include more than one rectangular wool rug without violating the second condition. Thus, in addition to the one silk rug, the selection must consist of two oval rugs and one rectangular rug.

(B) is therefore the correct answer.

The Correct Answer:

B   If there is only one silk rug selected, that rug must be rectangular (to avoid violating the third condition). All of the remaining rugs must be selected from among the two oval wool rugs and the three rectangular wool rugs. Both of the oval wool rugs must be selected (to satisfy the first condition, which requires that at least two oval rugs be selected). To bring the required total number of rugs to at least four and to meet the second condition (which limits the number of wool rugs to a maximum of three), exactly one of the rectangular wool rugs must also be selected. So if exactly one silk rug is selected, the remaining rugs selected must be two oval rugs and one rectangular rug.

The Incorrect Answer Choices:

A, E   Since the silk rug mentioned in the question cannot be an oval rug, (A) violates the first condition, which requires that at least two oval rugs must be selected. (E) also violates the first condition.

C, D   (C) and (D) each violate the part of the second condition that says there cannot be more than three wool rugs among the rugs selected. (C) would require that four wool rugs be selected, and (D) would require that five wool rugs be selected.

- *Difficulty Level: 3*

Question 22

What you need to keep in mind for this question: In each of the answer choices, you are told both how many rectangular rugs have been selected and whether those rectangular rugs are made of silk or of wool. However, all you are told about any oval rugs is the total number that have been selected, not what they are made of. Thus, for at least some of the answer choices, there may be more than one selection of four rugs that satisfies the description given. If **one** of those selections satisfies all three conditions, then that answer choice describes an acceptable selection of rugs (and so is the correct answer), even if **some other selection** that also satisfies that description violates one or more of the conditions.

Overview: You will probably see right away that limiting the total number of rugs selected to four doesn't help much in finding the right answer. And since there are only three conditions to satisfy, it is probably most efficient to move straight to considering each answer choice in turn, eliminating those that don't satisfy all three conditions.

> **Note.** As mentioned in "A Guide to Analytical Reasoning Questions," you should always be aware that since all of the questions in a set are based on the same conditions, you may have discovered things in responding to earlier questions that might be helpful when dealing with a question that comes later. This question might be a case in point. You may remember using the acceptability of an overall selection of four rugs that included three oval rugs and one rectangular silk rug to eliminate incorrect answer choices in question 20. If so, you may, as a bonus of having worked question 20 correctly, be able to spot answer choice (C) of this question as correct, without having to work this question "from the ground up." It is not in general advisable to waste time going over the solutions to other questions to try to find useful pointers for dealing with the question currently before you, but if you do happen to remember information that you can exploit, you should take full advantage of it.

The Incorrect Answer Choices:

A, E   Any selection that does not include at least two oval rugs violates the first condition. Therefore, neither (A) nor (E) describes an acceptable selection.

B   Two selections of four rugs satisfy the description in (B):

(1) a selection consisting of two oval wool rugs and two rectangular wool rugs

or

(2) a selection consisting of one oval silk rug, one oval wool rug, and two rectangular wool rugs.

The first of these selections includes a total of four wool rugs, and so violates the second condition. The second includes an oval silk rug as the only silk rug and so violates the third condition. Thus neither of the selections described in (B) is acceptable.

D Only three oval rugs are available: two wool and one silk. Therefore you know that any selection that includes three oval rugs has to include one oval silk rug. So to satisfy the third condition, it would also have to include a rectangular silk rug. But since the only rectangular rug in the selection described in (D) is a wool rug, (D) does not describe an acceptable selection.

The Correct Answer:

C This selection includes three oval rugs and so satisfies the first condition. Since there are only three oval rugs available for selection in the first place, you know exactly what they are: two oval wool rugs (which are enough to satisfy the second condition) and one oval silk rug. And since this selection includes a rectangular silk rug as well as the oval silk rug, it also satisfies the third condition. So (C) describes an acceptable selection.

- *Difficulty Level: 3*

Question 23

What you need to keep in mind for this question: Be careful to note that this question requires you to find the rug, or group of rugs, that cannot be added to the three silk rugs to make up an acceptable selection. So if the rug, or group of rugs, listed in an answer choice plus the three silk rugs would make up a selection that does satisfy all of the conditions, that answer choice is **incorrect**.

Remember also that for each answer choice, what you are considering is the possible acceptability of a selection consisting of the three silk rugs plus **all** of the rugs on that list **and no other rugs**.

Overview: You can tell right away that selecting all three silk rugs means that, no matter which other rugs are added, the third condition will be satisfied. Since all of the answer choices add from one to three additional rugs, they are all going to produce selections that are the right size. Since one of the silk rugs is an oval rug, the addition of even one other oval rug will produce a selection that satisfies the first condition. And the second condition will be satisfied if two or more wool rugs are added to the silk rugs. So what you are looking for is an answer choice that adds only rectangular rugs (thus violating the first condition) or adds only one wool rug (thus violating the second condition).

The Correct Answer:

A Since (A) adds only one wool rug to the three silk rugs, the "Overview" above show that the rug listed in (A) **cannot** be added to the three silk rugs to produce an acceptable selection.

The Incorrect Answer Choices:

B, C, D, E   Each of these answer choices adds either two or three wool rugs, thus satisfying the second condition. Since in each case at least one of those additional rugs is oval, all of these choices also satisfy the first condition. Therefore, the lists of rugs in (B), (C), (D), and (E) would all produce acceptable selections.

- *Difficulty Level: 3*

Question 24

Overview: Since there are only three silk rugs available, any selection of six rugs will have to include at least three of the wool rugs. The second condition, however, rules out including more than three wool rugs. So to get a total of six rugs, an acceptable selection will have to include all three silk rugs (thus satisfying the third condition) and three wool rugs. Since there is only one oval silk rug, at least one of those three wool rugs must be an oval rug to satisfy the first condition (and at least one will be rectangular because there are only two oval wool rugs). So there are two possibilities for an acceptable six-rug selection:

(1) one oval silk, two rectangular silk, one oval wool, two rectangular wool

or

(2) one oval silk, two rectangular silk, two oval wool, one rectangular wool

The Correct Answer:

C As you can see, the "Overview" above lead directly to (C) as the correct answer. Both acceptable selections of six rugs include the two rectangular silk rugs, so the two rectangular silk rugs **must** be included.

The Incorrect Answer Choices:

A, E These answer choices can be eliminated because both violate the first condition. In each case, there would only be one oval rug selected, rather than the minimum of two.

B, D Answer choices (B) and (D) do not violate any of the setup conditions and so, unlike (A) and (E), cannot be eliminated on those grounds. Indeed, if you look at the two acceptable six-rug selections at the end of the "Overview" above, you will see that selection (2) includes both (B)'s two oval wool rugs and (D)'s exactly three rectangular rugs. But selection (1) is also an acceptable six-rug selection and neither (B) nor (D) is included in selection (1). So (B) and (D) can be eliminated because, although they **can** be included in an acceptable six-rug selection, they do not **have** to be included.

■ *Difficulty Level: 3*

Question 1

Overview: The passage makes two comparisons: At pre-school age, children who spend the day in day-care nurseries are ill more often than those who do not. By school age, the situation is reversed; it is the children who had not spent the day in day care during their pre-school years who are ill more often than their classmates who had. The passage suggests that the difference between the preschool-age children can be explained by the fact that the children in day care are exposed to many common illnesses. But school-age children almost all attend school and so are all equally likely to be exposed to illnesses at school. So if it is more frequent exposure to illnesses that explains why children in day care are ill more often than children of the same ages who are not in day care, you might reasonably expect that, contrary to what the passage reports, school-age children would all tend to be ill at about the same rate.

You are asked to select a statement that helps to explain this apparent discrepancy.

The Correct Answer:

C This answer choice suggests that the very factor—exposure to many common illnesses—that causes the high frequency of illness among preschool children in day care also results in those same children becoming immune to many of those illnesses. Pre-school children who were not in day care had less exposure to common illnesses and so did not develop immunity to as many common illnesses. Thus, when these children do go to school, they are less likely to be immune to the illnesses to which they are exposed. They are therefore more likely to become ill than their classmates who had been in day care are. Thus, (C) explains the apparent discrepancy in the information given in the passage.

The Incorrect Answer Choices:

A This answer choice explains why school-age children might be expected to become ill fairly often. But it does not explain why school-age children who had been in day care as preschoolers tend to become ill less frequently than their classmates do.

B If (B) is true, it provides an explanation for why some children tend to become ill more often than others. But this explanation has no connection to the tendencies reported in the passage, such as the tendency of school-age children who were not in day care to be ill more often.

Thus, (B) does nothing to explain the apparent discrepancy in the information given in the passage.

D If (D) is true, it provides a reason to expect that illnesses would be more prevalent among school-age children than among children in day care. But (D) provides no reason to expect that school-age children who had not been in day care as preschoolers would be ill more often than their classmates who had.

E This statement tells us something about the nature of the illnesses that children in day care contract. But (E) provides no information about the frequency of illnesses among school-age children and so can do nothing to explain the apparent discrepancy in the information given in the passage.

■ *Difficulty Level: 1*

Question 2

Overview: The conclusion of the argument is, "The vision test for obtaining a driver's license should not be limited to measuring the adequacy of vision in daylight conditions." This conclusion is supported by information that suggests that people with adequate daylight vision can have vision that is inadequate for safe night driving and by information that stresses the importance of drivers' having adequate night vision.

The Correct Answer:

A The argument explicitly concludes that the vision test for a driver's license should not be limited to testing vision in daylight conditions. The support for this conclusion strongly suggests that adequate night vision is very important for safe driving and that current vision testing practices do too little to ensure that drivers have adequate night vision. It is therefore fair to say that the main point of the argument is that the vision test for obtaining a driver's license should also measure the adequacy of vision in night conditions.

The Incorrect Answer Choices:

B The argument seems to take for granted that the current driver's license vision test does reduce the problem of drivers with inadequate vision. But the argument focuses on the drawbacks of not testing night vision, not on the benefits of testing daylight vision. Thus, (B) is not a point the argument is trying to establish.

C, E The argument explicitly states that many people whose daylight vision is adequate have night vision that is inadequate for safe night driving. Its concern is that the current vision test fails to screen for these cases. But both (C) and (E) are about drivers whose vision is adequately tested by the current vision test, so neither (C) nor (E) presents a point that concerns the argument.

D All that concerns the argument is that inadequate vision plays some role in the majority of car accidents that occur at night. It makes no effort to establish that inadequate vision is the primary factor. So (D) is not the main point of the argument.

■ *Difficulty Level: 2*

Question 3

Overview: The passage presents some information about pit vipers. It gives us both the standard scientific view and one researcher's alternative hypothesis about the use pit vipers make of their infrared sensors.

The question asks for support for this alternative hypothesis, which is that infrared sensors serve primarily to assist pit vipers in judging the size of approaching predators and how far away they are.

The Correct Answer:

B This statement compares pit vipers with closely related vipers without pits, and presumably without infrared sensors. What (B) tells us strongly suggests that having infrared sensors affects the way vipers react in the presence of predators, but does not affect the way they react in the presence of prey. (B), therefore, strongly supports the researcher's hypothesis.

The Incorrect Answer Choices:

A This statement lists certain respects in which male and female pit vipers do not differ from each other, but this information is neutral, favoring neither the standard view nor the researcher's hypothesis.

C, D Both of these answer choices provide further information about pit vipers but nothing that bears on the issue of the use pit vipers make of their infrared sensors. Thus, neither (C) nor (D) supports the researcher's hypothesis over the standard view.

E This statement says that certain pit vipers use rattles to intimidate predators. This information, however, has no bearing on whether or not they also use their infrared sensors in dealing with predators. Thus, (E) does not support the researcher's hypothesis over the standard view.

■ *Difficulty Level: 2*

Questions 4–5

Overview: The argument's conclusion is that a certain explanation for medieval authorities' persecution of minority groups is "highly questionable." The explanation that the argument challenges is that "official persecutions of various minority groups were undertaken very reluctantly by medieval authorities and only in order to soothe popular unrest caused by underlying popular hostility to the groups in question." Two points are presented in support of this challenge.

Question 4

To answer this question, you have to decide which of the answer choices best describes how the argument goes.

The Correct Answer:

D The first point that the argument makes in support of its challenge to the scholars' explanation is that there is inadequate evidence that the popular hostility presupposed by the scholars' explanation actually existed. The second point in support of the challenge suggests an alternative to that explanation by providing evidence for a motive that would account for the persecutions on different grounds. Thus, (D) is a good description of the way the argument proceeds.

The Incorrect Answer Choices:

A The argument says that many scholars hold a certain view. However, the point of the argument is not to show that this view is correct, but to show that it is questionable. (A), therefore, does not describe how the argument proceeds.

B The argument concludes that a certain explanation concerning events in the distant past—the Middle Ages—is "highly questionable." It bases that conclusion on evidence it presents concerning that same period. Thus, contrary to (B), the argument proceeds by treating conclusions based on such evidence as reliable.

C The argument does not mention, let alone criticize, any "particular comparison" between events. So (C) is not a good description of how the argument proceeds.

E The argument challenges a certain historical explanation by presenting two pieces of evidence against it. No effort is made to establish any general principle, nor is any general principle appealed to in order to justify any conclusion. (E), therefore, does not describe how the argument proceeds.

Question 5

To answer this question, you need to determine which answer choice provides information that would most strengthen the case already made against the view that medieval authorities were reluctant to persecute minority groups and did so only to soothe popular unrest caused by underlying popular hostility to the groups in question. That is, you should pick the answer choice that, when combined with the two points already made in the argument, makes the strongest case **against** that view.

The Correct Answer:

A This answer choice strongly suggests that medieval authorities who persecuted minorities were motivated by their own ill will toward those minorities. This fits very well with the second point that the argument raised—that medieval authorities carried out persecutions that targeted exactly those groups that most effectively disputed the authorities' right to govern. And most importantly, (A) directly undercuts the view that official persecutions were carried out reluctantly by authorities who sought only to soothe popular unrest caused by underlying popular hostility. If the authorities were concerned with soothing this popular unrest, they would not launch propaganda campaigns that are presumably aimed at encouraging popular hostility. Since the scholars held that medieval authorities were reluctant to persecute minorities, (A) strengthens the case against the scholars' belief.

The Incorrect Answer Choices:

B This statement suggests that medieval minority communities might have needed to be protected against the hostility of various elements of the population. But in that case, it is more likely that popular hostility to minorities was a persistent problem and, therefore, more likely that the authorities undertook persecutions of minority groups reluctantly and only in order to soothe such unrest. So (B) does not strengthen the argument's case against the scholars' belief, but actually weakens it.

C This answer choice suggests that popular hostility toward a group could result in serious public unrest. This could have given medieval authorities an incentive for acting in ways that would soothe such unrest. So (C) reinforces the scholars' view rather than strengthening the argument against it.

■ *Difficulty Level: 2*

D　This statement provides some support for the view that the medieval authorities themselves were not hostile to minority groups. And it thus provides some support for the scholars' view that the authorities were reluctant to undertake the persecution of such groups.

E　The issue in the argument is whether certain scholars have correctly explained medieval authorities' persecutions of minority groups. Information to the effect that convicted felons were not considered victims of persecution tells us nothing about how minority groups came to be victims of official persecution. So (E) does nothing to strengthen the argument against the scholars' view.

■ *Difficulty Level: 3*

Question 6

Overview: In this passage you are given various pieces of information about the recent discovery in a glacier of an ancient, well-preserved body of a man. The passage simply makes a number of statements without drawing a conclusion from those statements.

To answer the question associated with this passage, you must decide which of the answer choices is most strongly supported by the information in the passage.

The Correct Answer:

C　The passage tells us that the man's body was well preserved. It also tells us that the body wouldn't have been well preserved if it hadn't been sealed in the glacier shortly after the man died, or if it had thawed. So we can infer that the man's body was sealed in the glacier shortly after his death, that is, at least 4,000 years ago. We can also infer that this glacier has been continuously frozen for at least the past 4,000 years. Thus, (C) is very strongly supported by the information in the passage.

The Incorrect Answer Choices:

A　The passage tells us that the artifacts found on the body show that the man lived at least 4,000 years ago. That means that none of those artifacts could have been less than 4,000 years old, since the body, along with its artifacts, had been sealed up, undisturbed from the time the man died. So the artifacts could well be somewhat more than 4,000 years old. Therefore, (A) is not supported by the information in the passage.

B　Nothing in the passage tells us anything about how the man died. All we know is that he was on or very near a glacier when he died. So he might have frozen to death, or he might have died from other causes. So (B) is not supported by any information provided in the passage.

D　The passage tells us that the body would not still be preserved if it had not been frozen. However, the only thing we know about the artifacts found with the body is that they are probably at least 4,000 years old. The passage tells us nothing that would indicate what those artifacts were made of. Some artifacts, like those made of animal skins, may need to be frozen in order to be preserved. Other artifacts, like those made of stone or metal, might well have been preserved even if they had not been frozen. So, although (D) might be true, the passage does not support it.

E The passage gives us good reason to believe that the climate at the location of the glacier is warmer now than it was 4,000 years ago. But there is no reason to think that changes in temperature at a single spot on the globe are good indicators of changes in the global climate as a whole. So (E) is not supported by the information in the passage.

- *Difficulty Level: 2*

Question 7

Overview: In this argument, the results of an experiment are presented as supporting a hypothesis. This result, as it is reported, does not provide much support for the hypothesis. It is true that in this experiment, the composition that people preferred was one that they had already heard earlier that day. However, for all we know, "Study I" may be a more appealing musical composition than "Study II" and would have been preferred by a substantial majority of people even if "Study II" had been the composition they heard once before. So the results presented by the argument, by themselves, provide little evidence that "Study I" was preferred because it had been heard before.

To strengthen this argument, then, what you need is evidence that makes it more likely that the people in the experiment preferred "Study I" primarily because they had heard it before rather than because of the kind of music it is or for some other reason.

The Correct Answer:

D (D) reports the results of an experiment much like the one cited in the argument except that in this case, the composition heard in the morning was "Study II." In the experiment described in (D), a very substantial majority (70 out of 80) preferred "Study II." (D), therefore, makes it more likely that hearing one of the compositions on an earlier occasion, rather than the relative merits of the compositions themselves, determined the subjects' preferences.

The Incorrect Answer Choices:

A The results of the experiment reported in (A) show, at the very least, that people's preferences are strongly influenced by something in addition to an earlier exposure to one of the compositions. Moreover, these results provide no evidence that earlier exposure to a composition has any influence on people's preferences.

B (B) strongly indicates that, taking the two compositions on their merits, "Study I" is more appealing than "Study II" is. Such a result actually undermines the view that the preference shown for "Study I" among the people in the experiment cited in the argument had something to do with their having heard it earlier.

C Since the hypothesis seems to be about people with no special musical expertise, including professional music critics in the study raises questions about the study. This questionable aspect of the study, if anything, weakens the support for the hypothesis. Other than this, (C) has no effect on the strength of the argument.

E   (E) suggests that the study described in the argument might not have been well conducted, though even this is not clear. But if the complaints are indications of a real problem, (E) still tells us nothing about how this problem may have affected people's preferences. So (E) does not strengthen the case for the hypothesis; it may very well weaken that case by raising questions about whether the results of the study can be trusted.

- *Difficulty Level: 2*

Questions 8–9

Overview: The main conclusion of the argument is that in areas that have been hit by natural disasters, retailers that raise prices on new shipments of plywood to well above predisaster prices are not taking advantage of the disaster to make more money on each sheet of plywood that they sell. We are given one piece of evidence in support of this conclusion: that transporting plywood into devastated areas is difficult and expensive. The argument infers from this evidence that plywood's cost to retailers is higher than it was before the disaster. And this inference is the basis for the argument's main conclusion.

The inference on which the main conclusion is based seems fairly safe. If shipping costs go up, the overall cost to the retailer for new shipments of plywood is almost certainly going to go up as well. So to avoid making less on each sheet of plywood than before, retailers will have to raise prices by enough to cover the increased shipping costs. But the argument's main conclusion is that the retailers' profit on each sheet of plywood is **no** higher than before. For that to be true, the price increase cannot be greater than the increase in the retailers' costs.

Question 8

The Correct Answer:

E   As the discussion in the "Overview" indicates, (E) is an assumption on which the argument depends. If (E) were not true—that is, if the increase in the price charged by retailers exceeded the increase in those retailers' costs—then the retailers would be making more money on each sheet of plywood sold, and the argument would fail.

The Incorrect Answer Choices:

A   The issue of residents' ability to pay has implications for total sales and, thus, total profits for plywood retailers. The argument, however, is not about retailers' total profits, but about their profit on each individual sheet of plywood sold. And as long as the increased per-sheet price does no more than reflect the increased per-sheet shipping costs, the retailers are not going to make more money per sheet than before the disaster. So (A) has no bearing on the argument.

B The argument tells us that retailers do raise the price they charge for a sheet of plywood. But the argument concludes that retailers do not make more profit per sheet as a result, because shipping costs have also increased. So the argument depends on assuming that at least some of the increase in shipping costs is paid by the retailers. But as far as the argument is concerned, the companies that supply the plywood to the retailers might bear some of the increased shipping costs. As long as the retailers do not increase their per-sheet price by more than the increase in shipping costs that they themselves pay, they will not make more money on each sheet of plywood. So the argument does not assume that retailers must pay the full amount of any increase in shipping costs.

C If (C) is false, some retailers make so much money per sheet of plywood that they could absorb an increase in shipping costs without raising prices for a long time. When such retailers sell plywood after a natural disaster, which increases the plywood's cost to them, they may very well make **less** money per sheet of plywood than before the disaster even if they raise their prices. So the conclusion of the argument—that retailers who raise their prices on plywood after a natural disaster do not make **more** money on each sheet of plywood than they did before the disaster—can still hold even if (C) is false. Thus the argument doesn't depend on (C).

D If (D) were true, retailers would presumably have less plywood to sell after the disaster than before. But since the argument only concerns the retailers' per-sheet profits, the total amount of plywood involved is irrelevant.

- *Difficulty Level: 4*

Question 9

The Correct Answer:

C From the discussion in the "Overview," you see that the clause "the plywood's cost to retailers is higher than it was before the disaster" is an intermediate conclusion that the argument draws from a certain piece of evidence. And this intermediate conclusion is then used to support the main conclusion of the argument. (C) is therefore a good description of the role played by the clause.

The Incorrect Answer Choices:

A The argument as a whole is directed to countering the accusation that certain retailers take advantage of a disaster to make more money on each sheet of plywood sold. It does not do this, however, by giving a counterexample—an example that would undermine the support for the accusation.

B The argument as a whole is directed toward the main conclusion that in areas that have been hit by natural disasters, retailers that raise prices on new shipments of plywood to well above predisaster prices are not taking advantage of the disaster to make more money on each sheet of plywood that they sell. The clause at issue only supports the main conclusion.

D The argument does not treat the position it argues against as implausible. Rather, the argument takes that position seriously and attempts to make a reasoned case against it. The clause at issue is part of a careful attempt at a rebuttal, not an example used to illustrate the implausibility of the position being argued against.

E As illustrated in the "Overview," the statement that plywood's cost to retailers is higher than it was before the disaster plays a central role in how the argument goes. It is not there to provide background information.

- *Difficulty Level: 5*

Question 10

Overview: The conclusion of the argument is that the results of a certain study support the hypothesis that "much of the nitrous oxide that contributes to air pollution originates from the burning of organic matter in forest fires." In the study in question, smoke samples from many forest fires were collected and bottled. When these bottled smoke samples were later analyzed in a laboratory, they were all found to contain high concentrations of nitrous oxide.

On the face of it, the argument appears to be quite strong. The evidence produced by the study appears to be relevant. And since the hypothesis makes a fairly modest claim, it seems to be well supported by the study. Thus to undermine this argument you need to find something that seriously challenges the significance of the study to the hypothesis.

The Correct Answer:

D (D) strongly suggests that the high concentrations of nitrous oxide found in the smoke samples were at least largely the result of the smoke having been kept in bottles before being analyzed. That means that finding high concentrations of nitrous oxide in the bottled samples is no indication that there are high concentrations of nitrous oxide in the smoke from forest fires that is dispersed in the atmosphere. So as a test of the hypothesis, the study was fundamentally flawed. Since the argument rests entirely on the results of the study, (D) completely undermines the argument.

The Incorrect Answer Choices:

A The hypothesis does not say that the burning of organic matter in forest fires is responsible for all, or even most, of the nitrous oxide in the atmosphere. The hypothesis merely says that "much of the nitrous oxide" comes from such fires. So 10 percent of the nitrous oxide in the atmosphere coming from a source other than forest fires presents no difficulty for the hypothesis. Whatever support the hypothesis receives from the results of the study is thus unaffected by (A).

B The industrial scientists' hypothesis is narrowly focused on where nitrous oxide as a component of air pollution comes from. (B) tells us that nitrous oxide is not the only pollutant present in the atmosphere and that forest fires are not the only way that organic materials can end up contributing to air pollution. But neither of these factors has a bearing on whether forest fires release significant amounts of nitrous oxide into the atmosphere or whether the study shows that they do.

C (C) tells us that forest fires may be indirectly responsible for even more of the nitrous oxide in the atmosphere than smoke can account for. So (C) can be taken as providing some independent support for the hypothesis, but it does not undermine the support that the study provides for the hypothesis.

E (E) suggests an alternative way of doing the study. But the fact that the study could be done differently is not in itself a reason to think that the actual study was defective in any way. So (E) does nothing to undermine the argument.

- *Difficulty Level: 1*

Question 11

Overview: The argument's conclusion is that the size and shape of a fossilized leaf provide enough information to determine the altitude at which the plant grew. This conclusion is based on two claims: (1) that the size and shape of a fossilized leaf indicate the climate at which the plant grew and (2) that the climate at a given location depends on the altitude.

How good an argument is this? If both (1) and (2) are true, does the conclusion also have to be true? Well, (1) says that if you know the size and shape of a leaf, you can determine the climate. So if (2) said that if you know the climate you can determine the altitude, the truth of (1) and (2) would ensure that the conclusion is also true.

But that is not what (2) says. All (2) actually says is that the climate at a given location **depends on** the altitude. This means that altitude is a factor in determining the climate but this is not to say that if you know the climate, you can determine the altitude. (2) says nothing to rule out two different locations having the same climate but entirely different altitudes. For this reason, the argument fails to establish that the size and shape of a fossilized leaf is enough to determine the altitude at which it grew.

The Correct Answer:

B As you can see from the discussion in the "Overview," the argument leaves open the possibility that locations at different altitudes can have the same climate. And if locations at different altitudes can have the same climate (as, in fact, they can), then the reasoning in the argument fails. So (B) points out a way in which the reasoning is vulnerable to criticism.

The Incorrect Answer Choices:

A Nothing in the argument depends on whether or not plant species can survive violent changes in their environments. The issue is whether, given only the size and shape of a fossilized leaf, it is possible to determine the altitude at which the plant that produced that particular leaf had grown. So (A) is not a relevant basis for criticizing the reasoning.

C The argument claims that if you know the size and shape of a fossilized leaf, then you can determine the climate in which the leaf grew. But in doing this, the argument does not commit itself to size and shape being the only physical characteristics of a leaf that depend on climate. There may be other such characteristics, but there is no need to consider them in the argument because they would not be relevant to the line of reasoning pursued there. So (C) does not provide a basis for criticizing the reasoning.

D The argument takes it for granted that the size and shape of a leaf can be determined from the fossil of that leaf. But this is not to say that the reasoning relies on there being any similarity or analogy between a leaf and the fossil of a leaf. Thus (D) does not accurately describe what the argument's reasoning does, so it cannot serve as grounds for criticizing that reasoning.

E (E) would be a telling criticism if the argument claimed that the size and shape of a leaf was enough information to determine the climate (and consequently the altitude) **at the location where the leaf was found**. But the argument is focused on determining the climate and altitude **where the leaf grew**. So (E) is not an effective criticism.

■ *Difficulty Level: 3*

Question 12

Overview: This passage presents you with two pieces of information: the first says that, overall, box office receipts at movie theaters increased significantly last year; and the second says that the number of movie theaters that went bankrupt last year increased sharply. The first piece of information, as the passage points out, seems to indicate that the film industry overall is prospering. The second clearly points in the opposite direction. So there is an apparent discrepancy between what is indicated by the two pieces of information.

To answer the question, you need to pick out the piece of information that helps to explain why the increase in bankruptcies and the overall increase in box office receipts occurred during the same period.

The Correct Answer:

C (C) tells us that last year's box office success was not widely distributed among movie theaters but was enjoyed only by a select group of theaters. So even though box office receipts increased 40 percent last year, most theaters were not in a position to benefit from this increase. At the same time, (C) suggests that a large number of theaters had a bad year last year because the films they showed were not successful. So it is not surprising that a lot of movie theaters went bankrupt at the same time that box office receipts **taken as a whole** went up and the film industry **overall** made high profits.

The Incorrect Answer Choices:

A Since it is reasonable to think that at least some of the increased cost of producing a film would be passed on to movie theaters, (A) suggests that movie theaters probably have to pay more for a film now than they did 10 years ago. This might help explain why, even with high box office receipts, movie theaters now might have more difficulty making a profit than they did 10 years ago. But the change described in (A) took place over a 10-year period. It does not explain why **last year**—a year in which overall box office receipts increased 40 percent **from the previous year**—twice as many movie theaters went bankrupt **as in the preceding 2 years combined**.

B If many of the theaters that went bankrupt last year were theaters at which ticket prices fell, then we might have at least a partial explanation of why those theaters went bankrupt. (B), however, doesn't tell us this. Moreover, (B) leaves it completely mysterious why movie theaters on the verge of bankruptcy would have lowered their ticket prices in a year when people were spending far more money on movie tickets than they had in the previous year. So (B) does not help to resolve the apparent discrepancy.

D Greatly increased film advertising might explain why overall box office receipts went up last year. But since, according to (D), most of the costs of that advertising were absorbed by the producers and distributors of the films and not by the theater owners, (D) makes it even more puzzling why theater bankruptcies increased so much last year.

E (E) suggests that movie theaters would have greater profits from sales of soft drinks and snack foods in years with increased box office receipts. Thus, (E) makes last year's increase in bankruptcies even more puzzling, heightening the apparent discrepancy rather than resolving it.

■ *Difficulty Level: 2*

Question 13

Overview: This passage first describes the circumstances confronting someone who has to decide whether to sign a consent form permitting her father to receive a kidney transplant. And then it tells us that she decides not to sign the form.

Each answer choice consists of a principle, a rule for how people should act in particular situations. To answer this question you have to decide which principle backs up the decision made by Mr. Smith's daughter. That is, given the circumstances described in the passage, you need to determine which one of the principles directs Mr. Smith's daughter to not sign the consent form.

The Correct Answer:

E According to (E), people have an obligation to go along with a patient's preferences concerning treatment. And in cases like that described in the passage, where patients cannot communicate their own preferences, (E) says that others have an obligation to go along with what they can infer that the patient's preferences would be, based on their general knowledge of the patient's commitments, beliefs, and desires.

In the case of Mr. Smith, his daughter knew that her father "strongly objected" to transplantation of organs from live donors. She also knew that his objection was based on his belief that such operations caused serious disability to the organ donor. The daughter herself thinks that this belief is mistaken in the case of kidney donors, but she knows that her father held that belief. So she can infer that, given his actual commitments and beliefs, her father would have strongly objected to having the transplant. So if she goes along with what she can infer to be her father's preferences concerning treatment, she will not consent to the surgery. Thus (E) says that Mr. Smith's daughter made the right decision.

The Incorrect Answer Choices:

A Under the circumstances, the best way to protect the life and health of her father would probably be for Mr. Smith's daughter to sign the consent form. And there is no reason to believe that Mr. Smith had explicitly prohibited her from doing so. So if we accept (A), we have to conclude that Mr. Smith's daughter should have decided to consent to the surgery. Thus her decision violates the principle set out in (A) rather than conforming to it.

B This principle says that, regardless of the circumstances, anyone making a medical decision concerning another person should always decide "according to what would most help promote that person's health." So, applied to the case at hand, (B) says that Mr. Smith's daughter should have decided to consent to the surgery. So her decision violates the principle set out in (B) rather than conforming to it.

C This principle says that if surgery is not likely to prolong the life of the patient, then there is no obligation to permit that surgery. So (C) is a principle that applies only in cases where the surgery is not likely to prolong the life of the patient. In Mr. Smith's case, however, there is every reason to think that a transplant would likely prolong his life. Thus, (C) has nothing to say about the decision that Mr. Smith's daughter should make.

D According to this principle, Mr. Smith's daughter would be justified in refusing to consent to the surgery if donating the kidney would seriously disable her father's cousin. We have been told that Mr. Smith believed that anyone donating a kidney would be seriously disabled. But according to the passage, the daughter knows that her father was wrong in this belief, and that, in fact, donating the kidney would not have seriously disabled the cousin. So (D) doesn't apply to the daughter's case and thus cannot justify her decision.

■ *Difficulty Level: 1*

Questions 14–15

Overview: The letter writer wants to show that a claim made in last Thursday's editorial is false. In order to show this, the writer offers an argument for the conclusion that a large percentage of burglars will be caught. Two premises are presented in support of this conclusion: (1) at least 70 percent of people who commit crimes are caught; and (2) all burglars are criminals. But these two premises actually provide little, if any, support for the conclusion.

(1) indicates that criminals in general are caught at a high rate, and the argument concludes from this that burglars are also caught at a high rate. But nothing in the two premises indicates that the rate at which burglars are caught is at all similar to the rate for criminals in general. The premises don't even guarantee that any burglars at all are among the 70 percent of criminals who are caught. So the argument is flawed because it assumes that if a large percentage of the members of a group (criminals) have a certain property (getting caught), then a large percentage of any part of that group (burglars) will also have that property.

Question 14

To answer this question you have to decide which of the arguments has the same type of flaw as the letter writer's argument.

The Correct Answer:

A The conclusion of the argument in (A) is that a large percentage of nurses are self-employed. This conclusion is based on two claims: (1) that a large percentage of professional persons are self-employed and (2) that all nurses are professional persons. Thus it mistakenly assumes that if a large percentage of the members of a group (professional persons); has a certain property (being self-employed), then a large percentage of the members of any part of that group (nurses) will have that property. So (A) exhibits the same flawed pattern of reasoning that the letter writer's argument does.

The Incorrect Answer Choices:

B The conclusion of the argument in (B) is that some people who have social-work training also have medical training. It bases this conclusion on two claims: (1) a large percentage of psychiatrists have social-work training; and (2) all psychiatrists have medical training. But in this case, if both (1) and (2) are true, then the conclusion must also be true, so the reasoning in (B) is not flawed at all.

C The conclusion in (C), "all professional persons who have changed their careers required new training," is a claim about professional persons in the past. But there is no reason to think that the crucial premise in this argument, "career changes require new training," applies to the past. So the argument draws a conclusion about the past that is well supported only for the present. This is the only logical flaw in (C), and it is not the same type of flaw as the one in the letter writer's argument.

D The argument in (D) also puts forward two claims: (1) that a large percentage of doctors are specialists; and (2) that all specialists have training beyond the usual medical curriculum. (D)'s conclusion, that many doctors have training beyond the usual medical curriculum, logically follows from these two claims. So the reasoning in (D) is not flawed at all.

E The conclusion of the argument in (E) is that many engineers need training in management. This conclusion is based on two claims: (1) that many engineers are employed in management positions; and (2) that anyone in a management position needs training in management. But in this case, if both (1) and (2) are true, then the conclusion must also be true, so the reasoning in (E) is not flawed at all.

■ *Difficulty Level: 3*

Question 15

The Correct Answer:

E As you saw in the "Overview," the letter writer's argument does not conclude that all burglars will be caught, only that a large percentage of burglars will eventually be caught. So the letter writer can concede that some burglars will not be caught without in any way undermining the argument's conclusion. The claim that some burglars will undoubtedly escape does just that. So (E) correctly describes the role that claim plays in the letter writer's argument.

The Incorrect Answer Choices:

A From the discussion in the "Overview," you can see that the claim that some burglars will escape is not part of the evidence for the conclusion. That claim simply makes it clear that the letter writer is not maintaining that all burglars will be caught, only that a large percentage of them will be caught. So (A) does not correctly describe the role the claim plays in the letter writer's argument.

B The letter writer provides no evidence for the claim that some burglars will escape.

So that claim cannot be the conclusion of any argument expressed in the passage, even a subsidiary argument. Thus the claim does not play the role described in (B).

C The letter writer's argument focuses on how frequently burglars are caught or not caught. It does not discuss any particular case or kind of case. So nothing in the letter writer's argument could possibly do what (C) describes.

D The letter writer's argument as a whole is directed against the editorial's position that someone who commits a burglary runs almost no risk of being caught. Saying that some burglars will undoubtedly escape does not restate this position; it is a point on which the letter writer and the editorial agree.

- *Difficulty Level: 2*

Question 16

Overview: This passage consists of a number of statements about carcinogenic chemicals and about studies of the carcinogenicity of food additives. The task is to decide which of the five answer choices gets the most support from the statements in the passage.

The Correct Answer:

B The passage tells us that almost any chemical is carcinogenic if taken in doses that are large enough to kill cells. It also tells us that until now studies to determine whether food additives are carcinogenic involved giving the test animals doses of additives that are "massive enough to kill large numbers of cells in the animals." So we can conclude that in most cases such studies would find that the additive being tested causes cancer in the test animal. But the first two sentences of the passage strongly imply that many chemicals are not carcinogenic if taken in small doses. So we can also conclude that in many cases the additive might not have caused cancer in test animals if it had been given in smaller doses.

The passage indicates that doses as large as those used in studies until now are larger than anything humans might be exposed to. Studies that used smaller doses, therefore, would better represent the levels of human exposure to food additives. And we have already seen that such studies would conclude less often that food additives are carcinogenic. Hence the passage supports (B).

The Incorrect Answer Choices:

A The passage tells us that until now studies of the carcinogenicity of food additives have always involved administering to the test animals doses of the additive that are "massive enough to kill large numbers of cells in the animals." So the passage provides no support for (A).

C The passage does not tell us about the effects of small doses of chemicals. It does, however, tell us that although almost any chemical is carcinogenic in doses massive enough to kill cells, a few chemicals are carcinogenic even without causing cell death. The passage does not use the term "truly carcinogenic chemicals," but if there are any chemicals that deserve to be called "truly carcinogenic chemicals," it would probably be the ones that are carcinogenic without causing cell death. Perhaps these chemicals are carcinogenic in small doses, but they cause cancer without causing cell death. So the passage provides no support for (C).

D The passage tells us that studies of the carcinogenicity of food additives have until now "involved administering to test animals doses of additives larger than the largest possible human exposure levels." But this tells us nothing about amounts of carcinogenic chemicals usually absorbed in the natural environment. As far as the passage is concerned, those amounts may be small, large, or somewhere in between. So the passage provides no support for (D).

E The passage provides some support for the view that in many cases, the cancer rate observed in carcinogenicity studies is higher than it would be if the test animals had been given a dose of the additive that was more in line with typical human exposure levels. But it provides no support for thinking that any of the additives that are now banned because of carcinogenicity could be safely used in smaller doses. In part, this is because the passage does give us details about why any of these additives have been banned. So the passage provides no support for (E).

- *Difficulty Level: 4*

Question 17

Overview: The conclusion of the argument is that "if the tolls are eliminated, then the entire cost of maintaining the highways will have to be paid for by an increase in general taxes." This conclusion is supported by two considerations: first, that Holston has no choice but to maintain its highways, and second, that toll revenue has in the past been the sole source of the money used to pay for highway maintenance.

Notice that the argument's conclusion goes beyond what the argument gives evidence for. Specifically, it might not be necessary to increase general taxes by an amount that covers the entire cost of maintaining the highways. One significant alternative that the argument does not consider is that Holston might reduce public expenditures in some other area and use the resulting savings to cover at least part of the cost of highway maintenance.

The Correct Answer:

B If (B) were false, the amount of money saved by eliminating the costs associated with collecting tolls would be available to cover part of the total cost of maintaining the highways. In that case, the fact that toll revenue has until now covered all of the expenses for highway maintenance no longer strongly supports the argument's conclusion. So if (B) were false, the support for this conclusion would be undermined. (B) is thus an assumption of the argument.

The Incorrect Answer Choices:

A The argument does assume that work on highway maintenance will be paid for from a revenue stream such as tolls or taxes, but it doesn't specify that the revenue must be collected before the work can be authorized. It is thus consistent with the argument that Holston would authorize work on highway maintenance before the money to pay for it has been collected. So (A) is not assumed.

C If (C) were false, then preventive maintenance would be as important after the abolition of tolls as before. This would affect how much money would be required for highway maintenance, but it does not affect the central issue of the argument: whether money for maintaining highways can only be raised by increasing general taxes. So (C)'s being false would not interfere with how well the argument works.

D The argument concludes that general taxes would have to increase if tolls were abolished. But it does not conclude this because highway maintenance would become more expensive. Rather, general taxes would have to be increased because general tax revenue would have to cover a cost that it did not need to cover before—the cost of maintaining the highways. So (D) is not assumed.

E The argument concludes that eliminating highway tolls would require a tax increase that covers the entire cost of maintaining Holston's highways. The argument does not require that there would not simultaneously be other governmental needs that would have to be covered by raising general taxes. Thus, as far as the argument is concerned, general taxes might have to be increased even if the highway tolls were not eliminated. (E), therefore, is not assumed.

- *Difficulty Level: 4*

Questions 18–19

Overview: Efraim makes an argument for the conclusion that "disregarding journalists' advice about reducing health risks is bound to pose less of a health risk than does trying to follow any such advice." He presents two points as support for this conclusion. First, that by seeking to avoid health risks, people inevitably become anxious. And second that anxiety poses a major health risk.

Felicity responds by offering a counterexample to Efraim's conclusion: Many people stopped smoking because of journalists' advice and led longer and healthier lives as a result.

Question 18

To answer this question, you have to decide which answer choice most accurately expresses a point that, given what they actually say, Felicity and Efraim would have to disagree about.

The Correct Answer:

D Efraim's position is that "disregarding journalists' advice about reducing health risks" is bound to be less of a health risk than trying to follow their advice would be. So, according to Efraim, no one can reduce the overall risks to his or her health by following the advice of articles in the popular press on such matters.

Felicity's counterexample is presented to show that there are people—people who stopped smoking in response to journalists' warnings about the health risks of smoking—who did reduce risks to their health by heeding the advice of articles in the popular press.

So (D) expresses a point at issue between the two.

The Incorrect Answer Choices:

A Felicity's response shows that she believes that, at least in the case of smoking, journalists have been correct in describing certain products and practices as posing health risks. Efraim says that it is healthier to disregard journalists' advice about avoiding products and practices that pose health risks than to try to follow it. However, Efraim does not think this because he believes that the products and practices people are being advised to avoid are actually safe, but because he regards them as posing **less** risk to health than is posed by the anxiety that results from attempting to follow such advice. So Efraim and Felicity do not necessarily disagree about (A).

B According to Efraim, there is some connection between a person's likelihood of trying to avoid health risks and that person's likelihood of suffering anxiety. But this does not mean that Efraim thinks that the people most likely to suffer anxiety in stressful situations are also the people most likely to try to avoid health risks. Efraim doesn't address this rather strong claim, and neither does Felicity, who merely tries to present a counterexample to Efraim's conclusion. So (B) is not a point at issue between Efraim and Felicity.

C The fact that Efraim bothers to present his argument strongly suggests that he thinks that too many people heed journalists' advice about avoiding health risks. And Felicity's comments about smoking suggest that she thinks that too many people ignore journalists' advice about avoiding health risks. But both could agree that some people ignore that advice.

E Efraim's argument depends both on anxiety actually resulting from attempts to follow journalists' advice to avoid various health risks and on that anxiety itself posing a major health risk. So if that anxiety can be overcome, his argument would be seriously weakened. Felicity does not dispute Efraim's claim that anxiety results from efforts to avoid health risks, or his claim that anxiety itself poses a major health risk. However, nothing she says commits her to believing that such anxiety even exists, much less to having any view about whether, if it exists, it can be overcome. So, although (E) is an issue for Efraim, it is not a point at issue between Efraim and Felicity.

■ *Difficulty Level: 2*

Question 19

The Correct Answer:

D In his argument, Efraim contends that when journalists warn the public about health risks, the health risks posed by anxiety over these warnings is greater than that posed by the health risks that the journalists advise us to avoid. But what if disregarding journalists' advice also produces anxiety? And what if that anxiety is at least as great as the anxiety that results from seeking to avoid those risks? Then as far as the health risk posed by anxiety is concerned, it is pretty much the same whether or not you disregard the journalists' advice. But heeding the advice can presumably reduce the health risk posed by things other than anxiety, such as smoking or poor diet. So heeding the advice would result in lowering health risks overall whereas disregarding it would not. Therefore if (D) is false, the case for the conclusion of Efraim's argument is very weak at best. Efraim's argument thus depends on assuming (D).

The Incorrect Answer Choices:

A Efraim's argument, essentially, is that in trying to avoid a health risk you inevitably create another health risk (in the form of anxiety) that is bigger than the health risk you are trying to avoid. (A) says that you might not be able to eliminate all of the health risk you are trying to avoid by following the journalists' advice. So if (A) is true, it does make Efraim's argument stronger. However, all his argument requires is that any reduction in health risks achieved by following journalists' advice is outweighed by the health risk posed by the anxiety that results from following that advice. Thus, Efraim's argument does not depend on assuming (A).

B Efraim's argument does not depend on assuming (B). Suppose that journalists do not use needlessly alarming language. Efraim's argument would still carry weight in this case, because even if journalists report health risks in neutral language, trying to avoid those risks could still produce anxiety in people and subject them to health risks as a result.

C Efraim's argument takes it for granted that some journalists recommend that people avoid at least some health risks. Nothing, however, depends on whether the popular press is unanimous in its recommendations about health risks. Thus, Efraim's argument does not depend on assuming (C).

E According to Efraim's argument, in attempting to avoid health risks, you are, at best, trading a smaller health risk for a larger one that comes in the form of anxiety. If there were strategies for eliminating personal anxiety that do not themselves cause additional personal anxiety and are **effective**, this would undermine the argument. But we are given no reason to believe that there are any effective strategies for eliminating personal anxiety. So even if most strategies for dealing with personal anxiety do not themselves induce anxiety, Efraim's argument is not undermined. Thus his argument does not depend on assuming (E).

- *Difficulty Level: 4*

Question 20

Overview: The argument claims that its conclusion—that a recently discovered orchid species "is one that is pollinated solely by insects"—**follows** from the evidence presented in its support. One piece of evidence is that all orchid species that are pollinated solely by insects have features that attract insects. The other piece of evidence demonstrates that the recently discovered orchid species has just such insect-attracting features.

The question tells you that this argument is flawed, so you know that the conclusion does not really follow from the evidence presented. To answer the question, you have to decide which of the answer choices best describes what is wrong with the logic of the argument.

The Correct Answer:

D The first piece of evidence tells us something about one class of orchid species, the ones that are pollinated solely by insects. It tells us that every single orchid species of that class has insect-attracting features. So we know that if an orchid species is discovered that does **not** have insect-attracting features, then that species is **not** one that is pollinated solely by insects. But does that mean that if an orchid species **does** have insect-attracting features then it **does** fall into that class? No, because, for all we have been told, there might well be other classes of orchid species that also have insect-attracting features—for example, species that are pollinated partly by insects and partly in other ways.

If the argument told us that orchid species that are solely pollinated by insects are the only class of orchid species that have insect-attracting features, the conclusion would follow from the evidence. But the argument gives us no reason to think this is true. The argument is thereby proceeding as if a characteristic (having insect-attracting features) known to be true of one class of things (orchid species pollinated solely by insects) is not true of any other class of things. This is the reasoning flaw that (D) describes.

The Incorrect Answer Choices:

A The only two classes of things for which the argument could be construed as pointing out a shared characteristic are orchid species pollinated solely by insects on the one hand and the recently discovered orchid species on the other. The argument does claim that they share a characteristic (having features that attract insects) but it does not claim that this is their only common feature. So the argument does not make the unwarranted assumption described in (A).

B The argument does assume that having insect-attracting features is a characteristic that distinguishes orchid species that are pollinated solely by insects from orchid species that aren't pollinated solely by insects. But as far as the argument is concerned, there might be any number of other characteristics that distinguish these two classes of orchid species from each other. So the argument is not flawed in the way described in (B).

C To make the mistake that (C) describes, the argument would have to do something like jump from a premise that having insect-attracting features is unique to a particular type of orchid to a conclusion that having insect-attracting features is unique to an unrelated type of orchid. The argument clearly does nothing like this, so it is not flawed in the way described by (C).

E The argument only makes one generalization that might be described as broad: "All orchid species that are pollinated solely by insects have features that attract insects." But it does not do this on the basis of anything else in the argument. It is presented as one of the argument's basic premises. So (E) is clearly not an accurate description of the argument.

- *Difficulty Level: 5*

Question 21

Overview: This passage presents an argument for accepting a certain explanation. What needs to be explained is why none of the contemporary Portuguese accounts of the Moroccan defeat of the Portuguese in 1578 mention that Portugal's King Sebastian died on the battlefield. The passage concludes that the omissions must have had a psychological cause. In support of this conclusion, the passage provides evidence to show that an alternative explanation—that none of the people writing the accounts knew of the king's death—can be ruled out.

You're being asked to identify the role played in this argument by the passage's discussion of two Portuguese officers.

The Correct Answer:

A According to the passage, the two officers wrote accounts of the battle in which King Sebastian was killed, and they wrote those accounts in a Moroccan prison where they "actually shared their cells with the Portuguese soldiers who identified the king's body to Moroccan officials." The passage thus suggests the officers would have known that the king had been killed. So the discussion of the two officers presents evidence that at least two of the accounts of the defeat were written by people who knew of the king's death. Thus, the role of that discussion is to provide grounds for eliminating simple ignorance of the king's death as an explanation for its never being mentioned. So (A) correctly describes the way that discussion functions in the argument.

The Incorrect Answer Choices:

B The only death with which the argument is concerned is the king's death, and whether the king actually died is never in dispute. Since there is no disputed death, (B) cannot correctly describe anything that goes on in the argument.

C An "apparent contradiction" is too strong a description of the relationship between the argument's main premises. The closest thing to an apparent contradiction is probably the tension between certain facts that the argument brings together—people who wrote battlefield accounts of the Portuguese defeat failed to mention an extremely important feature of that defeat, namely King Sebastian's death in battle, even though at least some of those writers were in a position to have known of the king's death. But even this tension is not resolved by the discussion about the two officers; it is resolved by the explanatory hypothesis that the Portuguese found Sebastian's death so humiliating that they could not bring themselves to write about it. Thus (C) is not an accurate description of the role played by the discussion of the two officers.

D If there is "a general psychological principle" on which the main conclusion is based, it is that people are unable to bring themselves to write about something if they are sufficiently humiliated by it. But no such principle is **explicitly** presented as grounds for the conclusion. Moreover, the discussion about the two officers does not support such a principle. It tells us nothing about how humiliated they felt by the king's death or why they did not write about it. The case of the two officers is not evidence for the principle; rather, it is part of a puzzle that the principle is used to explain.

E Nothing in the passage suggests that there are any historical reports that conflict with the argument's main conclusion. The discussion about the two officers is presented to rule out the possibility that none of the people who wrote about the battle knew of the king's death. That discussion is not presented to counter evidence that they were not humiliated by the king's death. Thus, (E) does not correctly describe anything that goes on in the argument.

■ *Difficulty Level: 5*

Question 22

Overview: This passage consists of a number of facts about the reproduction of a species of thrips. You are asked to select the answer choice that, given those facts, can be inferred to be true about the reproduction of thrips.

The Correct Answer:

C The passage says that there are about as many female thrips who reach adulthood as there are male thrips who reach adulthood. It also says that female offspring survive to adulthood at a much lower rate than male offspring do. For females to match males reaching adulthood in overall numbers in spite of the higher rate of deaths for females between birth and early adulthood, there must be more female births overall. Since all females are hatched from eggs and all males are live-born, it follows that, across the species, more of the offspring are born by hatching from eggs than are born live. So if the information presented in the passage is true, (C) must also be true.

The Incorrect Answer Choices

A The passage does say that the particular species of thrips is the first species to have been identified as being capable of reproducing by the two different methods mentioned. The passage does not claim or imply, however, that no other species uses those two methods. And it says nothing about whether there may be other combinations of two methods of reproduction that some species or other might use. Consequently, (A) cannot be inferred.

B The passage tells us only that for any one instance of reproduction, a given female will use only one method of reproduction. But this claim is consistent with a wide range of possibilities. For example, it could be that some females reproduce only by laying eggs, some only by bearing live young, and some by different methods on different occasions. Thus (B) cannot be inferred.

D The passage does not provide enough information to support the claim in (D). For all we are told in the passage, there could be **more** live-born broods over time than broods hatched from eggs. The passage tells us that there are fewer individuals in live-born (i.e., all male) broods than in the (all female) broods hatched from eggs. This is counteracted to some degree by the higher survival rate for males, but we don't know how much. If the higher survival rate for males doesn't fully compensate for the fewer individuals in the live-born broods, then the even ratio of adult males to adult females could only be accounted for if there are more live-born broods over time than broods hatched from eggs.

Furthermore, for all we are told in the passage, there could be **fewer** live-born broods over time than broods hatched from eggs. If the higher survival rate for males overcompensates for the fact that there are fewer individuals in live-born broods, then the even ratio of adult males to adult females could only be accounted for if there are fewer live-born broods over time than broods hatched from eggs.

E The passage does not provide enough information for (E) to be properly inferred. The passage tells us that "for any one instance of reproduction, a given female will use only one of the two methods," but tells us nothing that suggests that some females use only one method during their lifetimes.

- *Difficulty Level: 4*

Question 23

Overview: This argument gives two pieces of information—"the zoo has more animals than enclosures" and "every animal lives in an enclosure"—as the basis for concluding that "at least one of the enclosures contains more than one animal."

This argument works by establishing that one type of thing (enclosures at the zoo) **contains** every one of another type of thing (zoo animals) and that there are **more** of the second type of thing than there are of the first. It concludes that **at least one** thing of the first type **must contain** more than one individual of the second type.

The Correct Answer:

D The conclusion of the argument in (D) is that "at least one of the families in Herndon has more than one child." This conclusion is based on two pieces of information: that there are fewer families in Herndon than there are children, and that in Herndon every child is a member of a family. This argument works just like the argument about the zoo, as revealed in the "Overview." It establishes that one type of thing (families in Herndon) **contains** every one of another type of thing (children in Herndon) and that there are **more** of the second type of thing than there are of the first. And from this, it concludes that **at least one** thing of the first type **must contain** more than one individual of the second type.

The Incorrect Answer Choices:

A The conclusion presented in (A) is that some people who have no brothers or sisters have more parents than their parents have children. In (A), this conclusion is drawn from a single premise, namely that every person has two biological parents. The fact that every person is outnumbered by their biological parents is a crucial element of this argument, and this element has no analogue in the argument about the zoo. This, in itself, is enough to show that the pattern of reasoning in (A) is not parallel. In addition, this argument lacks the crucial features of argument about the zoo, such as a premise asserting that one type of thing contains every one of another type of thing.

B The conclusion presented in (B) is that there must be some marriages that will not end in divorce. (B) presents this conclusion as following from the claim that every year there are more marriages than divorces. Suppose you treat that claim as being parallel to the claim that, in the zoo, there are more animals than enclosures. If you try to extend this parallel to the conclusion in (B), you would end up concluding that there must be at least one divorce that ends more than one marriage. This absurd conclusion is very different from what (B) actually concludes. So the pattern of reasoning in (B) is not parallel to that in the argument about the zoo.

C The conclusion presented in (C) is that at least one girl under ten has more than one brother under ten. (C) presents this conclusion as following from two pieces of information. The first of these—that there are more boys under ten than there are girls under ten—is the only one that could be parallel to the statement that there are more animals at the zoo than enclosures. (Notice that boys under ten would be parallel to animals and girls under ten parallel to enclosures.) The second piece of information—that some families have more than one child under ten—would then have to be parallel to the statement that every animal lives in an enclosure. But this does not work. For one thing, the statement about families is about **some** families whereas the statement about animals is about **all** animals. For another, nothing in the argument about the zoo corresponds to the category of "child under ten."

E The conclusion presented in (E) is that there must be fewer families that include teenagers than there are teenagers belonging to such families. In (E), this conclusion is drawn from the premise that there is at least one family that includes more than one teenager. Looking at the argument about the zoo, you can see that neither of that argument's premises—the two pieces of information on which that argument is based—correspond with the premise in (E). You may notice that the premise in (E) is a close match to the conclusion of the argument about the zoo, but this similarity is nothing like a parallel pattern of reasoning.

■ *Difficulty Level: 5*

Question 24

Overview: This passage gives you information about how the size of the offices on the first, third, and fourth floors of the Hartshorn Building compare with the size of the offices on the second floor. Note that the comparisons between the fourth and second, and the second and first, are quite stark: every fourth-floor office is larger than any second-floor office, and every second-floor office is larger than any first-floor office.

Your task is to select the answer choice that **must** be true if the information you have been given in the passage is true. It is probably best to approach this question by considering each of the answer choices in turn. If, given the information in the passage, an answer choice could be false, then you can rule that choice out.

The Correct Answer:

D The passage tells you that every fourth-floor office is bigger than even the largest second-floor office, and it tells you that some of the offices on the third floor are not bigger than the largest second-floor offices. So you know that every fourth-floor office is bigger than some of the third-floor offices. That is, some third-floor offices are smaller than every fourth-floor office. So if the statements in the passage are true, (D) must be true.

The Incorrect Answer Choices:

A The passage tells you that the fourth-floor offices are all larger than any second-floor office. And it tells you that every second-floor office is larger than even the largest first-floor office. We can conclude from this that the smallest fourth-floor office is bigger than even the largest first-floor office. This contradicts what (A) says. Therefore, not only can (A) be false if the statements in the passage are true, (A) must be false.

B, C (B) says that the largest first-floor offices are as big as the smallest third-floor offices. And (C) says that the largest first-floor offices are bigger than the smallest third-floor offices. So both (B) and (C) could be false if it is possible that the smallest third-floor office is bigger than the largest first-floor office.

The first statement in the passage tells you that the smallest third-floor office is no bigger than the largest second-floor office. But as far as this statement is concerned, the smallest third-floor office might be a lot bigger than some of the smaller second-floor offices. The passage also tells you that **every** second-floor office is bigger than even the largest first-floor office. That means that, as far as the information in the passage is concerned, the smallest third-floor office might be much bigger than the largest first-floor office. So both (B) and (C) can be false.

E According to (E), the largest third-floor offices are bigger than the smallest fourth-floor offices. This could be false if it is possible that every fourth-floor office is bigger than every third-floor office (including the largest).

The second statement in the passage tells you that every office on the fourth floor is bigger than any second-floor office, but it doesn't say how much bigger they are. So as far as this statement is concerned, every fourth-floor office might be many times as large as the largest second-floor office. The first statement in the passage tells you that most of the third-floor offices are bigger than every second-floor office. But as far as this statement is concerned, even the largest third-floor office might be only slightly larger than the largest second-floor office. Thus, as far as the information in the passage is concerned, every office on the fourth floor could be much bigger than even the largest third-floor office. So (E) does not have to be true.

▪ *Difficulty Level: 5*

Question 25

Overview: Louis' conclusion is that people's intentions cannot be, on the whole, more bad than good. He bases this conclusion on an argument that considers the consequences of believing that people's intentions are more bad than good. He basically argues that because there would be very negative consequences if this were widely believed, it cannot be true.

The Correct Answer:

A Louis claims that if we held the belief that people's intentions were more bad than good, certain negative consequences would result—society would lack the mutual trust that is necessary for its survival. From this he concludes that this belief is false. Louis' argument makes little sense, however, unless you understand that he is assuming that believing in something that is true will not bring about negative consequences. But Louis does nothing to back up this assumption, and this assumption certainly requires some sort of justification. So Louis' argument is vulnerable to the objection that nothing he says shows that holding a true belief cannot have deleterious consequences.

The Incorrect Answer Choices:

B Louis' argument focuses on the consequences of a certain view being believed. It does not make any logical moves from the impossibility of two claims both being true to the impossibility of their both being false. So (B) simply does not describe what goes on in Louis' argument, so it is not a criticism that the argument is vulnerable to.

C Louis' argument does challenge the truth of a potential claim—that people's intentions can, on the whole, be more bad than good. But he does not suggest that anyone actually holds this belief. So the issue of "the motives of those who profess that they believe it to be true" does not arise. Louis' argument, therefore, is not vulnerable to the criticism in (C).

D At certain points in the argument, Louis implicitly deals with situations with two possible outcomes: for example, society surviving and society not surviving. But he never assumes that the most negative will inevitably occur. His argument actually takes it for granted that positive outcomes (such as society surviving) can occur. So the argument is not vulnerable to the criticism in (D).

E   Louis' argument is very general: it is about people, their beliefs, and the effects of those beliefs on society. Louis does not focus on particular groups of individuals. In particular, he does not make any inferences from what is true about one group of individuals to what is true about some other group of individuals. So his argument is not vulnerable to the criticism in (E).

- *Difficulty Level: 5*

General Directions for the LSAT Answer Sheet

The actual testing time for this portion of the test will be 2 hours 55 minutes. There are five sections, each with a time limit of 35 minutes. The supervisor will tell you when to begin and end each section. If you finish a section before time is called, you may check your work on that section <u>only</u>; do not turn to any other section of the test book and do not work on any other section either in the test book or on the answer sheet.

There are several different types of questions on the test, and each question type has its own directions. <u>Be sure you understand the directions for each question type before attempting to answer any questions in that section.</u>

Not everyone will finish all the questions in the time allowed. Do not hurry, but work steadily and as quickly as you can without sacrificing accuracy. You are advised to use your time effectively. If a question seems too difficult, go on to the next one and return to the difficult question after completing the section. MARK THE BEST ANSWER YOU CAN FOR EVERY QUESTION. NO DEDUCTIONS WILL BE MADE FOR WRONG ANSWERS. YOUR SCORE WILL BE BASED ONLY ON THE NUMBER OF QUESTIONS YOU ANSWER CORRECTLY.

ALL YOUR ANSWERS MUST BE MARKED ON THE ANSWER SHEET. Answer spaces for each question are lettered to correspond with the letters of the potential answers to each question in the test book. After you have decided which of the answers is correct, blacken the corresponding space on the answer sheet. BE SURE THAT EACH MARK IS BLACK AND COMPLETELY FILLS THE ANSWER SPACE. Give only one answer to each question. If you change an answer, be sure that all previous marks are <u>erased completely</u>. Since the answer sheet is machine scored, incomplete erasures may be interpreted as intended answers. ANSWERS RECORDED IN THE TEST BOOK WILL NOT BE SCORED.

There may be more questions noted on this answer sheet than there are questions in a section. Do not be concerned but be certain that the section and number of the question you are answering matches the answer sheet section and question number. Additional answer spaces in any answer sheet section should be left blank. Begin your next section in the number one answer space for that section.

LSAC takes various steps to ensure that answer sheets are returned from test centers in a timely manner for processing. In the unlikely event that an answer sheet(s) is not received, LSAC will permit the examinee to either retest at no additional fee or to receive a refund of his or her LSAT fee. THESE REMEDIES ARE THE EXCLUSIVE REMEDIES AVAILABLE IN THE UNLIKELY EVENT THAT AN ANSWER SHEET IS NOT RECEIVED BY LSAC.

Score Cancellation

Complete this section only if you are absolutely certain you want to cancel your score. A CANCELLATION REQUEST CANNOT BE RESCINDED. IF YOU ARE AT ALL UNCERTAIN, YOU SHOULD NOT COMPLETE THIS SECTION; INSTEAD, YOU SHOULD CONSIDER SUBMITTING A SIGNED SCORE CANCELLATION FORM, WHICH MUST BE RECEIVED AT LSAC WITHIN 9 CALENDAR DAYS OF THE TEST.

To cancel your score from this administration, you **must:**

A. fill in both ovals here ..... ◯ ◯

AND

B. read the following statement. Then sign your name and enter the date.
YOUR SIGNATURE ALONE IS NOT SUFFICIENT FOR SCORE CANCELLATION. BOTH OVALS ABOVE MUST BE FILLED IN FOR SCANNING EQUIPMENT TO RECOGNIZE YOUR REQUEST FOR SCORE CANCELLATION.

I certify that I wish to cancel my test score from this administration. I understand that my request is irreversible and that my score will not be sent to me or to the law schools to which I apply.

_____

Sign your name in full

_____

Date

HOW DID YOU PREPARE FOR THE LSAT?
(Select all that apply.)

Responses to this item are voluntary and will be used for statistical research purposes only.

◯ By studying the sample questions in the *LSAT Registration and Information Book.*
◯ By taking the free sample LSAT in the *LSAT Registration and Information Book.*
◯ By working through *The Official LSAT Prep Test(s) and/or TriplePrep.*
◯ By using a book on how to prepare for the LSAT **not** published by LSAC.
◯ By attending a commercial test preparation or coaching course.
◯ By attending a test preparation or coaching course offered through an undergraduate institution.
◯ Self study.
◯ Other preparation.
◯ No preparation.

CERTIFYING STATEMENT

Please write (DO NOT PRINT) the following statement. Sign and date.

I certify that I am the examinee whose name appears on this answer sheet and that I am here to take the LSAT for the sole purpose of being considered for admission to law school. I further certify that I will neither assist nor receive assistance from any other candidate, and I agree not to copy or retain examination questions or to transmit them in any form to any other person.

_____

_____

_____

_____

_____

_____

_____

_____

_____

_____

SIGNATURE: _____   TODAY'S DATE: ____/____/____
                                                                    MONTH DAY YEAR

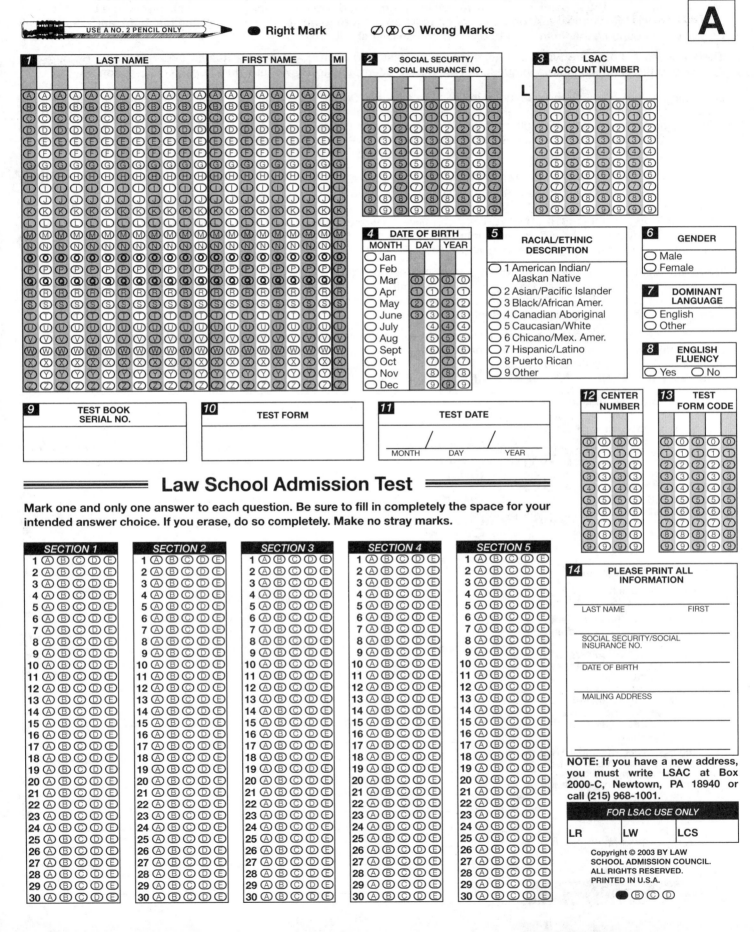

PrepTest B Table of Contents

1

SECTION I

Time—35 minutes

26 Questions

<u>Directions:</u> The questions in this section are based on the reasoning contained in brief statements or passages. For some questions, more than one of the choices could conceivably answer the question. However, you are to choose the <u>best</u> answer; that is, the response that most accurately and completely answers the question. You should not make assumptions that are by commonsense standards implausible, superfluous, or incompatible with the passage. After you have chosen the best answer, blacken the corresponding space on your answer sheet.

Questions 1–2

Tennyson's line of poetry "nature, red in tooth and claw" is misconstrued by many evolutionists as a reference to Darwin's theory of evolution. The poem in which the line appears was published in 1850, but Darwin kept his theory closely held until publishing it in 1859. In addition, in view of the context provided by the rest of the poem, the line was clearly meant to refer to the dominant biological theory of the early nineteenth century, which was a creationist theory.

1. Which one of the following most accurately expresses the main point of the argument?

   (A) The line of Tennyson's poetry cannot now be construed as an apt description of Darwin's theory of evolution.
   (B) The dominant biological theory in the early nineteenth century was a creationist theory.
   (C) Tennyson's line of poetry was written well before Darwin had published his theory of evolution.
   (D) Darwin's theory of evolution was not the dominant biological theory in the early nineteenth century.
   (E) Tennyson's line of poetry was not a reference to Darwin's theory of evolution.

2. The claim about the publication dates of Tennyson's poem and Darwin's theory plays which one of the following roles in the argument?

   (A) It casts doubt on whether the theory of evolution should be attributed to Darwin alone.
   (B) It supports the claim that creationist theories of biology were dominant in the early nineteenth century.
   (C) It provides reason to believe that Tennyson did not know about Darwin's theory when the poem was published.
   (D) It suggests that Tennyson's line provided Darwin with the inspiration for developing his theory.
   (E) It implies that Tennyson knew little about the dominant biological theories of the nineteenth century.

3. Space programs have recently suffered several setbacks with respect to their large projects, and much money has been lost. Consequently, these grand projects should be abandoned in favor of several small ones.

Which one of the following, if true, provides the most support for the reasoning above?

   (A) The cost of starting a space project increases every year.
   (B) It is just as easy to revise, and even scrap, small projects as it is large ones.
   (C) Large projects are intrinsically more likely to fail and so are more financially risky than small projects.
   (D) Project managers prefer to work on small projects rather than large ones.
   (E) Large space projects can explore a few places thoroughly, while small projects can investigate more regions, though less thoroughly.

GO ON TO THE NEXT PAGE.

4. In an experiment testing whether hyperactivity is due to a brain abnormality, the brain activity of 25 hyperactive adults was compared to the brain activity of 25 adults who were not hyperactive. The tests revealed that the hyperactive adults had much less brain activity in the premotor cortex, a region of the brain believed to control action, than did the nonhyperactive adults. The experimenters concluded that diminished activity in the premotor cortex is one cause of hyperactivity.

Which one of the following, if true, most undermines the conclusion drawn by the experimenters?

(A) Some of the nonhyperactive adults in the study had children who suffer from hyperactivity.

(B) The hyperactive adults who participated in the experiment varied in the severity of their symptoms.

(C) The neuropsychologists who designed the experiment were not present when the tests were performed.

(D) All of the hyperactive adults in the study had been treated for hyperactivity with a medication that is known to depress activity in some regions of the brain, while none of the nonhyperactive adults had been so treated.

(E) The test was performed only on adults because even though the method by which the test measured brain activity is harmless to adults, it does require the use of radiation, which could be harmful to children.

5. Large discount chains can make a profit even while offering low prices, because they buy goods in large quantities at favorable cost. This creates a problem for small retailers. If they try to retain their customers by lowering prices to match those of large discount chains, the result is a lower profit margin. But small retailers can retain their customer base without lowering prices if they offer exceptional service. Hence, small retailers that are forced to compete with large discount chains must offer exceptional service in order to retain their level of profitability.

The reasoning is flawed because it fails to take into account the possibility that

(A) not all large discount chains do in fact make a profit

(B) some large discount chains have lower profit margins than do some small retailers

(C) small retailers are often motivated by things other than the desire for profit

(D) not all small retailers are forced to compete with large discount chains

(E) exceptional service is not the only reason customers prefer small retail stores

6. We should do what will make others more virtuous and not do what will make others less virtuous. It is an irony of human existence that praise makes those who are less virtuous more virtuous, while it makes those who are more virtuous less virtuous. And, of course, none except the more virtuous deserve praise.

From the statements above, if true, which one of the following can be properly inferred?

(A) We should withhold praise from those who deserve it least.

(B) We should not fail to praise those who deserve it most.

(C) We should praise those who do not deserve it and withhold praise from those who deserve it.

(D) We should praise everyone, regardless of whether or not they deserve it.

(E) We should withhold praise from everyone, regardless of whether or not they deserve it.

7. Generic drugs contain exactly the same active ingredients as their brand-name counterparts, but usually cost much less to develop, produce, and market. So, generic drugs are just as effective as their brand-name counterparts, but cost considerably less.

Which one of the following, if true, most strengthens the argument?

(A) The ingredients used in the manufacture of brand-name drugs cost no more than the ingredients used to produce their generic counterparts.

(B) Generic drugs are no more likely than brand-name drugs to suffer from defects in composition.

(C) Generic drugs are just as likely as brand-name drugs to be readily available in pharmacies.

(D) The higher costs of brand-name drugs underwrite drug companies' heavy investment in research.

(E) Because of advertising, doctors frequently prescribe brand-name drugs by their brand name, rather than by their chemical name.

GO ON TO THE NEXT PAGE.

8. Economist: In the interaction between producers and consumers, the only obligation that all parties have is to act in the best interests of their own side. And distribution of information about product defects is in the best interests of the consumer. So consumers are always obligated to report product defects they discover, while producers are never obligated to reveal them.

Which one of the following is an assumption required by the economist's argument?

(A) It is never in the best interests of producers for a producer to reveal a product defect.
(B) No one expects producers to act in a manner counter to their own best interests.
(C) Any product defect is likely to be discovered by consumers.
(D) A product defect is more likely to be discovered by a consumer than by a producer.
(E) The best interests of consumers never coincide with the best interests of producers.

9. All potatoes naturally contain solanine, which is poisonous in large quantities. Domesticated potatoes contain only very small amounts of solanine, but many wild potatoes contain poisonous levels of solanine. Since most of the solanine in potatoes is concentrated in the skin, however, peeling wild potatoes makes them at least as safe to eat as unpeeled domesticated potatoes of the same size.

Which one of the following, if assumed, allows the conclusion above to be properly drawn?

(A) The proportion of a potato's solanine that is contained in its skin is larger in wild potatoes than in domesticated potatoes.
(B) The amount of solanine concentrated in the skin of a wild potato is large enough by itself to be poisonous.
(C) There is no more solanine in a peeled wild potato than in an unpeeled domesticated potato of the same size.
(D) There are no poisonous substances in domesticated potatoes other than solanine.
(E) Wild potatoes are generally much smaller than domesticated potatoes.

10. The consequences of surgical errors can be devastating, and no one would want to risk surgery unless it was performed by someone highly competent to perform surgery. General surgeons have special training and expertise that make them extremely competent to perform surgery. Therefore, surgery at the hands of anyone other than a general surgeon involves highly undesirable risks.

The reasoning in the argument is flawed because the argument fails to consider the possibility that

(A) there are general surgeons who are incompetent
(B) general surgeons are not the only doctors competent to perform surgery
(C) the competence of the doctor performing surgery does not guarantee a successful outcome
(D) risk is not the only factor in deciding whether to have surgery
(E) factors in addition to competence are relevant when choosing a doctor

11. Although the concept of free will is essential to that of moral responsibility, its role in determining responsibility is not the same in all situations. We hold criminals morally responsible for the damage they cause, assuming that they freely chose their activities. But we do not hold someone who has a heart attack while driving morally responsible for the damage caused, if any, even when we have good reason to believe that the heart attack could have been prevented by eating different foods and that one's choice of diet is made freely.

The claim that a choice of diet can affect whether or not one has a heart attack plays which one of the following roles in the argument?

(A) It is a subsidiary conclusion of the argument.
(B) It is used to show that we should hold someone morally responsible for damages caused by having a heart attack while driving.
(C) It is cited as evidence that our concept of moral responsibility should be the same in all situations.
(D) It is used to disprove the claim that we should not hold criminals morally responsible for damages.
(E) It is used in support of the conclusion of the argument.

GO ON TO THE NEXT PAGE.

12. Alice will volunteer to work on the hospital fund-raising drive only if her brother Bruce also volunteers and a majority of the others working on the drive promise to select Bruce to manage the drive. However, although Bruce is willing to volunteer, none of the others working on the drive will promise to select Bruce to manage the drive. Thus it is certain that Alice will not volunteer.

In which one of the following arguments is the pattern of reasoning most similar to the pattern of reasoning in the argument above?

(A) Bill and Steve will work together at the bake sale tomorrow only if Bill has enough time. However, since Bill has quite a few errands to run tomorrow, it is likely that Steve will work alone at the sale.

(B) Leon will go to the picnic only if Vera also goes. However, according to his friends Leon does not plan to go to the picnic; so it is certain that Vera is not planning to go.

(C) Jim will go to the party only if both Sam and Elaine also go. Sam is going to the party, but Elaine is not going. So it is certain that Jim will not go to the party.

(D) If Paula works with Elise, then Jane will work with Arthur only. However, if Paula does not work, Elise will also work with Jane. So if Paula does not work, Arthur will work with both Jane and Elise.

(E) Therese will work in the yard tomorrow only if Maria helps her and it is not raining. Although Maria does not like working in the yard, she will help Therese. So unless it rains tomorrow, Therese will certainly work in the yard.

Questions 13–14

If an artist receives a public subsidy to support work on a specific project—e.g., making a film—and if this project then proves successful enough to allow the artist to repay the subsidy, is the artist then morally obliged to do so? The answer is clearly yes, since the money returned to the agency distributing the subsidies will be welcome as a source of support for other artists deserving of public subsidies.

13. The passage tries to establish an artist's obligation by arguing that

(A) this person has benefited from other people's acting in just this way in the past

(B) acting this way would allow others to obtain a benefit such as the one that this artist has obtained in the past

(C) this person had in fact, at an earlier time, made a tacit promise to act this way

(D) not acting this way would be a small benefit to the person in the short term but a substantial detriment to the person in the long run

(E) this person, by acting this way, would provide general benefits with a value exceeding the cost to the person of acting this way

14. Which one of the following principles, if established, most helps to justify the conclusion in the passage?

(A) An artist has a moral duty to urge deserving fellow artists to try to obtain public subsidies, especially if those artists' projects promise to be financially successful.

(B) A financially successful artist should acknowledge that financial success is not solely a function of artistic merit.

(C) A subsidy should be understood as creating a debt that, though routinely forgiven, is rightly forgiven only if either the debtor is unable to repay it or the creditor is not interested in repayment.

(D) The provider of a subsidy should judge as most deserving of subsidies those whose projects are most likely to turn into financial successes.

(E) An artist requesting a subsidy for a potentially profitable project should be required to make a reasonable effort to obtain a bank loan first.

GO ON TO THE NEXT PAGE.

1

1

15. Jessica: The budget surplus should be used only to increase government payments to those who are unemployed.

Marcie: A better use of the money would be for a public works project that would create jobs.

On the basis of their statements, Jessica and Marcie are committed to disagreeing about the truth of which one of the following?

(A) Using the budget surplus to increase government payments to those who are unemployed is putting the money to good use.

(B) The public deserves to have jobs created when there are many people who are unemployed.

(C) When there is a choice between increasing payments to the unemployed and funding a public works project, the latter should usually be chosen.

(D) Creating jobs through a public works project will ultimately benefit the public.

(E) There is a better way to use the budget surplus than increasing government payments to those who are unemployed.

16. In a town containing a tourist attraction, hotel and restaurant revenues each increased more rapidly over the past year than did revenue from the sale of passes to the attraction, which are valid for a full year. This led those in charge of the attraction to hypothesize that visitors were illicitly selling or sharing the passes.

Each of the following, if true, helps to undermine the hypothesis of those in charge of the tourist attraction EXCEPT:

(A) During the past year other tourist attractions have opened up in the area.

(B) Those possessing passes made more frequent trips to the attraction last year than in previous years.

(C) While the cost of passes is unchanged since last year, hotel and meal prices have risen.

(D) The local board of tourism reports that the average length of stay for tourists remained unchanged over the past year.

(E) Each pass contains a photograph of the holder, and during the past year these photographs have usually been checked.

17. The difference between manners and morals is that the former are necessarily social in nature whereas the latter are not necessarily social in nature. So the rules of etiquette do not apply when one is alone.

The statements above, if true, most strongly support which one of the following inferences?

(A) One could be immoral without ever having caused any other person any harm.

(B) No immoral act could be a violation of the rules of etiquette.

(C) The rules of morality apply only when one is alone.

(D) It is more important to be moral than to have good manners.

(E) What is social in nature could not be a matter of morality.

18. Sociologist: The intended function of news is to give us information on which to act. But in a consumer society, news becomes a product to be manufactured and dispensed to the consumer. An enormous industry for the production and consumption of news has evolved, and we ingest news with an insatiable appetite. Under such circumstances, news is primarily entertaining and cannot, therefore, serve its intended function.

Which one of the following is an assumption on which the sociologist's argument depends?

(A) News that serves its intended function should not be entertaining.

(B) Most viewers prefer that news be entertaining.

(C) News has only one important function.

(D) News that primarily entertains does not give us information on which to act.

(E) A news industry that aims to make a profit inevitably presents news as entertainment.

GO ON TO THE NEXT PAGE.

19. Paleontologist: It is widely, but falsely, held that life
    began in the ocean and did not exist on land until
    half a billion years ago. Traces of carbon 14 have
    been found throughout certain 1.2-billion-year-old
    rocks in North America. Carbon 14 is extracted by
    plants and microbes from the atmosphere to fuel
    their chemical reactions, and is then released when
    the plants and microbes die.

Each of the following, if true, provides additional
support for the paleontologist's conclusion EXCEPT:

(A) According to one dating technique, a few fossils
     of plants that lived on land are more than half a
     billion years old.

(B) The severity of conditions in the primordial
     oceans would have made it difficult for life to
     begin there.

(C) Research suggests that some portions of the
     1.2-billion-year-old rocks were at one time
     submerged in water, though other portions
     clearly never were.

(D) The 1.2-billion-year-old rocks were formed from
     soil containing very small amounts of carbon 14
     that entered the soil directly from the
     atmosphere.

(E) Uranium testing has been used to confirm that the
     age of the rocks is 1.2 billion years.

20. The nature of English literature reflects the rich and
    diverse vocabulary of the English language, which
    resulted from the dual influence of the Anglo-Saxon and,
    later, French languages. The French language, though, is
    a direct descendant of Latin, with few traces of the Celtic
    language spoken by the pre-Roman inhabitants of the
    area; the hallmark of French literature is its simplicity
    and clarity.

Which one of the following can be most reasonably
inferred from the information above?

(A) The origin of English played a role in shaping
     English literature.

(B) The vocabulary of the Anglo-Saxon language was
     richer than that of the French language.

(C) The vocabulary of English is larger than the
     vocabulary of French.

(D) Simple and clear literature cannot be written in a
     language with a rich and diverse vocabulary.

(E) English literature and French literature have had
     little influence on one another.

21. Two doctrines have been greatly influential in this
    century. The first holds that the explanation of any
    historical event must appeal to economic factors. The
    second attempts to account psychologically for all
    historical events, especially in terms of early childhood
    experience. Both doctrines, however, are mistaken.
    Certainly there have been events that were due both to
    economic forces and to the nature of the early childhood
    experiences of the major participants in the event.

The argument depends on assuming which one of the
following?

(A) The first doctrine precludes any noneconomic
     factors in explanations of historical events.

(B) The second doctrine places importance only on
     childhood experiences.

(C) Historical events are influenced as much or as
     little by economic factors as by psychological
     factors.

(D) One is likely to find that both economic and
     psychological explanations have been proposed
     for any given historical event.

(E) Appeals to both economic and psychological
     factors are needed to understand any historical
     event properly.

GO ON TO THE NEXT PAGE.

22. Editorial: Supporters of the proposed law that would require bicyclists to wear helmets are seriously misguided. The number of pedestrians who die yearly as a result of accidents involving automobiles is five times the number of deaths resulting from bicycle accidents, and drunken driving exacts a much higher toll than both combined. Yet there are no calls for a ban on alcohol or walking down the street.

Which one of the following exhibits a pattern of flawed reasoning most similar to that in the argument above?

(A)   It is silly to recommend that test pilots give up cigarette smoking. Their risk of death from other causes is so high that it is unlikely they will live long enough to develop lung cancer.

(B)   It is foolish to require lab workers to wear safety goggles when working with acids and other dangerous liquids. No one suggests that people stop eating or socializing, even though more people become ill due to food poisoning and contagious diseases than are injured in laboratory accidents.

(C)   The proposal to introduce foreign language study to students in their first years of school is misguided. Young students should master their own language first and learn basic mathematics before studying a foreign language. No one suggests teaching calculus before arithmetic.

(D)   The recommendation that this company replace the radio communication system in our fleet of trucks with an entirely new system is unwise. Most of our trucks are scheduled to be replaced by the end of next year, so updating the communication system then would be more cost effective.

(E)   The mayor's directive that all city employees be tested for Lyme disease is inefficient. Not one case of the disease has been reported among office workers. The directive should apply only to those employees who work outside and may have been exposed to the ticks that carry the disease.

23. Deep tillage is even more deleterious to the world's topsoil supply than previously believed. For example, farmers who till deeply are ten times more likely to lose topsoil to erosion than are farmers who use no-till methods. Results like these make it clear that farmers who now till deeply should strive, by using other topsoil aeration techniques, to incorporate no-till methods instead.

The argument depends on assuming which one of the following?

(A)   Topsoil erosion does not make farmers want to till more deeply.

(B)   In deep-tillage farming, the deeper one tills, the greater the susceptibility to topsoil erosion.

(C)   Tilling by any method other than deep tillage is not a viable option.

(D)   The most expensive farming methods employ topsoil aeration techniques other than deep tillage.

(E)   On average, topsoil that is no-tilled is more aerated than topsoil that is tilled deeply.

24. Editorial: Our society has a vested interest in maintaining a political system in which candidates are free to adhere to their principles. Yet campaigning for elected office is extremely costly, and because only the wealthiest individuals are able to finance their own political campaigns, most candidates must seek funding from private sources. In so doing, the candidates are almost invariably obliged to compromise their principles. Thus, government itself should assume the cost of candidates' campaigns.

Which one of the following principles, if valid, most helps to justify the conclusion as it is drawn in the argument?

(A)   Candidates should not run for elected office if doing so would compel the candidates to compromise their principles.

(B)   Candidates wealthy enough to finance their own political campaigns should not be permitted to raise additional funds from private sources.

(C)   Voters should not support a candidate if that candidate is known to have accepted funding from private sources.

(D)   The government should finance a given activity if doing so will further a vested interest of society.

(E)   Private funding for political campaigns should be encouraged only if it redresses an imbalance among candidates' financial means.

GO ON TO THE NEXT PAGE.

25. A clothing manufacturer reports that unsalable garments, those found to be defective by inspectors plus those returned by retailers, total 7 percent of the garments produced. Further, it reports that all of its unsalable garments are recycled as scrap, but the percentage of garments reported as recycled scrap is 9 percent.

Which one of the following, if true, could contribute most to explaining the discrepancy between the reported percentages?

(A) Garments with minor blemishes are sent to wholesale outlets for sale at discounted prices and are not returned for recycling.
(B) The percentage of garments returned by retail outlets as unsalable includes, in addition to defective merchandise, garments in unacceptable styles or colors.
(C) Some inspectors, in order to appear more efficient, tend to overreport defects.
(D) The total number of garments produced by the manufacturer has increased slightly over the past year.
(E) Unsalable garments are recorded by count, but recycled garments are recorded by weight.

26. Marion knows that the bridge on her usual route is closed and that, unless she takes the train instead of driving, she can get to work on time only by leaving at least 45 minutes early. She must go to her neighborhood bank before leaving for work, however, and the bank will not be open in time for her to do so if she leaves 45 minutes early. Therefore, since she hates taking the train, Marion cannot avoid being late for work.

The reasoning in the argument is flawed because the argument

(A) mistakes a situation that almost certainly affects many people for one that affects a particular person alone
(B) ignores the fact that people often know that something is the case without considering all the consequences that follow from its being the case
(C) assumes without justification that because people generally have an interest in avoiding a given result, any particular person will have an interest in avoiding that result
(D) treats evidence that someone will adopt a particular course of action as though that evidence excluded the possibility of an alternative course of action
(E) overlooks the possibility that someone might occasionally adopt a given course of action without having a good reason for doing so

S T O P

IF YOU FINISH BEFORE TIME IS CALLED, YOU MAY CHECK YOUR WORK ON THIS SECTION ONLY.
DO NOT WORK ON ANY OTHER SECTION IN THE TEST.

2

SECTION II

Time—35 minutes

24 Questions

Directions: Each group of questions in this section is based on a set of conditions. In answering some of the questions, it may be useful to draw a rough diagram. Choose the response that most accurately and completely answers each question and blacken the corresponding space on your answer sheet.

Questions 1–6

Exactly eight boats—Jewel, Kashmir, Neptune, Ojibwa, Pacific, Spain, Tornado, and Valhalla—arrived at a dock. No boat arrived at the same time as any other boat. The boats arrived in an order consistent with the following conditions:

Tornado arrived before Spain but after Jewel.
Neptune arrived before Tornado.
Kashmir arrived after Jewel but before Spain.
Spain arrived before Ojibwa.

1. If Neptune arrived after Kashmir, which one of the following must be false?

    (A) Jewel was the second of the boats to arrive.
    (B) Kashmir was the fifth of the boats to arrive.
    (C) Neptune was the third of the boats to arrive.
    (D) Ojibwa was the sixth of the boats to arrive.
    (E) Spain was the seventh of the boats to arrive.

2. Which one of the following must be true?

    (A) At least two of the boats arrived before Neptune.
    (B) At least five of the boats arrived before Pacific.
    (C) At least four of the boats arrived before Spain.
    (D) At least three of the boats arrived before Tornado.
    (E) At least two of the boats arrived before Valhalla.

3. Of the eight boats, what is the maximum number that could have arrived before Jewel?

    (A) none
    (B) one
    (C) two
    (D) three
    (E) four

4. Of the eight boats, if Valhalla was the second to arrive, then which one of the following CANNOT be true?

    (A) Jewel was the third to arrive.
    (B) Jewel was the first to arrive.
    (C) Kashmir was the third to arrive.
    (D) Pacific was the third to arrive.
    (E) Tornado was the third to arrive.

5. If Valhalla arrived before Neptune but after Pacific, which one of the following could be true?

    (A) Tornado arrived before Valhalla.
    (B) Kashmir arrived before Pacific.
    (C) Ojibwa was not the last of the boats to arrive.
    (D) Spain arrived before Valhalla.
    (E) Spain was not the seventh of the boats to arrive.

6. Of the boats, what are, respectively, the minimum number and the maximum number that could have arrived before Kashmir?

    (A) one, five
    (B) two, five
    (C) three, five
    (D) one, six
    (E) two, six

GO ON TO THE NEXT PAGE.

Questions 7–12

A park contains at most five of seven kinds of trees—firs, laurels, maples, oaks, pines, spruces, and yews—consistent with the following conditions:

> If maples are in the park, yews are not.
> If firs are in the park, pines are not.
> If yews are not in the park, then either laurels or oaks, but not both, are in the park.
> If it is not the case that the park contains both laurels and oaks, then it contains firs and spruces.

7. Which one of the following could be a complete and accurate list of the kinds of trees in the park?

   (A) firs, maples
   (B) firs, laurels, oaks
   (C) firs, laurels, pines, spruces
   (D) firs, laurels, spruces, yews
   (E) firs, maples, oaks, spruces, yews

8. If neither maples nor spruces are in the park, then which one of the following could be true?

   (A) Exactly four kinds of trees are in the park.
   (B) Exactly five kinds of trees are in the park.
   (C) Laurels are not in the park.
   (D) Oaks are not in the park.
   (E) Yews are not in the park.

9. Which one of the following could be true?

   (A) Neither firs nor laurels are in the park.
   (B) Neither laurels, oaks, nor yews are in the park.
   (C) Neither laurels nor spruces are in the park.
   (D) Neither maples nor yews are in the park.
   (E) Neither oaks nor spruces are in the park.

10. If firs are not in the park, then which one of the following must be true?

    (A) Maples are not in the park.
    (B) Spruces are not in the park.
    (C) Yews are not in the park.
    (D) Pines are in the park.
    (E) Spruces are in the park.

11. If pines are in the park, then which one of the following must be true?

    (A) Exactly four kinds of trees are in the park.
    (B) Exactly five kinds of trees are in the park.
    (C) Neither firs nor maples are in the park.
    (D) Neither firs nor oaks are in the park.
    (E) Neither laurels nor maples are in the park.

12. Each of the following could be an accurate, partial list of the kinds of trees in the park EXCEPT:

    (A) oaks, spruces
    (B) oaks, yews
    (C) firs, laurels, oaks
    (D) firs, maples, oaks
    (E) laurels, maples, oaks

GO ON TO THE NEXT PAGE.

Questions 13–18

Four married couples—Francisco and Gabrielle, Kyoko and Lee, Olivia and Peter, Raymond and Simone—will dine together at the same circular table. Each person will sit in a different one of the eight chairs evenly spaced around the table. The chairs are numbered from 1 through 8 with successively numbered chairs next to each other and chair 1 next to chair 8. Seating arrangements must meet the following conditions:

No person sits next to her or his spouse.
Simone sits in chair 1 and Raymond sits in chair 4.
Neither Peter nor Olivia sits next to Raymond.
Neither Kyoko nor Lee sits next to Gabrielle.

13. Which one of the following could be the list of people sitting in chairs 5 through 8, respectively?

   (A)   Francisco, Olivia, Gabrielle, Peter
   (B)   Francisco, Gabrielle, Peter, Lee
   (C)   Olivia, Gabrielle, Peter, Kyoko
   (D)   Gabrielle, Lee, Olivia, Kyoko
   (E)   Lee, Olivia, Francisco, Kyoko

14. Each of the following could be true EXCEPT:

   (A)   Peter and Gabrielle sit in chairs 2 and 3, respectively.
   (B)   Peter and Kyoko sit in chairs 1 and 3, respectively.
   (C)   Francisco, Kyoko, and Peter sit in chairs 5, 6, and 7, respectively.
   (D)   Gabrielle, Olivia, and Kyoko sit in chairs 5, 6, and 7, respectively.
   (E)   Gabrielle, Peter, and Lee sit in chairs 5, 6, and 7, respectively.

15. If Francisco sits in chair 2 and Olivia sits next to Simone, Gabrielle must sit next to which one of the following persons?

   (A)   Francisco
   (B)   Olivia
   (C)   Lee
   (D)   Raymond
   (E)   Peter

16. If neither Gabrielle nor Lee sits next to Raymond, which one of the following must be true?

   (A)   Francisco sits next to Raymond.
   (B)   Olivia sits next to Simone.
   (C)   Francisco sits in chair 3.
   (D)   Olivia sits in chair 6.
   (E)   Olivia sits in chair 7.

17. If Lee sits in chair 2, which one of the following must be true?

   (A)   Peter sits next to Gabrielle.
   (B)   Kyoko sits next to Simone.
   (C)   Francisco sits next to Lee.
   (D)   Gabrielle sits in chair 5.
   (E)   Olivia sits in chair 6.

18. If both Francisco and Gabrielle sit next to Raymond, which one of the following is a complete and accurate list of people any one of whom could sit next to Olivia?

   (A)   Francisco, Gabrielle, Kyoko
   (B)   Lee, Simone, Kyoko
   (C)   Lee, Gabrielle, Kyoko
   (D)   Francisco, Lee, Gabrielle, Kyoko
   (E)   Lee, Simone, Gabrielle, Kyoko

GO ON TO THE NEXT PAGE.

Questions 19–24

Zeno's Unfinished Furniture sells exactly five types of furniture—footstools, hutches, sideboards, tables, and vanities. Irene buys just four items, each of a different type, and each made entirely of one kind of wood—maple, oak, pine, or rosewood. The following conditions govern Irene's purchases:

Any vanity she buys is maple.
Any rosewood item she buys is a sideboard.
If she buys a vanity, she does not buy a footstool.
If Irene buys a footstool, she also buys a table made of the same wood.
Irene does not buy an oak table.
Exactly two of the items she buys are made of the same kind of wood as each other.

19. Which one of the following could be an accurate list of the items Irene buys?

(A) maple footstool, maple hutch, rosewood sideboard, maple table
(B) oak hutch, rosewood sideboard, pine table, oak vanity
(C) rosewood hutch, maple sideboard, oak table, maple vanity
(D) pine footstool, rosewood sideboard, pine table, maple vanity
(E) maple footstool, pine hutch, oak sideboard, maple table

20. If Irene buys one item made of rosewood and two items made of maple, then which one of the following pairs could be two of the items she buys?

(A) a rosewood sideboard and an oak footstool
(B) an oak hutch and a pine sideboard
(C) an oak hutch and a maple table
(D) a maple sideboard and a maple vanity
(E) a maple hutch and a maple table

21. Which one of the following is a complete and accurate list of all the woods any footstool that Irene buys could be made of?

(A) maple, oak
(B) maple, pine
(C) maple, rosewood
(D) maple, oak, pine
(E) maple, oak, pine, rosewood

22. Suppose Irene buys a footstool. Then which one of the following is a complete and accurate list of items any one of which she could buy in maple?

(A) footstool, hutch, sideboard, table, vanity
(B) footstool, hutch, sideboard, table
(C) footstool, hutch, sideboard
(D) footstool, hutch
(E) footstool

23. Which one of the following CANNOT be the two items Irene buys that are made of the same wood as each other?

(A) footstool, hutch
(B) hutch, sideboard
(C) hutch, table
(D) sideboard, vanity
(E) table, vanity

24. If Irene does not buy an item made of maple, then each of the following must be true EXCEPT:

(A) Irene buys a footstool.
(B) Irene buys a pine hutch.
(C) Irene buys a rosewood sideboard.
(D) Irene buys exactly one item made of oak.
(E) Irene buys exactly two items made of pine.

S T O P

IF YOU FINISH BEFORE TIME IS CALLED, YOU MAY CHECK YOUR WORK ON THIS SECTION ONLY.
DO NOT WORK ON ANY OTHER SECTION IN THE TEST.

SECTION III

Time—35 minutes

26 Questions

Directions: Each passage in this section is followed by a group of questions to be answered on the basis of what is stated or implied in the passage. For some of the questions, more than one of the choices could conceivably answer the question. However, you are to choose the best answer; that is, the response that most accurately and completely answers the question, and blacken the corresponding space on your answer sheet.

Until recently, many biologists believed that invertebrate "schools" were actually transient assemblages, brought together by wind, currents, waves, or common food sources. Jellyfish groupings,
(5) for example, cannot be described as schools—cohesive social units whose members are evenly spaced and face the same way. However, recent research has found numerous cases in which crustaceans and other invertebrates form schools as fish do. Schooling
(10) crustaceans such as krill regularly collect in such massive numbers that they provide abundant food for fish, seabirds, and whales.

Like schooling fish, invertebrates with sufficient mobility to school will swim in positions that are
(15) consistent relative to fellow school members, and are neither directly above nor directly below a neighbor. The internal structure of such a school changes little with external physical disruption but dramatically with the advent of a predator.
(20) Since schooling is an active behavior, researchers assume that it must bring important benefits. True, schooling would appear to make animals more visible and attractive to predators. However, schooling leaves vast tracts of empty water, thereby reducing a
(25) predator's chances of picking up the school's trail. A large group maintains surveillance better than an individual can, and may discourage predation by appearing to be one massive animal. And although an attacking predator may eat some of the invertebrates,
(30) any individual school member has a good probability of escaping.

In addition to conferring passive advantages, schooling permits the use of more active defense mechanisms. When a predator is sighted, the school
(35) compacts, so that a predator's senses may be unable to resolve individuals, or so that the school can execute escape maneuvers, such as freezing to foil predators that hunt by detecting turbulence. If the predator attacks, the school may split, or may employ "flash
(40) expansion"—an explosive acceleration of animals away from the school's center. When large predators threaten the entire school, the school may attempt to avoid detection altogether or to reduce the density of the school at the point of attack; when small predators
(45) threaten the margins, school members may put on dazzling and confusing displays of synchronized swimming.

Schooling may also enable invertebrates to locate food—when one group member finds food, other
(50) members observe its behavior and flock to the food

source. On the other hand, competition within the school for food may be intense: some mysids circle around to the back of the school in order to eat food particles surreptitiously. Schooling can facilitate the
(55) search for mates, but as a school's numbers rise, food may become locally scarce and females may produce smaller clutches of eggs, or adults may start to feed on the young. Thus, circumstances apparently dictate the optimal size of a school; if that size is exceeded, some
(60) of the animals will join another school.

1. Which one of the following best expresses the main idea of the passage?

(A) The optimal size of a school of invertebrates is determined by many different circumstances, but primarily by issues of competition.

(B) The internal structure of a group of invertebrates determines what defensive maneuvers that group can perform.

(C) Although in many respects invertebrate schools behave in the same way that fish schools do, in some respects the two types of schools differ.

(D) Certain invertebrates have been discovered to engage in schooling, a behavior that confers a number of benefits.

(E) Invertebrate schooling is more directed toward avoiding or reducing predation than toward finding food sources.

2. According to the passage, each of the following is characteristic of an invertebrate school EXCEPT:

(A) The number of members in a school is influenced by external circumstances.

(B) A school's members are arranged directly above and below one another.

(C) A school's members arrange themselves so that they all face in the same direction.

(D) The individual members of a school maintain regular spacing from member to member.

(E) Population increase in a school can diminish reproduction by individual school members.

GO ON TO THE NEXT PAGE.

3. If substituted for the word "resolve" in line 36, which one of the following words would convey the same meaning in the context of the passage?

(A) control
(B) answer
(C) reconcile
(D) distinguish
(E) pacify

4. Which one of the following best describes the final paragraph of the passage?

(A) Arguments for opposing points of view are presented and then reconciled.
(B) The disadvantages of certain types of choices are outlined and alternative choices are proposed.
(C) Two different interpretations of a phenomenon are evaluated and one is endorsed as the more plausible.
(D) The disadvantages of an action are enumerated and the validity of that action is called into question.
(E) Advantages and disadvantages of a behavior are discussed and some actions for avoiding the adverse consequences are mentioned.

5. According to the passage, jellyfish are an example of invertebrates that

(A) do not engage in schooling behavior
(B) form groups with evenly spaced members
(C) assemble together only to feed
(D) form schools only when circumstances are advantageous
(E) collect in such large numbers as to provide abundant food

6. It can be inferred from the passage that if cannibalism were occurring in a large school of crustaceans, an individual crustacean encountering the school would

(A) try to stay at the edge of the school in order to obtain food
(B) be more likely to be eaten if it were fully grown
(C) be unlikely to join that particular school
(D) try to follow at the back of the school in order to escape predators
(E) try to confuse school members by executing complex swimming maneuvers

7. Which one of the following, if true, would most clearly undermine the assumption about schooling mentioned in the first sentence of the third paragraph?

(A) Observation reveals that many groups of invertebrates are unable to execute any defensive maneuvers.
(B) Biologists find that some predators can always tell the difference between a school and a single large animal.
(C) Research demonstrates that the less an invertebrate associates with others of its species, the better its chances of survival.
(D) Biologists confirm that predators are more likely to notice a nearby school of invertebrates than to notice a single invertebrate.
(E) Researchers determine that the optimal school sizes for numerous species have each declined in previous years.

GO ON TO THE NEXT PAGE.

Many of us can conceive of penalties that seem disproportionate to the crimes they are intended to
(5) punish. A sentence of probation for a person convicted of a brutal murder is one example of such an imbalance. At the other extreme is a sentence of twenty years in prison for shoplifting. But what is the source of these commonsense intuitions about the appropriateness of punishments?

There are two main rationales for punishing
(10) criminals. The first rationale justifies a punishment in terms of its benefit to society. Society is said to benefit whenever the fear of punishment deters a person from committing a crime, or when a convicted criminal is removed from contact with society at large. The second
(15) rationale is that a punishment is justified by the severity of the crime, independent of any benefit to society. This rationale is controversial because some find it difficult to see how a punishment can be justified if it brings no societal benefit; without such
(20) benefit, punishment would appear to be little more than retribution. But from the retributivist point of view, the question to be asked about punishment is not whether it is beneficial, but whether it is just—that is, appropriate.

One problem with the social-benefit rationale is
(25) that it is possible that very harsh penalties even for minor offenses may have great benefit to society. For example, if shoplifters faced twenty-year jail sentences, shoplifting might be deterred. Yet something leads us to say that in such cases the penalty far outweighs the
(30) crime. That is, there appears to be something intuitively wrong, or unjust, about these punishments. And it would seem that this intuition can only find support in a retributive conception of punishment, under which certain types of punishments are
(35) inherently more appropriate than others. The notion of appropriateness is absent from the first rationale, which could conceivably allow for any sort of punishment as long as it benefits society. Retributive considerations, on the other hand, allow for proportionality between
(40) punishments and crimes. This is what fuels our notion of just (as opposed to beneficial) punishment.

However, it can be argued that our intuition of the injustice of an overly harsh punishment is based on our sense that such a punishment is more harmful to the
(45) criminal than beneficial to society; and, similarly, that our intuition that a punishment is just is based on our sense that this punishment fairly balances societal benefit against harm to the criminal. In this way the second rationale can be seen as grounded in the first
(50) and its retributive nature disappears. Thus it seems that even our so-called intuitive notions of the appropriateness of punishments have their basis in the concept of benefit.

8. Which one of the following most accurately states the main point of the passage?

(A) Of the two main rationales for justifying punishing criminals, the retributivist rationale can be shown to be more fundamental, since our sense of the social benefit of punishments can be explained by our intuitions about justice and injustice.

(B) Although social benefit appears to be a reasonable rationale for punishing criminals, the fact that it can justify very harsh penalties for even minor offenses shows its inadequacy and argues for the alternative retributivist rationale.

(C) Because the retributivist rationale for punishing criminals allows for proportionality between punishments and crimes, it is able to support our intuitions that certain penalties are disproportionate to their crimes in a way that the social-benefit rationale cannot.

(D) Because the rationale that punishment is justified by the severity of the crime amounts to no more than retribution, punishment of a criminal can be justified only if it produces a social benefit that outweighs the harm it brings to the criminal.

(E) Although it appears better able to support our intuitions about just and unjust punishment than the social-benefit rationale, the rationale that punishments ought to fit crimes may, in the end, be itself grounded in the concept of benefit.

GO ON TO THE NEXT PAGE.

9. According to the passage, the second rationale for punishing criminals is controversial because it

 (A) does not employ the notion of social benefit
 (B) allows for disproportionately severe punishments
 (C) conflicts with our intuitions about justice
 (D) implies that punishment does not deter criminals
 (E) arises from intuition rather than logic

10. Based on the passage, the "retributive nature" of the second rationale for punishing criminals (line 50) consists in that rationale's

 (A) equating social benefit with harm to criminals
 (B) regarding punishment as justified by the severity of the crime
 (C) support for sentences disproportionate to the crimes they punish
 (D) belief that any punishment that benefits society is just
 (E) favoring harsher sentences over more lenient ones

11. The author states that our intuition of the injustice of an overly harsh punishment may be based on which one of the following notions?

 (A) Such punishment brings no benefit to society at large.
 (B) Such punishment is potentially harmful to the criminal.
 (C) Such punishment benefits society less than it harms the criminal.
 (D) Such punishment harms the criminal less than it benefits society.
 (E) Such punishment attempts to reconcile social benefit with harm to the criminal.

12. It can be inferred from the passage that the author would be most likely to agree with which one of the following characterizations of the second rationale for punishing criminals?

 (A) It is more widely accepted than the first rationale.
 (B) It does not have the same potential unfairness as the first rationale.
 (C) It justifies more kinds of punishments than the first rationale.
 (D) It is used just in those cases where the first rationale violates our intuitions.
 (E) It inherently allows more lenient punishment than the first rationale.

13. As expressed in the passage, the author's attitude toward very harsh penalties for minor offenses is most accurately described as

 (A) reluctant approval of the deterrence they offer against crime
 (B) mild skepticism that they ultimately benefit society
 (C) detached indifference toward their effects on criminals
 (D) scholarly neutrality on whether they are justified
 (E) implicit disapproval of their moral injustice

14. As described in the second paragraph, the second rationale for punishing criminals is most consistent with which one of the following principles?

 (A) The correctness of an action depends not on its consequences but on its inherent fairness.
 (B) The correctness of an action depends not on its consequences but on what society deems correct.
 (C) The correctness of an action depends partly on its consequences and partly on its inherent fairness.
 (D) The correctness of an action depends partly on its consequences and partly on its intuitive rightness.
 (E) The correctness of an action depends entirely on its consequences.

GO ON TO THE NEXT PAGE.

Despite the great differences among the cultures from which we spring, there is a trait shared by many Hispanic-American writers: the use of a European language, Spanish, transplanted to the Western
(5) hemisphere. This fact has marked our literature profoundly and radically. We Hispanic Americans who write in Spanish have attempted from the beginning to break the ties of dependency that linked us with the literature of Spain. We have pursued this goal of ever-
(10) increasing independence through a twofold movement, seeking to adopt the literary forms and styles in vogue in other European and North American literatures, and endeavoring to describe the nature of the United States and give voice to the Hispanic peoples who live there.
(15) These often conflicting tactics can be described as cosmopolitanism and nativism, respectively.

The opposition between cosmopolitanism and nativism has divided the Hispanic-American literary consciousness for generations. For example, the work
(20) of one Mexican-American novelist was praised by some Hispanic-American critics for its skillful adaptation of European literary techniques but criticized for its paucity of specifically Mexican-American settings or characters. On the other hand, a
(25) Cuban-American novel was admired by other Hispanic-American critics for the vivid portrayal of its characters' daily lives but faulted for its "roughness" of form and language.

Cosmopolitanism is the venturing forth into the
(30) public or mainstream culture; nativism, the return to the private or original culture. There are periods in which the outward-oriented sensibility predominates, and others in which tendencies toward self-absorption and introspection prevail. An example of the former
(35) was the rich period of the avant-garde between 1918 and 1930. This was a time of searching and experimentation, when successive European movements from expressionism to surrealism— movements that were also inspiring other North
(40) American writers—had a profound influence on many Hispanic-American poets and novelists. This phase, which produced a number of outstanding works of exceptional boldness of expression, was followed by another characterized by a return to our peoples and
(45) our colloquial dialects, by the creation of works less indebted to current trends in the mainstream culture. Throughout our history, a concern for novelty and experimentation has been followed by a return to origins.
(50) We contemporary Hispanic-American writers who write in Spanish live somewhere between the European tradition and the reality of the Americas. Our roots may be European, but our horizon is the land and history of the Americas. This is the challenge that we confront
(55) each day: in order to appreciate the value of one's own culture, one must first venture forth into the public sphere; in order not to disappear into the mainstream, one must return to one's origins. In this way, we attempt to reconcile the opposing tendencies of
(60) cosmopolitanism and nativism.

15. Which one of the following statements most accurately expresses the passage's main point?

(A) Although differing in culture, style, and content, the various branches of Hispanic-American literature are linked by their shared use of the Spanish language, a condition that gives them a strong connection to their European heritage.

(B) Many Hispanic-American writers have attempted to separate their literature from that of Spain through a mixture of cosmopolitanism and nativism, conflicting tendencies that alternately dominate Hispanic-American literature.

(C) Many Hispanic-American writers attempt to reconcile the opposing tendencies of cosmopolitanism and nativism by beginning their careers writing European-influenced novels and later switching to works that utilize specifically Hispanic-American settings.

(D) Despite statements by literary critics to the contrary, the cosmopolitanist and nativist tendencies in Hispanic-American literature do not compete with one another for dominance even though they occur concurrently.

(E) If Hispanic-American literature is to achieve its full potential, it must reconcile the conflicting tendencies of cosmopolitanism and nativism that have isolated writers of differing cultures from one another.

16. According to the passage, many of the Hispanic-American literary works produced between 1918 and 1930 were especially notable for their

(A) unusual expressiveness
(B) use of colloquial language
(C) unprecedented reliance on Spanish literary forms
(D) introspective quality
(E) reduced emphasis on current trends in mainstream North American culture

GO ON TO THE NEXT PAGE.

17. According to the passage, the nativist tendency represents an attempt to

    (A) experiment with form and style to illustrate the range of Hispanic-American literary achievement

    (B) adapt the forms and styles of other literatures to the exploration of Hispanic-American themes

    (C) transform the Spanish language into an apt vehicle for any theme

    (D) align Hispanic-American literature with other North American literary movements

    (E) depict the experiences of various Hispanic peoples in U.S. settings

18. It can be inferred from the passage that the Hispanic-American literature written in Spanish in the period immediately following 1930 was most likely characterized by

    (A) narrative experimentation

    (B) expressionistic tendencies

    (C) surreal imagery

    (D) use of mainstream literary forms

    (E) greater naturalness of expression

19. The author of the passage suggests that contemporary Hispanic-American writers who write in Spanish are

    (A) continually confronted by cosmopolitanist and nativist influences

    (B) writing more works in the nativist mode than in the cosmopolitanist mode

    (C) unaffected by the debate between cosmopolitanism and nativism that previous generations experienced

    (D) uncertain whether cosmopolitanism and nativism will help achieve their literary goals

    (E) cleanly and strongly divided into cosmopolitanist and nativist camps

20. Based on the passage, the author's attitude toward nativism in Hispanic-American literature is most likely

    (A) enthusiastic support

    (B) general approval

    (C) reluctant acceptance

    (D) strong skepticism

    (E) clear disapproval

21. The primary purpose of the passage is to

    (A) illustrate a general problem of literature by focusing on a particular culture's literature

    (B) illuminate a point of tension in a particular culture's literature

    (C) summarize the achievements of a particular culture's literature

    (D) provoke a discussion of the political aspect of literature by focusing on a particular culture's literature

    (E) refute a prevailing assumption about the development of a particular culture's literature

GO ON TO THE NEXT PAGE.

In the past, students of Renaissance women's education extolled the unprecedented intellectual liberty and equality available to these women, but recently scholars have presented a different view of

(5) Renaissance education and opportunity for women. Joan Gibson argues that despite more widespread education for privileged classes of women, Renaissance educational reforms also increased restrictions on women. Humanist education in the

(10) Renaissance was based on the classical division of the liberal arts into seven categories, including the three language arts: grammar, dialectic, and rhetoric. Although medieval monastic education, also based on the classical division, had stressed grammar and

(15) languages in preparation for a life devoted to meditation on religious literature, humanist education revived the classical emphasis on rhetoric—the art of persuasive and declamatory speech—in the context of training for public service in legal and political debate.

(20) All students began with elementary study of grammar and progressed to stylistics and literary criticism. But rhetorical training, which was increasingly undertaken only at the university level, could lead in different directions—to study of composition and oral

(25) expression or to study of persuasion, in conjunction with a dialectic concerned with broad principles of logic and argumentation. Male students routinely learned material through rhetorical, argumentative role-playing, and although many Renaissance authors

(30) expressed horror at their aggressive wrangling, such combativeness was thought still less appropriate for women, who were not supposed to need such preparation for public life.

Thus, humanist education for women encompassed

(35) literary grammatical studies in both classical and vernacular languages, while dialectic and rhetoric, the disciplines required for philosophy, politics, and the professions, were prohibited to women. Even princesses lacked instruction in political philosophy or

(40) the exercise of such public virtues as philanthropy. The prevailing attitude was that girls needed only a generalist education conducted in a family setting and directed toward private enjoyment and the eventual teaching of very young children. Unlike either dialectic

(45) or rhetoric, grammar training cast students in the role of an audience, striving to understand authors and teachers. Women were to form an audience, not seek one; for them, instruction in speaking was confined to books of courtesy.

(50) The coupling of expanded linguistic and literary education for women with the lack of available social roles for educated women led to uneasy resolutions: exceptionally learned women were labelled as preternatural or essentially masculine, or were praised

(55) as virtuous only if they were too modest to make their accomplishments public. Some Italian humanist women gave fashionable oratorical performances, but these were ceremonial in nature rather than designed to influence public affairs. Renaissance women educated

(60) along humanist lines did not tend to write works of

philosophy; instead they became most notable for literary achievements, particularly translations, poetry, and tales in the vernacular or correspondence and orations in Latin.

22. Which one of the following best expresses the main idea of the passage?

(A) Although previous scholarship portrayed the Renaissance as a time of expanded education for women, recent scholarship has shown that fewer women received an education during the Renaissance than in medieval times.

(B) The differences in the Renaissance educational curricula for males and females reflected expectations about how the members of each gender would apply their education.

(C) The education of women during the Renaissance did not prepare them for careers in literature, but many of these women managed to contribute noteworthy literary works.

(D) The division of language arts from other liberal arts in the Renaissance reinforced gender-based differences in terms of curriculum.

(E) Even though their respective curricula eventually diverged, males and females in the Renaissance engaged in the same studies during first stages of their educations.

23. Each of the following aspects of Renaissance humanist education is mentioned in the passage EXCEPT:

(A) a method used for rhetorical training
(B) an educational goal
(C) a sequence of subjects that were studied
(D) types of schools for grammar studies
(E) prerequisites for certain careers

GO ON TO THE NEXT PAGE.

24. Which one of the following statements about women's roles during the Renaissance can be inferred from information given in the passage?

   (A)   Women played an important role in providing advanced grammar training despite their lack of access to universities.
   (B)   Women became increasingly acceptable as orators due to the humanists' interest in classical rhetoric.
   (C)   The accepted roles of female students diverged from those of male students at the point when study of stylistics and literary criticism began.
   (D)   The women who were acclaimed as authors were those who managed to study subjects omitted from the usual curriculum for female students.
   (E)   Women who demonstrated intellectual attainment tended to be regarded as anomalies rather than as models for other women.

25. Which one of the following, if true, would most weaken the distinction between training in grammar and training in dialectic and rhetoric that is drawn in lines 44–47 of the passage?

   (A)   Grammar students were encouraged to emulate the compositional techniques used by certain authors and to avoid those of other authors.
   (B)   Students of dialectic and rhetoric were encouraged to debate on set subjects rather than on subjects they themselves proposed.
   (C)   Grammar training had a different place in the sequence of studies followed by male students than in that followed by female students.
   (D)   Grammar training included exercises designed to improve a student's skill at articulating his or her own ideas.
   (E)   Training in dialectic and rhetoric focused more on oral expression than on written expression.

26. Which one of the following situations is most analogous to the one introduced in the second sentence of the passage?

   (A)   As a new segment of the population is registered to vote, the entire election process is undermined by a government that manipulates the results.
   (B)   At the same time that more people become able to afford a certain product, supplies dwindle and the product becomes harder to obtain.
   (C)   Although additional workers are employed in an industry, they are prevented from rising above a certain level.
   (D)   When a new group of players joins in a game, the original participants become more aggressive in response to the increased competition.
   (E)   Even though an increasing number of people are becoming familiar with a new technology, that technology is growing more complicated to master.

S T O P

IF YOU FINISH BEFORE TIME IS CALLED, YOU MAY CHECK YOUR WORK ON THIS SECTION ONLY.
DO NOT WORK ON ANY OTHER SECTION IN THE TEST.

SECTION IV

Time—35 minutes

25 Questions

<u>Directions:</u>   The questions in this section are based on the reasoning contained in brief statements or passages. For some questions, more than one of the choices could conceivably answer the question. However, you are to choose the <u>best</u> answer; that is, the response that most accurately and completely answers the question. You should not make assumptions that are by commonsense standards implausible, superfluous, or incompatible with the passage. After you have chosen the best answer, blacken the corresponding space on your answer sheet.

1. Shortly after Isaac Newton circulated some of his theories of light in 1672, his colleague Robert Hooke claimed that most of those theories were based on Hooke's own work. A modern reader might interpret Newton's famous comment, "if I have seen further it is by standing on the shoulders of giants," as a conciliatory gesture acknowledging indebtedness to Hooke and other contemporary scientists for some of his theories. Conciliatory gestures acknowledging indebtedness were uncharacteristic of Newton, however, and in his day such allusions to "giants" typically referred to the ancient Greeks, not to contemporary scientists.

The statements in the passage, if true, most strongly support which one of the following?

(A) Newton did not intend the quoted comment to be an acknowledgment that his theories of light were largely derived from Hooke's.

(B) Newton did not take credit for any advances that Hooke made in the theory of light.

(C) Newton did not believe that any of Hooke's theories of light were based on those of the ancient Greeks.

(D) Newton intended to credit some contemporary scientists other than Hooke for some of the advances that Newton made in the theory of light.

(E) Newton was not familiar with Hooke's work on the theory of light.

2. The blues is a modern musical form whose lyrics usually address such topics as frustration, anger, oppression, and restlessness. Yet blues musicians claim to find joy in performing, and the musicians and fans alike say that the blues' overall effect is an affirmation of life, love, and hope.

Each of the following, if true, helps to resolve the apparent conflict in the passage EXCEPT:

(A) The sharing of blues music serves to create a cohesive, sympathetic social network.

(B) Blues musicians who do not draw on their personal tragedies are no more successful than blues musicians who do.

(C) The irony and wit found in the blues provide a sense of perspective on life's troubles.

(D) The realization that other people share one's plight is helpful in dealing with life's problems.

(E) The conversion of personal sorrow into an artistic work can have a cathartic effect on artists and their audiences.

GO ON TO THE NEXT PAGE.

3. Nutritionist: A study revealed that although most adults estimated their diets to correspond closely with the recommendations of standard nutritional guidelines, most of their diets did not come close to those recommendations. Both women and men underestimated the amount of fat in their diets and overestimated their intake of most other foods. In most food categories, especially fruits and vegetables, women's diets did not meet the recommendations. Men underestimated their fat intake by half, and though they met the recommendations for breads, they fell short in all other categories.

Which one of the following is most strongly supported by the information offered by the nutritionist?

(A)   Both men and women in the study misjudged their compliance with the nutritional guidelines in every food category.

(B)   In the study, more men than women were aware that in some food categories their diet failed to reflect the recommendations closely.

(C)   Women in the study were more aware than men were of the recommended intake of breads.

(D)   Men in the study estimated their daily intake of fruits and vegetables to be significantly lower than it in fact was.

(E)   Most men in the study did not consume the amounts of fruits and vegetables that the nutritional guidelines recommend.

4. Maude is incessantly engaging in diatribes against people who are materialistic. But her hypocrisy is evinced by the sentimental treatment of the watch her grandmother gave her. She certainly is very fond of the watch—she worries about damaging it; in fact she always sets it carefully in a special box before going to bed.

Which one of the following is an assumption on which the argument depends?

(A)   Possessions that come from relatives are treated with better care than those that do not.

(B)   Sentimental attachment to a single possession indicates being materialistic.

(C)   People who care about material things in general tend to take special care of all their possessions.

(D)   Maude's watch is not the only material thing she especially cares for.

(E)   People who are not materialistic tend to have merely sentimental attachments to things.

5. The most reliable way to detect the presence of life on a planet would be by determining whether or not its atmosphere contains methane. This is because methane completely disappears from a planet's atmosphere through various chemical reactions unless it is constantly replenished by the biological processes of living beings.

Which one of the following statements, if true, most seriously weakens the argument?

(A)   There are other ways of detecting the presence of life on a planet.

(B)   Not all living beings have the ability to biologically produce methane.

(C)   We are incapable at present of analyzing a planet's atmosphere for the presence of methane.

(D)   Some living beings biologically produce only very small amounts of methane.

(E)   Earth is the only planet whose atmosphere is known to contain methane.

GO ON TO THE NEXT PAGE.

4

Questions 6–7

Willett: Lopez and Simmons, a married couple, have both been offered jobs at Evritech Corporation. Because Evritech has a rule against hiring more than one member of the same family, Lopez and Simmons have decided to reveal their marriage to Evritech. Their decision is foolish, however, since it will mean that one of them will have a job offer withdrawn. After all, they could easily keep their marriage secret initially and, if they want, later claim to have married after they were hired: Evritech has no policy of terminating one of two employees who marry each other.

6. The main conclusion of Willett's argument is that

(A) Lopez and Simmons should not both have applied for jobs at Evritech Corporation

(B) Evritech Corporation's rule against hiring more than one member of the same family is often not enforced

(C) Lopez and Simmons would be unwise to reveal their marriage to Evritech Corporation without already having started to work there

(D) Evritech Corporation should be willing to employ two members of the same family if it is willing to retain two of its employees who marry each other

(E) Evritech Corporation is not likely to discover the marital status of Lopez and Simmons if they do not volunteer the information

7. Which one of the following principles, if valid, most helps to support the reasoning in Willett's argument?

(A) Corporations that have rules against hiring more than one member of the same family should also prohibit their employees from marrying one another.

(B) Corporations should adopt a policy of refusing to hire more than one member of the same family if that policy promotes overall fairness in its hiring practices.

(C) Job applicants are no more entitled to withhold information that is requested on application forms than they are entitled to lie on such application forms.

(D) Job candidates should refuse to accept positions in corporations whose personnel policies they cannot adhere to.

(E) Job candidates have no obligation to reveal to a prospective employer personal information such as marital status, regardless of the employer's policies.

8. Linguist: Only if a sentence can be diagrammed is it grammatical. Any grammatical sentence is recognized as grammatical by speakers of its language. Speaker X's sentence can be diagrammed. So, speaker X's sentence will be recognized as grammatical by speakers of its language.

The linguist's reasoning is flawed because it fails to consider the possibility that

(A) most people are unable to diagram sentences correctly

(B) some ungrammatical sentences are diagrammable

(C) all sentences recognized as grammatical can be diagrammed

(D) all grammatical sentences can be diagrammed

(E) some ungrammatical sentences are recognized as ungrammatical

9. To allay public concern about chemicals that are leaking into a river from a chemical company's long-established dump, a company representative said, "Federal law requires that every new chemical be tested for safety before it is put onto the market. This is analogous to the federal law mandating testing of every pharmaceutical substance for safety."

Which one of the following, if true, most seriously weakens the representative's implied argument that the public need not be concerned about the leak?

(A) When pharmaceutical substances are tested for safety pursuant to federal requirements, a delay is imposed on the entry of potentially lifesaving substances onto the market.

(B) Leakage from the dump has occurred in noticeable amounts only in the last few months.

(C) Before the federal law requiring testing of nonpharmaceutical chemicals went into effect recently, there were 40,000 such chemicals being manufactured, many of them dangerous.

(D) The concentration of the chemicals leaking into the river is diluted, first by rainwater and then by the water in the river.

(E) The water in the river is murky because of the runoff of silt from a number of nearby construction projects.

GO ON TO THE NEXT PAGE.

10. In the course of his reading, George Orwell probably encountered certain storytelling conventions over and over again, and these are the devices he would have most likely used in his work. That is why it does not follow that, even though his *1984* resembles other books of its futuristic genre, Orwell read those books; it is possible that he and the other authors were simply drawing on the same body of literary conventions.

Which one of the following most closely illustrates the principle that the passage illustrates?

(A) A novel that is directly influenced by Gothic novels is likely to fall into the Gothic genre.

(B) A mystery novel may not resemble novels from other genres, even though it was directly influenced by such novels.

(C) To direct an effective movie within the cowboy genre, a director must study previously successful cowboy movies.

(D) A recent film that involves car chases, explosions, and clever villains is not necessarily directly influenced by other films of the action genre.

(E) A historical romance novel does not fit into its literary genre unless it employs certain kinds of conventions.

11. On the basis of research with young children, a developmental psychologist hypothesized that the skills involved in copying curves must be developed before the skills involved in copying angles can be developed.

Which one of the following, if true, supports the developmental psychologist's hypothesis?

(A) All of the children who can copy curves can also copy straight lines.

(B) All of the children who can copy angles can also copy curves.

(C) The ability to discriminate angles must be developed before angles can be copied.

(D) Some of the children who cannot copy curves can copy angles.

(E) Young children have the cognitive processes involved in copying angles.

12. Nearly everyone has complained of a mistaken utility bill that cannot easily be corrected or of computer files that cannot readily be retrieved. Yet few people today would tolerate waiting in long lines while clerks search for information that can now be found in seconds, and almost no one who has used a word processor would return to a typewriter.

The information above conforms most closely to which one of the following principles?

(A) The fact that people complain about some consequences of technology cannot be taken as a reliable indication that they would choose to live without it.

(B) If people do not complain about some technology, then it is probably not a significant factor in their daily lives.

(C) The degree to which technologies elicit complaints from people is always an accurate measure of the extent to which people have become dependent on them.

(D) The complaints people make about technological innovations are more reliable evidence of the importance of those innovations than the choices people actually make.

(E) The less willing people are to do without technology the more likely they are to complain about the effects of technology.

13. Television allows us to transmit images of ourselves that propagate into space. The earliest of these transmissions have by now reached all of our neighboring star systems. None of these transmissions, so far as we know, has been recognized; we have yet to receive any messages of extraterrestrial origin. We must conclude that there is no extraterrestrial intelligence in any of our neighboring star systems.

The reasoning in the argument is questionable because the argument

(A) fails to provide an adequate definition of the word "messages"

(B) infers that there is no extraterrestrial intelligence in neighboring star systems from the lack of proof that there is

(C) assigns too little importance to the possibility that there is extraterrestrial intelligence beyond our neighboring star systems

(D) neglects to mention that some governments have sent meticulously prepared messages and recordings on spacecraft

(E) overlooks the immense probability that most star systems are uninhabited

GO ON TO THE NEXT PAGE.

14. Citizen: Our legislators need to act quickly to counter the effects of the recession, especially the present level of unemployment, which is the highest ever. We urgently need a major tax cut for our upper-income citizens. There would then be a correspondingly large increase in investment that would create new jobs. If this measure is not taken, investment will not grow.

The citizen's argument depends on the assumption that

(A)   the recession in the citizen's country is the worst one in its history

(B)   the greater the tax cut given to a group of people, the more likely it is that members of that group will invest the money

(C)   upper-income citizens have invested more money in total than have lower-income citizens

(D)   upper-income citizens would use the money gained from the tax cut in ways that increase investment

(E)   in the past, tax cuts for certain groups of people have tended to create new jobs

15. Ideally, scientific laws should display the virtues of precision and generality, as do the laws of physics. However, because of the nature of their subject matter, laws of social science often have to use terms that are imprecise; for example, one knows only vaguely what is meant by "republicanism" or "class." As for generality, laws that apply only in certain social systems are typically the only ones possible for the social sciences.

Which one of the following statements is most strongly supported by the information above?

(A)   All else being equal, a precise, general scientific law is to be preferred over one that is not general.

(B)   The social sciences would benefit if they redirected their focus to the subject matter of the physical sciences.

(C)   Terms such as "class" should be more precisely formulated by social scientists.

(D)   Social scientists should make an effort to construct more laws that apply to all societies.

(E)   The laws of social science are invariably not truly scientific.

16. The miscarriage of justice in the Barker case was due to the mistaken views held by some of the forensic scientists involved in the case, who believed that they owed allegiance only to the prosecuting lawyers. Justice was thwarted because these forensic scientists failed to provide evidence impartially to both the defense and the prosecution. Hence it is not forensic science in general that should be condemned for this injustice.

Which one of the following, if true, most strengthens the argument?

(A)   Most forensic scientists acknowledge a professional obligation to provide evidence impartially to both the defense and the prosecution.

(B)   The type of injustice that occurred in the Barker case has occurred in other cases as well.

(C)   Most prosecuting lawyers believe that forensic scientists owe a special allegiance to the prosecution.

(D)   Many instances of injustice in court cases are not of the same type as that which occurred in the Barker case.

(E)   Many forensic scientists do not believe that any miscarriage of justice occurred in the Barker case.

17. Everyone who is excessively generous is not levelheaded, and no one who is levelheaded is bold.

Which one of the following is strictly implied by the above?

(A)   Everyone who is excessively generous is not bold.

(B)   Everyone who is not bold is excessively generous.

(C)   No one who is not bold lacks excessive generosity.

(D)   If someone is levelheaded, then that person is neither bold nor excessively generous.

(E)   If someone is not levelheaded, then that person is either bold or excessively generous.

GO ON TO THE NEXT PAGE.

18. In a study in which secondary school students were asked to identify the teachers they liked the best, the teachers most often identified possessed a personality type that constitutes 20 percent of the general public but only 5 percent of teachers. Thus something must discourage the people who would be the best-liked teachers from entering this profession.

Which one of the following, if true, most weakens the argument?

(A) People with the personality type constitute 5 percent of the medical profession.

(B) People with the personality type constitute 5 percent of college students pursuing a degree in education.

(C) Students of teachers with the personality type are intensely recruited for noneducational professions.

(D) Students with the personality type are more likely to be liked by teachers than those with other personality types.

(E) Teachers with the personality type are more likely to quit teaching than those with other personality types.

19. A successful chess-playing computer would prove either that a machine can think or that chess does not involve thinking. In either case the conception of human intelligence would surely change.

The reasoning above is most vulnerable to criticism on the grounds that it does not consider the possibility that

(A) the conception of intelligence is inextricably linked to that of thought

(B) a truly successful chess program may never be invented

(C) computer programs have been successfully applied to games other than chess

(D) a successful chess-playing computer would not model a human approach to chess playing

(E) the inability to play chess has more to do with lack of opportunity than with lack of intelligence

20. James: Chemists have recently invented a new technique for extracting rhodium, an element necessary for manufacturing catalytic converters for automobiles, from nuclear waste. Catalytic converters function to remove noxious gases from automobile exhaust. The use of nuclear power is therefore contributing in at least one way to creating a cleaner environment.

Marta: The technique you mention, though effective, is still at an experimental stage, so there has been no shift in the sources of the rhodium currently used in manufacturing catalytic converters.

Marta responds to James's argument by

(A) casting doubt on the accuracy of the claims made by James in support of his conclusion

(B) questioning the credibility of advocates of nuclear power

(C) indicating that James is assuming the truth of the conclusion that he intends to establish

(D) pointing out a fact that James, in drawing his conclusion, did not take into account

(E) pointing out that James's premises are no more plausible than is his conclusion

21. Ethicist: A person who treats others well is more worthy of praise if this treatment is at least partially motivated by feelings of compassion than if it is entirely motivated by cold and dispassionate concern for moral obligation. This is so despite the fact that a person can choose to do what is morally right but cannot choose to have feelings.

If the ethicist's statements are true, then each of the following could be true EXCEPT:

(A) Only actions that are at least partially the result of a person's feelings should be used in measuring the praiseworthiness of that person.

(B) If a person feels compassion toward the people affected by that person's actions, yet these actions diminish the welfare of those people, that person does not deserve praise.

(C) Only what is subject to a person's choice should be used in measuring the praiseworthiness of that person.

(D) Someone who acts without feelings of compassion toward those affected by the actions is worthy of praise if those actions enhance the welfare of the people affected.

(E) If someone wants to have compassion toward others but does not, that person is worthy of praise.

GO ON TO THE NEXT PAGE.

22. Children fall into three groups—nontasters, regular tasters, and supertasters—depending on how strongly they experience tastes. Supertasters strongly prefer mild cheddar cheese to sharp, regular tasters weakly prefer mild to sharp, and nontasters show no preference. Also, the more bitter a food tastes, the less children like it. Thus, supertasters experience sharp cheddar as tasting more bitter than mild cheddar, but nontasters experience sharp cheddar as tasting no more bitter than mild cheddar.

Which one of the following, if assumed, enables the conclusion above to be properly inferred?

(A) Supertasters like mild cheddar cheese more than do regular tasters.

(B) The age of the child is the most important factor in determining whether that child is a nontaster, a regular taster, or a supertaster.

(C) The sweeter a food tastes, the more children like it.

(D) Bitterness is the only factor relevant to how strongly children prefer sharp cheddar cheese to mild cheddar cheese.

(E) Nontasters tend to like a wider variety of foods than do regular tasters, who in turn like a wider variety of foods than do supertasters.

23. Donna claims to have found the museum's current exhibition of bronzes from Benin less interesting than many of the other exhibitions recently put on by the museum. According to all the critical reviews, however, the Benin exhibition is more interesting than any other exhibition that the museum has put on in years. Therefore, Donna's claim must be false.

Which one of the following arguments contains flawed reasoning that is most similar to the flawed reasoning in the argument above?

(A) Alice claims to have completed her assignment. According to her supervisor, however, the task that Alice was assigned to do has not yet been completed. Alice's claim, therefore, must be false.

(B) Morris claims to have seen the famous fire at the Charles Theater. According to all the news reports, however, that fire took place in 1982 and Morris was out of the country during all of 1982. Morris's claim, therefore, must be false.

(C) Denise claims to have gone to the party only to please Albert. Albert, however, insists that he went to the party only to please Denise. Denise's claim, therefore, must be false.

(D) Loren claims to like the taste of the fish at the Diggin's Diner. However, since according to everyone who knows anything about food, the fish at the Diggin's Diner tastes dreadful, Loren's claim must be false.

(E) Douglas claims to have climbed the tallest mountain in the country. According to the atlas, however, the country contains two other mountains that are taller than the one Douglas climbed. Douglas's claim, therefore, must be false.

GO ON TO THE NEXT PAGE.

24. If an external force intervenes to give members of a community political self-determination, then that political community will almost surely fail to be truly free, since it is during the people's struggle to become free by their own efforts that the political virtues necessary for maintaining freedom have the best chance of arising.

The reasoning above conforms most closely to which one of the following principles?

(A) Political freedom is a virtue that a community can attain through an external force.

(B) Self-determination is not the first political virtue that the members of a community achieve in their struggle to become free.

(C) A community cannot remain free without first having developed certain political virtues.

(D) Political self-determination is required if a community is to remain truly free.

(E) Real freedom should not be imposed on a community by external forces.

25. Some residents of Midville claim that Midville is generally more expensive to live in than nearby towns are, but these people are mistaken. They focus on Midville's relatively high tax rate while ignoring the services paid for by their taxes. Only Midville provides residents with trash removal, rent- and mortgage-assistance programs, and reasonably priced public transportation. In nearby towns individuals pay for their own trash removal, and housing and transportation costs are high in comparison to Midville.

Which one of the following is the main point of the argument?

(A) Midville is generally no more expensive to live in than nearby towns are.

(B) Some of the residents of Midville consider their taxes to be too high.

(C) Services funded by a municipality are generally less expensive than those services would be if privately funded.

(D) Some residents of Midville are unaware of many of the services that Midville provides.

(E) Most of the residents of Midville make use of all of the services the town provides.

S T O P

IF YOU FINISH BEFORE TIME IS CALLED, YOU MAY CHECK YOUR WORK ON THIS SECTION ONLY.
DO NOT WORK ON ANY OTHER SECTION IN THE TEST.

SIGNATURE _____   __/__/__
                                          DATE

LSAT WRITING SAMPLE TOPIC

The principal of a public secondary school has narrowed her choice for a math teacher to two candidates, Asano and Gonzales. Write an argument favoring one candidate over the other based on the following considerations:

• The school is seeking a teacher who can develop a math program that effectively integrates the curriculum with a work-study project with local businesses.

• The school wants to improve its math program, mainly by greatly expanding the program's use of computers.

Gonzales attended an internationally recognized research institution, where he received a bachelor's degree in math education and a master's degree in economics. He was a teaching assistant in graduate school but has not taught full time. For the first three years after earning his master's degree, Gonzales was assistant budget director at a book publisher. For the last ten years, he has been a financial analyst at a local securities brokerage, where he also directs computer training for new staff. He has been promoted several times while at the brokerage but now finds the pressure and competitiveness increasingly unrewarding. A few years ago he was a volunteer tutor in a community outreach program designed to decrease math anxiety. He found this stimulating as well as fulfilling and has decided to teach full time.

Asano earned a bachelor's degree in math from a local university and a master's degree in education from a prestigious program at a large university. He was a teaching assistant in graduate school and has taught secondary school for six years. In the three schools in which he has taught, he was widely regarded, by both students and colleagues, as a good teacher and an effective leader of diverse extracurricular activities. In their letters of reference, the principals of each of the three schools praised his competence and dedication to teaching. Asano left each of his previous teaching jobs seeking increased professional opportunities. At his most recent job, he was the chairperson of a math department with five full-time teachers. He has recently completed a six-semester series of courses entitled "Computers in Education."

Directions:

1. Use the Answer Key on the next page to check your answers.

2. Use the Scoring Worksheet below to compute your raw score.

3. Use the Score Conversion Chart to convert your raw score into the 120-180 scale.

Scoring Worksheet

1. Enter the number of questions you answered correctly in each section.

	Number Correct
Section I	_____
Section II	_____
Section III	_____
Section IV	_____

2. Enter the sum here: _____
   This is your Raw Score.

Conversion Chart
For Converting Raw Score to the 120-180 LSAT Scaled Score
LSAT Form 9LSS42

Reported Score	Raw Score Lowest	Raw Score Highest
180	97	101
179	96	96
178	95	95
177	94	94
176	93	93
175	92	92
174	91	91
173	90	90
172	89	89
171	87	88
170	86	86
169	85	85
168	84	84
167	82	83
166	81	81
165	79	80
164	78	78
163	76	77
162	75	75
161	73	74
160	72	72
159	70	71
158	69	69
157	67	68
156	65	66
155	64	64
154	62	63
153	61	61
152	59	60
151	57	58
150	56	56
149	54	55
148	52	53
147	51	51
146	49	50
145	47	48
144	46	46
143	44	45
142	43	43
141	41	42
140	39	40
139	38	38
138	36	37
137	35	35
136	33	34
135	32	32
134	31	31
133	29	30
132	28	28
131	27	27
130	25	26
129	24	24
128	23	23
127	22	22
126	21	21
125	20	20
124	19	19
123	18	18
122	16	17
121	--*	--*
120	0	15

* There is no raw score that will produce this scaled score for this form

SECTION I

1. E	8. A	15. E	22. B
2. C	9. C	16. D	23. C
3. C	10. B	17. A	24. D
4. D	11. E	18. D	25. E
5. E	12. C	19. D	26. D
6. C	13. B	20. A	
7. B	14. C	21. A	

SECTION II

1. B	8. A	15. E	22. B
2. C	9. D	16. A	23. A
3. D	10. A	17. C	24. B
4. E	11. C	18. E	
5. B	12. E	19. E	
6. A	13. E	20. C	
7. D	14. B	21. B	

SECTION III

1. D	8. E	15. B	22. B
2. B	9. A	16. A	23. D
3. D	10. B	17. E	24. E
4. E	11. C	18. E	25. D
5. A	12. B	19. A	26. C
6. C	13. E	20. B	
7. C	14. A	21. B	

SECTION IV

1. A	8. B	15. A	22. D
2. B	9. C	16. A	23. D
3. E	10. D	17. D	24. C
4. B	11. B	18. E	25. A
5. B	12. A	19. D	
6. C	13. B	20. D	
7. E	14. D	21. C	

Questions 1–2

Overview: The argument begins by stating the position that it is arguing for: a claim about a line of poetry being misconstrued. This is followed by two separate lines of reasoning in support of that claim.

Question 1

The Correct Answer:

E The main point of the argument is what the two lines of support are presented to establish—specifically, that the construal of Tennyson's line of poetry as a reference to Darwin's theory of evolution is wrong. So (E) accurately expresses the main point of the argument.

The Incorrect Answer Choices:

A The question of how appropriate Tennyson's line is as a description of Darwin's theory is not even addressed in the argument, so (A) could not be an accurate expression of the argument's main point.

B (B) is part of a line of reasoning advanced in support of the position being argued for. Thus (B) plays a role in establishing the main point of the argument, but it does not express that main point.

C, D (C) is an unstated intermediate conclusion in one line of support for the position being argued for. (D) is part of the other line of support. Thus (C) and (D) each play a role in establishing the main point of the argument, but neither expresses that main point.

- *Difficulty Level: 1*

Question 2

The Correct Answer:

C One line of reasoning in the argument works by trying to show that Tennyson's line of poetry did not refer to Darwin's theory because Tennyson could not have known about Darwin's theory. The claim about the publication dates of Tennyson's poem and Darwin's theory is a crucial part of this reasoning. Thus, (C) accurately describes the role this claim plays in the argument.

The Incorrect Answer Choices:

A The claim about publication dates establishes that Tennyson's poem was published before Darwin's theory. However, there is no reason to infer from this that Tennyson, or anyone other than Darwin, was at all responsible for the theory of evolution. So (A) does not describe the role that the claim about publication dates plays.

B The claim that the dominant theory of biology in the early nineteenth century was a creationist theory is simply asserted in the argument. No support is offered for the truth of that assertion. Thus, not only does the claim about publication dates not play the role described in (B), nothing else does either.

D The claim about publication dates, which establishes that Tennyson's poem was published before Darwin's theory, does not rule out Darwin's theory having been inspired by Tennyson's poem, but the claim about the dates also does nothing to suggest that this was the case.

E The argument never makes a connection between the publication dates and Tennyson's knowledge of the dominant biological theories of the nineteenth century. So the claim about publication dates doesn't play the role described by (E).

- *Difficulty Level: 1*

Question 3

Overview: The conclusion of the argument is a recommendation: large space-program projects should be abandoned in favor of several smaller projects. The only reason given for this recommendation is that recently large projects have suffered setbacks resulting in the loss of much money.

As it stands, this is a very weak argument. It is true that less money is at risk with an individual small project compared to a large project. But notice that there actually isn't any evidence offered that less money would be lost overall if several small projects were funded instead of one large one. Nor does the argument give any reason to think that the recent setbacks suffered by large projects are a good indication of how large projects typically fare.

The Correct Answer:

C   (C) addresses both of the argument's shortcomings mentioned above. It states that large projects are intrinsically more likely to fail than small ones, which provides evidence that the recent setbacks suffered by large projects are not anomalous. Also, it states that large projects are financially riskier than small ones, supporting the claim that less money would be lost overall if several small projects were funded rather than one large one. So (C) strengthens the argument.

The Incorrect Answer Choices:

A   (A) tells us that the amount of money at risk in space projects is increasing. But it says nothing to suggest that this is less of a problem with small projects than with large ones. So (A) does nothing to strengthen the argument.

B   (B) says that small projects and large projects are about equal in terms of how easy it is to revise or scrap them. Since (B) talks only about a respect in which small projects are the same as large ones, it provides no support for the argument's conclusion that small projects should be favored over large ones.

D   Project managers might prefer to work on small projects rather than large ones for reasons that have nothing to do with their likelihood of success. Without knowing the reason for the project managers' preference, the mere fact that they have such a preference does not strengthen the argument.

E   The argument says nothing about whether it is better for space programs to explore a few places thoroughly or to explore more places less thoroughly. Therefore, the information provided in (E) does not tell us whether small or large projects better serve the objectives of the space program.

■ *Difficulty Level: 1*

Question 4

Overview: This passage recounts an experiment and the conclusion drawn by the experimenters. The experiment showed that, compared to nonhyperactive adults, hyperactive adults had much less brain activity in a region of the brain believed to control action. The experimenters concluded that this abnormality in the brains of hyperactive adults is one cause of hyperactivity.

The question asks what would undermine this conclusion. The only thing the experiment firmly establishes is a correlation between hyperactivity and diminished activity in a certain region of the brain. The experimenters' conclusion is one possible explanation for that correlation. So anything that points to an alternative explanation of the observed correlation would undermine the experimenters' conclusion.

The Correct Answer:

D (D) tells us that the differences in brain activity found in the experiment could well have been caused by the medication taken by the hyperactive adults but not by the nonhyperactive adults. So (D) points to an explanation of the experimental results that gives us a clear alternative to the conclusion that the experimenters reached.

The Incorrect Answer Choices:

A The experimenters' conclusion was based on tests performed on hyperactive and nonhyperactive adults. Information about the children of any of these adults has no bearing on what can be concluded from those tests.

B Variation in the severity of symptoms of hyperactivity would be expected in any random sample of hyperactive people. (B) gives us no reason to think that the experimenters had any difficulty in clearly distinguishing between adults who were hyperactive and those who were not. So (B) does nothing to challenge the experiment and thus does nothing to undermine the conclusion based on it.

C As long as an experiment was competently carried out, it makes no difference to the outcome whether the people who actually designed the experiment were present or not. (C) provides no reason to think that the experiment was not competently carried out. Thus (C) does nothing to undermine the conclusion based on the outcome of that experiment.

E (E) explains why the experimental subjects were all adults. It does not call into question the reliability of the results obtained by the experiment. Nor does it challenge the conclusion based on those results.

- *Difficulty Level: 1*

Question 5

Overview: The argument concludes that small retailers competing with large discount chains cannot retain their level of profitability unless they offer exceptional service. This conclusion is based on two considerations: first, that lowering prices in order to retain customers will result in lower profits, and second, that customers can be retained without lowering prices if exceptional service is offered.

The question tells you that this argument is flawed because there is a possibility that it fails to take into account.

The Correct Answer:

E   The argument tells us about a strategy for dealing with competition from large discount chains—offering exceptional service—that will enable small retailers to retain both customers and profitability. From this the argument concludes that unless exceptional service is offered, profitability will not be retained. But to legitimately draw this conclusion, the argument would have had to establish that there is no other strategy that would enable retailers to retain both customers and profitability. Since the argument fails to do this, as (E) points out, the argument's reasoning is flawed.

The Incorrect Answer Choices:

A   Large discount chains that do not make a profit will presumably not continue in business indefinitely. But that has no bearing on the difficulty faced by small retailers who are competing with such discount chains while those chains are in business. So overlooking (A) is not a flaw in the argument.

B   According to the argument, the problem that large discount chains pose for small retailers is that the large chains can offer low prices. In proposing a strategy for dealing with this problem, the argument need not concern itself with how the profits of large discount chains compare with those of small retailers. So not taking the possibility of (B) into account is not a flaw in the reasoning.

C   The argument is concerned only with what small retailers must do in order to retain their level of profitability. Whether or not there are small retailers who are not, or not solely, motivated by the desire for profit is irrelevant to the argument. So the argument is not flawed because it overlooks the possibility that (C) is true.

D   The argument is concerned only with small retailers who are forced to compete with large discount chains. Thus, the possibility of (D) is not something that the argument needs to take into account.

- *Difficulty Level: 3*

Question 6

Overview: Here you are presented with a number of statements and asked what can be properly inferred from them. The first statement is a general moral principle, namely that we should do whatever makes others more virtuous and we should not do anything that makes others less virtuous. Then you are told of the effects that praise has on people: it makes people who are not so virtuous more virtuous, and it makes highly virtuous people less virtuous. The passage finally presents another statement that amounts to saying that the highly virtuous deserve praise and the not-so-virtuous do not.

The Correct Answer:

C The moral principle together with the statement about the effects of praise imply that we should praise the not-so-virtuous and should not praise those who are highly virtuous. When we combine this with the statement about who deserves praise, we can draw the surprising conclusion that we should not praise those who actually deserve praise but should instead praise those who don't deserve praise. So (C) can be properly inferred from the statements in the passage.

The Incorrect Answer Choices:

A The passage implies that those who don't deserve praise should be praised. Thus (A) runs counter to what can be inferred from the passage.

B The passage implies that those who deserve praise should not be praised. Thus (B) runs counter to what can be inferred from the passage.

D, E (D) and (E) both say that we should extend praise equally to those who deserve praise and those who do not deserve praise. This is in sharp contrast to what can be inferred from the passage.

- *Difficulty Level: 4*

Question 7

Overview: The conclusion of this argument has two parts: (1) that generic drugs are just as effective as their brand-name counterparts and (2) that generic drugs cost less than their brand-name counterparts. Separate evidence is provided for each part of the conclusion. The evidence for (1) is that generic drugs contain exactly the same active ingredients as their brand-name counterparts. The evidence for (2) is that generic drugs are less expensive to develop, produce, and market. So any additional information that strengthens either side of this two-pronged argument would strengthen the argument as a whole.

The Correct Answer:

B The evidence for part (1) of the conclusion is that generic drugs contain exactly the same active ingredients as their brand-name counterparts. But the effectiveness of a drug depends not only on its having certain active ingredients but also on the drug being correctly manufactured so that it has the right composition. (B) tells us that generic drugs are no more likely to be defective in their composition than brand-name drugs are, thereby strengthening the argument for part (1) of the conclusion.

The Incorrect Answer Choices:

A We already know that generic drugs contain the same active ingredients as their brand-name counterparts. So the fact that the ingredients used in the manufacture of brand-name drugs are no more expensive than those used in the manufacture of generic drugs provides no additional evidence concerning the effectiveness of generic drugs. And (A) clearly does not add support for the conclusion that generic drugs cost less than their brand-name counterparts.

C (C) establishes that generic drugs are as easy to obtain in pharmacies as brand-name drugs. Though this ready availability might make generics more convenient for consumers to obtain, it provides no additional support for either the effectiveness or the lower cost of generic drugs as compared to their brand-name counterparts.

D Part of the evidence the argument gives for brand-name drugs costing more is that they cost much more to develop. (D) just provides details about this greater development cost. So (D) provides no additional support for the conclusion that brand-name drugs are more expensive.

E If (E) is true, it indicates one way in which advertising helps brand-name drugs compete against generic drugs. But it doesn't address the issues of effectiveness or cost, so (E) does not provide any additional support for the argument's conclusion.

■ *Difficulty Level: 4*

Question 8

Overview: The conclusion of the economist's argument is that consumers are always obligated to reveal product defects and producers are never obligated to reveal product defects. The grounds on which this conclusion is based are twofold. The first is a general principle according to which producers' and consumers' only obligation is to act in the best interests of their own side. The second is the claim that distribution of information about product defects is in the best interests of consumers. Strictly speaking, this last point supports only the part of the conclusion that deals with the obligation of consumers to distribute information about product defects.

The Correct Answer:

A Suppose that (A) were false, and that it is sometimes in the best interests of a producer to reveal a product defect. Then, according to the general principle cited by the economist, producers would have an obligation to reveal that product defect. So if (A) were false, part of the economist's conclusion would be false. This shows that (A) is an assumption required by the argument.

The Incorrect Answer Choices:

B The economist's argument is based on a principle about what producers are obligated to do, not about what people expect or don't expect producers to do. So (B) is not an assumption required by the argument.

C, D The conclusion drawn is not about who is likely to discover a defect or whether most defects are even likely to be discovered. It is about consumers' and producers' obligations **when** they discover a product defect. So either (C) or (D) could be false without affecting the argument.

E The economist's argument focuses on the issues of what is in the best interests of producers and consumers regarding the reporting of product defects. So if (E) is false only because the best interests of consumers and producers do coincide with respect to some other issue—for example, lowering sales taxes—the economist's argument would not be affected. So (E) is not an assumption required by the argument.

■ *Difficulty Level: 4*

Question 9

Overview: The conclusion of this argument is that peeling wild potatoes makes them at least as safe to eat as unpeeled domesticated potatoes of the same size. This conclusion is supported by three premises: (1) Domesticated potatoes—which we know are not poisonous—contain very small amounts of solanine. (2) Many wild potatoes contain poisonous levels of solanine. (3) Most of the solanine in potatoes is concentrated in the skin.

The Correct Answer:

C We know from the passage that solanine, at poisonous levels, is what makes unpeeled wild potatoes unsafe to eat. Thus if there is no more solanine in a peeled wild potato than in an unpeeled domesticated potato of the same size, then a peeled wild potato is just as safe as an unpeeled domesticated potato of the same size. So if (C) is assumed, the conclusion can be properly drawn.

The Incorrect Answer Choices:

A The passage does not give specific information about how much of the solanine in potatoes is located in the skin; it merely says that most of the solanine is concentrated in the skin. So (A) doesn't tell us much more than we already know regarding how much of a wild potato's solanine is in its skin. Thus (A) doesn't give us enough information to conclude that peeling a wild potato will make it as safe as an unpeeled domesticated potato.

B Wild potatoes may contain so much solanine that even if the amount in the skin is large enough by itself to be poisonous, the amount of solanine in the rest of the potato could also be large enough by itself to be poisonous. So assuming (B) does not enable us to properly draw the conclusion.

D Assuming that solanine is the only poisonous substance in domesticated potatoes would not help establish the argument's conclusion. As long as wild potatoes also contain no poisonous substance other than solanine, then the conclusion can be properly drawn if it is established that peeled wild potatoes contain no more solanine than unpeeled domesticated potatoes. But that latter claim has not been established by the argument stated in the passage, and (D) does nothing to help establish it.

E The conclusion drawn is about the relative safety of wild and domesticated potatoes **of the same size**. Thus no assumption about the relative sizes of wild potatoes and domesticated potatoes is relevant to the argument.

■ *Difficulty Level: 3*

Question 10

Overview: This argument rests on two claims: (1) if surgery is not performed by someone extremely competent to perform surgery, then it involves undesirable risks; and (2) general surgeons have training and expertise that makes them extremely competent to perform surgery. The conclusion drawn on the basis of these two premises is that any surgery performed by someone other than a general surgeon involves undesirable risks.

The question tells you that the reasoning in this argument is flawed because there is a possibility that the argument fails to consider.

The Correct Answer:

B Claim (1) would allow the conclusion to be properly drawn if we knew that the only people who are extremely competent to perform surgery are general surgeons. Claim (2), however, does not tell us this. It tells us that general surgeons are extremely competent to perform surgery, but it does not tell us that there aren't other people who are also extremely competent to perform surgery. Claim (2) leaves open the possibility that specialist surgeons, for example, are also extremely competent to perform surgery. And unless we know that they are not, the conclusion cannot legitimately be drawn.

The Incorrect Answer Choices:

A The conclusion of the argument is that having surgery performed by someone who is not a general surgeon involves highly undesirable risks. It doesn't say that surgery conducted by a general surgeon never involves highly undesirable risks. So the possibility that there are general surgeons who are incompetent does not challenge the conclusion actually presented, and failing to consider this possibility is thus not a flaw in the argument.

C The conclusion drawn is that surgery performed by someone other than a general surgeon involves undesirable risks. The conclusion is not that surgery performed by a general surgeon will guarantee a successful outcome. So the possibility that (C) is true is not relevant to the argument's reasoning.

D The conclusion drawn concerns the risks involved in surgery. It is not a flaw in the **reasoning** in the argument—how well its premises support its stated conclusion—that it does not consider other issues that might be important in making decisions about surgery.

E   The argument concludes that choosing anyone other than a general surgeon involves highly undesirable risks. So the argument is concerned only with categories of doctors. The argument is not concerned with how to decide which particular surgeon should perform a particular operation. So the factors involved in that decision are not relevant to the argument.

- *Difficulty Level: 3*

Question 11

Overview: This question asks you to identify the role played in the argument by a claim about the connection between diet and heart attacks. To answer the question, you have to understand how the argument goes.

The main conclusion of the argument is presented in the first sentence. It is that the role of free will in determining moral responsibility is not the same in all situations. In support of this position, two contrasting cases are presented. In each of these cases, freely chosen actions ultimately lead to damage. But in only one of the cases does the fact that these actions were freely chosen incline us to hold the person morally responsible for the damage. The two cases support the conclusion of the argument because they are **alike** in involving freely chosen actions but **unlike** in the judgments we make about the moral responsibility of those who freely chose to act in a way that resulted in damage.

The Correct Answer:

E   The claim that a choice of diet can affect whether or not one has a heart attack combined with the claim that the choice of diet is made freely is used to establish that the second case is one in which freely chosen actions result in damage. Thus its role is to show that the two cases are alike with respect to damage resulting from the exercise of free will. This ultimately supports the conclusion of the argument, as outlined in the "Overview."

The Incorrect Answer Choices:

A   The claim that the heart attack could have been prevented by eating different foods is asserted without any support being offered for it. Thus it is not a subsidiary conclusion of the argument.

B   The argument does not attempt to show that we should hold someone morally responsible for damages caused by having a heart attack while driving. So the claim is not used in the way described by (B).

C   The argument tries to establish that our actual concept of moral responsibility assigns different roles to the concept of free will in different situations. The argument does not try to establish that our concept of moral responsibility should be the same in all situations. So the claim in question cannot be used as evidence that our concept of moral responsibility should be the same in all situations.

D The argument never tries to disprove the claim mentioned in (D)—that we should not hold criminals morally responsible for damages. The argument simply takes it for granted that we do hold criminals morally responsible for the damages they cause. So the claim mentioned in the question could not be doing what (D) indicates.

- *Difficulty Level: 4*

Question 12

Overview: The structure of the argument in the passage is as follows: Someone (Alice) will act in a certain way only if both of two conditions are satisfied. We are told that one of those conditions will be satisfied but the other will not. So it is concluded that the person (Alice) will not act in that way. In this argument the conclusion is guaranteed by the reasons given in support of it.

To answer the question you need to identify the answer choice that presents an argument with the same structure.

The Correct Answer:

C In this argument, someone (Jim) will act in a certain way (go to the party) only if both of two conditions are satisfied: Sam goes to the party and Elaine goes to the party. One of those conditions is satisfied (Sam will go), but the other is not (Elaine will not go). And it is concluded that the person (Jim) will not act in that way (go to the party). Thus the structure of the argument in (C) is the same as that in the argument in the passage. Note also that in the argument in (C), just as in the argument in the passage, the conclusion of this argument is guaranteed by the reasons offered in its support.

The Incorrect Answer Choices:

A In this argument, two people (Bill and Steve) will act in a certain way (work together) only if a condition about Bill is satisfied. That condition is unlikely to be satisfied. So it is concluded that it is unlikely that the two people will act in that way. This argument differs from the argument in the passage in several ways. Only one condition is involved (Bill having enough time). It is only unlikely that the condition won't be satisfied, not certain, as in the argument in the passage. And the conclusion is about what is likely to happen, not about what is certain to happen. So this argument is less similar in structure to the argument in the passage than the argument in (C) is.

B Here we are told to expect a certain outcome (Leon will go to the picnic) only if a condition is met. But rather than offering evidence about whether the condition will be met, this argument offers evidence about whether the outcome will occur. The conclusion is about whether the condition will be met. Thus, the structure of this argument is unlike the structure of the argument in the passage. Moreover, this argument, unlike the argument in the passage, is flawed in its reasoning: its conclusion is not guaranteed by the reasons offered in its support.

D This argument, like the argument in the passage, presents two conditions. But it differs from the argument in the passage in many respects. For one thing, in the argument in the passage both of the conditions have to be satisfied in order for someone to act in a certain way. But in the argument in (D), each of the conditions is a condition for a different action, that is, one is a condition for Jane working with Arthur only, and the other is a condition for Jane working with Elise and Arthur. Also, the argument in (D) has a conditional conclusion; it concludes that a certain outcome will occur (Arthur will work with Jane and Elise) **if** a condition holds (Paula does not work).

E Here someone (Therese) will act in a certain way (work in the yard) only if two conditions are satisfied. One of those conditions (Maria helping) is satisfied. Then it is concluded that if the other condition is also satisfied (no rain), Therese will work in the yard. The structure of this argument differs importantly from that of the argument in the passage. One difference is that this argument has a conditional conclusion; it concludes that someone will act in a certain way **if** a condition is satisfied, whereas the conclusion of the argument in the passage does not contain any such condition. Another difference is that the reasoning in this argument is flawed. Suppose Therese wakes up with a headache. In that case, even if it isn't raining and Maria is willing to help (that is, even if both of the necessary conditions are satisfied), Therese might decide not to work in the yard. So in this argument the conclusion is not guaranteed by the reasons offered in its support.

- *Difficulty Level: 3*

Questions 13–14

Overview: This passage presents an argument for a certain position—that an artist who receives a public subsidy to support a project is morally obliged to repay that subsidy if the project proves successful enough to make repayment possible. The grounds offered in support are that the granting agency would welcome the repayment because it would provide a source of support for other deserving artists.

Question 13

This question asks how the passage tries to establish its position. That is, you are being asked to select the answer choice that best characterizes the support offered for that position.

The Correct Answer:

B The support offered is that repaying the subsidy would mean that other artists deserving of public subsidies would also be funded. Thus, as (B) correctly indicates, the passage argues that an artist has an obligation to repay the subsidy that supported a financially successful project because doing so would allow others to obtain a similar benefit.

The Incorrect Answer Choices:

A The passage presents no evidence that the source of the successful artist's subsidy was the repayment of a subsidy by a previous artist. So (A) does not correctly describe anything argued for in the passage.

C The passage says nothing about any promise—tacit or otherwise—made by the artist to repay the subsidy.

D, E Nothing in the passage bears on the issue of how any costs of repaying—or not repaying—compare with any benefits of doing so. So neither (D) nor (E) describes anything that goes on in the passage.

- *Difficulty Level: 1*

Question 14

For this question you are asked to select the principle that does the most to justify the position for which the passage argues. That is, you need to figure out which of the five principles, together with the grounds offered in the passage, would produce the strongest argument for that position.

The Correct Answer:

C The principle in (C) says that, with only two exceptions, subsidies should always be repaid. The two exceptions are: the person who received the subsidy can't afford to repay it or the granting agency isn't interested in being repaid. The artist under discussion in the passage can afford to repay the subsidy. And we are told that the subsidy-granting agency would welcome the repayment. So according to this principle, an artist who receives a public subsidy to support a project that ends up being financially successful is morally obligated to repay that subsidy.

The Incorrect Answer Choices:

A The passage neither says nor implies anything about whether an artist should urge other artists to try to obtain public subsidies. Thus there is nothing in the passage that the principle in (A) could help to justify.

B The passage is about artists' obligation to repay subsidies that funded projects that turned out to be financially successful. The passage is not concerned with how successful artists view their success. So the principle in (B) does not engage a concern that plays a role in the argument.

D, E The passage is not concerned with what providers of subsidies should do or with conditions that should be placed on artists seeking subsidies. Therefore, neither (D) nor (E) provides any support for the position that the passage is trying to justify.

- *Difficulty Level: 3*

Question 15

Overview: In this passage, two speakers each make a statement about how budget surplus money should be spent. The question asks you to pick out the statement that the two speakers are committed to disagreeing about. That is, one of the speakers must be committed to this statement being false while the other speaker is committed to its being true.

The Correct Answer:

E By saying what she does, Jessica is committed to (E) being false. If, as she says, the **only** thing that the budget surplus should be used for is to increase government payments to those who are unemployed, then there cannot be a better way to use the budget surplus. Marcie, on the other hand, says that there is a better way to use the budget surplus, namely, for a public works project to create jobs. So Marcie is committed to (E) being true.

The Incorrect Answer Choices:

A Since Jessica says that increasing government payments to those who are unemployed is the only thing that the budget surplus should be used for, she undoubtedly thinks that using the money this way would be putting it to good use. But Marcie could very well agree with Jessica that (A) is true. All Marcie says is that using it for a public works project would be a better use of the money. By saying this she doesn't deny that increasing those government payments would be a good use; she merely denies that it would be as good as the use she advocates.

B, D Since Marcie advocates using the budget surplus for a public works project to create jobs, she almost certainly agrees with both (B) and (D). However, nothing Jessica says indicates that she holds strong views about either (B) or (D). Her statement commits her to only one thing with respect to job creation: jobs shouldn't be created **by using the budget surplus**. So it leaves open the possibility that she believes that creating jobs through a public works project—as long as it is not done by using the budget surplus—would ultimately benefit the public.

C Both Jessica and Marcie are addressing a very specific issue: how a certain budget surplus should be used. The claim made in (C) is not restricted in this way. It proposes a general rule about where money, regardless of its source, should be spent. So neither speaker is committed to any particular position on (C).

- *Difficulty Level: 5*

Question 16

Overview: This passage presents some facts and then reports a hypothesis that was offered to explain those facts. The idea behind the hypothesis is that people come to visit the town to see the tourist attraction. They buy a pass, stay in hotels, and eat in restaurants. Then some of them give or sell their passes—which are good for the whole year—to other tourists, who come to town, stay in hotels, and eat in restaurants, but don't buy passes.

The question asks you to select the one answer choice that does not help to undermine the hypothesis.

The Correct Answer Choice

D The longer tourists stay in town, the more their visit will contribute to hotel and restaurant revenues. However, since a pass is good for an entire year, a visitor will buy only one pass however long he or she stays. So if the average length of stay had increased, that would explain the greater increase in hotel and restaurant revenues compared to revenues from passes. But (D) says that there was no increase in average length of stay. So (D) doesn't even begin to undermine the hypothesis; it actually supports the hypothesis by ruling out an alternative explanation.

The Incorrect Answer Choices:

A If other tourist attractions have opened up in the area during the past year, more tourists might be coming to the town, staying in hotels, and eating in restaurants, without going to the tourist attraction selling the passes. This would provide an alternative explanation for the comparatively small increase in pass revenues. So (A) helps to undermine the hypothesis.

B If people who bought passes last year made a greater number of trips to the town to visit the attraction, they probably spent more money on hotels and restaurants than in previous years. But since the pass is good for the entire year, they wouldn't have spent more money on passes. So (B) provides an alternative explanation and thus helps to undermine the hypothesis.

C If hotel and meal prices have risen, then we would expect hotel and restaurant revenues to have increased more rapidly than the number of visitors to the tourist attraction. Moreover, if the price of a pass has not risen, then revenue from sale of the passes would not have increased more rapidly than the number of visitors. So (C) could help explain the relatively large increase in hotel and restaurant revenues, thereby helping to undermine the hypothesis.

E (E) tells us that illicitly sharing passes isn't likely to work. Thus (E) undermines the hypothesis by directly challenging its viability.

- *Difficulty Level: 4*

Question 17

Overview: This passage first draws a distinction between manners and morals: Manners necessarily involve a social element; morality does not necessarily involve a social element. Then the passage spells out what this means in the case of manners. You are asked to identify the answer choice that is most strongly supported by these statements.

The Correct Answer:

A The passage claims that the rules of etiquette— manners—are necessarily social in nature, that is, they apply only when other people are involved. And it claims that morals differ from manners in that morals are not necessarily social in nature, that is, morals can apply when no other people are involved. So it must be possible to violate the rules of morality when no other people are involved. And if no other people are involved, no other people are harmed. So (A) is supported by the statements in the passage.

The Incorrect Answer Choices:

B According to the passage, manners are necessarily social in nature, but morals are not necessarily social in nature. This leaves open the possibility that immoral acts are sometimes social in nature. So the passage leaves open the possibility that there are immoral acts that are also violations of the rules of etiquette.

C The passage, by saying that morals do not necessarily involve other people, implies that there are cases in which the rules of morality apply when a person is alone, but the passage does not support the position that those rules apply only then.

D The passage does not differentiate between morality and manners in terms of their importance. Thus the statements do not support (D).

E The passage says that morals are not necessarily social in nature, which leaves open the possibility that some things that are social in nature are subject to the rules of morality.

- *Difficulty Level: 4*

Question 18

Overview: The argument's conclusion is based on two claims. The first claim is that the intended function of news is to give us information on which to act. The second claim is that under the present circumstances, news is primarily entertaining. The sociologist's conclusion is that under the present circumstances, news cannot serve its intended purpose.

As it is stated, this argument contains a significant gap. The premises provide support for the conclusion only if news that is entertaining cannot at the same time provide us with information on which to act.

The Correct Answer:

D If news can be primarily entertaining and still provide us with information on which to act, then the sociologist's argument fails. (D) rules out this possibility and thus is an assumption on which that argument depends.

The Incorrect Answer Choices:

A The sociologist's argument depends on it being impossible for news that is primarily entertaining to serve its intended function. However, the argument leaves open the possibility that news that does serve its intended function could still be somewhat entertaining. So (A) is not an assumption on which the sociologist's argument depends.

B The sociologist gives an account of how news has become something that is primarily entertaining. But this account does not depend on most consumers preferring that news be entertaining nor does any other part of the sociologist's argument.

C The claim that the intended function of news is to provide us with information on which to act means that someone, such as the journalists who report news, intend for it to serve this function. But this and the rest of the argument is perfectly compatible with news actually serving other important functions that it was not intended to serve. So the argument does not depend on assuming (C).

E The sociologist makes certain claims about how news is regarded in current consumer societies. The conclusion drawn is one about the fate of news in such societies. But the sociologist's argument would not fail if there were other kinds of societies in which the news industries aimed to make a profit and yet did not present news as entertainment. So (E) is not an assumption on which the sociologist's argument depends.

- *Difficulty Level: 3*

Question 19

Overview: The paleontologist's conclusion is that a certain widely held view is false. That view is that life began in the ocean and did not exist on land until half a billion years ago. The evidence offered for this conclusion is the existence of traces of carbon 14 throughout certain 1.2 billion-year-old rocks. This provides evidence for the conclusion because, as we are told in the last sentence of the passage, carbon 14 indicates the existence of plants and microbes. The argument evidently presumes that the rocks containing carbon 14 formed where the plants and microbes lived.

The question tells us that all but one of the answer choices present additional support for the conclusion that life began on land more than half a billion years ago. Your task is to identify the one answer choice that does **not** provide any such additional support.

The Correct Answer:

D The evidence about the existence of carbon 14 in the 1.2 billion-year-old rocks supports the paleontologist's conclusion only if that carbon 14 came from plants and microbes that died where the rocks were formed. (D), however, tells us that the carbon 14 in the rocks entered the soil from which the rocks were formed directly, without involving plants or microbes. Thus (D) does not support the paleontologist's conclusion; it seriously weakens the support for that conclusion.

The Incorrect Answer Choices:

A Part of the view against which the paleontologist is arguing is that plants did not exist on land until half a billion years ago. Thus, any fossil evidence that plants lived on land more than half a billion years ago provides additional support for the paleontologist's conclusion. (A) is a statement of such evidence.

B The paleontologist argues against a view that life began in the ocean and later moved to land. (B) supports the view that life did not begin in the ocean. Thus (B) provides additional support for the paleontologist's conclusion.

C The evidence cited by the paleontologist is the existence of carbon 14 **throughout** certain rocks. If those rocks had ever been entirely submerged in the ocean, then they might have acquired the carbon 14 from life in the ocean rather than from life on land. If that were true, it would seriously undermine the support given to the paleontologist's conclusion. But (C) tells us that at least some portions of those rocks were never submerged in water. (C) thus strengthens the paleontologist's conclusion by ruling out an alternative explanation for the presence of carbon 14 in the 1.2 billion-year-old rocks.

E The paleontologist's conclusion rests on a claim about the age of the rocks containing the carbon 14. (E) tells us that there is scientific confirmation of the correctness of that claim. (E) thus supports the paleontologist's conclusion.

- *Difficulty Level: 5*

Question 20

Overview: The passage contrasts the origin of the English language to that of French. It also discusses certain characteristics of English and French literature. In the case of English literature, it relates the nature of that literature to the vocabulary of the English language and attributes the nature of English's vocabulary to the language's origin.

The Correct Answer:

A The passage tells us that the nature of English literature reflects the rich and diverse vocabulary of the English language. It also tells us that this rich and diverse vocabulary resulted from the way the English language developed from two source languages, Anglo-Saxon and French. From these two claims we can infer that the way the English language developed had an effect on its vocabulary and thus on the nature of English literature. (A), therefore, can be reasonably inferred from the information in the passage.

The Incorrect Answer Choices:

B We know from the passage that modern English has a rich and diverse vocabulary that resulted from the dual influence of the Anglo-Saxon and French languages. But we have no basis for inferring that the vocabulary of Anglo-Saxon was richer than that of French. So (B) cannot be inferred.

C Given what the passage says, (C) could well be false. The passage tells us that English has a rich and diverse vocabulary that is a result of the language's origin. But the passage never says that such an origin is the only possible source of a rich and diverse vocabulary, so French could also have a rich and diverse vocabulary. Also, diversity is not necessarily linked to size of vocabulary. So even if we could conclude that the vocabulary of French is not as rich and diverse as that of English, we couldn't necessarily conclude that the vocabulary of French is smaller. Thus (C) cannot be inferred as reasonably as (A) can.

It may seem that the passage suggests that (C) is true, since French is contrasted with English, and we are told that English has a rich and diverse vocabulary. Also, the passage says that a hallmark of French literature is its simplicity, and you might think that literature written in a language with a limited vocabulary would tend to be simple. However, while the passage may suggest that (C) is true, it provides very strong support for (A). So (A), rather than (C), is the answer choice that can be **most reasonably** inferred.

D According to the passage, simplicity and clarity is the hallmark of French literature. This suggests that simplicity and clarity are not characteristic of English literature to the same extent, but we cannot infer that no English literature is simple and clear. Thus, (D) cannot be inferred from the information in the passage.

E We know from the passage that the French language had an influence on the development of the English language, and thus, indirectly, on the nature of English literature. But we are told nothing about what influence French literature may have had on English literature, or vice versa. Thus, the passage provides no basis for inferring (E).

- *Difficulty Level: 3*

Question 21

Overview: The conclusion of this argument is that both of two doctrines are mistaken. The first doctrine is presented as holding that the explanation of any historical event must appeal to economic factors. The second doctrine, we are told, attempts to account psychologically for all historical events. The support offered for the conclusion is that there have been historical events that were due both to economic forces and to the early childhood experiences of the major participants in the events.

The Correct Answer:

A The argument depends on each of the two doctrines holding that its preferred mode of explanation—economic on the one hand, psychological on the other—cannot be successfully employed together. As described, the first doctrine is committed only to the position that any adequate historical explanation must **include** an appeal to economic factors, thereby leaving open the possibility that noneconomic factors are relevant in some cases. For the argument to succeed, this possibility must be ruled out. (A) does this and is thus an assumption on which the argument depends.

The Incorrect Answer Choices:

B The argument says that for the second doctrine, early childhood experiences are especially important in accounting for historical events. By saying "especially important," the argument strongly suggests that, in at least some cases, other psychological factors are also important. So (B) is not assumed.

C, E The argument depends on there being events that can be explained only by reference to both economic and psychological factors. But it doesn't depend on those factors being of equal importance in historical events. Nor does it depend on both economic and psychological factors being needed to explain every historical event. So the argument does not depend on assuming either (C) or (E).

D Suppose that (D) is false and that, for most historical events, one kind of explanation or the other, but not both, have been offered. Would the argument fail? No. What the argument relies on to show that both doctrines are mistaken is that at least some historical events are, in fact, the result both of economic forces and of the psychological experiences of major participants in those events. So (D) is not an assumption on which the argument depends.

■ *Difficulty Level: 5*

Question 22

Overview: The argument concludes that measures to reduce a certain risk (that of head injury to bicyclists) are ill-advised because the incidence of other more common accidents (pedestrians being hit by automobiles and drunken driving accidents) would be reduced if certain measures were taken, but no one proposes taking those measures.

This argument has at least two flaws. First, the measure proposed in the one case and the measures that no one is actually proposing are quite different in the burden they impose. Requiring bicyclists to wear helmets narrowly and specifically addresses the risk of head injuries to bicyclists. Prohibiting people from walking down the street to keep pedestrians from being hit by automobiles would be far more like prohibiting bicycle riding altogether than like requiring bicyclists to wear helmets. Another flaw is that the argument compares the **number** of deaths resulting from bicycle accidents with the number of deaths resulting from the other causes. But what seems most relevant to whether bicyclists should be required to wear helmets is the **risk** of death resulting from each of these causes.

The Correct Answer:

B In (B) a measure to reduce the risk in working with dangerous liquids in labs is dismissed on the grounds that more serious risks remain unaddressed. But the contention that these other risks are more serious is based on a comparison of the total number of harmful incidents, not on a comparison of the likelihood of being harmed when participating in these activities. In addition, requiring lab workers to wear safety goggles when working with dangerous liquids has the same narrow and appropriate focus as requiring bicycle riders to wear helmets. Stopping people from eating to reduce the risk of food poisoning, however, is an extremely ill-focused remedy, just as keeping pedestrians from walking down the street to reduce the risk of their being killed by automobiles is an extremely ill-focused remedy. So (B) matches the argument in the passage very closely and exhibits the same flawed pattern of reasoning.

The Incorrect Answer Choices:

A (A) is like the argument in the passage in that it rejects a recommendation to reduce a certain risk. But the support offered for this rejection is that the risk of lung cancer from smoking is very low for test pilots because of their high risk of death from other causes. The argument does not support its conclusion by pointing out that other activities cause more deaths and that the risk posed by these activities is not being addressed, as the argument in the passage does. So the argument does not exhibit the same pattern of reasoning as that found in the argument in the passage.

C (C), like the argument in the passage, rejects a proposal. In (C), the grounds offered for rejecting the proposal are that there is an alternative to the rejected proposal that is better. The alleged problem with the rejected proposal is then illustrated by a comparison to a proposal that is clearly bad and is supposed to be parallel to the rejected proposal. In the argument in the passage, the grounds offered for the rejection of the proposal are not that there is a better alternative proposal, but that cases that would be more worthy of being attended to haven't even been addressed. So the kinds of grounds offered in (C) are quite different from those offered in the argument in the passage.

D (D), unlike the argument in the passage, is a fairly reasonable argument, exhibiting no clearly flawed reasoning. A proposal is rejected as unwise on the grounds that an alternative proposal costs less to implement and would involve only a relatively short delay in achieving the desired result. By comparison, the argument in the passage does not reject a proposal on the grounds that a superior alternative is available. Thus, the pattern of reasoning in (D) is quite different from that in the argument in the passage.

E (E) is like the argument in the passage in rejecting a proposal that addresses a risk. But unlike the argument in the passage, (E) argues for an alternative proposal. Moreover, this alternative proposal is simply a more limited version of the original proposal. And the reason for preferring the alternative proposal is that the original proposal was too sweeping, since it would have applied to people who were unlikely to be at risk. Thus, the pattern of reasoning in (E) is quite unlike that in the argument in the passage.

- *Difficulty Level: 4*

Question 23

Overview: The argument in the passage is basically the following: No-till methods are significantly better at preserving topsoil than deep tillage is. Therefore, farmers who now practice deep tillage should make an effort to adopt no-till methods.

The Correct Answer:

C Suppose (C) were false, that is, some tillage method is a viable alternative to both deep tillage and no-till methods. In that case the argument would fail, because it offers no reason to prefer no-till methods over this alternative method of tillage. (C), therefore, is assumed by the argument.

The Incorrect Answer Choices:

A Suppose (A) were false. Then there would be a vicious cycle: deep tillage causes erosion which in turn prompts even more deep tillage which in turn causes even more erosion, and so on. This would make it even more important for farmers to turn to methods other than deep tillage. So (A)'s being false would lend more urgency to the argument, rather than causing it to fail. Thus, the argument does not depend on assuming (A).

B In order to infer its conclusion that farmers should switch from deep tillage to no-till methods, the argument needs the claim—which is made by one of its premises—that deep tillage is bad, as far as susceptibility to topsoil erosion goes. But the fact that the argument needs that claim provides no reason to think that it depends on the stronger claim stated in (B), namely, that the deeper you till, the worse the topsoil erosion will be.

D Suppose (D) were false, that is, the most expensive farming methods employ deep tillage. This would suggest that farmers should avoid certain deep-tillage methods because they are so expensive. This would certainly not cause the argument to fail. If anything, it would strengthen the argument by providing an additional reason why some deep-tillage methods are less advantageous than no-till methods.

E The argument assumes that no-till methods are not substantially worse than deep tillage in important respects other than erosion control. But it doesn't have to assume that no-till methods are **better** than deep tillage in such respects.

- *Difficulty Level: 5*

Question 24

Overview: The conclusion of the argument in the editorial is that the government should assume the cost of candidates' campaigns. This conclusion rests on three points: (1) campaigning for elected office is so expensive that—in the absence of government funding—most candidates must seek funding from private sources; (2) in almost all cases, candidates have to compromise their principles to secure funding from private sources; and (3) society has a vested interest in maintaining a political system in which candidates don't have to compromise their principles.

The Correct Answer:

D The three points on which the conclusion rests, taken together, imply that the dependence on private funding for campaigns works against a vested interest of society. But we cannot infer from this that the government should pay for candidates' campaigns unless we also know that furthering a vested interest of society justifies government funding. (D) tells us that if an activity furthers a vested interest of society, that justifies government funding of that activity. So (D) helps justify the argument's conclusion.

The Incorrect Answer Choices:

A, B, C You are looking for a principle that helps support the argument's conclusion, which is about what the government should do, not about what voters or candidates should do. Since neither (A), nor (B), nor (C) is concerned with what the government should do, none of these answer choices can help justify the argument's conclusion.

E The principle in (E) allows that private funding for political campaigns is justified in certain limited circumstances. This principle, therefore, does not help justify the editorial's position that there should be no private funding for political campaigns under any circumstances.

- *Difficulty Level: 3*

Question 25

Overview: The passage tells us that that 7 percent of a certain manufacturer's garments are reported as unsalable and defines "unsalable garments" as those found to be defective by inspectors plus those returned by retailers. It then tells us that all of this manufacturer's unsalable garments are recycled as scrap. Finally it tells us that 9 percent of that manufacturer's garments are reported as being recycled as scrap.

You are asked to select the answer choice that could contribute most to explaining the discrepancy between the reported 7 percent of the garments being unsalable and the reported 9 percent of them being recycled.

The Correct Answer:

E We're looking for an explanation of why unsalable garments comprise 7 percent of total garments whereas recycled garments comprise 9 percent of total garments. (E) tells us that unsalable garments are measured by count but recycled garments are measured by weight. So if heavier garments are more likely to be considered unsalable, (E) would explain the discrepancy.

The Incorrect Answer Choices:

A The garments described in (A) have not been found defective by inspectors nor will they be returned by retailers. Thus none of these garments are unsalable. This means that none of these garments are recycled as scrap. So (A) has no bearing on the figures reported and cannot contribute to an explanation of the discrepancy between them.

B (B) tells us something about the kind of garments that are returned by retailers as unsalable. But since the passage tells us that all unsalable garments are recycled as scrap—regardless of why they are considered unsalable—(B) cannot contribute to an explanation of the different percentages reported for unsalable garments and for recycled garments.

C (C) tells us why some of the garments are reported as defective by inspectors. But since the passage tells us that all garments reported as defective by inspectors are recycled—regardless of why the inspectors report them as defective—(C) cannot contribute to an explanation of the different percentages reported for unsalable garments and for recycled garments.

D If the increase in the number of garments produced by the manufacturer over the past year affected either figure, it would equally affect the other. So (D) cannot help explain the difference in the percentages reported.

- *Difficulty Level: 5*

Question 26

Overview: We are told that Marion cannot avoid being late for work unless she takes the train instead of driving. And the argument provides evidence that supports a prediction that Marion will not take the train. Thus the argument could legitimately conclude that there is a good chance that Marion will be late for work. However, the conclusion the argument actually draws is that Marion cannot avoid being late for work. That conclusion would follow only if Marion's hating to take the train made it impossible for her to take the train. But we know that people frequently do things they deeply dislike doing.

The question asks you to identify the answer choice that best characterizes what has gone wrong in this argument.

The Correct Answer:

D   The argument is flawed because it treats evidence that supports the prediction that Marion will drive (i.e., the fact that she hates taking the train) as though it was evidence that absolutely rules out the possibility that Marion will take the train. (D) thus correctly characterizes the flaw in the reasoning of the argument.

The Incorrect Answer Choices:

A   The argument is concerned with a certain situation only as it affects Marion, but it does not treat that situation as though it affected Marion alone. The fact that others would have been affected by the closing of the bridge has no bearing on the argument. Thus (A) does not describe anything that the argument does.

B   In order for (B) to describe a flaw in the argument, the argument would have to infer, from a claim that Marion knows that something is the case, that she is aware of some consequence of that thing being the case. The only things that the argument claims Marion knows are that the bridge is closed and that unless she takes the train, she will have to leave for work at least 45 minutes early in order to get there on time. But the argument does not infer that Marion is aware of any consequences of these things. So (B) does not accurately describe the argument.

C   The argument does not reason from something that is true of people generally to a conclusion about what is true of Marion or any other particular person. So (C) does not describe anything that happens in the argument.

E   In the circumstances considered in the argument, Marion has strong reasons for adopting either of the courses of action open to her. So the possibility mentioned in (E) is not relevant to the reasoning of the argument.

■ *Difficulty Level: 3*

Analytical Reasoning: Questions 1–24

Questions 1–6

What the setup tells you: This group of questions has to do with the order in which eight boats arrived, one at a time, at a dock. The conditions tell you when certain boats arrived relative to other boats. Putting the conditions together, you get the following arrangement:

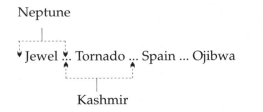

One of the most important things to note is that two of the boats—Pacific and Valhalla—are completely unrestricted by the conditions. That means that they could have arrived anywhere in the sequence.

Question 1

Overview: This question asks you to find the one answer choice that **cannot** be true if Neptune arrived after Kashmir. So the incorrect answer choices will all be things that can be true under those conditions.

From the setup, you know that Neptune had to arrive before Tornado, and Kashmir had to arrive after Jewel. So if Neptune arrived after Kashmir, the relative order in which six of the boats had to arrive is

...Jewel...Kashmir...Neptune...Tornado...Spain...Ojibwa...

Setting aside Pacific and Valhalla for the moment, the boats would have the numbered positions shown above.

What effect would taking account of Pacific and Valhalla have? Suppose they both arrived after Ojibwa. The numbered positions of the other six boats would remain exactly the same. Now, if Pacific and Valhalla both arrived before Jewel—which would put them in positions 1 and 2—the other six boats would be shifted down exactly two places (Jewel would be in position 3, Kashmir in position 4, and so on). And in fact, no matter where either Pacific or Valhalla is in the sequence, none of the other six boats will shift more than two places down. For example, Jewel could have arrived either first, second, or third, Neptune could have arrived either third, fourth, or fifth, and so on.

With this in mind, you can turn to the individual answer choices and directly determine which can and which cannot be true.

The Correct Answer:

B   As discussed above, Kashmir could have arrived second, third, or fourth. Since (B) has Kashmir arriving fifth, you know that (B) can't be true.

The Incorrect Answer Choices:

A   As discussed above, Jewel could have arrived first, second, or third. So (A) can be true.

C   As discussed above, Neptune could have arrived third, fourth, or fifth. So (C) can be true.

D   As discussed above, Ojibwa could have arrived sixth, seventh, or eighth. So (D) can be true.

E   As discussed above, Spain could have arrived fifth, sixth, or seventh. So (E) can be true.

■ *Difficulty Level: 2*

Question 2

Overview: In this question, you're asked what must be true on the basis of the setup alone.

You know from "What the setup tells you" that Pacific and Valhalla could have arrived anywhere in the sequence. Thus, there is nothing that must be true of either one. So you can immediately rule out (B) and (E).

That leaves only three answer choices to check. Since you know that Spain must have arrived relatively late in the sequence, (C) is a good answer choice to check first.

The Correct Answer:

C   From what the setup conditions tell you, you know that Jewel, Neptune, Kashmir, and Tornado all arrived before Spain did. So whether or not Pacific or Valhalla also arrived before Spain, you know that there are at least four boats that must have arrived before Spain. You are now done. There's no need to check the other answer choices.

The Incorrect Answer Choices:

A, D   The following outcome violates none of the setup conditions and shows that neither (A) nor (D) has to be true:

Neptune, Jewel, Tornado, Kashmir, Spain, Ojibwa, Pacific, Valhalla

In this sequence, there are no boats arriving before Neptune and there are only two boats arriving before Tornado.

B, E   (B) describes a restriction involving Pacific, and (E) describes a restriction involving Valhalla. However, these boats are not restricted by the conditions. So given just the setup conditions alone, there is nothing that must be true of either Pacific or Valhalla. Both boats can appear anywhere in the sequence.

■ *Difficulty Level: 1*

Question 3

Overview: Essentially what this question is asking is the following: If as many boats as possible arrived before Jewel, how many boats is that?

The Correct Answer:

D   Neptune could have arrived before Jewel, and Pacific and Valhalla could have arrived anywhere in the sequence, so you know that at least those three boats could have arrived before Jewel. The remaining boats—Kashmir, Tornado, Spain, and Ojibwa—all arrived after Jewel, so there's a maximum of just three boats that could have arrived before Jewel.

The Incorrect Answer Choices:

A, B, C   None of these answer choices is correct, because each is smaller than the maximum of "three."

E   This answer choice is incorrect because it is larger than the maximum of "three."

■ *Difficulty Level: 2*

Question 4

Overview: Keep in mind that this question asks you what **cannot** be true if Valhalla was the second of the eight boats to arrive.

The Correct Answer:

E According to the question, Valhalla arrived second. Both Neptune and Jewel had to arrive before Tornado. That means that at least three boats—Neptune, Jewel, and Valhalla—all arrived before Tornado. Thus Tornado cannot have been the third to arrive.

The Incorrect Answer Choices:

A Jewel could have arrived third, as the following outcome shows:

Neptune, Valhalla, Jewel, Kashmir, Tornado, Spain, Ojibwa, Pacific

B, C Both (B) and (C) are possible, as the following outcome shows:

Jewel, Valhalla, Kashmir, Neptune, Tornado, Spain, Ojibwa, Pacific

D Pacific can go anywhere in the sequence, and here only the second position is specifically taken. So Pacific could have arrived third.

■ *Difficulty Level: 1*

Question 5

Overview: If Valhalla arrived before Neptune and after Pacific, then the positions of six of the boats relative to one another are fixed:

...Pacific...Valhalla...Neptune...Tornado...Spain...Ojibwa

Now check the answer choices. You can immediately rule out (A) and (D): both Tornado and Spain must have arrived **after** Valhalla.

You don't know exactly where Jewel and Kashmir fit into the sequence. But you do know that both of them arrived before Spain. Thus, Spain must have been the seventh to arrive, and Ojibwa must have been the eighth (last). Checking the remaining answer choices, you can now eliminate (C) and (E) because both must be false. You are done. You know that (B) is the correct answer.

The Correct Answer:

B The following outcome, which satisfies the conditions and the specific requirement of the question itself, demonstrates that (B) can be true:

Jewel, Kashmir, Pacific, Valhalla, Neptune, Tornado, Spain, Ojibwa

In this sequence, Kashmir arrived before Pacific.

The Incorrect Answer Choices:

A, D The information provided by the setup conditions and the question itself determines the relative positions of six of the boats, as follows:

...Pacific...Valhalla...Neptune...Tornado...Spain...Ojibwa

Neither (A) nor (D) is satisfied here, and so neither could be true of the final outcome either.

C, E If the sequence above were completed by adding Jewel and Kashmir, both would have to be placed somewhere before Spain. This means that Spain must have been seventh and Ojibwa must have been last. Thus, neither (C) nor (E) could be true.

■ *Difficulty Level: 2*

Question 6

In this question, you're asked to determine both the minimum and the maximum number of boats that could have arrived before Kashmir. Any answer choice that gets one of these numbers wrong can be eliminated.

Since only Jewel had to arrive before Kashmir (the third condition says that Jewel arrived before Kashmir), the minimum number is one.

Turning to the answer choices with this in mind, you can immediately rule out (B), (C), and (E), since none of them lists "one" as the first number.

This means that the choice is between (A) and (D). Since one has "five" where the other has "six", you know that at least five boats could have arrived before Kashmir. So the question reduces to the following: Could there have been six boats arriving before Kashmir? If so, then the correct answer is (D). If not, then the correct answer is (A).

For six boats to come before Kashmir in the sequence, Kashmir would have to be seventh. But Kashmir has to be before Spain, and Spain has to be before Ojibwa. So there are at least two boats that must **follow** Kashmir. Since there are only eight boats in all, that leaves just five boats that could possibly be before Kashmir. Thus (D) can be eliminated, and you know that (A) is the correct answer.

The Correct Answer:

A   Jewel is the only boat that necessarily arrived before Kashmir (as specified by the third condition). Thus, the minimum number of boats that could have arrived before Kashmir is one. What is the maximum number of boats that could have arrived before Kashmir? Both Neptune and Tornado could have arrived before Kashmir. In addition to Jewel, that makes three. Pacific and Valhalla could have arrived anywhere in the sequence and so could have arrived before Kashmir, making five. The remaining boats—Spain and Ojibwa—must have arrived after Kashmir. Thus, there are a maximum of five boats that could have arrived before Kashmir.

The Incorrect Answer Choices:

B   (B) is incorrect because it lists "two" as the minimum rather than "one."

C   (C) is incorrect because it lists "three" as the minimum rather than "one."

D   (D) is incorrect because it lists "six" as the maximum rather than "five."

E   (E) is incorrect because it lists "two" as the minimum rather than "one", and it lists "six" as the maximum rather than "five."

■ *Difficulty Level: 2*

Questions 7–12

What the setup tells you: This group of questions is about the different kinds of trees in a park. The park is said to have at most five kinds of trees. The phrase "at most" lets you know that five is the maximum, and it also lets you know that there might be fewer than five kinds of trees in the park.

The first condition means that the park can't have both maples and yews: it can have maples, or yews, or neither, but not both. The same is true of firs and pines in the second condition.

The third condition tells you what happens in case yews are not in the park (it doesn't tell you anything about what happens in case yews **are** in the park). If the park doesn't have yews, then it must have either laurels or oaks, but not both and certainly not neither. And so it also tells you that there are two conditions under which the park must contain yews: if it has both laurels and oaks and if it has neither.

The fourth condition tells you what circumstances indicate that both firs and spruces are in the park. There are three such circumstances: The first is if the park has laurels but not oaks. The second is if the park has oaks but not laurels. And the third is if the park has neither laurels nor oaks (if it has neither, it certainly doesn't have both). Conversely, if the park doesn't have firs and spruces, then it must have both laurels and oaks.

Question 7

Overview: This question asks you to identify the list of trees that meets all the requirements of the setup. So just take the conditions in turn and eliminate answer choices as soon as you detect a violation.

First, scan the answer choices for any in which maples and yews are both included. (E) is such an answer choice. It violates the first condition and gets crossed out.

Next, check for answer choices among (A) through (D) that include both firs and pines. (C) is such an answer choice, and it gets crossed out.

Now, with the third condition, remember what kind of option would present a violation: a list that includes no yews and that either includes both laurels and oaks or, alternatively, neither laurels nor oaks. (A) is one such answer choice: no yews, but no laurels and no oaks either. Therefore, cross out (A). Going on to (B), you find that it too violates the third condition, though in the other way: no yews, but both laurels and oaks. So (B) gets crossed out.

You've now crossed out (A), (B), (C), and (E). So you're left with (D) as the correct answer. In other words, you're done.

Note that you haven't checked any of the answer choices against the fourth condition. There was no need to do so, since using this method you were able to rule out all but one of the answer choices using only the first three conditions.

The Correct Answer:

D   This answer choice violates none of the requirements of the setup, and so it could be a list of the kinds of trees in the park.

The Incorrect Answer Choices:

A   (A) can be eliminated because it violates the third condition. Yews are not in the park, and in this case the third condition requires that either laurels or oaks be in the park. (A) has neither laurels nor oaks. Alternatively, (A) can be eliminated because it violates the fourth condition. The park has neither laurels nor oaks, and in this case the fourth condition requires that it have both firs and spruces. (A) violates this condition because it doesn't have firs and spruces.

> **Note.** Although (A) can be eliminated on the basis of more than one condition, it is enough to detect a single violation. In the actual test, you would be wasting time if you were to verify every possible violation for a given answer choice.

B   (B) violates the third condition. Although yews are not in the park, both laurels and oaks are.

C   (C) violates the second condition. The list contains both firs and pines.

E   (E) violates the first condition. The list contains both maples and yews.

▪ *Difficulty Level: 1*

Question 8

Overview: Here you start with the information that there are no maples and no spruces in the park. The absence of maples does not immediately give you any useful leads. (Don't interpret the first condition as telling you that if there are no maples in the park, then there must be yews. Remember that the first condition is consistent with there being neither maples nor yews in the park.)

The absence of spruces is a much more immediately useful piece of information. Take a look at the fourth condition. Note that if there are no spruces in the park, then the pairing of spruces with firs is also not in the park. And that means that the circumstances that would require that both firs and spruces be in the park cannot be present. In other words: since there are no spruces in the park, both laurels and oaks must be in the park.

You have your first new result. A quick check of the answer choices against this result shows that (C) and (D) are both false. So both (C) and (D) can be eliminated.

This new result can now be usefully employed to draw further inferences. Consider the third condition. If both laurels and oaks are in the park, then the circumstances that would make this impossible cannot be in place. So yews must be in the park.

Checking the remaining answer choices shows that (E) is false and can be eliminated.

So at this point you're left with the choice between (A) and (B). Either there are four kinds of trees in the park, or there are five kinds. You've already established that the following three kinds of trees must be in the park: laurels, oaks, and yews. There are two remaining to consider: firs and pines. This would make five kinds of trees. But the second condition rules out the possibility that the park has both firs and pines, so the park can't have five kinds of trees and (B) can be crossed out.

You are done. (A) must be the correct answer.

The Correct Answer:

A   The following is a list of four trees that includes neither maples nor spruces and that violates none of the setup conditions:

firs, laurels, oaks, yews

This outcome shows that (A) could be true.

The Incorrect Answer Choices:

B If spruces are not in the park, then the park must have both laurels and oaks (by the fourth condition). If both laurels and oaks are in the park, then yews must be (by the third condition). That makes three kinds of trees so far: laurels, oaks, and yews. The question itself tells you that the park has neither maples nor spruces, and so there remain two kinds of trees to consider: firs and pines. The park can't have both firs and pines, since that is ruled out by the second condition. Therefore, the park can't have five kinds of trees.

C According to the fourth condition, if spruces are not in the park, then the park must have both laurels and oaks. So (C) can't be true.

D According to the fourth condition, if spruces are not in the park, then the park must have both laurels and oaks. So (D) can't be true.

E According to the fourth condition, if spruces are not in the park, then the park must have both laurels and oaks. And, according to the third condition, if both laurels and oaks are in the park, then yews must be. So (E) can't be true.

- *Difficulty Level: 4*

Question 9

Overview: The question asks which one of the answer choices could be true. In order to eliminate an answer choice, you have to show that it can't be true. In this case, you need to be especially alert because the answer choices that you're trying to show are not true are themselves all negative statements. For example, how would you show that it can't be true that neither firs nor laurels are in the park? You would do this by showing that at least one of the two—either firs or laurels or both—must be in the park. If you can demonstrate that this is so, eliminate the answer choice.

There are occasions when you can look at a question and realize at the outset that you've already done some of the work that goes into answering it. This is a case in point. Eliminating the incorrect answer choices of the previous question involved showing that if spruces are not in the park, then laurels, oaks, and yews must be. This result allows you to eliminate (C) and (E) of this question without doing any new work at all.

The answer choices are all about kinds of trees that are not in the park. Two of the conditions—the third and fourth—talk about what happens if certain kinds of trees are not in the park, so these are the ones to check first. Take the third condition, for instance. (B) says that yews are not in the park, so by the third condition the park has to have either laurels or oaks. But (B) also says that neither laurels nor oaks are in the park. So (B) can't be true and can thus be crossed out.

Now turn to the fourth condition. The fourth condition applies to (A): the park doesn't have both laurels and oaks (because it doesn't have laurels). This means that the park would have to have both firs and spruces. But (A) says that the park doesn't have firs, so it can't be true because it violates the fourth condition.

You've now eliminated (A), (B), (C), and (E). And you're done. The correct answer must be (D).

The Correct Answer:

D The following list of trees includes neither maples nor yews and meets all of the requirements of the setup:

firs, laurels, spruces

This outcome shows that (D) could be true.

The Incorrect Answer Choices:

A According to the fourth condition, if the park doesn't have both laurels and oaks, then it has both firs and spruces. (A) tells you that the park doesn't have laurels (so it doesn't have both laurels and oaks) and that it doesn't have firs. This state of affairs violates the fourth condition, so (A) can't be true.

B According to the third condition, if the park has neither laurels nor oaks, then it must have yews. (B) violates the third condition because it has neither laurels nor oaks, but it does have yews. So (B) can't be true.

C According to the fourth condition, if the park doesn't have both laurels and oaks, then it has both firs and spruces. (C) tells you that the park doesn't have laurels (so it doesn't have both laurels and oaks) and that it doesn't have spruces. This state of affairs violates the fourth condition, so (C) can't be true.

E According to the fourth condition, if the park doesn't have both laurels and oaks, then it has both firs and spruces. (E) tells you that the park doesn't have oaks (so it doesn't have both laurels and oaks) and that it doesn't have spruces. This state of affairs violates the fourth condition, so (E) can't be true.

- *Difficulty Level: 4*

Question 10

Overview: The question asks what must be true if there are no firs in the park. The fourth condition mentions firs, and it is of use here. If there are no firs in the park, then the pairing of firs with spruces is also not in the park. That means that the circumstances that would require that both firs and spruces be in the park cannot be present. In other words, since there are no firs in the park, the park must contain both laurels and oaks. (The second condition, although it mentions firs, specifies a consequence of the presence of firs, not of their absence. So the second condition doesn't yield any useful inferences here.)

A quick check of the answer choices against this result shows that so far none of them can be eliminated. However, this result can now be employed to draw further inferences. Consider the third condition. If both laurels and oaks are in the park, then the circumstances that would make this impossible cannot be in place. So yews must be in the park.

Checking the answer choices again, you find that your newest result shows (C) to be false. The fact that yews are in the park yields a further result: by the first condition, if yews are in the park, then maples are not. And this is what (A) says, so (A) is the correct answer. You are done.

It is also possible to answer this question by using a shortcut. The question asks what must be true if firs are not in the park. You may have noticed that, as far as the application of the first, third, and fourth conditions is concerned, firs behave structurally exactly as spruces do. Anything that is true of firs is true of spruces, and vice versa. (The exception is where the second condition is concerned—it mentions firs but not spruces—but the second condition doesn't come into play in this question.) In answering question 8, you've already worked out the implications of there being no spruces in the park. Those implications are: laurels, oaks, and yews are in the park, and maples are not. The absence of firs from the park has exactly the same implications. This means that you already have your answer, "Maples are not in the park," which in this question is (A). You're done. Recourse to such shortcuts is not something you can always rely on having available to you. But where the opportunity presents itself, you can certainly take advantage of it.

The Correct Answer:

A If firs are not in the park then, by the fourth condition, both laurels and oaks are. If both laurels and oaks are in the park then, by the third condition, yews are also in the park. If yews are in the park then, by the first condition, maples are not. Thus, (A) must be true.

The Incorrect Answer Choices:

B, C, D   The following is an acceptable outcome that doesn't include firs and that conforms to all the requirements of the setup:

laurels, oaks, spruces, yews

Since the list contains spruces, it shows that (B) doesn't have to be true. Since the list contains yews, it shows that (C) doesn't have to be true. (One of the results noted in the "Overview" is that if firs are not in the park, then yews must be in the park. So in fact (C) **must** be false.) Finally, since the list doesn't contain pines, it shows that (D) doesn't have to be true.

E   If spruces are removed from the list above, the resulting outcome is also acceptable:

laurels, oaks, yews

Since this list doesn't contain spruces, it shows that (E) doesn't have to be true.

- *Difficulty Level: 5*

Question 11

Overview: As usual, you start with the supposition introduced by the question: pines are in the park. This has an immediate consequence in view of the second condition: if pines are in the park, then firs can't be in the park (because if firs were in the park, pines couldn't be). Now, firs not being in the park is exactly the circumstance addressed by the previous question. So all the inferences you drew there apply here. In particular, they are: if there are no firs in the park, then laurels, oaks, and yews are in the park, and maples are not in the park.

At this point, check these results against the answer choices. You will find that you are done. You've shown that if pines are in the park, then neither firs nor maples are in the park. That is, you've shown that (C) must be true.

The Correct Answer:

C   If pines are in the park, then (by the second condition) there are no firs in the park. If there are no firs in the park, then of course it can't be that firs and spruces are in the park. But that means (according to the fourth condition) that the circumstances that require that both firs and spruces be in the park cannot be present. In other words: since there are no firs in the park, the park must have both laurels and oaks.

According to the third condition, if both laurels and oaks are in the park, then the circumstances that would make this impossible—there being no yews in the park—cannot be in place. So yews must be in the park.

And (by the first condition) if there are yews in the park, maples can't be in the park. Thus (C) is true: if pines are in the park, then neither firs nor maples can be in the park.

The Incorrect Answer Choices:

A, B   If pines are in the park, then laurels, oaks, and yews must also be in the park. This has been established in the "Overview." So far you know that there are at least four kinds of trees in the park: laurels, oaks, pines, and yews. But note that spruces could be added to this list without any conditions being violated, so there could be either four or five kinds of trees in the park. Thus, neither (A) nor (B) is something that **must** be true.

D   According to the second condition, if pines are in the park then firs can't be. And according to the fourth condition, if firs are not in the park then oaks must be. So (D) must be false.

E According to the second condition, if pines are in the park then firs can't be. And according to the fourth condition, if firs are not in the park then laurels must be. So (D), which says that laurels are not in the park, can't be true.

- *Difficulty Level: 5*

Question 12

Overview: This question asks you to identify a combination that **cannot** be part of any acceptable list of trees in the park. First, notice that none of the answer choices is in direct violation of a condition. For example, none of them contain the pair firs and pines, which would be ruled out by the second condition. Finding the correct answer, therefore, depends on deducing additional information that can then be shown to lead to a violation.

The Correct Answer:

E If maples are in the park, then yews are not in the park. And if yews are not in the park, then laurels and oaks cannot both be in the park (though one of them must be). So the park can't have maples together with both laurels and oaks. (E), therefore, is an unacceptable partial list, which makes it the correct answer to this question.

The Incorrect Answer Choices:

A, B, C The following is an acceptable outcome:

firs, laurels, oaks, spruces, yews

Since (A), (B), and (C) are all drawn from this list, each of them could be an accurate, partial list of the kinds of trees in the park.

D The list in (D) is an acceptable partial list, because it can be turned into an acceptable outcome by the addition of spruces. The resulting list satisfies all the requirements of the setup:

firs, maples, oaks, spruces

- *Difficulty Level: 5*

Questions 13–18

What the setup tells you: The setup is about a seating arrangement for eight people around a table. Two people have been assigned to specific seats, and the eventual seating arrangement is also subject to some conditions that deal with who can sit next to whom. If you decide to represent the circular arrangement as just a straight line in your diagram, remember that chair 8 is next to chair 1.

The conditions are clearly stated, and there do not seem to be any hidden complexities here. So you should turn to the questions without delay.

Question 13

Overview: This question asks you to find a seating arrangement for chairs 5 through 8 that could be part of a complete seating arrangement. The incorrect answer choices will be partial seating arrangements that directly violate the conditions as they are, or that can't be completed in a way that meets all the requirements of the setup.

(B) is an example of a partial arrangement that directly violates a condition: it places Francisco and Gabrielle in chairs that are next to each other. But since they are married to each other, this violates the first condition. (D) is another example of a condition being violated within the partial arrangement. (D) places Gabrielle in chair 5 and Lee in chair 6, in violation of the fourth condition. So both (B) and (D) can be crossed out right away.

The other reason that a partial arrangement can be ruled out is if the remaining chairs can't be assigned to people without violating some condition. (C) works this way. Olivia is placed in chair 5. But you know from the setup that Raymond sits in chair 4 and would thus end up sitting next to Olivia, in violation of the third condition. So (C) can be crossed out.

(A) is a little more complex. In addition to knowing who sits in chairs 5 through 8, you know that Simone and Raymond sit in chairs 1 and 4. This tells you who has to be in chairs 2 and 3: the two remaining people, Kyoko and Lee. But since Kyoko and Lee are married to each other, they can't end up in chairs that are next to each other. So any completion of (A) would violate the first condition, and (A) can be crossed out.

The only answer choice that hasn't been crossed out is (E), so you know that (E) must be the correct answer. At this point, you're done.

The Correct Answer:

E That (E) could be the people sitting in chairs 5 through 8 is shown by the following acceptable outcome:

Simone, Peter, Gabrielle, Raymond, Lee, Olivia, Francisco, Kyoko

The Incorrect Answer Choices:

A According to the second condition, chairs 1 and 4 are taken by Simone and Raymond. That leaves Kyoko and Lee to occupy chairs 2 and 3. But Kyoko and Lee are married and so, as given by the first condition, they can't sit next to one another. Since there is no acceptable completion of (A), it can't be the list of people sitting in chairs 5 through 8.

B In (B), the married couple Francisco and Gabrielle are sitting next to one another, in violation of the first condition.

C (C) can be ruled out because it violates the third condition. In (C), Olivia sits in chair 5. You know from the second condition that Raymond sits in chair 4. But the third condition prohibits Olivia from sitting next to Raymond, so this answer choice can be ruled out.

D This answer choice violates the fourth condition, since it has Gabrielle sitting next to Lee.

■ *Difficulty Level: 4*

Question 14

Overview: This question is similar to the previous question in that it presents you with partial seating arrangements. In this case, however, you are to find the one that **cannot** be part of an acceptable outcome.

As before, you can begin by checking to see whether any of the answer choices violates a condition directly. This turns out to be the case with (B): (B) places Peter in chair 1, and this violates the second condition, according to which it is Simone who sits in chair 1. Since you were looking for a partial seating arrangement that is unacceptable, you are done.

The Correct Answer:

B The partial seating arrangement described by (B) can't be true. According to the second condition, Simone sits in chair 1, but (B) places Peter in chair 1.

The Incorrect Answer Choices:

A (A) could be part of the following seating arrangement: Simone, Peter, Gabrielle, Raymond, Lee, Olivia, Francisco, Kyoko.

C (C) could be part the following seating arrangement: Simone, Olivia, Gabrielle, Raymond, Francisco, Kyoko, Peter, Lee.

D (D) could be part of the following seating arrangement: Simone, Peter, Lee, Raymond, Gabrielle, Olivia, Kyoko, Francisco.

E (E) could be part of the following seating arrangement: Simone, Kyoko, Francisco, Raymond, Gabrielle, Peter, Lee, Olivia.

■ *Difficulty Level: 1*

Question 15

Overview: This question appears to be one in which drawing inferences one at a time, and checking each result against the answer choices, offers the best promise of success.

There are several inferences that follow immediately from the fact that Francisco is in chair 2. First, in order for Olivia to sit next to Simone, she must sit in chair 8 (since chair 2 is occupied by Francisco). So at this point, what you've got is the following partial seating arrangement:

Simone	Francisco	?	Raymond	?	?	?	Olivia
1	2	3	4	5	6	7	8

Next, since Gabrielle is Francisco's spouse, she can't sit in chair 3. So the chairs that remain as possibilities for Gabrielle are 5, 6, and 7. Neither Kyoko nor Lee can sit next to Gabrielle. How can we place Gabrielle so that she doesn't sit next to Kyoko or Lee? Gabrielle can't be in chair 6, because she would end up sitting next to one of them (the chairs left for Kyoko and Lee would be 3, 5, and 7). Similarly, in order to make sure that neither Kyoko nor Lee sits next to Gabrielle, neither one can sit in chair 6. So it is Peter, the only remaining person, who must sit in chair 6. For Gabrielle, then, there are two options: she will be in chair 5 (the first outcome below) or chair 7 (the second outcome below). For Kyoko and Lee, one of them will be in chair 3 and the other will be in either chair 7 (the first outcome) or chair 5 (the second outcome).

Simone	Francisco	Lee/Kyoko	Raymond	Gabrielle	Peter	Kyoko/Lee	Olivia
1	2	3	4	5	6	7	8

Simone	Francisco	Lee/Kyoko	Raymond	Kyoko/Lee	Peter	Gabrielle	Olivia
1	2	3	4	5	6	7	8

With this much established, you're now in a position to check the answer choices and select the correct answer. Gabrielle must sit next to Peter, and the correct answer is thus (E).

The Correct Answer:

E The question tells you that Olivia sits next to Simone, which means that she must sit in chair 2 or chair 8. Since the question also tells you that chair 2 is taken by Francisco, you know that Olivia must sit in chair 8. Gabrielle can't sit in chair 3, since that would place her next to Francisco, in violation of the first condition. Gabrielle is limited to chair 5 or chair 7, since if she were in chair 6 she would end up sitting next to either Kyoko or Lee, in violation of the fourth condition. Of Kyoko and Lee, one is in chair 3 and the other is in either chair 5 or chair 7, so that neither is sitting next to Gabrielle. So it is Peter who sits in chair 6. This means that Gabrielle must sit next to Peter, because she sits in either chair 5 or chair 7.

The Incorrect Answer Choices:

A (A) is ruled out directly by the first condition. Since Francisco is Gabrielle's spouse, Gabrielle can't sit next to Francisco.

B With chair 2 taken by Francisco, Olivia must sit in chair 8 in order to be next to Simone. Because she can't sit next to either Kyoko or Lee, Gabrielle sits in either chair 5 or chair 7, so that Kyoko and Lee will both have places that are not adjacent to Gabrielle. She **can** sit next to Olivia if she sits in chair 7, but as she can alternatively sit in chair 5, she doesn't **have** to sit next to Olivia.

C (C) is ruled out directly by the fourth condition. According to the fourth condition, Gabrielle can't sit next to Lee.

D It was established in the "Overview" that Gabrielle sits in either chair 5 or chair 7. According to the second condition, Raymond sits in chair 4. Gabrielle **can** sit next to Raymond if she sits in chair 5. But since she can also sit in chair 7, she doesn't **have** to sit next to him.

■ *Difficulty Level: 4*

Question 16

Overview: What you notice first about this question is that it places a significant restriction on who can sit next to Raymond: neither Gabrielle nor Lee. What makes this so significant is that the setup already heavily restricts who can sit next to Raymond: Peter and Olivia are ruled out by the third condition, and Simone is ruled out by both the first and second conditions. This means that, all together, there are five people barred from sitting next to Raymond. The two left—namely, Francisco and Kyoko—must be the ones who sit next to Raymond.

If you check this result against the answer choices, you will find that you're done. (A) must be true.

The Correct Answer:

A The following people cannot sit next to Raymond: Simone (by either the first or the second condition), Peter and Olivia (by the third condition), and Gabrielle and Lee (by the question itself). Who's left? Just Francisco and Kyoko, both of whom must be the ones who sit next to Raymond. So (A) must be true.

The Incorrect Answer Choices:

B, C, D The following seating arrangement, which meets all of the requirements of the setup and the question, shows that none of (B), (C), or (D) must be true, since none of them is true in this outcome.

Simone, Peter, Kyoko, Raymond, Francisco, Lee, Olivia, Gabrielle

E The following seating arrangement, which meets all of the requirements of the setup and the question, shows that (E) doesn't have to be true. In this outcome, (E) is false.

Simone, Olivia, Kyoko, Raymond, Francisco, Lee, Peter, Gabrielle

■ *Difficulty Level: 3*

Question 17

Overview: This question asks you to determine what must be the case if Lee sits in chair 2. You already know that Simone sits in chair 1 and Raymond sits in chair 4. Continue to fill out the seating assignment. Who can sit in chair 3? You know that it can't be Simone, Raymond, or Lee. The third condition tells you that it can't be Peter or Olivia either. So far, that leaves Francisco, Gabrielle, and Kyoko. But Gabrielle can't sit in chair 3, because that would place her next to Lee, which is ruled out by the fourth condition. And Kyoko can't sit there, because that would place her next to her spouse Lee, which is ruled out by the first condition. That leaves Francisco as the only person who can sit in chair 3, next to Lee in chair 2.

If you check this result against the answer choices, you find that you're done. (C) must be true.

The Correct Answer:

C   The following diagram describes the complete possibilities for the seating arrangement in case Lee sits in chair 2:

Simone 1	Lee 2	Francisco 3	Raymond 4	Kyoko or Gabrielle 5	Peter or Olivia 6	Gabrielle or Kyoko 7	Olivia or Peter 8

If Lee sits in chair 2, then Francisco must sit in chair 3. So then it must be true that Francisco sits next to Lee.

The Incorrect Answer Choices:

A, B   The following seating arrangement shows that neither (A) nor (B) must be true:

Simone, Lee, Francisco, Raymond, Gabrielle, Olivia, Kyoko, Peter

D, E   This seating arrangement shows that neither (D) nor (E) must be true:

Simone, Lee, Francisco, Raymond, Kyoko, Peter, Gabrielle, Olivia

▪ *Difficulty Level: 5*

Question 18

Overview: If Francisco and Gabrielle sit next to Raymond, they must sit in chairs 3 and 5, although you don't know yet exactly who sits where. Which chairs does that leave to fill, and who will fill them? It leaves chairs 2, 6, 7, and 8, and it leaves two couples—Kyoko and Lee, and Peter and Olivia—to fill them. According to the first condition, spouses cannot sit next to one another. So one couple will have to occupy chairs 6 and 8, and the other couple will have to occupy chairs 2 and 7. This is the only way to distribute the two couples so as not to violate the first condition.

With the structure thus clarified, you can now track what can happen to Olivia. She could sit in chair 2. This has two immediate implications. Her spouse, Peter, would then sit in chair 7, as explained above. And Olivia would be sitting next to Simone, who sits in chair 1 according to the second condition. So this tells you that any complete list of people who can sit next to Olivia must include Simone.

If you check this result against the answer choices, you find that (A), (C), and (D) can all be crossed out, because none of them includes Simone.

That leaves (B) and (E), which differ only in that (E) includes Gabrielle. What you need to do, therefore, is to check whether Gabrielle can sit next to Olivia. (Checking whether Lee and Kyoko can sit next to Olivia would be a waste of time because they are both included in (B) as well as in (E).)

Since you have already started working through the assignment with Olivia in chair 2, continue that way. Peter, her spouse, remains in chair 7. Gabrielle can sit next to Olivia in chair 3. This puts Francisco in chair 5, and Kyoko and Lee in chairs 6 and 8. So, there is a possible seating arrangement with Olivia seated next to Gabrielle.

At this point, you're done. (B) can be ruled out because it doesn't include Gabrielle. So the correct answer has to be (E).

The Correct Answer:

E If Francisco and Gabrielle sit next to Raymond, they must sit in chairs 3 and 5. The remaining couples are Kyoko and Lee, and Olivia and Peter. According to the first condition, spouses cannot sit next to one another. So one couple will have to occupy chairs 2 and 7, and the other couple will have to occupy chairs 6 and 8. In addition, recall that the fourth condition prohibits Gabrielle from sitting next to Lee or Kyoko. So you eliminate any cases that would create such a violation: If Kyoko or Lee is in chair 6, then Gabrielle can't be in chair 5. And if Kyoko or Lee is in chair 2, then Gabrielle can't be in chair 3. The following two diagrams describe all the possible seating arrangements if Francisco and Gabrielle sit next to Raymond.

Olivia and Peter in chairs 2 and 7, and Kyoko and Lee in chairs 6 and 8:

Simone 1	Olivia/ Peter 2	Gabrielle 3	Raymond 4	Francisco 5	Kyoko/ Lee 6	Peter/ Olivia 7	Lee/ Kyoko 8

Kyoko and Lee in chairs 2 and 7, and Olivia and Peter in chairs 6 and 8:

Simone 1	Kyoko/ Lee 2	Francisco 3	Raymond 4	Gabrielle 5	Olivia/ Peter 6	Lee/ Kyoko 7	Peter/ Olivia 8

From these diagrams, you can see that each of Lee, Simone, Gabrielle, and Kyoko can sit next to Olivia, and there's no one else who can. (E) is complete because it lists all four of these people, and it is accurate because it doesn't include anyone who can't sit next to Olivia.

The Incorrect Answer Choices:

A (A) is inaccurate because it contains Francisco, and it is incomplete because it fails to list Simone and Lee.

B (B) is incomplete because it fails to list Gabrielle.

C (C) is incomplete because it fails to list Simone.

D (D) is inaccurate because it contains Francisco, and it is incomplete because it fails to list Simone.

■ *Difficulty Level: 5*

Questions 19–24

What the setup tells you: This group of questions involves Irene's purchase of four different pieces of furniture. These pieces are selected from five types of furniture, so there is one type of furniture that she doesn't buy. The third condition tells you that the type Irene doesn't buy is either a footstool or a vanity. The condition states that if she buys a vanity, she doesn't buy a footstool; and since she has to buy four different types of furniture, if she doesn't buy a vanity, she must buy a footstool. So she buys a table, a hutch, and a sideboard, together with either a footstool or a vanity.

The other task is to determine what kind of wood the items are made of. The sixth condition tells you that regardless of which items are purchased, exactly three out of the four available types of wood will be represented among them.

The fourth and the fifth conditions taken together tell you that neither the table nor the footstool can be oak. The first condition tells you that the vanity must be maple. So the hutch and the sideboard are the only items that can be made of oak.

The second condition says that only one kind of item—the sideboard—can be made of rosewood. None of the others can be rosewood. (Notice that the second condition does not say that a sideboard has to be rosewood. If she buys a sideboard, it can be made of any of the four kinds of wood.)

Question 19

Overview: For this question, an orientation type of question, your task is to find the one answer choice that represents an acceptable selection of furniture. You can start by taking the conditions in turn and crossing out any answer choice that violates that condition. When you've crossed out all but one answer choice, you're done; you've found the correct answer.

So start with the first condition. Cross out any answer choice that includes a vanity made of some wood other than maple. This eliminates (B).

Then go on to the second condition. Out of the four remaining answer choices, cross out any that includes an item other than a sideboard that is made of rosewood. This lets you cross out (C) because it includes a rosewood hutch. (Note that the fact that (C) includes a maple sideboard does not violate the second condition.)

Then check (A), (D), and (E) to see whether any of them violates the third condition, by including both a vanity and a footstool. (D) does, so it can be crossed out.

Neither (A) nor (E) violates either the fourth or the fifth conditions. (A) does, however, violate the sixth condition since it includes three items made of maple. So you're left with (E) as the correct answer.

The Correct Answer:

E   (E) conforms to all of the requirements of the setup, and so could be an accurate list of the items Irene buys.

The Incorrect Answer Choices:

A   (A) violates the sixth condition because it contains three items made of maple.

B   (B) violates the first condition because it contains a vanity made of something other than maple.

C   (C) violates the second condition because it contains a rosewood item that is not a sideboard.

D   (D) violates the third condition because it contains both a vanity and a footstool.

■ *Difficulty Level: 4*

Question 20

Overview: This question asks you to suppose that, of the items that Irene buys, one is rosewood and two are maple. Then you're asked to determine which pair of items could be among her purchases.

You know (from the second condition) that the item made of rosewood has to be the sideboard. And you know (from the third condition) that the selection will include either a footstool or a vanity. If it's a footstool, you know (from the fourth and fifth conditions) that the two maple items have to be the footstool and the table. If it's a vanity, you know (from the first condition) that the vanity has to be one of the two maple items.

These are probably all the readily available inferences you can draw from the information introduced in the question in combination with the setup conditions. So now turn to the answer choices.

Starting with (A), you find that you can rule it out because it includes a footstool that is not made of maple. You can cross out both (B) and (D) because they each include a sideboard that is not made of rosewood. Finally, you can also rule out (E) because, as discussed above, the two maple items must either be the footstool and the table, or they must include a maple vanity. Any selection including the items in (E)—a maple table and a maple hutch—would have to include three maple items, because it would also have to include either a maple footstool or a maple vanity. That leaves (C) as the only answer choice not crossed out, so (C) must be the correct answer.

The Correct Answer:

C   The following are acceptable outcomes in which two items are made of maple and one is made of rosewood (as the question requires) and that include the oak hutch and maple table specified in (C). Each one demonstrates that (C) can be a pair of items that Irene buys.

maple footstool, **oak hutch**, **maple table**, rosewood sideboard

or

maple vanity, **oak hutch**, **maple table**, rosewood sideboard

The Incorrect Answer Choices:

A (A) is ruled out by the fourth and fifth conditions. The fourth condition tells you that if Irene buys a footstool, she also buys a table made of the same wood. (A) lists an oak footstool, which means that Irene would also have to buy an oak table, but an oak table is ruled out by the fifth condition. So (A) could not be a pair of items she buys.

B (B) can be ruled out on the basis of the second condition together with information provided by the question. The question asks you to suppose that Irene buys a rosewood item. By the second condition, you know that any rosewood item she buys is a sideboard. But instead of a rosewood sideboard, (B) lists a pine sideboard.

D (D) can be ruled out on the basis of the second condition together with information provided by the question. The question asks you to suppose that Irene buys a rosewood item. By the second condition, you know that any rosewood item she buys is a sideboard. But instead of a rosewood sideboard, (D) lists a maple sideboard.

E This answer choice lists a hutch and a table as the two maple items that Irene buys. Since she also buys a rosewood item, you know by the second condition that she buys a rosewood sideboard. The fourth item she buys will then be either a hutch or a vanity. If she buys a vanity, it must be made of maple (by the first condition), which would result in her buying three maple items, in contradiction to the specific supposition of the question. If she buys a footstool, it must be made of the same wood as the table (by the fourth condition), which again results in her buying three maple items. So (E) cannot be a pair of items that Irene buys.

■ *Difficulty Level: 5*

Question 21

Overview: What you need to do in order to answer this question is to take each type of wood and ask, "Can Irene buy a footstool made of this type of wood?" If she can, then that type of wood must appear on the list. If she can't, then it shouldn't appear on the list.

You know (from the second condition) that no footstool can be made of rosewood. So you can immediately cross out (C) and (E). And you know (from the fourth and fifth conditions taken together) that no footstool can be oak, which allows you to cross out (A) and (D). (The fact that (E) could also have been ruled out for this reason is beside the point, since you've already crossed (E) off.)

Thus, you're done. The only remaining answer choice, (B), has to be the correct answer.

The Correct Answer:

B Irene can buy a maple footstool or a pine footstool, but not a footstool of any other type. To see that both possibilities exist, consider the following two outcomes, each of which satisfies all of the setup conditions:

maple footstool, oak hutch, rosewood sideboard, maple table

and

pine footstool, maple hutch, oak sideboard, pine table

She can't buy an oak footstool, because by the fourth condition this would require that she also buy an oak table, which is ruled out by the fifth condition. She can't buy a rosewood footstool, because the second condition requires that any rosewood item she buys be a sideboard.

The Incorrect Answer Choices:

A (A) is inaccurate because it includes oak and incomplete because it fails to include pine.

C (C) is inaccurate because it includes rosewood and incomplete because it fails to include pine.

D (D) is inaccurate because it includes oak.

E (E) is inaccurate because it includes oak and rosewood.

■ *Difficulty Level: 3*

Question 22

Overview: This question asks you to suppose that Irene buys a footstool. What you need to do in order to answer this question is to take each type of furniture and ask, "If Irene buys a footstool, can this item be among the items Irene buys and be made of maple?" If it can, then that item must appear on the list. If it can't, then it shouldn't appear on the list.

Keep in mind that, for this question, all of the items in the correct answer will be items made of maple. A quick glance at the answer choices shows that all five of them list a footstool. So it must be possible for an acceptable outcome to include a maple footstool. (As it turns out, you know already, from answering the previous question, that there are outcomes that include a maple footstool. Although the question requires inclusion of a footstool, the footstool mentioned in the question is not necessarily a maple one. But since Irene could buy a maple footstool, a footstool has to be one of the items on the list.) You also know (by the fourth condition) that any acceptable outcome that includes a maple footstool has to include a maple table. So you can cross off any answer choice that doesn't include a table. Accordingly, you cross off (C), (D), and (E), and you're left with just (A) and (B) to choose between.

The only difference between (A) and (B) is that (A) includes a vanity. But you know from the third condition that no acceptable outcome that includes a footstool can include a vanity. So (A) can be ruled out.

Since you've eliminated all of the answer choices except (B), you're done. (B) has to be the correct answer.

The Correct Answer:

B To show that (B) is an accurate list, you would need to show that for each item listed in (B), there's at least one acceptable outcome that includes this item in maple. Each of the following selections shows this:

maple footstool, **maple table**, oak hutch, pine sideboard

pine footstool, pine table, **maple hutch**, rosewood sideboard

pine footstool, pine table, oak hutch, **maple sideboard**

To show that (B) is a complete list, you would need to show that no acceptable selection can include a maple vanity. The vanity is ruled out on the basis of the third condition—Irene can't buy both a footstool and a vanity.

The Incorrect Answer Choices:

A (A) is incorrect because it includes a vanity.

C (C) is incomplete because it fails to include a table.

D (D) is incomplete because it fails to include a sideboard and a table.

E (E) is incomplete because it fails to include a hutch, a sideboard, and a table.

- *Difficulty Level: 5*

Question 23

Overview: Keep in mind that in this question you're being asked to find two items that **cannot** be the ones that are made of the same wood. All of the incorrect answer choices will be pairs that **can** be made of the same wood.

The Correct Answer:

A   You know (by the fourth condition) that if Irene buys a footstool, she also buys a table that is made of the same wood. So the pair of items that are made of the same wood can't consist of a footstool together with an item other than a table. Therefore, the pair in (A)—a footstool and a hutch—can't be the pair of items that are made of the same wood.

The Incorrect Answer Choices:

B   The following outcome violates none of the setup conditions and demonstrates that the pair in (B) could be made of the same wood:

oak hutch, **oak sideboard**, maple vanity, pine table

C   The following outcome violates none of the setup conditions and demonstrates that the pair in (C) could be made of the same wood:

pine hutch, **pine table**, maple vanity, rosewood sideboard

D   The following outcome violates none of the setup conditions and demonstrates that the pair in (D) could be made of the same wood:

maple sideboard, **maple vanity**, pine table, oak hutch

E   The following outcome violates none of the setup conditions and demonstrates that the pair in (E) could be made of the same wood:

maple table, **maple vanity**, rosewood sideboard, pine hutch

- *Difficulty Level: 5*

Question 24

Overview: To answer this question, you have to select the answer choice that does **not** have to be true if none of the items Irene buys is made of maple. So the answer choices you cross off here are those that must be true in this circumstance.

Since none of the items selected is made of maple, the vanity can't be selected. So you know that the selection will consist of the following items:

a footstool, a table, a hutch, a sideboard

With this result, look at the answer choices and see if any can be eliminated. (A) can be eliminated because a footstool must be selected.

If none of the items is maple, then that leaves three kinds of wood—oak, pine, and rosewood. Two items will be made of the same kind of wood, and the other two will be made of two different kinds of wood. Since rosewood will have to be one of the woods appearing in the outcome, and since (by the second condition) any rosewood item must be a sideboard, Irene must buy a rosewood sideboard. This eliminates (C).

Since the table can never be made of oak or rosewood, and it isn't made of maple, then it has to be made of pine. Therefore, the footstool will also have to be made of pine (by the fourth condition). Thus (E) must be true and can be eliminated.

That leaves oak as the only wood that the hutch could be made of. This means that (D) has to be true and so can be eliminated. You're left with (B) as the only remaining answer choice. (Because the hutch must be made of oak, it can't be made of pine, which shows that (B) **must** be false.) So you're done.

The Correct Answer:

B   Putting together all of the inferences drawn in the "Overview" above, you can see that, if Irene doesn't buy an item made of maple, there's only one acceptable selection:

pine footstool, pine table, oak hutch, rosewood sideboard

This selection doesn't include a pine hutch. (B), therefore, doesn't have to be true. (In fact, it must be false.)

The Incorrect Answer Choices:

A   If Irene doesn't buy an item made of maple, then she can't buy a vanity (because the first condition says that if she buys a vanity, it's a maple vanity). So the items she buys must be a footstool, a table, a hutch, and a sideboard. Therefore, she must buy a footstool. So (A) must be true and thus can't be the correct answer.

C   If nothing that Irene buys is made of maple, then oak, pine, and rosewood must be the woods that the items she buys are made of. Since the rosewood item must be a sideboard, (C) must be true.

D   If Irene doesn't buy an item made of maple, then oak, pine, and rosewood must be the woods that the items she buys are made of. By the first condition, she doesn't buy a vanity (because it would have to be made of maple), so she must buy a footstool, a hutch, a sideboard, and a table. The second condition requires that the footstool and the table be made of the same type of wood. Since by the second condition neither can be made of rosewood, and since by the fifth condition the table can't be made of oak, these two items must be made of pine. The sideboard, by the second condition, must be made of rosewood. By the sixth condition, you know that there are just two items that are made of the same wood. That leaves one item, the hutch, to be made of oak. Therefore, (D) must be true.

E   If Irene doesn't buy an item made of maple, then oak, pine, and rosewood must be the woods that the items she buys are made of. By the first condition, she doesn't buy a vanity (because it would have to be made of maple), so she must buy a footstool, a hutch, a sideboard, and a table. The second condition requires that the footstool and the table be made of the same type of wood. Since by the second condition neither can be made of rosewood, and since by the fifth condition the table can't be made of oak, these two items must be made of pine. By the sixth condition, you know that there are just two items that are made of the same wood, so (E) must be true.

■ *Difficulty Level: 5*

Reading Comprehension: Questions 1–26

Questions 1–7

Synopsis: The passage begins by making the point that an earlier view held by biologists—the view that no invertebrates form schools—has been abandoned in the face of evidence that there are numerous cases of invertebrates that do form schools. Evidence that these truly are cases of schooling is presented in the second paragraph. The first sentence of the third paragraph presents the central thesis of the passage, namely, that schooling brings benefits. The rest of the third paragraph focuses mainly on benefits that are enjoyed passively by the school, such as giving the appearance of a single large creature and thereby discouraging predation, while the fourth is concerned with the advantages enjoyed by a school in actively defending itself against predators. The final paragraph turns to potential survival advantages of schooling that are related to feeding and breeding, but it also discusses what may happen when a school gets too large for the available food supply.

Question 1

The Correct Answer:

D As you can see from the synopsis, the passage begins by making the point that there are invertebrates that form schools. Most of the rest of the passage presents benefits that schooling invertebrates may derive from their schooling behavior. Choice (D) accurately captures both of these aspects of the main point.

The Incorrect Answer Choices:

A The passage strongly suggests that the optimal size of a school of invertebrates is determined by how much food is available. But the passage is not primarily concerned with analyzing what determines the optimal size of a school. The passage mentions the issue of optimal size only as part of its discussion of the survival benefits of schooling in the areas of feeding and breeding.

B The passage discusses defensive maneuvers only as part of its account of one of the benefits of schooling. Thus, how defensive maneuvers work provides evidence for one of the main ideas of the passage, but it is not itself the main focus of the passage. Moreover, (B) does not correctly describe what the passage says about defensive maneuvers. The passage does not relate specific defensive maneuvers to aspects of the internal structure of the school.

C The passage compares schooling invertebrates to schooling fish only to make the point that their schools have highly similar internal structures. The passage does not mention any dissimilarities between schools of fish and schools of invertebrates. So (C) is not correct.

E The passage mentions both protection from predation and finding food as benefits that schooling provides for invertebrates, but it does not discuss the issue of the relative importance of these two benefits. So (E) does not describe an idea that can be found in the passage.

■ *Difficulty Level: 1*

Question 2

Keep in mind that what we are looking for here is something that is **not** presented by the passage as a characteristic of an invertebrate school. So if something is presented in the passage as a characteristic of an invertebrate school, it cannot be the correct answer to this question.

The Correct Answer:

B The passage does not say that members of an invertebrate school are arranged directly above or below one another. (In fact, it says just the opposite in lines 15–16.) So (B) is not a characteristic of invertebrate schools, according to the passage.

The Incorrect Answer Choices:

A The passage explains how a local scarcity of food (lines 55–59) can keep the size of an invertebrate school down. Since scarcity of food is an external circumstance, (A) is characteristic of invertebrate schools, according to the passage.

C, D In lines 5–7, the passage defines schools as "cohesive social units whose members are evenly spaced and face the same way." Hence, it implies that any school, including any invertebrate school, must have these characteristics. It follows that, according to the passage, both (C) and (D) are characteristic of invertebrate schools.

E The passage says, in lines 54–57, "Schooling can facilitate the search for mates, but **as a school's numbers rise**, food may become locally scarce and **females may produce smaller clutches of eggs** . . ." [emphasis added]. (E) captures accurately what the emphasized clauses taken together say. So according to the passage, (E) is characteristic of invertebrate schools.

▪ *Difficulty Level: 1*

Question 3

Since this question asks which word could replace the word "resolve" in line 36 without a change in meaning, it is essential to understand how the word "resolve" actually functions in line 36. The sentence in which "resolve" occurs says, "When a predator is sighted, the school compacts, so that a predator's senses may be unable to resolve individuals . . ." (lines 34–36). So what the predator may be unable to do, as the school contracts to one big blob, is pick out any one individual from the rest of the school. This is a fairly common use of "resolve" in connection with sensory perception. When people speak of the "resolution" of an image, it is this sense of "resolve" that they have in mind.

The Correct Answer:

D As indicated above, we are looking for a word that means something like "pick out" or "tell apart," and of the available answer choices, only (D)—"distinguish"—fits this description. When it is substituted for "resolve" in line 36, the meaning of the original text is preserved.

The Incorrect Answer Choices:

A The word "resolve" has a variety of different meanings, but none of them is even close to any meaning of "control." In fact, if you substitute "control" for "resolve," as the question directs you to do, the result you get is ". . . a predator's senses may be unable to control individuals." With this substitution, the sentence appears to be more or less nonsense. In any case, it is clear that it doesn't mean the same thing as the original sentence with "resolve" left in place.

B Again, the intended sense of "resolve" is not close to any of the usual senses of "answer." Moreover, the sentence that results from actually making the substitution is more or less nonsense.

C The word "reconcile" may be a tempting candidate for a substitution because there are contexts in which its meaning comes close to the meaning of "resolve." For example, there is a rough equivalence between speaking of "resolving a dispute" and speaking of "reconciling the two sides in a dispute with each other." But notice that in the sense in which "reconcile" comes close to a meaning of "resolve," it is about making differences disappear or at least seem less important. The sense of "resolve" to be matched, however, goes in exactly the opposite direction: it is a matter of discerning differences, of telling where one individual leaves off and another one begins. Thus in the specific context of line 36, "reconcile" is not a good substitute for "resolve."

E This is another case like (A) and (B) above. The intended sense of "resolve" is not close to any sense of "pacify." And the result of actually making the substitution is more or less nonsense.

- *Difficulty Level: 1*

Question 4

The Correct Answer:

E The final paragraph mentions two advantages of invertebrate schooling behavior, namely, that it enables invertebrates to find food and that it facilitates the search for mates. These advantages can lead to an increase in the size of the school. The downside is that the school can get too large for the local food supply, so that it faces starvation. The paragraph ends by pointing out reactions on the part of the school that have the effect of reducing its size, thereby eliminating the imbalance between population size and food supply. Thus (E) is the correct answer, since it mentions all three salient points: advantages of schooling, disadvantages of schooling, and responses by the school to avoid adverse consequences.

The Incorrect Answer Choices:

A The final paragraph is written from only one point of view: the point of view of someone trying to explain that invertebrate schooling behavior is, on balance, of benefit to the invertebrates. There is no mention in this paragraph, or anywhere else in the passage, of any opposing point of view on this matter.

B The final paragraph describes a variety of behaviors on the part of schooling invertebrates. All of these behaviors are best described purely as reactions determined by environmental circumstances, and not as involving any element of choice. But even if one does, metaphorically, call these behaviors "choices," it is not accurate to say that the last paragraph proposes alternative choices.

C It is not clear what it would mean to "interpret" a phenomenon like invertebrate schooling. But, in any case, no alternative interpretation is discussed or evaluated. So (C) fails to be correct for reasons similar to those for which (A) does.

D The final paragraph does suggest that schooling can have the disadvantageous result of making a population too large for the available food supply. But the last paragraph does not question the claim that, overall, schooling is beneficial.

- *Difficulty Level: 2*

Question 5

The Correct Answer:

A The passage says that jellyfish groupings—and this is the only mention of jellyfish in the passage—"cannot be described as schools" (line 5). Thus, jellyfish are an example of invertebrates that do not engage in schooling behavior.

The Incorrect Answer Choices:

B The passage denies that jellyfish groupings are schools (line 5), and immediately goes on to characterize schools as "cohesive social units whose members are evenly spaced." So, the passage presents jellyfish as examples of invertebrates that do **not** form groups with evenly spaced members.

C The passage does not say that jellyfish are brought together in groups **only** by the availability of a common food source. The passage also explicitly mentions wind, currents, and waves as giving rise to such groups.

D As mentioned in the discussion of choice (A), the passage explicitly denies that jellyfish groupings are schools. Thus, since jellyfish do not form schools at all, they are not examples of invertebrates that form schools only when circumstances are advantageous.

E The passage does describe krill as collecting in such massive numbers that they provide abundant food, but it does not describe jellyfish this way. The passage neither comments on the size of jellyfish groupings nor on whether such groupings are a rich food source for predators.

- *Difficulty Level: 1*

Question 6

The Correct Answer:

C The passage makes it clear that the kind of cannibalism that can occur in a school of crustaceans—adults feeding on the young (lines 57–58)—is triggered by scarcity of food. A school that suffers from a shortage of food is not an attractive school for an unattached individual crustacean to join. In fact, such schools are so unattractive that some of their members leave and join other schools (lines 59–60). Thus, the passage provides support for (C).

The Incorrect Answer Choices:

A According to the passage, cannibalism tends to occur in schools that suffer from a shortage of food. It is unlikely that there would be much food available at the edge of such a school. So it would be highly unlikely that an individual crustacean encountering such a school would attach itself to the edge of that school specifically in order to obtain food.

B Cannibalism in schools of crustaceans is specifically described as a matter of adults feeding on the young. So it would be reasonable to infer the opposite of (B), namely, that an individual crustacean would be **less** likely to be eaten if it were fully grown.

D As the discussion of the correct answer suggests, the most likely reaction on the part of an individual crustacean encountering a school that does not have enough to eat is to avoid that school. As shown by the fact that some members leave a school whose food supply is inadequate, the protection from predation that a school provides is less important than having enough to eat.

E The passage does mention complex swimming maneuvers executed by members of invertebrate schools. These swimming maneuvers are not presented as a means of confusing members of the school but rather as a means of baffling small predators. So the passage provides no grounds for inferring (E).

- *Difficulty Level: 2*

Question 7

The Correct Answer:

C   The assumption mentioned in the first sentence of the third paragraph is that schooling, since it is an active behavior, must bring important benefits. The rest of the passage makes it clear that the important benefits provided by schooling are those that promote survival. But (C) implies that schooling diminishes an invertebrate's chances of survival. Hence, (C), if true, undermines the stated assumption.

The Incorrect Answer Choices:

A   If (A) said that many groups of **schooling invertebrates** are unable to execute any defensive maneuvers, then, if true, it would negate one of the benefits claimed for schooling by the passage and thus undermine the assumption to some degree, though perhaps not to the same degree as (C). But in fact (A) says only that many groups of **invertebrates** are unable to execute such maneuvers, and this does not undermine the assumption at all, since the invertebrates in question may all be of nonschooling varieties. (It is implicit in the first sentence of the second paragraph that some invertebrates lack sufficient mobility to school, and hence, presumably, to execute defensive maneuvers.)

B   One important benefit discussed in the passage is the benefit of protection from predation. One of the ways in which schools discourage predation is by appearing to be one massive animal. (B) says that there are some predators that would not be fooled in this way. But even if (B) is true, this mechanism might still discourage a majority of predators. Moreover, this is only one of the ways in which schooling provides protection against predators, and nothing in the passage suggests that it is necessarily even the most important one. So even if (B) is true, schooling would still bring the important benefit of helping to foil predators.

D   The passage essentially acknowledges that (D) is true (lines 21–23). However, it suggests that this drawback of schooling is outweighed by the fact that schooling reduces the chances of an encounter between the invertebrates in a school and a predator (lines 23–25).

E   The last paragraph indicates that the optimal size of a school depends mainly on the availability of food. So what choice (E) suggests most strongly is that in general there has been a decline in the richness of sources of food. But this does not mean that schools are not an efficient way of exploiting such sources of food as there are, or that they do not confer the other benefits claimed for them, such as protection from predators.

■ *Difficulty Level: 3*

Questions 8–14

Synopsis: The first paragraph of the passage asks what is the basis for our intuitions concerning the proper balance between the seriousness of a crime and the severity of the punishment for that crime. To help answer this question, the second paragraph distinguishes between two kinds of rationale for punishing criminals. The first, or "social-benefit," rationale holds that punishment is justified to the extent that it benefits society by helping to deter criminals from committing crimes, either by fear of the punishment or by removing them from society for some period of time. The second rationale holds that the punishment meted out to a criminal is justified by the seriousness of the crime committed, independent of any benefit to society. This rationale is controversial because it seems to make punishment consist in retribution.

The third paragraph points out that the social-benefit rationale would seem to favor extremely harsh punishments even for minor offenses, since such punishments would have a greater deterrent effect than milder ones. This rationale thus appears unable to account for our intuition that such punishments would be unjustly harsh. It could thus be argued that retributive considerations, which demand that punishment be proportional to the crime, must be the source of intuitions about when a punishment is just.

In the final paragraph, however, the author proposes another possible analysis: intuitions about just, or appropriate, punishment have to do with the balance such punishment strikes between harm to the criminal and societal benefit. Thus the author suggests that the second rationale, that the punishment ought to fit the crime, is grounded in the same concept of benefit that underlies the first rationale, and not on purely retributive considerations.

Question 8

The Correct Answer:

E As the discussion above makes clear, the passage argues that although the rationale that the punishment ought to fit the crime appears to correspond more closely to our intuitions about just punishment than does the social-benefit rationale, in the end it too is grounded in the concept of social benefit.

The Incorrect Answer Choices:

A According to the final paragraph of the passage, "the second rationale can be seen as grounded in the first and its retributive nature disappears" (lines 48–50). Thus (A) misinterprets the passage both in regard to which rationale is the more fundamental and in regard to whether the second rationale is ultimately retributivist in nature.

B The statement in (B) can be considered a summary of an argument considered in the third paragraph. But the passage does not endorse this argument, and in the final paragraph it comes to a conclusion at odds with it.

C The statement in (C) is the conclusion of the argument considered in the third paragraph, but, as noted above in our discussion of (B), the passage ultimately comes to quite a different conclusion. The phrase "it would seem that" (line 32) might, in another context, indicate tentative endorsement, but the final paragraph makes it clear that here it indicates a view that the author considers attractive at first glance, but ultimately false.

D The passage suggests that a punishment is unjust if it is more harmful to the criminal than beneficial to society (lines 44–45). However, the passage does not insist that for a punishment to be just, the social benefit from that punishment must **outweigh** the harm it does to the criminal, but only that there must be a fair balance between the two (lines 47–48). So (D) misrepresents the view advocated by the author of the passage.

■ *Difficulty Level: 2*

Question 9

The Correct Answer:

A   The passage comments on the controversial nature of the second rationale explicitly: "This rationale is controversial because some find it difficult to see how a punishment can be justified if it brings no societal benefit" (lines 17–19). In other words, the second rationale is said to be controversial because it does not employ the notion of social benefit.

The Incorrect Answer Choices:

B   The risk of disproportionately severe punishments is associated by the passage with the first, or social-benefit, rationale (lines 24–31). The second rationale, on the other hand, is said to allow for proportionality between punishments and crimes (lines 38–40).

C   The passage does not call the second rationale controversial because it conflicts with our intuitions about justice. In fact, the passage introduces the second rationale as one that conforms to our intuitions about justice better than the social-benefit rationale does.

D   The passage describes the second rationale as controversial because that rationale regards the justice of punishment as "independent of any benefit to society" (lines 16–17). In other words, the second rationale is controversial because in justifying a punishment it makes no appeal to any social benefits—such as deterring criminals—that this punishment might bring. But this does not mean that the second rationale implies that punishment has no deterrent effect.

E   In discussing the rationales for punishment, the passage does not contrast intuition with logic. It makes no reference to logic at all. So (E) cannot be a good description of why, according to the passage, the second rationale is controversial. The passage does talk about intuitions in the third paragraph; specifically, it mentions our intuitions about the justice or injustice of punishments. And the fact that the second rationale supports those intuitions is presented as a strong point of this rationale, not as something that makes it controversial.

■ *Difficulty Level: 1*

Question 10

The question asks about the phrase "retributive nature," which appears in the passage only in line 50. This does not mean, however, that the meaning of that phrase can be determined from what is said in or around line 50. Rather, the phrase refers to a concept that has been introduced and developed much earlier in the passage, in the discussion of the second rationale (lines 14–23).

The Correct Answer:

B   The passage says of the second rationale that it justifies a punishment "by the severity of the crime, independent of any benefit to society" (lines 15–17), and goes on to say that, without such benefit, "punishment would appear to be little more than retribution" (lines 20–21). So the passage sees the retributive nature of the second rationale as consisting in the fact that this rationale regards punishment as justified solely by the severity of the crime. This is confirmed in line 50, where it is asserted that this retributive nature "disappears," in other words, that the second rationale only appeared to be retributive. The reason given is that when this rationale is understood properly, it is seen to base the severity of the punishment not purely on the severity of the crime, but on whether its benefit to society warrants the amount of harm done to the criminal.

The Incorrect Answer Choices:

A   The second rationale relies, in part, on the notion of harm to criminals. It claims that, for a punishment to be just, the harm to the criminal—that is, the severity of the punishment—must be proportionate to the seriousness of the crime. But this does not **equate** social benefit with harm to criminals; doing so would lead to the absurd conclusion that the greater the harm to criminals, the greater the benefit to society.

C   According to the passage, retributive considerations, unlike considerations of social benefit, "allow for proportionality between punishments and crimes" (lines 38–40). So according to the second rationale, sentences that are disproportionate to the crimes they punish would be unjust punishments.

D According to the passage, the second rationale treats punishments as just or unjust independent of whether they benefit society (line 16). And the passage argues that, unlike the first rationale, the second rationale would not license excessive punishments merely because they are beneficial to society. So the second rationale runs counter to the belief that any punishment that benefits society is just.

E The passage does not state that the second rationale is biased toward harsh punishments. The key notion that characterizes just punishments, under the second rationale, is appropriateness, not harshness.

- *Difficulty Level: 4*

Question 11

The Correct Answer:

C The author says, in lines 42–45, "[that] it can be argued that our intuition of the injustice of an overly harsh punishment is based on our sense that such a punishment is more harmful to the criminal than beneficial to society." The statement in (C), "Such punishment benefits society less than it harms the criminal," is merely an alternative way of saying that the harm to the criminal outweighs the benefit to society. So (C) correctly restates the author's point.

The Incorrect Answer Choices:

A By saying that an overly harsh punishment is one that is "more harmful to the criminal than beneficial to society" (lines 44–45), the author is not saying that such punishment brings **no** benefit to society at large. What makes the punishment overly harsh is that the harm to the criminal is greater than the benefit to society.

B The author readily grants that overly harsh punishment is harmful to the criminal, but this is not presented by the author as the basis for our intuition of the injustice of such a punishment. That intuition is based on the notion that the harm to the criminal is greater than any benefit to society. (B) misses this important point.

D Since (C) is the correct answer for the reasons dicussed above, and since (D) is its opposite, (D) cannot be correct.

E The author says that "our intuition that a punishment is just is based on our sense that this punishment fairly balances societal benefit against harm to the criminal" (lines 46–48). So a punishment that attempts to reconcile social benefit with harm to the criminal is one that attempts to be just. Our intuition of the injustice of an overly harsh punishment is therefore based on its **not** being a punishment of the sort described in (E).

- *Difficulty Level: 4*

Question 12

The Correct Answer:

B The author says explicitly, referring to the first rationale, that it can lead to instances of penalties that far outweigh the crime (lines 29–30); in other words, penalties that are grossly unfair to the criminal being punished. The second rationale, on the other hand, is presented by the author as demanding proportionality between punishments and crimes. So we can infer that the author presumably does not believe that the second rationale has the same potential unfairness as the first.

The Incorrect Answer Choices:

A The author neither says nor implies anything about how widely accepted either rationale is. So nothing in the passage suggests that the author would be likely to agree that the second rationale for punishing criminals is more widely accepted than the first.

C The author mentions certain specific punishments, but only in passing. In line 3 the author mentions a "sentence of probation," and in lines 5–6, a "sentence of twenty years in prison." But the author gives no systematic account of kinds of punishment and does not compare the two rationales in terms of how many different kinds of punishments each justifies.

D The second rationale is not presented as a sort of backup rationale, applicable to cases in which the first rationale would produce an unsatisfactory result. The author presents the second rationale as a conceptual alternative to the first, and presents each as an attempt to account for the full range of our intuitions about which punishments are just and which are not.

E According to the author, what characterizes the punishments that are in keeping with the second rationale is that they exactly fit the crime; that is, they are neither too lenient nor too harsh. In contrast, with regard to the first rationale, the author argues that it could allow for excessively harsh punishments. So it is unlikely that the author would agree with (E).

- *Difficulty Level: 4*

Question 13

The Correct Answer:

E The author's attitude toward very harsh penalties for minor offenses is revealed in the third paragraph. One thing the author says is that such penalties represent a "problem" (line 24) for the social-benefit rationale. More telling is what the author says in lines 28–31, namely, "something leads us to say that in such cases the penalty far outweighs the crime. That is, there appears to be something intuitively wrong, or unjust, about these punishments." The second comment is more revealing about the author's attitude because the author says, "something leads us to say," making clear that the author would be included among those who say so. And the terms used, "wrong" and "unjust," are clear indications of disapproval of moral injustice.

The Incorrect Answer Choices:

A The author explicitly grants that such penalties might deter crime (line 28). But while conceding deterrence as a potential fact, the author gives no indication of approval, however reluctant, of such penalties. Rather the author suggests that these penalties are intuitively wrong, and there is no indication that this negative judgment of the penalties is in any way offset by the effect that might be achieved.

B The author explicitly grants that it is possible that such penalties "may have great benefit to society" (line 26). The author does not hint at any skepticism regarding these potential benefits. What the author is skeptical about, and not just mildly, is the justice of such penalties as a means for bringing about these benefits.

C Calling such penalties "intuitively wrong, or unjust" (line 31) is not a matter of expressing detached indifference toward their effects on criminals, but rather strikes a note of moral concern. So (C) misrepresents the attitude expressed by the author.

D The author strongly suggests that such penalties are wrong and unjust. The author does not present any alternative positions. The attitude conveyed by the author is one of moral disapproval and not scholarly neutrality.

- *Difficulty Level: 5*

Question 14

The Correct Answer:

A As stated in the second paragraph, the second rationale is "that a punishment is justified by the severity of the crime, independent of any benefit to society" (lines 15–17). In other words, what is important according to this rationale is thus the inherent fairness of the punishment, not its social consequences. Hence, the second rationale is most consistent with principle (A).

The Incorrect Answer Choices:

B According to the second rationale, a punishment is justified entirely by the inherent seriousness of the crime itself. This is clearly independent of what society deems correct, as shown by the fact that the punishment deemed appropriate by sociey for the very same crime can change over time. Hence, the rationale is certainly less consistent with (B) than it is with (A).

C, D, E The second rationale is very clear in making justice, or fairness, the only relevant consideration. It is also very clear in denying that considerations of societal benefits have any role in justifying punishments. So any principle like (C), (D), or (E) that assigns any weight to the consequences of an action in determining its correctness is inconsistent with the second rationale.

- *Difficulty Level: 5*

Questions 15–21

Synopsis: The passage is concerned with a challenge faced by Hispanic-American writers: how to establish independence from the literature of Spain in light of the fact that many of them write in Spanish. The author, who is a Hispanic-American writer himself or herself, claims that Hispanic-America authors have pursued this goal through two often conflicting responses, cosmopolitanism and nativism. Cosmopolitanism seeks its models in North American literature and European literatures other than that of Spain. Nativism concentrates on the lives of the Hispanic peoples who live in the United States and seeks to give them voice.

The author then asserts that the tension between nativism and cosmopolitanism has shaped Hispanic-American literature for a number of generations. To illustrate the tensions between these two tendencies, the author contrasts two works by Hispanic American writers. The first was praised for its use of European literary techniques but criticized for its lack of specifically Hispanic-American settings or characters; the second was praised for its vivid portrayal of its Hispanic-American characters' daily lives but criticized for its lack of literary polish.

According to the author, the period from 1918 to 1930 was a predominantly cosmopolitan one. This period was followed by "a return to our peoples and our colloquial dialects" (lines 44–45). "Throughout our history," the author adds, "a concern for novelty and experimentation has been followed by a return to origins" (lines 47–49). The author closes by declaring that contemporary Hispanic-American writers who write in Spanish face a unique challenge. In order to appreciate the value of Hispanic-American culture, these writers must venture out into the broader, mainstream culture; by the same token, in order not to disappear into the mainstream, they must return to their origins. "In this way," the author concludes, "we attempt to reconcile the opposing tendencies of cosmopolitanism and nativism" (lines 58–60).

Question 15

The Correct Answer:

B The main point of the passage is to describe the ways Hispanic-American writers have tried to "break the ties of dependency" (line 8) that linked them with the literature of Spain. The passage says that Hispanic-American writers have used two tactics in their pursuit of this goal, cosmopolitanism and nativism, which are said to have alternately dominated Hispanic-American literature. Thus (B) accurately captures the chief focus of the passage.

The Incorrect Answer Choices:

A What (A) says is generally supported by the passage, but (A) does not express the main point of the passage. (A) can be regarded as an accurate description of the situation that creates the challenge faced by Hispanic-American writers, but the main point of the passage concerns the conflicting tactics for confronting this challenge.

C The passage does not say or imply that Hispanic-American writers tend to follow the pattern described in (C). Rather, the passage makes clear that the approaches of individual writers vary (see the second paragraph), and that one or the other of the two tendencies prevails in different eras.

D None of the **critics** described in the passage is presented as claiming that cosmopolitanism and nativism compete with each other for dominance. On the other hand, in the third paragraph the **author** suggests that the two tendencies compete with each other.

E The passage does not say that the conflicting tendencies of cosmopolitanism and nativism have isolated writers of differing cultures from one another. On the contrary, the author suggests that despite the great differences among the cultures from which they spring (lines 1–3), Hispanic-Americans share in the "attempt to reconcile the opposing tendencies of cosmopolitanism and nativism" (lines 59–60).

- *Difficulty Level: 4*

Question 16

The Correct Answer:

A The author describes the period between 1918 and 1930 as "the rich period of the avant-garde" (line 35). In addition, according to the passage, this period "produced a number of outstanding works of exceptional boldness of expression" (lines 42–43). In other words, many works produced in this period were especially notable for their unusual expressiveness.

The Incorrect Answer Choices:

B The phrase "a return . . . to our colloquial dialects" (lines 44–45) does not apply to works produced between 1918 and 1930 but rather applies to works produced during the nativistic phase that began after 1930.

C The passage does not describe any works by Hispanic-American writers as notable for their unprecedented reliance on Spanish literary forms. The literary forms that are said to have had "a profound influence on many Hispanic-American poets and novelists" between 1918 and 1930 (lines 40–41) are characteristic of European movements. But the first paragraph describes cosmopolitanism as characterized by an effort to "adopt the literary forms and styles in vogue in other European and North American literatures" (lines 11–12), where "other" means non-Spanish.

D According to the passage, "There are periods in which the outward-oriented sensibility predominates, and others in which tendencies toward self-absorption and introspection prevail" (lines 31–34). But the passage goes on to say that the period between 1918 and 1930 was marked by an outward-oriented sensibility and thus not by introspection.

E The period that is described in the passage as being characterized by the creation of works "less indebted to current trends in the mainstream culture" (lines 45–46) is the period immediately **after** that of 1918 to 1930. This reduced emphasis is what distinguishes the later period from the 1918–1930 period; the earlier period was characterized by experimentation and openness to "movements that were also inspiring other North American writers" (lines 39–40). So works produced between 1918 and 1930 are ot the ones said to be notable for their reduced emphasis on current trends in mainstream North American culture.

- *Difficulty Level: 3*

Question 17

The Correct Answer:

E   The author characterizes nativism in various ways. In lines 13–14, the author refers to the endeavor "to describe the nature of the United States and give voice to the Hispanic peoples who live there." The author also speaks of "the return to the private or original culture" (lines 30–31), and of "a return to our peoples and our colloquial dialects" (lines 44–45). Thus according to the passage, nativism does indeed represent an attempt to depict the experiences of various Hispanic peoples in U.S. settings.

The Incorrect Answer Choices:

A   The passage clearly associates experimentation with cosmopolitanism (see lines 36–38 and lines 47–48). Nativism, on the other hand, is characterized by "a return to origins" (lines 48–49) and is explicitly contrasted with the cosmopolitan quest for novelty and experimentation.

B   In the first paragraph, the author describes one approach taken by Hispanic American writers: "seeking to adopt the literary forms and styles in vogue in other European and North American literatures" (lines 11–12). In the next sentence, the author characterizes this approach as cosmopolitanism. Thus while the exploration of Hispanic themes described in (B) might be typical of nativism, the adoption of forms and styles from other literatures is not.

C   The passage does not say or imply that Hispanic-American writers (whether predominantly cosmopolitan or nativist in orientation) attempt to transform the Spanish language.

D   The passage states that the attempt on the part of Hispanic-American writers to align their work with other North American literatures characterizes cosmopolitanism (lines 10–11) rather than the nativist tendency.

■ *Difficulty Level: 4*

Question 18

The Correct Answer:

E   According to the passage, the period from 1918 to 1930 was marked by searching and experimentation inspired by European literary movements. This phase, the author says, produced a number of works of "exceptional boldness of expression" (line 43). The period following 1930 was marked by a return to origins—that is, it was "characterized by a return to our peoples and our colloquial dialects, by the creation of works less indebted to current trends" (lines 44–46). It can thus be inferred that in the period after 1930, Hispanic-American writers abandoned experimentation and boldness of expression in favor of a greater naturalness of expression that flows, at least in part, from the use of colloquial language.

The Incorrect Answer Choices:

A   Narrative experimentation is a variety of literary experimentation. As we noted in the explanation of the correct answer, literary experimentation is characteristic of cosmopolitanism. On the other hand, the period immediately following 1930 is described in the passage as a time in which nativism predominated. Accordingly, works produced in the period immediately following 1930 were characterized by the "return to our peoples and our colloquial dialects" (lines 44–45), and not by narrative experimentation.

B, C   The passage mentions both expressionism and surrealism as examples of European literary movements that inspired the cosmopolitanism of 1918 to 1930. The period immediately following 1930 was characterized by the abandonment of the forms and styles of such movements. Thus it can be inferred that Hispanic-American literature during the period after 1930 was **not** characterized by expressionistic tendencies or by surreal imagery.

D   The passage states that the period immediately following 1930 was characterized by "the creation of works less indebted to current trends in mainstream culture" (lines 45–46). So it can be inferred that this period was **not** characterized by use of mainstream literary forms.

■ *Difficulty Level: 4*

Question 19

The Correct Answer:

A In the final paragraph, the author identifies himself or herself as belonging to the group asked about in this question, "We contemporary Hispanic-American writers who write in Spanish ... " (lines 50–51). The author also says that there is a challenge that "we confront each day" (lines 54–55). That is, in order to appreciate the value of Hispanic culture, these writers must venture forth into the public sphere of mainstream culture, a process the author identifies with cosmopolitanism in lines 29–30; and in order not to disappear into the mainstream, they must return to their origins, which the author identifies with nativism in lines 44–46. The author concludes by saying, "In this way, we attempt to reconcile the opposing tendencies of cosmopolitanism and nativism" (lines 58–60). All of this together suggests that Hispanic-American writers who write in Spanish continually feel the influence of both the cosmopolitanist and nativist traditions.

The Incorrect Answer Choices:

B When discussing contemporary Hispanic-American writers who write in Spanish, the author tells us only that they "attempt to reconcile the opposing tendencies of cosmopolitanism and nativism" (lines 59–60). Nothing is said about how this attempt is reflected in the works they actually produce. Moreover, the third paragraph makes it clear that cosmopolitanism and nativism alternate in prevalence, but the author does not say which might currently be dominant.

C The author presents contemporary Hispanic-American writers who write in Spanish as being confronted each day by "the opposing tendencies of cosmopolitanism and nativism" (lines 59–60). This suggests that these contemporary writers are in fact strongly affected by the opposition between cosmopolitanism and nativism that has divided the Hispanic-American literary consciousness for generations (lines 18–19).

D The author says that Hispanic-American writers who write in Spanish have in fact exemplified these tendencies, but makes no suggestion about whether these authors believe that doing so will help them achieve their literary goals.

E There is no indication that contemporary writers are divided into two camps. In fact, the author says that contemporary Hispanic-American writers who write in Spanish try to reconcile the opposing tendencies of cosmopolitanism and nativism in their work, and the author suggests that each writer does this in his or her own work.

- *Difficulty Level: 2*

Question 20

The Correct Answer:

B   The passage is largely descriptive and has few explicit indications of the author's attitude toward nativism, but inasmuch as any attitude is indicated, it is generally positive. Among other things, the author describes nativism as "endeavoring to . . . give voice to the Hispanic peoples" (lines 13 and 14) who live in the United States. As a Hispanic American, the author would almost certainly believe this endeavor to be good. In the final paragraph the author strongly suggests that together with cosmopolitanism, nativism is a necessary factor in a successful Hispanic-American literature: Nativism reaffirms Hispanic Americans' cultural origins and thus keeps them from disappearing into the mainstream. The use of a phrase like "self-absorption" in line 33 might normally be taken to indicate a negative attitude, but here the phrase is best understood as establishing a contrast with the "outward-oriented sensibility" ascribed to cosmopolitanism in line 32; ultimately, the phrase refers to the "return to origins," as it is described later in the passage (lines 48-49). Thus, all the indications available in the passage suggest that the author's attitude is generally a positive one.

The Incorrect Answer Choices:

A   The passage gives us no reason to think that the author's attitude toward nativism is one of enthusiastic support. Words like "outstanding" and "exceptional," which the author uses in connection with cosmopolitanism, might very well be taken to indicate an enthusiastic attitude. The author, however, does not use any such language when talking about nativism.

C   The passage gives every indication that the author's overall attitude toward nativism is positive. So "acceptance" is accurate as far as it goes. But the author does not express any reservations about nativism that could indicate that this acceptance is reluctant. The author perhaps appears to favor cosmopolitanism more strongly, but this apparent preference cannot be taken to mean that the author is reluctant to accept the value of nativism.

D, E   Attitudes such as strong skepticism and clear disapproval are both definitively negative. There is no language in the passage that would indicate such strong disapproval of nativism on the part of the author.

■ *Difficulty Level: 3*

Question 21

The Correct Answer:

B   As the synopsis makes clear, the passage is primarily concerned with the tension between cosmopolitanism and nativism in Hispanic-American literature. The passage explains why this tension arose, how it has figured in Hispanic-American literature for generations, and what significance it has for contemporary Hispanic-American writers who write in Spanish. So (B) accurately describes the primary purpose of the passage.

The Incorrect Answer Choices:

A, D   The passage maintains an unwavering focus on the challenge faced by Hispanic-American writers who write in Spanish. It does not relate the problems faced by this group of writers to any problem of literature in general, contrary to (A). Nor is it concerned with the political aspect of literature in general, contrary to (D).

C   The passage is not a summary of the achievements of Hispanic-American literature written in Spanish. Its main concern is with how Hispanic-American writers writing in Spanish have responded to the challenge of creating a literature that is independent of that of Spain, and with the tensions their responses have created.

E   The passage does not explicitly or implicitly address anything that is presented as a prevailing assumption about Hispanic-American literature. Nor does it contain anything that could be considered a refutation. So there is no basis for thinking that (E) describes the primary purpose of the passage.

■ *Difficulty Level: 2*

Questions 22–26

Synopsis: This passage discusses recent scholarly work on the educational opportunities that were available to women of privileged classes in Renaissance Europe. According to some recent scholars, Renaissance women's educational opportunities were more restricted in scope than earlier scholars had believed, though they were still more expansive than the educational opportunities that had previously been available to women. In the first paragraph, the passage provides some necessary background information about education in the Renaissance by describing the three language arts—grammar, dialectic, and rhetoric—that were central to the humanist education of the Renaissance.

Recent scholars assert that both men and women received training in grammar and progressed to stylistics and literary criticism, but only men went on to receive training in dialectic and rhetoric—disciplines required for politics, philosophy, and the professions—because these subjects were regarded as inappropriate for women. This difference is presented as having its roots in the prevailing attitude that women, unlike men, had no role to play in public life. Women were seen as needing only a generalist education directed toward private enjoyment and the teaching of very young children.

The final paragraph briefly describes some uneasy outcomes arising from the combination of expanded education for women and the lack of significant public roles for educated women. Highly educated women were labeled as unnatural or masculine, or they were praised only if they were exceedingly modest about their accomplishments. Some women in Italy gave public addresses, but these were purely ceremonial in nature, and not meant to influence public affairs. Finally, Renaissance women did not typically write philosophy, but were noted instead for accomplishments only in literature.

Question 22

The Correct Answer:

B   As the synopsis makes clear, the passage is primarily about how, during the Renaissance, women's educational opportunities were restricted compared to those of men. The passage accounts for these differences by pointing to prevailing attitudes regarding women, who had no significant public roles available to them and thus were not thought to need preparation for public life. (B) thus describes the main point of the passage.

The Incorrect Answer Choices:

A   The passage does not present recent scholars as differing from earlier ones on the claim that educational opportunities were greater for women during the Renaissance than during medieval times. Joan Gibson, one recent scholar, is presented as agreeing that women had more access to education in the Renaissance than was the case before (lines 6–8). Where Gibson disagrees with previous scholarship is in her argument that the education women received was not intellectually equal to that of men. So (A) gets the central point of the passage wrong.

C   According to the passage, the education of women in the Renaissance included the study of grammar, languages, stylistics, and literary criticism. None of the educational opportunities that women were denied had anything to do with literature. So, in fact, to the extent that women's education prepared them for any career, it prepared them for careers in literature. This is borne out by the discussion of educated women who became notable for their literary achievements (lines 60–65).

D   In the first paragraph we are told that "education in the Renaissance was based on the classical division of the liberal arts into seven categories, including the three language arts: grammar, dialectic, and rhetoric" (lines 9–12). The gender-based differences in curriculum that the passage is concerned with, however, were differences of curriculum **within** the language arts. The passage does not relate the distinction between the three language arts and the other liberal arts to any gender-based differences in terms of curriculum.

E   This answer is basically correct in saying that women's and men's curricula were similar in the early stages of their education and diverged later. But the emphasis in (E) does not match that of the passage. (E) stresses that in the Renaissance, males and females followed much the same curriculum during the early stages of their education. In contrast, the passage seeks mainly to explain why, after that early stage, the curricula for males and females were **not** the same. So (E) gets the main focus of the passage wrong.

■ *Difficulty Level: 4*

Question 23

Overview: For this question it is important to keep in mind that you are looking for the answer choice that **is not** mentioned anywhere in the passage. It is generally easier to show that something **is** explicitly mentioned in a particular place in the passage than that it **is not** mentioned anywhere in the passage. So the best strategy in a case like this is probably to eliminate each incorrect answer choice by confirming that it is explicitly mentioned in the passage (either by finding where it is mentioned or, if you are confident of your memory of one or more of the answers, by relying on your memory). The answer that is left at the end of this process is the correct answer.

The Correct Answer:

D The passage is concerned with the kinds of things that formed grammar studies, but it says nothing at all about types of schools for those studies.

The Incorrect Answer Choices:

A A method used for rhetorical training is mentioned in lines 27–29.

B An educational goal for men is mentioned in line 19, and an educational goal for women is mentioned in lines 43–44.

C A sequence of subjects that were studied is mentioned in lines 20–27.

E Prerequisites for certain careers are mentioned in lines 17–19 and in lines 36–38.

■ *Difficulty Level: 5*

Question 24

The Correct Answer:

E In the last paragraph the passage says that "exceptionally learned women were labelled as preternatural or essentially masculine" (lines 53–54). This very strongly suggests that such women were regarded as anomalies and that they were not regarded as suitable models for other women.

The Incorrect Answer Choices:

A In lines 41–44 we are told that the prevailing attitude during the Renaissance was "that girls needed only a generalist education . . . directed toward private enjoyment and the eventual teaching of very young children." This strongly suggests that, contrary to (A), women did not play an important role in providing **advanced** grammar training.

B The disciplines required for public life (and hence for public speaking as well) were dialectic and rhetoric, and women were excluded from studying both of these disciplines during the Renaissance. The passage does mention women as orators in lines 56–59, where it say, "Some Italian humanist women gave fashionable oratorical performances, but these were ceremonial in nature rather than designed to influence public affairs." In context, this sentence suggests that such women were the exception rather than the rule. So the passage provides little, if any, support for (B).

C In lines 20–21 the passage tells us that both male and female students "began with elementary study of grammar and progressed to stylistics and literary criticism." Thus, it can be inferred from the passage that (C) is false.

D The passage tells us that as writers, women "became most notable for literary achievements, particularly translations, poetry, and tales in the vernacular or correspondence and orations in Latin" (lines 61–64). Lines 34–36 state that "humanist education for women encompassed literary grammatical studies in both classical and vernacular languages." So contrary to (D), there is no evidence that women who were acclaimed as authors studied subjects omitted from the usual curriculum for female students.

■ *Difficulty Level: 3*

Question 25

Overview: According to the passage, rhetoric—the art of persuasive and declamatory speech—was taught to men as part of their training for "public service in legal and political debate" (lines 17–19). The passage adds that "rhetorical training…could lead in different directions—to study of composition and oral expression or to study of persuasion, in conjunction with a dialectic concerned with broad principles of logic and argumentation" (lines 22–27). So, as the passage describes it, training in dialectic and rhetoric was training in the effective and persuasive expression of ideas and opinions. In lines 44–47 we are told, "Unlike either dialectic or rhetoric, grammar training cast students in the role of an audience." Thus, grammar training—in contrast to training in dialectic and rhetoric—is presented as training in understanding what other people said and wrote, not training in the formulation and expression of one's own ideas and opinions. This question asks you to identify which piece of evidence would, if true, weaken this distinction.

The Correct Answer:

D If (D) were true, training in grammar would cast students in a less passive role than is suggested by lines 44–47. Instead of casting students exclusively in the role of an audience trying to understand the writing or orations of others, grammar training would also cast students in the active role of articulating their own ideas. This would make grammar training much more like training in dialectic and rhetoric than lines 44–47 suggest, and the distinction drawn there would therefore be weakened.

The Incorrect Answer Choices:

A This answer might seem to diminish the distinction in question to some extent since it suggests that grammar students were encouraged to write compositions. But here students are encouraged to imitate existing models of expression, whereas the correct answer emphasizes the articulation of the students' own ideas. Thus (D) weakens the distinction more than (A) does.

B As long as students of dialectic and rhetoric are formulating and expressing their own ideas and arguments about the subject under debate, engaging in that debate provides them with training in the skilled formulation of their own ideas. It doesn't matter whether the subject they are debating is one they have chosen themselves or one that has been set by their teachers—either way, (B) doesn't weaken the distinction drawn in the passage.

C We have been given no reason to think that the character of grammar training would be affected by where it occurred in the sequence of studies. So there is no reason to think that (C) could weaken the distinction the passage draws between training in dialectic and rhetoric and training in grammar.

E The distinction at issue is that between training that makes a student a good audience for the ideas of others and training that improves students' abilities to express their own views to an audience. Whether those ideas are expressed in speech or in writing is irrelevant in this context. So (E) has no significant impact on the distinction between training in dialectic and rhetoric and training in grammar.

- *Difficulty Level: 4*

Question 26

Overview: The second sentence describes the following situation: There are more women who are being educated; at the same time educational reforms have made it impossible for women to go beyond the first level of training in the language arts. So the situation is one in which more people participate in an activity than was the case previously. This activity can be pursued at different levels, from less advanced to more advanced. At the same time, the additional people who are now participating in the activity are prevented from pursuing it beyond a certain level. This question asks you to identify the response that is most similar to this situation in all of these relevant ways.

The Correct Answer:

C   In (C) more people than before participate in some activity (in this case, employment in a particular industry). The jobs range from low-level jobs to high-level jobs. And at the same time, the newly hired workers in that industry are prevented from pursuing that activity beyond a certain level. So the situation in (C) is similar to the situation described in the second sentence of the passage.

The Incorrect Answer Choices:

A   In (A) more people are being allowed to participate in something (voting) but voting is not something that has higher and lower levels, as education does. In addition, in (A) the new participants are not being kept from participating fully in the election process. What is happening in (A) is that the entire election process is being undermined for all participants.

B   In (B) more people than before can participate in an activity (trying to purchase a certain product). But that product becomes scarcer and thus harder for **everyone** to acquire, not just for those who have recently become able to afford it.

D   In (D) more people participate in a certain activity (a game), but there is no mention of any levels of this activity, nor are the new players restricted from full participation.

E   In (E) more people are participating in something (use of a new technology). But **everyone** is finding full participation (mastery of the technology) increasingly difficult.

- *Difficulty Level: 4*

Logical Reasoning: Questions 1–25

Question 1

Overview: The passage tells us what a modern reader might make of Newton's comment, "if I have seen further it is by standing on the shoulders of giants." The passage goes on to give two reasons why the modern reader would most probably be wrong in seeing this comment as a conciliatory gesture acknowledging indebtedness to Hooke and other contemporary scientists. First, such gestures were uncharacteristic of Newton, and second, in Newton's day, the allusion to "giants" typically referred to ancient Greeks.

The Correct Answer:

A (A) is a way of saying that Newton did not have the intention that modern readers might think he had, and this is what the two reasons described in the "Overview" go toward establishing.

The Incorrect Answer Choices:

B The passage says that Hooke claimed that Newton took credit for some advances that Hooke made in the theory of light. The passage does not address the issue of whether Newton in fact took credit for advances that Hooke made; it merely addresses the issue of whether Newton's comment should be taken as an acknowledgment of indebtedness to Hooke. So (B) is not supported by the passage.

C The passage tells us nothing about what beliefs Newton may have had about the origins of Hooke's theories of light. The passage suggests that Newton might have wanted to give the impression that his own theories of light owed something to the ideas of the ancient Greeks, but there is nothing in the passage to indicate whether Newton believed that Hooke owed any debt of this kind.

D The passage says that conciliatory gestures acknowledging indebtedness were uncharacteristic of Newton. This applies to conciliatory gestures to other contemporary scientists as much as it does to conciliatory gestures to Hooke. So the passage lends no support to (D).

E The passage does not support the idea that Newton was unfamiliar with Hooke's theories. It merely makes the point that even if Newton was indebted to Hooke, Newton's comment was not likely to have been intended as a conciliatory gesture acknowledging this indebtedness.

- *Difficulty Level: 1*

Question 2

Overview: The passage helps you to identify the apparent conflict by using the term "yet" in introducing the second sentence. What "yet" tells us is that the second sentence is going to say things that are contrary to expectations that have been set up by the first sentence. And in fact, whereas the content of the blues has been characterized as emotionally negatively charged in the first sentence, we are told in the second sentence that both performers and audiences have a strongly positive reaction to the blues.

The correct answer to this question is the one answer choice that does **nothing** to resolve this conflict between the content and the reaction.

The Correct Answer:

B (B) tells us that success as a blues musician is not connected to whether you draw on personal tragedies for your inspiration. But the passage is not concerned with the question of what makes a blues musician successful. So (B) is largely irrelevant to the passage and does not help explain how blues music produces a positive reaction from seemingly negative subject matter.

The Incorrect Answer Choices:

A (A) helps to resolve the conflict in the passage since it tells us that sharing blues music with an audience creates the kind of social network that is readily associated with the idea of affirmation of life.

C If (C) is true, the effect of the blues on an audience is to make life's troubles seem less immediate. This would make people feel better, making more room for hope and for the affirmation of life. So (C) reduces the conflict in the passage by suggesting a positive effect that the blues can have on audiences.

D The passage tells us that blues lyrics are about life's problems. So hearing the blues helps people realize that other people have the same kinds of problems that they have. According to (D), people find such a realization helpful in dealing with these problems. So (D) helps to resolve the conflict in the passage by indicating how the blues, with its seemingly negative subject matter, is nonetheless life-affirming.

E To say that there is a cathartic effect is to say that something like release of tension or spiritual renewal is brought about. (E) thus helps to explain how blues music can transform personal sorrow into an affirmation of life.

- *Difficulty Level: 1*

Question 3

Overview: The question is concerned with identifying a claim that receives strong support from what the nutritionist says. It is important to recognize that some of what the nutritionist says concerns the accuracy of men's and women's **estimates of their consumption** of various categories of food: for example, both men and women underestimate the amount of fat in their diets. Other things that the nutritionist says concerns how men's and women's **actual consumption** in these food categories diverges from nutritional recommendations: for example, women's diets did not meet nutritional recommendations in most food categories, especially fruits and vegetables.

The Correct Answer:

E   As indicated at the end of the nutritionist's report, men consume too little of every category of food other than fat and breads. In particular, therefore, they consume lower amounts of fruits and vegetables than the nutritional guidelines recommend.

The Incorrect Answer Choices:

A   According to the nutritionist, men met the nutritional guidelines for one category—breads. So, in order to misjudge their compliance with the guidelines in every food category, men would have to think that they don't meet the guidelines for bread consumption. But the nutritionist says nothing to suggest that men think this. In fact, the nutritionist says that adults in general estimate their diets to correspond closely to the guidelines. So the nutritionist's information actually suggests that (A) is false, and that information certainly doesn't support (A).

B   According to the nutritionist, "most adults estimated their diets to correspond closely with the recommendations of standard nutritional guidelines." So the nutritionist implies that relatively few people were aware of not complying with the guidelines. The nutritionist says nothing, however, about how many of these relatively few people were men, or about how many were women.

C   The nutritionist doesn't give specific information about the awareness the men and women in the study have with respect to the nutritional recommendations for the various food categories. The nutritionist tells us that men, in their diets, met the recommendations for breads, but doesn't tell us whether the men, or the women, knew what those recommendations were. So there is no basis for concluding (C).

D   The nutritionist says that men overestimated their consumption in most food categories. The nutritionist indicates that men underestimated their fat consumption but says nothing to indicate that they underestimated their fruit and vegetable consumption. So (D) is not supported.

- *Difficulty Level: 4*

Question 4

Overview: The question asks you to identify an assumption on which the argument depends, but first you need to identify the conclusion of the argument and the support offered for that conclusion. Although this argument does not present its conclusion neatly packaged in a separate sentence, it is evidently directed toward the conclusion that Maude is hypocritical in constantly denouncing people for being materialistic. The evidence that is presented in support of this conclusion is Maude's sentimental treatment of one particular material possession, namely, the watch her grandmother gave her.

The Correct Answer:

B The argument tries to show that Maude is hypocritical in her criticism of others. That is, it tries to show that Maude has exactly the same faults as those she criticizes. Since Maude criticizes others for being materialistic, the evidence that the argument presents must be evidence that Maude is herself materialistic. The only evidence presented is evidence about Maude's sentimental treatment of a single possession, so the argument must be assuming (B), that "sentimental attachment to a single possession indicates being materialistic."

The Incorrect Answer Choices:

A The fact that the watch that Maude is very fond of was given to her by her grandmother is a descriptive detail with no special importance in the argument. The argument would have had exactly the same force if the watch had been given to Maude by an old friend rather than a relative. The important point is the special, sentimental treatment that the watch receives. So assuming (A) makes no difference to the argument.

C The argument that Maude is materialistic, and therefore hypocritical, is based on her treatment of one particular possession and says nothing about how she treats her other possessions. (C) is irrelevant to this argument because it links caring about material things with a tendency to take special care of all of your possessions.

D The argument takes Maude's sentimental treatment of one particular object—a watch—to be sufficient evidence to show Maude to be hypocritical. As the argument makes its case, therefore, it does not depend on there being other material things that Maude especially cares for.

E The case for Maude's being materialistic clearly does not assume the truth of (E). Assuming (E) would actually make Maude's sentimental treatment of the watch consistent with her **not** being materialistic.

- *Difficulty Level: 1*

Question 5

Overview: The argument concludes that testing for methane in a planet's atmosphere would be the most reliable way of detecting life on that planet. The grounds offered for this conclusion are that without the biological processes of living beings generating methane, any methane on the planet would disappear.

The question asks for the answer choice that most weakens this argument.

The Correct Answer:

B   If there are living beings that cannot produce methane through their biological processes, then a planet with no methane in its atmosphere might nonetheless support life. So the absence of methane in a planet's atmosphere would not in itself prove that there is no life on that planet. Thus (B) calls the reliability of the methane test into question.

The Incorrect Answer Choices:

A   The argument would be undermined if other ways of detecting the presence of life on a planet were more reliable than the methane test. But (A) does not tell us this. It says that there are other ways, but says nothing about their reliability.

C   The argument concludes that checking for the presence of methane would be the most reliable way to detect the presence of life. The "would be" in this formulation signals that this is a hypothetical claim; that is, if we could detect the presence of methane in a planet's atmosphere, then this would be the most reliable way of telling whether there were living beings on that planet. The argument doesn't presuppose that we actually can do the required analysis, so (C) doesn't weaken this argument.

D   The methane test that is mentioned would determine whether atmospheric methane is present or absent, not how much methane is present. If methane were present, the quantities involved would be irrelevant. Therefore, (D) does not weaken the argument.

E   (E) doesn't say that Earth is the only planet in the universe that contains methane, just that we don't **know** of any other such planet. But what we know or don't know about the planets in the universe is irrelevant to the issue that the argument addresses—the reliability of the methane test as a means of detecting life on a planet. Clearly then, (E) does not weaken the argument.

• *Difficulty Level: 1*

Questions 6–7

Overview: Willett argues that Lopez and Simmons, in deciding to tell Evritech that they are married to each other, have made a foolish decision. The decision is bad, according to Willett, because letting the corporation know that the two are a married couple would have a negative consequence: the job offers that they have from Evritech would not both remain on the table. Willett underscores the point that the decision is poorly conceived by pointing out that there is an alternative to the course of action they have decided on.

Question 6

The Correct Answer:

C   As the" Overview" shows, Willett's main conclusion is that Lopez and Simmons would be foolish if, prior to joining Evritech's staff, they tell Evritech that they are married. In other words, Willett's main conclusion is (C).

The Incorrect Answer Choices:

A   Willett's argument suggests that Lopez and Simmons should take action that would allow both of them to accept and hold jobs with Evritech. Thus it seems that Willett does not object to both of them having applied for jobs there, contrary to what (A) says.

B   Willett does not suggest that Evritech does not consistently enforce its rule against hiring more than one member of the same family. On the contrary, Willett says flatly that if Evritech finds out, prior to hiring Lopez and Simmons, that the two are married, "one of them will have a job offer withdrawn."

D   Willett does not argue about what Evritech's policies should be. Willett's argument basically accepts Evritech's policies and works out how Lopez and Simmons can evade a certain negative consequence of those policies.

E   Willett says that Lopez and Simmons "could easily keep their marriage secret initially," meaning until after they were hired. So Willett's argument does seem to presuppose the truth of (E), at least for the short term. But (E) is not the main conclusion of Willett's argument.

• *Difficulty Level: 2*

Question 7

The Correct Answer:

E Willett's alternative to Lopez and Simmons revealing their marriage is that they conceal it, at least until some time after they are both hired. But from Willett's argument alone it is not actually clear that Lopez and Simmons are free to do this. There may be an ethical or legal reason that job candidates such as Lopez and Simmons should reveal their marital status. The principle in (E) denies that there is any such obligation on the part of job candidates to reveal their marital status. By pushing aside this potential obstacle, (E) provides support for Willett's reasoning.

The Incorrect Answer Choices:

A Willett's argument simply takes Evritech's rules as they stand. The fact that those rules are in violation of the principle put forward in (A) plays no role in Willett's argument.

B (B) concerns what policies corporations should have, but Willett's argument is directed toward helping Lopez and Simmons deal with certain implications of those policies. So (B) does not help Willett's reasoning.

C This principle is not applicable to the situation that Willett's reasoning addresses because Lopez and Simmons both have job offers and are past the stage of filling out application forms.
    The general idea behind (C)—that withholding relevant information is wrong—would actually work against Willett's reasoning, which treats the withholding of relevant information as a viable choice. So there is no way that (C) helps to support Willett's reasoning.

D Lopez and Simmons would not be adhering to Evritech's policy if they both accepted positions with Evritech. But Willett wants to enable both to accept positions with Evritech anyway. So Willett's objective is inconsistent with the principle in (D).

- *Difficulty Level: 1*

Question 8

Overview: The linguist concludes that since speaker X's sentence can be diagrammed, it will be recognized as grammatical by speakers of the language. The linguist's argument is designed to proceed in two steps: (1) we are to infer that a sentence is grammatical if it is diagrammable, and (2) we are to infer that a sentence will be recognized as grammatical if it is grammatical.
    Step 2 is in fact justified by the generalization, "Any grammatical sentence is recognized as grammatical by speakers of its language." The other generalization in the linguist's argument—"Only if a sentence can be diagrammed is it grammatical"—is not adequate justification for step 1, however. This generalization ensures that all grammatical sentences are diagrammable, but not that all diagrammable sentences are grammatical.

> **Cross-reference:** *The reasoning error in this argument is an example of a confusion between "sufficient conditions" and "necessary conditions." For a more detailed discussion, see "Necessary Conditions and Sufficient Conditions" on pages 24–25.*

The Correct Answer:

B As noted, step 1 does not ensure that all diagrammable sentences are grammatical. Another way of saying this is to say that it leaves open the possibility that some ungrammatical sentences are diagrammable. (B) identifies what is missing in step 1, and thus reveals the flaw in the linguist's reasoning.

The Incorrect Answer Choices:

A The linguist's argument does depend on the idea that sentences, including speaker X's sentence, "can be diagrammed." But a sentence can be diagrammed if just one or two people can diagram it. So if most people can't diagram sentences correctly, it makes no difference to the linguist's argument.

C To be recognized as grammatical, a sentence would actually have to be grammatical. The linguist's first statement says that any grammatical sentence would have to be diagrammable. It follows that any sentence that is recognized as grammatical is diagrammable. So, rather than failing to consider (C) as a possibility, the linguist's reasoning is actually committed to the truth of (C).

D   As explained in the "Overview" and in the discussion of option (C), the linguist in effect claims that all grammatical sentences can be diagrammed. So the flaw in the linguist's reasoning cannot be that it fails to consider the possibility that (D) is true.

E   Not considering a possibility is only a flaw in the reasoning of an argument if that possibility interferes with how the argument is meant to go. The possibility characterized in (E) is not relevant to either of the two steps in the linguist's argument, so it cannot reveal a flaw in that argument.

■ *Difficulty Level: 1*

Question 9

Overview: Since the task here is to find something that would weaken the representative's implied argument, the first step is to spell out this implied argument. The company representative's only stated premise is that federal law requires that every new chemical be tested for safety before it is put on the market. To reach the conclusion that the public need not be concerned about chemicals leaking from a chemical company's dump, we need to make a few assumptions. We need to assume that the company complies with the federal law. We also need to assume that the chemicals that leak from the dump have all passed safety tests. Anything that challenges one of these assumptions would weaken the implied argument.

The Correct Answer:

C   (C) suggests that it is not just chemicals that testing has shown to be safe that are leaking from the dump. Since the dump has been there for a long time, it might well contain a large number of dangerous chemicals that came on the market before the legislation requiring testing of new chemicals went into effect. So (C), by calling into question a crucial assumption of the representative's argument, weakens that argument.

The Incorrect Answer Choices:

A   Though (A) is only about the testing of pharmaceutical substances, the general point it makes is that testing takes time and that during that time, some opportunities for beneficial applications of what is being tested can be lost. This particular potential disadvantage of safety testing, however, has no bearing on the issue addressed by the representative's argument: whether the requirement that new chemicals be tested ensures that the chemicals leaking from the dump are safe.

B   The issue that the representative's implied argument addresses is whether what is leaking from the dump is safe. There is no reason to think that the fact that the leakage is quite recent would be relevant to safety. So (B) does not engage this issue.

D   The representative's implied argument is based on trying to establish that the chemicals in the dump are safe. (D) does nothing to call the safety of the chemicals in the dump into question, nor does it give any other reason to think that the leak poses no threat to the public. Dilution may make some chemicals safe, but it doesn't make safe chemicals unsafe. So (D) doesn't weaken the argument.

E (E) points out that there are problems with the river's water aside from any chemicals leaking into it. This does not, however, address the question of whether the public should be concerned about those chemicals, and is thus irrelevant to the representative's argument.

- *Difficulty Level: 2*

Question 10

Overview: The task here is to form at least a rough idea of the principle that underlies the reasoning in the passage, and then to identify the answer choice that illustrates that same principle at work. The reasoning in the passage relies on a principle that might be stated as follows: similarities among different works in a given genre do not necessarily point to a direct influence by one work on another within that genre, since all those works might have drawn on the same broader artistic conventions.

The Correct Answer:

D (D) illustrates the principle sketched out in the "Overview": similarities among different works in a given genre—in this case, the genre of action movies—do not necessarily point to a direct influence of one work on another within that genre.

The Incorrect Answer Choices:

A, E The principle that underlies the reasoning in the passage is not relevant to how one might identify the genre into which a particular work falls. It is thus unlike the principles illustrated by (A) and (E), which do concern themselves with this question.

B The principle underlying (B) is, broadly, that a work belonging to a particular genre that was directly influenced by works outside that genre is **not** necessarily similar to any of the works it was influenced by. The principle underlying the reasoning in the passage is quite different from this in that it deals with works that **are** similar to each other without necessarily having directly influenced each other.

C The passage is not concerned with what accounts for an author's success with a work within a given genre, whereas accounting for a director's success is the central concern of (C). It is thus evident that the passage and (C) do not illustrate the same principle.

- *Difficulty Level: 4*

Question 11

Overview: Here you are given a hypothesis, with no indication of what specifically it is based on. The reference to "research with young children" does suggest that there is some support for the hypothesis, but not what it is. Your task is to select the answer choice that provides specific support.

The Correct Answer:

B (B) supports the developmental psychologist's hypothesis because it quite clearly conforms to that hypothesis and, perhaps more importantly, rules out a very serious potential challenge to that hypothesis. If there were children who had the ability to copy angles but who could not copy curves, the hypothesis could no longer be maintained. But (B) says that this particular challenge will not materialize, and thereby allows the hypothesis to be maintained.

The Incorrect Answer Choices:

A (A) suggests that the ability to copy straight lines develops before the ability to copy curves.

It's not clear whether this says anything at all about the connection between developing the ability to copy curves and the ability to copy angles. So (A) neither supports nor challenges the hypothesis.

C The ability to discriminate angles is likely to be one of the skills involved in copying angles and would thus naturally have to be developed before angles can be copied. But appreciating this fact doesn't support any position concerning whether the ability to copy curves is developed before the ability to copy angles.

D As discussed in the explanation of the correct answer, the statement in (D) is a direct challenge to the hypothesis rather than something that supports it.

E Since the hypothesis is said to be based on research with young children, it should not be surprising if (E) is true. But (E) says nothing of relevance to the issue addressed by the hypothesis.

■ *Difficulty Level: 1*

Question 12

Overview: This question asks about a principle underlying the situation described in the passage. The situation described is one in which people complain about certain aspects of computer technology but have come to rely on other aspects. The passage indicates that people's reliance on computer technology outweighs their frustrations, insofar as most people would be unwilling to give up this technology.

The Correct Answer:

A The situation in the passage is a very close fit with the principle in (A). The situation presents an example in which people complain about a particular kind of technology, but their dissatisfaction is not so deep that they would like to do without that technology. (A) presents a broader statement about all types of technology, indicating that complaints about the consequences of technology are not good evidence that people would like to see that technology eliminated. Thus (A) is the correct answer.

The Incorrect Answer Choices:

B The passage has nothing to say about technologies that people do not complain about, so a principle about such technologies does not fit the information in the passage.

C, E Both (C) and (E) are principles that relate the frequency of complaints about a technology to the extent that people depend on that technology. The information in the passage, however, does not compare different technologies either with respect to the degree to which they elicit complaints or with respect to people's dependence on them. Thus neither (C) nor (E) is a good fit for the information in the passage.

D The information in the passage does not conform to (D). The passage doesn't address the issue of which technological innovations are more important than others. A principle like that in (D), which offers guidance in determining which innovations are more important, is therefore out of step with the passage.

■ *Difficulty Level: 2*

Question 13

Overview: The conclusion that this argument draws is far more extreme than anything that its premises might justify, and it is open to several objections. One objection is that it fails to concede that there could be extraterrestrial intelligence that is unwilling or unable to make contact. Another objection is that it does not consider whether, though there has been time for signals from Earth to reach all the neighboring star systems, there has been enough time for a possible response to reach Earth. Even though this argument is vulnerable to several objections, your task is to pick the answer choice that gives the best account of why the argument is questionable.

The Correct Answer:

B (B) describes in very general terms how the argument does, in fact, proceed. The argument specifies one way in which proof of extraterrestrial intelligence has failed to materialize. From this consideration alone, it concludes that there is no extraterrestrial intelligence in neighboring star systems. This way of arguing can be a very problematic way of establishing a conclusion, as the discussion in the "Overview" shows. So (B) is a good general account of why the reasoning in the argument is questionable.

The Incorrect Answer Choices:

A It is true that the argument does not provide a definition of the word "messages," but it doesn't depend on any particular decision about whether to call something a message or not. So a precise definition of "messages" is not required.

C Given what the argument is trying to show, it would be pointless to consider star systems beyond our neighboring systems. So while the possibility of extraterrestrial intelligence beyond neighboring star systems may be an important issue, it is not an issue that is relevant to the reasoning in the argument, and the fact that the argument does not address the issue is clearly not a problem.

D The argument does not, in fact, mention any of these governmental messages. But even if it had, the argument would not be affected. If the argument mentioned these messages and added that there has been no extraterrestrial response, it would still be vulnerable to the same serious objections.

E It is true that the argument doesn't take note of it being immensely probable that most star systems are uninhabited. But that information is largely irrelevant to the argument. The argument isn't based on anything having to do with the probability of star systems being inhabited. It is based on the lack of messages coming from neighboring star systems. So (E) does not point to any problem with the reasoning in the argument.

■ *Difficulty Level: 2*

Question 14

Overview: The citizen presents an argument for the conclusion, "We urgently need a major tax cut for our upper-income citizens." The two sentences following that conclusion specifically support the choice of a tax cut as the means of achieving a decrease in unemployment. According to the argument, a tax cut, and nothing else, would stimulate investment, and the increase in investment would create jobs.

This argument makes a number of substantial assumptions. For example, it assumes that the projected extra investment would not go toward business practices that actually reduce the number of employees. The question asks you to identify one such assumption.

The Correct Answer:

D   Suppose that (D) were false, in which case the money from the tax cut would not be invested. Then there would be no creation of new jobs driven by investment, and the tax cut would fail to decrease unemployment. The case the argument presents for the tax cut would fall apart. Thus, the argument depends on assuming (D).

The Incorrect Answer Choices:

A   While the argument is motivated by the notion that the current recession is a very serious one, the argument does not need to assume that the recession is the worst one in the country's history. Any recession that brings about high unemployment could be enough to require the government to develop economic policies meant to counteract its effects; it doesn't have to be the worst recession in the country's history.

B   The citizen's argument doesn't depend on assuming (B) because (B) is a generalization that applies to all groups of people, but the citizen's argument only concerns the effects of a tax cut on investment by upper-income citizens. So the citizen's argument could still work even if the generalization in (B) were false: if (B) is false because it is not true of middle- or lower-income citizens, then the citizen's argument is not affected.

C   If (C) were false, and lower-income citizens had invested more money in total than upper-income citizens, the citizen's case for the tax cut would not fall apart. That case depends on how much money upper-income citizens would invest if they received a tax cut, not on whether upper-income citizens as a group account for more current investment than lower-income citizens do. The total amount that each income group has invested is probably not a good indicator of how much each group would invest if they received a tax cut.

E   The citizen's argument need not assume (E). The argument would work just as well even if there had never been a tax cut in the citizen's country. (E) gives one possible way of supporting an important premise of the argument—that tax cuts for upper-income citizens would tend to create jobs—but that premise could be supported in other ways. For example, it could be supported by theoretical economic models.

- *Difficulty Level: 2*

Question 15

Overview: Most of the passage is concerned with noting that, and in part explaining why, the laws of social science fall short with respect to two virtues of scientific laws: precision and generality. The passage makes clear that, in this respect, social science laws fall short of being ideal scientific laws. Your task is to select the answer choice that is most strongly supported by what the passage says.

The Correct Answer:

A   The first sentence of the passage indicates that generality is a virtue of scientific laws. This implies that greater generality makes one scientific law preferable to a competing scientific law, provided that the competing law is not superior in terms of some other virtue. So (A) is strongly supported by the information in the first sentence.

The Incorrect Answer Choices:

B   The passage doesn't take issue with the choice of subject matter in the social sciences. The passage acknowledges that the social sciences' subject matter prevents the laws of social science from being ideal scientific laws. But the passage says nothing relevant to the topic of a shift in subject matter for the social sciences.

C   The passage mentions "class" as an example of a term that is imprecise. But the passage suggests that imprecise terms like this are part of the essence of the subject matter. The passage does not suggest that social scientists can do anything to increase the precision of such terms.

D   The passage suggests that any effort of the sort that (D) describes would be wasted. The passage says explicitly that laws that apply only in certain social systems are typically the only ones possible for the social sciences, so the passage does not support (D).

E   Even though the passage says that, by and large, the laws of social science fall short of being ideal scientific laws, the passage does not suggest that these laws are not truly scientific. The passage does not even broach the subject of what is truly scientific, so (E) is not supported.

- *Difficulty Level: 5*

Question 16

Overview: The conclusion of the argument is that the injustice in a particular court case should not be blamed on forensic science in general. In supporting this conclusion, the argument defends an alternative thesis: the injustice is due to the mistaken views of certain forensic scientists involved in the case. The argument says that the scientists' error lies in their believing that they ought to provide evidence preferentially to the prosecution, rather than providing evidence impartially to both the defense and the prosecution.

The Correct Answer:

A   The argument gives us some reason to believe that certain forensic scientists are responsible for the miscarriage of justice, but it does little or nothing to exonerate forensic science in general. To do a good job of supporting the conclusion, the argument needs to do something to shift blame away from forensic science. (A) does this. It supports the idea that the forensic scientists with "the mistaken views" were out of step with forensic science in general.

The Incorrect Answer Choices:

B   (B) means that if the argument's conclusion is correct with respect to the injustice in the Barker case, then the same reasoning is likely to apply to other cases as well. But this sheds no light on whether the argument's conclusion is, in fact, correct about the injustice in the Barker case.

C   What prosecuting lawyers believe may or may not reflect the truth, but since they are an interested party in this matter, we have some reason to doubt the accuracy of this belief. The impact of (C) on the argument is therefore unclear. But even if the prosecuting lawyers' belief were accepted as true, it would undermine the argument rather than strengthen it.

D   If (D) is true, the type of injustice in the Barker case is not the only type that occurs in court cases. This would certainly not be surprising. But it has no relevance to the argument, which is concerned with determining responsibility for the injustice in the Barker case only.

E   The argument takes it for granted that there was a miscarriage of justice in the Barker case, and it attempts to explain that miscarriage of justice. By calling into question whether there was any miscarriage of justice, (E) raises doubt about whether there is anything for the argument to explain. This suggests that the argument is pointless because it rests on a misconception; it does nothing to strengthen the argument.

- *Difficulty Level: 3*

Question 17

Overview: The second statement in the passage says no one who is levelheaded is bold. The first statement can be rephrased in a parallel fashion: no one who is levelheaded is excessively generous.

The Correct Answer:

D   The two statements in the passage can be combined to say that no one who is levelheaded is either bold or excessively generous. This is just what (D) says. So (D) is strictly implied by the information given.

The Incorrect Answer Choices:

A, B, C   (A), (B), and (C) are each concerned with the relationship between being excessively generous and being bold. The passage, however, doesn't say or imply anything about whether anyone who is excessively generous is bold. The passage is compatible with all excessively generous people being bold, with some excessively generous people being bold, and with no excessively generous people being bold.

E   The two statements in the passage can be combined to say that no one who is levelheaded is either bold or excessively generous. This means that all bold people and all excessively generous people are not levelheaded. But it could still be true that some people who are not levelheaded are neither bold nor excessively generous. Thus, the statements in the passage do not guarantee the truth of (E), which means that (E) is not strictly implied by those statements.

- *Difficulty Level: 4*

Question 18

Overview: The conclusion of the argument is that there must be something that keeps certain people—those with a specific personality type—from entering the teaching profession. This conclusion is basically a way of accounting for the anomaly that people with this personality type are only 5 percent of teachers but fully 20 percent of the general public.

The Correct Answer:

E   (E) weakens the argument by offering an alternative account of why people with the personality type at issue constitute such a low proportion of teachers. The proportion is not low because they enter the profession in disproportionately low numbers, but because they leave the profession in disproportionately high numbers.

The Incorrect Answer Choices:

A   (A) tells us that people with the personality type are underrepresented to the same extent in the medical profession. But this has no effect on the argument's explanation of the personality type's underrepresentation in the teaching profession. (A) merely presents us with something else to be explained.

B   (B) is consistent with the position taken by the argument. If people with the personality type are being discouraged from entering the teaching profession, they may be discouraged before they even pursue degrees in education. So (B) does nothing to undermine the explanation that we find in the argument; it may even help that explanation by ruling out certain alternative explanations, such as the one in (E).

C   (C) describes something that would probably keep many students of teachers with the personality type from becoming teachers themselves. But (C) does not tell us anything about the personality types of the students who are successfully recruited into noneducational professions. So the impact of (C) on the argument cannot be evaluated.

D   (D) suggests that, whatever discourages students with the personality type from becoming teachers, it is not their experience with their own teachers. But this does not weaken the case for the argument's conclusion that there must be something that discourages people with the personality type from going into teaching.

- *Difficulty Level: 4*

Question 19

Overview: The argument sets out a basic dichotomy: a computer that plays chess successfully would prove either that machines can think or that thinking is not part of playing chess. Either of these possibilities, it is argued, would change our conception of human intelligence. So we are left to draw the conclusion that a computer that plays chess successfully would change our conception of human intelligence.

This argument is highly compressed. It doesn't give a justification for the dichotomy that it sets out and it doesn't provide details about how a change in our conception of human intelligence follows from either part of the dichotomy. Given that the question directs us to look for grounds on which the reasoning is vulnerable to criticism, we should look for a possibility that undermines either the dichotomy or the connection between the dichotomy and a change in our conception of human intelligence.

The Correct Answer:

D   If, as (D) says, a chess-playing computer would not play chess in the same way that humans do, then the existence of a chess-playing computer would not force a choice between the alternatives in the dichotomy that the argument sets out. If the human approach to playing chess is different from the computer approach, then perhaps only the human approach involves thinking. In that case, a successful chess-playing computer would not prove that a machine can think, but chess could still involve thinking, at least when it is played by humans. So (D) is a possibility that points the way to another alternative, and thereby shows how the reasoning has gone wrong.

The Incorrect Answer Choices:

A   The argument treats the idea that the conception of intelligence is intrinsically linked to that of thought not just as a possibility but as an obvious fact. Changes in what we believe to be true about human thinking are said to lead to changes in our conception of human intelligence. So the possibility in (A) is certainly **not** one that the argument fails to consider.

B   The possibility in (B) is left open by the argument, rather than not being considered by it. The idea of a successful chess-playing computer is presented purely hypothetically, indicating a belief that such a computer might never actually become a reality. (As an aside, you may find this answer choice confusing because you are aware that successful chess programs have been invented. But you should note that this question is from a test that was administered several years ago.)

C The argument does not consider the possibility in (C). But this is not a weakness or an error in the reasoning. Those other games might be relatively simple games. So computers being able to play them successfully might not have an impact on our conception of human intelligence, which is the focus of the argument.

E Presumably this answer choice is addressing the issue of why some people are unable to play chess, because it seems very odd to talk about a computer having the opportunity to play chess. This issue is very far, however, from the issue that the argument is concerned with—what a chess-playing computer implies about human intelligence. So failing to consider the possibility in (E) is not a weakness in the reasoning.

- *Difficulty Level: 4*

Question 20

Overview: Marta, in responding to James, grants that his news about the new technique for extracting rhodium and his claim about the major use of rhodium are both correct. She disagrees, however, with James's unstated assumption that rhodium extracted from nuclear waste with the new technique is already being used in catalytic converters. She claims that no catalytic converters have been manufactured using rhodium derived from nuclear waste.

In asking how Marta responds to James's argument, the question is asking for a description of how Marta's response connects to James's reasoning.

The Correct Answer:

D In her response to James, Marta points out that the extraction of rhodium from nuclear waste, though successful in experiments, has not yet become part of the industrial production of catalytic converters. The fact that there is this lag between experimental success and industrial application had not been taken into account by James in drawing his conclusion.

The Incorrect Answer Choices:

A As the "Overview" indicates, Marta does not question the accuracy of any of the claims that James makes in support of his conclusion. Rather, she questions an unstated assumption of James's argument. (A), therefore, misdescribes how Marta responds to James.

B James does not introduce anyone into the conversation who could be called an advocate of nuclear power and whose credibility Marta might be questioning. Marta herself does not talk about nuclear power or its advocates at all. So (B) is clearly inaccurate.

C As mention in the discussion of (A) above, Marta does concern herself with an assumption that James makes. Although this assumption is crucial to establishing the conclusion of James's argument, Marta does not claim that James is assuming the conclusion itself. So (C) misdescribes Marta's response to James.

E As the "Overview" indicates, Marta rejects James's conclusion, but she fully accepts the premises that he presents. So while her response does ultimately cast doubt on James's conclusion, she does not question the plausibility of his premises.

- *Difficulty Level: 3*

Question 21

Overview: According to the ethicist's position, something that people have no choice about—feelings of compassion—makes them more worthy of praise than something people have control over—whether or not to honor moral obligations.

The question asks you to identify a statement that cannot be true if the ethicist's statements are true; that is, a statement that is inconsistent with the ethicist's position.

The Correct Answer:

C (C) squarely runs counter to the basic point of the ethicist's position. (C) states that only things about which people have a choice are relevant to the question of whether a person is praiseworthy, but for the ethicist something that is **not** subject to a person's choice—feelings—contributes to a person's praiseworthiness. So (C) is inconsistent with the ethicist's position.

The Incorrect Answer Choices:

A (A) represents the ethicist's position taken to an extreme: people are worthy of no praise at all for actions motivated by nothing but dispassionate concern for moral obligation whereas people can only be worthy of praise for actions motivated at least in part by their feelings. While (A) is extreme, it is consistent with the ethicist's position.

B The ethicist's statements are exclusively about the praiseworthiness of people who treat others well. (B), on the other hand, is about the praiseworthiness of people whose actions diminish the welfare of others. Since the ethicist's statements do not say anything about the kinds of cases addressed by (B), there is no reason to think that there is any conflict between the ethicist's position and (B).

D According to the ethicist's position, a person who treats others well but does so entirely out of cold and dispassionate concern for moral obligation is **less** worthy of praise than a person who treats others well at least partially out of feelings of compassion. But the ethicist does not deny that a person acting only out of concern for moral obligation may still be worthy of praise.

E The ethicist's position, as it is developed in the passage, does not cover the issue of whether people are worthy of praise merely for a desire to have compassion, even if that desire remains unsatisfied. There is thus nothing in the passage to rule out (E), and (E) is consistent with the ethicist's position.

■ *Difficulty Level: 5*

Question 22

Overview: The argument presents a general premise: the more bitter a food tastes, the less children like it. In addition, the argument describes taste preferences between two kinds of cheddar cheese for three different groups of children. And the argument concludes that there are differences between two of the groups of children in whether they experience one kind of cheddar as more bitter than the other.

There is an important gap in this argument. To draw the kind of conclusion it does, the argument has to assume some sort of relationship between the children's taste preferences between the two kinds of cheese and how bitter those cheeses taste to them.

The Correct Answer:

D Assume that bitterness is the only factor that determines the children's taste preferences regarding the different types of cheddar cheese. Then the supertasters' strong preference for the mild cheese over the sharp would have to indicate that they found the mild cheese to be less bitter. There would be no other explanation available. At the same time, the nontasters' lack of preference for either cheese would indicate that they found no difference in bitterness. So assuming (D) would enable us to reach the conclusion, because it would be the only available explanation for what we are told about the children's taste preferences.

The Incorrect Answer Choices:

A (A), if assumed, would provide a refinement of some of the evidence. It would tell us that the differences in the children's taste preference do not all come from how much, or how little, they like sharp cheddar. This refinement, however, is irrelevant to the gap in the argument, which has to do with the connection between the children's taste preferences and how bitter the cheeses taste to them.

B The differing intensity with which the three groups experience taste is a central fact in the argument. Whatever predisposes children to fall into one of these groups rather than another is not relevant to the reasoning in the argument, however.

C (C) suggests that it might not be differences in bitterness, but differences in sweetness, that account for the facts about taste preferences. So if (C) were assumed, it would suggest an alternative to the conclusion. Thus, it would challenge the conclusion rather than allowing the conclusion to be properly inferred.

E   The argument deals solely with differing strengths of children's taste experiences and with relative taste preferences. The argument is not concerned with the question of what variety of foods children tend to like or dislike. So (E) has no impact on the reasoning in the argument and thus cannot close the gap in that reasoning.

- *Difficulty Level: 4*

Question 23

Overview: Donna says that she found a certain exhibition to be among a museum's less interesting recent efforts. Professional critics, however, disagree with Donna's view. From this, the argument concludes that Donna's claim is false. But how can a claim about one's own subjective reactions be false? The only way is if someone, for some reason or another, misrepresents those reactions. But if we assume that Donna isn't misrepresenting her own reactions, she may be wrong about whether the exhibition is relatively uninteresting, but she cannot be wrong about whether she **finds** the exhibition uninteresting. The reasoning in the argument is therefore flawed because it treats a report about an inherently subjective matter as though it can be undermined by outside opinion to the contrary.

You are asked to identify an argument in which the reasoning is flawed in most nearly the same way as it is in the argument in the passage. So you should look for an argument in which someone's claim about their inherently subjective viewpoint on a particular matter is at odds with other people's views on that matter.

The Correct Answer:

D   Loren's claim concerns an inherently subjective matter—a certain food tasting good to Loren. Loren's opinion about the taste of that food is at odds with that of a group of supposed experts ("everyone who knows anything about food"). Because Loren's opinion diverges from the expert consensus, the argument concludes that Loren's claim about a subjective experience is false. This argument has exactly the same general structure, and thus exhibits the same flaw in reasoning, as the argument in the passage.

The Incorrect Answer Choices:

A, B, E   (A), (B) and (E) are each about a claim that concerns a factual matter, not a matter of subjective judgment. That is, they are claims that can be objectively established as either true or false. Moreover, (A), (B), and (E) each offer evidence that actually helps to show that the claim at issue is false. So neither (A), (B), nor (E) contains reasoning that is flawed in the same way that the reasoning in the argument in the passage is flawed.

C (C) is similar to the argument in the passage in that people's claims about their motivation are reasonably considered to be subjective. But the argument in (C) differs from the earlier argument in at least one important respect. While the earlier argument pits one person's opinion against the opinions of a group of experts, nothing like this occurs in (C). (C) pits one person's claim against another's, and neither person is more authoritative than the other. So the argument in (C) doesn't attempt to undermine a report of one person's subjective experience by appealing to the opinion of authorities, which is an important part of the flaw in the earlier argument.

■ *Difficulty Level: 3*

Question 24

Overview: The passage presents an argument for one particular view about how a political community that lacks political self-determination can become and then remain truly free. What such a community has to have, according to the passage, are certain political virtues that are necessary for maintaining freedom. And, according to the argument, these virtues have a far better chance of arising if the community wins its freedom through its own struggle than if freedom is bestowed on it by an external force.

The question asks you to identify the principle that can most reasonably be said to underlie the reasoning in the argument.

The Correct Answer:

C The argument refers to "the political virtues necessary for maintaining freedom." These virtues are said to have the best chance of arising in situations in which a people struggle to become free by their own efforts, and this is a central consideration in the support for the argument's conclusion. So the reasoning ultimately presupposes that a community must develop certain political virtues in order to maintain its freedom. (C) expresses this presupposition, and thus expresses a principle that underlies the reasoning.

The Incorrect Answer Choices:

A The reasoning in the passage doesn't conform to the principle stated in (A). In fact, the argument raises serious questions about whether (A) is even true, claiming that a community that attains political freedom through an external force is almost certain not to become truly free.

B Nothing in the reasoning hinges on there being some political virtue that members of a community, in their struggle to become free, achieve before they achieve self-determination. The passage is centrally concerned with the circumstances under which certain political virtues are likely to arise, and not at all with the order in which they arise.

D The only thing that the reasoning in the passage refers to as a requirement for maintaining freedom is the development of certain political virtues. These virtues, according to the passage, have virtually no chance of arising when people attain self-determination through an external force. So clearly, the passage does not regard self-determination itself as one of those virtues. (D), therefore, does not state a principle to which the reasoning conforms.

E One point that the argument makes is that it is virtually certain that intervention by an external force cannot bring true freedom. And if real freedom **cannot** come about this way, it is pointless to maintain, as (E) does, that it **should not** be brought about this way. Therefore (E) is not a principle that could play any role in the reasoning.

- *Difficulty Level: 5*

Question 25

Overview: The first sentence of the passage asserts that a certain claim—that Midville is generally more expensive to live in than nearby towns—is false. The rest of the passage presents a case for that claim being false. So the denial of that claim is the conclusion of the argument.

You are asked to identify the main point of the argument, or in other words, the conclusion that the argument draws.

The Correct Answer:

A As the "Overview" indicates, the conclusion of the argument is the denial of a claim that "Midville is generally more expensive to live in than nearby towns are." (A) is the denial of that claim and is thus the main point of the argument.

The Incorrect Answer Choices:

B The argument says that some of Midville's residents consider their taxes to be "relatively high." This doesn't necessarily mean that they find those taxes to be "too high." And in any event, the argument is not directed toward supporting the view that some residents find their taxes to be too high.

C The argument doesn't take a position on (C). The argument does suggest that Midville residents are getting good value for their taxes, but this does not mean that services such as trash removal are less expensive if they are municipally funded than they are if they are privately funded. So (C) is not a point that the argument makes, and it is certainly not its main point.

D The argument claims that some Midville residents, in judging Midville to be expensive to live in, ignore the services paid for by their taxes. This means that in making their calculations they don't take the value of those services sufficiently into account. It doesn't mean that they are unaware of the actual services. So in talking about services being ignored, the argument does not make the point in (D), nor does the argument make that point anywhere else.

E (E) actually seems to be inconsistent with what the argument says. Two of the services cited are rent-assistance and mortgage-assistance, and it is unlikely that people who make use of one also make use of the other. So it is unlikely that most Midville residents make use of **all** of the services Midville provides. But in any case, the argument is directed toward establishing a point about how expensive it is to live in Midville, not toward establishing the point that (E) makes.

- *Difficulty Level: 2*

General Directions for the LSAT Answer Sheet

The actual testing time for this portion of the test will be 2 hours 55 minutes. There are five sections, each with a time limit of 35 minutes. The supervisor will tell you when to begin and end each section. If you finish a section before time is called, you may check your work on that section only; do not turn to any other section of the test book and do not work on any other section either in the test book or on the answer sheet.

There are several different types of questions on the test, and each question type has its own directions. Be sure you understand the directions for each question type before attempting to answer any questions in that section.

Not everyone will finish all the questions in the time allowed. Do not hurry, but work steadily and as quickly as you can without sacrificing accuracy. You are advised to use your time effectively. If a question seems too difficult, go on to the next one and return to the difficult question after completing the section. MARK THE BEST ANSWER YOU CAN FOR EVERY QUESTION. NO DEDUCTIONS WILL BE MADE FOR WRONG ANSWERS. YOUR SCORE WILL BE BASED ONLY ON THE NUMBER OF QUESTIONS YOU ANSWER CORRECTLY.

ALL YOUR ANSWERS MUST BE MARKED ON THE ANSWER SHEET. Answer spaces for each question are lettered to correspond with the letters of the potential answers to each question in the test book. After you have decided which of the answers is correct, blacken the corresponding space on the answer sheet. BE SURE THAT EACH MARK IS BLACK AND COMPLETELY FILLS THE ANSWER SPACE. Give only one answer to each question. If you change an answer, be sure that all previous marks are erased completely. Since the answer sheet is machine scored, incomplete erasures may be interpreted as intended answers. ANSWERS RECORDED IN THE TEST BOOK WILL NOT BE SCORED.

There may be more questions noted on this answer sheet than there are questions in a section. Do not be concerned but be certain that the section and number of the question you are answering matches the answer sheet section and question number. Additional answer spaces in any answer sheet section should be left blank. Begin your next section in the number one answer space for that section.

LSAC takes various steps to ensure that answer sheets are returned from test centers in a timely manner for processing. In the unlikely event that an answer sheet(s) is not received, LSAC will permit the examinee to either retest at no additional fee or to receive a refund of his or her LSAT fee. THESE REMEDIES ARE THE EXCLUSIVE REMEDIES AVAILABLE IN THE UNLIKELY EVENT THAT AN ANSWER SHEET IS NOT RECEIVED BY LSAC.

Score Cancellation

Complete this section only if you are absolutely certain you want to cancel your score. A CANCELLATION REQUEST CANNOT BE RESCINDED. IF YOU ARE AT ALL UNCERTAIN, YOU SHOULD NOT COMPLETE THIS SECTION; INSTEAD, YOU SHOULD CONSIDER SUBMITTING A SIGNED SCORE CANCELLATION FORM, WHICH MUST BE RECEIVED AT LSAC WITHIN 9 CALENDAR DAYS OF THE TEST.

To cancel your score from this administration, you **must**:

A. fill in both ovals here ..... ◯◯
    AND

B. read the following statement. Then sign your name and enter the date.
    YOUR SIGNATURE ALONE IS NOT SUFFICIENT FOR SCORE CANCELLATION. BOTH OVALS ABOVE MUST BE FILLED IN FOR SCANNING EQUIPMENT TO RECOGNIZE YOUR REQUEST FOR SCORE CANCELLATION.

I certify that I wish to cancel my test score from this administration. I understand that my request is irreversible and that my score will not be sent to me or to the law schools to which I apply.

_____
Sign your name in full

_____
Date

HOW DID YOU PREPARE FOR THE LSAT?
(Select all that apply.)

Responses to this item are voluntary and will be used for statistical research purposes only.

◯ By studying the sample questions in the *LSAT Registration and Information Book*.
◯ By taking the free sample LSAT in the *LSAT Registration and Information Book*.
◯ By working through *The Official LSAT Prep Test(s) and/or TriplePrep*.
◯ By using a book on how to prepare for the LSAT **not** published by LSAC.
◯ By attending a commercial test preparation or coaching course.
◯ By attending a test preparation or coaching course offered through an undergraduate institution.
◯ Self study.
◯ Other preparation.
◯ No preparation.

CERTIFYING STATEMENT

Please write (DO NOT PRINT) the following statement. Sign and date.

I certify that I am the examinee whose name appears on this answer sheet and that I am here to take the LSAT for the sole purpose of being considered for admission to law school. I further certify that I will neither assist nor receive assistance from any other candidate, and I agree not to copy or retain examination questions or to transmit them in any form to any other person.

_____
_____
_____
_____
_____
_____
_____
_____
_____

SIGNATURE: _____ TODAY'S DATE: ____ / ____ / ____
                                                              MONTH DAY YEAR

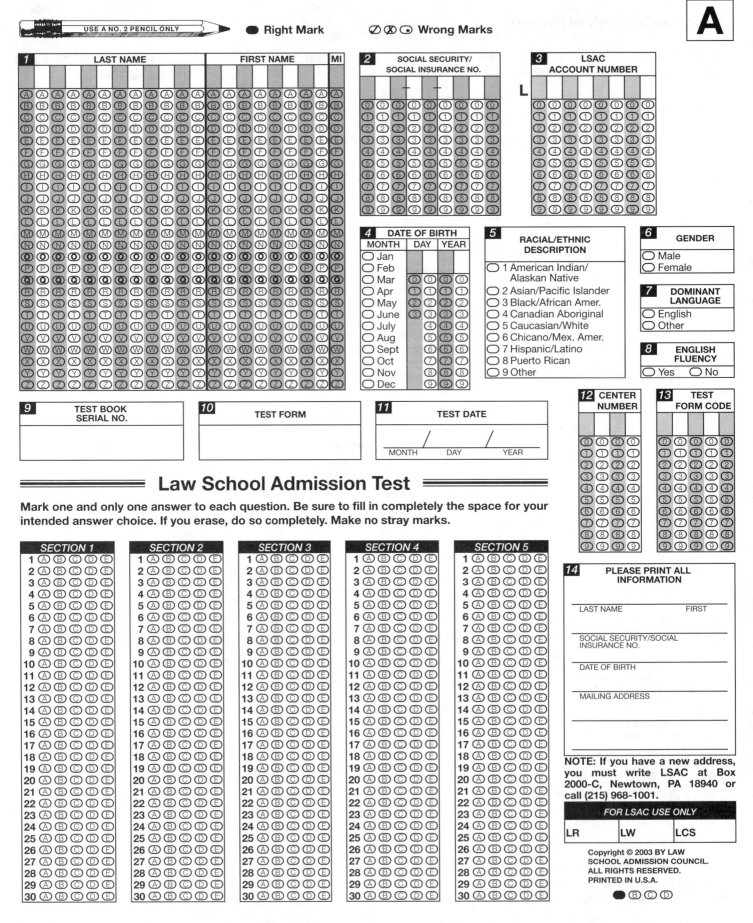

The PrepTest Table of Contents

1

SECTION I

Time—35 minutes

24 Questions

Directions: Each group of questions in this section is based on a set of conditions. In answering some of the questions, it may be useful to draw a rough diagram. Choose the response that most accurately and completely answers each question and blacken the corresponding space on your answer sheet.

Questions 1–5

At a water carnival, each of the eight lifeguards—J, K, L, M, P, Q, R, and S—will participate in two events, a boat race and a rescue exercise. For each of these events the eight lifeguards are grouped into four two-person teams, subject to the following rules:

If two lifeguards are teammates in the boat race, they cannot also be teammates in the rescue exercise.
L and Q are teammates in the boat race.
K and L are teammates in the rescue exercise.
R and S are not teammates in either event.

1. Which one of the following could be a list of the four teams participating in the boat race?
   - (A) J and L; K and S; M and Q; P and R
   - (B) J and M; K and P; L and Q; R and S
   - (C) J and M; K and R; L and S; P and Q
   - (D) J and M; K and S; L and Q; P and R
   - (E) J and P; K and L; M and R; Q and S

2. Which one of the following is a pair of lifeguards who cannot be teammates in the rescue exercise but who could be teammates in the boat race?
   - (A) J and P
   - (B) K and R
   - (C) L and S
   - (D) P and M
   - (E) P and Q

3. If M and P are teammates in the boat race and J and R are teammates in the rescue exercise, which one of the following is a pair that must be teammates in the boat race?
   - (A) J and K
   - (B) J and S
   - (C) K and L
   - (D) K and S
   - (E) Q and R

4. If P and K are teammates in the boat race and P and Q are teammates in the rescue exercise, then each of the following lists a pair of lifeguards who must be teammates in one of the two events EXCEPT:
   - (A) J and M
   - (B) J and R
   - (C) J and S
   - (D) M and R
   - (E) M and S

5. If J and P are teammates in the boat race, then M could be the teammate of
   - (A) K in the boat race and S in the rescue exercise
   - (B) L in the boat race and S in the rescue exercise
   - (C) R in the boat race and L in the rescue exercise
   - (D) S in the boat race and K in the rescue exercise
   - (E) S in the boat race and P in the rescue exercise

GO ON TO THE NEXT PAGE.

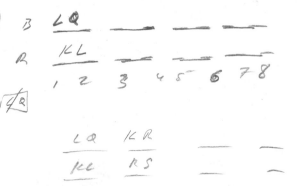

1

Questions 6–12

A critic ranks exactly seven restaurants—Lautrec, Medici, Pastilla, Robusto, Scheherazade's, Tantoko, and Vistula— from highest (best) to lowest (worst). The ranking must meet the following conditions:
  Pastilla ranks higher than Lautrec but lower than Robusto.
  Medici ranks higher than Vistula but lower than Tantoko.
  If Scheherazade's ranks higher than Pastilla, Medici ranks higher than Scheherazade's.
  If Medici ranks higher than Scheherazade's, Scheherazade's ranks higher than Pastilla.
  There are no ties.

6. Which one of the following could be an accurate ranking of the restaurants, from highest to lowest?

  (A) Tantoko, Medici, Scheherazade's, Pastilla, Vistula, Robusto, Lautrec
  (B) Robusto, Pastilla, Tantoko, Medici, Scheherazade's, Vistula, Lautrec
  (C) Tantoko, Medici, Scheherazade's, Robusto, Vistula, Pastilla, Lautrec
  (D) Tantoko, Robusto, Medici, Vistula, Pastilla, Scheherazade's, Lautrec
  (E) Robusto, Pastilla, Scheherazade's, Medici, Vistula, Tantoko, Lautrec

7. If Pastilla ranks second highest, then which one of the following is a complete and accurate list of restaurants any one of which could be ranked fourth highest?

  (A) Lautrec
  (B) Lautrec, Vistula
  (C) Scheherazade's, Lautrec
  (D) Scheherazade's, Lautrec, Medici
  (E) Scheherazade's, Lautrec, Tantoko

8. Which one of the following is the lowest ranking that Medici could have?

  (A) second highest
  (B) third highest
  (C) fourth highest
  (D) fifth highest
  (E) sixth highest

9. If Medici ranks lower than Lautrec, then which one of the following must be true?

  (A) Lautrec ranks higher than Tantoko.
  (B) Scheherazade's ranks higher than Vistula.
  (C) Pastilla ranks higher than Tantoko.
  (D) Tantoko ranks higher than Scheherazade's.
  (E) Tantoko ranks higher than Pastilla.

10. If Vistula ranks higher than Robusto, then which one of the following restaurants could be ranked fifth highest?

  (A) Tantoko
  (B) Medici
  (C) Scheherazade's
  (D) Vistula
  (E) Pastilla

11. Which one of the following CANNOT be true?

  (A) Pastilla ranks second highest.
  (B) Vistula ranks third highest.
  (C) Lautrec ranks third highest.
  (D) Robusto ranks fifth highest.
  (E) Scheherazade's ranks sixth highest.

12. If Tantoko is ranked third highest, then which one of the following CANNOT be true?

  (A) Lautrec is ranked fourth highest.
  (B) Pastilla is ranked fifth highest.
  (C) Medici is ranked fifth highest.
  (D) Scheherazade's is ranked fifth highest.
  (E) Medici is ranked sixth highest.

GO ON TO THE NEXT PAGE.

Questions 13–19

Each of exactly three parks—Jessup, Island, and Hilltop—has at least one attraction. Each attraction is exactly one of five different types: fountain, garden, museum, playground, or theater. Among the three parks at least one of each type of attraction is included. No two attractions of the same type are included in any park. The following conditions must apply:

Each of exactly two parks has a garden.
Jessup has a museum but not a theater.
Island has exactly one attraction.
No park has both a playground and a fountain.
Each park that has a theater also has a garden.
Each park that has a museum also has a playground.

13. Which one of the following could be a complete and accurate matching of each park to its attractions?

(A) Jessup: garden, museum; Island: playground; Hilltop: garden, theater
(B) Jessup: museum, theater; Island: garden; Hilltop: fountain, garden, playground, theater
(C) Jessup: garden, museum, playground; Island: theater; Hilltop: garden, museum, playground
(D) Jessup: garden, museum, playground; Island: fountain; Hilltop: garden, theater
(E) Jessup: museum, playground; Island: fountain, garden; Hilltop: garden, theater

14. Which one of the following CANNOT be true?

(A) Neither Island nor Hilltop has a museum.
(B) Neither Island nor Hilltop has a playground.
(C) Neither Jessup nor Hilltop has a fountain.
(D) Neither Jessup nor Island has a garden.
(E) Neither Jessup nor Island has a theater.

15. If each of exactly two of the parks has a fountain, then which one of the following could be true?

(A) Island does not have a fountain.
(B) Jessup does not have a garden.
(C) Jessup has exactly two attractions.
(D) Hilltop has exactly three attractions.
(E) Hilltop has exactly four attractions.

16. If Jessup has exactly three attractions, then it is possible to determine the exact set of attractions featured by which of the parks?

(A) Island only
(B) Jessup only
(C) Island and Hilltop only
(D) Island and Jessup only
(E) Jessup, Island, and Hilltop

17. If the attraction included in Island is of the same type as an attraction included in Jessup, then which one of the following must be true?

(A) Hilltop has a playground.
(B) Island has a museum.
(C) Island has a fountain.
(D) Island has a garden.
(E) Jessup has a garden.

18. Which one of the following could be true?

(A) Both Hilltop and Island have a garden.
(B) Both Hilltop and Island have a playground.
(C) Both Hilltop and Island have a theater.
(D) Both Island and Jessup have a fountain.
(E) Both Island and Jessup have a garden.

19. If Hilltop has exactly three attractions, then each of the following could be true EXCEPT:

(A) Hilltop has a museum.
(B) Hilltop has a playground.
(C) Island does not have a fountain.
(D) Island has a garden.
(E) Jessup has a garden.

GO ON TO THE NEXT PAGE.

Questions 20–24

Each year for the next three years, Dynamic Motors will assemble four new automobile models—the Volante, the Whisper, the Xavier, and the Ziggurat—in exactly five of its factories—F, G, H, J, and K. Each factory will assemble exactly one model in each year. Because of contractual obligations Dynamic will assemble all four models each year according to the following constraints:

No model is manufactured in the same factory in consecutive years.
Neither Volantes nor Whispers are assembled in any factory in which Xaviers were assembled the previous year.
Neither Volantes nor Xaviers are assembled in any factory in which Ziggurats were assembled the previous year.
In any year, only one factory assembles Ziggurats.

20. Which one of the following could be the assembly schedule for factories F and G for the first two years?

(A)　year 1: Volantes in F, Ziggurats in G
　　　year 2: Xaviers in F, Whispers in G
(B)　year 1: Whispers in F, Xaviers in G
　　　year 2: Whispers in F, Ziggurats in G
(C)　year 1: Xaviers in F, Volantes in G
　　　year 2: Ziggurats in F, Ziggurats in G
(D)　year 1: Xaviers in F, Xaviers in G
　　　year 2: Whispers in F, Ziggurats in G
(E)　year 1: Ziggurats in F, Whispers in G
　　　year 2: Volantes in F, Volantes in G

21. If in the first year Volantes and Whispers are assembled in F and G, respectively, the models that are assembled in the second year in F and G, respectively, could be

(A)　Volantes and Whispers
(B)　Whispers and Volantes
(C)　Whispers and Ziggurats
(D)　Ziggurats and Whispers
(E)　Ziggurats and Ziggurats

22. Which one of the following must be true?

(A)　Xaviers are assembled in exactly two of the factories in the first year.
(B)　Xaviers are assembled in exactly one of the factories in the second year.
(C)　Xaviers are assembled in exactly two of the factories in the second year.
(D)　Xaviers are assembled in exactly one of the factories in the third year.
(E)　Xaviers are assembled in exactly two of the factories in the third year.

23. If in the second year Ziggurats are assembled in F, which one of the following must be true?

(A)　Volantes are assembled in exactly one of the factories in the third year.
(B)　Whispers are assembled in exactly one of the factories in the third year.
(C)　Volantes are assembled in F in the first year.
(D)　Whispers are assembled in F in the first year.
(E)　Xaviers are assembled in F in the first year.

24. If in the second year Volantes and Whispers are assembled in F and G, respectively, the models that are assembled in the first year in F and G, respectively, could be

(A)　Whispers and Volantes
(B)　Whispers and Xaviers
(C)　Xaviers and Volantes
(D)　Xaviers and Ziggurats
(E)　Ziggurats and Volantes

S T O P

IF YOU FINISH BEFORE TIME IS CALLED, YOU MAY CHECK YOUR WORK ON THIS SECTION ONLY.
DO NOT WORK ON ANY OTHER SECTION IN THE TEST.

2

SECTION II

Time—35 minutes

24 Questions

Directions: The questions in this section are based on the reasoning contained in brief statements or passages. For some questions, more than one of the choices could conceivably answer the question. However, you are to choose the best answer; that is, the response that most accurately and completely answers the question. You should not make assumptions that are by commonsense standards implausible, superfluous, or incompatible with the passage. After you have chosen the best answer, blacken the corresponding space on your answer sheet.

1. Jorge: It is obvious that a shift in economic policy is needed, so why not proceed with the necessary changes all at once? If one wants to jump over a chasm, one would do it with one leap.

    Christina: I disagree with your view, even though I agree that a shift in economic policy is needed. If one wants to teach a horse to jump fences, one should train it to jump lower heights first.

    Jorge and Christina disagree over whether

    (A)   a shift in economic policy is not needed
    (B)   revising current economic policy incrementally is like teaching a horse to jump fences
    (C)   the faster current economic policy is revised, the less painful the initial changes will be
    (D)   the economic changes should not all be made at the same time
    (E)   the current economic situation is grave

2. John: For 40 years, fluoride has been added to public drinking water. According to a study, fluoridated public drinking water when given to laboratory rats causes bone cancer. Ninety percent of all the male rats in the test sample were affected, but the female rats were unaffected. Even though I am healthy now, I should nevertheless stop drinking fluoridated water; only then will I be sure not to develop bone cancer.

    Which one of the following is the strongest criticism of John's reasoning?

    (A)   John does not consider how others besides himself are affected by fluoridation of water.
    (B)   John does not consider whether fluoridated water causes other diseases.
    (C)   John does not consider whether there were any brief periods during the 40 years in which fluoride was not added to the water.
    (D)   John does not focus on the positive effects that fluoridated water has on people.
    (E)   John does not consider the possibility of other causes of bone cancer.

3. Columnist: Polls can influence voters' decisions, and they may distort the outcome of an election since their results are much less reliable than the public believes. Furthermore, the publication of polls immediately prior to an election allows no response from those wishing to dispute the polls' findings. A ban on publishing polls during the week prior to an election only minimally impairs freedom of expression, and thus should be implemented.

    Which one of the following, if true, most seriously weakens the columnist's argument?

    (A)   Few people are influenced by the results of polls published during the two weeks immediately prior to an election.
    (B)   The publication of poll results would not decide the winner of an uneven election race.
    (C)   The publication of poll results may remove some voters' motivation to vote because of the certainty that a particular candidate will win.
    (D)   The publication of poll results in the last weeks before an election draws attention to candidates' late gains in popularity.
    (E)   Countries in which such a ban is in effect do not generally have better informed citizens than do countries in which such a ban is not in effect.

GO ON TO THE NEXT PAGE.

4. High cholesterol levels are highly correlated with cardiovascular disease. In the Italian town of Limone, however, each of the residents has had high cholesterol levels for many years, and yet they have not developed cardiovascular disease.

Which one of the following, if true, most helps to explain the unusual health condition of the residents of Limone?

(A) Persons who come from families that have enjoyed great longevity tend not to develop cardiovascular disease.

(B) The stress and pollution found in large cities exacerbate existing cardiovascular disease, but there is little stress or pollution in Limone.

(C) The residents of Limone have normal blood sugar levels, and very low blood sugar levels tend to cancel out the cardiovascular effects of a high cholesterol level.

(D) The residents of Limone inherited from common ancestors a blood protein that prevents vascular blockage, which is a cause of cardiovascular disease.

(E) Olive oil is a staple of the diet in some parts of Italy, but unlike butter, olive oil is a monosaturated fat, and monosaturated fats do not contribute to cardiovascular disease.

5. Smith's new grazing land consists entirely of fescue grass. Half of the grass contains a species of fungus that makes cows ill when they eat it. Smith's cows will most likely learn to graze exclusively on the grass that does not contain the fungus, since, like many other animals, cows will avoid eating a patch of grass if they sense a substance in it that has made them ill.

Which one of the following is an assumption required by the argument?

(A) At least one other species of fungus is contained in the fescue grass that does not contain the fungus that makes cows ill.

(B) At least some cows that have been made ill by the fungus are capable of sensing the fungus in fescue grass.

(C) The fungus that makes cows ill cannot be found in any variety of grass other than fescue grass.

(D) The cows are the only animals grazing on the new land who become ill after eating the fungus contained in the fescue grass.

(E) The fungus that is contained in the fescue grass cannot be eradicated without destroying the grass itself.

6. News item: The result of a recent public survey has been called into question because one of the pollsters admitted to falsifying data. The survey originally concluded that most people in the country favor investing more money in information technologies. Because falsified data were included in the survey, its conclusion is not true; a majority does not favor more investment in information technologies.

The news item's argument is vulnerable to criticism because it fails to consider the possibility that

(A) the conclusion of the survey would be verified if the falsified data were excluded

(B) the conclusion of the survey will be accepted by the public even though falsified data were used

(C) other pollsters in other surveys also may have falsified data

(D) some people who responded to the survey were lying

(E) people's opinions about investing in information technologies can change as new technologies develop

7. When an invading insect threatens an ant colony's territory or food sources, the ants will vigorously swarm over the invader, biting or stinging it. This defensive tactic can effectively deter even aggressive flying insects, such as wasps. Ants do not attack all insects within their territory, however. For example, riodinid caterpillars commonly live harmoniously among South American ants. These caterpillars, which are a favorite prey of wasps, produce secretions the ants consume as food.

Which one of the following is most strongly supported by the information above?

(A) The secretions produced by riodinid caterpillars are chemically identical to substances secreted by plants on which South American ants also feed.

(B) South American ants are more likely to be successful in defending their food sources and territory against intruders than are ants that live elsewhere.

(C) With the sole exception of riodinid caterpillars, South American ants will vigorously attack any organism that enters an area they inhabit.

(D) Among insect species that inhabit South America, wasps are the only kinds of organism other than ants that use riodinid caterpillars as a source of food.

(E) Riodinid caterpillars in South America that live among ants are less likely to be attacked successfully by wasps than those that do not live among ants.

8. The traditional way to define the difference between rural and urban lifestyles is geographically. But with the impact of communications technology it makes more sense to draw the distinction in informational terms. People who rarely communicate electronically with anyone are living rural lifestyles, irrespective of where they live, while people who communicate daily with dozens of people via fax or modem are living urban lifestyles, even if they live in the country.

The situation described above most closely illustrates which one of the following propositions?

(A) Frequency of electronic communication with others is superseding geographical considerations in defining our lifestyles.

(B) Many people who use electronic technology find urban lifestyles more satisfying than they find rural lifestyles.

(C) People who live rural lifestyles communicate less frequently than do people who live urban lifestyles.

(D) We are unable to foresee the magnitude of the changes that the information revolution may have in defining our lives.

(E) People are choosing to live in different regions of the nation than previously because of the impact of electronic communications technology.

9. Very powerful volcanic eruptions send large amounts of ash high into the atmosphere, blocking sunlight and causing abnormally cold temperatures for a year or more after the eruption. In 44 B.C. there was a powerful eruption of Mount Etna in Sicily. In the following year, Chinese historians recorded summer frosts and dimmed sunlight in China, thousands of miles east of Sicily. If these phenomena were caused by volcanic ash in the atmosphere, then the ash sent into the atmosphere by Mount Etna's eruption must have spread over great distances.

In evaluating the support given for the conclusion advanced in the last sentence of the passage, it would be most important to determine whether

(A) modern monitoring equipment can detect the precise path of volcanic ash in the atmosphere

(B) the abnormal weather in China lasted for a full year or longer

(C) temperatures in Sicily were abnormally cold after Mount Etna erupted

(D) there were any volcanic eruptions near China around the time of Mount Etna's eruption

(E) subsequent eruptions of Mount Etna were as powerful as the one in 44 B.C.

Questions 10–11

Mario: The field of cognitive science is not a genuinely autonomous discipline since it addresses issues also addressed by the disciplines of computer science, linguistics, and psychology. A genuinely autonomous discipline has a domain of inquiry all its own.

Lucy: Nonsense. You've always acknowledged that philosophy is a genuinely autonomous discipline and that, like most people, you think of philosophy as addressing issues also addressed by the disciplines of linguistics, mathematics, and psychology. A field of study is a genuinely autonomous discipline by virtue of its having a unique methodology rather than by virtue of its addressing issues that no other field of study addresses.

10. Lucy responds to Mario by

(A) questioning Mario's expertise in cognitive science

(B) demonstrating that Mario confuses the notion of a field of study with that of a genuinely autonomous discipline

(C) showing that some of Mario's beliefs are not compatible with the principle on which he bases his conclusion

(D) disputing the accuracy of Mario's description of cognitive science as addressing issues also addressed by other disciplines

(E) establishing that Mario is not a philosopher

11. On the basis of their statements, Mario and Lucy are committed to disagreeing about the truth of which one of the following?

(A) If a field of study that has a unique methodology lacks a domain of inquiry all its own, it can nonetheless be a genuinely autonomous discipline.

(B) If a field of study is not a genuinely autonomous discipline, it can still have a unique methodology.

(C) All fields of study that are characterized by a unique methodology and by a domain of inquiry all their own are genuinely autonomous disciplines.

(D) Any field of study that is not a genuinely autonomous discipline lacks both a unique domain of inquiry and a unique methodology.

(E) Any field of study that is not a genuinely autonomous discipline addresses issues also addressed by disciplines that are genuinely autonomous.

GO ON TO THE NEXT PAGE.

12. Undoubtedly, one's freedom is always worth the risk of losing one's life. Consider a person who is locked in a bare cement room with no hope of escape. This person is not really living and has nothing to lose.

A flaw in the argument's reasoning is that the argument

(A) presumes, without providing justification, that nothing can have greater value than one's own freedom

(B) fails to consider that it is not always possible to rebel physically against an encroachment on one's freedom

(C) generalizes inappropriately from a single extreme case to a universal claim

(D) fails to establish that the freedom of others is worth taking risks for

(E) overlooks the possibility that some people do not have the courage to take risks for freedom

13. Ramona: One of the primary values of a university education is the intellectual growth that results from exposure to a wide range of ideas. Too many students miss this because they choose technical majors only to improve their chances on the job market. Recent pressures to graduate as quickly as possible only make matters worse.

Martin: But we have to be realistic. My brother graduated last year as an English major, but he's working as a waiter. Anyway, you are forgetting that even students in technical majors are required to take some liberal arts classes.

The conversation most strongly supports the claim that Ramona and Martin agree with each other that

(A) students are stimulated to grow intellectually only in English classes

(B) only graduates with degrees in technical subjects get good jobs

(C) not every university class exposes students to a wide range of ideas

(D) intellectual growth is more important than financial security

(E) financial security is more important than intellectual growth

14. Essayist: Some researchers criticize British governmental security agencies for not releasing enough information about sightings of unidentified flying objects (UFOs) made by these military and intelligence agencies. Requests for information by civilian researchers are brushed aside. This leads one to suspect that there have been spacecraft sighted near Earth that are extraterrestrial in origin.

Which one of the following, if true, would most strengthen the essayist's argument?

(A) The British government is generally not forthcoming with secure information.

(B) The British government would withhold information pertaining to UFOs only if it were established that they were from other planets.

(C) The British government would deny the requests by civilian researchers to have access to data only if this government had something to hide.

(D) The British government is less trusting of civilian researchers than it is of military researchers.

(E) The British government has always attempted to deny the existence of UFOs.

GO ON TO THE NEXT PAGE.

15. Each of two drugs, S and T, greatly reduces the effects of potentially fatal heart attacks if given as soon as possible after the attack begins, but a trial has shown that use of drug T instead of drug S would prevent death in one additional case out of 120. Drug T, however, costs $2,000 more per treatment than drug S. Therefore society is presented with a stark policy decision: whether or not to pay the $240,000 it would cost to use drug T in order to save one additional patient.

Which one of the following is an assumption on which the argument relies?

(A) Drug S has certain side effects not shared by drug T.

(B) Drug T is much newer than drug S, and had far higher development costs.

(C) After a heart attack, drug T remains relatively effective if given at a time at which drug S is no longer effective.

(D) There is no quick, practical, and relatively inexpensive way of telling for any individual case whether drug S will be as effective as drug T.

(E) Drug T works significantly faster than drug S.

16. Researcher: Results indicate that the higher their educational level, the better are students' mathematical skills. These results do not prove that education improves mathematical skills, however, since it is possible that students who have better mathematical skills to start with are the students who reach higher educational levels.

The reasoning of the researcher's argument is most similar to that of which one of the following arguments?

(A) Results indicate that the quality of papers submitted for publication varies significantly from university to university. This may say nothing about the quality of education offered at different schools, but may only reflect a defect in the review process.

(B) Results from competition indicate that professional athletes outperform amateur athletes. These results do not prove that becoming a professional athlete improves one's athletic performance, since it is possible that the athletes who become professionals are those whose performance is better to begin with.

(C) Studies indicate that students who graduate from more prestigious schools often get good jobs. These studies do not show that these schools prepare students well for the job market, since it is possible that employers are impressed by the mere fact that the students are from more prestigious schools.

(D) Surveys indicate that politicians with law degrees are better at what they do than politicians without law degrees. These surveys do not prove that having a law degree makes one a better politician, since it is possible that many politicians without law degrees were left out of the survey.

(E) Studies suggest that some people who are gifted in higher mathematics are inept at performing simple arithmetical calculations. These studies do not show that being good at mathematics precludes being good at arithmetic, since there are also many people who are good at both.

GO ON TO THE NEXT PAGE.

17. Two hundred randomly selected subjects were asked, "Have you ever awakened, seemingly paralyzed, with a sense of a strange presence in the room?" Forty percent answered yes. A randomly selected control group of 200 different subjects in the same study were asked simply if they remembered ever waking up seemingly paralyzed. Only 14 percent of the control group answered yes.

Which one of the following statements is most supported by the information above?

(A) Experiencing a sense of a strange presence in a room in some way causes subjects to feel as though they are paralyzed.

(B) The number of subjects who had awakened with a sense of a strange presence in the room was greater in the first group than in the control group.

(C) If the reports of the first group of subjects were accurate, approximately 60 percent of them had never awakened with a sense of a strange presence in the room.

(D) At least some of the randomly selected subjects of the study gave inconsistent reports.

(E) The tendency of subjects to report a recollection of an event can sometimes be increased by suggesting circumstances that accompanied the event.

18. Sid: The sign says "Keep off the grass."

Micki: I know, but just one person walking across the grass doesn't hurt it.

Sid: Your statement is false. If everyone believed as you do, everyone would walk across the grass, and the grass would die.

Sid's argument is questionable in that it

(A) attempts to use a statement about the consequences of actions to disprove a statement about the actions themselves

(B) treats a statement about the consequences of an action as though it were instead about the consequences of everyone believing the statement

(C) contradicts itself by treating a statement that the arguer does not believe as though it were a statement believed by everyone

(D) discounts the fact that there may be circumstances under which hurting the grass is justified

(E) attempts to undermine a statement by calling into question the character of the person making the statement

19. Newspaper editorial: Many pharmaceutical companies develop "me too" drugs, drugs designed to duplicate, more or less, the effect of another company's product that is already on the market. Some critics object that such development constitutes an unnecessary, redundant use of resources that provides no new benefits to consumers. However, the entry of "me too" drugs into the market can result in a price reduction for the drugs they resemble. Therefore, "me too" drugs can indeed benefit consumers.

Which one of the following, if true, most strengthens the editorial's argument?

(A) Some "me too" drugs turn out to be more effective than the drugs they were designed to imitate.

(B) If "me too" drugs were prohibited, more money would be available for the development of innovative drugs.

(C) Pharmaceutical companies often make more money on a "me too" drug than on an original drug.

(D) If all pharmaceutical companies developed "me too" drugs, fewer innovative drugs would be developed.

(E) Some pharmaceutical companies lose money on the development of innovative drugs because of the development by other companies of "me too" drugs.

GO ON TO THE NEXT PAGE.

20. One of the most important events for modern astronomy was the series of collisions, during a single week in 1994, of more than a dozen large objects with Jupiter. The collision of these objects, which once formed most of the comet Shoemaker-Levy 9, resulted in formations that showed no signs of water. There was thus no water involved in the collisions, so we know that none of the comet's fragments penetrated to Jupiter's lower atmosphere and that the comet was composed of rock rather than ice.

Which one of the following is an assumption on which the argument depends?

(A) Comets tend to be composed largely of ice while asteroids are composed mainly of rock.

(B) If Jupiter's lower atmosphere had been penetrated by the comet's fragments, the resulting formations would show signs of water.

(C) A larger explosion would occur upon collision with Jupiter if Shoemaker-Levy 9 were composed of rock than if it were composed of ice.

(D) The post-collision analysis of Jupiter showed that the formations all had exactly the same composition.

(E) The deeper the explosion occurred in Jupiter's atmosphere, the more difficult it would be to detect from Earth.

21. The experts who now assure us that genetically engineered plants are harmless are the same experts who claimed that introducing non-native plants into the wild was a good idea. It is too late to be skeptical now that some non-native plants have become a serious problem. But we should conclude, while we still have time, that genetically engineered plants will also be harmful.

The flawed reasoning in which one of the following most closely parallels the flawed reasoning in the argument above?

(A) The same people who complain that taxes are too high complain that the government does not provide enough services. We should conclude that high taxes and big government go together.

(B) The film critics who called Meisner's last film brilliant are the same ones who are calling her new film confused and boring. But because Meisner's last film was excellent I conclude that this one will be also.

(C) The economists who tell us that the current economic expansion will soon be over are the same economists who failed to predict the end of the last recession. Wise investors will conclude that the expansion will continue for some time.

(D) Children who beg and plead with their parents to buy them trendy toys are the same children who begged for trendy toys last year. I conclude that parents ought to ignore such pleadings and simply buy traditional toys.

(E) The population experts who are predicting world food shortages in the next decade are the same ones who have erroneously predicted such shortages in the past. Therefore, if there are food shortages in the next decade, it will not be because population experts predicted them.

GO ON TO THE NEXT PAGE.

22. One can be at home and be in the backyard, that is, not in one's house at all. One can also be in one's house but not at home, if one owns the house but rents it out to others, for example. So one's being at home is not required for one's being in one's own house.

Which one of the following most accurately describes the relationship between the argument's conclusion and its claim that one can be at home without being in one's house?

 (A) The claim is required to establish the conclusion.
 (B) The claim represents the point the conclusion is intended to refute.
 (C) The claim is compatible with the truth or falsity of the conclusion.
 (D) The claim points out an ambiguity in the phrase "at home."
 (E) The claim inadvertently contradicts the conclusion.

23. Economist: In any country, inflation occurs when the money supply grows more than the production of goods and services grows. Similarly, deflation occurs when the production of goods and services grows more than does the money supply. In my country, gold anchors the money supply, so the money supply is very stable. Hence, my country is very unlikely to experience significant inflation or deflation.

Which one of the following is an assumption on which the economist's argument depends?

 (A) Having stability in the production of goods and services is the most effective means of preventing inflation or deflation.
 (B) Having an anchor such as gold is necessary for the stability of a country's money supply.
 (C) The production of goods and services in the economist's country is unlikely to grow markedly.
 (D) Inflation is no more likely to occur in the economist's country than is deflation.
 (E) A stable money supply is the most effective means of preventing inflation.

24. Agricultural economist: We can increase agricultural production without reducing biodiversity, but only if we abandon conventional agriculture. Thus, if we choose to sustain economic growth, which requires increasing agricultural production, we should radically modify agricultural techniques.

Which one of the following principles, if valid, most helps to justify the agricultural economist's reasoning?

 (A) Agricultural production should be reduced if doing so would increase biodiversity.
 (B) Economic growth should not be pursued at the expense of a loss of biodiversity.
 (C) Economic growth should be sustained only as long as agricultural production continues to increase.
 (D) Preserving biodiversity is no more important than increasing agricultural production.
 (E) Agricultural techniques should be radically modified only if doing so would further the extent to which we can increase agricultural production.

S T O P

IF YOU FINISH BEFORE TIME IS CALLED, YOU MAY CHECK YOUR WORK ON THIS SECTION ONLY.
DO NOT WORK ON ANY OTHER SECTION IN THE TEST.

SECTION III

Time—35 minutes

26 Questions

<u>Directions:</u> The questions in this section are based on the reasoning contained in brief statements or passages. For some questions, more than one of the choices could conceivably answer the question. However, you are to choose the <u>best</u> answer; that is, the response that most accurately and completely answers the question. You should not make assumptions that are by commonsense standards implausible, superfluous, or incompatible with the passage. After you have chosen the best answer, blacken the corresponding space on your answer sheet.

1. Despite the best efforts of journalists to be objective, it is inevitable that their own biases will enter their reporting, even if inadvertently. Therefore, it is imperative that a trained editor look over journalists' work with an eye toward detecting and removing their biases, so as to make reporting as objective as possible.

   Each of the following is an assumption on which the argument depends EXCEPT:

   (A) Journalists do not eliminate all of the biases that enter their reporting.
   (B) It is imperative that reporting be as objective as possible.
   (C) Objectivity in reporting is undermined by the presence of journalists' biases.
   (D) Trained editors are able to detect at least some biases of journalists.
   (E) Journalists' reporting that is not objective is not taken seriously by trained editors.

2. Astronomer: Mount Shalko is the perfect site for the proposed astronomical observatory. The summit would accommodate the complex as currently designed, with some room left for expansion. There are no large cities near the mountain, so neither smog nor artificial light interferes with atmospheric transparency. Critics claim that Mount Shalko is a unique ecological site, but the observatory need not be a threat to endemic life-forms. In fact, since it would preclude recreational use of the mountain, it should be their salvation. It is estimated that 200,000 recreational users visit the mountain every year, posing a threat to the wildlife.

   Which one of the following, if true, most weakens the astronomer's argument?

   (A) More than a dozen insect and plant species endemic to Mount Shalko are found nowhere else on earth.
   (B) A coalition of 14 different groups, as diverse as taxpayer organizations and hunting associations, opposes the building of the new observatory.
   (C) Having a complex that covers most of the summit, as well as having the necessary security fences and access road on the mountain, could involve just as much ecological disruption as does the current level of recreational use.
   (D) The building of the observatory would not cause the small towns near Mount Shalko eventually to develop into a large city, complete with smog, bright lights, and an influx of recreation seekers.
   (E) A survey conducted by a team of park rangers concluded that two other mountains in the same general area have more potential for recreational use than Mount Shalko.

GO ON TO THE NEXT PAGE.

3. The local fair held its annual photography contest and accepted entries from both amateurs and professionals. The contest awarded prizes in each of several categories. As it turned out, most of the prizes in the contest were won by amateurs.

Each of the following, if true, could by itself constitute an explanation of the outcome of the photography contest EXCEPT:

(A) Many more of the entries in the contest were from amateurs than were from professionals.

(B) The judges in the contest were amateurs, and amateurs tend to prefer photographs taken by other amateurs.

(C) Amateurs tend to enter their best photographs while professionals tend to save their best work for their clients.

(D) Each category in the contest was restricted to amateurs only or professionals only, and there were more categories open to amateurs.

(E) Three times as many amateurs entered the contest as had entered in any previous year.

4. The average 40-year-old North American will have watched more than one million TV commercials in his or her lifetime. We may safely conclude, therefore, that the TV commercial has influenced North American habits of thought.

The conclusion above follows logically if which one of the following is assumed?

(A) The habits of thought that people develop are largely determined by external influences.

(B) Anything people are exposed to in great quantity will influence their habits of thought.

(C) It is impossible to avoid or ignore television commercials.

(D) Some people find television commercials more interesting to watch than the programs themselves.

(E) Certain forms of communication to which people are subjected will affect their habits of thought.

5. Researchers have developed a membrane that quickly removes the oxygen from a refrigerator, thereby killing bacteria and enabling food to be stored almost indefinitely. Since food need not be kept as cold to prevent spoilage, energy costs will be greatly reduced. Thus, over the long run, oxygen-removing refrigerators will prove far less expensive than current models.

The reasoning in the argument is most vulnerable to criticism on the grounds that it does not

(A) address the expense of building or refitting a refrigerator with the new technology

(B) address the possibility of consumer discomfort with the new refrigerators

(C) explain the technology that enabled the oxygen-removing membrane to be developed

(D) take into account the effectiveness of current refrigerator technology in preventing food spoilage

(E) take into account the inconvenience caused by food spoilage in current refrigerators

6. Shortly after the power plant opened and began discharging its wastewater into the river, there was a decrease in the overall number of bass caught by anglers downstream from the plant.

Each of the following, if true, could explain the decrease described above EXCEPT:

(A) The discharged wastewater made the river more attractive to fish that are the natural predators of bass.

(B) The discharged water was warmer than the normal river temperature, leading the bass to seek cooler water elsewhere.

(C) Because of the new plant, access to the part of the river downstream from the plant was improved, leading to an increase in the number of anglers fishing for bass.

(D) Because of the new plant, the level of noise downstream increased, making that section of the river a less popular place for anglers to fish.

(E) The discharged wastewater created turbulence that disrupted the vegetation of the river downstream, destroying some of the bass's natural habitat.

GO ON TO THE NEXT PAGE.

7. The existing works of ancient literature, science, and philosophy do not represent the most original work produced in ancient times. The most compelling evidence for this view is that the existing works frequently refer to other works that we no longer have.

Which one of the following statements, if added to the argument, most helps to justify its conclusion?

(A) Works that contain frequent references to other works tend to be derivative.

(B) Many extant works have laudable things to say about the missing works.

(C) A surprisingly large number of ancient texts have been irretrievably lost.

(D) Subversive ideas tend to be suppressed whenever they are proposed.

(E) Most current ideas regarded as original were already proposed in ancient times.

8. A metaphor is the application of a word or phrase to something to which it does not literally apply in order to emphasize or indicate a similarity between that to which it would ordinarily apply and that to which it is—nonliterally—being applied. Some extremists claim that all uses of language are metaphorical. But this cannot be so, for unless some uses of words are literal, there can be no nonliteral uses of any words.

Which one of the following most accurately expresses the main conclusion of the argument?

(A) It is not the case that all uses of language are metaphorical.

(B) Either all uses of words are literal or all uses of words are metaphorical.

(C) Nonliteral meaning is possible only if some uses of words employ their literal meanings.

(D) Metaphors are nonliteral uses of language that can be used to suggest similarities between objects.

(E) The ordinary meanings of words must be fixed by convention if the similarities between objects are to be representable by language.

9. In a recent poll of chief executive officers (CEOs) of 125 large corporations, the overwhelming majority claimed that employee training and welfare is of the same high priority as customer satisfaction. So the popular belief that the top management of large corporations behaves indifferently to the needs and aspirations of employees is unfounded.

The argument is most vulnerable to criticism on the grounds that it

(A) fails to define adequately the term "top management"·

(B) presumes, without giving justification, that one is not indifferent to something that one considers a top priority

(C) presumes, without giving justification, that the CEOs' priorities tend to be misplaced

(D) presumes, without giving justification, that the CEOs' claims are reflected in actual practice

(E) makes a generalization based on an unrepresentative sample

10. Many people joke about Friday the thirteenth being an unlucky day, but a study showed that in one year approximately 17 percent of people scheduled to fly canceled or did not show up for their flights on Friday the thirteenth—a rate higher than that on any other day and date in that year. This shows that a significant percentage of the population would rather disrupt their travel plans than risk flying on a supposedly unlucky day.

Which one of the following statements, if true, most seriously weakens the argument?

(A) People who fly tend to be professionals who as a group are less superstitious than the general public.

(B) Surveys show that less than 5 percent of the population report that they believe that Friday the thirteenth is an unlucky day.

(C) Weather conditions at several major airports were severe on the Fridays that fell on the thirteenth in the year of the study.

(D) In the year of the study, automobile traffic was no lighter on Friday the thirteenth than on other Fridays.

(E) The absentee rate among airline workers was not significantly higher than normal on the Fridays that fell on the thirteenth in the year of the study.

GO ON TO THE NEXT PAGE.

11. The everyday behavior of whales is particularly difficult to study because introducing novel stimuli, such as divers or submarines, into the whales' environment causes whales to behave in unusual ways. Some biologists plan to train sea lions to carry video cameras on their backs and, on command, to swim along with whales. They argue that since whales are accustomed to there being sea lions nearby, using the sea lions to film the whales would allow biologists to study the everyday behavior of whales.

Which one of the following is an assumption on which the biologists' reasoning depends?

(A) Whales will often react aggressively in the presence of divers and submarines although aggressive behavior is unusual for whales.

(B) The behavior of the sea lions under human command will be within the range of sea lion behavior to which the whales are accustomed.

(C) The trained sea lions will not be aware that they are carrying video cameras on their backs.

(D) Sea lions carrying video cameras will be able to film whales at a much closer range than divers can.

(E) Whales prefer the presence of sea lions to that of either divers or submarines.

12. Geologist: A geological fault in the mountain under which the proposed nuclear waste storage facility would be buried could, after a few thousand years, cause the contents to seep out or water to seep in. Since nuclear waste remains dangerous for up to 25,000 years, such seepage would be disastrous. So we should not place a nuclear waste storage facility under this mountain until scientists investigate whether this mountain has any geological faults.

Which one of the following, if true, most strengthens the geologist's argumentation?

(A) In a few thousand years, human civilization may no longer exist.

(B) The scientists' investigation would conclusively show whether or not the mountain has any geological faults.

(C) The proposed facility was not initially intended to be used for the storage of nuclear waste.

(D) The scientists' investigation would increase dramatically the cost of storing nuclear waste under the mountain.

(E) Nuclear waste could be stored in the proposed facility on a temporary basis.

13. Mall manager: By congregating in large groups near the stores in our mall, teenagers create an atmosphere in which many adult shoppers feel uncomfortable. As a result, the adults have begun to spend less time shopping than they have in the past. The mall's goal in this situation is to prevent a significant loss in overall sales, so merchants should do their utmost to discourage teenagers from congregating near stores.

Merchant: But the amount spent by teenagers who congregate near mall stores constitutes a significant percentage of the total amount spent in those stores.

The merchant's response to the manager's argument is most accurately described as

(A) disputing the truth of claims the manager offers as support for the recommendation

(B) giving information that pertains to the relation between the manager's recommendation and the mall's goal

(C) suggesting that the mall's goal is an undesirable one

(D) contending that the manager's recommendation is sound but for reasons other than those given by the manager

(E) using the information cited by the manager to make an additional recommendation that would help achieve the mall's goal

14. Wu: Jurgens is dishonest and so should not be elected mayor.

Miller: I disagree with your conclusion. Jurgens should be elected mayor. Honest people usually are not tough enough to run a city.

Miller's questionable reasoning in which one of the following dialogues is most closely parallel to Miller's questionable reasoning in the dialogue above?

(A) Wu: We should not go back to that restaurant. The service is too slow.
   Miller: Yes, we should. Food that is served quickly is often of poor quality.

(B) Wu: Bailey should not be the company spokesperson. He is too aggressive.
   Miller: Yes, he should. Aggressive people generally do not get pushed around.

(C) Wu: We should not paint the office this shade of yellow. It's too bright.
   Miller: Yes, we should. Bright colors keep people feeling wide awake.

(D) Wu: We should not upgrade the software. It's too expensive.
   Miller: Yes, we should. The best normally costs more.

(E) Wu: This job applicant should be hired. She has experience.
   Miller: No, we should hire Lyons instead. Everyone lacks experience when first starting out.

GO ON TO THE NEXT PAGE.

3

15. A survey of historians shows that most believe written texts to be the best source for historical understanding. None of the historians regarded painting, architecture, music, dance, or culinary arts as the best source for historical understanding. So these historians neglect many important repositories of historical knowledge.

The reasoning in the argument is flawed because the argument takes for granted that

(A) there are no potential sources for historical understanding other than written texts and the arts

(B) painting, architecture, music, dance, and culinary arts are important only as sources for historical understanding

(C) there are no sources for historical understanding that are neither considered best by historians nor neglected by them

(D) something other than written texts is the best source for historical understanding

(E) the other sources for historical understanding mentioned by the historians surveyed are not important repositories of historical knowledge

16. To act responsibly in one's professional capacity, one must act on the basis of information that one has made a reasonable effort to make sure is accurate and complete.

Which one of the following judgments most closely conforms to the principle cited above?

(A) Peggy acted responsibly in ordering new computers for the school last year because they turned out to be needed due to an unexpected increase in enrollment this year.

(B) Mary acted responsibly in firing John, for she first examined the details of his work record and listened to negative reports from some of his supervisors and coworkers.

(C) Toril did not act responsibly in investing the company's money in Twicycled Ink, for, though the investment yielded a large return, she had not investigated the risks associated with that investment.

(D) Conchita did not act responsibly in hiring Helmer to do the company's bookkeeping because Helmer made a mistake that cost the company a lot of money, though he had never been known to make such a mistake in the past.

(E) Jennifer did not act responsibly in deciding where to go on her vacation because, instead of carefully weighing her options, she waited until the last minute and decided on impulse.

17. Radial keratotomy (RK), a surgery that is designed to reshape the cornea so that light focuses correctly on the retina, is supposed to make eyeglasses or contact lenses that correct for nearsightedness unnecessary. Yet a study of patients who have undergone RK shows that some of them still need to wear glasses or contact lenses.

Each of the following, if true, would help to resolve the apparent discrepancy in the information above EXCEPT:

(A) As the eye heals from an operation to correct nearsightedness, it may in fact overcorrect, causing the person to be farsighted.

(B) The more severe a patient's nearsightedness, the less effective the corneal reshaping of RK will be in correcting the problem.

(C) Occasionally an RK patient's eyes may heal differently, causing a difference in the two eyes' visual acuity that can be overcome only with corrective lenses.

(D) RK patients who originally suffered from only mild nearsightedness may, if the cornea does not heal evenly, develop an astigmatism that requires corrective lenses.

(E) Those who choose to undergo RK tend to be as nearsighted before this operation as those who choose not to undergo RK.

18. Chelas and Stelma are required to leave their respective stations immediately to pursue any prisoner who attempts to escape from their sector. Furthermore, unless they are pursuing such a prisoner, Chelas and Stelma are forbidden to leave their stations until their replacements have arrived. On May 11 at 9 P.M., when Chelas and Stelma finished the four-hour shift in their sector and their replacements arrived, it was discovered that Chelas had violated these rules and Stelma had not.

If the statements above are true, each of the following could be true EXCEPT:

(A) Chelas and Stelma were at their respective stations at 9 P.M.

(B) Stelma left her station before 9 P.M. but Chelas did not.

(C) Chelas left his station before 9 P.M. but Stelma did not.

(D) A prisoner attempted to escape from Chelas and Stelma's sector at 7 P.M. and neither Chelas nor Stelma left his or her station before 9 P.M.

(E) A prisoner attempted to escape from Chelas and Stelma's sector at 7 P.M. and both Chelas and Stelma left their stations before 9 P.M.

GO ON TO THE NEXT PAGE.

19. Faden: Most of our exercise machines are still in use after one year. A recent survey of our customers shows this.

Greenwall: But many of those customers could easily be lying because they are too embarrassed to admit that they don't exercise anymore.

Faden: You have no way of showing that customers were lying. Your objection is absurd.

Which one of the following most accurately describes a flaw in the reasoning above?

(A) Greenwall takes for granted that many customers have stopped using the equipment but are too embarrassed to admit it.

(B) Greenwall presumes, without giving justification, that most people are dishonest about their personal habits.

(C) Faden presumes, without providing justification, that the more conclusive the evidence is for a claim, the less believable the claim becomes.

(D) Faden presumes, without providing justification, that the evidence for a claim has not been undermined unless that evidence has been proven false.

(E) Greenwall ignores the possibility that some people stopped using the equipment but were not embarrassed about it.

20. Sarah: Reporters, by allotting time to some events rather than others, are exercising their judgment as to what is newsworthy and what is not. In other words, they always interpret the news.

Ramon: Reporters should never interpret the news. Once they deem a story to be newsworthy, they are obliged to relay the facts to me untainted.

Sarah and Ramon's remarks provide the most support for holding that they disagree about the truth of which one of the following statements?

(A) Reporters actually do interpret the news every time they report it.

(B) Reporters should exercise their own judgment as to which events are newsworthy.

(C) Reporters' primary responsibility is to see that people are kept informed of the facts.

(D) Reporters should not allot time to reporting some events rather than others.

(E) Reporting on certain events rather than others qualifies as interpreting the news.

21. Advertisement for a lactase supplement: Lactase, an enzyme produced by the body, aids in the digestion of lactose, a natural sugar found in dairy foods. Many subjects in an experiment who drank a liter of milk on an empty stomach showed signs of lactose intolerance—difficulty in digesting dairy products because of insufficient lactase. Thus, extrapolating from the number of subjects adversely affected, at least 50 million people in North America alone should take lactase supplements.

Which one of the following statements, if true, most seriously weakens the argument?

(A) Eating solid food when drinking milk can decrease the amount of lactase produced by the body.

(B) Most people who consume dairy products consume less lactose at each meal than the amount found in a liter of milk.

(C) The production of lactase by the human body increases with age.

(D) Lactose intolerance can interfere with proper nutrition.

(E) Some dairy foods, such as cheese, contain a form of lactose more difficult to digest than that found in milk.

22. Jim: I hear that the company is considering giving Fred and Dorothy 25 percent raises. That would make their salaries higher than mine. Since I have worked here longer than they have, it would be unfair to raise their salaries unless mine is raised to at least what theirs will be.

Tasha: Thirty-five employees have been here the same length of time you have and earn the same salary you earn. It would be unfair to raise your salary without raising theirs.

Which one of the following principles most helps to justify both parties' statements?

(A) In order to be fair, a business must pay identical salaries to employees with identical duties.

(B) In order to be fair, a business must pay an employee a salary commensurate with his or her experience in the field.

(C) In order to be fair, a business must always pay one employee more than another if the first employee has worked for the company longer than the second has.

(D) In order to be fair, a business must never pay one employee more than another unless the first employee has worked for the company longer than the second has.

(E) In order to be fair, a business must always pay employees a salary commensurate with the amount of time they work every day.

GO ON TO THE NEXT PAGE.

23. Commentator: A political constitution that provides the framework for the laws of a nation must be interpreted to apply to new situations not envisioned by its authors. Although these interpretations express the moral and political beliefs of the interpreters, they are usually portrayed as embodying the intentions of the authors. This fiction is vital because without it the illusion, so necessary for political stability, that laws are the bequest of a long tradition rather than the preferences of contemporary politicians would vanish.

Which one of the following is most strongly supported by the commentator's statements, if they are true?

(A) If the people of a nation do not believe that the laws under which they live express the intentions of their political leaders, that nation will become more politically unstable.

(B) Political instability will increase if the people of a nation cease to believe that their constitution is being interpreted consistently with the intentions of its authors.

(C) Political instability will ensue if people come to believe there is a divergence between the beliefs of the authors of their constitution and those of their present political leaders.

(D) A written constitution preserves the illusion that laws are the bequest of a long tradition rather than the creations of modern politicians.

(E) The perceived lack of a long legal tradition in a nation makes the political stability of that nation dependent upon the fiction that its present political leaders share the intentions of the authors of the constitution of that nation.

24. Only if a family manages its finances wisely will it obtain fiscal security. But without realistic projections of financial obligations, a functional budget cannot be devised. So, if either fiscal security is to be obtained or a workable budget devised, finances must be managed wisely or financial obligations must be projected realistically.

Which one of the following arguments is most similar in its pattern of reasoning to that in the argument above?

(A) Without continued use of pesticides it is not possible to grow enough food for the world's people. But only when researchers develop pesticides harmless to humans will persistent health problems be reduced. Thus, pesticide use must continue or pesticides harmless to humans must be developed if enough food is to be produced or persistent health problems are to be reduced.

(B) Reasonably healthy people who wish to lose weight must alter their balance of caloric intake and caloric burn off. But without benefit of medical supervision, drastic changes in diet or exercise patterns would be harmful. So, one who wishes to lose weight but does not want to risk health problems should seek medical supervision before beginning a diet or exercise program.

(C) Many popular, low-maintenance houseplants are available. Yet some of these plants, because they are toxic, are unsuitable for homes where pets are kept indoors. As a result, pet owners should either select nontoxic plants or keep the plants out of a pet's reach if they want low-maintenance houseplants or cannot keep their pets outside.

(D) Only employees who work diligently will be retained in this company until they are eligible for retirement. Also, we can retain only those employees who fit the new organizational structure of our proposed redesign process. So, if this redesign process is carried out, any employee who seeks continuing employment here must work diligently and fit the new organizational structure.

(E) A successful charity drive requires detailed planning. Volunteers must be recruited and trained, and equipment and facilities must be prepared months before the drive is to begin. Thus, if a group is organizing a charity drive, the group must formulate a detailed plan well ahead of time or it can expect failure.

GO ON TO THE NEXT PAGE.

Questions 25–26

Anthropologist: After mapping the complete dominance hierarchy for a troupe of vervet monkeys by examining their pairwise interaction, we successfully predicted more complex forms of their group behavior by assuming that each monkey had knowledge of the complete hierarchy. Since our prediction was so accurate, it follows that the assumption we used to reach it was in fact true.

Primatologist: Although I agree that your assumption helped you make those predictions, your conclusion does not follow. You might as well argue that since we can predict the output of some bank cash machines by assuming that these machines actually want to satisfy the customers' requests, these cash machines must really have desires.

25. The primatologist uses which one of the following argumentative techniques in countering the anthropologist's argument?

(A) citing various facts that could not obtain if the anthropologist's conclusion were correct

(B) offering another argument that has as its premise the denial of the thesis that the anthropologist defends

(C) applying one of the anthropologist's reasoning steps in another argument in an attempt to show that it leads to an absurd conclusion

(D) attacking the anthropologist's expertise by suggesting the anthropologist is ignorant of the analogy that can be drawn between animals and machines

(E) suggesting that the anthropologist's argument relies on a misinterpretation of a key scientific term

26. Which one of the following is a point about which the anthropologist and the primatologist are committed to disagreeing?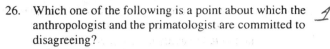

(A) whether the anthropologist successfully predicted the behavior of individual monkeys by use of the map of the troupe's dominance hierarchy

(B) whether the output of a bank cash machine can be accurately predicted on the basis of knowledge of the requests made to it by customers

(C) whether vervet monkeys can have knowledge of the complete hierarchy of dominance relations that exists within their own troupe

(D) whether the fact that the anthropologist's assumption led to such successful predictions provides sufficient grounds for the claim that the vervet monkeys had knowledge of their dominance hierarchy

(E) whether the behavior exhibited by vervet monkeys in experimental situations can be used as the basis for a generalization concerning all vervet monkeys

S T O P

IF YOU FINISH BEFORE TIME IS CALLED, YOU MAY CHECK YOUR WORK ON THIS SECTION ONLY.
DO NOT WORK ON ANY OTHER SECTION IN THE TEST.

SECTION IV

Time—35 minutes

27 Questions

Directions: Each passage in this section is followed by a group of questions to be answered on the basis of what is <u>stated</u> or <u>implied</u> in the passage. For some of the questions, more than one of the choices could conceivably answer the question. However, you are to choose the <u>best</u> answer; that is, the response that most accurately and completely answers the question, and blacken the corresponding space on your answer sheet.

Naturalists have long studied the ability of North American forest birds to survive extremely cold overnight temperatures in winter. For example, nuthatches sleep in cavities such as tree hollows or
(5) holes dug into snowdrifts, retaining heat closer to the body and thus saving energy by reducing the need for shivering. Chickadees <u>induce torpor</u>, saving energy by allowing their body temperatures to decline drastically. Grosbeaks stay close to trees whose seeds contain
(10) sufficient <u>fat to fuel</u> shivering. But the survival of one species, the <u>kinglet, remains something of a mystery.</u>

There are two reasons for this. First, although kinglets are tiny—about 9 cm long including the tail—they maintain extremely high body temperatures at
(15) conditions well below freezing. According to the physical laws of heating and cooling, kinglets would lose heat at a rate about <u>75 percent faster than</u> birds <u>twice their mass</u>—chickadees, for example—and so would have to consume and burn 75 percent more food
(20) per unit of body mass than the larger birds to maintain the same body temperature. The insulation provided by feathers, which, similarly to other northern birds, make up about 25 percent of the kinglet's mass, accounts for some of its heat-retaining capability but does not
(25) explain how kinglets manage to survive as well in cold climates as do the larger birds. Because smaller birds have a lesser absolute amount of insulation than larger birds, they would cool even faster than predicted by body mass alone.
(30) The second reason kinglet survival is so remarkable is that, unlike most bird species that remain in cold climates during winter, their diet consists exclusively of insects. Researchers wonder how it is possible for kinglets, birds that do not cache food and
(35) are known not to forage at night, to gather and consume the <u>necessary amount of insects each short winter day.</u> The question is more vexing considering that a kinglet's stomach when filled to capacity contains only enough food to keep it warm for one
(40) hour.

A partial explanation is that kinglets store fat; kinglet body fat can <u>triple in the course of a day.</u> Nevertheless, this increase accounts for only about half the energy needed to maintain the kinglet's body
(45) temperature overnight. Researchers once theorized that torpor might make up the difference, but found no <u>evidence of torpor in kinglets.</u> Another theory, which is still untested but which may be borne out by a recent <u>study of goldcrests,</u> a related species, is that kinglets
(50) cluster together at night. Kinglets flock in groups of

twos and threes during the day; while such small groups alone could not maintain such high body temperatures, it is hypothesized that after nightfall several groups in a region may find each other by
(55) means of calling and consolidate in a central location.

1. Which one of the following most accurately states the central idea of the passage?

(A) Kinglets are able to survive the coldest winter nights despite a size, physiology, and behavior that should make them vulnerable to low temperatures.

(B) Researchers have tested several theories in their attempts to answer the question of how kinglets survive very low temperatures.

(C) Kinglets are unique among small birds due to a survival rate in extremely low temperatures that is twice that of larger birds.

(D) The kinglet's tiny size complicates the attempts by researchers to observe how it survives the extremely low temperatures of winter nights.

(E) Researchers do not yet fully understand the behavioral and physiological factors that allow kinglets to survive the coldest winter nights.

GO ON TO THE NEXT PAGE.

2. Which one of the following generalizations best captures the reasoning behind the rejection of the theory that torpor explains the kinglet's ability to survive extremely cold overnight temperatures?

(A) Absence of evidence for a behavior can be taken as evidence for absence of the behavior.
(B) Dissimilar species tend to exhibit dissimilar behaviors.
(C) The existence of evidence for a theory is not enough to establish the theory as true.
(D) A theory can be taken as false if several initial tests fail to produce conclusive results.
(E) Acceptance of a theory requires a consensus in the scientific community.

3. According to the passage, the physical laws of heating and cooling suggest that in order to maintain body temperature in winter, kinglets must

(A) consume more food per unit of body mass than any other bird of equivalent mass does
(B) consume enough food to keep their stomachs continuously filled to capacity
(C) consume more food than larger birds do
(D) consume more food per unit of body mass than birds twice their mass do
(E) consume less food per unit of body mass than larger birds with less insulation do

4. The passage suggests that the author most likely regards the hypothesis that groups of kinglets cluster together on cold winter nights as

(A) almost certainly true, since all other explanations have been eliminated
(B) feasible given that kinglets flock in groups during the day
(C) a possibility that, though unlikely, is the only option left to explore
(D) well established by a recent study of goldcrests
(E) the hypothesis most widely discussed in the scientific community

5. The author cites all of the following as contributing to the mystery of kinglet survival in extremely cold overnight winter temperatures EXCEPT:

(A) the kinglet's stomach capacity
(B) the kinglet's relation to goldcrests
(C) the kinglet's limited diet
(D) the kinglet's small body mass
(E) the kinglet's lack of night foraging

6. The author mentions nuthatches, chickadees, and grosbeaks primarily to

(A) introduce various methods of surviving extremely cold overnight temperatures employed by North American forest birds
(B) identify which North American forest birds successfully cope with extremely low overnight temperatures
(C) show that adaptation to extremely cold overnight temperatures is found only among North American forest birds
(D) present strategies of surviving extremely cold overnight temperatures also employed by kinglets
(E) prove that each bird species employs a unique approach to surviving extremely cold overnight temperatures

7. The passage suggests that the author would most likely agree with which one of the following?

(A) Naturalists have yet to achieve much understanding of the ability of small birds to survive extremely cold temperatures overnight.
(B) The kinglet's diet may be found to be high enough in fat to provide sufficient energy to account for its survival.
(C) The behavior of kinglets includes calls that trigger the impulse to flock with other members of its species.
(D) Nocturnal behavior observed in species related to kinglets might reasonably be presumed to occur also among kinglets.
(E) The kinglet adapts to extremely low temperatures by drastically reducing its body temperature.

GO ON TO THE NEXT PAGE.

Much of mainstream thinking concerning juvenile delinquency in Canada and the United States is based on the assumption that if uncorrected it automatically leads to adult crime and should thus be severely
(5) punished, usually by some form of incarceration, before it becomes an ingrained behavior pattern. While there is some connection between juvenile delinquency and adult criminality, some criminologists argue that this can actually be explained by the actions of the
(10) justice system itself: research by these criminologists suggests that incarceration may have the perverse effect of ensuring that the young offenders will continue to perform delinquent acts. This is an interesting point, but a difficult one to translate into
(15) policy—and the criminologists do not make an attempt to do so, in part because taken to its extreme their research suggests that the best form of law enforcement intervention might be none.

The criminologists' unwillingness to attempt to
(20) articulate a policy also stems from their failure— perhaps mirroring that of law enforcement—to distinguish sufficiently between what the young adults themselves think of as criminal behavior and what they consider merely "fun" even while acknowledging that
(25) it is illegal. Many of the subjects of the criminologists' research used just this word to explain why they indulged in delinquent behavior as juveniles. This suggests that while young adults who engage in occasional delinquent activity think of that activity as
(30) illegal, they do not think of themselves as criminals— and that once they become officially recognized by law enforcement as criminals deserving incarceration the young adults may change their opinion of themselves. The strongest support for this view is that most
(35) youthful offenders who escape detection by law enforcement stop their delinquent behavior by age 18, and that only 8 percent of these report that they did so out of the fear of getting caught. Perhaps a policy that encourages maturation, rather than routinely imposing
(40) incarceration, may be the most effective form of rehabilitation for young offenders.

The problem of juvenile delinquency certainly ought to be dealt with, but the question is one of approach. The conventional wisdom has held that it is
(45) essential to make youthful offenders understand that their actions are absolutely impermissible, even if this requires incarceration. However, we do not need to remove delinquents from the community, but rather rehabilitate them when they do wrong. Might it not
(50) make a difference, for instance, if a young adult caught stealing from a store is made to return the merchandise and apologize to the store owner rather than being incarcerated as a thief? We should be trying to ensure that youthful offenders learn the values of the larger
(55) society by the time they reach maturity. This should be the goal when dealing with juvenile delinquency, and it can be achieved without either inflicting incarceration or allowing young offenders to escape penalty.

8. Which one of the following most accurately expresses the main idea of the passage?

(A) The prevailing law enforcement view of illegal juvenile behavior differs from the way in which many young offenders view their own behavior.

(B) Criminologists should refocus their research methodology so as to gain a better idea of the causes of juvenile delinquency.

(C) Criminologists and law enforcement personnel must cooperate if the problem of juvenile delinquency is to be solved.

(D) Juvenile delinquency is a significant problem and a threat to social stability in Canada and the United States.

(E) Timely rehabilitation of juvenile delinquents can be achieved without resorting to incarceration of those who do wrong.

9. The author's opinion about the work of the criminologists discussed in the first paragraph can most accurately be described by which one of the following?

(A) They advocate the right policies despite errors in their research.

(B) Their advocacy of mistaken policies has led them to distort their research findings.

(C) Their research findings are useful, but they advocate policies that are incompatible with them.

(D) Their research findings are useful, but they have failed to draw any policy conclusions from them.

(E) The errors in their research findings have led them to advocate mistaken policies.

10. It can be inferred from the passage that the author holds which one of the following views regarding juveniles who view their delinquent activities as "fun"?

(A) They believe that there is never a moral difference between so-called right and wrong behavior.

(B) They have not sufficiently learned some of the values of society.

(C) They do so primarily because of the policy of treating delinquency as serious criminal behavior.

(D) They should be sentenced to the same punishments as adults.

(E) They should be rehabilitated through expanded programs and facilities in the prisons.

GO ON TO THE NEXT PAGE.

11. The author's attitude toward current law enforcement policies dealing with juvenile delinquency can most accurately be described as

    (A) optimistic that these policies result in high detection rates
    (B) certain that these policies cause further juvenile delinquent acts
    (C) confident that these policies promote the good of society
    (D) convinced that these policies should be revised
    (E) confident that these policies have no effect on juvenile delinquency

12. In relation to lines 10–13 of the passage, the author's purpose in lines 49–53 is to

    (A) describe a policy with which the author wishes to take issue
    (B) illustrate and support a proposal that is motivated partly by the point made in lines 10–13
    (C) provide an example that confirms what the author refers to as mainstream thinking regarding juvenile delinquency
    (D) show an interpretation of data that is opposed to the interpretation given in lines 10–13
    (E) reiterate the flaws inherent in the methodology of criminologists

13. Which one of the following is most closely analogous to the purported relationship in the passage between incarceration and criminologists' research findings?

    (A) Since medical research shows that untreated melanoma almost invariably leads to more-serious and generalized lesions, it is a common policy to treat all detected melanomas quickly and aggressively.
    (B) It was once a common policy to treat sore throats by removing the tonsils, but medical research has shown that tonsillectomy is generally not effective for that purpose and can be harmful.
    (C) It is a common policy to treat viral sore throats with antibiotics, but medical research shows that antibiotic therapy can have undesirable side effects.
    (D) It is a common policy to treat heartburn with antacids, but medical research shows that the use of antacids often leads to rebound acidity, causing the very condition that it treats.
    (E) Since medical research shows that allergic sinusitis treated with decongestant therapy has several accompanying side effects, it is now a common policy to let less serious cases of sinusitis go untreated.

14. The passage includes information regarding each of the following EXCEPT:

    (A) how juvenile delinquents perceive themselves and their actions
    (B) which illegal acts are generally committed by juveniles but not by adults
    (C) a recommended policy of law enforcement to be used in dealing with juvenile delinquents
    (D) the effects of incarceration on juvenile delinquents
    (E) an age by which most juveniles cease delinquent behavior without legal intervention

15. The primary purpose of the passage is to

    (A) prove that law enforcement officials have not understood the true causal roots of juvenile delinquency
    (B) discuss how juvenile delinquents view their own behavior and illegal activities
    (C) examine the validity of the contention that juvenile delinquency inevitably leads to adult criminality
    (D) explain the causes of juvenile delinquency in Canada and the United States and its treatment by law enforcement officials
    (E) argue that a different method of treating juvenile delinquents could yield better results for society

GO ON TO THE NEXT PAGE.

Robin D. G. Kelley's book *Hammer and Hoe* explores the history of communism in the U.S. state of Alabama. Kelley asks not whether the Communist Party was ideologically correct, but how it came to
(5) attract a substantial number of African-American workers and how these workers could embrace and use the Communist Party as a vehicle for organizing themselves. He insists on measuring communism not by its abstract tenets but by its ability to interact with a
(10) culture to generate bold class organization.

Most scholarship that has offered a defense of the Communist Party in the 1930s and 1940s (a period known as the party's Popular Front) has tended to emphasize its attempts to draw on democratic political
(15) traditions, and to enter meaningful political alliances with liberal political forces. While this is an understandable viewpoint among historians searching for models of unity between radicals and liberals, Kelley's interest is in African-American organizing.
(20) From that point of view the Popular Front appears as much less of a blessing.

Indeed Kelley argues that the wild, often sectarian Third Period that preceded the Popular Front better undergirded organization among African-American
(25) farmers and industrial workers. The extreme rhetoric of the Third Period communists was not taken seriously by African-American party members, who avoided posturing and confrontation whenever possible. But on another level, rhetoric regarding a "new world"
(30) resonated among African Americans, whose traditions emphasized both a struggle for survival and the transcendent hope of deliverance. Help from a powerful ally, even one as far away as Moscow, seemed a source of power and possibility. The
(35) worldwide efforts of the communist-led International Labor Defense in mobilizing against lynch law in the United States helped to establish the party's image as such an ally.

The Popular Front saw African-American
(40) participation in the Communist Party decline. A retreat from attacks on white chauvinism and a tendency to de-emphasize, however slightly, involvement in local African-American issue–oriented politics made the party seem less an instrument of deliverance. The
(45) party's increasing cautiousness, born of a desire to appeal to moderates, doubtless made it a less attractive alternative in interracial conflicts.

Even so, Kelley is far from claiming that the change to a Popular Front line was the sole reason for
(50) the decline of African-American communism. The Popular Front initially appealed to African-American communists because it seemed to open new strategies for blunting repression. Kelley's rounded portrait of the decline emphasizes not the absence of a "correct line"
(55) but the presence of factional battles and of transformations in the agriculture industry caused by market changes and U.S. federal government intervention.

16. Which one of the following most accurately characterizes the passage's main point?

(A) By spending little time discussing ideological controversies, *Hammer and Hoe* fails to fully explicate the relationship between the Communist Party and African-American workers during the 1930s and 1940s.

(B) The relationship between the Communist Party and African-American workers during the 1930s and 1940s makes it clear that ideological purity and consistency are not essential to effecting political change.

(C) *Hammer and Hoe* constitutes a valuable tool for the modern historian who is attempting to search for models of unity between radicals and liberals.

(D) The true measure of the success of the Communist Party at organizing African-American workers was not its ability to change people's thinking but to interact with their culture.

(E) *Hammer and Hoe* offers new insights into the nature of the relationship, in the 1930s and 1940s, between the Communist Party and African-American workers.

17. The passage's characterization of the Communist Party in Alabama before the 1930s includes each of the following EXCEPT that the party

(A) refrained from attacking white chauvinism
(B) benefited from the goodwill created by the actions of the International Labor Defense
(C) inspired some African Americans with its rhetoric
(D) failed to convince some of its African-American members that confrontation was an acceptable political stance
(E) was involved in local African-American political issues

GO ON TO THE NEXT PAGE.

18. The primary purpose of the second paragraph is to

   (A) contrast Kelley's viewpoint on the Popular Front with that of previous historians
   (B) defend the Popular Front from Kelley's attacks on it
   (C) question the political usefulness of searching for common ground between radicals and liberals
   (D) enumerate the differences between the Popular Front and the Third Period
   (E) argue that one valid way to approach the study of communism in the United States is to discuss its impact on African-American workers

19. It can be inferred from the passage that Kelley would most likely agree with which one of the following assertions about the Popular Front?

   (A) The Popular Front introduced factors that hampered the political appeal of communism for African Americans.
   (B) The Popular Front was inherently inimical to African-American interests from its inception.
   (C) The increasing cautiousness of the Popular Front appealed to most African-American party members.
   (D) The Popular Front was viewed by African Americans as an improvement over the rhetoric of the Third Period.
   (E) The extreme posturing and confrontation of the Popular Front alienated many African Americans.

20. Based on the passage, which one of the following statements is more likely to have been made by a Communist Party organizer during the Third Period than during the Popular Front?

   (A) African Americans and whites must join together under the common banner of communism.
   (B) Workers everywhere must revolt to bring about the final global victory over capitalist oppression.
   (C) African Americans should strive to overcome racism in the highest levels of government.
   (D) The goals of communism have much in common with those of more liberal causes.
   (E) One should not expect too much progress too quickly when attempting to change the prevailing social order.

GO ON TO THE NEXT PAGE.

Darwin's conception of early prehistoric humans as confident, clever hunter-gatherers has long dominated anthropology. His theory has been reinforced by an accident of history: the human fossil record has been
(5) found largely in reverse order. Remains of humans' most recent forebears, who lived 35,000 to 100,000 years ago, were discovered in 1856; over the next century, discoveries yielded fossils of hominids from progressively earlier eras. Because the first-discovered
(10) fossil hominids, the Neanderthals, genuinely resembled modern humans, anthropologists from Darwin on have confused the life-styles of today's nonindustrial peoples with those of our distant hominid forebears. These anthropologists have failed to consider both the
(15) sophistication of modern hunter-gatherer societies (including their use of fire, clothing, shelter, weapons, tools, language, and complex strategies) and the ways in which their environments differ from prehistoric ones (for example, in containing fewer large animal
(20) predators).

Recent intellectual developments, such as the new field of taphonomy, have called into question the traditional hypothesis that early hominids outsmarted the predators with whom they competed for meat and
(25) that they mastered their world through hunting. Taphonomy investigates the transformation of skeletal remains into fossils—it asks, for example, whether bone piles have been deposited by predators, hunters, or floodwaters, and whether hyenas' teeth scar animal
(30) bones differently than do human tools.

Taphonomy has been utilized by some researchers in studying a group of animal fossils, hominid fossils, and stone tools that were almost two million years old. By comparing the microscopic features of linear
(35) grooves on the fossilized animal bones with similar grooves on modern bones, the researchers found that cut marks made by stone tools differed from the marks of other taphonomic agents, such as carnivores' teeth or sedimentary abrasion. They also found that the
(40) markings of stone tools on many of the fossilized animal bones did not occur systematically at the joints and that toothmarks of animal carnivores often underlay rather than overlay the cut marks.

The researchers hypothesized from this evidence
(45) that early hominids were scavengers of meat left from carnivore kills, rather than hunters of live prey. From patterns of wear on fossilized hominid teeth, the researchers further deduced that early hominids, like other scavengers, ate fruit primarily and meat only
(50) occasionally. Early hominids could have been well adapted for scavenging: agility in climbing trees helped them escape predators and gain superior vantage points, and an upright mode of walking enabled them to scan the ground for carcasses and to
(55) carry useful scavenging tools. According to these researchers, Darwin's vision of early prehistoric hunters may be familiar and appealing, but the fossil record suggests a revised picture of less-confident early hominids who often perched in trees and who foraged
(60) and scavenged alone or in small groups.

21. Which one of the following most accurately expresses the main idea of the passage?

(A) With the aid of new research methods, a group of anthropologists has been able to refute Darwinian theories about the social organization of modern hunter-gatherer societies.

(B) The recent development of new techniques for conducting anthropological research has begun to challenge the traditional methodologies used by anthropologists.

(C) Although most anthropologists have long accepted Darwin's conception of prehistoric humans, new research techniques are providing support for an alternative view of early hominids.

(D) Anthropologists' mistaken conception of prehistoric humans as successful hunters has arisen from and been reinforced by historical circumstances.

(E) Because of recent discoveries about the environment in which prehistoric humans lived, anthropologists are revising their picture of the relationship that existed between these humans and large animal predators.

22. It can be inferred from the passage that the author would encourage the anthropologists mentioned in line 14 to do which one of the following types of research on modern hunter-gatherer societies?

(A) apply the methodologies of taphonomy to study these societies

(B) investigate the similarities of life-styles and environments among the various societies

(C) contrast the competition for food faced by these societies with the competition faced by prehistoric societies

(D) examine the life-styles of hunter-gatherer societies who lived in the previous century

(E) analyze how the world's increasing industrialization is changing the survival strategies used by these societies

GO ON TO THE NEXT PAGE.

23. It can be inferred from the passage that in reaching their conclusions, the researchers mentioned in line 44 interpreted the taphonomic analysis of marks on animal fossils in which one of the following ways?

    (A) The fact that the marks of stone tools did not occur at the joints of the animals indicated that the early hominids hunted and butchered animals less skillfully than did hominids in subsequent eras.

    (B) The fact that the marks of stone tools did not occur in a systematic manner indicated that the early hominids might have been working hastily in order to complete their task before a competing group of hominids arrived.

    (C) The fact that the marks of stone tools overlay those of animal carnivores indicated that early hominids did not move quickly enough to hunt animals and then butcher them.

    (D) The fact that the toothmarks of animal carnivores underlay the marks of stone tools indicated that the early hominids came upon the remains of an animal already killed by an animal predator.

    (E) The fact that the toothmarks of animal carnivores accompanied the marks of stone tools indicated that both animal predators and early hominids tended to prefer large prey animals.

24. The author cites the early hominids' "upright mode of walking" (line 53) primarily in order to

    (A) counter anthropologists' previous hypotheses about how early hominids walked

    (B) provide an example of how the hominids were suited to their method of gathering food

    (C) explain why early hominids subsisted on a diet that included more fruit than meat

    (D) increase the reader's appreciation for the resemblance between early hominids and modern humans

    (E) contrast early hominids and other mammals with whom they competed in hunting live prey

25. Which one of the following situations is most analogous to the discovery of fossil hominids as described in the first paragraph?

    (A) Traces of an ancient civilization are found, and scholars conclude that its people occupied the site for only a short period; however, further excavations reveal that the civilization had flourished in this area for several centuries.

    (B) Art historians who know the late paintings of an artist find similar paintings done by the artist a few years prior to the late paintings, and conclude that the artist's first paintings, as yet unrecovered, must have been done in the same style.

    (C) Two manuscripts written by an anonymous medieval author are discovered many years apart; when the second manuscript is found, historians realize that the manuscripts are far older than they had first believed.

    (D) Pottery dating back thousands of years is found, and scholars determine that these pieces bear a striking resemblance to some made only a few hundred years ago.

    (E) A fossil of an unknown prehistoric plant is discovered, and botanists seek to find in it characteristics that are similar to those seen in the fossils of other, better-known prehistoric plants.

26. Each of the following is mentioned in the passage as determinable by taphonomic investigation into the marks on fossilized bones EXCEPT the

    (A) order in which certain marks were placed

    (B) characteristic physical differences among the marks

    (C) approximate age of fossils on which the marks are found

    (D) agents that have left the marks

    (E) similarities to marks on modern bones

27. The author's primary purpose in writing the passage is to

    (A) differentiate between outdated and contemporary research methods

    (B) expose the preconceptions behind previous research

    (C) present a narrative of how historical events might have unfolded

    (D) explain the basis for a revisionary approach to a subject

    (E) describe how a new theory has replaced the traditional one

S T O P

IF YOU FINISH BEFORE TIME IS CALLED, YOU MAY CHECK YOUR WORK ON THIS SECTION ONLY.
DO NOT WORK ON ANY OTHER SECTION IN THE TEST.

SIGNATURE _____ _/_ /_
DATE

LSAT WRITING SAMPLE TOPIC

Jonathan Parks, a student of fashion design, must choose one of two summer internships. Write an argument in favor of his taking one internship rather than the other based on the following criteria:

- Jonathan wants to make contacts that will help his career after he graduates.
- Jonathan wants to learn as much as possible about the process of developing a creative idea into a marketable product.

Wearhouse Inc. has offered Jonathan one of the ten internships it offers every summer to promising design students. Wearhouse is a well-established clothing company with offices around the world. The interns work in the company's headquarters. Jonathan would be part of a large team working on a line of children's casual clothing to be marketed the following spring. Wearhouse has one of the oldest internship programs in the industry, and many former interns have gone on to illustrious and successful careers in the fashion world.

Marina Vertucci has offered Jonathan an internship at her fledgling clothing company. Only a few years out of school herself, Vertucci has already attracted attention for her bold, innovative designs. Sales of her clothing have increased dramatically over the last year, and her work was recently featured in a major fashion magazine. Jonathan would be the only intern in Vertucci's small company. In addition to working on a line of clothing that Vertucci has promised to produce for a major department store, Jonathan would also be expected to help with whatever projects come their way over the summer.

Directions:

1. Use the Answer Key on the next page to check your answers.

2. Use the Scoring Worksheet below to compute your raw score.

3. Use the Score Conversion Chart to convert your raw score into the 120-180 scale.

Scoring Worksheet

1. Enter the number of questions you answered correctly in each section.

Number Correct

Section I . . . . _____

Section II . . . . _____

Section III . . . . _____

Section IV . . . . _____

2. Enter the sum here: _____
   This is your Raw Score.

Conversion Chart
For Converting Raw Score to the 120-180 LSAT Scaled Score
LSAT Form 0LSS48

Reported Score	Raw Score Lowest	Raw Score Highest
180	98	101
179	97	97
178	96	96
177	95	95
176	94	94
175	93	93
174	92	92
173	90	91
172	89	89
171	88	88
170	87	87
169	85	86
168	84	84
167	82	83
166	81	81
165	79	80
164	78	78
163	76	77
162	75	75
161	73	74
160	71	72
159	70	70
158	68	69
157	67	67
156	65	66
155	63	64
154	62	62
153	60	61
152	58	59
151	57	57
150	55	56
149	53	54
148	52	52
147	50	51
146	49	49
145	47	48
144	45	46
143	44	44
142	42	43
141	41	41
140	39	40
139	38	38
138	36	37
137	35	35
136	33	34
135	32	32
134	31	31
133	29	30
132	28	28
131	27	27
130	26	26
129	24	25
128	23	23
127	22	22
126	21	21
125	20	20
124	19	19
123	17	18
122	16	16
121	15	15
120	0	14

* There is no raw score that will produce this scaled score for this form

SECTION I

1. D	8. E	15. D	22. B
2. B	9. B	16. B	23. E
3. B	10. C	17. E	24. A
4. A	11. E	18. A	
5. E	12. B	19. A	
6. C	13. D	20. A	
7. E	14. D	21. B	

SECTION II

1. D	8. A	15. D	22. C
2. E	9. D	16. B	23. C
3. A	10. C	17. E	24. B
4. D	11. A	18. B	
5. B	12. C	19. A	
6. A	13. C	20. B	
7. E	14. B	21. C	

SECTION III

1. E	8. A	15. C	22. D
2. C	9. D	16. C	23. B
3. E	10. C	17. E	24. A
4. B	11. B	18. D	25. C
5. A	12. B	19. D	26. D
6. C	13. B	20. E	
7. A	14. A	21. B	

SECTION IV

1. E	8. E	15. E	22. C
2. A	9. D	16. E	23. D
3. D	10. B	17. A	24. B
4. B	11. D	18. A	25. B
5. B	12. B	19. A	26. C
6. A	13. D	20. B	27. D
7. D	14. B	21. C	

Questions 1–5

What the setup tells you: This setup requires you to take eight lifeguards and arrange for their participation in two different events—a boat race and a rescue exercise. The task that you have to carry out is this: for each of the two events, you must divide the eight people into pairs. There is one general restriction on pairs: no one can be paired with the same person in both events. There are also some more specific restrictions: there are exactly two people who simply cannot be paired with each other in either event and, for each event, one of the pairs has already been fixed. What your task comes down to is taking the remaining six people in each event and dividing them into three pairs.

Question 1

Overview: This question asks you to identify an acceptable way of pairing up people for the boat race. Since the correct answer will simply be a pairing up that doesn't violate any of the setup conditions, the best approach is probably to take the conditions one by one and cross out any answer choices that violate a condition. There will be one answer choice that doesn't get crossed out, and that's the correct answer.

The first condition may at first look like an unpromising one to check. How could the pairs for the boat race violate a condition that seems primarily to be concerned with restricting pairings for the rescue exercise? Actually, though, the first condition can be applied here, provided it's used in conjunction with the third condition. We'll return to this after we've discussed the other conditions.

Checking each one of the answer choices for compliance with the second condition, you find that (A), (C), and (E) violate the condition that L and Q are teammates in the boat race. So all three are crossed out.

For the moment, let's skip the third condition, which is about the rescue exercise and not the boat race. In order for the third condition to provide any information about the boat race, it must be taken in conjunction with the first condition, and we'll return to that below.

This leaves (B) and (D) to be checked against the fourth condition. (B), by including R and S as teammates, violates the fourth condition, so (D) must be the correct answer.

Now let's return to the first and third conditions. When considered together, they do tell you something about the boat race. The third condition requires that a certain pair—K and L—be in the rescue exercise. So that means (by the first condition) that K and L cannot also be a pair in the boat race. This would allow you to cross out (E), since (E) shows K and L as a pair in the boat race.

The Correct Answer:

D As shown in the "Overview," (D) violates none of the conditions for pairing people in the boat race. It therefore describes a possible outcome for the boat race and so is the correct answer.

The Incorrect Answer Choices:

A (A) can be eliminated because it violates the second condition. According to the second condition, L and Q are teammates in the boat race, but (A) pairs L with J and Q with M.

B (B) can be eliminated because it violates the fourth condition. According to the fourth condition, R and S are not teammates in either event. So (B) can be ruled out because it shows R and S as teammates in the boat race.

C (C) can be eliminated because it violates the second condition. (C) pairs L with S and Q with P in the boat race, but according to the second condition, L and Q are teammates in the boat race.

E (E) can be eliminated because it violates the second condition. According to the second condition, L and Q are teammates in the boat race, but (E) pairs L with K and Q with S.

An incorrect answer choice can often be eliminated in a number of different ways. As described in the "Overview," (E) can also be eliminated because it makes a violation of either the first or the third condition inevitable. Here's how it works. (E) pairs K and L in the boat race. The third condition requires that K and L be paired in the rescue exercise. But that would mean that the first condition is violated, since K and L would be teammates in both the boat race and the rescue exercise. You can't avoid a violation of the first condition by not pairing K and L in the rescue exercise, because that would violate the third condition. So (E) is not a possible outcome for the boat race.

Keep in mind, however, that in the interest of managing your testing time effectively, you should avoid doing any more than you need to do in order to identify the correct answer. This means that once an answer choice has been eliminated, you shouldn't concern yourself with any other ways that it might be eliminated.

■ *Difficulty Level: 1*

Question 2

Overview: This question asks you to look for a pair of lifeguards that has two properties: the pair cannot be in the rescue exercise but could be in the boat race.

The task that confronts you here is how to choose an effective strategy for finding the correct answer. Should you try to zero in on the correct answer directly, or should you try to isolate the correct answer by eliminating the incorrect answer choices? A principle that you can apply to the task is this: generally, it takes much less time to show that a condition is being violated than it does to show that something conforms to all of the conditions. So you should first try eliminating the incorrect answer choices.

To show that an answer is incorrect, you can show either that the pair can be teammates in the rescue exercise, or that the pair cannot be teammates in the boat race, or both. First, identify the pairs that, if included among those participating in the rescue exercise, would cause a rule violation. The correct answer must be one of these, because it must be a pair that cannot participate in the rescue exercise. Second, see which of these answer choices, if included among the pairs participating in the boat race, would trigger a rule violation. Cross out those pairs, because the correct answer must be a pair that could participate in the boat race.

Following this approach, you'll find that both (B) and (C) are pairs that cannot participate in the rescue exercise. For the rescue exercise, K must be paired with L, so neither (B)—K paired with R—nor (C)—L paired with S—can be a pair in the rescue exercise. Since none of (A), (D), or (E) violates a condition having to do with the rescue exercise, you've narrowed the search for the correct answer to a choice between (B) and (C). Which of these can be a pair in the boat race? (C) violates the requirement that L is paired with Q in the boat race, because (C) pairs L with S. So you cross out (C), and you are left with (B) as the correct answer.

The Correct Answer:

B The strategy suggested in the "Overview" leads to (B) as the answer choice that has to be correct. And when taking the test, all you want to do is identify the correct answer. If you have already identified the correct answer by eliminating the incorrect answers, you would gain nothing by painstakingly demonstrating its correctness more directly, and you would lose valuable time by doing so.

Even though you should almost certainly not do so during the test, the correctness of (B) can of course be demonstrated directly. K and R cannot be teammates in the rescue exercise, because by the third condition K must be teammates with L in the rescue

exercise. The other half of the demonstration—the proof that K and R can be teammates in the boat race—consists in finding at least one acceptable outcome that has K paired with R in the boat race. The following is such an outcome:

Boat race: J and P; K and R; L and Q; M and S
Rescue exercise: J and S; K and L; M and R; P and Q

The Incorrect Answer Choices:

A You can show that (A) is incorrect by showing that J and P can be teammates in the rescue exercise. The following outcome, in which J is paired with P in the rescue exercise, provides that proof.

Boat race: J and R; K and S; L and Q; M and P
Rescue exercise: J and P; K and L; M and R; Q and S

C (C) is incorrect because L and S cannot be teammates in the boat race. According to the second condition, L's teammate in the boat race is Q.

D By the same reasoning you used for (A), the fact that P can be paired with M in the rescue exercise shows (D) to be incorrect.

Boat race: J and K; L and Q; M and S; P and R
Rescue exercise: J and S; K and L; M and P; Q and R

E Using the same reasoning as in (A) and (D), the following, with P and Q paired in the rescue exercise, shows (E) to be incorrect.

Boat race: J and K; L and Q; M and S; P and R
Rescue exercise: J and S; K and L; M and R; P and Q

Alternatively, you can rule out (E) because it is a pair that cannot participate in the boat race. The second condition requires that L and Q be teammates in the boat race, but in (E) Q is paired with P.

- *Difficulty Level: 2*

Question 3

Overview: This question provides relatively rich information—it fixes one pair for each of the events, and with the additional pairs fixed by the setup, you now have two pairs for each of the events fixed at the outset. The question asks you to identify a pair that must be in the boat race.

You know from the second condition that L and Q are a pair in the boat race. The question itself asks you to suppose that M and P are another pair in that event. As for the rescue exercise, the third condition tells you that K and L are a pair and the question asks you to suppose that J and R are also a pair. So far, you know the following:

Boat race: L and Q; M and P
Rescue exercise: K and L; J and R

The Correct Answer:

B   As discussed in the "Overview," four of the eight pairs are fixed at the outset—the two fixed by the conditions and the two fixed by the question itself. What else can you learn from the conditions? The fourth condition tells you that R is going to be in one of the remaining pairs in the boat race, and S is going to be in the other. Since, according to the question, J is paired with R in the rescue exercise, J cannot also be paired with R in the boat race, as that would violate the first condition. Consequently, the only other option is for J to be paired with S in the boat race, which leaves R to be paired with K.

Boat race: L and Q; M and P; J and S; K and R
Rescue exercise: K and L; J and R

Now all that is left for you to do is to check which of these two pairs—J and S, or K and R—is listed among the answer choices, and you'll have found the correct answer. The correct answer is (B), which contains J and S.

The Incorrect Answer Choices:

A   The question asks you to suppose that M and P are one of the pairs in the boat race. By the second condition, L and Q are another pair in the boat race. By the fourth condition, one of the remaining two pairs must include R and the other must include S.

Boat race: M and P; L and Q; R and ?; S and ?

This means that J cannot be paired with K in the boat race, because one of them must be paired with S and the other with R.

C   Since by the second condition L must be paired with Q in the boat race, L cannot be paired with K in the boat race.

D   The question asks you to suppose that M and P are one of the pairs in the boat race. By the second condition, L and Q are another pair in the boat race. By the fourth condition, one of the remaining two pairs must include R and the other must include S.

Boat race: M and P; L and Q; R and ?; S and ?

Since, according to the question, J is paired with R in the rescue exercise, J cannot be paired with R in the boat race, by the first condition. This means that J must be paired with S in the boat race, and so K cannot be paired with S in the boat race.

E   Since by the second rule Q must be paired with L in the boat race, Q cannot be paired with R in the boat race.

■ *Difficulty Level: 2*

Question 4

Overview: This question is similar to the preceding one in that it provides relatively rich information. In addition to the two pairs that are fixed by the second and third conditions, it asks you to suppose that two more pairs are fixed. The question asks you to pick out the one pair that does **not** have to be in one of the two events.

You know from the setup conditions that L and Q are a pair in the boat race and that K and L are a pair in the boat race. The question asks you to suppose that P and K are another pair in the boat race and that P and Q are another pair in the rescue exercise. In both events, one of the remaining pairs will include R and the other S, as required by the fourth condition.

> Boat race: L and Q; K and P; R and ?; S and ?
> Rescue exercise: K and L; P and Q; R and ?; S and ?

The teammates of R and S will be J and M and, as required by the first condition, they will be paired differently for the two events (for example, R with J in one and R with M in another).

The Correct Answer:

A   The "Overview" discusses the parts of the outcome that can be determined on the basis of the setup and the information in the question. Once you have established those things, there is not much more to figure out about the possible outcomes. Since you've already figured out which lifeguards must be teammates in one or the other of the two events, all that's left to do is to check the answer choices to see which one isn't among them. In the circumstances established by this question, J and M don't have to be a pair in either event (and in fact they cannot be a pair). So (A) is the correct answer.

The Incorrect Answer Choices:

B, C   By the second condition, L and Q are one of the pairs in the boat race. The question asks you to suppose that P and K are another one of the pairs in the boat race. By the third condition, K and L are one of the pairs in the rescue exercise. The question asks you to suppose that P and Q are another one of the pairs in the rescue exercise. In both events, one of the remaining pairs will include R and the other will include S, as required by the fourth rule. Since by the first rule J cannot be paired with the same person in both events, J must be paired with R in one of the two events and with S in the other. So both (B)—J paired with R—and (C)—J paired with S—contain pairs that must be teammates in one of the two events.

D, E   By the second condition, L and Q are one of the pairs in the boat race. The question asks you to suppose that P and K are another one of the pairs in the boat race. By the third condition, K and L are one of the pairs in the rescue exercise. The question asks you to suppose that P and Q are another one of the pairs in the rescue exercise. In both events, one of the remaining pairs will include R and the other will include S, as required by the fourth rule. Since by the first rule M cannot be paired with the same person in both events, M must be paired with R in one of the two events and with S in the other. So both (D)—M paired with R—and (E)—M paired with S—contain pairs that must be teammates in one of the two events.

- *Difficulty Level: 2*

Question 5

Overview: In this question, you're not asked what must be true, only what could be true. The best approach, therefore, is probably to proceed by process of elimination.

You know from the setup rules that L and Q are a pair in the boat race. The question itself asks you to suppose that J and P are another pair in the boat race. The fourth rule tells you that R will be in one of the remaining pairs for the boat race, and S in the other. Their teammates will be K and M, the remaining two lifeguards.

    Boat race: L and Q; J and P; R and ?; S and ?

Checking the answer choices in light of this result, you find that you can cross out both (A) and (B). M cannot be paired with either K or L in the boat race, but (A) lists M and K and (B) lists M and L.

You also know from the setup rules that K and L are a pair in the rescue exercise. This means that M cannot be paired with either K or L in the rescue exercise.

Checking the answer choices in light of this result, you find that you can cross out both (C) and (D). (C) pairs M with L in the rescue exercise and (D) pairs M with K in the rescue exercise.

This means that you're done. There's only one answer choice left that you haven't crossed out, and that is (E).

The Correct Answer:

E   That (E) is the correct answer can be shown by the following outcome, in which J and P are teammates in the boat race and M is paired with S in the boat race and P in the rescue exercise:

Boat race: J and P; L and Q; M and S; K and R
Rescue exercise: J and R; K and L; M and P; Q and S

The Incorrect Answer Choices:

A   (A) can be eliminated because it would lead to a violation of the fourth condition. By the second condition, L and Q are teammates in the boat race. So if J and P are also teammates in the boat race, K and M cannot be teammates in the boat race. If they were, the fourth pair would have to be R and S, in violation of the fourth condition.

B   (B) can be eliminated because it violates the second condition. M cannot be the teammate of L in the boat race, because by the second condition L's teammate in the boat race is Q.

C   (C) can be eliminated because it violates the third condition. M cannot be the teammate of L in the rescue exercise, because by the third condition L's teammate in the rescue exercise is K.

D   (D) can be eliminated because it violates the third condition. M cannot be the teammate of K in the rescue exercise, because by the third condition K's teammate in the rescue exercise is L.

■ *Difficulty Level: 2*

Questions 6–12

What the setup tells you: This group of questions has to do with ranking seven restaurants, from highest (best) to lowest (worst). The last condition tells you that in this ranking there are no ties: each restaurant occupies a different place in the ranking. The first two conditions are equally straightforward: each fixes the ranking of three of the seven restaurants, but only relative to one another. The first condition gives you R > P > L, or

... Robusto ... Pastilla ... Lautrec ...

This condition doesn't tell you what specific rank any of these three restaurants has and it doesn't tell you anything about where the other four restaurants are ranked in relation to these three.

The same is true of the second condition, which gives you T > M > V, or

... Tantoko ... Medici ... Vistula ...

The third and fourth conditions are both about the ranking of the restaurants Medici, Pastilla, and Scheherazade's relative to each other. The third condition considers the case in which Scheherazade's ranks higher than Pastilla and tells you that in this case, Medici ranks higher than Scheherazade's. (Or, if S > P then M > S > P.)

Another possibility is that Scheherazade's ranks lower than Pastilla. Is there any information about that case? Yes, and it is provided by the fourth condition, which can be reproduced in shorthand as if M > S, then S > P. This conditional statement can be recast as follows: "If Scheherazade's ranks lower than Pastilla, Medici ranks lower than Scheherazade's." (Or, if P > S then S > M.) So these two conditions, taken together, boil down to this: whether Medici is ranked higher than Pastilla or vice versa, Scheherazade's is always ranked somewhere in between them.

The third and fourth conditions, taken together, tell you that there are exactly two possibilities for the relative rankings of Medici, Pastilla, and Scheherazade's: M > S > P and P > S > M, or

... Medici ... Scheherazade's ... Pastilla ...

and

... Pastilla ... Scheherazade's ... Medici ...

Like the diagrams reflecting the first two conditions, these diagrams don't tell you the specific rank of any of the three restaurants.

At this point, you've represented to yourself in a readily usable form what the conditions say. In practice, this is probably as far as it is efficient to go before tackling individual questions.

It is, however, possible to derive additional information by considering the diagrams together. Consider the third diagram, which depicts the case of Pastilla being ranked lower than Scheherazade's, and add to it information from the first diagram. You know from the first diagram that Pastilla ranks higher than Lautrec. You also know that Robusto ranks higher than Pastilla, but you don't know exactly where it ranks in relation to Medici and Scheherazade's.

Robusto
... Medici ... Scheherazade's ... Pastilla ... Lautrec ...

Next, you could add the information from the second diagram:

You have now diagrammed the complete set of possibilities for the case in which Medici is ranked higher than Pastilla.

In the other case—the case of Pastilla being ranked higher than Scheherazade's—a similar process will give you the complete set of possibilities:

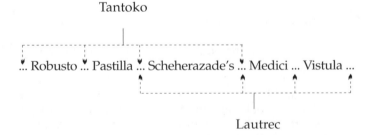

These last two diagrams capture in compressed form all of the information that can be extracted from the setup.

Question 6

Overview: This question asks you to choose the ranking that violates none of the conditions. One way to go about doing this is to eliminate the incorrect answer choices by showing that each one violates at least one of the conditions. So start by taking the conditions in turn, checking each answer choice against them, and crossing out answer choices as soon as a violation is detected. Once you have crossed out an answer choice, there's no need to check it against other conditions.

The first condition is violated by (A), since (A) has Pastilla ranked higher than Robusto. So (A) gets crossed out.

The second condition is violated by (E), since (E) has Medici ranked higher than Tantoko. So (E) gets crossed out.

None of (B), (C), or (D) violates the third condition. Both (B) and (D), however, have Scheherazade's ranked lower than Medici and Pastilla. So both (B) and (D) violate the fourth condition and can thus be crossed out. The correct answer is (C), the only one you haven't crossed out.

The Correct Answer:

C   As shown in the "Overview," (C) violates none of the conditions and so is a possible ranking of the restaurants.

The Incorrect Answer Choices:

A   (A) can be eliminated because it violates the first condition. (A) ranks Pastilla higher than Robusto, but by the first condition Pastilla ranks lower than Robusto.

B, D   Both (B) and (D) rank Medici higher than Scheherazade's, and Scheherazade's lower than Pastilla, but by the fourth condition, if Medici ranks higher than Scheherazade's, Scheherazade's has to rank higher than Pastilla. So both (B) and (D) can be eliminated because they violate the fourth condition.

E   (E) can be eliminated because it violates the second condition. (E) ranks Medici higher than Tantoko, but by the second condition Medici ranks lower than Tantoko.

■ *Difficulty Level: 1*

Question 7

Overview: This question asks you to take the case in which Pastilla is ranked second highest and identify which restaurants could be ranked fourth highest in that situation. To do this, you'll need to consider more than one possible ranking.

Here is one way to go about determining what the possible rankings are. From the first condition, you can infer that if Pastilla is ranked second highest, Robusto has to be ranked highest. (The only constraint on Lautrec is that it be ranked lower than Pastilla, but since Lautrec appears in every one of the answer choices, you know anyway that Lautrec must be one of the restaurants that could be ranked fourth highest.)

The second condition tells you that Tantoko, Medici, and Vistula have to be ranked in just that order (Tanoko, Medici, Vistula). And since Scheherazade's has to be ranked somewhere between Pastilla and Medici (as explained in "What the setup tells you"), you get the following summary of possible rankings:

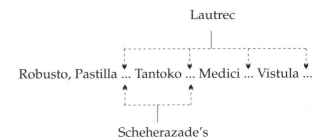

This summary shows that there are two other restaurants besides Lautrec that could be ranked fourth highest, namely, Tantoko and Scheherazade's. This is the answer given in (E): Scheherazade's, Lautrec, Tantoko.

Notice that this diagram also shows that Medici is ranked no higher than fifth and that Vistula is ranked no higher than sixth.

The Correct Answer:

E   There are three restaurants that could be ranked fourth if Pastilla is ranked second, namely, Lautrec, Scheherazade's, and Tantoko. The following are some possible outcomes that demonstrate this fact:

Robusto, Pastilla, Tantoko, **Lautrec**, Scheherazade's, Medici, Vistula

Robusto, Pastilla, Tantoko, **Scheherazade's**, Medici, Vistula, Lautrec

Robusto, Pastilla, Lautrec, **Tantoko**, Scheherazade's, Medici, Vistula

There is no other restaurant that can be ranked fourth, if Pastilla is ranked second. The question fixes Pastilla as second highest, and by the first condition Robusto must be first. By the second condition, Vistula must be ranked somewhere below Medici. Medici must be ranked somewhere below Scheherazade's because here Pastilla is ranked above Scheherazade's. (E) is the only list that includes Lautrec, Scheherazade's, and Tantoko. So (E) is a complete and accurate list of restaurants any one of which could be ranked fourth highest.

The Incorrect Answer Choices:

A   (A) can be eliminated because it's not a complete list of restaurants that could be ranked fourth highest if Pastilla is ranked second highest. In particular, Scheherazade's and Tantoko, each of which could be ranked fourth highest, are missing from (A). The ranking "Robusto, Pastilla, Tantoko, Scheherazade's, Medici, Lautrec, Vistula"—with Pastilla ranked second highest and none of the conditions violated—shows that Scheherazade's could be ranked fourth highest. The same ranking, with only the ranks of Tantoko and Scheherazade's reversed, shows that Tantoko also could be ranked fourth highest.

B   (B) is not complete because it fails to include Scheherazade's and Tantoko, each of which could be ranked fourth highest. And it is not accurate because it includes Vistula, which could be ranked sixth or seventh highest, but not fourth highest.

C   (C) can be eliminated because Tantoko, which could be ranked fourth highest, is missing. The ranking "Robusto, Pastilla, Scheherazade's, Tantoko, Medici, Lautrec, Vistula"—with Pastilla ranked second highest and none of the conditions violated—shows that Tantoko could be ranked fourth highest.

D   (D) can be eliminated because it fails to include Tantoko, which could be ranked fourth highest (as shown in the discussion of (C) above). And (D) is not accurate because it includes Medici, which cannot be ranked any higher than fifth and thus cannot be ranked fourth highest.

■ *Difficulty Level: 3*

Question 8

Overview: This question asks you what the lowest ranking is that Medici could have. From answering the previous question, you already know that it is possible for Medici to be ranked lower than any of the seven restaurants except Vistula (because, by the second condition, Medici always ranks higher than Vistula). So you know that Medici can be ranked sixth highest, but not seventh. Thus, you can answer this question without doing any further work.

The Correct Answer:

E   What specific information about Medici can be inferred from the conditions? From the discussion in "What the setup tells you," you know that Medici can be ranked lower than both Scheherazade's and Pastilla (that is, the relative ranking P > S > M is possible). The other condition that mentions Medici is the second condition. So only the second condition limits how **low** in the ranking Medici can be: Vistula must be ranked below Medici. Thus Medici could be ranked sixth highest, above Vistula, but not seventh.

The Incorrect Answer Choices:

A, B, C, D   As the discussion in "The Correct Answer" shows, the lowest rank Medici could have is sixth. (A), (B), (C), and (D), which are all ranks higher than sixth, are incorrect.

■ *Difficulty Level: 2*

Question 9

Overview: For this question, you're looking for something that must be true if Medici ranks lower than Lautrec. So you start with that assumption, and then use the conditions to draw further inferences.

The first condition tells you that Pastilla (and so, Robusto) must rank above Lautrec. And, by the second condition, Vistula must rank lower than Medici. This gives you the following partial ranking.

Robusto ... Pastilla ... Lautrec ... Medici ... Vistula

Since each of the answer choices is concerned with the ranking of either Scheherazade's or Tantoko, or both, the partial ranking above doesn't allow you to evaluate any of the answer choices yet.

What are the constraints, if any, on Tantoko's ranking? The second condition tells you that Tantoko can have **any** ranking above Medici's; beyond that, its ranking is not further constrained. Thus Tantoko could be ranked highest, which rules out both (A) and (C). Or Tantoko could be ranked somewhere below Scheherazade's and above Medici. That rules out (E).

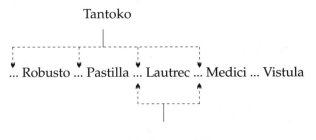

The remaining two answer choices—(B) and (D)—mention Scheherazade's. As discussed in "What the setup tells you," Scheherazade's can be ranked anywhere between Medici and Pastilla. This information allows you to rule out (D), since it is not necessary for Tantoko to be ranked higher than Scheherazade's. The correct answer is (B), the only remaining answer choice.

You can also see directly from this diagram that Scheherazade's must be ranked higher than Vistula, which is exactly what (B) states.

The Correct Answer:

B A consideration of the information provided by the question itself (Medici ranks lower than Lautrec) and the information contained in the first and second conditions yields the following partial ranking:

Robusto ... Pastilla ... Lautrec ... Medici ... Vistula

Since Scheherazade's must be ranked in between Medici and Pastilla, as discussed in the "Overview" above, it must be ranked higher than Medici here. By the second condition, you can infer that Scheherazade's must also be ranked higher than Vistula, and this is what (B) states. So (B) must be true.

The Incorrect Answer Choices:

A, C The ranking "Tantoko, Robusto, Pastilla, Lautrec, Scheherazade's, Medici, Vistula"—with Medici ranking lower than Lautrec and none of the conditions violated—shows that Tantoko could be ranked first. That proves that neither (A) nor (C) must be true.

D, E The ranking "Robusto, Pastilla, Lautrec, Scheherazade's, Tantoko, Medici, Vistula"—with Medici ranking lower than Lautrec and none of the conditions violated—shows that Tantoko could be ranked lower than Scheherazade's (contrary to (D)) and lower than Pastilla (contrary to (E)). That proves that neither (D) nor (E) must be true.

- *Difficulty Level: 4*

Question 10

Overview: If Vistula is ranked higher than Robusto, then it is possible to use the first two conditions to determine the relative rank of all the restaurants except Scheherazade's:

Tantoko ... Medici ... Vistula ... Robusto ... Pastilla ... Lautrec

You know that Scheherazade's has to be ranked between Pastilla and Medici (as discussed in "What the setup tells you"). That means that there are three possible outcomes in which Vistula ranks higher than Robusto:

Tantoko, Medici, **Scheherazade's**, Vistula, Robusto, Pastilla, Lautrec

Tantoko, Medici, Vistula, **Scheherazade's**, Robusto, Pastilla, Lautrec

Tantoko, Medici, Vistula, Robusto, **Scheherazade's**, Pastilla, Lautrec

Thus, either Robusto or Scheherazade's could be ranked fifth highest. (Robusto is not listed among the answer choices, but Scheherazade's is.) The correct answer is (C) Scheherazade's.

The Correct Answer:

C You can construct the following relative ranking using just the information in the question itself and the first two conditions:

Scheherazade's

Tantoko ... Medici ... Vistula ... Robusto ... Pastilla ... Lautrec

Because Scheherazade's could appear in any position between Medici and Pastilla, you next determine that either Scheherazade's or Robusto could be ranked fifth highest. Robusto is not one of the answer choices but Scheherazade's is, so Scheherazade's is the correct answer.

The Incorrect Answer Choices:

If Vistula is ranked higher than Robusto, you can use the first two conditions to determine the relative rank of all the restaurants except Scheherazade's. And you know from the third and fourth conditions that Scheherazade's has to be ranked somewhere between Pastilla and Medici.

Scheherazade's

Tantoko ... Medici ... Vistula ... Robusto ... Pastilla ... Lautrec

A Working from the diagram above, you can determine that Tantoko must be ranked highest and thus cannot be ranked fifth highest.

B The diagram above allows you to determine that Medici must be ranked second highest and thus cannot be ranked fifth highest.

D The diagram above shows that Vistula must be ranked either third or fourth highest and thus cannot be ranked fifth highest.

E The diagram above shows that Pastilla must be ranked sixth highest and thus cannot be ranked fifth highest.

■ *Difficulty Level: 4*

Question 11

Overview: This question asks you to select the one answer choice that can't be true. In this kind of question, the answer choices that **don't** violate the setup conditions are the ones that are incorrect.

The Correct Answer:

E   From the discussion in "What the setup tells you," you know that Scheherazade's has to occur in between Medici and Pastilla in the ranking. So it must rank higher than one of them. For Scheherazade's to rank sixth highest of the seven restaurants, either Medici or Pastilla would have to rank seventh (the lowest in the ranking). But (by the second condition) Vistula has to rank lower than Medici, and (by the second condition) Lautrec has to rank lower than Pastilla. Therefore, neither Medici nor Pastilla can rank seventh highest, and so Scheherazade's cannot rank sixth highest.

The Incorrect Answer Choices:

A, C   "Robusto, Pastilla, Lautrec, Tantoko, Scheherazade's, Medici, Vistula" is an acceptable ranking of the seven restaurants. It shows that Pastilla can be ranked second highest and Lautrec can be ranked third highest.

B, D   "Tantoko, Medici, Vistula, Scheherazade's, Robusto, Pastilla, Lautrec" is an acceptable ranking of the seven restaurants. It shows that Vistula can be ranked third highest and that Robusto can be ranked fifth highest.

   This question can also be approached via a shortcut. When a question asks what **cannot** be true on the basis of the setup conditions alone, the incorrect answer choices will all be things that, according to the setup conditions, **can** be true. In the course of answering previous questions, you will have already determined many things that **can** be true, and this information may be helpful in ruling out answer choices in a question such as this one. You cannot always count on previous questions to provide information that will be useful, but it can be worth your while to quickly check back to see whether some of your previous work can be used. In this particular case—depending on how you figured out the answers to various questions—you might actually find that all the work has already been done:

- (A) and (C) can both be ruled out because the work you did to answer question 7 shows that each of them could be true.

- (B) and (D) can both be ruled out because the work you did to answer question 10 shows that each of them could be true.

> **Note.** Do not use this shortcut unless you are confident that you answered earlier questions in this group correctly. If one of your previous answers was wrong, it could mislead you here.

- *Difficulty Level: 4*

Question 12

Overview: In this question, you're looking for something that can't be true if Tantoko is ranked third highest.

If Tantoko is ranked third highest, then exactly two of the other restaurants are ranked above it. Neither Medici nor Vistula can be ranked higher than Tantoko (by the second condition). Lautrec can't be ranked higher, because (by the first condition) there are at least two other restaurants that must rank higher than Lautrec. With just two available slots, there is not enough room for Lautrec and two other restaurants to rank above Tantoko.

So Medici, Vistula, and Lautrec are all ranked lower than Tantoko. Of the remaining three restaurants—Pastilla, Robusto, and Scheherazade's—there is room for only two of them to rank higher than Tantoko.

The Correct Answer:

B If Tantoko is third, two restaurants will be ranked higher than Tantoko. By using the first and second conditions, you can narrow down the candidates for those two positions to Pastilla, Robusto, and Scheherazade's. What else do you know about these three restaurants? By the first condition, you know that Robusto ranks higher than Pastilla. You also know, from the "Overview," that Scheherazade's must occur somewhere in between Pastilla and Medici in the ranking. Logically, there are three ways that Pastilla, Robusto, and Scheherazade's can be arranged around Tantoko. But only the first one conforms to the conditions:

R	P	T	... S ...	OK
S	R	T	... P ...	Does not conform
R	S	T	... P ...	Does not conform

In the first ranking, Tantoko is ranked third highest, Robusto is higher than Pastilla in the ranking, and Scheherazade's occurs somewhere in between Pastillo and Medici. So Pastilla must be ranked second highest, and it cannot have any other rank. Thus (B), which says that Pastilla is ranked fifth highest, can't be true and it is the correct answer.

The Incorrect Answer Choices:

A, D, E The following is an acceptable outcome in which Tantoko is ranked third highest:

Robusto, Pastilla, Tantoko, Lautrec, Scheherazade's, Medici, Vistula

Thus, (A), (D), and (E) are all answer choices that could be true.

C The following is an acceptable outcome in which Tantoko is ranked third highest.

Robusto, Pastilla, Tantoko, Scheherazade's, Medici, Vistula, Lautrec

Thus, (C) could be true.

- *Difficulty Level: 4*

Questions 13–19

What the setup tells you: This group of questions has to do with three parks and the different attractions that they have. There are five types of attractions, and each one of them must be in at least one of the parks. Similarly, each park has to have at least one attraction (since no park is without an attraction). Your task involves determining which parks have what attractions.

The second and third conditions give you information about specific parks, and the remaining conditions give you more general information about how the attractions are distributed.

What conclusions can you draw at the outset? From the second and sixth conditions, you know that Jessup has both a museum and a playground, but no theater. From the third condition, together with the fifth and sixth conditions, you know that Island has neither a theater nor a museum. Since neither Jessup nor Island has a theater, Hilltop has to have one. This in turn means that (by the fifth condition) Hilltop also has to have a garden.

The following table summarizes what you've got so far:

Jessup	Island	Hilltop
museum		theater
playground		garden

In addition, you know (from the fact that each attraction must be in at least one park) that at least one fountain must be added to the table. You know from the first condition that exactly one more garden must be added, for a total of two gardens. You know from the fourth condition that the fountain cannot be in Jessup, and so there must be a fountain in either Island or Hilltop, or both. And since no park can have two attractions of the same type you know that the second garden has to be in either Jessup or Island, since Hilltop already has one. The following is a summary of these observations:

- As far as Jessup is concerned, the only uncertainty is whether or not it has a garden. Either Jessup or Island, but not both, will have the second garden.

- As far as Island is concerned, it might have a garden, as noted above. Alternatively, it might have a fountain. The third alternative is that it has a playground.

- As far as Hilltop is concerned, if Island has either a garden or a playground, then Hilltop will have to have a fountain (and therefore no playground). If Island has a fountain, Hilltop could have either a fountain or a playground, but not both, although it doesn't have to have either one. If Hilltop has a playground, then it could also have a museum (whereas, by the sixth condition, if it has a museum, then it must have a playground).

Thus, from the setup, you know that the attractions are distributed among the parks as follows:

Jessup	Island	Hilltop
museum	fountain/garden/playground	theater
playground		garden
[garden]		[fountain/playground]
		[museum and playground]

Question 13:

Overview: This question asks you to pick an acceptable outcome from among the five answer choices. An efficient way to approach this type of question is to take the conditions in turn and check the answer choices against them, eliminating any answer choice as soon as you detect a violation of a condition. There's no need to recheck an answer choice once you've crossed it out.

Since all of the answer choices have exactly two gardens, none of them violates the first condition.

In (B), Jessup has a theater, in violation of the second condition. So (B) can be crossed out.

In (E), Island has two attractions, in violation of the third condition. So (E) can be crossed out.

The fourth condition is not violated in any of the remaining options (A), (C), and (D). (It is violated in (B) but that doesn't matter, since you've already crossed out (B)).

Checking the fifth condition against (A), (C), and (D), you find that you can cross out (C). Your choice comes down to (A) and (D).

(A) violates the sixth condition, and this leaves you with (D). Since only (D) remains, you know that it has to be the correct answer and you are done.

You may also notice that in (A) and (C) none of the parks has a fountain. Both (A) and (C) could be crossed out because they don't conform to the basic setup, which requires that at least one of each type of attraction be included among the three parks.

The Correct Answer:

D The "Overview" shows by process of elimination that (D) is the correct answer.

The following provides an independent demonstration that (D) is an acceptable outcome. (D) satisfies the basic setup: each of the parks has at least one attraction, none of the parks has two attractions of the same type, and all five attractions appear somewhere. And (D) doesn't violate any of the first three conditions: both Jessup and Hilltop have a garden; Jessup has a museum but no theater; and Island has only one attraction, a fountain. None of the parks has both a fountain and a playground, and so the fourth condition isn't violated. Hilltop is the only park with a theater and it also has a garden. So the fifth condition isn't violated. And Jessup, which is the only park with a museum, also has a playground. So the sixth condition isn't violated.

The Incorrect Answer Choices:

> **Tip:** Keep in mind that in the interest of managing your test time effectively, you should avoid doing any more than necessary to identify the correct answer. So, for example, the fact that (A), (B), and (C) each exhibit more than one violation is a fact that you can, and should, ignore.

A   (A) can be eliminated because it violates both the basic setup and the sixth condition. (A) violates the basic setup because none of the three parks has a fountain, whereas the basic setup provides that "among the three parks at least one of each type of attraction is included." (A) violates the sixth condition by listing Jessup as having a museum but no playground.

B   (B) can be eliminated because it violates the second, fourth, fifth, and sixth conditions. It violates the second condition by listing Jessup as having a theater. It violates the fourth condition by listing Hilltop as having both a fountain and a playground. It violates the fifth condition by listing Jessup as having a theater but no garden. And it violates the sixth condition by listing Jessup as having a museum but no playground.

C   (C) can be eliminated because it violates both the basic setup and the fifth condition. (C) violates the basic setup because none of the three parks has a fountain, whereas the basic setup provides that "among the three parks at least one of each type of attraction is included." (C) violates the fifth condition by listing Island as having a theater but no garden.

E   (E) can be eliminated because it violates the third condition by listing Island as having two attractions, not just one.

▪ *Difficulty Level: 1*

Question 14

Overview: This question asks you to select the answer choice that is **ruled out** by the setup conditions. You want to eliminate any answer choice that could be true.

The Correct Answer:

D   According to the first condition, exactly two of the parks have a garden. This means that there is only one park without a garden. So (D) cannot be true and is therefore the correct answer.

The Incorrect Answer Choices:

A   In order to eliminate this answer choice, you need to demonstrate that it could be true that neither Island nor Hilltop has a museum. Since each attraction must appear at least once, you also need to demonstrate that at the same time Jessup could have a museum. (Otherwise, an outcome in which none of the parks has a museum would fail to conform to the requirements of the setup.) You know from the third and sixth conditions that Island cannot have a museum. There is no requirement that Hilltop have a museum. And since, by the second condition, Jessup has a museum, the requirement that at least one park have a museum is satisfied. Since it could be true that neither Hilltop nor Island has a museum, (A) could be true and so can be ruled out.

B   If neither Island nor Hilltop has a playground, then Jessup must have one. (Otherwise, an outcome in which none of the parks has a playground would fail to conform to the requirements of the setup.) You know from the second and sixth conditions that Jessup has a playground and thus that the requirement that at least one park have a playground is satisfied. There is no requirement that either Island or Hilltop have a playground. So, both Island and Hilltop could be without a playground. Thus (B) could be true.

C   If neither Jessup nor Hilltop has a fountain, then Island must have one (because it is required that at least one of each attraction be among the three parks). You know from the second and fourth conditions that Jessup cannot have a fountain. This means that either Island or Hilltop must have a fountain. And if Island has a fountain, then Hilltop doesn't have to have one. There is no requirement that Hilltop have a fountain. So (C) could be true.

E   If neither Jessup nor Island has a theater, then Hilltop must have one (because it is required that at least one of each attraction be among the three parks). You know from the second condition that Jessup doesn't have a theater. And you know from the third and fifth conditions that Island cannot have a theater. So (E) could be true. (In fact, it must be true.)

- *Difficulty Level: 3*

Question 15

Overview: This question asks you what could be true in case there are exactly two parks with a fountain. You know from the discussion in "What the setup tells you" that if two parks have a fountain, those two parks have to be Island and Hilltop. Jessup cannot have a fountain because it has a museum, which means that it also has a playground. (No park has both a playground and a fountain.) So (A), which says that Island has no fountain, can't be true and it gets crossed out. You also know that if Island has a fountain, Jessup has to have a garden along with its museum and playground. So (B), which says that Jessup has no garden, and (C), which says that Jessup has exactly two attractions, cannot be true. Consequently, (B) and (C) get crossed out.

That leaves (D) and (E). You know from the discussion in "What the setup tells you" that Hilltop has both a theater and a garden. So if Hilltop has a fountain, it has to have at least three attractions. Could it have four attractions? If it did, it would have to have either a playground or a museum. It can't have a playground because it has a fountain (by the fourth condition). But that means that (by the sixth condition) it can't have a museum either, because a park that has a museum must also have a playground, and you have just ruled out the possibility of a playground for Hilltop. So Hilltop can't have four attractions, and thus (E) can be crossed out. (D), the only remaining answer choice, is the correct answer.

The Correct Answer:

D   As shown in the "Overview," if two of the parks have a fountain, then Hilltop has exactly three attractions. If exactly two parks have a fountain, then those two parks are Island and Hilltop. In addition, you know from the discussion in "What the setup tells you" that Hilltop has both a theater and a garden. Hilltop is not required to have any other attraction. So Hilltop can have exactly three attractions—a fountain, a theater, and a garden—and (D) is the correct answer.

The Incorrect Answer Choices:

If exactly two parks have a fountain, then those two parks are Island and Hilltop. This is so because Jessup cannot have a fountain: Jessup has a museum, which means that it also has a playground, and no park that has a playground can also have a fountain.

A   (A) can be eliminated because if exactly two of the parks have fountains, one of the two must be Island. So (A) cannot be true.

B Since Island's one attraction must be a fountain, Jessup must have one of the gardens. This means that (B) can be eliminated.

C Since Island's one attraction must be a fountain, Jessup must have one of the gardens. As discussed in "What the setup tells you," Jessup must also have a museum and a playground. Thus, (C) can be eliminated, because in fact Jessup must have at least three attractions.

E It was shown in the "Overview" that Hilltop can have exactly three attractions: a fountain, a garden, and a theater. But can it have four? If Hilltop has a museum, then it must also have a playground. That would make five attractions, not four. Hilltop cannot have a playground, because no park has both a playground and a fountain. Hilltop can have three attractions, but no more than three, and this rules out (E).

- *Difficulty Level: 3*

Question 16

Overview: This question asks you to consider what else you know about the possible outcomes if you know that Jessup has exactly three attractions. With the information that Jessup has exactly three attractions, you will be able to determine the outcome for some or all of the parks, and the question asks you to identify those parks. You already know (from the discussion in "What the setup tells you") that it is possible to determine the exact set of attractions featured by Jessup in this case. Specifically, if Jessup has exactly three attractions, those three attractions have to be a museum, a playground, and a garden. So you know that any answer choice that doesn't include Jessup can be eliminated. Turning to the answer choices, you can immediately cross out (A) and (C). Both Island and Hilltop are mentioned in the remaining answer choices, so you need to find out whether it is now possible to determine what the exact set of attractions is for either of these parks.

The next question you might ask is: does the outcome for Jessup determine which attraction Island has? You know that Island cannot have a garden, and that it can have either a fountain or a playground. But since either is possible, it is not possible to determine the exact set of attractions for Island. The next question is: do the outcomes for Jessup and Island determine the outcome for Hilltop? It turns out that they don't: if Island doesn't have a fountain, then Hilltop could. So just by knowing that Jessup has exactly three attractions, we can determine exactly what Jessup's attractions are, but there is still more than one possible outcome for Island and Hilltop. These options are depicted in the following two diagrams.

Jessup	Island	Hilltop
museum	playground	theater
playground		garden
garden		fountain

Jessup	Island	Hilltop
museum	fountain	theater
playground		garden
garden		

So you can cross out any remaining options in which Island or Hilltop appear. This means that both (D) and (E) can be crossed out. Only (B) is left, and you're done.

The Correct Answer:

B The discussion in the "Overview" shows that (B) is the correct answer. If Jessup has exactly three attractions, then those attractions are a garden, a museum, and a playground. So you know that it is possible to determine the exact set of attractions featured by Jessup. You also know that Island may have either a fountain or a playground, and that Hilltop may or may not have a fountain in addition to its garden and theater. So any answer choice that includes Island or Hilltop is incorrect: you can't determine the exact set of attractions for either one.

The Incorrect Answer Choices:

A, C (A) and (C) can be eliminated because neither includes Jessup. If Jessup has exactly three attractions, it's possible to tell exactly which three attractions those are, namely, a museum, a playground, and a garden.

D, E (D) and (E) can be eliminated because each of them includes Island. If Jessup has exactly three attractions, Island's one attraction could be either a fountain or a playground; in other words, it isn't possible to tell exactly which attraction it will have. The inclusion of Hilltop in (E) is an additional reason for eliminating (E). If Jessup has exactly three attractions, there is still more than one possible outcome for Hilltop.

- *Difficulty Level: 4*

Question 17

Overview: This question asks you to determine what must be true if Island and Jessup have an attraction of the same type. The only attractions Jessup can have are a museum, a playground, and a garden; and the only attractions Island can have are a fountain, a playground, and a garden (as shown in "What the setup tells you"). Therefore, if Island and Jessup have an attraction of the same type, that attraction has to be either a garden or a playground. But it can't be a garden. From "What the setup tells you," you also know that Hilltop has a garden. By the first condition, you know that there are only two gardens in all three parks. So Island and Jessup can't both have a garden, as that would bring the count to three. Since the type of attraction that Island and Jessup have in common can't be a garden, it must be a playground.

Turning to the answer choices, then, you can immediately rule out (B), (C), and (D), since each one of them says that Island has something other than a playground.

Since Jessup has a playground, no other park is required to have one. And there is no requirement that Hilltop have a playground. So (A) can also be crossed out.

You're done. (E) must be the correct answer.

The Correct Answer:

E As explained in the "Overview," the only type of attraction that Jessup and Island can have in common is a playground. And if Island's one attraction is a playground, then it doesn't have a garden. According to the first condition, exactly two parks have a garden. If Island doesn't have a garden, then Hilltop and Jessup each have to have one. So Jessup must have a garden.

The Incorrect Answer Choices:

A As discussed in "What the setup tells you," Jessup cannot have a fountain. If Jessup and Island have an attraction in common, that attraction must be a playground, as shown in the "Overview." So in this circumstance, Island's one attraction is a playground (not a fountain). But there must be a fountain in at least one park, so that park must be Hilltop. But by the fourth condition, no park has both a fountain and a playground, so Hilltop can't have a playground. (A) can therefore be eliminated.

B, C, D As discussed in the "Overview," if Jessup and Island have an attraction in common, that attraction must be a playground. By the third condition, Island has only one attraction. Since this attraction must be a playground, it cannot be a museum, a fountain, or a garden, and (B), (C), and (D) can thus be eliminated.

- *Difficulty Level: 4*

Question 18

Overview: This question asks what could be true given the information in the setup. The incorrect answer choices will be ones that cannot be true under any circumstances.

The Correct Answer:

A From the discussion in "What the setup tells you," you know that Hilltop must have a garden and that although Jessup could have a garden, it doesn't have to. Suppose Jessup doesn't have a garden. In that case, both Island and Hilltop have a garden. In addition, if both Island and Hilltop have a garden, all of the requirements of the setup can be met.

Jessup	Island	Hilltop
museum	**garden**	theater
playground		**garden**
		fountain

So (A) describes something that could be true and thus is the correct answer.

The Incorrect Answer Choices:

B This answer choice can be ruled out on the basis of the fourth condition. Since Jessup has no fountain (as shown in "What the setup tells you"), either Island or Hilltop (or both) must have a fountain. But, by the fourth condition, no park can have both a fountain and a playground. Because you know that either Island or Hilltop (or both) must have a fountain, you also know that they cannot both have a playground. Thus (B) cannot be true.

C You know, by the third condition, that Island has only one attraction. You also know, by the fifth condition, that any park that has a theater also has a garden. So Island cannot have a theater, and (C) cannot be true.

D You know from "What the setup tells you" that Jessup has no fountain. So (D) cannot be true.

E From the discussion in "What the setup tells you," you know that Hilltop must have a garden. The first condition requires that exactly two parks have a garden, and so that means that either Jessup or Island—but not both—will have a garden. So (E) cannot be true.

■ *Difficulty Level: 4*

Question 19

Overview: The correct answer to this question will be something that can't be true of any outcome in which Hilltop has exactly three attractions. The incorrect answers will all be things that could or must be true.

From the discussion in "What the setup tells you," you know that Hilltop has to have a theater and a garden and could also have either a playground, a fountain or a museum as a third attraction. But if Hilltop has a museum, then (by the sixth condition) it would also have to have a playground, making a total of four attractions. So if Hilltop has exactly three attractions, then the third attraction cannot be a museum.

Turning to the answer choices, you can immediately select (A) as the correct answer and you're done.

The Correct Answer:

A As shown in the "Overview," if Hilltop has a museum, it must have four attractions: a theater, a garden, a museum, and a playground. Thus, if Hilltop has exactly three attractions, it can't have a museum. So (A) is the answer choice that can't be true.

The Incorrect Answer Choices:

B, E The following is an acceptable outcome in which Hilltop has exactly three attractions.

Jessup	Island	Hilltop
museum	fountain	theater
playground		garden
garden		playground

This outcome, in which Hilltop has a playground and Jessup has a garden, demonstrates that (B) and (E) each could be true.

C, D The following is an acceptable outcome in which Hilltop has exactly three attractions.

Jessup	Island	Hilltop
museum	garden	theater
playground		garden
		fountain

Since in this outcome Island has a garden and doesn't have a fountain, you have demonstrated that (C) and (D) each could be true.

■ *Difficulty Level: 4*

Questions 20–24

What the setup tells you: The task here is to work out a three-year production schedule for four models of automobiles. Cars will be produced in five factories, one model per factory per year. In each of the three years, all four models will be produced. Since there are five factories and four models, this means that each year two of the factories will be producing the same model, with the other three factories producing the other three models. According to the last condition, the Ziggurat can never be the model that is produced in two factories in the same year.

What needs to be determined, for each of the three years, is which models are to be manufactured in which factories. Here's a diagram that captures this relationship:

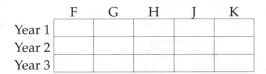

When you turn to the questions, you will find that none of them requires you to fill out the entire diagram. Instead, it will be enough to focus on just part of the diagram in answering the questions that follow.

The first three conditions give constraints on which models can follow one another within a given factory. The most general of these conditions (the first one) says that, within a given factory, the same model cannot be assembled twice in a row.

The next two conditions mention specific models. The second condition says, essentially: Volantes and Whispers never follow Xaviers. Recall that, by the first condition, the Xavier cannot follow itself. One way to represent this information in shorthand is: *XV, *XW, *XX. Since there are only four models in all, this means simply: if a model follows the Xavier, that model must be the Ziggurat (in shorthand, X__ → XZ). Or very concisely: *only Ziggurats after Xaviers.*

Notice that *only Ziggurats after Xaviers* has a very specific implication when taken together with the fourth condition, which requires that in any year only one factory assembles Ziggurats. This implication is that in each of the first two years, the Xavier can be assembled in only one factory (namely, the one in which the Ziggurat will be assembled in the following year). Since there is only one factory that produces Ziggurats in any given year, that one production of Ziggurats has to be preceded by a production of Xaviers.

Here's how it works: Every time the Xavier is produced (except for the third year), it must be followed by a production of the Ziggurat. The Xavier must be produced at least once in each year. Since there is only one Ziggurat production in any year, a production of the

Xavier has to precede that production of Ziggurats. This means that there cannot be any Ziggurats that follow any model other than the Xavier (__Z→ XZ). Or very concisely: *only Xaviers before Ziggurats.*

The third condition boils down to this: if a model follows a Ziggurat, that model must be a Whisper (Z__ → ZW). Or very concisely: *only Whispers after Ziggurats.* Notice here, however, that since the Whisper is not limited to being produced in only one factory per year, it is possible for there to be an occasion in which the Whisper follows a model other than the Ziggurat. (So there is no restriction here that would correspond to *only Xaviers before Ziggurats.*)

In summary, you have derived the following rules from the second and third conditions:

> *only Ziggurats after Xaviers*
> *only Xaviers before Ziggurats*
> *only Whispers after Ziggurats*

At this point, you have recast in an accessible format much of the information given in the setup, and you can now turn to the individual questions.

Question 20

Overview: The question asks about an acceptable partial assembly schedule, covering only two years and two factories. Since none of the factories has been given any specific properties in the setup, you can ignore the fact that this question mentions factories F and G **in particular**. The reference to F and G just helps you keep track of "the same factory."

The best approach to finding the one acceptable assembly schedule is probably to take the conditions one by one, see for each condition whether any of the proposed schedules violates it, and cross out any schedule that does produce a violation.

So, beginning with the first condition, you check to see if a model is manufactured in the same factory in both years. In (B), you find that Whispers are scheduled to be manufactured in factory F in years 1 and 2. So (B) violates the first condition and gets crossed out.

Next, look for violations of the second condition. In (D), Whispers are to be assembled in factory F in the second year even though Xaviers are supposed to be assembled in F in the first year. But recall the gist of the second condition: *only Ziggurats after Xaviers.* So (D) violates the second condition and gets crossed out.

The third condition is violated by the proposed schedule in (E), since Volantes are to be assembled in F in the second year even though the Ziggurat would be assembled in F in the first year. This violates the restriction *only Whispers after Ziggurats.* So (E) gets crossed out.

Finally, (C) gets crossed out because it violates the fourth condition. The fourth condition rules out any schedule in which Ziggurats are assembled in more than one factory in a single year, which is what the schedule in (C) proposes.

The only proposed schedule that you haven't found to be in violation of any condition is (A). This means that you're done: (A) is the correct answer.

The Correct Answer:

A As detailed in the "Overview," (A) is the only answer choice that conforms to the requirements of the setup. So you know that the partial schedule in (A) could be part of a complete assembly schedule.

A demonstration that (A) could be the assembly schedule for factories F and G is provided by showing that the partial schedule exhibited in (A) can indeed be incorporated in an acceptable overall schedule for all three years and all five factories (but remember that, in order to save time, you should probably not undertake such a demonstration when taking the test):

	F	G	H	J	K
Year 1	V	Z	X	V	W
Year 2	X	W	Z	W	V
Year 3	Z	X	W	V	X

The Incorrect Answer Choices:

B (B) can be eliminated because it violates the first condition. The Whisper is scheduled to be manufactured in factory F in years 1 and 2, in violation of the condition that no model is manufactured in the same factory in consecutive years.

C (C) can be eliminated because it violates the fourth condition. The Ziggurat is scheduled to be manufactured in year 2 in both factory F and factory G, in violation of the condition that in any year only one factory assembles the Ziggurat. ((C) also violates the restriction that follows from the interaction between the second and the fourth conditions: *only Xaviers before Ziggurats*.)

D (D) can be eliminated because it violates the second condition. The Whisper is scheduled to be manufactured in year 2 in factory F, where the Xavier is scheduled to be manufactured in year 1. This violates the condition *only Ziggurats after Xaviers*.

E (E) can be eliminated because it violates the third condition. The Volante is scheduled to be manufactured in year 2 in factory F, where the Ziggurat is scheduled to be manufactured in year 1. This violates the condition *only Whispers after Ziggurats*.

Question 21

Overview: This question asks you to determine what could happen in the second year for two factories that in the first year assemble Volantes and Whispers, respectively. This is again a question about just a portion of the three-year assembly schedule, and what was said in the "Overview" applies here too: The fact that the question mentions factories F and G in particular, rather than other factories, is irrelevant. The references to F and G are merely there to help you track "the same factory." The best approach is the same as the one adopted for the previous question: check the answer choices against each condition in turn, and cross out any answer choice that produces a violation.

The first condition is violated by (A), since (A) has factories F and G manufacturing the same model in two consecutive years. So (A) gets crossed out.

The first condition is also violated by (D), since factory G would be manufacturing Whispers in two consecutive years. So (D) gets crossed out.

Now consider the second condition and the restrictions it implies: *only Ziggurats after Xaviers* and *only Xaviers before Ziggurats*. It is the restriction *only Xaviers before Ziggurats* that rules out (C) and (E).

Since only (B) is left, you know that (B) is the correct answer. You're done. There is no need to check the third or fourth conditions.

The Correct Answer:

B A demonstration that (B) could indeed be true is provided by showing that the partial schedule given in (B) can be incorporated in an acceptable overall schedule for all three years and all five factories (but remember that, in order to save time, you should probably not undertake a thorough demonstration such as this when taking the test):

	F	G	H	J	K
Year 1	V	W	X	Z	W
Year 2	W	V	Z	W	X
Year 3	V	X	W	X	Z

The Incorrect Answer Choices:

A (A) can be eliminated because it violates the first condition. In (A), the Volante is scheduled to be manufactured in factory F in the first two years, and the Whisper is scheduled to be manufactured in factory G in the first two years. Both of these scheduling decisions are in violation of the first condition.

C   (C) can be eliminated because it violates the restriction you derived from the interaction of the second and fourth conditions: *only Xaviers before Ziggurats*. Scheduling the Whisper to precede the Ziggurat in factory G is the violation here.

D   (D) can be eliminated because it violates the restriction *only Xaviers before Ziggurats*, in this case by scheduling the Volante to precede the Ziggurat in factory F. In addition, (D) violates the first condition because the Whisper is scheduled to be manufactured in factory G in the first two years.

E   (E) can be eliminated because it violates the restriction *only Xaviers before Ziggurats*. The violation lies in having the Volante precede the Ziggurat in factory F, and having the Whisper precede the Ziggurat in factory G. In addition, and more obviously, (E) violates the fourth condition, by scheduling the Ziggurat in two factories in the second year.

- *Difficulty Level: 5*

Question 22

Overview: This question asks you to identify an answer choice that must be true. In this case, all of the options are about the Xavier. For this reason, it is probably a good idea to start with what you know about that model specifically. There are two rules that summarize what the setup has to say about the Xavier: *only Ziggurats after Xaviers* and *only Xaviers before Ziggurats*.

The Correct Answer:

B   Within a given factory, the Xavier must be followed by the Ziggurat, and the Ziggarut must be preceded by the Xavier. Because only one factory assembles the Ziggurat in any given year, the Xavier can be assembled in only one factory in the first and second years of the three-year period. (This consideration does not apply to the third year, since there is no fourth year following it in the schedule.) It follows that in the second year the Xavier must be assembled in exactly one factory.

The Incorrect Answer Choices:

A, C   As discussed in the "Overview" and "The Correct Answer," there is exactly one production of Xaviers in the first year and exactly one production of Xaviers in the second year. So neither (A) nor (C) must be true. In fact, what has been shown is that neither can be true.

D   An effective demonstration that (D) does not have to be true is an acceptable three-year schedule in which (D) is, in fact, not true. Such a schedule appears in the discussion of the correct answer to Question 21 and is reproduced here for convenience:

	F	G	H	J	K
Year 1	V	W	X	Z	W
Year 2	W	V	Z	W	X
Year 3	V	X	W	X	Z

In this schedule, which meets all of the requirements of the setup, the Xavier is assembled in two factories in the third year. So it does not have to be true that the Xavier is assembled in only one factory in the third year.

Notice that the rule *only Ziggurats after Xaviers* does not limit Xaviers to being produced in only one factory in the third year, for the simple reason that in the production schedule there is no fourth year. So in this schedule nothing at all comes after the Xaviers that are scheduled for the third year, which is consistent with the rule *only Ziggarats after Xaviers*.

E   An effective demonstration that (E) does not have to be true is an acceptable three-year schedule in which (E) is not true. The following is such a schedule:

	F	G	H	J	K
Year 1	V	W	X	Z	W
Year 2	W	V	Z	W	X
Year 3	V	W	W	**X**	Z

In this schedule, which meets all of the conditions, the Xavier is assembled in only one factory in the third year. So it does not have to be true that the Xavier is assembled in two factories in the third year.

- *Difficulty Level: 5*

Question 23

Overview: In this question, the answer is dependent on the second-year assembly of the Ziggurat. It would therefore be useful to concentrate on the restrictions on assembly of the Ziggurat. There are three such restrictions: *only Ziggurats after Xaviers*, *only Xaviers before Ziggurats*, and *only Whispers after Ziggurats*.

The Correct Answer:

E   If in the second year Ziggurats are assembled in F, the rule *only Xaviers before Ziggurats* tells you that in the first year Xaviers are assembled in F. So (E) must be true.

The Incorrect Answer Choices:

A   An effective demonstration that (A) doesn't have to be true is an acceptable three-year schedule in which (A) is not true. The following is such a schedule:

	F	G	H	J	K
Year 1	X	Z	W	V	W
Year 2	Z	W	V	W	X
Year 3	W	**V**	X	**V**	Z

In this schedule, which meets all of the conditions, the Volante is assembled in two factories in the third year. So it doesn't have to be true that the Volante is assembled in exactly one factory in the third year.

B   An effective demonstration that (B) doesn't have to be true is an acceptable three-year schedule in which (B) is not true. The following is such a schedule:

	F	G	H	J	K
Year 1	X	Z	W	V	W
Year 2	Z	W	V	W	X
Year 3	**W**	V	**W**	X	Z

In this schedule, which meets all of the conditions, the Whisper is assembled in two factories in the third year. So it doesn't have to be true that the Whisper is assembled in exactly one factory in the third year.

C, D   The rule *only Xaviers before Ziggurats* requires that the Xavier be assembled in factory F in the first year, if the Ziggurat is assembled there in the second year: production of the Xavier must precede production of the Ziggurat. This means that the model assembled in factory F in the first year cannot be the Volante (which rules out (C)) and it cannot be the Whisper (which rules out (D)).

- *Difficulty Level: 5*

Question 24

Overview: This question is about the models assembled in two of the factories, F and G, in the first two years. The question itself tells you that in the second year, Volantes are assembled in F and Whispers are assembled in G, and you are to pick the answer choice that represents a possible schedule for the first year.

A quick scan of the answer choices shows that none of them violates the first condition: none of them proposes that Volantes be assembled in F in the first year, and none of them proposes that Whispers be assembled in G in the first year. Similarly, there are no violations of the fourth condition: in neither the first nor the second year is it proposed that Ziggurats be assembled in both F and G.

So any violations will be violations of one of the following rules, derived from the second and third conditions:

only Xaviers before Ziggurats
only Ziggurats after Xaviers
only Whispers after Ziggurats

The first of these rules is violated by none of the answer choices.

(B), (C), and (D) all violate the second rule. In (B), Whispers are scheduled to come after Xaviers. In both (C) and (D), Volantes are scheduled to come after Xaviers. But the rule requires *only Ziggurats after Xaviers*.

(E) violates the third rule. In (E), Volantes are scheduled to come after Ziggurats, but this violates the rule *only Whispers after Ziggurats*.

The remaining answer choice, (A), is the correct answer.

The Correct Answer:

A A demonstration that (A) could indeed be true is provided by showing that the information in (A) can be incorporated into an acceptable overall schedule for all three years and all five factories (but remember that, in order to save time, you probably shouldn't undertake any such demonstration when taking the test). The following is such a schedule:

	F	G	H	J	K
Year 1	**W**	**V**	X	Z	W
Year 2	**V**	**W**	Z	W	X
Year 3	X	V	W	X	Z

The Incorrect Answer Choices:

B (B) can be eliminated because it violates the second condition. In (B), Xaviers are assembled in factory G in a year immediately preceding a year in which Whispers are assembled there, which is in direct violation of the second condition.

C, D (C) and (D) can be eliminated because they violate the second condition. According to both (C) and (D), Xaviers are assembled in factory F in a year immediately preceding a year in which Volantes are assembled there, which is in direct violation of the second condition.

E (E) can be eliminated because it violates the third condition. According to (E), Ziggurats are assembled in factory F in a year immediately preceding a year in which Volantes are assembled there, in direct violation of the third condition.

Difficulty Level: 5

Logical Reasoning: Questions 1–24

Question 1

Overview: The exchange between Jorge and Christina covers two points. One they agree about: that a shift in economic policy is needed. The other they disagree about: whether this shift should be made to happen all at once or more gradually. They use metaphors to illustrate their respective positions.

The question asks you what they disagree about, so you need to look for the answer choice that deals with the pacing of the shift in economic policy.

The Correct Answer:

D   As discussed in the "Overview," the disagreement between Jorge and Christina concerns the issue of whether economic policy should be changed all at once or in a number of steps. (D) best captures this disagreement.

The Incorrect Answer Choices:

A   Christina explicitly says that she agrees with Jorge that a shift in economic policy is needed, so they clearly do not disagree about (A).

B   Teaching a horse to jump fences by starting with lower heights is Christina's metaphor for changing economic policy incrementally. Christina obviously thinks this metaphor is apt, but there's no way to tell whether Jorge would agree or disagree.

C   Neither Jorge nor Christina expressly considers the pain that may initially be involved when economic policy is revised. So it is impossible to tell from their exchange whether they disagree about (C).

E   Although Jorge and Christina agree that a shift in economic policy is needed, neither of them says anything about why a shift is needed. Therefore, there is no particular reason to think that one of them considers the current economic situation to be grave and the other does not.

- *Difficulty Level: 1*

Question 2

Overview: John's argument goes as follows: Male laboratory rats, when given fluoridated public drinking water to drink, developed bone cancer in a very high proportion of cases. Females were not affected. So John, being male, proposes to stop drinking fluoridated water, reasoning that this is the only way to make sure he won't develop bone cancer.

The question asks what the strongest criticism of John's reasoning is. The argument appears to be badly flawed: there is little or no real support for concluding that no longer drinking fluoridated water would offer complete protection from bone cancer. So the strongest criticism of John's reasoning is bound to be a very serious one.

The Correct Answer:

E   John concludes that if he stops drinking fluoridated water he can make sure that he won't develop bone cancer. But even if the consumption of fluoridated water is indeed a cause of bone cancer in human males, this does not mean that there couldn't be a variety of other causes of bone cancer. Since not drinking fluoridated water wouldn't necessarily protect John from developing bone cancer from one of those other causes, John's reasoning can properly be faulted for not considering this possibility.

The Incorrect Answer Choices:

A   The conclusion John draws is just about what he should do. Since John's conclusion does not make any claims about how others are affected by fluoridated water, there's no need for the reasoning leading to that conclusion to consider how others are affected. So (A) does not provide an effective criticism of John's reasoning.

B   It is true that John does not consider whether fluoridated water causes diseases besides bone cancer. But since his reasoning is focused on what he should do to avoid developing bone cancer, any other diseases that fluoridated water might cause are not relevant to the adequacy of John's reasoning.

C   If fluoridated water did cause bone cancer, John's earlier exposure would certainly be relevant to his risk of developing bone cancer. But the possibility that there were short intervals when he was **not** exposed would not materially affect the situation. So (C) does not provide an effective criticism of John's reasoning.

D Whether John's conclusion—that the only way of being sure to avoid bone cancer is to stop drinking fluoridated water—is correct has nothing to do with whatever positive effects fluoridated water might have. So not taking any such positive effects into account is not a flaw in John's reasoning.

■ *Difficulty Level: 1*

Question 3

Overview: The columnist's argument describes how polls can distort elections. According to the columnist, polls influence voters' choices, but poll results are not as reliable as people think. This becomes a special problem when poll results are published right before an election, because there is not enough time for people who might wish to dispute those results to do so. The columnist concludes that there should be a ban on publishing polls within a week of an election since the distorting effects of polls outweigh the minor negative consequence— a slight impairment of the freedom of expression— of the ban.

The question asks which of five additional observations weakens the columnist's argument.

The Correct Answer:

A If poll results published within two weeks of an election influence few people, then the evidence used by the columnist—that polls can influence voters' decisions—does not argue very strongly in favor of banning the publication of poll results within one week of an election. Also, the fact that there might not be time to dispute late-breaking poll results would not be as strong a point in favor of a ban. So the information in (A) significantly weakens the argument for the columnist's conclusion.

The Incorrect Answer Choices:

B (B) points out that there could be cases in which the ban that the columnist argues for would be irrelevant. But as long as there are cases in which it is relevant—in which there is a real risk that the outcome of an election will be distorted—the strength of the columnist's argument is undiminished.

C The possibility that (C) points out does not weaken the columnist's argument. On the contrary, it would provide additional support for the proposed ban. After all, if people decide not to vote as a result of the polling information they're exposed to, this would be another way that polls distort the outcome of an election, which is the risk that the ban is meant to reduce.

D (D) could be part of an explanation of how polls influence an election. Perhaps there is a sort of bandwagon effect: as polls call attention to a candidate's late gain in popularity, voters who had been hesitant to support that candidate because of pessimism about his or her chances of winning decide to vote for the candidate. This explanation would not in any way weaken the argument, however; it would just explain why one of its premises is true.

E How well informed people are in general is not the issue that the argument addresses. The issue is whether poll results published very close to the date of an election distort the results of that election. The columnist proposes the ban not as a way to produce better-informed citizens, but only as a way to produce election results that are not distorted by polls. Thus (E) does not weaken the support for the argument's conclusion that such a ban is justified.

■ *Difficulty Level: 2*

Question 4

Overview: The passage presents a mystery of sorts: despite the generally high correlation between high cholesterol levels and cardiovascular disease, the Italian town of Limone is free from cardiovascular disease even though cholesterol levels are high there.

The question asks which of the answer choices helps explain the atypical case of that town's residents.

The Correct Answer:

D (D) identifies a factor that provides significant protection from cardiovascular disease to all of the residents of Limone. Moreover, it is the kind of factor that could account for its being common to the residents of Limone but relatively rare elsewhere. This helps explain why residents of Limone have high cholesterol levels but no cardiovascular disease in spite of the high correlation between high cholesterol levels and cardiovascular disease among people in general.

The Incorrect Answer Choices:

A The passage provides no independent evidence that people in Limone have generally lived to an old age. Moreover, if there is a causal connection between longevity and absence of cardiovascular disease, it is probably the absence of cardiovascular disease that contributes to longevity, rather than the other way around. So (A) does not help explain the unusual situation in Limone.

B The factors described in (B) are relevant only to people who already have cardiovascular disease, so (B) cannot explain why residents of Limone have not developed cardiovascular disease in the first place.

C (C) describes a factor—very low blood sugar levels—that can account for the absence of cardiovascular disease despite high cholesterol levels. But (C) also says that this factor is not present among the residents of Limone. So (C) does not help explain the unusual health condition of Limone residents.

E (E) tells us that olive oil is a dietary staple in some parts of Italy, but it does not tell us whether Limone is one of those parts. So (E) couldn't possibly explain the exceptional pattern found in Limone.

■ *Difficulty Level: 3*

Question 5

Overview: The argument concludes that Smith's cows will most likely learn to graze solely on the grass that is free of the fungus that makes cows ill. This conclusion is based partly on the claim that cows avoid eating grass in which they sense a substance that has made them ill.

The Correct Answer:

B The claim that cows avoid eating grass in which they sense a substance that has made them ill would provide no support at all for the argument's conclusion if the fungus that makes Smith's cows ill can't be sensed by grazing cows. So the argument must be assuming that it is possible for at least some cows to sense that fungus in fescue grass.

The Incorrect Answer Choices:

A As far as fungi contained in the fescue grass on Smith's new grazing land are concerned, the argument's sole focus is on the one fungus that makes cows ill when they eat it. So if, contrary to (A), no other fungi were present on the fescue grass on the new grazing land, the argument would not be affected. Thus the argument does not depend on assuming that there are other fungi present on any of the fescue grass.

C The argument states that fescue is the only kind of grass on Smith's new grazing land. So it is completely irrelevant to the argument whether other varieties of grass contain the fungus that makes cows ill.

D Suppose (D) were false and there were sheep grazing on Smith's land as well, and the fungus also made the sheep ill. This would not affect the case that the argument makes about the cows learning to graze only on grass that does not contain the fungus. So the argument does not require the assumption that (D) is true.

E The argument assumes that the fungus will not be eradicated, at least not right away. But the argument need not assume that the fungus **cannot** be eradicated without destroying the grass. Perhaps Smith will not eradicate the fungus because doing so would be very expensive.

- *Difficulty Level: 3*

Question 6

Overview: The argument attempts to assess the impact of the fact that one of the pollsters in a public survey falsified data. According to the opening sentence, the result of the survey—that most people in the country favor investing more money in information technologies—"has been called into question." But the final assessment is much stronger: the conclusion of the survey is said to be false. The argument for this stronger assessment is vulnerable to criticism.

The Correct Answer:

A Without more information about the falsified data, it is impossible to say what impact it had on the survey result. It could be that even without the falsified data, a majority of survey respondents would have been in favor of investing more money in information technologies, in which case the basic result of the survey would be true. This means that without ruling out the possibility that the survey would be verified if the falsified data were excluded, the argument cannot legitimately conclude that the survey results are false. So the argument is vulnerable to criticism because it did not consider the possibility described in (A).

The Incorrect Answer Choices:

B The argument focuses on the question of whether the conclusion of the survey is true, not on whether it will be accepted by the public. So there is no reason to criticize the argument for not considering the possibility raised in (B).

C The argument is concerned with assessing what damage to this particular survey's result was done by the pollster who falsified data in this particular case. The possibility that other pollsters in other surveys also may have falsified data is not relevant to that assessment. It would therefore not be a valid criticism of the argument to point out that it overlooked the possibility raised in (C).

D The possibility that some people who responded to the survey were lying might provide yet more grounds for doubting the correctness of the survey result. But the argument already concludes that the survey result is not true. This makes any additional reasons there might be for doubting the accuracy of that result inconsequential. The argument is thus not vulnerable to the criticism described in (D).

E   The argument tries to set the record straight on what current public opinion is in the face of irregularities in a recent public survey. The possibility that public opinion might change in the future, as new technologies emerge, has nothing to do with evaluating the effect of those irregularities on the survey results. So there is no reason for the argument to consider that possibility.

- *Difficulty Level: 2*

Question 7

Overview: The passage tells us that riodinid caterpillars live harmoniously among South American ants. This suggests that the caterpillars and the ants each get something out of the living arrangement. The passage makes it clear what the ants get: the caterpillars produce secretions that the ants use for food. The passage does not explicitly say what the caterpillars get out of the arrangement, but it does tell us that the caterpillars are a favorite prey of wasps. The passage also says that the ants have tactics for defending their food sources that can deter even aggressive flying insects like wasps.

The Correct Answer:

E   From the statements that the caterpillars are a favorite prey of wasps and that the ants can deter wasps, we can infer what the caterpillars get out of the living arrangement: a measure of protection against wasp attacks. In other words, the riodinid caterpillars that live among ants fare better against wasps than caterpillars that do not live among ants.

The Incorrect Answer Choices:

A   The passage gives no indication as to whether the riodinid caterpillars' secretions are chemically unique, or if not, what other substance the secretions might be similar or identical to. So (A) is not supported by the information in the passage.

B   The passage indicates that ants in general have some success in defending their food sources. But it says nothing to suggest that South American ants have more success than ants that live elsewhere.

C   The passage cites riodinid caterpillars as an example of insects that ants do not attack, suggesting that riodinid caterpillars are not the only insects that ants do not attack. Moreover, the passage doesn't say anything at all about how ants might react to organisms other than insects that enter ant territory. So the information in the passage provides no support for (C).

D   The passage definitely claims that both ants and wasps use the riodinid caterpillars as a source of food, though in different ways. The fact that no other insect species are mentioned as using those caterpillars as a source of food, however, does not imply that there aren't any other insect species that prey on the caterpillars.

- *Difficulty Level: 2*

Question 8

Overview: The passage proposes a shift in how the difference between urban and rural lifestyles is defined. Traditionally, the definition is in terms of geography—living in a city versus living in the country. According to the passage, the difference should be defined in informational terms—communicating daily electronically with many people versus rarely communicating electronically with anyone.

The question asks which general proposition this proposal illustrates.

The Correct Answer:

A (A) puts forward a general proposition according to which our lifestyles are increasingly being determined by frequency of electronic communication with others instead of by geographical considerations. The view that it "makes more sense to draw the distinction [between rural and urban lifestyles] in informational terms" is an instance of what (A) describes in more general terms.

The Incorrect Answer Choices:

B The passage is concerned solely with how one can tell what certain people's lifestyles are. It says nothing about how satisfying anyone finds his or her lifestyle. The passage cannot, therefore, illustrate a general proposition about people finding one lifestyle more satisfying than another.

C Notice that (C) talks about the frequency of communication in general, whereas the passage is concerned only with the frequency of **electronic** communication. As far as the passage is concerned, people with rural lifestyles could communicate more often in total than people with urban lifestyles do. So there is no way that the situation in the passage could illustrate (C).

D The passage does not concern itself with our ability to foresee future changes stemming from the information revolution. The passage claims that a development that has already occurred prompts a shift in how certain lifestyles are defined. Since the passage does not deal with the concerns of (D), it cannot illustrate those concerns.

E The passage says nothing about people choosing to live in different regions than before. Thus, the passage does not illustrate (E).

■ *Difficulty Level: 1*

Question 9

Overview: The passage begins with a general account of how the ash emitted by very powerful volcanic eruptions affects temperatures. It then presents two historical events: a powerful eruption of Mount Etna in Sicily in 44 B.C., and summer frosts and dimmed sunlight in China a year later. It then concludes that, if volcanic ash caused the cold weather in China, then the ash from Mount Etna must have spread over great distances.

The question asks what sort of information would be useful to have for the purpose of evaluating the strength of the support that the main conclusion receives.

The Correct Answer:

D Suppose that (D) is true, that is, there were volcanic eruptions near China around the time of Mount Etna's eruption. In that case, even if we assume that volcanic ash caused the cold weather, we would have little reason to conclude that the ash from Mount Etna spread over great distances and blocked the sun in China. It would be much more plausible to conclude that the ash from the eruption near China spread a fairly short distance and blocked the sun. So if (D) is true, the support provided in the passage for the conclusion is quite weak. Thus, knowing whether (D) is true is very important in evaluating the support given for the conclusion.

The Incorrect Answer Choices:

A Modern monitoring equipment could provide information only about the path of volcanic ash under **current** atmospheric conditions. Since there is no reason to think that modern atmospheric conditions are similar to conditions that prevailed over 2,000 years ago, (A) would not be an important piece of information.

B If the argument asserted that the cold weather in China was caused by volcanic ash, then a negative answer to (B) would cast doubt on that assertion. But the argument neither makes, nor depends on, any such assertion. The argument confines itself to drawing out the consequences that would follow **if** volcanic ash was responsible for China's cold weather. The reasoning can be evaluated without regard to whether the supposition actually is true. Knowing whether (B) is true, therefore, would not be useful in evaluating the argument.

C　Information about whether temperatures in Sicily were abnormally cold after Mount Etna erupted might tell us something about the movement of volcanic ash in the atmosphere near the site of the eruption. However, it would be unlikely to have any bearing on whether the ash could have spread great distances.

E　The passage gives no indication that ash from any eruptions of Mount Etna after 44 B.C. affected the weather in China. Thus, in evaluating the argument, it would not be helpful to know whether these later eruptions were as powerful as the one in 44 B.C.

- *Difficulty Level: 2*

Questions 10–11

Overview: The issue that Mario raises—and that Lucy disagrees with him about—is whether a discipline (cognitive science, in particular) can be genuinely autonomous if it doesn't have a subject matter all to itself. Mario says no, and Lucy says yes. Lucy, moreover, accuses Mario of being inconsistent in this matter since he thinks philosophy is autonomous but does not think the same of cognitive science even though neither has a subject matter all to itself. Lucy further claims that having a unique methodology is the defining characteristic of a genuinely autonomous discipline.

Question 10

The Correct Answer:

C　The principle on which Mario bases his conclusion is that a genuinely autonomous discipline must have a subject matter not shared with any other discipline. Lucy points out that Mario's belief that philosophy is a genuinely autonomous discipline is inconsistent with this principle, since he thinks of philosophy as addressing issues also addressed by other disciplines. So (C) accurately describes how Lucy responds to Mario.

The Incorrect Answer Choices:

A　The only things that Lucy questions are the general principle on which Mario bases his assessment of cognitive science as not being a genuinely autonomous discipline, and thus also the assessment itself. Neither of these is a matter of expertise in cognitive science. So (A) does not describe Lucy's response to Mario.

B　Both Mario and Lucy treat "field of study" as the more general category, and "genuinely autonomous discipline" as a special subcategory—even though they do not agree on how the subcategory should be defined. The issue of confusing one with the other does not arise.

D　Lucy implicitly accepts the accuracy of Mario's description of cognitive science as addressing issues also addressed by other disciplines. What she disputes is Mario's conclusion that this characteristic of cognitive science means that it is not a genuinely autonomous discipline. So (D) misdescribes Lucy's response to Mario.

E　The issue of Mario's field of study never comes up. Lucy mentions philosophy only to show that Mario's belief about philosophy is inconsistent with the principle on which he bases his conclusion about cognitive science.

- *Difficulty Level: 3*

Question 11

The Correct Answer:

A Mario's position is that to be a genuinely autonomous discipline, a field of study must have a domain of inquiry all its own. So Mario must hold that (A) is false. Lucy, on the other hand, claims that all that a field of study requires to be a genuinely autonomous discipline is a unique methodology. So Lucy would accept that (A) is true. Thus Mario and Lucy are committed to disagreeing about (A).

The Incorrect Answer Choices:

B, D Since Mario says nothing at all about unique methodologies, he is not committed to any view about the truth of either (B) or (D). Thus, Mario and Lucy cannot be committed to disagreeing about either (B) or (D).

C Lucy is committed to the truth of (C), because for her, having a unique methodology is all it takes for a field of study to be a genuinely autonomous discipline. Mario's statements, on the other hand, do not commit him to a position on (C). He explicitly denies that a field can be a genuinely autonomous discipline if it does not have a domain of inquiry all its own. But from Mario's statements we can't tell whether he is committed to the belief that all fields that have a unique methodology and a domain of inquiry all their own are genuinely autonomous disciplines. So Mario's statements do not commit him to agreeing or to disagreeing with Lucy about (C).

E Lucy's statements commit her to only one thing regarding fields of study that are not genuinely autonomous disciplines: they lack a unique methodology. Thus nothing Lucy says commits her to any view about the truth of (E). Therefore, Mario and Lucy cannot be committed to disagreeing about (E).

- *Difficulty Level: 3*

Question 12

Overview: The argument states its conclusion first: it is always worthwhile to risk losing one's life in order to preserve or gain one's freedom. This conclusion is supported by means of an example that is meant to show that if one were stripped of one's freedom, one's life would have so little value that it could not really be called a life.

You are asked to identify a flaw in this line of reasoning.

The Correct Answer:

C The argument bases its conclusion on an example it gives of a loss of freedom: being locked in a bare cement room with no hope of escape. This is clearly an extreme case of loss of freedom. It could well be that it would be worth risking one's life to avoid this extreme case yet not be worth risking one's life to ward off less severe limitations of one's freedom. So it is certainly a flaw in the argument that it jumps from consideration of a single extreme case to the universal claim that one's freedom is **always** worth the risk of losing one's life.

The Incorrect Answer Choices:

A The argument's conclusion clearly places a very high value on freedom: it is so valuable that it is worth the risk of losing one's life. But freedom's having very high value is not incompatible with something else having even higher value.

B The argument's conclusion implies that one should not shy away from trying to preserve or gain one's freedom just because doing so would put one's life at risk. But this does not mean that the argument assumes that it is always possible to rebel physically against a restriction of one's freedom.

D The argument is concerned with the risks that are worthwhile for preserving one's freedom. The question of what risks should be taken to preserve the freedom of others is irrelevant to the argument that is presented.

E The argument is an attempt to establish that risking one's life for one's freedom is always justified. The argument does not go into the issue of who is likely to take this risk, so it cannot be committing the reasoning error that (E) describes.

- *Difficulty Level: 3*

Question 13

Overview: Ramona says that one of the things that make a university education valuable is the intellectual growth that is stimulated by exposure to a wide range of ideas. She claims that an entire category of students attend universities without receiving this benefit: students who choose technical majors in order to do well on the job market.

Martin makes two points in responding to Ramona. First, he cities the example of his brother to show that students who do not choose technical majors can end up with jobs that they could have gotten without a university education. And second, students who choose technical majors do not entirely forego the benefits of being exposed to ideas from outside of those majors.

You are asked to evaluate the exchange between Ramona and Martin and identify something that they probably agree about, given what each of them says.

The Correct Answer:

C   Both Ramona and Martin appear to think that the classes that form the core of technical majors are classes that do not expose students to a wide range of ideas. So they are probably in agreement on (C). Ramona is very direct about this: she says that students who choose technical majors miss the intellectual growth that results from exposure to a wide range of ideas. Martin disagrees with her that they miss this growth entirely, but this is because, according to Martin, they have to take some liberal arts classes.

The Incorrect Answer Choices:

A   Based on what Ramona and Martin say, they very likely agree with each other that (A) is false, rather than that it is true. Martin apparently believes that liberal arts classes in general, not just English classes, can stimulate intellectual growth. Ramona does not mention any specific category of classes as stimulating intellectual growth, but she seems to view any classes associated with nontechnical majors as potentially providing opportunities for intellectual growth.

B   Neither Ramona nor Martin says anything that commits either of them to a position on what sorts of graduates actually get good jobs. Ramona claims that many students who choose technical majors do so because they would like to get good jobs. Martin talks about his brother, whose job Martin does not seem to regard as a good job. But their conversation leaves open the possibility that they believe that some graduates with degrees in nontechnical subjects get good jobs.

D   There is no strong indication that either Ramona or Martin accepts what (D) says. Ramona calls intellectual growth one of the primary values of a university education, and she does not like to see any students missing out on this. But she does not say that intellectual growth is more important than financial security. Martin certainly seems willing to grant that intellectual growth is of value, but his statements are even less specific than Ramona's with regard to how great that value is.

E   Neither Ramona nor Martin says anything that could be taken as an indication of how important either of them thinks financial security is. They both grant that financial security is important to certain students, and at least Ramona seems to feel that those students rate financial considerations too highly. But Ramona's and Martin's own assessment of the importance of financial security is not revealed in their conversation.

- *Difficulty Level: 5*

Question 14

Overview: The essayist's conclusion is presented as a suspicion that there might have been spacecraft sighted near Earth that are extraterrestrial in origin. The essayist provides only a rather slender basis for this very specific suspicion: British governmental security agencies have not been forthcoming with information about sightings of UFOs made by these agencies, and requests by a civilian researcher for more information have been brushed aside.

The question asks for something that would strengthen the essayist's argument. Clearly this argument, as it stands, needs something to connect the fact that the security agencies are so secretive with the idea that the UFOs were extraterrestrial in origin. Without such a connection, the essayist's conclusion is essentially unsupported.

The Correct Answer:

B (B) supplies the connection, discussed in the "Overview," between government secretiveness and the idea that the UFOs were extraterrestrial. Since the British government apparently is withholding information about UFOs, it follows from (B) that those UFOs have been established to be from somewhere other than Earth.

The Incorrect Answer Choices:

A The assertion that the British government is generally not forthcoming with secure information suggests that there is nothing unusual about its reluctance to provide information about UFOs. So that reluctance gives us no reason to infer anything about the nature of the UFOs. Thus (A) certainly does not strengthen the essayist's argument.

C Even if having something to hide about UFOs were the British government's only motive for not giving civilian researchers access to data, as (C) suggests, this alone does not indicate what it is about UFOs that the government doesn't want people to know. In particular, it doesn't indicate that the British government wishes to hide knowledge that UFOs are extraterrestrial in origin. So (C) does not provide the needed connection between government secrecy and UFOs being from other planets.

D (D) suggests that the British government's refusal to provide information about UFOs could well be due to a general distrust of civilian researchers rather than because it is trying to conceal the extraterrestrial origin of the UFOs. So (D) does not strengthen the essayist's argument.

E If the British government has always attempted to deny the existence of UFOs, whether or not they were extraterrestrial, then its continued reluctance to release information about sightings of UFOs appears simply a continuation of this general pattern, rather than specifically pointing to sightings of extraterrestrial spacecraft.

- *Difficulty Level: 5*

Question 15

Overview: The argument compares two drugs—S and T—each of which is effective in reducing the severity of heart attacks that are otherwise potentially fatal. T costs $2,000 more per patient than S, but it also saves one additional patient in every 120 patients treated. From these figures the argument concludes that it would cost $240,000 (that is, 120 times $2,000) to save one additional life. The argument embeds this conclusion in its own, further conclusion that the decision society has to make is whether to pay this price for one additional life saved.

The question asks you to identify an assumption on which this argument relies.

The Correct Answer:

D   The argument, in arriving at the figure of $240,000, assumes that, on average, drug T would have to be given instead of drug S to 120 patients in order for one extra life to be saved. But suppose that there were an easy way to determine for each patient whether drug S would improve his or her chances of survival as much as drug T does. If this were possible, then drug T would be given only where it made the difference. So saving the one extra life would not cost $240,000 but something closer to $2,000. (D) is a statement of the assumption that there is no such possibility.

The Incorrect Answer Choices:

A   The argument does not consider side effects for either drug. The only measure the argument uses to compare the effects of the two drugs is number of lives saved. If, contrary to (A), drug T had all the side effects that drug S has, the argument would not be affected. So the argument does not rely on assuming that (A) is true.

B   For the argument it does not matter when the two drugs were developed. All that matters is that currently both are available. And even though the argument does rely on the information that drug T costs $2,000 more per treatment than drug S, it does not matter from the point of view of the argument whether any of that higher cost has to do with higher development costs. So the argument does not rely on assuming either part of (B).

C   Suppose that, contrary to (C), drug S and drug T both have to be given within the same amount of time after a heart attack in order to be effective. Would the argument be affected? No, not as long as the cost of each drug and the proportion of patients whose lives they save does not change, and there's no reason to think these would change. So the argument does not rely on assuming (C).

E   The argument neither directly nor indirectly touches on the issue of how quickly either drug works. The only fact that, for purposes of the argument, distinguishes the effects of drug T from those of drug S is that drug T saves more lives than drug S does. So the argument does not depend on assuming (E).

■ *Difficulty Level: 3*

Question 16

Overview: The researcher notes that there is a strong positive correlation between students' educational level and their mathematical skills. The researcher cautions that it would be wrong to conclude that education improves mathematical skills. This is because students with better mathematical skills might be the ones who tend to reach higher educational levels.

Stripped to its basics, the reasoning is as follows: a strong positive correlation between levels of A and levels of B does not prove that A is a causal factor in producing B, since it is possible that what really explains the correlation is B being a causal factor in producing A.

The question is, which of five arguments is most similar in its structure to the researcher's argument.

The Correct Answer:

B This argument is closely parallel to the argument in the passage. Rephrasing the argument makes this clear: "The strong positive correlation between being a professional athlete and superior athletic performance does not prove that being a professional athlete is a causal factor in producing the superior athletic performance, since it is possible that superior athletic performance is a causal factor in an athlete's turning professional."

The Incorrect Answer Choices:

A This argument speaks of results that suggest a correlation between universities and the quality of certain papers produced there. But instead of considering two different explanations of this observed correlation, this argument says that there is no need for an explanation because there might not actually be a correlation. The apparent correlation might be due to an error that is reflected in the results. So the structure of this argument is not parallel to that of the argument in the passage.

C This argument, like the argument in the passage, notes a strong positive correlation, in this case between graduating from a prestigious school and getting a good job. But, in contrast to the argument in the passage, this argument does not suppose that either of the two facts that are correlated could just as well have been the causal factor. The argument assumes that getting a good job could only have been an effect, and it goes on to justify a skeptical stance toward one explanation of this effect by presenting another possible explanation. So the pattern of reasoning is different from the pattern in the argument in the passage.

D This argument would be very similar to the argument in the passage if at the end it said, "since it is possible that those who have a knack for politics are more likely to get a law degree than people who are not good at politics." Instead, this argument casts doubt on the data from which the survey results were derived, thereby calling into question whether there is a genuine correlation to be explained.

E This argument, rather than presenting some general correlation and then speculating about how to explain it, just presents a fact about a particular group of people. The argument warns against jumping to a particular conclusion in trying to explain this fact, pointing out that there are further data that disconfirm that conclusion. Thus this argument, unlike the argument in the passage, does not deal with a general correlation at all.

■ *Difficulty Level: 1*

Question 17

Overview: The passage describes the results of a study in which two groups of people are asked different versions of a question. The version that asks, "Have you ever awakened seemingly paralyzed?" is the more general of the two. The more specific version asks, "Have you ever awakened seemingly paralyzed, with a sense of a strange presence in the room?" Since anyone who ever awakened seemingly paralyzed under the more specific circumstances would have awakened seemingly paralyzed, one would expect at least as many yes-responses to the more general version as to the more specific version. The actual results suggest that just the opposite is true: the more specific version of the question elicits a yes-response much more frequently than the general version of the question.

The Correct Answer:

E The only difference between the two questions is that the one question suggests a specific context in which the event to be recalled—awakening seemingly paralyzed—was embedded. So it is reasonable to hypothesize that this difference is responsible for the surprising outcome. (E) essentially says this.

The Incorrect Answer Choices:

A The information in the passage does not support any specific hypothesis about whether feeling a strange presence causes one to feel paralyzed, or vice versa. (A) isn't supported any more strongly than the claim that waking up seemingly paralyzed causes people to experience a sense of a strange presence in the room. Moreover, (A) sheds no light on why subjects' responses should differ depending only on whether they're asked the more general or the more specific version of the question.

B All we know about the control group is that only 14 percent reported that they remembered waking up seemingly paralyzed. So we know nothing about how many of the members of the control group remembered waking up with a sense of a strange presence in the room. For all we know, more than 40 percent of the members of the control group—that is, more than for the first group—remembered waking up with a sense of a strange presence in the room.

C For the information in the passage to support (C), there would have to be some indication in the passage that there were few, if any, people who had awakened with a sense of a strange presence in the room **without** seeming to be paralyzed. But since the passage gives no indication about any such people, (C) is not supported.

D The passage explicitly says that the 200 subjects in the control group were different from the ones in the experimental group. So, as far as we can tell from the passage, each of the randomly selected subjects of the study answered only a single question. There was consequently no opportunity for any of them to give inconsistent reports.

- *Difficulty Level: 2*

Question 18

Overview: Micki asserts that the consequence of a certain action—one person walking across the grass—is that the grass doesn't get hurt. Sid responds to Micki by arguing that if everyone believed as she does, everyone would walk across the grass, with the result that the grass would be hurt.

The question asks you to identify the best account of what makes Sid's argument questionable.

The Correct Answer:

B Sid's argument attempts to trace the consequence of everyone believing Micki's statement that the grass won't be hurt if just one person walks across it. He concludes that the consequence of everyone believing this statement is that everyone walks across the grass and the grass in turn gets hurt. Sid apparently regards his argument as a refutation of Micki's statement. But Micki has merely made a claim about the consequences of one person's actions; she said nothing about the consequences of everyone believing this claim. So in his effort to disprove Micki's statement, Sid treats that statement—which is about the consequence of an action—as though it were about the consequences of everyone believing the statement. This makes Sid's argument questionable because he has disproved a different statement than the one he argued against.

The Incorrect Answer Choices:

A Sid's argument attempts to disprove a statement Micki makes, but Micki's statement is about the consequences of an action and not about the action itself. So (A) does not describe what Sid's argument does.

C Sid's argument explores what would happen if everyone believed the statement that one person walking across the grass doesn't hurt it. But this is not the same as treating that statement as though it were believed by everyone. So (C) does not describe what Sid's argument does.

D Sid's argument just tries to disprove Micki's claim that a certain action would not hurt the grass. Whether there are circumstances under which hurting the grass is justified is not relevant to Micki's claim or to Sid's argument against it.

E Sid's argument tries to undermine Micki's statement solely by developing a line of reasoning that shows that the statement is false. His argument does not attack Micki's character.

■ *Difficulty Level: 3*

Question 19

Overview: The editorial argues that "me too" drugs can provide new benefits to consumers, since their entry into the market can result in a price reduction for the drugs they resemble.

The question asks what would strengthen this argument, that is, make it more likely that the argument's conclusion is true.

The Correct Answer:

A If, as (A) says, some "me too" drugs are more effective than the drugs they were designed to duplicate, then their entry into the market can benefit consumers by providing them better alternatives to previously existing drugs. The support for the conclusion that "me too" drugs can benefit consumers is thus strengthened.

The Incorrect Answer Choices:

B According to (B), a prohibition on "me too" drugs would make more money available for the development of innovative drugs. Since innovative drugs would benefit consumers, allowing "me too" drugs deprives consumers of a benefit if (B) is true.

C If pharmaceutical companies often make more money on a "me too" drug than on an original drug, this may be good news for those companies and their shareholders, but it is not a benefit to the consumers of drugs.

D It seems unlikely that (D) would have any effect on the editorial's argument since there is no indication that all pharmaceutical companies would develop "me too" drugs. But if all pharmaceutical companies did develop those drugs, that would certainly weaken the argument because consumers would be deprived of the benefit of some innovative drugs.

E If (E) is true, the development of "me too" drugs means that pharmaceutical companies cannot recoup their investment in some innovative drugs. But if pharmaceutical companies lose money on the development of innovative drugs, their incentive to keep developing such drugs will weaken, to the detriment of consumers.

■ *Difficulty Level: 2*

Question 20

Overview: The argument draws a dual conclusion: none of the Shoemaker-Levy 9 fragments penetrated to Jupiter's lower atmosphere, and Shoemaker-Levy 9 was composed of rock rather than ice. This conclusion is based on an intermediate conclusion: the collision between the Shoemaker-Levy 9 fragments and Jupiter involved no water. This intermediate conclusion in turn is based on the observation that the collision of the Shoemaker-Levy 9 fragments with Jupiter resulted in formations that showed no signs of water.

The question asks you to identify an assumption on which the argument depends.

The Correct Answer:

B If, contrary to (B), Jupiter's lower atmosphere could be penetrated without there being any signs of water in the resulting formations, then the absence of formations containing water could not be evidence that the lower atmosphere had not been penetrated. The argument, as far as it is concerned with whether the comet fragments penetrated to Jupiter's lower atmosphere, would then fail. Thus, since (B) has to be true if the argument is to succeed, the argument depends on assuming (B).

The Incorrect Answer Choices:

A The argument describes Shoemaker-Levy 9 as a comet and infers that it was composed of rock, not ice. And Shoemaker-Levy 9 is the only comet that is considered in the argument. So there is clearly no need for the argument to assume that comets tend to be composed largely of ice. And since the argument doesn't even mention asteroids, there is no need to assume anything about their composition.

C The argument does not relate the inference that Shoemaker-Levy 9 was composed of rock to the size of the explosion that resulted from the collision between Shoemaker-Levy 9 and Jupiter. Rather, the argument bases this inference on the observation that there was no water involved in the collision. Thus (C), while it may be consistent with the argument, is not an assumption on which it depends.

D The argument asserts that all the formations were the same in one respect: none of them showed any signs of water. The argument is based entirely on this feature of the formations. So the argument does not assume that there are any other similarities among the formations.

E There is no indication in the argument that detection of the explosion from Earth presented any difficulties. So while (E) may be true in theory, it is not something that has any bearing on the reasoning in the argument.

■ *Difficulty Level: 2*

Question 21

Overview: The argument goes roughly as follows: Certain experts used to say that introducing non-native plants into the wild was a good idea. They were subsequently proved wrong. Now the same experts say that genetically engineered plants are harmless. We should conclude that they are wrong this time, too.

The flaw in this argument is that it overgeneralizes from a single error. The argument assumes something like: once in error, always in error.

You are asked to identify flawed reasoning that is closest in structure to the flawed reasoning in the argument in the passage.

The Correct Answer:

C   In this argument, we are told that certain economists were in error in not predicting the end of the last recession. Now the same economists say that the current economic expansion will soon be over. So it is concluded that the expansion will go on for some time. This conclusion implies that the economists will be proven wrong a second time.

The reasoning here is closely parallel to that in the argument in the passage: one past failing in someone's professional judgment is the basis for predicting that, in a new case, the judgment of those same professionals will be in error.

The Incorrect Answer Choices:

A   This argument describes people as complaining both that taxes are too high and that there are too few government services. The argument concludes that high taxes and big government go together. While it is not clear how the conclusion is supposed to follow from the premise, it is clear that the flaw is not that of inferring, from a claim that certain people have been wrong once before, that they are wrong now. So the flawed reasoning in (A) is not parallel to the flawed reasoning in the argument in the passage.

B   This argument lacks the element of overgeneralizing from an error in someone's professional judgment. This argument does not assume that film critics are consistently wrong. So the flawed reasoning in this argument is not parallel to that in the argument in the passage.

D   It's not clear why the reasons that this argument presents for ignoring children's pleadings for trendy toys should be compelling. But it is clear that this argument doesn't try to prove its point by exposing an error in a past professional judgment and arguing that subsequent professional judgment must also be in error. Consequently, the reasoning in (D) is not similar to the reasoning in the argument in the passage.

E   This argument tells us that certain population experts have erroneously predicted food shortages in the past and now the same population experts are predicting food shortages again. The argument concludes that if these experts are right this time around, it won't be because their predictions somehow caused the food shortages.

For the reasoning in (E) to be parallel to that in the argument in the passage, (E) would have to have had a different conclusion. If the conclusion had read, "This time around, they'll be wrong again," there would have been a close parallel. But the actual conclusion in (E) does not match anything in the argument in the passage.

■ *Difficulty Level: 4*

Question 22

Overview: The argument presents two situations in which "being at home" and "being in one's house" don't coincide. It then concludes that one's being at home is not required for one's being in one's own house.

A close look at the argument shows that only one of the two situations presented is actually relevant to the conclusion. The conclusion, slightly restated, just says that one can be in one's own house without being at home. And that is the point made in the second sentence and illustrated by the case of one's house being rented out to others, so that it does not serve as one's home. The point made in the first sentence—that one can be at home without being in one's house—is irrelevant to the conclusion.

You are asked to identify an accurate description of the relationship between the first sentence of the argument and the argument's conclusion.

The Correct Answer:

C   The claim that the question alludes to—that one can be at home without being in one's house—is presented in the first sentence of the passage. This claim is compatible with the truth of the conclusion. If it were not, it would undermine the conclusion, and it clearly doesn't. And the claim is also compatible with the falsity of the conclusion. If it were not, it would be a compelling reason for accepting the conclusion as true. The only conclusion that can be drawn from the claim, however, is that being in one's house is not a requirement for being at home. This is the reverse of the conclusion drawn in the argument.

The Incorrect Answer Choices:

A   As the "Overview" points out, the first sentence plays no role in establishing the conclusion. In particular, then, it is not required to establish the conclusion.

B   The only thing that the conclusion could refute is the claim that being in one's home is required for one's being in one's own house. The first sentence clearly does not represent this claim.

D   The claim used the phrase "at home" and the conclusion does as well. But the claim doesn't point out anything about this phrase or even draw attention to it.

E   As mentioned in the discussion of (C), the truth of the first sentence is compatible with the truth of the conclusion, which means that the first sentence does not contradict the conclusion.

■ *Difficulty Level: 5*

Question 23

Overview: According to the economist, whether inflation or deflation occurs depends on how fast the money supply grows relative to the growth of the production of goods and services. The economist then argues that since the money supply in the economist's country is very stable, that country is unlikely to experience significant inflation or significant deflation.

The question asks about an assumption on which the economist's argument depends.

The Correct Answer:

C   Note that the economist says that deflation occurs when the production of goods and services grows more than the money supply does. So if the production of goods and services grew markedly, significant deflation would result. Thus, the argument for the conclusion that the economist's country is unlikely to have significant inflation or deflation depends on the assumption that the production of goods and services is unlikely to grow markedly.

The Incorrect Answer Choices:

A, E   Given how the economist depicts both inflationary and deflationary economic conditions, it is clear that what must be kept stable is the balance between the growth of the money supply and the increase in goods and services produced. Keeping only one side of this relationship stable does not protect against inflation or deflation if the other side is permitted to shift significantly. So the economist's argument does not depend on assuming either (A) or (E).

B   According to the economist, the fact that gold anchors the country's money supply is responsible for the stability of that money supply. But nothing the economist says suggests that having an anchor such as gold is the only way to have a stable money supply. Hence, there is no reason to think that the economist's argument depends on assuming (B).

D   Suppose (D) were false, and inflation were more likely than deflation to occur in the economist's country. Would the argument fail? No. The argument concludes that it is unlikely that either significant inflation or significant deflation will occur. But the argument would be unaffected if a tiny degree of inflation were more likely than a tiny degree of deflation. The argument would be similarly unaffected if, while both significant inflation and significant deflation are both very unlikely, significant inflation is the more likely of the two. So (D) is not an assumption on which the economist's argument depends.

■ *Difficulty Level: 5*

Question 24

Overview: The agricultural economist's argument is based on the claim that the only way to increase agricultural production without reducing biodiversity is to abandon conventional agriculture. From this the conclusion is drawn that if we choose to sustain economic growth, we should radically modify agricultural techniques, that is, abandon conventional agriculture.

The question asks what principle most helps justify the agricultural economist's reasoning.

The Correct Answer:

B The argument leaves open the possibility that, if we don't care what happens to biodiversity, then it might well be possible to increase agricultural production, and to sustain economic growth, by continuing to rely on conventional agriculture. And since the argument never says that we should care about biodiversity, it can't really properly infer its conclusion. (B) says that if we try to sustain economic growth, we should do so in a way that doesn't reduce biodiversity. Since sustaining economic growth requires increasing agricultural production, and since the only way to increase agricultural production without reducing biodiversity is to abandon conventional agriculture, it follows that we should abandon conventional agriculture. Thus (B), together with the information that the argument provides, justifies the agricultural economist's conclusion.

The Incorrect Answer Choices:

A The conclusion of the agricultural economist's argument concerns what we should do to increase agricultural production. Thus a principle like (A), which states a circumstance under which agricultural production should be reduced, cannot justify the argument.

C (C) says that we should not sustain economic growth if there is no increase in agricultural production. But according to the argument, sustaining economic growth requires increasing agricultural production. In other words, it's not even possible to sustain economic growth without increasing agricultural production. So (C) just tells us that we should not do something that it is impossible to do anyway. A principle like this cannot add anything to the argument.

D The premise of the agricultural economist's argument states that we can increase agricultural production and preserve biodiversity. Since no choice between the two needs to be made, the question whether one or the other is more important does not need to be addressed. The principle in (D), however, is concerned only with that question and is thus not relevant to the agricultural economist's reasoning.

E (E) says that agricultural techniques should not be radically modified unless doing so would help increase agricultural production. So (E) sets out a condition that must be met for it to be true that agricultural techniques should be radically modified. But this couldn't possibly enhance the case for the view that agricultural techniques should be radically modified, and that case needs to be enhanced in order to help justify the agricultural economist's reasoning.

■ *Difficulty Level: 5*

Question 1

Overview: The conclusion of the argument is that it is imperative that a trained editor look over journalists' work with an eye toward detecting and removing their biases in order to make reporting as objective as possible. The grounds offered for this conclusion are that journalists' biases will inevitably enter their reporting.

The argument leaves many things unstated. For example, it assumes that editors are effective at removing biases from reporting, but it doesn't state this explicitly.

The question tells you that all but one of the answer choices are assumptions on which the argument depends. Your task is to identify the answer choice that does **not** present such an assumption.

The Correct Answer:

E If (E) is true, then trained editors do not take a serious attitude toward reporting that is not objective. But the argument suggests that trained editors take a very serious attitude toward reporting that is not objective; after all, it is said that trained editors need to go over journalist's work to make that reporting as objective as possible. So (E) is far from being an assumption of the argument; it actually goes against one of the argument's central claims.

The Incorrect Answer Choices:

A If, contrary to (A), journalists did eliminate all the biases that enter their reporting, then there would be no need for trained editors to look over journalists' work with an eye toward detecting and removing those biases. The argument therefore depends on assuming (A).

B According to the argument, the reason it is imperative for trained editors to look over journalists' work with an eye toward detecting and removing biases is to make reporting as objective as possible. So if it weren't imperative that reporting be as objective as possible, there would be no reason to conclude that oversight by trained editors is imperative. Thus, the argument depends on assuming (B).

C If, contrary to (C), objectivity in reporting is not undermined by the presence of journalists' biases, then there would be no need for trained editors to attempt to remove those biases in order to make reporting as objective as possible. So the argument depends on assuming (C).

D Suppose that, contrary to (D), trained editors were unable to detect any of the biases in journalists' reporting. There would then be no point in editors looking over that reporting in order to remove those biases. Thus, the argument depends on assuming (D).

■ *Difficulty Level: 1*

Question 2

Overview: The astronomer makes a case for choosing Mount Shalko as the site for a proposed observatory. As part of that case, the astronomer argues against an objection from critics that the observatory would be a threat to life forms that are unique to Mount Shalko. Essentially, the astronomer's argument against this objection is that the observatory would be good for wildlife because it would remove an existing threat. The existing threat comes from recreational use of Mount Shalko, which would have to cease if the observatory were built.

The Correct Answer:

C   In responding to the critics, the astronomer claims that the observatory would eliminate a threat to Mount Shalko's ecology. However, removing an existing threat can produce a net benefit only if no equally serious threats are introduced in the process. According to (C), however, having the observatory on Mount Shalko could cause just as much ecological damage as continued recreational use would. Thus, (C) weakens the astronomer's argument.

The Incorrect Answer Choices:

A   (A) simply gives some details relevant to the claim that Mount Shalko is a unique ecological site. The astronomer's argument, however, grants the ecological importance of the site. So (A) does nothing to weaken the astronomer's argument.

B   (B) indicates that a certain coalition of groups "opposes the building of the new observatory," not that this coalition objects specifically to locating the new observatory on Mount Shalko. Since the astronomer's argument only addresses the issue of whether the observatory should be built on Mount Shalko, not the prior issue of whether it should be built at all, (B) is not relevant to that argument. But even if the coalition objected specifically to locating the observatory on Mount Shalko, this would not in itself weaken the astronomer's argument. For the astronomer's argument to be weakened, we would also have to be told something about of the substance of those objections.

D   (D) mentions one possible result of locating the observatory on Mount Shalko that would clearly pose a threat to endemic wildlife (as well as to the effective operation of the observatory). But (D) tells us that this particular result will not come about. So, if anything, (D) strengthens the astronomer's argument rather than weakening it.

E   (E) has no effect on the issue of the environmental impact of building the observatory on Mount Shalko. It has some effect on the broader issue of whether Mount Shalko should be chosen as the site of the observatory, because it is an effective rejoinder to the objection that recreational opportunities would be lost if the observatory is built on Mount Shalko. But this would strengthen the astronomer's argument, not weaken it.

- *Difficulty Level: 2*

Question 3

Overview: We are told that in a photography contest open to both amateurs and professionals, most of the prizes went to amateurs. This outcome may seem surprising because we naturally expect professional photographers to be better photographers, on average, than amateurs are.

We are told that all but one of the answer choices provide possible explanations of this outcome. The task is to identify the one answer choice that does **not** by itself provide such an explanation.

The Correct Answer:

E (E) compares the number of amateurs entering the contest this year with the number of amateurs entering the contest in previous years. If more amateurs had won prizes this year than had done so in previous years, (E) would help explain such an increase, but the outcome that needs to be explained is that more amateurs than professionals won prizes in this year's contest. By itself, (E) gives us no insight into why amateurs would win more prizes than professionals.

The Incorrect Answer Choices:

A If (A) is true, the amateur photographers in the contest had a certain strength in numbers. So even if the amateur photographers who entered the contest were not, on average, as good as the professionals who entered, the amateurs could still win more prizes simply because of their greater numbers. So (A) could explain why more amateurs than professionals won prizes.

B (B) supplies a straightforward explanation of the outcome. If the judges determined prizes on the basis of how appealing they themselves found the photographs, and if, in general, they preferred amateur photographs to professional ones, then it is not surprising that more amateurs than professionals won prizes.

C Even if the overall quality of professional photographs was higher than the overall quality of amateur photographs, the very best amateur photographs might well be better than most average-quality professional photographs. Thus, (C) could explain the outcome.

D (D) says that each category in the contest was open either to amateurs or to professionals but not to both. And, according to (D), there were more categories for amateurs than for professionals. So, because prizes were awarded in each category, it was inevitable that more prizes were won by amateurs.

- *Difficulty Level: 3*

Question 4

Overview: Here we are presented with a piece of information: the average 40-year-old North American will have watched more than one million TV commercials in his or her lifetime. And from this piece of information a conclusion is drawn: the TV commercial has influenced North American habits of thought.

As it stands, this conclusion does not follow logically from the information offered, because no link has been established between extensive exposure to TV commercials and habits of thought. Your task is to identify the answer choice that provides a suitable link.

The Correct Answer:

B Watching more than one million TV commercials is being exposed to TV commercials in great quantity. So if it is true, as (B) says, that **anything** that people are exposed to in great quantity influences their habits of thought, then it follows that the average North American's habits of thought are influenced by TV commercials.

The Incorrect Answer Choices:

A If, as (A) says, the habits of thought that people develop are largely determined by external influences, that doesn't mean that TV commercials are among the external influences that have this effect. Thus, the conclusion does not follow if (A) is assumed.

C, D Either (C) or (D), if assumed, might help explain the very large number of TV commercials North Americans watch on average. However, the argument requires some indication that watching these TV commercials has an influence on habits of thought. Neither (C) nor (D) provides any such indication, so the conclusion does not follow if either (C) or (D) is assumed.

E The argument requires a link between certain specific types of communication—TV commercials—and habits of thought. (E) says merely that such a link exists between **certain** forms of communication to which people are subjected and those people's habits of thought. Since (E) does not establish that TV commercials are among those forms of communication, the conclusion does not follow if (E) is assumed.

- *Difficulty Level: 1*

Question 5

Overview: The conclusion of the argument is that, over the long run, oxygen-removing refrigerators will prove far less expensive than current models. The grounds offered for this conclusion are that energy costs for an oxygen-removing refrigerator are lower than those for conventional refrigerators. The energy costs are said to be lower because the oxygen-removing refrigerators don't have to keep food as cold to prevent it from spoiling.

You are looking for something that the argument should have done in order to make a good case for its conclusion, but did not do.

The Correct Answer:

A The only basis for the argument's prediction that oxygen-removing refrigerators will be less expensive is their lower energy costs. But energy consumption is just one factor in determining the long-term expense of an appliance. Other factors may include purchase price, maintenance cost, and durability. Thus, the argument is vulnerable to the criticism that it overlooks expenses other than energy costs. So (A) expresses one thing that the argument doesn't do but should have done.

The Incorrect Answer Choices:

B The argument's sole concern is the relative expense, over the long run, of oxygen-removing refrigerators compared with current refrigerators. The issue of customer discomfort with the new oxygen-removing refrigerators is not relevant to this concern, so it is not legitimate to criticize the argument for not addressing this issue.

C The argument asserts that a membrane that can quickly remove oxygen from a refrigerator has been developed and goes on to compare the expenses associated with such refrigerators with those associated with current models of refrigerators. But to do this cost comparison it is not necessary to understand the technology that enabled the oxygen-removing membrane to be developed. So the argument cannot be legitimately criticized for not doing (C).

D The argument tells us that current refrigerators, in order to keep food from spoiling, have to be kept colder than oxygen-removing refrigerators. So by suggesting that current refrigerators are effective in preventing food spoilage if they are kept cold enough, the argument does, at least to some degree, take into account the effectiveness of current refrigerator technology. Thus, the argument cannot be faulted for not taking this into account.

E The argument is strictly about comparing costs associated with the two types of refrigerator. The issue of inconvenience associated with food spoilage does not enter into this comparison. Arguably, the cost associated with food spoilage is relevant, but (E) only addresses the issue of convenience. So although the argument does not do (E), it cannot legitimately be criticized for not doing so.

■ *Difficulty Level: 1*

Question 6

Overview: The passage tells us that there was a decrease in the overall number of bass caught downstream from a power plant shortly after the power plant opened and began discharging wastewater into the river. The task is to select the one answer choice that does not point to an explanation of this decrease.

The Correct Answer:

C The decrease to be explained is a decrease in the **total number** of bass caught by all the anglers combined. (C) tells us that there were more anglers fishing for bass. This might explain why each angler, on average, caught fewer bass, but it cannot explain why the combined catch was lower.

The Incorrect Answer Choices:

A, E Any decline in the total number of bass in the river could explain why the total number of bass caught by anglers declined. According to (A), the number of fish that prey on bass has increased in the river. According to (E), some of the bass's natural habitat has been destroyed. Both (A) and (E) make it likely that the total number of bass in the river has declined. So either (A) or (E) could explain the decrease.

B The situation (B) describes would be likely to reduce the number of bass in the particular part of the river in which the anglers fish, and fewer bass in that part of the river means that fewer bass are available for catching. So (B) could explain why the total catch in that area has declined.

D If fewer anglers are fishing for bass, it is reasonable to expect fewer bass overall to be caught—even though it might mean more bass caught per individual angler. Thus, (D) could explain the decrease described.

■ *Difficulty Level: 4*

Question 7

Overview: The argument draws an inference about the originality of existing works of ancient literature, science, and philosophy from the frequency with which those works refer to works that no longer exist. The argument evidently relies on a principle that connects a work's originality with the frequency with which it refers to other works.

You are asked to pick out the additional statement that, if added to the argument, would most help justify its conclusion.

The Correct Answer:

A The statement in (A), if added to the argument, would supply a principle that is crucial to the argument. (A) indicates that works that contain frequent references to other works tend to be derivative, that is, unoriginal. So the fact that the existing works make frequent references to other works is evidence that they are not very original. Thus, adding (A) to the argument helps justify the argument's conclusion that the existing works are not the most original work produced in ancient times.

The Incorrect Answer Choices:

B (B) gives us evidence that at least some of the missing works were laudable. But being laudable and being original are different things. Adding (B) to the argument could help justify its conclusion if the argument also provided a link between being laudable and being original, but the argument contains no such link.

C If a large number of ancient texts have been lost, it would seem likely that much original work was lost with them. But it doesn't make it any less likely that some of the existing works are among the most original. So adding (C) to the argument would not help justify its conclusion.

D (D) might suggest that books containing subversive ideas were more likely to be destroyed than books not containing such ideas. This would help to justify the argument's conclusion if it was accepted that subversiveness is evidence of originality. Nothing in the argument, however links subversiveness with originality. Without such a link, adding (D) to the argument does not help justify its conclusion.

E (E) raises questions about what should properly be called an original idea. But it raises these questions equally with respect to ancient works that still exist and ancient works that we no longer have. So (E) does not help justify the conclusion that the works we no longer have include work that is more original than anything in the ancient works that still exist.

■ *Difficulty Level: 4*

Question 8

Overview: The first sentence of the passage gives a definition of a metaphor, a term that figures importantly in the argument. The second sentence reports a claim and labels those who make it "extremists." The third sentence rejects the position of the so-called extremists, and then presents grounds to justify this rejection.

The question asks you to identify the main conclusion of the argument. Keep in mind that the main conclusion of an argument is the claim or position that the other parts of the argument are meant to support. The main conclusion can neither be something that is offered in support of something else stated in the argument nor something that is asserted without anything offered in its support.

The Correct Answer:

A The argument culminates in the first part of the third sentence, which says "But this cannot be so." This is the only conclusion in the argument, because it is the only part of the argument for which support is offered. In context, this statement says that it is not true that "all uses of language are metaphorical." Since (A) also says this, (A) accurately expresses the main conclusion of the argument.

The Incorrect Answer Choices:

B (B) cannot be the main conclusion because it is a position that the argument does not even endorse. The argument explicitly rejects the view that all uses of words are metaphorical, and it maintains only that **some** uses of words must be literal, not that all are.

C (C) is a rephrasing of the second part of the third sentence. Since that part of the argument is offered as support for another claim—the claim made in the first part of the sentence—it cannot be the main conclusion of the argument.

D (D) is a compressed version of the definition found in the argument. Since that definition is presented with no support from elsewhere in the argument, (D) is not the main conclusion of the argument.

E In what it says, (E) is similar to the second part of the third sentence. Since that part of the argument is not the main conclusion, neither is (E). Also note that (E) goes beyond what is stated in the argument; nothing in the argument, for example, talks about the meanings of words being fixed by convention. This is another reason why (E) cannot be the main conclusion.

■ *Difficulty Level: 5*

Question 9

Overview: The argument draws the conclusion that, contrary to popular belief, top management of large corporations do not behave indifferently to the needs and aspirations of employees. It bases this conclusion on the results of a recent poll of the CEOs of 125 large corporations. In that poll, the overwhelming majority of CEOs claimed to set a very high priority on employee training and welfare.

The question indicates the reasoning in this argument is vulnerable to criticism and asks you to pick the answer choice that describes what makes it problematic.

The Correct Answer:

D The conclusion of the argument is about how top management actually behaves. But this conclusion is not supported by evidence about behavior; the only evidence offered is what CEOs claim about their priorities in response to a poll. People's behavior, however, may very well fail to reflect the values they claim to hold. In light of this, some justification is required for treating a claim about priorities as a reliable indication of actual behavior in any particular case, and the argument can legitimately be criticized for not providing any such justification.

The Incorrect Answer Choices:

A The argument takes a sample of chief executive officers to be representative of top management. This is not controversial, so there seems to be no reason to give a precise definition of "top management." A precise definition of "top management," if one could be given, would not make the argument any clearer than it is. So the argument cannot legitimately be criticized on the grounds presented in (A).

B If someone actually considers something a "top priority," then that person cannot be "indifferent" to that thing. This simply follows from the meaning of the two terms. Thus, the argument cannot legitimately be criticized for presuming that people are not indifferent to something that they consider a top priority.

C The argument does not depend on any view about how appropriate the CEOs' priorities are. The argument's only concern about priorities is with CEOs' claims about their priorities and the connection between those claims and the behavior of top management. Thus, the argument does not do what (C) describes.

E The argument bases its generalization about how the top management of large corporations behaves on a sample of 125 CEOs of large corporations. There is no reason to think that such a sample is unrepresentative of top management of large corporations.

- *Difficulty Level: 2*

Question 10

Overview: The argument presents some interesting information: the percentage of people scheduled to fly on a Friday the thirteenth who cancelled or did not show up for their flights was higher than the percentage on other day/date combinations of that year. The argument concludes that this shows that a significant percentage of the population would rather disrupt their travel plans than risk flying on a supposedly unlucky day.

The Correct Answer:

C (C) tells us that there was something unusual about that particular year: the Fridays that fell on the thirteenth happened to be days on which there were severe weather conditions at several major airports. These weather conditions would likely cause an unusually high rate of cancellations and no-shows, regardless of the day and date. And it is unlikely that such severe weather conditions occurred on every instance of some other day/date combination (e.g., Thursdays that fell on the eighth). So (C), by giving an alternative explanation for the high percentage of people changing their travel plans, seriously weakens the argument.

The Incorrect Answer Choices:

A (A) indicates that the people who fly actually underrepresent the degree of superstition in the general public. This suggests that, if the cancellations and no-shows indicate anything about the prevalence of the belief that Friday the thirteenth is an unlucky day, they don't show the full extent of that phenomenon in the general public. So (A) actually helps to strengthen the argument rather than weaken it.

B The argument concludes that **a significant percentage** of the population would rather disrupt their travel plans than risk flying on Friday the thirteenth. There is no estimate in the argument of what that percentage might be. It is certainly far less than 17 percent; after all, the argument suggests that only some of the cancellations and no-shows occurred because people thought that Friday the thirteenth was unlucky. So the significant percentage that the conclusion alludes to may very well be less than 5 percent of the population. So even if the surveys mentioned in (B) are accurate and less than 5 percent of the population believe that Friday the thirteenth is unlucky, this is entirely consistent with the argument.

D Most people are more apprehensive about air travel than automobile travel. So, many people might well feel that air travel—unlike automobile travel—is normally so risky that any additional risk would make them avoid it altogether. Thus, the fact that automobile traffic was no lighter than usual does not call into question the argument's conclusion.

E The information that (E) provides about airline workers has little relevance to the argument. Many airline workers work only on the ground, so even the superstitious among those workers would have little reason to stay home on Friday the thirteenth. The airline workers who do fly as part of their job are probably more comfortable with air travel than the general public, and thus less likely to avoid it if they feel that the risk is higher than usual. So (E) does not weaken the argument.

■ *Difficulty Level: 1*

Question 11

Overview: We are told about a particular problem: it is difficult to study the behavior of whales because the typical means of observation expose the whales to novel stimuli that makes them behave in unusual ways. Some biologists reason that they could get around this problem by training sea lions—which whales are accustomed to having nearby—to carry video cameras on their backs and to swim along with the whales. The biologists are undoubtedly reasoning that since the presence of sea lions isn't unusual for whales, the video-equipped sea lions won't strike whales as out of the ordinary either.

The Correct Answer:

B If (B) is false, then there is no reason to think that the trained, video-equipped sea lions will not also be a novel stimulus. And in that case, there is no reason to expect whales to display their everyday behavior around those sea lions. So if (B) is false, the biologists' reasoning is suspect. (B), therefore, is an assumption on which that reasoning depends.

The Incorrect Answer Choices:

A (A) describes one way that whales' behavior might be unusual in the presence of novel stimuli. But the biologists' reasoning doesn't depend on whales acting in one specific way around novel stimuli.

C If the trained sea lions were aware that they are carrying video cameras, that might have no effect on how they act around whales. So the biologist's reasoning doesn't depend on the sea lions being unaware of the cameras.

D From the biologists' point of view, the problem with using divers to film whales is that the presence of divers causes whales to behave in ways that are unlike their everyday behavior. There is no reason to believe that divers can't film whales at a close enough distance. Therefore, the biologists' reasoning does not depend on sea lions being able to film whales at closer range than divers could.

E The biologists' reasoning depends on whales being more accustomed to sea lions than to either divers or submarines. It does not, however, depend on whales having a preference for sea lions. If whales did prefer the presence of sea lions, that preference might cause whales to behave in unusual ways while being videotaped, which would actually undermine the biologists' plan.

▪ *Difficulty Level: 2*

Question 12

Overview: The geologist's argument is straightforward. The conclusion is that a proposed nuclear waste storage facility should not be placed under a certain mountain until scientists have investigated whether the mountain has any geological faults. Two considerations are offered in support of this conclusion. First, if a mountain has a geological fault in it, such a fault could cause failures in the storage facility after a few thousand years. And second, nuclear waste remains dangerous for many thousands of years.

The Correct Answer:

B The geologist's argument doesn't indicate the likelihood of a conclusive result from the proposed scientific investigation. So, from what we are told, the investigation may have little benefit. (B) tells us that the investigation would yield a conclusive result, so it strengthens the argument by guaranteeing that some benefit would be gained by waiting until an investigation is completed.

The Incorrect Answer Choices:

A According to the geologist, a geological fault in a mountain under which nuclear waste is buried could result in seepage of that waste within a few thousand years. If human civilization no longer exists by then, such seepage would clearly not harm human civilization. Thus, (A) suggests that there is a possibility that such seepage wouldn't be as disastrous as the geologist says. (A), therefore, does not strengthen the argument but actually weakens it.

C The geologist's argument is that, given the enormous risks posed by nuclear waste, nuclear waste should not be buried under a mountain without thoroughly investigating that mountain for geological faults. The argument does not depend in any way on the nature of the facility in which the waste would be stored nor on the original purpose of that facility. So (C) neither strengthens nor weakens the argument.

D The geologist's argument focuses on safety, not cost. (D) could explain why there might be resistance to the investigation the geologist calls for, but it does not strengthen the geologist's argument for the necessity of such an investigation.

E The geologist seems to grant that, for a few thousand years, nuclear waste could safely be stored in the proposed facility. The geologist's argument bases its conclusion on the assumption that nuclear waste stored in the facility would remain there longer than that. (E) says that this assumption is not necessarily correct, thereby undermining the geologist's argument rather than strengthening it.

■ *Difficulty Level: 1*

Question 13

Overview: According to the mall manager, teenagers congregating in large numbers in the mall have caused adult shoppers to cut down the time they spend shopping in the mall. The manager recommends discouraging the teenagers from congregating in order to achieve the goal of preventing a significant loss in overall sales. The merchant responds to the manager by pointing out that much of the total amount spent in the mall comes from the teenagers who congregate there.

The question asks you to select the answer choice that most accurately describes the merchant's response.

The Correct Answer:

B The manager's recommendation is to keep teenagers from congregating near stores. The mall's goal is to prevent a significant loss in overall sales. The relation between these two is straightforward: the goal is to be achieved by implementing the recommendation. The merchant gives information to suggest that implementing the recommendation might not have the desired effect. Thus, the merchant's response can be accurately described as giving information that pertains to the relation between the manager's recommendation and the mall's goal.

The Incorrect Answer Choices:

A If you go through each of the claims that the manager makes in support of the recommendation, you will see that the merchant's response disputes none of them.

C The merchant does not take issue with the desirability of the mall's goal but merely with the manager's recommendation for achieving it.

D The merchant's response is a reason for disagreeing with the manager's recommendation as a way of achieving the mall's goal. Thus, (D) does not accurately describe the merchant's response.

E The merchant makes no recommendation. The merchant simply points out something that is relevant to the case for the manager's recommendation.

■ *Difficulty Level: 2*

Question 14

Overview: In the initial dialogue, Wu concludes that Jurgens should not be elected mayor on the grounds that Jurgens is dishonest. Miller responds with a counterargument: Jurgens should be elected mayor on the grounds that honest people often lack the toughness required for running a city.

Notice that Miller's counterargument is extremely weak. Miller draws the bold conclusion that Jurgens should be elected mayor but says nothing that actually supports that conclusion. The only justification Miller gives for electing Jurgens as mayor is that people with a character trait that is the opposite of the one Wu objects to in Jurgens are not likely to be good mayors. This reasoning is questionable because an argument against an alternative to something is not by itself an argument in favor of that thing.

The question asks you to identify the answer choice in which Miller displays the same kind of questionable reasoning as in the initial dialogue.

The Correct Answer:

A   In (A), Wu objects to slow service at a restaurant. In response, the only justification Miller gives for returning to the restaurant is that restaurants with the opposite characteristic to the one that Wu objects to (i.e., restaurants with quick service) are not likely to be good choices. So, in both (A) and the initial dialogue, Miller's reasoning is questionable because it treats an argument against an alternative to something as though it were by itself an argument in favor of that thing.

The Incorrect Answer Choices:

B   In (B), Miller responds to Wu's argument by pointing out an advantage of the very same personality trait (aggressiveness) that Wu objected to. To match Miller's reasoning in the initial dialogue, however, Miller's response would have to be that people who are not aggressive are likely to get pushed around. Thus, Miller's reasoning in (B) is not closely parallel to Miller's reasoning in the initial dialogue.

C   In (C), Miller responds to Wu's argument by pointing out an advantage of the very same quality (brightness) that Wu objected to. To match Miller's reasoning in the initial dialogue, however, Miller's response would have to be that dull colors usually decrease people's alertness. Thus, Miller's reasoning in (C) is not closely parallel to Miller's reasoning in the initial dialogue.

D   In (D), Miller responds to Wu's argument by indicating that the quality that Wu objected to (expense) is something you might expect in the best alternative. To match Miller's reasoning in the initial dialogue, however, Miller's response would have to be that inexpensive alternatives to a software upgrade are usually not the best. Thus, Miller's reasoning in (D) is not closely parallel to Miller's reasoning in the initial dialogue.

E   In (E), Wu argues that a certain person should be hired because she has experience. In context, this argument suggests that Lyons should not be hired because Lyons lacks experience. In response, Miller argues that Lyons should be hired since everyone lacks experience when first starting out. To match Miller's reasoning in the initial dialogue, however, Miller's response would have to be that people with experience are likely to have some particular unwanted characteristic. Thus, Miller's reasoning in (B) is not closely parallel to Miller's reasoning in the initial dialogue.

■ *Difficulty Level: 5*

Question 15

Overview: The conclusion of the argument is that the historians surveyed neglect many important repositories of historical knowledge. This conclusion is based on the finding that none of these historians regard painting, architecture, music, dance, or culinary arts as the best source for historical understanding.

The Correct Answer:

C The report of the survey results merely said that none of the historians regarded painting, architecture, music, dance, or culinary arts as the **best** source for historical understanding. Many of these historians may nevertheless regard one or more of these disciplines as an important source for historical understanding. But the argument doesn't take this possibility into account when it reaches the conclusion that the historians neglect many important repositories of historical knowledge. So the argument is flawed in the way that (C) describes.

The Incorrect Answer Choices:

A The argument is focused on the issue of whether the historians that were surveyed consider certain arts to be important sources for historical understanding. If there were potential sources for historical understanding other than written texts and the arts, this would not be relevant to this issue. Moreover, the argument doesn't take (A) for granted because it states merely that **most** historians believe written texts to be the best sources, strongly suggesting that there are historians who believe that some other type of source is the best.

B The argument is focused entirely on sources of historical understanding. Therefore, the fact that it does not mention other reasons that painting, architecture, music, dance, or culinary arts might be important does not mean that the argument assumes that they are unimportant except as sources of historical knowledge.

D The argument's conclusion is that historians neglect many important sources of historical knowledge. But the argument does not depend on the view that these neglected sources, or any other sources, are better than written texts. So the argument does not take (D) for granted.

E The argument assumes that written texts are not the only important sources for historical understanding. But it does not depend on there being any sources that aren't important. So there are no grounds for thinking that the argument takes anything like (E) for granted.

■ *Difficulty Level: 5*

Question 16

Overview: This passage presents a principle about how people have to act in order to act responsibly in their professional capacity. Each answer choice presents a judgment about whether someone acted responsibly or not. Your task is to decide which judgment most closely conforms to the principle.

Note that for this principle to apply at all, the person acting has to have done so in a professional capacity. Also note that the principle indicates what must be done in order to act responsibly; it does not lay out a condition that would guarantee that one has acted responsibly.

The Correct Answer:

C In (C) you are presented with a situation in which Toril invested the company's money. Toril was evidently acting in a professional capacity and so the principle applies. According to (C), Toril acted without having investigated the risks associated with that investment. Since the risks associated with an investment are pertinent to the decision, Toril's action was based on incomplete information. So, by the principle, Toril did not act responsibly. The fact that the investment yielded a large return doesn't have any effect on whether Toril acted responsibly because the principle doesn't say anything about the consequences of an act. So the judgment in (C) conforms to the principle.

The Incorrect Answer Choices:

A, B Both (A) and (B) make judgments that someone acted responsibly. As mentioned in the "Overview," however, the principle does not lay out a condition that can guarantee that someone has acted responsibly. Judgments like those in (A) and (B), therefore, cannot be justified by the principle alone.

D Conchita was evidently acting in a professional capacity when she hired the bookkeeper, and so the principle applies. The other question is whether Conchita based her hiring decision on information that she has made a reasonable effort to verify for accuracy and completeness. There is no reason to think that she did not, since (D) makes it clear that the person she hired had never been known to make a mistake that cost his employer a lot of money. So there is no grounds for judging, on the basis of the principle, that Conchita did not act responsibly. The fact that the person she hired made a mistake that cost the company a lot of money is irrelevant because the principle doesn't say anything about the consequences of an act.

E As described in (E), Jennifer was acting in a private, not in a professional, capacity when she decided where to go on vacation. The principle, therefore, has no application to Jennifer's action.

- *Difficulty Level: 5*

Question 17

Overview: The question tells us that four of the five answer choices help explain why some people still need to wear corrective lenses in spite of having undergone RK, a surgery that is designed to eliminate the need for corrective lenses. Your task is to identify the one answer choice that doesn't help explain this.

The Correct Answer:

E (E) tells us that the extent of the nearsightedness of people who choose to undergo RK is about average. This gives us some indication that the people who undergo RK are representative of the nearsighted population in general, but it doesn't help us to explain why the surgery doesn't always eliminate the need for corrective lenses.

The Incorrect Answer Choices:

A, C, D (A), (C), and (D) each present different ways in which RK sometimes causes patients to develop new conditions that make corrective lenses necessary. So each of these answer choices helps to explain why some people still need corrective lenses after undergoing RK.

B According to (B), RK might have the effect it is ideally supposed to have in all but the most extreme cases of nearsightedness. Since the cases reported in the study might be cases of extreme nearsightedness, (B) would help explain why some people whose nearsightedness was reduced by RK might still need corrective lenses.

- *Difficulty Level: 2*

Question 18

Overview: The passage presents two rules that Chelas and Stelma are obliged to obey. The first is a requirement: they must leave their respective stations to pursue any prisoner who attempts to escape from their sector. The second is a prohibition: they are forbidden to leave their stations until their replacements arrive unless they are required to do so by the first rule.

The passage then tells us that during a certain shift Chelas had violated these rules and Stelma had not violated these rules. Your task is to find the answer choice that **cannot** be true, given what the passage says. The incorrect answer choices will each be things that could be true.

The Correct Answer:

D (D) makes two claims: first, that a prisoner attempted to escape from Chelas and Stelma's sector during their shift, and second, that neither Chelas nor Stelma left their station during that shift. If the first claim in (D) were true, both Chelas and Stelma would have been required to leave their station, but the second claim in (D) says that they didn't. So if (D) is true, they both broke the rules. According to the information in the passage, however, Stelma did not violate the rules. So at least one of the claims in (D) must be false, and thus (D) as a whole cannot be true.

The Incorrect Answer Choices:

A Suppose that no prisoners attempted to escape during the shift and that Stelma stayed at her station throughout the shift but Chelas left his station once and then came back before 9 P.M. In this case, Chelas violated the second rule. This shows that (A) could be true together with every statement in the passage.

B Suppose that a prisoner attempted to escape from Chelas and Stelma's sector at 7 P.M., and that Stelma pursued the prisoner, as required by the first rule, but Chelas did not. This shows that (B) could be true together with every statement in the passage.

C Suppose that no prisoners attempted to escape during the shift and that Stelma stayed at her station throughout her shift but Chelas temporarily left his station during his shift. In this case, Chelas violated the second rule, but Stelma did not violate either rule. So (C) could be true together with every statement in the passage.

E Suppose that Chelas and Stelma both pursued the prisoner who attempted to escape from their sector at 7 P.M. and both were back at their stations for the shift change at 9 P.M. Also suppose that Stelma, except for pursuing the prisoner, remained at her station throughout her shift, but that Chelas temporarily left his station at 6 P.M. to buy a cup of coffee, thus violating the second rule. This shows that (E) could be true together with every statement in the passage.

■ *Difficulty Level: 5*

Question 19

Overview: Faden, who evidently works for a company that makes exercise machines, claims that most of those machines are still in use after one year and bases that claim on the results of a customer survey. Greenwall responds by suggesting a reason to doubt the survey results: customers might lie to avoid embarrassment. Faden then emphatically dismisses Greenwall's objection on the grounds that Greenwall can't prove that any customers were lying.

The question tells you that there is a problem with either Greenwall's or Faden's reasoning, but it doesn't tell you whose reasoning is flawed. So you have to choose an answer choice that accurately describes something that is wrong with the reasoning of one speaker or the other.

The Correct Answer:

D Greenwall responds to Faden's original argument by presenting grounds for thinking that it would be unwise simply to take the survey results at face value, as Faden seems to do. Greenwall does not claim to have proved that the evidence from the survey actually fails to reflect the facts. But proof that evidence is false is not required in order to call the evidence into question. All that is required to raise a legitimate concern about taking survey results at face value is a plausible account of why those results might be misleading.

In responding to Greenwall's alternative account, Faden proceeds as though the only grounds for not accepting the evidence offered for a particular claim is proof of that evidence being false. (D) accurately describes this flaw in Faden's reasoning.

The Incorrect Answer Choices:

A Greenwall does not take it for granted that the customers are in fact lying but instead provides reason to think that customers might be lying. Thus, (A) does not accurately describe Greenwall's response.

B Greenwall provides a specific reason why some people might not tell the truth about how much they exercise. This does not mean that Greenwall assumes that most people are dishonest about their personal habits generally. Thus, (B) does not accurately describe Greenwall's response.

C The only evidence Faden cites is the results of a recent survey. Faden treats that evidence as conclusive and treats the claim based on it as believable. So Faden never presumes that more conclusive evidence makes a claim less believable.

E The issue raised by Greenwall is whether people who claim to still be using the exercise equipment are generally telling the truth. Greenwall never denies that some people who are no longer using the exercise equipment admitted this without embarrassment. Thus, (E) does not accurately describe Greenwall's response.

■ *Difficulty Level: 4*

Question 20

Overview: Sarah says that in deciding which events should be covered, reporters are interpreting the news. Ramon says that reporters should not interpret the news. He then clarifies what this means by telling us that reporters, after selecting a story, have an obligation to relay the facts untainted. In doing this, Ramon conveys the message that the opportunity to interpret the news arises only after a reporter has already deemed a story to be newsworthy.

Your task is to select the answer choice that, given what the two speakers say, is most likely to be accepted as true by one but be rejected by the other.

The Correct Answer:

E As the "Overview" indicates, Sarah and Ramon identify different points at which interpretation occurs. Sarah thinks that the choice of which events to report on involves interpretation of the news. Ramon thinks that the issue of interpretation arises only after this choice has been made, when the facts of a given story are reported. Thus, Sarah accepts (E) as true, whereas Ramon's remarks imply that he rejects (E).

The Incorrect Answer Choices:

A Sarah straightforwardly says that reporters always interpret the news. Ramon says that reporters shouldn't interpret the news. But Ramon's position is consistent with believing that, in actual fact, reporters always interpret the news. So Sarah and Ramon could agree that reporters actually do interpret the news every time they report it.

B Both Sarah and Ramon say that reporters do in fact exercise their own judgment about which events are newsworthy. But neither of them has anything to say about whether this should be so. So from what they say there is no reason to think that Sarah and Ramon disagree about (B).

C Ramon's remarks indicate that he believes that reporters have a responsibility to keep people informed of the facts, but it isn't clear that he thinks this is their primary responsibility. Sarah's remarks, on the other hand, indicate nothing at all about what she believes a reporter's responsibilities to be. So from what they say there is no reason to think that Sarah and Ramon disagree about (C).

D Both Sarah and Ramon indicate that it is reporters who choose to report on some events but not others. Neither seems to take issue with this practice. And both would presumably agree that no reporter can report on all events. So, from what they say, Sarah and Ramon are unlikely to disagree with each other about (D).

- *Difficulty Level: 4*

Question 21

Overview: The argument in the advertisement is based on the results of a single experiment in which subjects consumed a liter of milk and a certain percentage of them did not have enough of the enzyme lactase to easily digest the lactose in the milk. Based on applying this percentage to the North American population (presumably to the part of that population that consumes dairy products), the argument concludes that at least 50 million people in North America should take lactase supplements; that is, at least 50 million people have lactose intolerance that is severe enough to warrant their taking these supplements.

Since this argument uses experimental findings to reach a conclusion about people in their everyday environments, the strength of the argument depends on how closely the conditions in the experiment match the real-life conditions under which people consume dairy products.

The Correct Answer:

B According to (B) most people who consume dairy products don't consume as much lactose in one sitting as the people in the experiment did. So (B) weakens the argument by showing that the conditions in the experiment are not conditions that most dairy-product-consuming people in North America are likely to experience.

The Incorrect Answer Choices:

A In real life, unlike in the experimental conditions, people often drink milk while also consuming solid food. Thus, according to (A), most people are likely to have even less lactase available to help them digest milk than the experimental subjects did. So if (A) is correct, it suggests that the proportion of North Americans who need lactase supplements may be greater than the experimental results indicated. So (A) strengthens the argument rather than weakening it.

C If (C) is true, it is important that the experimental subjects were a representative sample with respect to age. But there is no indication that the sample wasn't representative in this respect. So (C) doesn't weaken the argument.

D (D) suggests that lactose intolerance can be a serious problem if it is not remedied. But this does nothing to weaken the argument, which focuses on the issue of how many people are lactose intolerant.

E (E) suggests that for many people, the need for lactase supplements might be greater than the experimental results indicated. So (E) does nothing to weaken the argument.

■ *Difficulty Level: 3*

Question 22

Overview: This question is based on two separate claims regarding fairness in determining salaries. Your task is to identify the principle that most helps to justify both of these claims.

Jim claims that it would not be fair to raise the salaries of two of his co-workers if his salary is not also raised enough to equal what theirs would be, since he has worked for the company longer than they have.

Tasha claims that raising Jim's salary would be fair only if the salaries of 35 other employees are raised to the same level, since those 35 employees have been working for the company as long as Jim has.

The Correct Answer:

D   (D) says that the only case in which a company can fairly pay one employee more than another is if the first employee has worked for the company longer than the second employee has. Thus, (D) rules out paying Fred and Dorothy more than Jim is paid and justifies Jim's claim. (D) also rules out paying Jim more than the 35 employees mentioned by Tasha and thus justifies Tasha's claim. So (D) justifies both Jim's and Tasha's claims.

The Incorrect Answer Choices:

A   The principle in (A) links pay to duties performed. Neither Jim nor Tasha says anything about the duties of any employee. They base their claims entirely on length of service. So (A) does not justify either Jim's or Tasha's claim.

B   The principle in (B) links pay to work experience. Neither Jim nor Tasha says anything about any employee's work experience. Each of them considers only the length of time employees have been working for one company. But an employee's work experience is not necessarily determined by how long that employee has worked for his or her present employer. So (B) does not justify either Jim's or Tasha's claim.

C   Tasha's claim concerns employees who have all worked at Jim's company for the same length of time as he has. But (C) has nothing to say about what is fair regarding pay for employees with equal lengths of service. So (C) does not justify Tasha's claim.

E   The principle in (E) links pay to the amount of time worked per day. Both Jim and Tasha, however, are concerned with how long an employee has been with a company. So (E) does not justify either Jim's or Tasha's claim.

■ *Difficulty Level: 4*

Question 23

Overview: The commentator contends that interpretations of a constitution are portrayed falsely but that this is a necessary fiction. The portrayal is false because these interpretations are usually portrayed as embodying the intentions of the constitution's authors, but they in fact express the beliefs of the interpreters. This fiction is necessary because political stability requires that laws be perceived as the bequest of a long tradition rather than something devised by contemporary politicians.

You are asked to select the answer choice that is most strongly supported by what the commentator says.

The Correct Answer:

B   If the commentator is correct, political stability requires that people believe that their laws are the bequest of a long tradition, which in turn requires that they believe that when their constitution is interpreted to apply to new situations, it is interpreted consistently with the intentions of its authors. So it follows that if people in a nation with some degree of political stability stop having this belief, then political stability in that nation will decrease. Since this is essentially what (B) says, (B) is strongly supported by the commentator's statements.

The Incorrect Answer Choices:

A   The commentator's statements give us no information about the effect of people not believing that their country's laws express the intentions of their political leaders. The commentator does indicate that political stability will suffer if people don't believe that the constitution is being interpreted in keeping with the intentions of its authors, but does not draw a similar connection between political stability and the perception that laws reflect the intentions of current political leaders.

C   The only threat to political stability that the commentator talks about comes from people no longer believing that their laws are the bequest of a long political tradition. The commentator says that people would lose this belief if they thought that the intentions of the constitution's authors are not being followed in the way the constitution is now being interpreted. But if people think that present political leaders and the authors of the constitution differ in some of their beliefs, they can still believe that the constitution is being interpreted in keeping with its authors' intentions and that laws are the bequest of a long political tradition. So (C) is not supported by the commentator's statements.

D The commentator does not distinguish between written constitutions and unwritten constitutions, and the commentator does not single out any characteristic of a constitution that preserves the illusion that laws are the bequest of a long tradition. The only thing that the author suggests preserves that illusion is portraying interpretations of a constitution as embodying the intentions of its authors.

E The commentator presents the perception that a nation's laws come out of a long legal tradition as a necessary condition for political stability. Thus, according to the commentator, a nation in which there is a perceived lack of such a tradition cannot be politically stable, no matter what people believe about the intentions of their political leaders. So (E) is not supported by what the commentator says.

- *Difficulty Level: 5*

Question 24

Overview: The initial argument has two premises: a family's fiscal security requires wise financial management, and a functional budget requires realistic projections of financial obligations. Each of these premises presents an outcome and a condition that must be met to achieve that outcome. The argument then draws the conclusion that if either of the two outcomes is to be achieved, one or the other of the conditions for achieving those outcomes has to be met. This conclusion, in effect, combines the two premises by bringing the two outcomes together as one either-or outcome and bringing the two requirements together as one either-or requirement.

To answer this question you have to decide which of the arguments in the answer choices has a pattern of reasoning that is most similar to that in the initial argument.

The Correct Answer:

A The first premise of this argument is that it is necessary to continue the use of pesticides if enough food is to be grown to feed the world's population. The second is that persistent health problems will be reduced only if researchers develop pesticides that are harmless to humans. Note that each premise presents an outcome and a condition that must be met to achieve that outcome. The argument then draws the conclusion that if either of the two outcomes is to be achieved, one or the other of the conditions for achieving those outcomes has to be met. So the pattern of reasoning in (A) is the same as the pattern of reasoning in the initial argument.

The Incorrect Answer Choices:

B While the first premise in this argument presents an outcome (weight loss) and something that must be done to achieve this outcome (change one's diet and exercise patterns), the second premise does not. That premise alerts us to a potential danger involved in not following proper safeguards (getting medical supervision). And while the conclusion of the initial argument brings together two outcomes and two requirements, the conclusion of this argument does not. Thus, the pattern of reasoning in (B) is not like that in the initial argument.

C This argument has only one premise: some popular, low-maintenance houseplants are toxic. The first sentence simply supplies background information and plays no role in the reasoning. The premise is presented in support of an intermediate conclusion (such houseplants are unsuitable for homes where pets are kept indoors). And the main conclusion is drawn from this intermediate conclusion. Thus, the pattern of reasoning in (C) is unlike that in the initial argument, even though the conclusion of this argument, considered in itself, has the same structure as the conclusion of the initial argument.

D This argument is like the initial argument in that it has two premises. Both of the premises, however, are about the same outcome (retaining an employee until retirement) and each sets out a different condition that has to be met for this outcome to be achieved. The conclusion that is drawn is that if that outcome is to be achieved, both conditions have to be met. Thus, the reasoning in (D) is not very similar to that in the initial argument.

E The argument in (E) is about a single outcome (conducting a successful charity drive). The first premise tells us one condition that has to be met (detailed planning) if that outcome is to be achieved. The second premise lists certain things that have to be done to achieve the outcome. These things have to be done well in advance, so the argument concludes that achieving the desired outcome—a successful charity drive—requires planning that is both detailed and done well in advance. Apart from the first premise, this argument is not at all similar to the initial argument.

- *Difficulty Level: 5*

Questions 25–26

Overview: In this exchange, an anthropologist reports that certain complex behavior among a troupe of vervet monkeys was successfully predicted on the basis of an assumption about what the individual monkeys knew. The anthropologist concluded that, since this assumption led to an accurate prediction, the assumption must actually be true.

The primatologist responds by arguing that the anthropologist's conclusion is not supported by sound reasoning. The primatologist's critique of the anthropologist's reasoning is based on an imaginary situation in which the reasoning involved is closely parallel to the reasoning used by the anthropologist—an assumption leads to a successful prediction—but in which the corresponding conclusion is obviously absurd.

Question 25

The Correct Answer:

C As discussed in the "Overview," the primatologist attempts to show that applying the anthropologist's reasoning to a different case leads to an absurd conclusion. This is done in an attempt to demonstrate that there is something wrong with that reasoning. So (C) is an accurate description of the primatologist's argumentative technique.

The Incorrect Answer Choices:

A The anthropologist's conclusion is that each vervet monkey in the troupe had knowledge of the complete dominance hierarchy for the troupe. The primatologist, contrary to what (A) says, does not cite facts that are inconsistent with this conclusion.

B The primatologist does not actually deny the anthropologist's thesis and thus, in particular, does not use the denial of the anthropologist's thesis as a premise in arguing against the anthropologist. The primatologist merely tries to show that the anthropologist, in arguing for that thesis, relied on faulty reasoning.

D The primatologist attacks the anthropologist's reasoning, not the anthropologist's expertise. Moreover, there is no suggestion that the anthropologist should have known about that particular analogy.

E The primatologist does not examine the anthropologist's use of scientific terms and does not criticize the anthropologist for misinterpreting any such term. The primatologist's critique is focused solely on the soundness of the anthropologist's method of reasoning.

- *Difficulty Level: 3*

Question 26

Here you are looking for a definite point of disagreement between the anthropologist and the primatologist. The correct answer choice will identify an issue on which the two are committed to opposing views.

The Correct Answer:

D   The anthropologist argues that the predictive success of the assumption that vervet monkeys have knowledge of their complete dominance hierarchy shows that assumption to be true. By making this argument, the anthropologist expresses the view that predictive success is sufficient grounds for the truth of the claim that vervet monkeys had knowledge of their dominance hierarchy. The primatologist, on the other hand, is committed to denying that the predictive success of the assumption provides sufficient grounds for the truth of this claim, because the primatologist's whole point is that the conclusion of the anthropologist's argument does not follow. So the anthropologist and the primatologist are committed to disagreeing on the issue raised by (D).

The Incorrect Answer Choices:

A   The anthropologist claims to have made accurate predictions of some complex group behaviors, but it is not clear whether any predictions of the behavior of individual monkeys were even attempted. And the primatologist makes no comment at all on the issue of whether the anthropologist's predictions actually succeeded. So there is no way of knowing either the anthropologist's or the primatologist's position on the issue raised by (A).

B   The primatologist seems to assume that at least some bank cash machines work with enough accuracy to enable us to predict their output on the basis of what customers request. The anthropologist's views on this matter cannot be determined from the dialogue since the anthropologist says nothing at all about bank cash machines. Thus, there is no way to tell if the two disagree about this point.

C   The anthropologist is committed to the view that vervet monkeys do have knowledge of the complete hierarchy of dominance relations in their own troupes: this is the point of the assumption that the anthropologist claims to have shown to be true. The primatologist, however, is not committed to denying that vervet monkeys have this knowledge. The primatologist merely denies that the anthropologist's argument proves that vervet monkeys have this knowledge. So the primatologist is not committed to disagreeing with the anthropologist about (C).

E   It is not clear whether the research on the behavior of the troupe of vervet monkeys was done in an experimental setting or in the wild. So there is no way to determine the anthropologist's view on the issue raised by (E). And since the primatologist is only responding to the anthropologist's argument, there is no way to determine the primatologist's view either.

■ *Difficulty Level: 4*

Questions 1–7

Synopsis: The subject matter of the passage is the limited success naturalists have had trying to explain the ability of kinglets, a North American species of forest bird, to survive the extremely cold nighttime temperatures of northern winters.

The purpose of the first paragraph is to draw a contrast: whereas naturalists understand fairly well how other North American forest birds make it through cold winters, they are somewhat baffled by the kinglet's survival.

The second and the third paragraphs tell why explaining the kinglet's survival is a special challenge. The second paragraph focuses on the unusual amount of energy—relative to their size—that kinglets must expend to survive cold winter nights. Kinglets are said to be subject to rapid heat loss both because of their small body mass and because of their having less insulation than larger birds in absolute terms. As a result—and also because of the extremely high body temperatures that they maintain—kinglets need to consume much more food per unit of body mass than other birds.

The third paragraph deepens the mystery. It focuses on the kinglet's energy intake. Unlike most birds that remain in cold climates during the winter, kinglets eat only insects. They forage only during the short daytime hours, and they do not store food for later consumption. And since their stomach holds only enough to keep them warm for an hour, it is hard to see how they could get enough food.

The theme of the fourth paragraph is perhaps best described as "groping for answers." Three theoretical possibilities are briefly considered. First, the kinglet's ability to quickly accumulate body fat is mentioned as at least a partial solution. Body fat will get kinglets through half a winter's night. Second, torpor is mentioned, but not as a viable explanatory hypothesis, but rather as a hypothesis now abandoned by researchers. Third, clustering together for warmth during the night is presented as a theoretical possibility for which there is some indirect evidence.

Question 1

The Correct Answer:

E   The unifying thread that runs through the passage is that naturalists would like to gain an understanding of the kinglet's survival in northern winters but have so far had only limited success. At present, two adaptations are hypothesized to be important parts of the story: one physiological adaptation—the ability to store fat—and one behavioral adaptation—the never-yet-observed clustering together of relatively large numbers of birds at night. But, as (E) correctly says, researchers do not yet have a full understanding.

The Incorrect Answer Choices:

A   The idea stated in (A) is essentially what the second and third paragraphs of the passage are concerned with. But the main point of the passage is not to establish that kinglets can survive cold winter nights despite formidable challenges. The main point is to show that researchers hoping to explain this phenomenon have not yet entirely succeeded.

B   That researchers have tested several theories is not the central idea of the passage. In fact, the only time the author mentions testing in connection with a theory is in the discussion of clustering in the final paragraph. What is said about that theory is that it is "still untested" (line 48).

C   This is not a statement supported by the passage. What the passage says is that "kinglets manage to survive as well in cold climates as do the larger birds" (lines 25–26). There is no mention anywhere in the passage of kinglets enjoying a superior survival rate.

D   The passage mentions the kinglet's tiny size as a special disadvantage that kinglets have to overcome in very cold winter temperatures. But nowhere is their tiny size mentioned as an impediment to observing them. So (D) is not a statement supported by the passage.

- *Difficulty Level: 3*

Question 2

The Correct Answer:

A   The only discussion of torpor in connection with kinglets is in lines 45–47: "Researchers once theorized that torpor might make up the difference, but found no evidence of torpor in kinglets." The use of the phrase "once theorized" indicates that researchers have given up on the torpor theory. And the reasoning behind the abandonment of this theory must have been that since there was no evidence of torpor, there was no torpor. (A) states a generalization that fits this reasoning.

The Incorrect Answer Choices:

B   The passage does not suggest that researchers rejected torpor as an explanation on the basis of a comparison between kinglets and some other species. Though chickadees are mentioned in lines 7–8 as a species that induces torpor to deal with cold temperatures and later, in line 18, contrasted with kinglets in size, there is no hint of an argument combining these facts along the lines suggested in (B).

C   We are told that researchers found no evidence of torpor in kinglets. So (C), which presupposes the existence of such evidence, does not apply here. Moreover, (C) would be a reason to withhold judgment regarding a theory, but not to reject it.

D   Since researchers found no evidence that kinglets even go into torpor, there was never an opportunity to test the theory that torpor helped kinglets survive bitter cold. Thus (D) cannot be the correct answer.

E   The passage strongly suggests that there is consensus in the scientific community to reject the torpor theory for kinglets. But the reason given for rejecting the theory is that there is no evidence in favor of it, not that the theory falls short of complete acceptance within the scientific community. So (E) does not capture the reasoning behind the rejection of the torpor theory for kinglets.

- *Difficulty Level: 2*

Question 3

The Correct Answer:

D   In the passage, kinglets are compared to chickadees, which are described as having twice the mass of kinglets. The passage says that, according to the physical laws of heating and cooling, kinglets would have to "consume and burn 75 percent more food per unit of body mass than the larger birds" (lines 19–20) to maintain body temperature. Hence, (D) correctly describes what kinglets must do to maintain body temperature in winter.

The Incorrect Answer Choices:

A   The passage does not mention any bird as having mass equivalent to that of a kinglet. If there are such birds, the account of the physical laws of heating and cooling given in the passage suggests that their food requirements must be the same as those of kinglets unless their body temperature is significantly different from that of kinglets.

B   The passage provides information that is inconsistent with (B). Specifically, the passage says that kinglets neither cache food nor forage at night, and it says that a kinglet's stomach, when filled to capacity, contains only enough food to keep it warm for one hour. This information strongly suggests that there are many hours during the night when the kinglet's stomach is not filled to capacity.

C   The passage specifically compares the kinglet's food consumption with that of only one other bird, the chickadee. The chickadee is described as having twice the kinglet's body mass. But although the chickadee thus has 100 percent more body mass than the kinglet, the kinglet is said to eat only 75 percent more food per unit of body mass than the chickadee. These numbers imply a lower total food consumption for the kinglet than for the chickadee.

E   According to the second paragraph, the amount of insulation as a percentage of body mass is approximately the same for all northern birds, around 25 percent. Consequently, smaller birds have less, not more, insulation in absolute terms than larger birds have, and must therefore consume more food per unit of body mass, contrary to what (E) says.

- *Difficulty Level: 4*

Question 4

The Correct Answer:

B In lines 50–55, the fact that kinglets naturally flock in small groups during the day is taken as encouraging the idea that several such small groups might gather together at night in a relatively large cluster. (B) is correct in characterizing this as bearing on the apparent reasonableness ("feasibility") of the hypothesis rather than as providing evidential support for it, since it is described as "still untested" (line 48).

The Incorrect Answer Choices:

A There is no indication that the author regards the clustering hypothesis as "almost certainly true." It is introduced in lines 47–48 as "another theory, which is still untested." In presenting it, the author seems to make a point of using the word "may." The hypothesis itself is that several groups of kinglets "may find each other," and it "may be borne out by a recent study of goldcrests." Nor is there any indication that "all other explanations have been eliminated." In fact, the author says that the kinglet's ability to store body fat provides a partial explanation (lines 41–42).

C The author treats clustering not as an unlikely possibility, but rather as a promising one, which "may be borne out by a recent study of goldcrests" (lines 48–49). And while it is reasonable to suppose that the author regards clustering as currently the most worthwhile option to explore, there is no indication that the author considers it the only option left to explore.

D As the discussion of (C) above suggests, the recent study of goldcrests is cited to indicate that clustering among kinglets is a real possibility, but not to show that clustering among kinglets is well established. The hypothesis is presented as conceptually promising but untested, with no solid evidence backing it up.

E The passage gives no indication of the extent to which any of the hypotheses it mentions are discussed in the scientific community, or may be thought by the author to be discussed in that community. So nothing in the passage suggests that (E) reflects the author's view of the clustering hypothesis.

■ *Difficulty Level: 2*

Question 5

Overview: The question asks you to identify something that is **not** among the factors cited by the author as contributing to the mystery of kinglet survival in extremely cold overnight winter temperatures. The incorrect answer choices are all factors that **are** so cited.

The Correct Answer:

B The fact that kinglets and goldcrests are related species is cited not as deepening the mystery of the kinglet's survival on cold winter nights, but, if anything, as suggesting a solution. If kinglets are like goldcrests in clustering together at night in large groups, heat loss in very cold temperatures might be reduced sufficiently to allow the kinglet's survival to be explained. So (B) is something that may help to make the kinglet's survival less mysterious.

The Incorrect Answer Choices:

A The kinglet's stomach, even when filled to capacity, "contains only enough food to keep it warm for one hour" (lines 39–40). This means that, since the kinglet doesn't feed at night, the kinglet's limited stomach capacity is a factor that contributes to the mystery of the kinglet's survival.

C According to the passage, the survival of kinglets is remarkable in part because, "unlike most bird species that remain in cold climates during winter, their diet consists exclusively of insects" (lines 30–33).

D In the second paragraph, the author explains how the kinglet's small body mass causes it to lose heat faster than larger birds, so that they have to consume more food per unit of body mass than larger birds if they are to maintain the same body temperature. This is another special handicap that kinglets have to overcome as they face cold winter nights.

E The fact that the kinglet does not forage at night (together with the fact that it does not cache food) means that it is completely dependent on food gathered and consumed during the short days of winter (lines 35–37). According to the passage, this is a fact that makes it harder to explain how kinglets can consume enough food to supply their energy needs.

■ *Difficulty Level: 3*

Question 6

The Correct Answer:

A In the first paragraph, nuthatches, chickadees, and grosbeaks are mentioned as species of North American forest birds that have developed special adaptations to survive extremely cold winter nights. The author takes considerable care to tell us how each of these species deals with extremely low overnight temperatures. So (A) is an accurate description of the author's intent in mentioning these species.

The Incorrect Answer Choices:

B Nuthatches, chickadees, and grosbeaks are mentioned as exemplifying different strategies for surviving extremely low overnight temperatures. They are merely representative. There is no indication that the author's purpose is to produce anything like an exhaustive list of those North American forest birds that are able to survive cold winter nights.

C The author's discussion is limited to North American forest birds, but there is nowhere any implication that they are the only birds that have been able to adapt to extremely cold overnight temperatures.

D The author's statement at the end of the first paragraph that "the survival of one species, the kinglet, remains something of a mystery" (lines 10–11), implies that none of the strategies ascribed to nuthatches, chickadees, and grosbeaks is known to be employed by the kinglet. There is no suggestion that kinglets employ the nuthatch's method of seeking out cavities. Torpor, the chickadee's method, appears to have been ruled out by researchers for lack of evidence (lines 46–47). And the consumption of fat-rich seeds, the grosbeak's method, does not apply to kinglets, which eat only insects.

E The fact that the author is interested in illustrating a certain diversity in the approaches taken by different birds does not mean the author's goal is to prove that each species has a unique method. That the author in fact has no such goal can be seen from the discussion in lines 47–55, which revolves around the suggestion, seemingly endorsed by the author, that for at least two different species, goldcrests and kinglets, the approach to surviving extremely cold overnight temperatures may be the same.

- *Difficulty Level: 2*

Question 7

The Correct Answer:

D The author would most likely agree with (D). The passage states that the hypothesis that kinglets cluster together at night "may be borne out by a recent study of goldcrests, a related species" (lines 47–50). The implication is that such behavior has actually been observed in goldcrests. In the following lines (50–55), the fact that kinglets flock in small groups during the day is taken as encouraging the hypothesis that they may form larger clusters at night. Thus the author would most likely agree that an inference from the nocturnal behavior of a species related to kinglets to similar behavior in kinglets, while hardly foolproof, would be reasonable. And this is all (D) requires.

The Incorrect Answer Choices:

A According to the author, naturalists "have long studied the ability of North American forest birds to survive extremely cold overnight temperatures in winter" (lines 1–3) and have apparently acquired a rather detailed understanding of this ability for a variety of birds. The only bird that is described as remaining "something of a mystery" (line 11) is the kinglet. And even here researchers apparently have at least a partial explanation (lines 41–42). So the author would most likely disagree with (A).

B The passage does not suggest that the author believes this. The only mention of a diet high in fat is in lines 9–10, where grosbeaks are described as staying "close to trees whose seeds contain sufficient fat to fuel shivering." This immediately precedes the statement that the kinglet's survival remains a mystery, which suggests that the author does not think the kinglet's diet is high in fat. Since the kinglet's diet is described (lines 32–33) as consisting solely of insects, this implies that insects are not high in fat (in fact they are not). Hence, the author apparently believes that the kinglet's diet is already well understood and is not high in fat. It is unlikely, then, that the author believes that it may be found to be high in fat.

C Kinglets are described as flocking in groups of two or three during the day, but how this flocking is initiated and maintained is not touched on in the passage. On the other hand, calls are hypothesized to be the means by which several such small groups may consolidate into larger clusters. That kinglets form such larger clusters is, however, presented by the author not as fact, but only as a promising hypothesis. So the author would most likely not agree with the flat claim, contained in (C), that calls **are** the means by which kinglets induce flocking behavior.

E The phenomenon of drastically reduced body temperature is referred to in the passage as torpor (lines 7–8), and the author seems fairly certain that torpor is not how kinglets deal with extremely low temperatures. Torpor had once been considered as a theoretical possibility, but as the author points out, no evidence of torpor in kinglets has ever been found. So the author would most likely disagree with (E).

- *Difficulty Level: 5*

Questions 8–15

Synopsis: This passage is about the sort of policy that should be adopted in dealing with the problem of juvenile delinquency. The general policy advocated by the author is presented as an intermediate one between two extremes, incarceration on the one hand and no penalty at all on the other hand.

The first paragraph presents the first of these two extremes as characteristic of much of mainstream law enforcement thinking, which favors severely punishing juvenile delinquents on the grounds that otherwise juvenile delinquency automatically leads to adult crime. The author then introduces research findings of certain criminologists. These findings suggest that the incarceration of young offenders might be counterproductive: incarceration might actually ensure that young offenders become adult criminals.

In the second paragraph, the author introduces a distinction between behavior that the young adults themselves think of as criminal behavior and behavior that they admit is illegal but think of as being merely "fun" and not as being criminal. This is a distinction that, according to the author, is not sufficiently appreciated by either the criminologists or law enforcement officials. But the author suggests that this category of behavior—behavior that juveniles consider illegal but not criminal—is important because it is behavior that most young offenders who escape detection by law enforcement naturally grow out of as they mature. Incarcerating young offenders for such behavior prevents this maturation process from occurring. These considerations lead the author to propose that a policy that encourages maturation replace that of routine incarceration.

The third paragraph elaborates on this proposal. Juvenile delinquency needs to be dealt with, not ignored. But young offenders should not be removed from the larger society and labeled as criminals. What should be done is to "ensure that young offenders learn the values of the larger society by the time they reach maturity" (lines 53–55). To illustrate how this rehabilitation might be approached, the author considers the case of a young adult caught stealing from a store. The author suggests that making the offender return the merchandise and apologize to the storeowner would inculcate the values of society more effectively than would incarcerating the offender as a thief.

Question 8

The Correct Answer:

E The author of the passage is primarily concerned to argue that the way to rehabilitate juvenile delinquents is to keep them in the larger society while helping them learn its values by the time they reach maturity (lines 53–58). That is, juvenile offenders can be rehabilitated without being incarcerated. (E) expresses this point and thus expresses the main idea of the passage.

The Incorrect Answer Choices:

A The idea in (A) is an important one in the passage. But it isn't the main point of the passage. The author introduces the distinction underlying (A) in order to argue that law enforcement's current approach to juvenile delinquency is counterproductive and that the young offenders' view of their own behavior is the key to an effective policy of rehabilitation.

B The author strongly suggests that the criminologists did not extract as much from their research as they could have (lines 19–27). The author uses the criminologists' actual research findings to argue for a particular approach for dealing with young offenders. It is with this alternative approach that the passage is primarily concerned, however, not with advising criminologists about how they should conduct their research.

C The issue of cooperation between criminologists and law enforcement personnel is never raised in the passage. The author is mainly concerned to advocate a policy for dealing with young offenders and does not go into much detail about how that policy should be implemented.

D The author does treat juvenile delinquency as a problem of some significance although nothing in the passage suggests that the author regards juvenile delinquency as a threat to social stability in Canada and the United States. But the seriousness of the problem is not the primary focus of the passage. What primarily concerns the author is the best way to rehabilitate young offenders.

■ *Difficulty Level: 1*

Question 9

The Correct Answer:

D The author draws heavily on the work of the criminologists discussed in the first paragraph in developing the policy advocated in the passage. So it can be inferred that the author regards that work as useful. But, according to the author, the criminologists themselves have not even made an attempt to translate their work into policy (lines 14–16). (D) thus accurately describes the author's opinion about the work of those criminologists.

The Incorrect Answer Choices:

A, B, C, E Each of answer choices (A), (B), (C), and (E) describes the author as holding some opinion about policies advocated by the criminologists. So (A), (B), (C), and (E) all presuppose that the author believes that the criminologists advocate policies. But the author explicitly says that those criminologists do not advocate any policies (lines 15–16). Thus none of (A), (B), (C), or (E) can be a description of an opinion that the author holds.

■ *Difficulty Level: 3*

Question 10

The Correct Answer:

B In the second paragraph, the author says that juvenile delinquents think of some of their delinquent behavior as "fun" rather than as criminal and suggests that this fact can partially explain the occurrence of such behavior. And according to the author, the best way to rehabilitate juvenile offenders engaging in such behavior is to ensure that they "learn the values of the larger society" (lines 53–54). Thus, it can be inferred that the author holds the view that juveniles who regard their delinquent behavior as "fun" rather than as criminal have not sufficiently learned some of the values of society.

The Incorrect Answer Choices:

A The author does not discuss the moral differences between so-called right and wrong behavior in general. Nevertheless the author does say that there are behaviors that even juveniles who view their delinquent activities as "fun" consider to be criminal (lines 23–24). It would seem that, on the author's view, anything these juveniles view as criminal they thereby regard as wrong and as morally different from so-called right behavior—behavior that is neither illegal nor criminal. Thus, the passage provides some support for holding that the author disagrees with (A).

C It can be inferred from the passage that the author believes that juveniles who view their delinquent activities as "fun" do so primarily because they are immature. Otherwise, the author would not suggest maturation as the most effective form of rehabilitation (lines 39–41). Thus, the passage does not support the view in (C). The author does attribute a consequence to the policy of treating delinquency as serious criminal behavior. But this consequence is that juveniles who had previously thought of themselves as noncriminals doing things that, although illegal, were merely "fun" come to think of themselves as criminals (lines 28–33).

D The author advocates dealing with juvenile delinquents without incarcerating them (e.g., lines 47–48, 50–53, and 57). There is no indication anywhere in the passage that the author believes that adult criminals should not be incarcerated. Thus (D) is not supported by the passage.

E The author advocates dealing with juvenile delinquents without incarcerating them. (e.g., lines 47–48, 50–53, and 57). Moreover, the author believes that juvenile delinquents do not have to be removed from the community to be rehabilitated (lines 47–49). Thus, it can be inferred that the author disagrees with (E).

■ *Difficulty Level: 1*

Question 11

The Correct Answer:

D The passage describes current law enforcement policies as entailing that juvenile delinquents should "be severely punished, usually by some form of incarceration" (lines 4–5). In contrast, the author's view is that the appropriate goal when dealing with juvenile delinquents is to ensure that they "learn the values of the larger society by the time they reach maturity"(lines 54–55) and that this can best be achieved without "inflicting incarceration" (line 57). Thus, the author can accurately be described as being convinced that current law enforcement policies should be revised.

The Incorrect Answer Choices:

A The passage mentions youthful offenders who escape detection by law enforcement (lines 35–36). So the author recognizes that current law enforcement does not achieve perfect detection rates for juvenile delinquents. However, the author says nothing about whether the actual detection rates achieved are high or not. So it cannot be determined whether (A) accurately describes the author's attitude.

B The author says that, according to some criminologists' research, "incarceration may have the perverse effect of ensuring that the young offenders will continue to perform delinquent acts" (lines 11–13). However, note that the language in which the author presents the implications of the criminologists' research is the language of supposition throughout. The author talks about what may or might be the case, or what is suggested, but never about what is certain to be the case. So there is no warrant for describing the author's attitude toward the implications of the criminologists' research as one of certainty.

C, E The author says both that current law enforcement policies favor the incarceration of juvenile delinquents (lines 1–5) and that research by criminologists suggests that incarceration may actually ensure that young offenders will continue to perform delinquent acts (lines 11–13). So the author's attitude cannot be described as one of confidence either that current law enforcement policies promote the good of society or that they have no effect on juvenile delinquency.

■ *Difficulty Level: 1*

Question 12

The Correct Answer:

B Lines 10–13 report research suggesting that incarceration may actually have the effect of ensuring that young offenders become adult criminals. The primary purpose of the passage is to argue that the best way of preventing juvenile delinquents from becoming adult criminals is to rehabilitate them by ensuring that they learn the values of the larger society and that this can best be done without incarcerating them. Lines 49–53 present an illustration of how this might be done: a young adult caught stealing from a store could be made to return the merchandise and apologize to the storeowner rather than being incarcerated as a thief. Thus the author's purpose in lines 49–53 is to illustrate and support a proposal motivated in part by lines 10–13, as (B) states.

The Incorrect Answer Choices:

A Lines 49–53 present an example of how the policy **advocated** by the author might actually be implemented in a specific case. Thus the author' purpose in lines 49–53 is not accurately expressed by (A).

C According to the author, mainstream thinking advocates incarcerating youthful offenders (lines 1–5). Thus lines 49–53 cannot be intended as an example that confirms this thinking.

D Lines 49–53 illustrate how the policy proposed by the author might be implemented. They do not present an interpretation of data. Moreover, the illustration in lines 49–53 does not oppose the interpretation given in lines 10–13, since both favor avoiding incarceration of youthful offenders. Thus (D) cannot describe the author's purpose in lines 49–53.

E The proposal made in lines 49–53 is motivated in part by the conclusion reported in lines 10–13. That conclusion is drawn from the criminologists' research findings, which the author thus appears to accept. Thus the author's purpose in lines 49–53 cannot be that described in (E).

■ *Difficulty Level: 2*

Question 13

Overview: The criminologists' research is said to suggest that incarceration might have an effect opposite the intended one. It might, according to the criminologists' research findings, actually contribute to adult criminality rather than preventing it. This is the point of saying that it might have a "perverse effect" (lines 11–12). Thus, in very general terms, the relationship is presented as one in which research indicates that a widely accepted treatment (here, incarceration) for a problem (here, criminal behavior) can actually result in further instances of the problem.

The Correct Answer:

D In (D) research indicates that a widely accepted treatment (antacids) for a problem (heartburn from excess stomach acidity) can actually result in further instances of that very problem. Thus (D) is closely analogous to the purported relationship in the passage between incarceration and criminologists' research findings.

The Incorrect Answer Choices:

A In (A) research indicates that a widely accepted policy (quick and aggressive treatment) for dealing with a problem (melanoma) is the best way to avoid more serious instances of that problem. The case in (A) is thus not closely analogous to the one in the passage.

B In (B) research shows that a once common treatment (removing the tonsils) for a problem (sore throats) is not effective and may be harmful. But since in this case, the treatment is not one that is currently widely accepted and the research is not said to indicate that the treatment actually led to more sore throats—once the patient recovered from the surgery—the case in (B) is not very closely analogous to the one in the passage.

C In (C) research indicates that a widely accepted treatment (antibiotics) for a problem (viral sore throat) can have undesirable side effects. But since the side effects are not specified as being of the same sort as the problem itself, there is nothing in (C) that corresponds to the "perverse effect" in the case in the passage. Thus (C) is not closely analogous to that case.

E In (E) research indicates that a certain treatment (decongestant therapy) has several side effects, and as a result, it has become common policy to avoid that treatment in less serious cases of the problem. The side effects in cases in which decongestant therapy continues to be used are not specified as being in any way similar to the problem that the therapy is used to treat. Thus (E) does not mention the sort of "perverse effect" that the passage mentions. So (E) is not closely analogous to the case in the passage.

■ *Difficulty Level: 2*

Question 14

Overview: The question asks you to identify something about which the passage does not include information. The incorrect answer choices will thus all be matters about which the passage does include information.

The Correct Answer:

B The only place in the passage where a specific type of illegal act is mentioned is in lines 49–53. There the author discusses a hypothetical case of a juvenile who steals from a store. The author says nothing to indicate that adult criminals don't steal from stores (and in fact, it is common knowledge that they do). Beyond this, the passage does not discuss specific kinds of illegal acts. Therefore, the passage provides no information about (B).

The Incorrect Answer Choices:

A The passage provides information about (A) in lines 22–33.

C The passage provides information about (C) in lines 47–58.

D The passage provides information about (D) in lines 10–13.

E The passage provides information about (E) in lines 34–36.

■ *Difficulty Level: 1*

Question 15

The Correct Answer:

E The passage is essentially an argument for a policy regarding the treatment of juvenile delinquents. This is a policy that is different from the one generally favored by law enforcement. The basis for advocating the proposed policy is that it reduces the likelihood that juvenile delinquents will continue to perform delinquent acts or become adult criminals. Thus (E) accurately describes the primary purpose of the passage.

The Incorrect Answer Choices:

A, D The author believes that law enforcement officials have failed to distinguish illegal behavior that young adults regard as genuinely criminal from illegal behavior that they consider merely "fun." The passage suggests that the fact that juveniles draw this distinction may help to explain some cases of juvenile delinquency. The passage also suggests that the fact that law enforcement officials do not draw this distinction may help to explain why they generally adopt a policy of incarcerating juvenile delinquents. But the author is not **primarily** concerned either with the true causal roots of juvenile delinquency or with law enforcement officials' understanding of those roots. Nor is the author **primarily** interested in explaining law enforcement's treatment of juvenile delinquency. Rather, these are subordinate to the author's main aim, which is to argue for an alternative policy as the best way of rehabilitating juvenile delinquents. Thus neither (A) nor (D) accurately describes the primary purpose of the passage.

B The author does discuss how juvenile delinquents view certain of their own illegal activities. The role this discussion plays in the passage is in arguing that these activities are products of immaturity rather than criminality, and therefore, that they should not be dealt with by incarceration. But the only reason the author discusses these matters is to lay the groundwork for the author's own policy proposal. Thus, (B) describes a subordinate, not the primary, purpose of the passage.

C The passage does not explicitly discuss the contention that juvenile delinquency inevitably leads to adult criminality, although it presents information that runs counter to that contention (lines 34–36). The passage does appear to accept the idea that **incarcerating** juvenile delinquents strongly encourages adult criminality. But the only reason the author discusses these matters is to lay the groundwork for the author's own policy proposal. Thus (C) does not describe the primary purpose of the passage.

- *Difficulty Level: 1*

Questions 16–20

Synopsis: The passage is about *Hammer and Hoe*, a book by Robin D. G. Kelley about the history of communism in Alabama. The passage is primarily concerned with Kelley's account of the relationship between African-American workers and the Communist Party during the party's Popular Front period, which extended through the 1930s and 1940s. The Third Period, which immediately preceded the Popular Front, is discussed mainly to bring the Popular Front into sharper focus.

The first two paragraphs focus on what is distinctive in Kelley's approach. The first paragraph tells us that Kelley, unlike most historians, does not engage in a critique of the ideology of communism, but rather examines how the Communist Party was instrumental in getting African-American workers and farmers to organize themselves. The second paragraph makes the point that most historians have defended the Communist Party of the Popular Front by emphasizing its attempts to ally itself with democratic political traditions and liberal political forces. Kelley, however, who has a different take on this period, focuses instead on the party's losing ground among African Americans.

The third paragraph lays the groundwork for Kelley's assessment of the Popular Front as a period in which African-American communism was in retreat. It presents Kelley's argument that it was really during the party's immediately preceding Third Period that the party was most successful in helping African-American farmers and industrial workers to organize. According to Kelley, this success owed nothing to the party's extreme confrontational stance at the time. What appealed to those groups was Communist Party rhetoric about a "new world," and the party's promise of a powerful ally in their struggle. The Communist Party's leadership in opposing lynch law in the United States was another strong point of attraction for African Americans.

The fourth paragraph presents Kelley's account of changes that the party underwent during the Popular Front. The party withdrew somewhat from specifically African-American concerns and from involvement in local African-American issue-oriented politics. In general, the party grew increasingly cautious as it tried to broaden its appeal. These changes made the party less attractive to African Americans.

The passage concludes by praising Kelley for his balanced account of the decline in African-American involvement with the Communist Party. The passage points out that Kelley by no means limits himself to an explanation in terms of what went on within the party, but duly recognizes the substantial role played by broad economic and political factors.

Question 16

Overview: The question is about the main point of the passage. One thing to keep in mind in considering this question is that the passage is about the views expressed by Kelley in his book. The views of the author of the passage are largely kept in the background. The main point of the passage is thus bound to be a point about Kelley or about Kelley's book. Another thing to keep in mind is that the main point of a passage may not actually be stated in any particular place in the passage. Instead, the main point may emerge from the structure of the passage and from various statements that contribute in different ways to a coherent theme.

The Correct Answer:

E The main point of the passage is that Kelley's book *Hammer and Hoe* breaks new ground by portraying the Communist Party's Popular Front (the period comprising the 1930s and 1940s) as a period of decline. Unlike other historians, Kelley measures the party's success by its ability to attract and organize substantial numbers of African-American workers. Kelley's detailed look at African-American involvement with the Communist Party in its Third Period shows that part of the reason for the decline during the Popular Front was that the party's public posture changed somewhat, in ways that made it less appealing to African-Americans. But Kelley is portrayed as also appreciating that this change in public posture was not the sole reason for the decline. So (E) provides the best characterization of the passage's main point.

The Incorrect Answer Choices:

A The passage acknowledges that *Hammer and Hoe* is not primarily concerned with ideological controversies, but it does not accuse Kelly of failing, for that reason, to fully explicate the relationship between the Communist Party and African-American workers during the 1930s and 1940s. Rather, the passage says that the book differs from most scholarship on the Communist Party's fortunes in those two decades in taking a close look at that very relationship and producing a "rounded portrait" (lines 53–54) of its decline.

B The passage does not address the question to which (B) could be taken as offering an answer. That is, the passage does not address the general question of whether ideological purity and consistency are essential to effecting political change. Nor is this a question that the passage describes Kelley as being concerned with. Kelley is portrayed as being specifically interested in what accounted for the appeal the Communist Party had for African-American workers in Alabama in the 1930s and 1940s.

C The passage mentions that some historians were "searching for models of unity between radicals and liberals" (lines 17–18) to explain why their interests differed from Kelley's. This suggests that Kelley was not searching for such models. Hence, one would not expect his work to be an especially valuable tool in this search, and the passage does not recommend it as such.

D (D) is neither a point that the passage itself makes, nor is it a point that it ascribes to Kelley. A different, though somewhat similar-sounding point is attributed to Kelley: that the true measure of the Communist Party's success was its ability, by interacting with their culture, to get African-American workers to organize themselves. But even this is not the main point of the passage. The main point is to show how Kelley accounts for the fact that the party's attractiveness to African-American workers declined during the 1930s and 1940s.

- *Difficulty Level: 4*

Question 17

Overview: The part of the passage that is straightforwardly just about the Communist Party in Alabama before the 1930s is the third paragraph (lines 22–38). But inferences about that period can also be drawn from comments in the fourth paragraph (lines 39–47), since some of those comments are concerned with ways in which the 1930s and 1940s were different from the period preceding the 1930s. The question asks you to identify a characteristic that the passage does not attribute to the Communist Party. Hence, each of the incorrect answer choices will be a characteristic that is so attributed.

The Correct Answer:

A   The passage mentions a retreat from attacks on white chauvinism as a characteristic of the period encompassing the 1930s and 1940s (lines 40–41). But retreat presupposes that there was something to retreat from, so the passage strongly suggests, contrary to (A), that the party attacked white chauvinism before the 1930s.

The Incorrect Answer Choices:

B   The passage says that "efforts of the communist-led International Labor Defense in mobilizing against lynch law in the United States helped to establish the party's image as such an ally" (lines 35–38). In context, "ally" here means an ally in African-American farmers' and industrial workers' struggle for survival. The benefit that resulted for the party in Alabama was that African-Americans joined the party in substantial numbers.

C   The passage suggests that there was party rhetoric that inspired some African Americans, in particular, the party's rhetoric regarding a "new world" (lines 29–32). So (C) accurately describes a characteristic that the passage says the Communist Party in Alabama had before the 1930s—even though it also says that there was other, extreme party rhetoric (lines 25–28) that African-American party members were inclined to discount.

D   The passage says that "the extreme rhetoric of the Third Period communists was not taken seriously by African-American party members, who avoided posturing and confrontation whenever possible." (D) accurately captures the fact that confrontation was not an acceptable political stance among African-American party members before the 1930s even though the passage suggests that this stance was officially promoted by the party.

E   The passage says that during the 1930s and 1940s, "a tendency to de-emphasize, however slightly, involvement in local African-American issue-oriented politics made the party seem less an instrument of deliverance" (lines 41–44). But involvement can be de-emphasized only where there is involvement. So the passage strongly suggests that the Communist Party in Alabama before the 1930s was indeed, as (E) says, "involved in local African-American political issues."

- *Difficulty Level: 5*

Question 18

The Correct Answer:

A The second paragraph is chiefly concerned with bringing out the differences between the way Kelley sees the Communist Party in its Popular Front period and the way the majority of historians do. The second paragraph tells us that Kelley concentrated on a different aspect of the party (namely, its usefulness in helping African-American workers organize themselves) than did most other scholars, and that this led to a more negative assessment of the Popular Front.

The Incorrect Answer Choices:

B The second paragraph says that, from Kelley's point of view, "the Popular Front appears as much less of a blessing" (lines 20–21) than it does from the point of view of most other scholars. However, the passage does not treat Kelley's account of the Popular Front as an attack but rather as a "rounded portrait" (line 53). The passage describes Kelley's account of that period without indicating any disagreement with it.

C The second paragraph refers to the Communist Party's attempts, during the 1930s and 1940s, to find common ground with liberals. But this reference is made in the context of explaining what most scholars—with the notable exception of Kelley—regard as interesting to study about the party in this period. The paragraph does not concern itself with the issue of whether the party's attempts to find common ground with liberals were politically useful to the Communist Party or to anyone else.

D The passage does not systematically enumerate the differences between the Popular Front and the Third Period anywhere. It does contain language that, both implicitly and explicitly, points to such differences. But these references to differences between the two periods are to be found primarily in the fourth paragraph and, to some extent, in the third. There are none in the second paragraph; at that point in the passage, the Third Period has not even been mentioned.

E The passage does not develop any argument such as the one described in (E). Rather, the passage takes it for granted that the approach characterized in (E) is valid while making the point, in the second paragraph, that most historians do not choose this approach. Kelley's work in *Hammer and Hoe*, which does take this approach, is plainly treated by the passage as respectable scholarly work, the validity of which does not need to be argued for.

■ *Difficulty Level: 3*

Question 19

The Correct Answer:

A According to the passage, Kelley argues that the Third Period of the Communist Party "better under-girded organization among African-American farmers and industrial workers" than the Popular Front did. The fourth paragraph is essentially a short list of factors that account for the diminishing appeal, among African Americans, of the Communist Party during the Popular Front. These factors involve changes that, according to Kelley, contributed to the decline of African-American communism, though Kelley by no means claims that they are the sole reason for that decline. So the passage provides support for the view that Kelley would agree with (A).

The Incorrect Answer Choices:

B Kelley holds the view, according to the passage, that "the Popular Front initially appealed to African-American communists because it seemed to open new strategies for blunting repression" (lines 50–53). Kelley gives no reason to think that there weren't, initially, possibilities for such strategies, and it is thus unlikely that Kelley would agree with the assertion in (B).

C The Communist Party's increasing cautiousness is mentioned as one of the factors Kelley considers responsible for the decline, during the Popular Front, in African-American participation in the Communist Party (lines 44–47). It is thus unlikely that Kelley would agree that the increasing cautiousness of the Popular Front appealed to most African-American party members.

D The passage suggests that the Popular Front was not in general viewed by African Americans as an improvement over the Third Period, since it tells us that during the Popular Front African-American communism declined. With regard to rhetoric in particular, we are told that, to the extent that African Americans took the rhetoric of the Third Period seriously, they viewed it favorably, in part because it struck the theme of deliverance. According to the passage, Kelley attributed the decline of African-American communism during the Popular Front to factors that "made the party seem less an instrument of deliverance" (lines 43–44). Hence, there is no reason to believe that Kelley would agree with (D).

E   The passage suggests that certain extreme Third Period rhetoric promoted posturing and confrontation. The Popular Front, by contrast, is characterized as a period of increasing cautiousness rather than as a period of extreme posturing and confrontation. So it is likely that Kelley would disagree with the assertion that "the extreme posturing and confrontation of the Popular Front alienated many African Americans," because he would disagree that these supposedly alienating factors were any part of the Popular Front. Moreover, when discussing extreme Third Period rhetoric, Kelley presents African Americans as not taking it seriously rather than as being alienated by it.

- *Difficulty Level: 4*

Question 20

Overview: This question asks you to select a statement that is more likely to have been made by Communist Party organizers during one period than during another. You are not asked to make a judgment about just how likely it is that any particular statement was made in either period. Rather, the idea is that the Third Period and the Popular Front are portrayed as being different in certain ways, and that those differences have implications that make some statements less likely to have been made in one period than in the other.

The Correct Answer:

B   (B) is a highly confrontational sort of statement. It portrays **revolt** as being necessary, it envisions a final global victory, and the enemy is oppression. It's also extreme: workers **everywhere** must revolt, and the revolt is to be sustained until **final** victory is achieved. Moreover, (B) calls for a **global** victory. The passage associates a confrontational approach, extreme rhetoric, and talk of a "new world" with the Third Period (lines 25–29), whereas it associates increasing cautiousness and moderation with the Popular Front (lines 45–46). So the passage supports the view that Communist Party organizers would have been more likely to have said things like (B) during the Third Period than during the Popular Front.

The Incorrect Answer Choices:

A   The passage gives us no reason to believe that this statement would be more likely to be made by a Communist Party organizer during the Third Period than during the Popular Front. Indeed, the note of inclusiveness struck by (A) might appear to fit the Popular Front even better than the more combative Third Period.

C   The sort of organizing that was done during the Third Period is grassroots organizing, among farmers and industrial workers (lines 23–25). Lines 42–43 imply that the Communist Party was more heavily involved in strictly local African-American issue-oriented politics during the Third Period than during the Popular Front. Therefore, fighting racism in the highest levels of government would have been less likely to have been emphasized by party organizers during the Third Period than during the Popular Front. There is thus no basis in the passage for thinking that (C) was more likely to have been said during the Third Period than during the Popular Front.

D According to the passage, the Communist Party was trying to enter meaningful political alliances with liberal political forces in the 1930s and 1940s (lines 12–16), so its organizers might well have made statements like (D). But the 1930s and 1940s were the period of the Popular Front, not the Third Period. Since the question asks about a statement that would have been more likely in the Third Period, (D) can be ruled out.

E (E) strikes the sort of judicious note of caution that, according to the passage, would have been more in keeping with the Communist Party line during the Popular Front than during the Third Period (line 45). Thus, Communist Party organizers would have been more likely to say things like (E) during the Popular Front than during the Third Period.

- *Difficulty Level: 5*

Questions 21–27

Synopsis: This passage attributes the widespread acceptance of Darwin's view of early prehistoric humans to a historical accident and argues that evidence found by researchers using recently developed techniques strongly supports an alternative conception.

The first paragraph contends that there are essentially two reasons for the long dominance of Darwin's conception of early prehistoric humans among anthropologists. First, the earliest discovered fossils of hominids happened to be fossils of humans' most recent forebears, who—unlike the hominids dating to far more distant eras—did genuinely resemble modern humans. This resemblance led anthropologists to follow Darwin in taking the lifestyles of today's hunter-gatherer societies as the model for the lifestyles of all of our hominid ancestors—even extending that model to the most distant forebears. And second, anthropologists have not sufficiently taken into account how advanced modern hunter-gatherers actually are and in what fundamental ways early prehistoric humans' lives must have been different from theirs.

The second paragraph introduces the recently developed field of taphonomy, which deals with the transformation of skeletal remains into fossils. The paragraph announces that taphonomy has yielded evidence that calls Darwin's conception into question.

The third paragraph provides a brief sketch of techniques involved in taphonomic research and reports two findings of taphonomic research on animal bones found among very early hominid fossils. First, stone-tool marks on the fossilized animal bones did not occur systematically at the joints. And second, tooth marks of animal carnivores often occurred under, rather than on top of, the stone-tool marks.

The last paragraph begins by reporting what these researchers take this evidence from animal bones to show, namely that early hominids were scavengers of meat left from carnivore kills rather than hunters of live prey. It then reports evidence gained from fossilized hominid teeth that further supports the idea that very early hominids were indeed scavengers. The passage ends with the conclusion that that the fossil evidence suggests a revised view of early hominids: they were less confident and clever than Darwin thought, often perching in trees to avoid predators and foraging and scavenging for food rather than hunting.

Question 21

The Correct Answer:

C As the discussion above indicates, the main idea of the passage is that new research techniques in anthropology—in particular, taphonomic techniques—have brought to light new evidence that supports an alternative to a long-accepted view about early hominids. This is essentially the idea expressed in (C).

The Incorrect Answer Choices:

A The new research method discussed in the passage —taphonomy—is a special way of looking at fossils. The passage says nothing to suggest that taphonomy has been applied (or how it could have been applied) in investigating modern hunter-gatherer societies. So (A) does not accurately describe an idea expressed in the passage.

B The passage is concerned with one new field of research—taphonomy—but says nothing about traditional methodologies or their limitations. The failure of anthropologists to consider the sophistication of modern hunter-gatherers and their environment (lines 14–20) is not presented as reflecting a methodological shortcoming but as an intellectual failure. Thus (B) does not accurately describe anything that can be found in the passage.

D The passage does discuss the idea expressed in (D). But this idea is mentioned only in the first paragraph (lines 3–13) as an introduction to the main concern of the passage, which is to discuss how a new field of research has found evidence suggesting an alternative conception of early hominids. Thus (D) does not describe the main idea of the passage, but only a subordinate idea.

E All of the recent discoveries that the passage is concerned with have to do with such things as the nature and placement of marks on fossil bones (lines 31–43) and the patterns of wear on fossilized hominid teeth (lines 46–50). These discoveries bear on hypotheses about the behavior of early hominids, namely, that they scavenged rather than hunted. The passage does not mention any discoveries about the environment in which early hominids lived. Thus the main idea of the passage cannot be that it was discoveries about that environment that prompted anthropologists to revise their thinking.

■ *Difficulty Level: 3*

Question 22

Overview: The anthropologists mentioned in line 14 are criticized by the author for their failure to appreciate certain differences between modern hunter-gatherers and prehistoric hunter-gatherers: differences in their sophistication in using fire, tools, language, and so on and differences in their environments. So it can be inferred from the passage that the author would be likely to encourage these anthropologists to engage in research that would sharpen their awareness of the differences between these two broadly defined groups. (Note that the question is framed in terms of research on modern hunter-gatherer societies, so when answer choices talk about "these societies" or "the various societies," they are referring to modern hunter-gatherer societies.)

The Correct Answer:

C One important feature of the environment for any society of hunter-gatherers is the competition that the society faces for food. So in order to appreciate how the environment of modern hunter-gatherers differs from that of prehistoric hunter-gatherers, it would be important to compare those environments in this respect. This is precisely the comparison that would result from doing the research described in (C).

The Incorrect Answer Choices:

A The passage tells us that taphonomy is concerned with fossils. The study of fossils is indispensable as a way of learning about prehistoric societies, because such societies, unlike modern hunter-gatherer societies, cannot be observed directly. Setting aside the question of whether enough time has gone by for any modern hunter-gatherer societies to have left any fossils, there is every reason to suppose that anyone studying them to learn about their lifestyles would learn more through direct observation or through historical records. Thus, the author would be highly unlikely to encourage the anthropologists to do (A).

B The author accuses the anthropologists of failing to distinguish modern hunter-gatherers from prehistoric hunter-gatherers. This failing would not be remedied by the investigation of similarities among the various modern hunter-gatherer societies. But it is the investigation of modern hunter-gatherer societies that (B) describes. Thus the passage provides no support for thinking that the author would encourage the anthropologists to do (B).

D The author accuses the anthropologists of failing to distinguish modern hunter-gatherers from prehistoric hunter-gatherers. This failing would not be remedied by merely investigating further the life-styles of modern hunter-gatherer societies. But the hunter-gatherer societies referred to in (D)—those who lived in the previous century—are modern rather than prehistoric. Thus the passage provides no support for thinking that the author would encourage the anthropologists to do (D).

E Analyzing how the survival strategies of modern hunter-gatherer societies are changing would provide no insight into how the situation of modern hunter-gatherer societies differs from that of prehistoric hunter-gatherer societies. So the passage provides no support for thinking that the author would encourage the anthropologists to do (E).

- *Difficulty Level: 5*

Question 23

Overview: The researchers mentioned in line 44 are said to have concluded that "early hominids were scavengers of meat left from carnivore kills, rather than hunters of live prey" (lines 45–46). According to the passage, they reached this conclusion on the basis of taphonomic analysis of marks on animal fossils. This analysis showed that "the markings of stone tools on many of the fossilized animal bones did not occur systematically at the joints" (lines 39–41), and that the cut marks from stone tools often occurred on top of toothmarks of animal carnivores (lines 42–43).

The Correct Answer:

D For the evidence cited to support the conclusion drawn, the researchers would have to have interpreted the evidence about toothmarks underlying tool marks as showing that carnivores got to the bones before tool-using hominids did. So it can be inferred that the researchers interpreted this sequence as indicating that the bones were those of an animal that had been killed by a carnivore that left its toothmarks on those bones, and that the early hominids later used tools on the remains of the animal that the carnivore had killed.

The Incorrect Answer Choices:

A The passage says that the researchers used the fact that the marks of stone tools did not occur systematically at the joints as evidence for their conclusion that early hominids were scavengers, rather than hunters (lines 44–46). It follows that the researchers did not interpret this fact as indicating anything about the skill with which early hominids hunted and butchered animals, contrary to (A).

B The passage says that the researchers used the fact that the marks of stone tools did not occur systematically **at the joints** as evidence for their conclusion that early hominids were scavengers, rather than hunters (lines 44–46). This is the only place in the passage that mentions tools not being used in a systematic manner. We are given no reason to believe that the researchers concluded from this or any other evidence that the early hominids were working hastily or that they were concerned about competing groups of hominids. Thus the passage provides no support for inferring that the researchers interpreted the evidence in the way (B) describes.

C According to the passage, the fact that the marks of stone tools overlay the toothmarks of animal carnivores was taken by the researchers to show that early hominids were scavengers rather than hunters. There is no indication in the passage that the researchers regarded any of the evidence gained by taphonomic analysis as explaining **why** early hominids were not hunters. Since (C) attributes just such an explanation to the researchers, it misrepresents the researchers' interpretation.

E The passage provides no reason to think that the researchers, in reaching their conclusion that early hominids were scavengers, considered the size of the animals whose fossils they analyzed to be of any importance. Thus there is no basis in the passage for inferring that the researchers interpreted the taphonomic evidence in the way (E) describes.

- *Difficulty Level: 2*

Question 24

The Correct Answer:

B In lines 53–55 the passage says that the early hominids' upright mode of walking "enabled them to scan the ground for carcasses and to carry useful scavenging tools." This is part of the case the researchers make for saying that "early hominids could have been well adapted for scavenging" (lines 50–51). The upright mode of walking is cited in the passage as one of two examples (the other being agility in climbing trees) suggesting that early hominids were well suited for scavenging—that is, well suited to the method of gathering food that the researchers hypothesized that they used.

The Incorrect Answer Choices:

A The passage says nothing about any previous hypothesis about how early hominids walked. Thus the author would not have cited their upright mode of walking in order to counter any such hypothesis.

C The passage presents no explanation for why early hominids "ate fruit primarily and meat only occasionally" (lines 49–50), but only for why researchers think they did. Researchers deduced the nature of the early hominid diet from wear patterns on fossilized hominid teeth (line 47), not from early hominids' upright mode of walking. Thus, the author's purpose in citing the upright mode of walking wasn't what (C) describes.

D The author thinks that a failure to appreciate how different early hominids were from modern humans is responsible for a mistaken view about the lifestyles of early hominids. Accordingly, the author does not to emphasize respects in which early hominids and modern humans were alike.

E The author's purpose in writing the passage is to explain, and not to criticize, the researchers' conclusion that early hominids were "scavengers of meat left from carnivore kills, rather than hunters of live prey" (lines 45–46). Since the contrast in (E) contradicts that conclusion, it is not one that the author would want to draw.

- *Difficulty Level: 2*

Question 25

Overview: The account given in the first paragraph of the discovery of hominid fossils goes essentially as follows: Anthropologists were acquainted with the lifestyles of modern hunter-gatherers before the first fossils of forebears of humans were discovered. Those fossils discovered first were of the hominids closest in time to modern humans. Since these most recent hominids genuinely resembled modern hunter-gatherers, it seemed likely that their lifestyles were similar. So anthropologists adopted the view that the lifestyles of all hominids, even the earliest ones, must have resembled those of modern hunter-gatherers. To answer this question you have to decide which of the answer choices presents a situation that has a structure similar to the structure of the situation involving the anthropologists and the discovery of hominid fossils.

The Correct Answer:

B   In the situation in (B) the art historians are acquainted with the late paintings of a certain artist. (This is analogous to the anthropologists' being acquainted with the lifestyles of modern hunter-gatherers.) Then some more paintings by the same artist were discovered, paintings that had been done just a few years before the paintings that the art historians already knew. (This is analogous to the first discovery of fossil hominids.) These newly discovered paintings were done in more or less the same style as the paintings they already knew. (This is analogous to the similarity between those first-discovered hominids and modern hunter-gatherers.) And on the basis of the similarity between these newly discovered paintings and the late paintings, the art historians concluded that all of this artist's paintings, even the earliest ones, must have been done in that same style. (This is analogous to the view adopted by the anthropologist about early hominids.) Thus, the structure of the situation in (B) is similar to the structure of the situation in the first paragraph of the passage.

The Incorrect Answer Choices:

A, C   The situation described in the first paragraph of the passage is one in which something is discovered that resembles something of the same general type that is already known. On the relevant time scale, the two things are close to each other. And the similarity between the two of them leads people to believe that this similarity extends to all things of the same general type, even those that are far older. Both (A) and (C), in contrast, describe situations in which there are two new discoveries. And in both (A) and (C), the second discovery is described as providing evidence that corrects a view formed on the basis of the initial discovery. In neither (A) nor (C) is a similarity between two things extended to other things that are of the same general kind but far distant in time. So neither the situation in (A) nor the situation in (C) is closely analogous to the situation in the first paragraph.

D   The situation in (D) is somewhat analogous to the situation in the first paragraph of the passage in that something very old is discovered and the determination is made that it closely resembles something much more recent. However, there is no mention in (D) of what, if any, conclusions were drawn on the basis of the resemblance. But in the situation described in the first paragraph of the passage, it is precisely the conclusion drawn on the basis of the resemblance that is of paramount importance, not the resemblance itself. So as described, the situation in (D) fails in important respects to be analogous to the situation described in the first paragraph.

E   In (E), scientists are trying to find a similarity between two things, both of which are known. And that is all that is going on in (E). In the situation described in the first paragraph of the passage, however, there is no doubt about the similarity between modern hunter-gatherers and Neanderthals. Moreover, this similarity is not the focus of the situation in the passage. Rather, the focus is on the conclusion that was drawn from this similarity. Thus the situation in (E) is not at all analogous to the situation described in the first paragraph of the passage.

■ *Difficulty Level: 5*

Question 26

Overview: To answer this question, the first thing you have to decide for each of the answer choices is whether the passage mentions what that answer choice describes. Then, if it does, you have to decide whether the passage explicitly says that the thing mentioned is something that can be determined by taphonomic investigation. What you are looking for is something that is either not mentioned at all or, if mentioned, is not mentioned as something that taphonomic investigation can determine.

The Correct Answer:

C   The passage says that the fossils on which researchers found the marks they investigated by taphonomic means were "almost two million years old" (line 33). But the passage does not indicate anything about how the age of those fossils was determined. Thus although (C) is mentioned in the passage, it is not mentioned as something that is determinable by taphonomic investigation.

The Incorrect Answer Choices:

A   In lines 42–43 the passage tells us that the order in which certain marks were made on the fossilized bones was determined by taphonomic investigation.

B   In lines 37–38 the passage tells us that taphonomic investigation can determine certain physical differences among the marks found on fossilized bones.

D   In lines 36–39 the passage tells us that taphonomic investigation can determine the agents that have left the marks on fossilized bones.

E   In lines 34–39 the passage tells us that taphonomic investigation can determine similarities between marks made on fossilized bones and marks made on modern bones.

- *Difficulty Level: 5*

Question 27

The Correct Answer:

D   Most of the passage is taken up with presenting discoveries made by taphonomy and showing how those discoveries form the basis for a view that is radically different from the view that the passage presents as the traditional one. Thus, (D) is a good description of the author's primary purpose in writing the passage.

The Incorrect Answer Choices:

A   The passage talks about only one research method—taphonomy. Taphonomy is described as a recent development, but it is not compared in any way to earlier methods. Thus (A) does not describe the author's primary purpose in writing the passage.

B   In the first paragraph, the author describes a preconception behind the standard view of the lifestyle of early hominids. And the author goes on to argue that this preconception is incorrect. But this preconception is not described as underlying previous research. So (B) does not accurately describe anything that the author actually does. Moreover, the author discusses this preconception only to clear the way for an alternative view based on recent research. So (B) does not describe the author's primary purpose in writing the passage.

C   The only narrative that the author presents is the account in the first paragraph of how the standard view of early hominids came about. The author's main concern, however, is to argue that recent research has provided the basis for a very different view of early hominids. Thus (C) is not a good description of the author's primary purpose in writing the passage.

E   The author presents evidence for a theory of how early hominids lived that differs significantly from what the passage describes as the traditional theory. But the author does not present this new theory as having actually **replaced** the traditional one. The evidence is presented as supporting the new theory, not as conclusively establishing it. In lines 21–23 the author says that recent developments "have called into question the traditional hypothesis . . ." And in lines 57–58 the author says that "the fossil record suggests a revised picture ..." Thus (E) is not an accurate description of the author's primary purpose in writing the passage.

- *Difficulty Level: 4*

Acknowledgment is made to the following sources from which material has been adapted for use in these tests.

Sandy Fritz, "Membrane Refrigerators." ©1993 by Popular Science.

Edward Hallett Carr, *What is History?* © by Edward Hallett Carr.

Feng-hsiung Hsu et al., "A Grandmaster Chess Machine." ©1990 by Scientific American, Inc.

Octavio Paz, *Convergences: Essays on Art and Literature*, tr. Helen Lane. ©1987 by Harcourt Brace Jovanovich, Inc.

David Roberts, "The Old Ones of the Southwest." ©1996 by the National Geographic Society.

Jonathan Rose, "The Invisible Sources of Nineteen Eighty-Four." ©1992 by the Journal of Popular Culture.

William Raspberry, "Maturity Ends Delinquency." ©1983 by Greenhaven Press, Inc.

Serious Tools for the Serious Law School Applicant

Law School Guides

- **LSACD™**

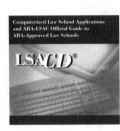

   (Windows®-compatible CD-ROM; Web version available via website only)
   Includes official applications for all ABA-approved law schools and searchable law school data.
   Web version: (available August 2004)
   CD-ROM: (available September 2004)

- **ABA-LSAC Official Guide to ABA-Approved Law Schools™**

   This is the only *official* guide to all the American Bar Association (ABA)-approved law schools in the United States, and it's the only one that contains up-to-date admission criteria and other essential admission information provided by the schools themselves. The *Official Guide* is the one book in which each school tells its story so that you can compare and decide which schools are best for you. Tuition, financial aid, special programs, and facilities are only some of the many categories covered in this handy guide.

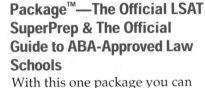

- **The *New* Whole Law School Package™—The Official LSAT SuperPrep & The Official Guide to ABA-Approved Law Schools**

   With this one package you can prepare for the LSAT and find the most accurate and up-to-date information about all ABA-approved law schools. Save money by buying the two books together.

- **So You Want to Be a Lawyer: A Practical Guide**

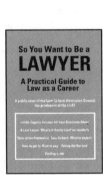

   This updated book can save you time and money by showing you how to identify what you should be looking for in a law school, and which ones may be looking for someone like you. Admission office insiders reveal what admission committees look for and how to make your application stand out amid the competition.

LSAT® Preparation

- **The Official LSAT SuperPrep™**
  Three new *PrepTests* with explanations for each item in all three tests.

- **10 Actual, Official LSAT PrepTests™**

- **10 More Actual, Official LSAT PrepTests™**

- **The Next 10 Actual, Official LSAT PrepTests™**

  Each of these books contains actual, previously administered LSATs. Each test includes an answer key, writing sample, and score conversion table.

◄ *(contains PrepTests 7, 9, 10, 11, 12, 13, 14, 15, 16, 18)*
This book contains *PrepTests* that are also featured in the *Official TriplePrep Plus*.

◄ *(contains PrepTests 19 through 28)*

◄ *(contains PrepTests 29 through 38)*
This book contains five tests (*PrepTests* 34-38) that can still be purchased individually.

- **The Official LSAT PrepTest With Explanations™**
  This great preparation tool includes a previously undisclosed official LSAT (February 1997), with explanations for each and every item in all four multiple-choice sections.

- **LSAT: The Official TriplePrep Plus™**
  (*PrepTests 11, 12, 13, explanations, extra writing samples*)
  TriplePrep Plus provides explanations for all three LSAT-item types. This book also contains 50 previously administered writing sample prompts in addition to three complete *PrepTests*.

- **LSAT: The Official TriplePrep®—Volume 1**
  (*PrepTests 2, 4, 5*)
  If you don't have time to take 10 practice tests, you can still save money by purchasing three. The *Official LSAT TriplePrep 1* contains three previously administered tests with answer keys, score-conversion tables, and 30 extra writing sample prompts for additional practice.

■ **The Official LSAT PrepTests®**

Each *PrepTest* is an actual LSAT administered on the date indicated. You can practice as if taking an actual test by following the test-taking instructions and timing yourself. In addition to actual LSAT questions, each *PrepTest* contains an answer key, writing sample, and score conversion table.

The Official LSAT PrepTest 34
June 2001 LSAT

The Official LSAT PrepTest 35
October 2001 LSAT

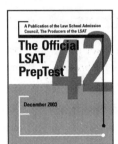

The Official LSAT PrepTest 36
December 2001 LSAT

The Official LSAT PrepTest 37
June 2002 LSAT

The Official LSAT PrepTest 38
October 2002 LSAT

The Official LSAT PrepTest 39
December 2002 LSAT

The Official LSAT PrepTest 40
June 2003 LSAT

The Official LSAT PrepTest 41
October 2003 LSAT

The Official LSAT PrepTest 42

December 2003 LSAT

The Official LSAT PrepTest 43
June 2004 LSAT
(available late July 2004)

The Official LSAT PrepTest 44
October 2004 LSAT
(available late November 2004)

The Official LSAT PrepTest 45
December 2004 LSAT
(available late January 2005)

Videos

■ Becoming a Lawyer: A Video Collection (DVD)

Contains the following six videos: *Getting There, Short Stories, Journeys, OUTlooks, Indian Lawyers, Believe and Achieve.*

■ Getting There: Four Paths to Law School

Four law school students from varied backgrounds recount their individual journey through the law school application process. (20 minutes)

■ Short Stories From the Real World of Law

A day-in-the-life view of five diverse, working lawyers. We glimpse how some lawyers balance their personal lives with demands of the profession. (20 minutes)

■ Journeys: Minorities and the Law School Experience

Only one in 25 lawyers in the United States is either Asian, Native American, Latino, or African American. In this video five minority law students offer their perspectives on the law school experience. (22 minutes)

■ OUTlooks

Law students and admission professionals talk candidly about the issues facing the gay or lesbian law school candidate. (27 minutes)

■ Indian Lawyers: Translators of Two Worlds

Native American lawyers tell their stories: what inspired them to pursue a law career and the successes and struggles that followed. The stories reflect the ways in which the attorneys forge connections between their cultural values and the law. (20 minutes)

■ Believe and Achieve: Latinos in the Law

Latino and Latina lawyers share their stories about how they chose law as a profession and how they achieved their current success. (20 minutes)

■ African American Lawyers: Role Models and Trailblazers (VHS/DVD)

Available September 2004
African American lawyers discuss the issues, triumphs, and rewards of pursuing a career in the legal profession. Legal education, professional opportunities, and mentoring are addressed.

■ Financing a Legal Education: Investing in Your Future (VHS/DVD)

Available September 2004
Law students and lawyers tell how they planned strategies for financing a legal education.

To Order: *Allow approximately three weeks for delivery of mail orders (use registration form in this book, pages I-1 through I-4). For faster delivery, order online at www.LSAC.org or by phone: 215.968.1001. Standard shipping is included in each price.* **All book and video sales are final.**

Note: *Prices and availability of all LSAC products are subject to change.*

FREE TIME
You'll have more of it if you apply to law school electronically.

cd-rom for windows

New Edition

cd on the web

The LSACD™

Updated annually in August

Choose the LSACD-ROM or LSACD on the Web to prepare your law school applications quickly and easily on your Windows®-compatible computer. Save time using the LSACD's common information form and flow-as-you-go technology—answer common questions only once, select the schools to which you want to apply and let the program place the answers in the proper fields. Once your applications are complete, you can print them out and mail them to the law schools yourself, or you can send them electronically to LSAC's electronic application clearinghouse for daily transmission to the law schools. Many schools will also accept application fees electronically by credit card. All ABA-approved law schools welcome applications prepared using the LSACD or LSACD on the Web.

LSACD on the Web

- Includes official applications for all ABA-approved law schools.

- Saves your application information on LSAC's secure central database so you can access it from any Windows®-compatible computer.

- Includes searchable data, photographs, descriptions, and links for each school accessible at no charge on LSAC's website.

LSACD-ROM for Windows®

- Includes official applications for all ABA -approved law schools.

- Saves your application information on your PC's hard drive.

- Includes searchable data, photographs, descriptions, and web links for each school.

Note: Prices and availability of all LSAC products are subject to change.

Visit our website: www.LSAC.org or call: 215.968.1001